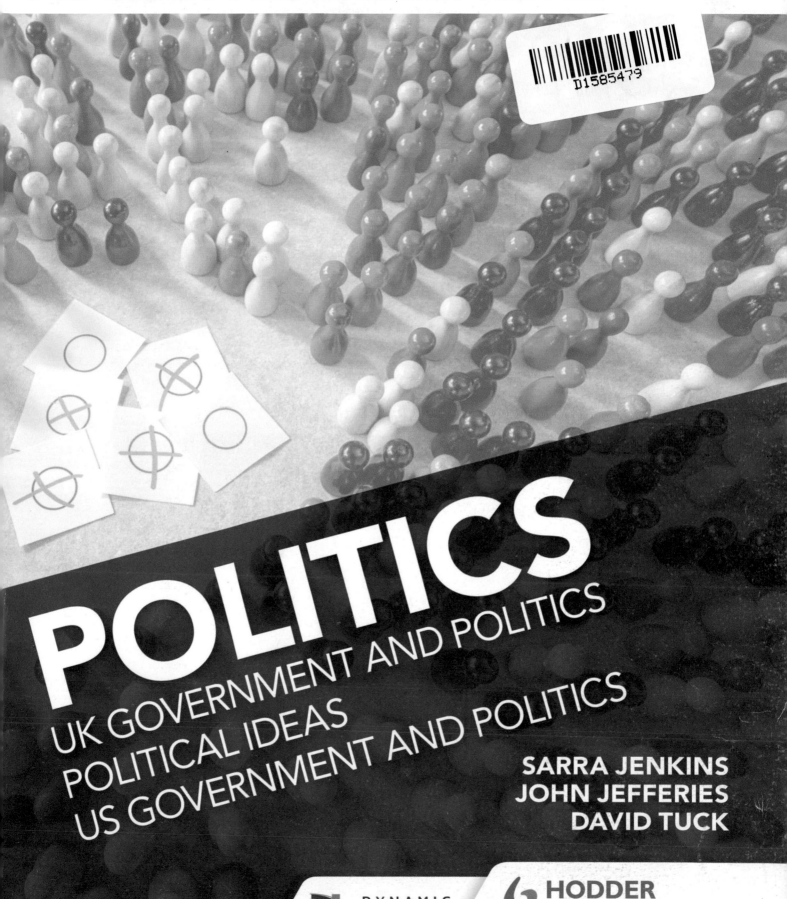

PEARSON EDEXCEL A LEVEL

POLITICS

UK GOVERNMENT AND POLITICS
POLITICAL IDEAS
US GOVERNMENT AND POLITICS

SARRA JENKINS
JOHN JEFFERIES
DAVID TUCK

DYNAMIC LEARNING

HODDER EDUCATION
AN HACHETTE UK COMPANY

In memory of Neil McNaughton

Hachette UK's policy is to use papers that are natural, renewable and recyclable products and made from wood grown in well-managed forests and other controlled sources. The logging and manufacturing processes are expected to conform to the environmental regulations of the country of origin.

Orders: please contact Bookpoint Ltd, 130 Park Drive, Milton Park, Abingdon, Oxon OX14 4SE. Telephone: (44) 01235 827827. Fax: (44) 01235 400454. Email education@bookpoint.co.uk

Lines are open from 9 a.m. to 5 p.m., Monday to Saturday, with a 24-hour message answering service. You can also order through our website: www.hoddereducation.co.uk

ISBN: 978 1 5104 4922 0

© Sarra Jenkins, John Jefferies and David Tuck 2019

First published in 2019 by

Hodder Education,
An Hachette UK Company
Carmelite House
50 Victoria Embankment
London EC4Y 0DZ

www.hoddereducation.co.uk

Impression number   10 9 8 7 6 5 4 3 2

Year   2023 2022 2021 2020 2019

Cover photo reproduced by permission of Ingo Bartussek – stock.adobe.com. For other photo credits, see page 564

Typeset by Integra Software Services Pvt. Ltd., Pondicherry, India

Printed in Italy

A catalogue record for this title is available from the British Library.

Get the most from this book

This textbook covers the key content of the Edexcel Government and Politics specification for teaching from September 2017.

Special features

Key terms
Concise definitions of key terms where they first appear.

Synoptic link
Explanation of links between important concepts in the specification.

In focus
A closer look at an example to support knowledge and understanding.

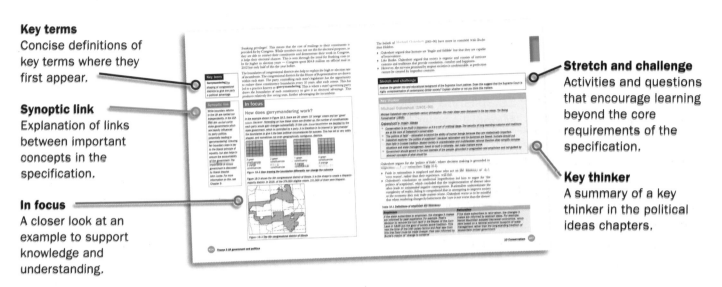

Stretch and challenge
Activities and questions that encourage learning beyond the core requirements of the specification.

Key thinker
A summary of a key thinker in the political ideas chapters.

Debate
Two sides of an argument to encourage evaluation and analysis.

Summary
A list of key questions at the end of every chapter against which you can check your knowledge.

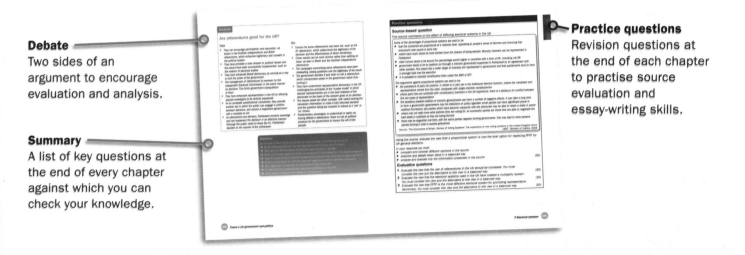

Practice questions
Revision questions at the end of each chapter to practise source evaluation and essay-writing skills.

Contents

Theme 1 UK government and politics

Theme 2 Political ideas

Theme 3 US government and politics

THEME 1

UK GOVERNMENT AND POLITICS

1 Democracy and participation

In 1947, in the House of Commons, Winston Churchill quoted the famous saying 'that democracy is the worst form of Government except for all those other forms'. Although his support for democracy might seem somewhat qualified, Churchill understood that the way in which democracy roots power in the people makes it the best form of government available. This is because the people hold their government accountable for what it does on their behalf and so choose the politicians whom they want to represent them. In autocratic forms of government, power is *permanently* vested in one individual or group, giving them ultimate power over their people.

The beginning of the UK's progression towards full democracy can be traced as far back as Magna Carta (1215) and possibly even to the Anglo-Saxon witan, giving the UK a good claim to have the longest history of democratic development in the world.

Runnymede, where King John sealed Magna Carta in 1215

In the USA, at the height of the American Civil War in 1863, President Abraham Lincoln (1861–65), in his Gettysburg Address, established the principle of democratic government as 'government of the people, by the people, for the people'.

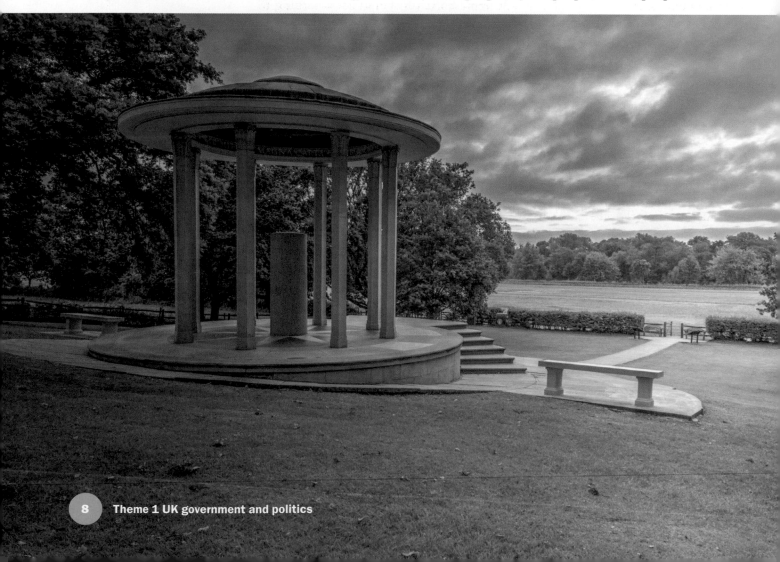

Current systems of democracy in the UK

Here we look at two forms of democracy in the UK — representative democracy and direct democracy.

Representative democracy

The UK is a **representative democracy**, which means that the voters elect politicians to make decisions on their behalf. There are so many complicated political decisions that need to be made in a modern democracy that it would be inconceivable for the public to have the time and understanding to vote on all of them. It is the job of professional politicians to acquire this sort of political understanding so that they can make informed decisions in the interests of the whole nation.

In a representative democracy, elected politicians are made accountable to the electorate in regular elections. This means that the voters ultimately retain sovereignty because they decide whether or not to renew the mandate of their representatives.

Representative democracy is based on the principle that elected politicians should represent the interests of all their constituents. As a result of this, MPs spend a significant amount of time in their constituencies listening to the concerns of their constituents in public meetings and surgeries. However, elected politicians should not simply act according to the wishes of their constituents. If they did this, they would be just a delegate. Instead, when making decisions, they should weigh up the feelings of the people they represent with their party's manifesto and their wider understanding of an issue. In other words, representatives should act according to their best judgement rather than slavishly following the voters' wishes.

The Westminster Parliament contains 650 MPs, all of whom are accountable to their constituents in regular general elections. Scotland, Wales and Northern Ireland also have their own devolved governments, while elected mayors and local councils provide another layer of representation for the public.

Advantages of representative democracy

The main advantage of representative democracy is that government is carried out by professional politicians who are required to be well informed about political issues. They are therefore more likely to make politically educated decisions than most members of the public, who may be swayed by emotion and may not fully understand the complexities of a question. For example, before a parliamentary bill is enacted it will have been carefully drawn up by ministers and civil servants, debated in both the House of Commons and the House of Lords, and been further analysed in committee stage when amendments may be added to it.

In a representative democracy, elected politicians balance conflicting interests when reaching decisions. This is important in protecting the rights of all citizens, especially minorities, and ensuring that the implications of a decision for all members of the community have been thoroughly examined. In direct democracy, in contrast, the public vote according to their self-interest without needing to consider the effect on others. This is more likely to encourage a majoritarian form of democracy, in which the rights and interests of the minority may be neglected.

> **Key term**
>
> **Representative democracy** A form of democracy in which voters elect representatives to make political decisions on their behalf. These representatives are then held accountable to the public in regular elections.

Table 1.1 Types of direct democracy

Example	Why they are used and the ways they can been criticised	When they have been used
Referendums A majoritarian form of democracy in which the public vote on a single issue. The side which gains over 50% of the vote wins outright	These allow the public to determine government policy on vital issues. However, by giving influence directly to the people referendums challenge the core principles of representative democracy	Scottish independence referendum (2014) UK membership of the EU referendum (2016)
Electronic petitions If a petition on the government website reaches 100,000 signatures it will be considered for debate in the House of Commons. This does not mean that legislation will have to be forthcoming	As a result of e-petitions, Parliament has had to engage with a number of issues which the public feel strongly about. Some e-petitions, such as two votes of no confidence in Jeremy Hunt when he was health secretary, though, have been criticised for not understanding how UK democracy works	Meningitis B vaccination to be made available to all children A second referendum on whether the UK should leave the European Union
Consultative exercises These can be set up when governing bodies want to assess the likely reaction to their proposed policies	These provide an important way of engaging with the public on issues that directly affect them. Since it is a consultative exercise, what the public says is not binding and the effectiveness of the exercise will depend on how representative the survey is	Communities which will be affected have been consulted over the expansion of Heathrow and the HS2 rail link
Open primaries A small number of constituencies have opted to select parliamentary candidates through open primaries, in which the public directly decide whom the candidate should be	Open primaries provide people with direct influence over whom the candidates for political office will be. This is a traditional part of democracy in the USA, enabling people from outside party politics, such as Donald Trump, to be elected. Whether or not this is a positive development divides opinion	The independent MP Sarah Wollaston became the Conservative candidate for Totnes in 2009 when she won an open primary
Election of the leadership of political parties All the main political parties now allow their membership to decide whom the leader of their party will be. This is a significant power since it may determine whom the prime minister will be	Supporters argue that this makes the leadership accountable to the whole party. This is an especially powerful argument in the Labour Party, which sees itself both as a political party and a popular movement. Critics respond that it gives too much influence to activists, who are often more radical than the electorate	In 2015, Jeremy Corbyn was elected leader of the Labour Party with 59.5% of the vote of party members. He was re-elected in 2016 with the support of 61.8% of party members
Recall of MPs Act 2015 Allows constituents to force a by-election	If an MP has been imprisoned, suspended from the House by the Committee of Standards or convicted of making false expenses claims then a petition by 10% of his or her constituents can trigger a by-election	In 2018 Ian Paisley Junior just survived a recall petition. He had been suspended from the House of Commons for not declaring two family holidays paid for by the Sri Lankan government. However, only 9.4% of his constituents signed the petition

Public trust in MPs

When Neil Kinnock became an MP, his father told him, 'Remember, Neil, MP stands not just for Member of Parliament, but also for Man of Principle.' Unfortunately, over the years a number of MPs have not lived up to these high standards. In 2009, MPs collectively were held up to contempt and ridicule over claims that they were overclaiming on their expenses. A former Labour cabinet member, Stephen Byers, was also secretly filmed telling a lobbying firm that he was 'like a cab for hire'. The way in which the media have focused on these cases has meant that public trust in MPs is low. In 2016, for example, Ipsos MORI recorded that the least trusted profession in the UK was politician, with just 21% of the population believing that politicians could be relied on to tell the truth.

Although the expenses scandal was in 2009, public trust in MPs remains low

Table 1.2 The turnout in British general elections, 1964–2017

General election date	Turnout (%)
1964	77.1
1966	75.8
1970	72
February 1974	78.8
October 1974	72.8
1979	76
1983	72.7
1987	75.3
1992	77.7
1997	71.4
2001	59.4
2005	61.3
2010	65.2
2015	66.1
2017	68.7

Supporters of direct democracy argue that it engages the public and makes politicians more responsive to what people really think. This therefore creates a closer connection between the public and political decision making. Critics of direct democracy respond that the general public are not always sufficiently well informed to make specific political decisions and that direct democracy gives too much influence to political activists, who can be more extreme in their political views than the average voter. The way in which the 2016 EU referendum created a conflict between the wishes of a majority of the public and those of parliament also suggests that direct democracy can have a destabilising impact on the political process.

From Table 1.2 it is clear that the numbers voting in general elections are, on average, lower than they have been. However, it would be misleading to suggest that this proves there is a **participation crisis**. Some general elections *do* inspire very high levels of turnout, such as the following.

- **1964** Harold Wilson's dynamic campaign aimed at ending '13 wasted years' of Conservative rule
- **February 1974** The 'Who Governs Britain?' crisis general election called by Edward Heath
- **1979** Margaret Thatcher challenging James Callaghan in the wake of the 'Winter of Discontent'
- **1992** John Major's soap box campaign against Labour's Neil Kinnock

Generally, though, turnout has been between about 70% and 75%. Voting dramatically decreased in 2001 when Tony Blair seemed assured of an easy victory and William Hague's leadership of the Conservative Party failed to generate much popular enthusiasm. However, voting steadily increased in the next four general elections.

If one compares the 1983 and 2017 general elections, when in each case radical socialist alternatives were being offered to a Conservative government, we can see that voting has declined by 4%. This is concerning, but it would be premature to call this a participation 'crisis'. Interestingly, there was an increase of 7.6% in voting in the two referendums on the UK's membership of the EEC/EU (Table 1.3).

Key term

Participation crisis A point at which the public has become disengaged from politics and voting levels have fallen so low that the legitimacy of elected governments can be questioned.

Table 1.3 Turnout in the 1975 and 2016 EEC/EU referendums

Referendum	Turnout (%)
1975 EEC referendum	64.6
2016 EU referendum	72.2

The turnout in national elections in the UK is significantly higher than that in US presidential elections. However, it is much less than in a number of other European democracies where voting is not compulsory, which suggests that politicians should not be complacent about voter participation (Table 1.4).

Table 1.4 Turnout in selected national elections

Election	Turnout (%)
2017 Dutch general election	81.9
2017 German federal election	76.2
2016 Second-round French presidential election	74.5
2017 British general election	68.7
2016 Spanish general election	66.5
2016 US presidential election	55.7

The membership of political parties (Table 1.5) is significantly lower than it was in the 1950s. However, this does not necessarily indicate a participation crisis, since floating voters are increasingly unlikely to fully identify with one party and therefore have little motivation to join one. The Labour Party actually increased its membership from 190,000 in 2014 to 552,000 in 2018. This has been due to the introduction of 'one member, one vote' by Ed Miliband and grassroots enthusiasm for the radical alternative offered by Jeremy Corbyn. The surge in party membership has also been helped by the rise of Momentum, a vibrant socialist movement whose members must also be members of the Labour Party.

Table 1.5 The membership of political parties in the UK, 2018

Party	Membership
Labour	552,000
Conservative	124,000
Liberal Democrat	101,000
Scottish National Party	118,000

Labour Party membership has dramatically increased under Jeremy Corbyn, suggesting that when the public is provided with a radical choice they can still choose to engage with politics

Membership of pressure groups remains high and the success of websites such as 38 Degrees shows how the public may now be choosing to participate in politics in different ways.

How convincing are proposals for the reform of UK democracy?

Although it would be premature to claim that the UK is suffering from a **democratic deficit** and a participation crisis, there are a number of ways in which it is claimed that politicians could be made more responsive to the public. These could encourage greater accountability and so lead to an increase in participation. All are controversial, however.

> ## Key term
>
> **Democratic deficit** When a democracy is not operating effectively because there is a lack of accountability among political bodies and not all citizens can claim equal influence over political decision making.

Further devolution

In order to encourage greater democratic participation, it has been suggested that more power should be devolved from Westminster, thereby giving people greater self-determination. The Scottish Parliament, the National Assembly for Wales and elected mayors show how decision making can be brought closer to the public.

However, turnout in elections for devolved assemblies is significantly lower than for the Westminster Parliament and has declined since they were established (Table 1.6).

Table 1.6 Turnout in assembly elections

Scottish Parliament	National Assembly for Wales	Northern Ireland Assembly
1999: 59.1%	1999: 46%	1998: 69.8%
2016: 55.6%	2016: 45.3%	2016: 54.9%

This suggests that providing another layer of government is not *that* effective a way of engaging the public. There is also little enthusiasm for an English Parliament and when, in 2004, the voters in the North East were given the opportunity to have their own assembly 78% of them voted against it. Elected mayors have similarly not succeeded in generating much enthusiasm from the electorate (Table 1. 7), and police and crime commissioners were elected in 2016 with, on average, a turnout of just 25%.

Creating further levels of government is, therefore, not an instant solution to encouraging greater voter participation. Indeed, some political commentators have even suggested that giving the public more voting opportunities can discourage participation by leading to democratic overload.

Table 1.7 Turnout in mayoral elections

Election	Turnout (%)
2016 London mayoral election	45.3
2017 Bristol mayoral election	29.7
2017 West Midlands mayoral election	26.7
2017 Manchester mayoral election	29.9

Power of recall

The Recall of MPs Act was passed in 2015, enabling voters to trigger a by-election if 10% of them sign a petition. However, the circumstances when this can happen — an MP would need to have been sentenced to prison or suspended from the House of Commons for at least 21 days — are quite extreme. Broadening the criteria on which power of recall could be demanded would give constituents considerably more power. In the USA, for example, 18 states have recall provisions and in 2003 the governor of California, Gray Davis, was recalled over his failure to balance the budget.

Critics of further reform point out that it would make MPs more like delegates, so limiting the Burkean principle of freedom of conscience.

House of Lords reform

The House of Lords is unelected and unaccountable. Its membership is selected through political patronage. When he left office in 2016, David Cameron appointed 13 peers from among his political allies. Making the Lords an elected chamber would mean that Westminster was fully democratically accountable. However, there is the danger that an elected Lords could become a rival to the Commons, thereby, potentially, creating constitutional gridlock. Given concerns about low electoral turnout, exchanging the expertise of the Lords for another elected chamber is controversial.

Digital democracy

Supporters of digital democracy argue that facilitating voting and encouraging electronic political discussion will encourage greater political engagement and higher turnout. Digital democracy is, however, problematic.

- Voting on your mobile phone at your convenience would be likely to encourage more voting, but it would also mean that voting was no longer carried out in secret and so the possibility of voter manipulation would increase.
- Allegations of cyber-interference in Western elections by Russia indicates that electronic voting is more open to fraud than traditional voting.
- The way in which politicians use Twitter can encourage populist sloganeering.
- The standard of debate on social media indicates that activists can use this as much to bully as to engage in considered debate.

Electronic petitions

The introduction of electronic petitions has contributed to UK democracy by giving the public more control over what is discussed in Parliament. E-petitions have led to important debates on the possible legalisation of cannabis and the extension of the meningitis B vaccination to all children. Making e-petitions more powerful, by making them automatically trigger a parliamentary vote, would make Parliament more accountable. However, this could bog Westminster down in unconstitutional and impractical debates.

- Some of the most popular e-petitions have called for banning Donald Trump from the UK, which is not even Parliament's right since the responsibility lies with the home secretary.
- In 2019, an e-petition calling on the UK to stay in the European Union gathered over 6 million signatures, making it the most popular e-petition since the process was introduced. This clearly demonstrated to Parliament how controversial the issue of Brexit remained.

In 2016, 4.1 million people signed an e-petition demanding a second EU referendum and in 2019 an e-petition calling for Brexit to be cancelled gained 6.1 million signatures. Both demonstrate how integral e-petitions have become to the ways in which UK democracy operates

Reform of the Westminster electoral system

The replacement of first-past-the-post (FPTP) with a proportional form of election would create a fairer connection between the votes a party receives and its representation in Parliament. Critics of FPTP claim that it discourages voting because it limits voter choice by over-rewarding the Labour and Conservative parties, ensuring that it is much more difficult for other parties to gain representation. By making votes count more, critics argue, 'wasted votes' and 'safe seats' would be eliminated and voters would have a greater incentive to vote.

- However, in 2011, 67.9% of the electorate voted in favour of *not* replacing FPTP with the additional vote (AV).
- Proportional representation would make coalition governments more likely, making it more difficult for political parties to fulfil their manifesto commitments.
- The claim that FPTP is no longer appropriate because the UK is becoming a multiparty democracy is challenged by the fact that in the 2017 general election the highest percentage of the electorate voted Conservative or Labour than at any general election since 1970 (Tables 1.8 and 1.9).

Table 1.8 General election results, 2015 and 2017

Party	2015 general election (%)	2017 general election (%)
Conservative	36.9	42.4
Labour	30.4	40
Liberal Democrat	7.9	7.4
Scottish National Party	4.7	3
UKIP	12.6	1.8

Table 1.9 Combined Labour and Conservative share of the vote, 2015 and 2017

	Conservative and Labour combined share of the vote (%)	Conservative and Labour combined share of seats in the House of Commons (%)
2015 general election	67.3	86
2017 general election	82.4	89

Widening the franchise and debates over suffrage

Historical perspective

The development of Britain as a democratic nation state can be traced far back into history. Some historians have claimed that the Anglo-Saxon witan, an assembly of aristocrats who advised their ruler, represented a rudimentary form of democracy. More usually, the origins of democracy are associated with King John (1199–1216) being forced by his barons to sign Magna Carta (1215). Although the barons were mostly interested in protecting their own powers from the King, they also inserted a number of clauses to protect the rights of *all* freeborn Englishmen from the arbitrary rule of the monarch. The three most iconic clauses in Magna Carta state that:

> 'In future no official shall place a man on trial upon his own unsupported statement, without producing credible witnesses to the truth of it'

(Paragraph 38)

> 'No free man shall be seized or imprisoned, or stripped of his rights or possessions, or outlawed or exiled, or deprived of his standing in any other way, nor will we proceed with force against him, or send others to do so, except by the lawful judgement of his equals or by the law of the land'

(Paragraph 39)

> 'To no one will we sell, to no one deny or delay right or justice'

(Paragraph 40)

Throughout the medieval period, Parliament developed the right to grant money to the Crown since it represented the nation's property holders, and Henry VIII (1509–47) used Parliament to provide his takeover of the English Church with legal validity.

However, it was not until the early seventeenth century that Parliament began to assert the right to protect the liberties of the English people against the increasingly autocratic Stuart monarchy. Edward Coke, the chief justice of James I (1603–25), laid down in the Petition of Right (1628) the principle that the Crown is not above the law, and during the English Civil War Parliament asserted its right to be the primary lawmaker against Charles I's belief in the 'divine right' of the King to rule alone. The violence and instability of the Civil War unleashed new democratic movements such as the Levellers, who stated that all men had the same right to elect their government, but such radical ideas were stamped out during the Protectorate of Oliver Cromwell (1653–58), who proved almost as unwilling as Charles I to work with Parliament.

Although Charles II was offered the Crown at the Restoration in 1660, his brother James II was suspected of trying to rule as a tyrant. In the Glorious Revolution of 1688, James was overthrown and Parliament invited William of Orange to become King of England. William III's agreement that he would cooperate with Parliament on the Bill of Rights (1689) is a key moment in the development of Britain's constitutional monarchy.

Key term

Franchise/Suffrage The right to vote. Throughout the nineteenth and twentieth centuries the franchise has gradually been extended so that now the UK has universal adult suffrage. This means that all men and women aged 18 and over have the right to vote in public elections unless they are mentally incapacitated, in prison or a member of the House of Lords.

However, Parliament remained the preserve of the rich and powerful, and it was only in the nineteenth century that a number of acts of parliamentary reform gradually opened up the **franchise**. The Reform Act 1832 enfranchised some members of the middle classes, while the Reform Acts 1867 and 1884 increasingly opened the vote to working-class householders in the boroughs and then the counties.

In focus

Early attempts at democracy

The inscription on a wall of St Mary's Church, the site of the Putney Debates

In 1647, during the Putney Debates, members of the New Model Army unsuccessfully put forward to Cromwell and the military command the case for manhood suffrage. Socialist politicians, in particular, regard these debates as a dramatic moment in the struggle for democracy.

'For really I think that the poorest he that is in England hath a life to live, as the greatest he; and therefore truly, Sir, I think it clear, that every Man that is to live under a Government ought first by his own Consent to put himself under that Government; and I do think that the poorest man in England is not at all bound in a strict sense to that Government that he hath not had a voice to put Himself under.'

Colonel Thomas Rainsborough
during the Putney debates, 1647

Stretch and challenge

In 1838, working-class movements across the country drew up a People's Charter demanding manhood suffrage. Some Chartists tried to provoke a national uprising in 1839 at Newport, in which 20 people were killed, and Chartism remained a worrying popular movement for the government until 1848. By the 1860s it had been succeeded by new radical groups such as the Reform League. Fear of the dangerous consequences of inaction was a major cause of nineteenth-century parliamentary reform.

Research popular movements for political change in the UK from the nineteenth century to today. How often have they achieved their objectives and to what extent do you think they have contributed towards British democracy?

In 1872, the Ballot Act made voting in secret compulsory, so protecting citizens' right to vote in any way they wished.

The Reform Acts of the nineteenth century had all been based on the principle that the right to vote depended on the ownership of property. Property owners had a stake in society and had thus 'earned' the right to vote. The principle of 'one person, one vote' was alien to these reformers and by the beginning of the twentieth century 40% of adult males could still not vote, as well as, of course, all women.

The suffragists, suffragettes and the Great War

Political reform has often been driven by popular pressure. In 1897 the National Union of Women's Suffrage Societies (NUWSS), also known as the suffragists, was established by Millicent Fawcett to lobby Parliament to extend the franchise to women. The efforts of the suffragists were not sufficient, though, for more militant women and in 1903 Emmeline Pankhurst established the Women's Social and Political Union (WSPU) under the slogan 'deeds not words'. The suffragettes, as they were known, engaged in much more disruptive and even violent action in order to draw attention to their cause. When imprisoned, some went on hunger strike and in 1913 one suffragette, Emily Davison, was killed when she tried to run in front of the King's horse in the Derby.

Although suffragette protests gained huge publicity, it was women's contribution to the Great War that was the immediate cause of some women gaining the franchise in 1918

At the outbreak of the First World War in 1914, the suffragettes suspended their activities. However, the sacrifices that both men and women made during the war changed the political atmosphere. Women did vital war work in factories, and 80,000 served as non-combatants in the armed forces. In 1916 male conscription was introduced and almost 750,000 men were killed in combat. In 1918, in recognition of this, the Representation of the People Act allowed all men aged 21 and over, and women aged 30 and over who fulfilled a property qualification, to vote in general elections. In 1928, a further Representation of the People Act extended the vote to men and women aged 21 and over, establishing universal suffrage.

Representation of the People Act 1969

In 1969 a third Representation of the People Act lowered the voting age from 21 to 18. This was in recognition of the way in which the opportunities and responsibilities of young people had developed. The extension of university education, greater sexual freedom provided by easier access to contraception, and the increased earning potential of young people all combined to make lowering the voting age to 18 relatively uncontroversial.

Contemporary debates on the further extension of the franchise

Although the UK elects the Westminster Parliament on the principle of universal suffrage, there are still some sections of society who are denied the vote. Some of these are uncontroversial, such as members of the House of Lords who, as members of the legislature, already have their interests represented. Those declared mentally incapacitated are also barred from voting.

Votes at 16

Support for lowering the voting age to 16 has significantly increased in recent years. The Votes at 16 Coalition was established in 2003 to bring together groups such as the National Union of Students and the British Youth Council to campaign for a lowering of the voting age. In the 2014 Scottish independence referendum, 16- and 17-year-olds were allowed to vote. In 2015, the Scottish Parliament then legislated to give 16- and 17-year-olds the vote in Scottish local and parliamentary elections. The Votes at 16 Coalition hopes that the rapidity of these developments will create an unstoppable momentum for change.

Votes at 16 arranges high-profile demonstrations such as the one above, placing them within the long history of those agitating for political reform

The tactics of the Votes at 16 Coalition are twofold:

1 In order to generate mass enthusiasm for reducing the voting age to 16 it is important to win as much positive publicity as possible. Given how much of their ideas young people now derive from social media, Votes at 16 has established a major presence on the internet through the imaginative use of Twitter, Facebook and #vote16. It also encourages school and college debates and its memorable slogan, 'Engage, empower, inspire', provides the movement with a coherent and powerful message of change.

2 The support of MPs is vital in winning parliamentary support for changes to the law. In 2017 and 2018, a Private Member's Bill to reduce the voting age to 16 failed in the House of Commons and so success depends on creating as much cross-party support as possible for change. The Votes at 16 website names all MPs and Lords who support its campaign in order to maintain high-profile momentum for change.

Debate

Should the age of voting be reduced to 16?

Yes

- At age 16, young people can exercise significant responsibility: they can engage in sexual relations, marry, pay tax and join the armed services, so it is irrational that they are regarded as not mature enough to vote.
- The introduction of citizenship lessons into the school curriculum means that young people are now better informed about current affairs and so can make educated political decisions.
- National Citizenship Service is encouraging young people to have a stake in society, which would be further entrenched by voting at 16.
- Most local education authorities (LEAs) hold elections for the UK Youth Parliament, which has been praised by politicians such as the speaker of the House of Commons, John Bercow, for its positive campaigning. In 2017, 955,000 young people aged 11–18 determined what the Youth Parliament would debate as part of the Make Your Mark campaign.
- The 2014 Scottish independence referendum demonstrated huge engagement by 16- and 17-year-olds. 75% of this age group voted and, according to Ruth Davidson, leader of the Scottish Conservatives, 'the democratic effect turned out to be entirely positive'.
- Since 16- and 17-year-olds can vote for the Scottish Parliament it is illogical that they cannot vote for the Westminster Parliament.
- Providing young people with the opportunity to vote earlier will encourage them to take their duties as citizens earlier; especially as these habits can be encouraged while they are still at school.

No

- Some of these claims are misleading. Parental permission is needed to join the army at 16 or 17 and, apart from in Scotland, parental permission is required to marry before 18.
- Young people are not regarded as responsible enough to be able to buy alcohol or cigarettes themselves until the age of 18, so it is disingenuous to claim that 16- and 17-year-olds are capable of exercising all adult responsibilities.
- Most 16- and 17-year-olds in the UK are still in full- or part-time education. They are therefore less likely to pay tax and so do not have the same 'stake' in society as those who are older.
- Voting turnout among 18- to 24-year-olds is lower than other age groups, so allowing 16- and 17-year-olds to vote could actually compound the problem of youth apathy. The Isle of Man has enfranchised 16- and 17-year-olds: the turnout in this age group has declined from 55.3% in 2006 to 46.2% in 2016.
- 16- and 17-year-olds have few adult life experiences on which to base their voting decisions. They are thus more likely to be manipulated into voting in a certain way by social media peer pressure.
- Although Scotland has reduced the voting age to 16, this does not mean it is the right thing to do. Very few countries allow voting at 16, so the UK is within the political mainstream by granting the franchise at 18.
- The Labour Party under Jeremy Corbyn has been so closely identifying itself with the youth vote that reducing the voting age to 16 now would be an act of political partisanship.

Prisoner voting

In the UK, prisoners are not entitled to vote. This is because they are regarded as having renounced the rights of citizenship for the duration of the time that they are incarcerated.

- The question of whether prisoners are being denied a fundamental human right gained some publicity in two cases brought by John Hirst against the British government. Hirst's claim, that although he was in prison he should be allowed to vote, was dismissed by the courts in 2001, but in 2004 the European Court of Human Rights declared that the blanket ban on prisoner voting was contrary to Article 3 of the First Protocol of the European Convention on Human Rights, which 'provides for the right to elections performed by secret ballot, that are also free and that occur at regular intervals'. The British government was, therefore, in defiance of the European Convention on Human Rights.
- Pressure groups such as Liberty and the Howard League for Penal Reform support prisoner voting. However, unlike voting at 16, there has been very little public pressure for a change in this law. When the issue was debated in the House of Commons in 2011 it also gained cross-party condemnation, with 234 MPs against prisoner voting and only 22 in favour.

The Hirst cases raised significant issues concerning the extent to which the British government can act in defiance of the European Court of Human Rights. Since 2004 this had been a constant source of friction with the court and so, in 2017, the government offered to allow the small numbers of prisoners on day release the right to vote in order to resolve the problem. This concession generated little public interest, which suggests that prisoner voting is unlikely to produce the sort of public enthusiasm necessary for the law to be changed.

Compulsory voting

Although voting is optional in the UK, 22 nation states have introduced some form of compulsory voting in order to ensure that voting rates are as high as possible.

- The first country to introduce compulsory voting was Belgium, in 1892. It is an accepted part of Belgian life and in the 2014 federal election turnout was 89%.
- Australia has required citizens to vote in national elections since 1924. In its 2016 federal elections, 91% of those eligible voted.

Supporters of compulsory voting argue that because it ensures that such a high percentage of the electorate engage in the democratic process, the outcome has enhanced legitimacy. In recent years voting has significantly decreased in many liberal democracies, so compulsory voting would address this pressing problem.

However, compulsory voting is also highly controversial since critics claim that it gives the state too much power to coerce its citizens. Some radical campaigners such as Russell Brand have even argued that the decision not to engage at any level with the voting process can be a powerful political statement of disapproval. In the 2017 French presidential runoff, for example, there was no socialist candidate, so the decision not to vote for either Emmanuel Macron or Marine Le Pen could have been an informed political decision.

Is compulsory voting necessary to increase voter turnout?

In 2015, David Winnick (Labour MP for Walsall North, 1979–2017) raised the need for compulsory voting in the House of Commons. According to Winnick, 'If we want our democracy to flourish, common sense dictates we should do what we can to get far more people to participate in elections than do at the moment.' The fact that just 44% of 18- to 24-year-olds voted in the 2010 general election seemed to provide a powerful case for reform. However, according to Ipsos MORI, in the 2017 general election, 64% of this age group voted. This is the highest turnout by young people since 1992 and suggests that if politicians provide radical enough alternatives people will be more likely to vote. However, this large increase is still at least 25% below national voting in Australia.

Should voting be made compulsory?

Yes

- Voting is a civic responsibility like jury service. If citizens are not required to fulfil the duties of citizenship then the principles of civic society are undermined.
- Political apathy is a problem in many liberal democracies. In the 2016 US presidential election, just 58% of the electorate voted. In the 2017 UK general election, turnout was 68.7% (in 1992 it had been 77.7%). Limited numbers of people voting can undermine the legitimacy of the result, especially if turnout falls beneath 50%.
- Those not voting are often from ethnic minorities, the poorest in society (D and E voters) and young people. This means that political decision making often favours older and wealthier voters. Compulsory voting would mean that politicians would have to be responsive to all shades of political opinion.
- Compulsory voting does not have to force people to make a choice. In Australia, for example, the voter can spoil their ballot if none of the candidates appeals to them. They must, though, attend a polling station.
- The legal requirement to vote can have an important educative role. If people have to vote, they will be more likely to inform themselves of the political choices open to them.

No

- The public has the right to choose whether or not to vote in an election. It is up to politicians to mobilise public enthusiasm by providing reasons to vote. Compulsory voting could, therefore, remove the incentive for politicians to engage with the public.
- The votes of politically disengaged citizens will carry less weight than the votes of those who take their civic responsibilities seriously. Random voting could undermine the legitimacy of the result.
- Compulsory voting is based on coercion, which is alien to the British political system. Voting is a civic right but it is not a duty such as the payment of taxes.
- According to liberal political theory, the extension of the power of the state over the individual ought to be resisted since it limits our right to act in the way we wish. The British state has traditionally intervened as little as possible in the liberties of its citizens. Nation Citizenship Service, for example, is voluntary.
- Not voting can be a positive decision to register dissatisfaction with the candidates or the process. Only 25% of the electorate voted for police commissioners in 2016, which may indicate that voters regard the post as insignificant. Forcing the public to vote for a choice they disagree with is an infringement of civic rights.

Pressure groups and other influences

The UK is a **pluralist democracy**, which means that political power and influence is widely distributed so that different groups can compete to influence the government in their favour. Therefore, as well as voting in elections, members of the public can participate in the political process by supporting pressure groups or becoming involved in online campaigns. Think-tanks, corporations, lobbying firms, professional bodies and religious movements can also put pressure on the government to act in a certain way, although they are not referred to as pressure groups.

Table 1.10 explains how pressure groups are categorised.

Table 1.10 Pressure group categorisation

Sectional/interest	Cause/promotional
Sectional pressure groups represent the interests of a particular group within society. For example, the Muslim Council of Britain specifically represents the interests of British Muslims and the National Union of Students (NUS) represents the interests of students. They therefore lobby government on behalf of these clearly defined social groups	Cause pressure groups promote a particular issue. Pressure groups such as Friends of the Earth and Greenpeace are cause pressure groups because their members are united by their shared interest in protecting the environment. Members of cause pressure groups can be drawn from across society
Insider	**Outsider**
An insider pressure group has privileged access to government decision making. The British Medical Association (BMA) represents doctors and so possesses specialist information which governments will wish to consult. The Howard League for Penal Reform is an impartial organisation which can supply the Home Office with important information concerning prison, policing and youth crime	Since outsider pressure groups do not possess access to political decision making, they need to achieve influence in other ways. This means that they have to gain the attention of the government by winning public support. The Gurkha Justice Campaign, for example, was an outsider group which achieved residency rights for Gurkhas who had served in the British military because of its high-profile campaign

Key term

Pluralist democracy In a pluralist democracy political influence is dispersed among a wide variety of elected and non-elected bodies, ensuring that there is fair and transparent competition between rival groups for influence.

How do pressure groups achieve success?

Insider status

Insider status can be vital in the success of a pressure group. If political decision makers decide that it is to their advantage to consult with a pressure group then the group's influence will be guaranteed. As a result of their specialist knowledge, groups such as the British Medical Association (BMA), the Confederation of British Industry (CBI) or the National Farmers' Union (NFU) will all be called on by governments. Since the administrations of Tony Blair (1997–2007) all governments have been keen to advance the rights of gay people and so, it could be argued, groups such as the LGBT Foundation are also achieving insider status as vital sources of information.

Whether a pressure group can claim insider status can also be determined by political circumstances. In the 1970s, trade unions in Britain were so powerful that Jack Jones, the general secretary of the Transport and General Workers' Union (TGWU) was often called 'the most powerful man in Britain' for the influence he wielded with prime ministers. Given the growing significance of environmental issues, contemporary politicians have become more likely to consult environmental groups for specialist information. Friends of the Earth, for example, is now regularly contacted by the Scottish government on its environmental strategy. Michael Gove, as environment secretary, has also been congratulated by the chief executive of Friends of the Earth, Craig Bennett, 'for listening to the experts' when deciding to ban bee-harming pesticides.

The smoking debate

Action on Smoking and Health (ASH) was established in 1971 and its campaigns have achieved significant successes such as banning smoking in enclosed workplaces, pubs and restaurants, removing displays of tobacco from the point of sale and introducing plain packaging with explicit images of the harm that tobacco can do. These successes have been facilitated by research by the BMA on the risks of smoking and the support of Parliament for stronger restrictions. In 2014, for example, a ban on smoking in cars containing children passed the House of Commons by 376 to 107 votes.

ASH has been considerably more successful than its main adversary FOREST (Freedom Organisation for the Right to Enjoy Smoking). What factors best explain the comparative success of ASH and the more limited success of FOREST?

- The political bias of the government will also determine which pressure groups are able to claim insider status. Trade unions which contribute funds to the Labour Party will be more likely to exercise insider influence during a left-wing Labour government than during a Conservative government. Conversely, pressure groups which represent big business, such as the Institute of Directors, or ones which emphasise small government, such as the Taxpayers' Alliance, will be more influential during a Conservative administration.
- Wealthy pressure groups which seek to access decision-making bodies will run offices as close as possible to those points of access. Brussels and Strasbourg are therefore full of the offices of powerful lobbying firms which seek to influence EU policy, while in the UK powerful pressure groups will often base their offices in key points of access such as London. The independent decision-making power of the London mayor also means that London is a prime point of contact for pressure groups. The devolution of decision-making powers has further meant that groups such as Friends of the Earth and ASH run offices in Edinburgh and Cardiff. The CBI has offices in leading commercial centres across the UK.

Other means of achieving success

- Other pressure groups seek to influence government by taking their case directly to the public. This can be because, like Greenpeace, they are reluctant to engage too closely with government since this could compromise their principles. It can also be because they do not have the necessary funds to directly lobby decision makers and so focus on mobilising support through real and online campaigns and high profile media events. Celebrity endorsement can provide an especially effective way of generating positive media coverage.

- Social media provide new opportunities for pressure groups to engage with the public. Groups such as Amnesty International, Oxfam and Friends of the Earth all appreciate the importance of having a considerable internet influence since this is where people increasingly access and spread ideas. Facebook, Twitter and hashtag campaigns provide a valuable way of keeping the public informed of a pressure group's activities and its website will usually provide opportunities to donate and sign online petitions, as well as up-to-date information on getting involved in national and regional campaigns.

- This way of mobilising public support has been called a 'clickocracy', since the internet enables the public to engage with pressure groups purely online. 38 Degrees, for example, was established in 2009 and provides a forum for its members to quickly choose and launch their own online campaigns. Its slogan is 'People, Power, Change' and it can focus public attention on local issues such as protecting green spaces or on national campaigns such as encouraging the government to introduce a drinks-container recycling scheme.

- Some pressure groups can choose to engage in civil disobedience in order to achieve their aims. This is a risky strategy, but it can create immediate publicity and even give rise to so much disruption that the government decides to back down or negotiate. In 1867, riots in Hyde Park demanding the extension of the franchise quickened the pace of parliamentary reform. In March 1990, the extraordinary violence of the poll tax riots in Trafalgar Square further undermined an already weakened Margaret Thatcher, contributing to her resignation in November and to her successor, John Major, swiftly abandoning the tax.

- Trade unions can, of course, deploy industrial action. The National Union of Rail, Maritime and Transport Workers (RMT) has, for example, called strikes in order to try to stop the introduction of driver-only operated trains which would jeopardise the jobs of conductors, as well as, the union argues, jeopardising passenger safety.

In focus

The UK and the Syrian refugee crisis

The way in which David Cameron's government changed its attitude towards taking Syrian refugees demonstrates how a combination of factors can lead to a sudden change in policy. Until 2015, government policy was not to admit significant numbers of Syrian refugees to the UK. Criticisms by pressure groups such as Amnesty International had done little to change government policy. However, when shocking images were broadcast across the media of a Syrian boy, Aylan Kurdi, drowned on a beach in Greece, this provoked outrage from MPs, religious leaders and council leaders eager for the government to provide a moral lead. As many as 4 million people signed an e-petition and the *Daily Mail* demanded action. So great was the pressure that Cameron announced the UK would take 20,000 refugees by 2020, stating 'Britain is a moral nation and we will fulfil our moral responsibilities.'

Examples of successful pressure group campaigns

Table 1.11 outlines the aims and campaign strategies of two UK pressure groups.

Table 1.11 Two successful pressure groups

Pressure group	Aims	Campaign strategy
The Gurkha Justice Campaign Gurkhas are Nepalese soldiers who have traditionally served in the British military. Only those who retired after 1997 were granted the right to live in Britain	The group was set up to extend the right to live in Britain to all retired Gurkhas	Popular actress Joanna Lumley provided the Gurkha Justice Campaign with powerful celebrity endorsement. Her leadership of a large delegation to present a petition signed by 250,000 to Downing Street generated highly positive media coverage and her constant pressure on the government of Gordon Brown created so much negative publicity for it that the government decided to grant equal rights of residency to all Gurkhas
Hillsborough Family Support Group/ Hillsborough Justice Campaign On 15 April 1989, 96 Liverpool fans lost their lives at Hillsborough football stadium when they were crushed to death in the overcrowded and fenced in stadium. It was the worst sporting disaster in British history. The families and survivors claimed that the tragedy had been caused by appalling crowd control by the South Yorkshire Police, but police blamed hooliganism and a verdict of 'accidental death' was recorded	The group was set up to demand a reopening of the case and to achieve justice	Pressure groups representing the families of the Hillsborough victims endorsed an e-petition, which gathered 130,000 signatures, demanding full disclosure of all relevant documents to an independent enquiry. The success of the e-petition created intense media interest, and government support of full disclosure contributed to a new inquest in which a verdict of 'unlawful killing' was reached, opening the way for the prosecution of those in charge of policing on the day Enthusiastic sporting and celebrity support for the families of the victims, as well as lobbying by Liverpool MPs and campaigning by the *Daily Mirror*, all contributed to the reopening of the case

The way in which Joanna Lumley was so closely associated with the Gurkha Justice Campaign shows how celebrity endorsement can be useful in helping a pressure group to secure its objectives

Why are some pressure groups more successful than others?

A useful mnemonic to understand the factors that contribute to pressure group success is RIPE:

- **R**esources
- **I**deological compatibility with the government
- **P**opularity
- **E**xpertise

A pressure group does not have to fulfil *all* of these criteria in order to be successful. However, it will have to demonstrate at least one of them if it is to achieve its objectives. For example, Migration Watch UK cultivated links with Theresa May's government because of their shared commitment to reducing immigration into the UK. The expertise of the BMA provides it with guaranteed insider status under any government, while the considerable resources of the Conservative and Labour Friends of Israel enable them to cultivate influence at Westminster. The popularity of the Gurkha Justice Campaign persuaded the Brown government to provide all Gurkhas with the automatic right of British residency.

However, if a pressure group does not fulfil *any* of these criteria then it is unlikely to be successful. Plane Stupid has opposed a third runway at Heathrow, and Stop HS2 opposes the new high-speed rail link between Birmingham and London, but both have failed because they have not been able to persuade the government that they have a powerful enough case or significant enough support. Table 1.12 illustrates why some campaigns are more successful than others.

Table 1.12 A successful and an unsuccessful pressure group campaign

Successful	Unsuccessful
Surfers Against Sewage Drinks-container recycling • Surfers Against Sewage's 'Message in a Bottle' campaign demonstrated growing public outrage at the way in which disposable plastic containers are blighting coastlines. Every day only half the 38.5 million plastic drinks containers bought are recycled • Other environmental groups such as the Council for the Preservation of Rural England also campaigned on the issue, as well as 38 Degrees, and in 2018 the government announced that it was going to introduce a deposit return scheme for all plastic, metal and glass containers • The success of this campaign was helped by the way in which the facts were objectively presented together with viable solutions to the problem. The cause was further helped by the way in which Prime Minister Theresa May and Environment Secretary Michael Gove were keen to move forward on the proposals and the way in which countries like Germany had shown success was possible	**Stop the War Coalition** War against Iraq 2003 • In 2003 the Stop the War Coalition organised the biggest demonstration in British history, in which as many as a million people marched through London to protest against Tony Blair's support for an American-led invasion of Iraq • Although the march was peaceful, was addressed by prominent anti-war activists such as Tony Benn, and made a powerful impact on the public, it did not change the policy of the government • The lack of success of this campaign was because Blair was committed to the overthrow of Saddam Hussein and, when Parliament voted on the justification for war, the Conservatives supported the government, giving Blair a substantial majority of 179. Therefore, Blair was safely able to ignore the protests and preparations for war continued

In focus

The Occupy Movement

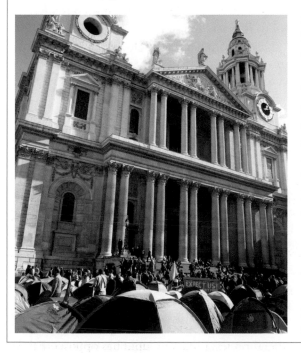

Sometimes it can be difficult to decide if a pressure group has achieved its goals. From 2011 to 2012, global sit-ins by the Occupy Movement were organised to protest against the inequalities of global capitalism. In London a major sit-in was organised outside St Paul's Cathedral, which gained a significant amount of media attention. However, the protestors' aims were criticised for being incoherent, ideologically extreme and unachievable, and protesters were moved on as a result of a court order. Supporters of Occupy have pointed out that its radical political programme created a powerful new critique of capitalism which has had an especially strong resonance with young people. This may have contributed to the 9.5% swing to Labour in the 2017 general election on its 'For the Many, Not the Few' manifesto.

From October 2011 to February 2012, an Occupy camp outside St Paul's Cathedral focused public attention on inequality in the UK

Case studies of pressure groups

Fathers4Justice

Fathers4Justice campaigns to change the law on behalf of fathers' rights in cases of divorce or separation. Founded in 2001 by Matt O'Connor, the organisation initially gained public attention through a number of high-profile stunts, often with a superhero theme. One member of Fathers4Justice scaled Buckingham Palace dressed as Batman and another climbed a crane dressed as Spiderman. In 2004, in its most high-profile exploit, two activists hurled purple flour bombs at Tony Blair during Prime Minister's Question Time.

Seeking to maintain the momentum of the campaign, later stunts became ever more outlandish and self-defeating, such as a naked protest in Marks and Spencer on Oxford Street, while one campaigner, Tim Haries, was given a 6-month jail sentence for spray painting 'Help' across a portrait of the Queen in Westminster Abbey — a shocking piece of vandalism. During his sentencing, Haries' supporters hurled abuse at the judge and Haries subsequently went on hunger strike.

These failures have meant that in recent years Fathers4Justice has focused more on engaging with the public through the positive use of social media and is trying to distance itself from violence and civil disobedience. Its website still has a 'superhero' theme, but the emphasis is now more on the personal and social importance of a child having a meaningful relationship with his or her father and on generating popular support through emotive images and news reports. It also focuses on providing advice on how to contact your MP and opportunities to sign online petitions and join online forums.

The group is still dogged by negative publicity. However, the way it is now attempting to campaign in a more sophisticated fashion demonstrates how the tactics, and possibly the fortunes, of a pressure group can change.

Liberty

Liberty exposes discrimination, highlights infringements of the Human Rights Act and fights attempts by the government to restrict civil liberties. It does this in a wide variety of contrasting ways, which gives it considerable influence in the political process. Like many outsider pressure groups, it engages directly with the public through online campaigns. The director of Liberty, Martha Spurrier, also regularly puts forward the case for civil liberties through the media.

However, Liberty also appreciates the importance of influencing decision makers. Therefore, like professional lobbying companies, Liberty works closely with like-minded MPs such as David Davis and Tom Watson, and Lords such as the former director of Liberty, Baroness Chakrabarti, to encourage cross-party support for civil liberties. It has encouraged MPs to oppose the introduction of identity cards and has campaigned to ensure that Brexit does not jeopardise any of the civil liberties enshrined in EU law. To this end it lobbied MPs in all parties to demand a 'People's Clause' in the repeal legislation underwriting all existing EU human rights legislation.

Liberty publishes reports and engages in consultative exercises in order to ensure that Parliament is fully informed about how legislation does or could affect civil liberties. These range from issues such as extradition, asylum and immigration to the right to take industrial action.

In addition, Liberty has launched judicial reviews in cases where it believes that the government has exceeded its powers and acted ultra vires (beyond its authority).

For example, in 2017, Liberty challenged the legality of the Investigatory Powers Act on the grounds that the European Court of Justice had declared its 'general and indiscriminate' approach to private individuals' data to be illegal.

Two other pressure groups

- **Human Rights Watch** monitors the extent to which governments around the world protect the human rights of their citizens. Its regular reports highlight abuses and its British office has focused on issues such as the extent to which government counterterrorism strategies conflict with civil liberties. Following the Grenfell Tower disaster, Human Rights Watch has also investigated the extent to which the civil liberties of those living in social housing have been compromised by inadequate safety standards.
- **Stonewall** is committed to 'acceptance without exception'. It focuses on lobbying Parliament to legislate to protect the rights of LGBT people and has helped to change the law so that gay people can serve in the military, as well as giving couples the same adoption rights as heterosexual couples. It is currently campaigning to ensure that laws ending discrimination of LGBT people are observed and that prejudice and intolerance are challenged.

Stonewall deploys a variety of methods to achieve its objectives: lobbying MPs and generating publicity through rallies, demonstrations and high-profile media events

Lobbyists, think-tanks, business and professional bodies

In addition to pressure groups, a number of other bodies seek to influence government. **Think-tanks** such as the right-wing Adam Smith Institute or the more left-wing Fabian Society work with the Conservative and Labour parties to develop policy. When he was leader of the Conservative Party, Iain Duncan Smith established the Centre for Social Justice in order to better advise his party on the problems faced by the most disadvantaged in society. Chatham House provides highly respected impartial analysis of global politics, which politicians consult, and Demos is a cross-party think-tank specialising in the development of social policy. Such groups contribute useful insights and ideas to the political debate and so play an important part in the political process.

More controversially, major corporations and **lobbying** firms seek to influence decision making by cultivating links with politicians. Powerful companies, such as

> **Key terms**
>
> **Think-tank** A group established in order to generate ideas. Political parties work closely with like-minded think-tanks in order to develop policy.
> **Lobbyist** Lobbyists represent the interests of a particular group or cause and seek to influence politicians in its favour.

Apple and Google, as well as the major interests such as banking, digital and media will all try to be as closely involved in the decision-making process as possible in order to advance their interests. In the same way, the Church of England, academic bodies such as universities, and the Office of Fair Trading (which protects the rights of consumers) will also seek to influence political debates which influence them.

Lobbying firms can also represent the interests of groups in society who are prepared to pay for their services. They have thus been criticised for enabling powerful interests to try to buy influence. In 2015, two former foreign secretaries, Jack Straw (Labour) and Malcolm Rifkind (Conservative), were secretly filmed offering to 'provide access for cash' to key political and diplomatic figures for a fake firm.

- Malcolm Rifkind told the fake company that he could provide 'useful access' to every UK ambassador in the world. He added that his usual fee per day was 'somewhere in the region of £5,000 to £8,000'.
- Jack Straw told the company that he operated 'under the radar' and had previously used his contacts and influence to change EU rules for a company which paid him a salary of £60,000 a year.

Lobbyists respond that they are necessary to democracy because they broaden the debate so that all sides are heard. Two examples may illustrate this:

- The Raptor Alliance, which represents pigeon fanciers, is a tiny organisation whose members argue that the Royal Society for the Protection of Birds has been so successful in protecting birds of prey that they are now killing off racing pigeons. Unable to gain public recognition, lobbyists have made their cause known in Parliament by encouraging the establishment of an All Party Parliamentary Group for Pigeon Racing and in 2018 organising the first Lords versus Commons pigeon race since 1928. After the event, the chairman of the group, Chris Davies MP, commented, 'The race was a huge success and we are delighted with the support already shown throughout Parliament.' During Prime Minister's Question Time, Theresa May even agreed to sponsor a bird.
- Lobbyists have also put forward the interests of gin drinkers. Since the Gin Act 1751, small-scale production had been forbidden in order to stop bootlegging. However, in 2008 lobbyists succeeded in having the Gin Act repealed and now boutique gin is becoming one of the UK's most enterprising new exports.

Rights in context

Human rights and civil liberties

As human beings we all possess the same universal human rights, such as the rights to life and liberty. However, it is not always possible to enforce human rights and so they are often referred to as a form of 'soft law'. Civil liberties are the rights that individuals possess in relation to the nation state and so are legally enforceable and represent 'hard law'.

Since the UK does not possess a codified constitution, the rights of British citizens have been determined and protected through constitutionally significant landmark events such as the signing of Magna Carta. In addition to this, judges have defined the nature of our civil rights in important common law cases, so setting a judicial precedent to be followed in future disputes. Specific Acts of Parliament have further developed the rights that UK citizens enjoy.

Therefore, the rights of the British public have traditionally been negative or residual rights. This means everything that is not expressly forbidden belongs to our rights, which means that they are not set out in one single document. Instead they derive from our rights as citizens and key constitutional and legal events such as the following:

- **Magna Carta 1215** This provides the foundation for British civil liberties by stating that the law should be impartial and that no freeman should be convicted of a crime unless he had been fairly tried.
- **Bill of Rights 1689** By accepting the Bill of Rights, William III agreed to govern with the consent of Parliament, thereby establishing the principle of a constitutional monarchy bound by the law.
- *Somerset v Stewart* **(1772)** Lord Mansfield stated that slavery within the UK was illegal since it had not been legislated for by an Act of Parliament and was unsupported by the common law. In his judgement he stated, 'It is so odious, that nothing can be suffered to support it, but positive law.' This far-reaching decision set the precedent for the elimination of slavery within Britain.
- *Entick v Carrington* **(1765)** In a case involving trespass, Lord Camden lay down the principle that government officials 'cannot exercise public power unless such exercise of it is authorised by some specific rule of law'. In short, the government can only act according to the law protecting the rights of citizens from despotic rule.
- **Representation of the People Act 1928** This established the principle of universal suffrage in the United Kingdom.

Anti-slavery seal by prominent abolitionist Josiah Wedgewood, 1787

The development of a rights-based culture since 1997

Since Tony Blair became prime minister in 1997, the approach towards British civil liberties has changed. Rather than primarily relying on common law decisions and constitutional conventions, there has been a greater emphasis on the codification of what the positive rights of British citizens are.

Human Rights Act 1998

Although the UK was fully involved in the drafting of the European Convention on Human Rights in 1950, it did not accept that the convention would be binding on British courts. However, in 1998 the Human Rights Act was passed, which incorporates the European Convention fully into British law. The Act entered into force in 2000. As a result, British citizens now possess a clear statement of their civil liberties, which is enforceable in British courts. Before the Human Rights Act came into force, UK civil liberties were grounded in specific statute and case law. This meant that the rights that British citizens could claim were not widely known or understood. The Human Rights Act is significant because it clearly establishes the positive rights that we are all equally eligible for, such as the right to life and the right to a fair hearing.

Freedom of Information Act 2000

This established a 'right of access' to information held by public bodies so long as it does not compromise national security. The Act, which came into force in 2005, provides the public with the opportunity to know more about the way in which public bodies such as the National Health Service operate, as well as being able to access information held about them. The MPs' expenses scandal in 2009 was exposed because journalists were able to demand access to this information because of the Freedom of Information Act.

Equality Act 2010

Although a number of Acts of Parliament have legislated in favour of equality, such as various Race Relations Acts and the Equal Pay Act 1970, it was not until the Equality Act 2010 that an Act of Parliament established equality before the law for all citizens. This Act consolidates existing legislation and states that in public life discrimination is illegal in nine recognised areas:

- Age
- Disability
- Gender reassignment
- Race
- Religion or belief
- Sex
- Sexual orientation
- Marriage and civil partnership
- Pregnancy and maternity

Civic responsibility and the restriction of civil liberties

As well as having rights, citizens also have responsibilities that can be enforced by law, such as paying taxes and serving on a jury. Other responsibilities are not legally enforceable, such as voting, but they are expected of citizens.

Terrorist attacks, such as the 2005 London bombings which killed 52 people, have been used to justify the restrictions of civil liberties in order to protect the collective rights of society

The public does not have the right to act in whatever way it wants and freedoms can be restricted if these are likely to endanger the collective good of society. This is most likely to happen when there is a threat to national security. Following the terrorist attacks on New York and Washington DC, in 2001 and London in 2005, a number of Acts of Parliament were passed to protect the public from further attack.

- The Anti-Terrorism Crime and Security Act 2001 gave the government the legal power to imprison foreign terrorist suspects indefinitely without trial.
- In 2005, the Serious Organised Crime and Police Act limited the right of protest outside Parliament and created a new offence of inciting religious hatred.
- The Terrorism Act 2006 extended the time terrorist suspects can be held without charge to 28 days and made 'glorifying terrorism' a crime.
- In 2016, Parliament passed the Investigatory Powers Act, which authorises the retention of personal electronic data and its access for law enforcement.

In focus

Identity cards

Post-9/11 concerns about terrorism convinced the Blair and Brown governments of the need to introduce identity cards. In 2006, the Identity Cards Act was passed, which created identity cards and a national identity register which would store information about citizens. Alan Johnson, Brown's home secretary, demonstrated his support for the scheme by allowing his photograph to appear on an official specimen identity card to publicise the initiative. But in 2010, the coalition announced that the Act would be repealed in order 'to reverse the substantial erosion of civil liberties under the Labour government and roll back state intrusion'.

The balance between collective and individual rights

There is naturally going to be tension between our rights as individuals and the need to protect the wellbeing of the community, and governments need to balance the needs of both. Especially since the terrorist attacks on New York, the Iraq War and the rise of extremist terrorist groups, a number of civil liberties groups, such as Liberty, have argued that the balance has shifted too far away from the individual to the government and that this has led to the erosion of civil liberties.

The Human Rights Act is important in providing people with greater protection by defining the positive rights to which they are entitled.

- In 2004, senior judges declared that the way in which *foreign* terrorist suspects were being held by the government was 'discriminatory' according to the European Convention on Human Rights. In the face of this legal challenge, the government released the detainees from Belmarsh Prison.
- Attempts by the government to deport Abu Qatada, an Islamist preacher who had entered the UK illegally, to face trial in Jordan were stopped for 8 years on the grounds that the evidence used against him might have been acquired through torture. This would have breached Articles 3 (freedom from torture) and 6 (right to a fair trial) of the Human Rights Act and Abu Qatada was not deported until 2014 when Jordan pledged that no such evidence would be used against him.
- In 2010, the Supreme Court declared that homosexuality could provide grounds for claiming asylum in the UK if the claimants were from countries where homosexuality was persecuted. Dismissing the argument that they could hide their sexuality, Lord Hope stated, 'To compel a homosexual person to pretend that his sexuality does not exist or suppress the behaviour by which to manifest itself is to deny his fundamental right to be who he is.'

How effectively are civil liberties protected in the UK?

Although the Human Rights Act has provided judges with significantly more power in protecting civil liberties, it is no different from any other Act of Parliament in that it can be suspended or repealed. It does not therefore represent a higher law, as would be the case if the UK had a codified constitution. As a result of this, Parliament remains the supreme law-making body and so can still enact legislation even if it conflicts with the European Convention on Human Rights on the principle that no parliament can bind its successor. For example, even though the Blair government accepted the release of the Belmarsh detainees following the High Court ruling, it quickly introduced legislation to keep them under close surveillance through control orders.

This means that judges have less power to protect the civil liberties of UK citizens than is the case for judges in liberal democracies which have a codified constitution and where judges can strike down legislation if it conflicts with the law of the constitution.

Therefore, civil liberties pressure groups are especially important in alerting the public to any erosion of their civil liberties, as well as raising awareness of the ways in which minorities may still be discriminated against. Liberty, for example, campaigns to increase public consciousness of ways in which the civil liberties of minorities might be challenged through, for example, the powers of surveillance contained in the Investigatory Powers Act.

It is important to appreciate that, as the representative of the public interest, Parliament itself can protect civil liberties.

- In 2005, the Blair government's attempt to increase the time that a terrorist suspect could be imprisoned to 90 days was defeated in the House of Commons by 323 votes to 290, with 49 Labour MPs voting against their government.
- In 2008, the Brown government's attempts to increase the number of days' detention to 42 days from 28 days was defeated in the House of Lords and the proposed legislation was subsequently shelved.
- The coalition in 2010 committed itself to the repeal of identity cards as an infringement of civil liberties.

However, the ferocity of terrorist attacks on big cities in the UK has also been used to justify the restriction of civil liberties. When he was mayor of London, Boris Johnson admitted, 'I'm not particularly interested in this civil liberties stuff when it comes to these people's emails and mobile phone conversations. If they are a threat to our society then I want them properly listened to.'

The argument that governments are undermining civil liberties is rejected by many politicians, who argue that some restrictions are necessary in order to protect the *collective* good of the nation. Also, the fact that only a few Acts, such as the introduction of identity cards, have generated much public outcry suggests the public may well accept that their collective good does require limitations to be put on their individual liberties.

A British Bill of Rights?

A number of Conservative politicians have signalled that they favour replacing the Human Rights Act with a British Bill of Rights. This is because the European Convention has been accused by Philip Hollobone MP of favouring 'the rights of bad people over the rights of good people'. A British Bill of Rights could also provide a clearer statement of the responsibilities which the individual owes to society as well as explicitly recognising parliamentary sovereignty over what constitutes a right.

Summary

By the end of this chapter you should be able to answer the following questions:
- → What is representative democracy and what are its advantages and disadvantages?
- → What is direct democracy and what are its advantages and disadvantages?
- → What evidence is there to suggest the UK is suffering from a participation crisis?
- → What are the key milestones in the development of British democracy?
- → In what ways could UK democracy be further improved?
- → In what ways might the franchise be further extended and why is this controversial?
- → How convincing is the case for compulsory voting?
- → How do pressure groups and other collective organisations access influence?
- → Why are some pressure groups/collective organisations more successful than others?
- → What is the significance of the distinction between individual and collective rights?
- → How effectively are human rights protected in the UK?

Source-based question

Direct democracy mechanisms, such as referendums, e-petitions, consultative exercises and recall votes, reinforce the fundamental principle of democratic self-governance, provide a check on the tendency of representatives to become disconnected from their electors, and can enhance the popular legitimacy underpinning key political decisions.

The days of representatives seated in national capitals making policy in relative isolation has been supplanted by a world where citizens can instantly communicate with elected leaders through online petitions, blogs, tweets and Facebook posts. Social media empowers citizens to organise and advocate. Results such as 'Brexit' are important examples of citizens expressing their viewpoints, and indeed educating their representatives on their visions regarding their countries' futures.

However, direct democracy is riddled with problems that obstruct the goals it seeks to achieve. When direct democracy is used, turnout is generally low and so calls into question the legitimacy of the result. There is also the danger that special interest groups or lobbyists, who specialise in certain issue areas and who have a broader political agenda, will spend lavishly on direct democracy initiatives. A lack of public understanding and the spread of misinformation can also have devastating consequences, not just in terms of the political result, but also for societal relations.

Source: adapted from an article published by the International Institute of Democracy and Electoral Assistance, 21 November 2016

Using the source, evaluate the view that direct democracy should be used more frequently in the UK.

In your response you must:
- *compare and contrast the different opinions in the source*
- *examine and debate these views in a balanced way*
- *analyse and evaluate only the information presented in the source* (30)

Evaluative questions

1 Evaluate the extent to which the UK is suffering from a participation crisis. *You must consider this view and the alternative to this view in a balanced way.* (30)
2 Evaluate the extent to which UK democracy is in urgent need of reform. *You must consider this view and the alternative to this view in a balanced way.* (30)
3 Evaluate the extent to which the tactics they deploy are the most important reason for the success or failure of pressure groups and other collective organisations. *You must consider this view and the alternative to this view in a balanced way.* (30)

2 Political parties

The functions and features of political parties

Features

The United Kingdom is a representative democracy, which means that we vote for MPs to make decisions on our behalf. They are then made accountable to us in regular general elections. In theory, it would be possible for voters to elect independent politicians with their own individual manifesto commitments, but since the English Civil War British politics has gradually developed according to a party system. In elections we generally select from a choice of political parties which represent the spectrum of political ideas from left to right (Table 2.1).

The UK's system of parliamentary democracy provides a wide range of political parties for the electorate to choose from

Table 2.1 The political spectrum in the UK

Left-wing political ideas	Right-wing political ideas
• Those on the left of British politics have a positive view of the state and a collectivist view of society	• The **right wing** of British politics focuses more on the importance of giving the individual as much control over their own life as possible
• They believe that the government should reduce inequality and encourage social cohesion by providing an extensive welfare state	• Right-wing politicians reject left-wing attempts to encourage greater equality and believe that the free market operates best when there is as little government interference as possible
• The wealthier in society should pay a higher share of the cost of this through redistributive taxation. The government should also play a major role in the economy through the nationalisation of key industries	• Governments should aim to keep taxation as low as possible and trade union influence needs to be limited in order to encourage the smooth operation of the market
• **Left-wing** politicians have generally enjoyed close relations with the trade union movement since the unions also represent the economic interests of the working class	• Companies operate most efficiently when there is competition, so nationalised firms are best privatised
• Socially, the left embraces multiculturalism. It is also socially libertarian and so supports giving alternative lifestyles equal status with more traditional ones	• Although economically libertarian, the right wing is socially conservative and so emphasises the importance of a shared national identity and encourages traditional lifestyles

---

Key terms

Right wing Right-wing political beliefs derive from liberal and conservative ideology. These include a liberal focus on the importance of limiting excessive government, keeping taxation low and protecting individual liberty. The right also emphasises conservative values such as law and order and the importance of national sovereignty and strong defence.

Left wing The left wing emphasises the importance of creating a fair and equal society through positive state intervention. This includes higher taxes on the wealthier, extensive welfare provision and greater state influence in the economy. The left wing is also socially progressive and favours an internationalist approach to global problems.

A political party comprises members who share a similar political ideology. This does not mean that they will agree about *every* political opinion, but their basic political ideology will be similar. For example, Conservatives are united in their belief that taxes should be kept as low as possible, because it is the individual's money rather than the state's, while members of the Labour Party all believe in the importance of the government encouraging social justice.

Within a party, different factions will emphasise different elements of the ideology. One-nation Conservatives, for example, are likely to be less economically libertarian and more socially libertarian than the New Right, moving them quite close to New Labour. The left of the Labour Party, represented by Jeremy Corbyn and Momentum, strongly favours redistributive taxation and nationalisation, which New Labour distanced itself from during the leadership of Tony Blair (1994–2007).

Between the main political parties, there will be varying degrees of agreement (Table 2.2).

Table 2.2 Consensus vs adversary politics

Consensus politics	Adversary politics
• Consensus politics means that there are many philosophical and policy similarities between the main political parties. The opposition may therefore be able to support some government policies • In the 1950s the shared commitment of the Labour chancellor of the exchequer, Hugh Gaitskell, and the Conservative chancellor of the exchequer, R.A. Butler, to full employment and a mixed economy led to the invention of the term 'Butskellism' • Tony Blair's embracing of traditionally Conservative principles such as the free market and low taxation made his time as Labour leader (1994–2007) a period of 'Butskellite' consensus	• When politics is adversary this means that the main parties are divided by fundamental philosophical and policy differences • The opposition will routinely oppose the policies of the government since they are so ideologically and practically opposed to them • The early 1980s provides a good example of adversary politics since the socialism of Labour leader Michael Foot (1980–83) was so fundamentally at odds with the free-market reforms of Margaret Thatcher. The leadership of Jeremy Corbyn has again made British politics adversary since, as a committed socialist, he is radically opposed to the policies of the Conservative Party

Functions

Selecting candidates

A key function of a political party is to select candidates to fight local, regional, mayoral and general elections. In order to contest a general election, applicants have to be a member of the party and then go through a national selection process to become an approved candidate. If they pass this, they can apply to a constituency party which will then choose the individual it considers to have the best chance of increasing the party's share of the vote.

Once a candidate wins a seat, he or she can claim to have an electoral **mandate** to represent that seat in the House of Commons. However, the local party can also deselect them from fighting the next general election if their views are too opposed to those of local activists. This gives the local party significant influence over whom the MP is likely to be, especially if it is a safe seat.

- In 2015 Tim Yeo, the Conservative MP for South Suffolk, did not fight the seat, having been denied the nomination by his local party for his pro–European Union views.
- Momentum is particularly in favour of using the prospect of deselection to ensure that Labour MPs at Westminster represent the interests of local party activists, who have generally been more favourable towards Jeremy Corbyn than the parliamentary party.

Providing the personnel of government

By providing candidates for election to public office, political parties contribute the personnel for government. This can be in a local, devolved or national executive. For example, in 2010 the membership of the parliamentary Conservative and Liberal Democrat parties provided the membership of the coalition government.

Electing a leader

The members of a political party also play an important role in the election of the party leader. In the Conservative Party, for example, the parliamentary party will agree on two MPs, whose names will then go forward to party members to decide between. In 2005, the party membership voted decisively for David Cameron over David

> **Key term**
>
> **Mandate** If a political party wins a general election it can claim the legitimate right, or mandate, from the electorate to try to implement its manifesto promises.

Davis. However, in 2016 the influence of party members was sidelined when Andrea Leadsom withdrew from the contest, ensuring that Theresa May became Conservative leader, and prime minister, unopposed.

Under Ed Miliband, the Labour Party also adopted one member, one vote. The current rules state that if an MP is able to secure the backing of 10% of the parliamentary Labour Party then their name will go forward to the party membership to vote on. In 2015, Jeremy Corbyn, who had only just scraped enough nominations from the parliamentary party as the 'token' left-winger, conclusively defeated his rivals when the party membership voted (Table 2.3).

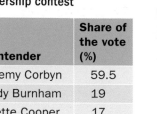

Table 2.3 2015 Labour leadership contest

Contender	Share of the vote (%)
Jeremy Corbyn	59.5
Andy Burnham	19
Yvette Cooper	17
Liz Kendall	4.5

Policy formulation (the manifesto)

Political parties determine the policy commitments that will be put in the party manifesto. In the Labour Party, a National Policy Forum consults with party members over the development of policy. Before the 2017 general election the National Policy Forum and the elected National Executive Council worked closely with the leadership and senior members of the parliamentary party to 'aggregate' a manifesto that fairly represented the political opinions of the Labour movement.

> At all levels the party will ensure that members, elected representatives, affiliated organisations and, where practicable, the wider community are able to participate in the process of policy consideration and formulation.
>
> Clause V, Labour Party Rule Book (2018)

The Conservative Party also encourages consultation and discussion among its membership, although the manifesto is more likely to be drawn up by senior members of the party. In 2017, Theresa May's joint chiefs of staff, Fiona Hill and Nick Timothy, played the key role in drawing up the party's controversial manifesto. More decentralised parties such as the Liberal Democrats and the Green Party give the party membership the final decision over what appears in the party manifesto. Table 2.4 summarises the path from manifesto to mandate.

Table 2.4 Manifesto and mandate

Manifesto	Mandate
• A political party will publish its manifesto during a general election campaign. This sets out what it will seek to achieve if it is able to form a government • If a party wins a parliamentary majority in a general election it can then claim the legitimacy to carry out its manifesto commitments • These manifesto promises will form the core of the Queen's Speech, which will be delivered by the monarch at the beginning of the new parliament	• If a political party has won a general election it can be said to have a mandate to govern the country. This means that it has the authority to try to enact its manifesto commitments. Having won a majority in the 2015 general election, David Cameron's government could legitimately seek to fulfil its manifesto commitments such as offering a referendum on the UK's membership of the EU • If no party has achieved a parliamentary majority then a coalition (2010) or a minority government (2017) will be established. In these circumstances the principle of the mandate does not operate smoothly since the government cannot rely on an unequivocal electoral mandate from the public • A government can also claim a 'doctor's mandate', which means that it can propose measures not included in its manifesto in response to changing political circumstances

Campaigning

The way in which political parties campaign during elections plays a key part in the democratic process. Party activists will deliver leaflets, canvass voters on the doorstep and arrange political hustings so that voters understand the choice between the candidates. The grassroots Labour movement, Momentum, in particular has appreciated the importance of getting its political message across through social media.

Political parties are increasingly using the internet to engage with voters between, as well as during, elections. They also invigorate democracy by campaigning on local issues.

Representation

Political parties also play a key representative function. This means that they ensure the opinions of everyone in society are given a mouthpiece. In the 2017 general election, 82.4% of those who voted felt that their political opinions were represented by the Conservative Party (42.4%) or the Labour Party (40%). There is also the opportunity to vote for a range of other political parties, ensuring that even the most radical political opinion has the chance of being heard. The way in which the Scottish Parliament, the Assembly for Wales, the London Assembly and the Northern Ireland Assembly are elected using proportional representation gives minority and nationalist parties a greater opportunity to achieve representative influence.

Debate

Do political parties help or hinder representative democracy?

Help

- Representative democracy could not function without political parties. If politicians simply represented their own individual views then it would be very difficult to establish a government since its members would not be united by one political ideology.
- Political parties develop/aggregate coherent political programmes through discussion. The way in which political parties then issue manifestos enables voters across the whole country to make the same rational choices about whom they will vote for.
- Without political parties, voting in elections would be more complicated because voters would no longer be able to associate a candidate with a particular party manifesto.
- Opposition political parties can hold a government accountable for its policies in a way that would be impossible for individual representatives.
- Political parties are vital in organising parliamentary business. If they did not exist representative bodies would become confused and disorganised.
- Political parties select suitable candidates to stand for election and to select their leader from. Without such mechanisms a representative democracy would not be able to function properly.

Hinder

- Political parties reduce voter choice by requiring voters to associate themselves with the manifesto of a political party even though that manifesto may not fully represent their political views. For example, in 2017 you might have voted Labour because you fully supported the party's policies on taxation and yet regarded their policies on nationalisation and defence much less favourably. A political party often only partially succeeds in being able to represent one's political views, so limiting the individual's choice.
- The freedom of action of MPs is reduced because, although they could argue that they have their own personal mandate, the party whips will expect them to support the programme of their political party. As Benjamin Disraeli once said, 'Damn your principles. Stick to your party.' Political parties can be criticised for suffocating genuine debate in a representative democracy by monopolising political decision making.
- The 'spirit of faction' which political parties create has also been criticised for creating a confrontational and negative approach to government, in which political parties too often focus on their differences and fail to work together for the good of the nation. This can create a dangerously polarised society. The gulf between the Democrats and Republicans in the USA today, which has even led to temporary shutdowns in government, illustrates how negative party animosities can be. On the other hand, the way in which the Conservative–Liberal Democrat coalition was able to last the full term of a parliament demonstrates what can be achieved when party differences are kept to a minimum.
- Political parties give excessive power to the party membership. By selecting the party leader, the membership effectively determines the choice of who will be prime minister in the general election.
- The way in which the main political parties benefit from disproportionate funding also ensures that they are able to monopolise political decision making.

Mobilising consent for government

Without the existence of political parties it would be difficult to form effective governments in representative democracies with large populations. Individual politicians, each with their own unique political opinions, would find it virtually impossible to quickly and effectively establish governments. The way in which parties combine elected politicians into recognisable groups creates favourable conditions for the establishment and survival of government.

How parties are funded

The way in which political parties are funded is highly controversial. In some countries the state itself funds its political parties. However, in the UK political parties have always relied on a great deal of private funding, although they do have some limited access to public funds to subsidise policy development and parliamentary scrutiny.

- Policy development grants allocate £2 million to all the main parties so that they can employ policy advisers.
- Short money, named after the Labour politician Ted Short, is allocated to the opposition parties for their work in the House of Commons on the basis of the number of seats they have (Table 2.5). The leader of the opposition is also funded almost £800,000 for the running of his or her office.
- Cranborne money, named after the Conservative peer Lord Cranborne, subsidises the work of scrutiny carried out by the opposition parties in the House of Lords.

Table 2.5 Short money allocation, 9 June 2017 to 31 March 2018

Opposition party	Short money
Labour Party	£6,222,106
Scottish National Party	£638,506
Liberal Democrats	£509,044
Green Party	£89,137
UKIP	£0 (in 2017 Douglas Carswell lost Clacton. This left UKIP without representation in the House of Commons and, consequently, no Short money)

These subsidies do not, however, cover campaigning and election expenses. For these, a political party will depend on the subscriptions of its party members, as well as individual donations from benefactors (Table 2.6). The Conservative Party has traditionally received large-scale donations from big business people who see a Conservative government as being in their best interests.

Critics of this way of funding political parties point out that it provides the Conservatives with a massive advantage over the other political parties. The Labour Party's close relationship with the trade union movement has meant that Labour gains significant financial support from the trade unions, leaving the Liberal Democrats and other minority parties severely disadvantaged.

The Trade Union Act 2016 has changed the laws regarding trade union membership so that a new union member must now 'opt in' if they wish their membership fee to go to the Labour Party. This suggests that the Conservative Party's advantage over Labour in terms of funding will further increase.

Table 2.6 Donations to political parties in the second quarter 2017, leading to the general election

Party	Donations
Conservative Party	£25 million
Labour Party	£10 million
Liberal Democrats	£5 million
UKIP	£170,000
Green Party	£150,000

The Political Parties, Elections and Referendum Act 2000 has provided the funding of political parties with greater transparency and fairness.

- An independent electoral commission was established to monitor how much money political parties spent on campaigns.
- The amount a political party can spend in a constituency during an election is limited to £30,000.
- Political parties must declare large-scale donations (over £5,000) to the electoral commission and must not accept donations from non-UK citizens.

Should the state fund political parties?

In 2007, the Phillips Report stated that there was now a strong case for political parties to be funded through taxation. The case had become particularly pressing because of the vast discrepancy in the amount of money different parties received, as well as a number of financial scandals which were undermining public faith in parliamentary democracy. In particular, controversy over 'cash for honours' (2006–07) gave force to the Phillips Report as it seemed to suggest that certain Labour donors had been elevated to the House of Lords by Tony Blair.

Further progress to reduce the discrepancy in party funding has been difficult because the Conservative Party, as the largest recipient of donations, is unwilling to lose that advantage over its rivals. Critics of state funding of political parties make the following arguments:

- In a free democracy, people should be able to financially support whatever cause they wish. Political parties are no different to charities or pressure groups.
- If the state was to fund political parties, as occurs in some countries, it would be controversial deciding how much each political party could claim.
- Philosophically, state funding might also suggest that political parties were somehow *servants* of the state — so, potentially, limiting their political independence.
- The funding of extremist political parties, such as the British National Party, which excludes certain groups from equal status in British society, would be extremely contentious.

Established political parties

The Conservative Party

Traditional conservatism

The origins of the Conservative Party can be traced back to the English Civil War. During this conflict, the royalist supporters of the monarchy and the established Church of England resisted giving Parliament greater influence and providing the public with greater freedom of worship. Those who supported the Crown were siding with the status quo against what they feared would become violent and destabilising change and innovation. This conservative fear of the violence that sudden change can unleash is reflected in Thomas Hobbes' masterpiece *Leviathan* (1651). Hobbes had lived through the Civil War and so knew at first hand what can happen when government breaks down. His view of human nature was also very negative and so he argued that if there was not a strong government to control its citizens and resist dangerous innovation then anarchy would ensue, ensuring that property would not be safe, violence would be endemic and 'the life of man solitary, poor, nasty, brutish and short'.

The dynamic new egalitarian principles of the French Revolution (1789) based on 'liberty, fraternity, equality' were in total conflict with traditional conservative principles. Horrified by the enthusiasm which some Britons were showing for the sudden upheaval of the French Revolution, the Whig MP Edmund Burke (1729–97) wrote *Reflections on the Revolution in France* (1790), in which he warned about the consequences of too rapid change. For Burke, the idealistic desire to change the world was dangerous and the safest course was always to approach problems pragmatically, respecting authority and tradition.

Closely associated with the monarchy and the Church of England, traditional conservatism was acutely aware of humanity's potential for 'mob rule' and so sought to resist radical changes to the British constitution. By the nineteenth century, Toryism was the party of:

- property
- pragmatism
- authoritarianism
- tradition
- stability

One-nation conservatism

According to Benjamin Disraeli (1804–81), traditional conservatism lacked the necessary dynamic to inspire men. In his 'Young England' novels, especially *Sybil* (1845), Disraeli, as an ambitious Tory backbencher, argued that conservatism must unite the nation in a collective reverence for those traditions and institutions that had made Britain great. Disraeli saw society as an organic body in which stability and prosperity could only be achieved through all classes and individuals appreciating their debt to each other and not putting their selfish interests above the wellbeing of the community. In the most famous passage in *Sybil*, Disraeli warns against Britain becoming 'Two Nations': 'THE RICH AND THE POOR', which is why the inclusive conservatism he argued for became known as '**one-nation** conservatism'.

> ### Key term
>
> **One nation** According to one-nation principles the Conservative Party should protect and advance the interests of the whole nation. One-nation conservatism is thus more inclusive and progressive than traditional conservatism.

Disraeli stated that the purpose of the Conservative Party was the 'elevation of the condition of the people'

Disraeli's 'one nation' sentiments were important in enabling the Conservatives to reach out to working-class support. As prime minister, he supported quite extensive social reforms and the Conservative Party went on to become the most successful modern vote-winning political party, and the main governing party for most of the twentieth century, by closely associating itself with one-nation principles.

Conservative prime ministers such as Stanley Baldwin (1923–24, 1924–29 and 1935–37), Harold Macmillan (1957–63) and Edward Heath (1970–74) all saw themselves within this tradition and sought to govern in the interests of the whole nation, accepting that the government had a major role to play in creating a more prosperous and inclusive society.

The New Right

By the 1970s, the effectiveness of one-nation conservatism was being undermined by large-scale industrial unrest. The way in which trade unions were increasingly demanding higher wages for their workers challenged the principle that a Conservative government could successfully unite all sections of society. When, in 1975, Margaret Thatcher defeated Edward Heath for the leadership of the Conservative Party, what became known as 'New Right principles' became the new dominant creed within Thatcherite conservatism.

Margaret Thatcher, Conservative prime minister 1979–90, with US president Ronald Reagan (1981–89). Their shared commitment to economic liberalism and strong national defence made them natural political allies

The New Right is an interesting combination of neo-liberalism and neo-conservatism. It is neo-liberal because, unlike one-nation conservatism, it is based on the principle that the economy best regulates itself with as little government intervention as possible: that businessmen and -women and entrepreneurs create wealth, rather than governments. This means that the role of government in the economy should be limited to making conditions as favourable as possible for the successful operation of the free market. This is what the classical economist Adam Smith (1723–90) referred to as the 'invisible hand of the market'. It should do this by:

- keeping taxation to a minimum in order to provide people with greater opportunities to take financial control of their lives
- reducing inflation and interest rates in order to encourage investment
- discouraging a 'dependency culture' based on too extensive a welfare state
- limiting the influence of trade unions since they disrupt the smooth operation of the free market by demanding excessive pay claims

However, the New Right is also influenced by neo-conservatism, which is more closely connected with the authoritarianism, fear of disorder and a sense of community associated with traditional conservatism. The New Right therefore sees a positive role for the state in encouraging social stability and security by:

- discouraging permissive and alternative lifestyles which threaten the traditional family unit as the basis for social harmony
- giving the government extensive powers to fight crime and disorder
- protecting the national interest by pursuing a strong defence policy
- emphasising the nation state as the ultimate source of the citizen's security (as a result of this the New Right is sceptical of regional organisations, such as the EU, which challenge the authority of the government)

Current Conservative ideas and policies

During the prime ministership of Margaret Thatcher (1979–90) a powerful criticism of the Conservative Party was that it had focused too much on free-market principles and allowed society to become divided. Indeed, in 2002, its authoritarianism and lack of commitment to social justice prompted Theresa May to admit that for many people the Conservatives had become the 'nasty party'. Conservative prime ministers such as John Major, David Cameron and Theresa May have tried to reposition the Conservatives as a more socially inclusive party. Modern conservatism combines elements of neo-liberalism and neo-conservatism, with a more tolerant attitude towards alternative lifestyles and a renewed focus on 'one-nation' inclusivity.

In focus

'Nice not nasty'

'As I said in the small hours of this morning, we will govern as a party of one nation, one United Kingdom. That means ensuring this recovery reaches all parts of our country, from north to south, from east to west.'

David Cameron, speaking after his general election victory, 8 May 2015

'The Conservatives are "a party not for the few, not even for the many, but for everyone who is willing to work hard and do their best".'

Theresa May, speaking at the Conservative Party conference, 3 October 2018

Neo-liberalism

- The Conservatives remain committed to low taxation as a way of maximising economic growth. In 2012, the chancellor of the exchequer, George Osborne, cut the top rate of taxation from 50p to 45p. In the 2017 general election, the Conservatives also pledged not to increase VAT, and by 2020 they aim to have cut corporation tax to 17%, making the UK one of the most competitive countries in the world to do business.
- In the 2017 general election, the Conservatives further demonstrated their commitment to reducing the burden of taxation by pledging to increase the threshold at which the top rate of taxation is paid to £50,000 by 2020, as well as increasing the personal tax allowance to £12,500.

- Since 2010 Conservative chancellors of the exchequer have pursued 'austerity' measures as a way of reducing the deficit, which had reached £100 billion when David Cameron took office, demonstrating the party's continued commitment to Thatcherite principles of 'good housekeeping'.

Neo-conservatism
- In its 2017 manifesto the Conservatives committed to cutting immigration to under 100,000 a year, demonstrating a neo-conservative emphasis on the importance of maintaining the nation state as a shared community.
- Theresa May committed her government to a strong national security policy. The Trident nuclear deterrent remains the cornerstone of Conservative defence policy.
- The way in which the Investigatory Powers Act 2016 expands the intelligence community's electronic surveillance powers demonstrated Theresa May's government's commitment to strong national defence, even though the Act has been labelled the 'snooper's charter' by civil liberties groups.
- The Conservative Party values constitutional traditions and so opposes further reform of the House of Lords as unnecessary.
- The Conservative emphasis on the central importance of the nation state has meant that euroscepticism has become increasingly influential within the party. During the 2016 referendum, 138 Conservative MPs signalled that they would vote to leave the EU compared to only ten Labour MPs.

One-nationism
- David Cameron's emphasis on a 'Big Society' had close similarities with Tony Blair's commitment to a 'Stakeholder Society'. The introduction by Cameron of a National Citizenship Qualification was a way of acknowledging the importance of our shared membership of society.
- Cameron used his authority as prime minister to commit the Conservative Party to supporting gay marriage, demonstrating the party's new commitment to tolerance and inclusivity.
- In 2016, the chancellor of the exchequer, George Osborne, introduced a national living wage which by 2020 should have risen to 60% of median earnings. This represents a significant intervention within the economy to protect the interests of the poorest in society.

'We do not believe in untrammelled free markets. We reject the cult of selfish individualism.'

Theresa May's foreword to the 2017 Conservative manifesto

- Theresa May surprised many free-market Conservatives by stating that one of her great political heroes is Joseph Chamberlain, a self-made businessman who was one of the great social reformers of the late nineteenth century. She has often referred to the positive role government can have in encouraging productivity, sharing wealth and protecting jobs. After the 2017 general election, for example, May established a new Department for Business, Energy and Industrial Strategy, which is designed to give the government an enhanced role in allocating funds in the most effective way to stimulate industrial growth.

Margaret Thatcher and Theresa May

Theresa May (Conservative prime minister 2016–19) always resisted comparisons between herself and Margaret Thatcher (Conservative prime minister 1979–90), remarking 'I think there can only ever be one Margaret Thatcher.'

Read the two passages below and explain the ways in which they suggest that Thatcher and May regard the relationship between the state and the individual differently.

'I think we've been through a period where too many people have been given to understand that if they have a problem, it's the government's job to cope with it. "I have a problem; I'll get a grant." "I'm homeless; the government must house me." They're casting their problems on society. And, you know, there is no such thing as society. There are individual men and women, and there are families. And no government can do anything except through people and people must look to themselves. It's our duty to look after ourselves and then also to look after our neighbour. People have got the entitlements too much in mind, without the obligations. There's no such thing as entitlement, unless someone has first met an obligation.'

Margaret Thatcher, in an interview with *Woman's Own*, 31 October 1987

'David Cameron has led a one-nation government and it is in that spirit that I plan to lead … That means fighting against the burning injustice that if you are born poor, you will die an average nine years earlier than others. If you're black, you're treated more harshly by the criminal justice system than if you are white. If you're a white working-class boy, you're less likely than anyone else in Britain to go to university. If you're at a state school, you're less likely to reach the top professions than if you were educated privately. If you are a woman, you will earn less than a man. If you suffer from a mental health problem, there's not enough help to hand.

If you're young you'll find it harder than ever before to own your own home … We will do everything we can to give you more control over your lives. When we take the big calls, we'll think not of the powerful but you.'

Theresa May's first speech as prime minister, 10 Downing Street, 13 July 2016

To what extent do you think that the Conservative Party today is more closely associated with the ideals expressed by Margaret Thatcher than those of Theresa May?

The Labour Party

Old Labour

The Labour Party was established in 1900 in order to represent the interests of the working class. Although its membership has included Marxists it has never been a Marxist party since it is not committed to the revolutionary overthrow of the capitalist free market. Instead, Labour has traditionally been a compromise between democratic socialism and social democracy. Democratic socialists, in the tradition of Beatrice Webb, believe that the capitalist state will inevitably be replaced by a socialist state as the working class achieve political power. According to Webb this represents 'the inevitability of gradualism'. Conversely social democrats, such as Anthony Crosland, have argued that a more socially just and equal society can be achieved by reforming *existing* capitalist structures.

> ### Key term
>
> **Old Labour** Old Labour is associated with left-wing principles of positive intervention to create a more equal society through higher taxes on the wealthy, nationalisation of public services and generous welfare provision.

At the core of Labour's socialist ideology is the principle of collectivism, whereby we achieve more by working together for the common good than by competing according to our own interests.

Labour governments have traditionally sought to create a more just and inclusive society through:

- nationalisation, whereby the government runs key industries in the interests of the workers and the nation
- redistributive taxation so that the wealthier in society pay a greater share of taxation
- supporting an extensive welfare state
- fostering close links with the trade unions since these, like Labour, were established to protect and advance the interests of the workers

The prime minister of the first majority Labour government (1945–51) was Clement Attlee. His governments are nostalgically remembered by many in the Labour Party as a high point of democratic socialism.

- In 1948, the health secretary, Aneurin Bevan, introduced the National Health Service, providing free healthcare for the nation.
- Approximately 20% of the economy was nationalised, including core industries such as steel, electricity and coal as well as the Bank of England.

As Labour prime minister 1964–70 and 1974–76, Harold Wilson believed that government should play a central role in the establishment of a dynamic economy and a more just and meritocratic society

The Labour governments of Harold Wilson (1964–70 and 1974–76) also attempted to create a fairer and more equal society based on government-led economic expansion. In 1963, Wilson argued that Labour would unleash the 'white heat of technology' in government and, as prime minister, he sought to associate Labour with progressive policies and industrial modernisation.

- In 1965, the deputy prime minister, George Brown, announced a National Plan for economic growth which would expand the economy by 25% by 1970.
- The maintenance grant was introduced to make it easier for young people from poorer backgrounds to attend university.
- The Open University was established to further open up higher education to those from poorer backgrounds.
- Wilson's governments were also committed to the expansion of comprehensive education at the expense of the grammar schools as a way of encouraging a more inclusive and less elitist society.
- Acts of Parliament were passed to encourage a fairer and more inclusive society, such as the Race Relations Act 1968, which made discrimination in the workplace illegal, and the Sex Discrimination Act 1975.
- In order to pay for a generous welfare state, taxes on the more wealthy dramatically increased under Labour. At its height in 1979, under Wilson's successor, James Callaghan (1976–79), the top rate of taxation reached 83%.

New Labour

In the 1979 general election, James Callaghan was defeated by the Conservative Party led by Margaret Thatcher. Following the election of Michael Foot as Labour leader in 1980, the party moved decisively to the left. In the 1983 general election, Labour's manifesto committed the party to further nationalisation, increased taxation of the wealthier in society, withdrawal from the European Economic Community and unilateral nuclear disarmament. One Labour MP, Gerald Kaufman, famously referred to the manifesto as 'the longest suicide note in history' and Labour's share of the vote collapsed from 36.9% in 1979 to 27.6% in the 1983 general election, handing Thatcher a landslide victory.

The scale of the 1983 general election defeat shocked Labour into abandoning its most socialist policies and, under the leadership of Neil Kinnock (1983–92) and John Smith (1992–94), Labour moved towards the centre. However, it was the election of Tony Blair as Labour leader in 1994 which most transformed Labour.

Blair was strongly influenced by the principles of the **'third way'**, which was developed by the political philosopher Anthony Giddens. According to Giddens, the third way represented a compromise between the extremes of socialism and capitalism. Labour governments ought not to commit themselves to ideological principles such as nationalisation, redistributive taxation and class conflict. Gone, too, was the socialist commitment to collectivism and equality. Instead, Labour should focus on the establishment of a 'stakeholder society' based on the principles of inclusion and communitarianism rather than trying to create a more equal society. Labour should enact policies which would encourage wealth creation rather than wealth redistribution, as well as loosen its ties with the trade union movement in a bid to become a less class-based party. In short, Labour should work for the achievement of social justice within a prosperous capitalist economy.

> **Key term**
>
> **New Labour (third way)**
> The third way combines a left-wing commitment to social justice with a right-wing emphasis on the value of free markets in encouraging economic prosperity.

So great was Blair's impact on the Labour Party that it became known as **New Labour**. A key moment in the development of New Labour was when, in 1995, Clause IV of the Labour Party Constitution (1918) was modified so that the party abandoned its commitment to nationalisation and accepted the economic benefits of a free-market economy. As prime minister (1997–2007), Blair's centrist policies put him starkly at odds with more left-wing members of the party such as Tony Benn and Jeremy Corbyn, who believed that New Labour was abandoning 'real' socialism.

> 'Socialism for me was never about nationalisation or the power of the state …
> it is a moral purpose to life, a set of values, a belief in society, in cooperation,
> in achieving together what we cannot achieve alone.'
>
> Tony Blair

- Margaret Thatcher's chancellor of the exchequer, Nigel Lawson, had lowered the top rate of taxation to 40% in 1988. Blair kept it at 40% on the basis that the wealthiest in society are wealth creators and that the economy would grow faster if their taxes were kept low.
- Greater emphasis was put on the state as an 'enabler' rather than a provider. State schools were given greater independence from local authorities and tuition fees were introduced so that students would have to contribute towards the cost of their higher education.
- New Labour introduced tough new laws such as anti-social behaviour orders (ASBOs) to combat crime.

As Labour leader 1994–2007, Tony Blair successfully broadened the party's appeal far beyond its traditional working-class core vote

- For Blair, a key element of New Labour was modernisation. In 1999, most of the hereditary peers were removed from the House of Lords. The European Convention on Human Rights was incorporated into British law in the Human Rights Act 1998 and an independent Supreme Court was established. Referendums paved the way for devolved assemblies in Scotland, Wales and Northern Ireland, dramatically altering the location of power in the United Kingdom.
- However, New Labour also remained committed to social justice and, like former Labour governments, tried to create a fairer and more inclusive society. In 1997, for instance, it introduced the minimum wage in order to help the lowest paid. The government also significantly increased spending on public services.

Current Labour ideas and policies

On the resignation of Tony Blair in 2007, Gordon Brown became prime minister. In response to the global economic crisis, his government (2007–10) attempted to stabilise public finances by introducing a 50 pence top rate of taxation on incomes over £150,000, as well as a partial bank nationalisation programme. Although these policies were primarily a reaction to the desperate economic situation, some political commentators predicted that they spelt the end of New Labour.

When Brown was defeated in the 2010 general election, his successor, Ed Miliband (2010–15), seemed to further distance the party from its recent Blairite past by maintaining its commitment to a 50p top rate of taxation, demanding an energy price freeze and drawing a distinction between 'predatory' finance capitalism and the 'producers' in industry.

Jeremy Corbyn and Momentum

However, it was the election of Jeremy Corbyn as Labour leader in 2015 that signalled the most striking shift in the direction of the Labour Party. A keen participant in socialist gatherings such as the Tolpuddle Martyrs' annual festival, and with a deep-seated belief in the importance of workers' solidarity, Corbyn was added to the list of candidates for the leadership by fellow MPs so that the left of the party would be represented in the ballot. However, under Ed Miliband, the party had changed the rules by which the Labour leader is elected to a one-member-one-vote system, and this resulted in Corbyn winning an unexpected landslide victory.

Soon after his election, a new group within Labour, known as Momentum, was established to sustain his leadership and encourage the spread of democratic socialist principles within the party, such as more government control of the financial sector, nationalisation and redistributive taxation. Momentum's principles of socialist equality and collective solidarity draw their inspiration from Karl Marx's optimistic vision of what human beings can achieve by working together, and their influence within the party can be seen in the slogan of the 2017 Labour election campaign: 'For the Many, Not the Few'.

As a result of its shift to the left, the current Labour Party is committed to a dramatically increased role for the government in advancing a fairer and more equal UK, as well as a close relationship with the trade union movement so that the interests of the working class are as fully represented as possible in government. The 2017 Labour Party manifesto was the most socialist since 1983.

- The top rate of taxation would be set at 50p for incomes above £123,000, since the very wealthiest in society should be expected to contribute more towards society. Those earning £80,000 would be expected to pay the 45% rate of taxation, and corporation tax would be increased to 26% by 2020. Responding to criticisms of these proposals, Corbyn has stated, 'There is a social crisis looming in Britain that cannot be resolved by continuing tax giveaways to the wealthiest in our society.'
- A Labour government would introduce an extensive programme of renationalisation. The railways and water companies would be taken back into public ownership and the privatisation of Royal Mail reversed. This is because, as essential services, they should be run in the public interest by the government rather than for profit.
- In the 2017 general election, Jeremy Corbyn stated that Labour will, 'never, ever apologise for the closeness of our relationship with the trade union movement': instead 'you are our family'. Labour is committed to repealing the Trade Union Act 2016, which requires 50% of the workforce to vote in a ballot if strike action is to be legal.
- Zero-hour contracts should be ended so that all workers will have a guaranteed number of hours that they work each week. The rights of workers would also be advanced by a £10 per hour minimum wage by 2020.
- The maintenance grant, which the Wilson government brought in, should be reintroduced and tuition and top-up fees will be abolished in order to encourage young people, especially from poorer backgrounds, to attend university.
- Labour would also provide free school meals for all primary school children, which would be paid for by the removal of the VAT exemption on private school fees — a policy which would further encourage a more equal society by discouraging parents from educating their children in the private sector. The introduction of a National Education Service would also provide the government with a greater role in coordinating a more uniform approach to education.
- A National Investment Bank would be established to provide a fund of £250 billion to invest in the UK's infrastructure. This commitment to giving the government a major role in stimulating economic activity demonstrates a significant return to Keynesian principles of government intervention.

Although most political commentators expected the 2017 Labour general election campaign to result in a crushing defeat like that of 1983, there was a 9.6% swing to Labour, suggesting that there is now considerable support for left-wing socialism among the electorate.

Jeremy Corbyn and Labour

However, it would not be true to say that Labour has entirely returned to its traditional values. The Labour manifesto in 2017 was only committed to increasing the top rate of taxation to 50p, rather than 83% where it had stood in 1979 when James Callaghan was defeated by Margaret Thatcher. Labour has also not sought to re-modify Clause IV and so is only committed to specific nationalisations rather than a wholesale renationalisation of British industry.

On the other hand, in a number of ways, Corbyn is more radical than old Labour has traditionally been. Corbyn, for example, supports unilateral nuclear disarmament, although the British nuclear deterrent was established by Clement Attlee. Corbyn has also favoured a soft Brexit, whereas leading Old Labour figures such as Michael Foot and Tony Benn were highly eurosceptic.

A united party?

It is important also to note that Jeremy Corbyn has opponents within the Parliamentary Labour Party. In 2016, following the EU referendum in which Corbyn had appeared an unenthusiastic Remainer, 172 Labour MPs supported a no confidence motion against him, and only 40 Labour MPs supported his leadership. Within Labour, there are still significant Blairite groups, such as Progress, and prominent centrist Labour MPs such as Stephen Kinnock and Hilary Benn have distanced themselves from Corbyn's leadership. Corbyn's personal success in the 2017 general election, in which Labour's share of the vote increased from 30.4% in 2015 to 40% has, however, provided him with a powerful mandate to continue the left-wing transformation of the party, in particular because he has such massive support among the party membership. In February 2019 the divisions within Labour were made even more starkly apparent when eight Labour MPs left the party and established their own Independent grouping.

Chuka Umunna MP, a prominent critic of Jeremy Corbyn, left the Labour Party to establish Change UK, before going on to join the Liberal Democrats

The Liberal Democratic Party

Origins — classical liberalism

Although the Liberal Democratic Party was established in 1988 and is the newest political party in the UK, its origins go far back into British history. In the 1850s, Whigs and radicals, who supported reform of Parliament and limits on royal authority, and supporters of the former prime minister Robert Peel, who had split the Conservative Party by repealing the protectionist Corn Laws, came together on the issue of free trade. Under the leadership of William Ewart Gladstone (1809–98), the Liberal Party became a dominant force in British politics, advocating not only free trade but lower taxes, balanced budgets, parliamentary and administrative reform and a more moral approach to foreign policy.

Gladstone had four periods of office as Liberal prime minister (1868–74, 1880–85, 1886 and 1892–94) and provided the party with a strong sense of moral purpose. According to Gladstone, 'Liberalism is trust of the people tempered by prudence. Conservatism is distrust of the people tempered by fear.'

1900 to today — modern liberalism

At the beginning of the twentieth century, the Liberal Party became increasingly influenced by the work of T.H. Green, John Hobson and William Beveridge, who argued that the government must provide adequate welfare provision for the most vulnerable in society. According to this 'New Liberalism', individual freedom and self-fulfilment required at least a basic standard of living, and during the governments of H.H. Asquith (1908–16), old-age pensions and sickness and unemployment insurance were introduced, which were partly paid for by higher taxes on the more wealthy.

> **Key term**
>
> **Modern liberalism** In addition to accepting the importance of civil liberties, the free market and limited government, modern liberalism also acknowledges that the government should play an important role in advancing social justice.

The rise of the Labour Party from 1900 provided a powerful alternative to the Liberal Party among the working class and, following the resignation of David Lloyd George as prime minister in 1922, the Liberal Party declined as Labour and the Conservatives shared power between them for the remainder of the twentieth century.

However, in the early 1980s the Liberal Party entered an electoral pact with former Labour MPs who had established the Social Democratic Party. Campaigning together as the Alliance, they fought the 1983 and 1987 general elections and merged to form the Liberal Democrats in 1988.

As a united party, the Liberal Democrats enjoyed growing success under Paddy Ashdown and, as a result of Charles Kennedy's principled opposition to the Iraq War, won 62 seats on 22% of the vote in the 2005 general election. Although their number of MPs dipped to 57 in the 2010 general election, their support proved necessary if David Cameron was going to be able to form a government — and so, under Nick Clegg, they re-entered government after years in the political wilderness.

The coalition agreement which Cameron and Clegg negotiated gave the Liberal Democrats five seats in the cabinet, including Nick Clegg's position as deputy prime minister. This was the most influence the party had enjoyed in government since David Lloyd George resigned as prime minister in 1922.

Current Liberal Democrat ideas and policies

Since the Liberal Democrats combines the values and principles of the Liberal and Social Democratic parties, its ideas cover a broad spectrum. There has often been conflict between those on the social democratic left of the party, such as Tim Farron, who emphasise the importance of social justice, and those who support a more neo-liberal approach to the economy, such as Nick Clegg. Those on the liberal side of the party are sometimes referred to as Orange Book liberals after a book published under that title in 2004, which argued that the Liberal Democrats should reconnect with their nineteenth-century commitment to free trade and free markets.

Nick Clegg's readiness to enter into coalition government with the Conservative Party from 2010 to 2015 frustrated many on the social democratic wing of the party, who viewed the Conservatives as a bigger threat than Labour. The election of Tim Farron (2015–17) and Vince Cable (2017–) as leaders of the Liberal Democrats suggests, however, that the party has moved back towards its more social democratic traditions. Under the leadership of Vince Cable, the Liberal Democrats' emphasis on social justice remains strong, although it continues to maintain a principled liberal support for limited government, constitutional reform, the European Union and a multinational approach to global politics.

- The emphasis on social justice means that the Liberal Democrats are prepared to increase taxes in order to improve the public services the government provides, especially for the more vulnerable. In the 2017 general election, the Liberal Democrats were committed to increasing all levels of income tax by 1p and increasing corporation tax to 20%. Vince Cable was also in favour of increasing capital gains tax and inheritance tax on the wealthier, arguing that 'too much inequality is bad for us all'.
- The Liberal Democrats oppose the opening of more grammar schools, which they regard as a threat to social cohesion since they give some children opportunities that others lack. Like Labour, the Liberal Democrats, in 2017, were committed to providing free school meals for all primary school children, further demonstrating their commitment to an extensive welfare state.
- As the most pro-European political party, the Liberal Democrats remain committed to the liberal values of international cooperation represented by the UK's membership of the European Union. They have demanded a second referendum on the terms of the Brexit deal that the government negotiates and consistently opposed leaving the single market and the customs union.
- In 2017 the Liberal Democrat manifesto was committed to taking 50,000 Syrian refugees by 2020. This is within the moral tradition of liberalism, which emphasises the importance of acting on principles that advance human rights rather than making decisions based on political expediency.
- The Liberal Democrats are also fully committed to the UK's continued membership of the European Convention on Human Rights as a core way of protecting our civil liberties. In coalition, Nick Clegg resisted attempts by David Cameron to repeal the Act as a challenge to parliamentary sovereignty.
- There has always been a strong tradition of parliamentary and constitutional reform within the Liberal Democrats and so they are committed to a democratic House of Lords and support further devolution as a way of making government more accountable to the public. They also support the introduction of proportional representation at Westminster in order to ensure that the Commons more fairly represents the way in which the UK votes.

Minority parties in the UK

Since the Second World War, UK politics has been dominated by the Conservative and Labour parties, with the Liberals/Liberal Democrats providing an alternative for those disillusioned with existing party dominance.

In addition to these three parties, a number of minor parties have achieved varying levels of political success. The Communist Party of Great Britain lasted from 1920 to 1991 and in the 1945 general election won two seats at Westminster. At the other extreme, the British National Party, under Nick Griffin, achieved 1.6% in the 2010 general election, as well as returning two MEPs in the 2009 European Parliament elections. Since then, however, its influence has steadily declined and its ten parliamentary candidates won just 4,642 votes between them in the 2017 general election.

However, other minority parties have been significantly more successful. For some this has been because they have achieved influence in Westminster or regional government. For others, it is because they have managed to set an agenda that the main political parties have decided to follow.

The Scottish National Party (SNP)

The Scottish National Party was established in 1934 and won its first parliamentary seat at the Hamilton by-election in 1967. Until the 2015 general election, the highest number of MPs the SNP had returned to Westminster had been 11 (October 1974). However, in 2015, the SNP won an extraordinary 56 of the 59 Scottish constituencies in the House of Commons on 50% of the popular vote in Scotland. In the 2017 general election its support fell back to 35 MPs with 36.9% of the vote in Scotland. This still meant, however, that the SNP was the third biggest party in the House of Commons following the general elections of 2015 and 2017.

56 SNP MPs with their leader Nicola Sturgeon at the Forth Bridge, after their landslide general election result in Scotland, 2015.

As a result of these general election successes, the SNP plays a significant role in contemporary British politics. Following the 2017 general election, for example, SNP MPs were elected to chair two House of Commons select committees (International Trade and Scottish Affairs). Its 35 MPs also provide the party with almost three times more voting influence than the 12 Liberal Democrat MPs elected in 2017. SNP MPs have been highly vocal in their criticism of Theresa May's decision to bomb President Assad's military installations and the way in which they voted had a dramatic impact on the government's ability to achieve the Brexit deal it wanted. However, the influence of the SNP at Westminster is limited by the unwillingness of the Labour Party to work too closely with a party that has supplanted it as the dominant political force in Scotland.

The most powerful influence of the SNP has been in the government of Scotland, where its policies have made a dramatic impact.

- Scotland has maintained free university tuition by not adopting the tuition fees that exist elsewhere in the UK.
- Prescription charges have been abolished.
- 16- and 17-year-olds are allowed to vote in local council elections and were allowed to vote in the Scotland independence referendum.

However, it is important not to exaggerate the influence of the Scottish National Party. Scotland is a part of the UK, and this puts significant restraints on what the SNP can achieve in government in Scotland. Although the SNP rejects nuclear weapons, national defence policy is determined at Westminster and so Trident is still based in Scotland. Also, in the Gina Miller case (2017), the Supreme Court established that the Scottish Parliament need not be consulted over legislation withdrawing the UK from the EU, even though Scotland voted decisively to remain in the EU.

Plaid Cymru

Plaid Cymru dates from 1925 and won its first seat at Westminster in the 1966 Carmarthen by-election. Unlike the success of the SNP across Scotland, Plaid Cymru's main basis of support has been in the Welsh-speaking parts of North Wales and it has never achieved an electoral breakthrough in Labour-dominated South Wales. In the 2017 general election Plaid Cymru won four of the 40 Welsh parliamentary seats, which is the most seats it has ever won and so its influence at Westminster has always been minimal.

On the National Assembly for Wales, Plaid Cymru has achieved more success and from 2007 to 2011 it formed a coalition with Labour on the agreement that there would be a referendum giving the Assembly further devolved powers. However, Labour's dominant influence in Wales has ensured that Plaid Cymru's influence has generally been limited both at Westminster and on the National Assembly.

United Kingdom Independence Party (UKIP)

The influence of UKIP on UK politics has been highly significant. Founded in 1993, it had little impact until the 2004 European Parliament elections, when it achieved 16.1% of the vote. Following the election of Nigel Farage as leader in 2006, it began to broaden its support among the white working class by opposing not only the UK's membership of the EU but also further immigration. The implications of the expansion of the EU in 2004 and 2007, and the resulting number of East Europeans coming into the UK, contributed to its growing electoral success. Farage's high-profile media presence and 'plain speaking' and 'common sense' criticism of establishment politicians further added to UKIP's influence. In the 2014 European Parliament elections, UKIP beat both Labour and the Conservatives with 26.6% of the vote and 24 seats.

The influence of UKIP in the Westminster Parliament, however, has always been tiny. In the 2015 general election, although it achieved an impressive 12.6% of the vote, it won only one seat, and in the 2017 general election, under a new leader, Paul Nuttall, it lost that seat as UKIP's support plummeted to just 1.8%. In the 2018 council elections, under another leader, Gerard Batten, UKIP lost 123 of its 126 seats.

However, UKIP's influence on British politics has been significantly greater than these results suggest. This is because David Cameron's manifesto commitment in the 2015 general election to offer the British public an in/out referendum on the UK's membership of the European Union was a response to the growing euroscepticism of British politics, which UKIP had done so much to fuel.

UKIP's high levels of support among traditional working-class Labour supporters in the 2015 general election also contributed to Labour achieving its worst share of the vote since 1987. For example, Labour lost several seats to the Conservatives because of a strong showing by UKIP. A much poorer showing by UKIP in 2017, consequently, was significantly to the advantage of Labour. The evidence in Table 2.7 shows how the changing fortunes of a minority party can have a defining impact on the outcome of a general election.

Table 2.7 Derby North general election results, 2015 and 2017

2015 (% votes won)	2017 (% votes won)
Conservative 36.7	Labour 48.5
Labour 36.6	Conservative 44.4
UKIP 14.6	Liberal Democrat 4.6
Liberal Democrat 8.6	UKIP 2.4

In addition, Nigel Farage played a defining role in the EU referendum campaign in 2016, placing uncontrolled immigration at the heart of the case for Brexit. This was highly effective in mobilising voters in traditional working-class parts of the country to vote Leave, in spite of Labour's support for Remain. In Middlesbrough, for example, which has always had a Labour MP, Leave won 65.5% of the vote. It could even be said that the way in which he increased popular opposition to the UK's membership of the EU makes Nigel Farage one of the most significant and controversial politicians of recent years, not just UKIP's most successful leader.

Even though UKIP has never achieved a breakthrough at Westminster, its impact on British politics has been incalculable. It helped to determine the result of the 2015 general election, secured a commitment from the Conservative Party to hold a referendum on the UK's membership of the EU and then helped to swing the vote towards Leave (Table 2.8).

Table 2.8 European Union referendum 2016 – the result

Leave	Remain
52%	48%

The Green Party

Like UKIP, the Green Party is a victim of first-past-the-post (FPTP) and so has achieved little success at Westminster. Originally known as PEOPLE, and then the Ecology Party, it changed its name to the Green Party in 1985. In 1989, the Greens achieved 15% in the European Parliament elections and in 2010 Caroline Lucas won Brighton Pavilion for the Greens, further increasing her share of the vote in the 2015 and 2017 general elections. In the 2015 general election over a million people voted Green, giving the party 3.6% of the vote but just one seat at Westminster. Then in the 2017 general election the Greens tactically helped to increase the Labour vote by not contesting a number of seats where there was a close contest between Labour and the Conservatives. For example, the Greens decided not to fight Ealing Central and Acton and put their support behind Labour (Table 2.9).

Table 2.9 Ealing Central and Acton general election results, 2015 and 2017

2015 (% votes won)	2017 (% votes won)
Labour 43.2	Labour 59.7
Conservative 42.7	Conservative 34.7
Liberal Democrat 6.1	Liberal Democrat 5.6
UKIP 3.8	
Green 3.6	

In 2010 Caroline Lucas won Brighton Pavilion for the Green Party, and she significantly increased her majority in the next two general elections. From 2016 to 2018 she led the Green Party

In spite of its modest electoral success, the Green Party has had a significant influence on British politics as an agenda setter, encouraging the main political parties to adopt more environmentally-friendly policies.

- In the 2017 general election, the shadow chancellor, John McDonnell, announced that the government's response to climate change required 'a transformation of our institutions and how our economies are run'.
- In 2018 Theresa May launched the government's 25 Year Environment Plan at the London Wetland Centre, in which she committed the government to drastically reducing plastic consumption.

Stretch and challenge

'As we leave the European Union, which for decades has controlled some of the most important levers of environmental policy, now is the right time to put the question of how we protect and enhance our natural environment centre stage. … It is a central priority for this government. Our mission is to build a Britain where the next generation can enjoy a better life than the one that went before it.'

Theresa May, speech at the London Wetland Centre, 2018

In what ways can minority parties influence the development and direction of British politics?

The Democratic Unionist Party (DUP)

The influence of the Democratic Unionist Party on British politics is in direct contrast to that of UKIP and the Greens. Founded in 1971 by the Reverend Ian Paisley, its priority is to keep Northern Ireland as part of the United Kingdom. It maintains strong links with the Free Presbyterian Church and its social conservatism and the intense Protestantism that it defends have ensured that it has had little impact on the manifestos of the main political parties.

However, the Democratic Unionists have played an indispensable role in the development of the peace process in Northern Ireland. Initially opposed to power sharing with republican parties, in the 2005 general election it became the largest unionist party at Westminster, as well as achieving the biggest share of the vote in elections to the Stormont Assembly (Table 2.10).

Table 2.10 Stormont Assembly results, 2016

Party	Share of the vote (%)	Description
Democratic Unionist Party	28	Unionist
Sinn Féin	27	Republican
SDLP	12	Republican
UUP	10	Unionist
Alliance	8	Non-sectarian
Green	2	Non-sectarian
Traditional Unionist Voice	1	Unionist
People Before Profit	1	Non-sectarian

The decision of Ian Paisley in 2007 to finally agree to power sharing with Sinn Féin was a pivotal event in the Northern Ireland peace process. However, the difficult relationship that the Democratic Unionists have with republican Sinn Féin has meant that it has not been easy for them to cooperate in government. This relationship is crucial since they are the two biggest parties in Northern Ireland, and yet in January 2017 power sharing between them broke down.

The DUP's increasingly strong presence at Westminster has provided it with influence disproportionate to its national vote. The ten seats that it won in the inconclusive 2017 general election made DUP support indispensable to the Conservatives if they were to reach the 326 MPs needed to avoid having to form a minority administration (Table 2.11).

Table 2.11 2017 general election results — seats won

Party	Number of seats
Conservatives	317
Labour	262
SNP	35
Liberal Democrats	12
Democratic Unionist Party	10
Plaid Cymru	4

By making a **confidence and supply** agreement with the Conservatives, the DUP agreed to vote with the government on key issues connected with Brexit and the Budget and to support the government in the event of a vote of confidence.

In return for this support, the DUP's leader, Arlene Foster:

- secured an extra £1 billion in funding in Northern Ireland
- achieved a parliamentary veto over the government's Brexit negotiations
- ensured that the Conservative government has not put pressure on the government of Northern Ireland to adopt the same-sex marriage legislation which exists elsewhere in the UK, or to allow abortion, even though the Republic of Ireland voted to allow this in a referendum in May 2018

Political parties in context

The development of a multiparty system and its implications

Barriers to entry for smaller parties

During most of the twentieth century, British politics was dominated by two main political parties. This can be referred to as a political duopoly, and was caused by the way in which the different social classes tended to identify with one or other of the main parties. As a result of class-based voting, the traditional working-class vote generally lined up behind Labour, with the middle classes and upper classes more likely to vote Conservative. This made it difficult for minority parties to achieve an electoral breakthrough.

The way in which the House of Commons is elected by FPTP means that smaller parties can find it difficult to gain representation. This is because smaller parties lack the depth of support that the larger parties can claim. The Liberals/Liberal Democrats have, for example, enjoyed significant breadth of support across the country but they lack the electoral strongholds of the Labour and Conservative parties. They have therefore historically been significantly underrepresented at Westminster (Table 2.12).

Table 2.12 1974 and 1983 general elections

General election	Conservatives	Labour	Liberal (1974) / SDP–Liberal Alliance (1983)
February 1974	37.9% 297 MPs	37.2% 301 MPs	19.3% 14 MPs
1983	42.4% 397 MPs	27.6% 209 MPs	25.4% 23 MPs

This has led to a self-fulfilling belief that a vote for a minority party is a wasted vote. In addition, minority parties have suffered from a lack of funding, since they have not been able to rely on the close financial links that Labour has had with the trade unions and the Conservatives with big business. As a result of Labour and Conservative dominance at Westminster for much of the postwar period, the UK was not a multiparty system.

In focus

Local and national success of the Lib Dems

The Liberal/Liberal Democrat Party has often achieved more success in local elections than in national elections. Thus even when the Labour and Conservative parties have dominated Westminster, local government has provided more of a multiparty system.

Has two-party dominance been eroded at Westminster?

Two-party dominance at Westminster began to be challenged in the 1980s, when the Social Democratic Party was established by former members of the Labour Party and formed an electoral alliance with the Liberal Party. This created a centrist party (the SDP–Liberal Alliance) with wider potential appeal and, following their merger as the Liberal Democrats in 1988, the party began to increase its influence at Westminster (Table 2.13).

Table 2.13 Liberal Democrat share of the national vote and representation at Westminster, 1992–2010

General election	Share of national vote (%)	Number of seats won
1992	17.8	20
1997	18.8	46
2001	18.3	52
2005	22	62
2010	23	57

The decline of the Westminster duopoly was also facilitated by growing partisan dealignment as voters increasingly voted on specific issues rather than according to class. The way in which the Liberal Democrats focused their efforts on certain key geographical areas which they had a good chance of winning, such as the South West, further maximised their influence at Westminster.

The consistent opposition of Liberal Democrat leader Charles Kennedy to the Iraq War (2003) further boosted Liberal Democrat support in the 2005 general election. Then in 2010 a strong campaign by his successor, Nick Clegg, combined with disappointing performances by David Cameron and Gordon Brown, provided the opportunity for the Liberal Democrats to form a coalition government with the Conservatives.

In comparison to the Liberal Democrats' slow progress, the SNP achieved its electoral breakthrough in the 2015 general election following its high-profile campaign in the 2014 Scottish independence referendum (Table 2.14).

Table 2.14 SNP share of the vote in Scotland and representation at Westminster, 1992–2015

General election	Share of vote in Scotland (%)	Number of Westminster seats won
1992	21.5	3
1997	22.1	6
2001	20.1	5
2005	17.7	6
2010	19.9	6
2015	50	56

The significance of the 2015 and 2017 general elections

The establishment of the Conservative–Liberal Democrat coalition in 2010 and the electoral breakthrough of the SNP in 2015 might suggest that the UK has now entered a two-and-a-half party model at Westminster. However, this would be premature. Although in the 2015 general election there was a dramatic increase in votes for the SNP, the Liberal Democrat vote went down by 15.1%, giving the Liberal Democrats just 7.9% of the popular vote — its smallest share of the vote in 45 years. In the 2017 general election its vote slipped even further, while the SNP also lost 21 seats. In comparison, the Labour and Conservative parties secured their highest share of the popular vote since the 1970 general election.

Tables 2.15 and 2.16 give breakdowns of the Lib Dem and SNP results in recent Westminster elections.

Table 2.15 Liberal/Liberal Democrat share of the national vote and number of seats at Westminster

General election	Share of national vote (%)	Number of seats won
1970	7.4	6
2015	7.9	8
2017	7.4	12

Table 2.16 SNP share of the vote in Scotland and number of seats at Westminster

General election	Results
2015	50% of the vote in Scotland 56 MPs
2017	36.9% of the vote in Scotland 35 MPs

The fortunes of UKIP plummeted in the 2017 general election under a new leader, Paul Nuttall, who lacked Nigel Farage's popular appeal. The Greens also fell back, which suggests that nationally the Conservative and Labour parties may have regained their traditional dominance. A key reason for this is likely to be the increasingly adversary nature of British politics, which means that voters now have a clear choice between Labour and Conservative and so are more likely to commit to one of these parties (Table 2.17).

Table 2.17 UKIP and the Green Party results in the 2015 and 2017 elections

General election	UKIP	Green Party
2015	12.6% of the popular vote 1 seat	3.8% of the popular vote 1 seat
2017	1.8% of the popular vote No seats	1.6% of the popular vote 1 seat

Multiparty democracy in the devolved assemblies

Although it could be strongly argued that the Conservative and Labour parties are still dominant at Westminster, the evidence suggests that the regional assemblies have encouraged the development of a multiparty democracy elsewhere in the UK.

As we can see from the evidence in Table 2.18, power is shared much more equally among the parties in all of the devolved assemblies. No two parties can be sure of being dominant and so, in the constituent parts of the UK, multiparty democracy does exist.

Table 2.18 Results in regional assemblies, 2016 (number of seats won)

Scottish Parliament election 2016	National Assembly for Wales election 2016	Northern Ireland Assembly election 2016
SNP 63	Labour 29	Democratic Unionist Party 38
Conservative 31	Conservative 14	Sinn Féin 28
Labour 24	Plaid Cymru 11	Ulster Unionist Party 16
Green 6	UKIP 7	Social Democratic and Labour Party (SDLP) 12
Liberal Democrat 5	Liberal Democrat 1	Alliance 8
		Green 2

Debate

Has the UK now become a multiparty democracy?

Yes

- In the devolved assemblies power is shared by more than two parties, so in the regions there is multiparty democracy.
- Smaller parties have been highly influential in recent general elections. In 2010 the Conservatives established a coalition with the Liberal Democrats and in 2017 the DUP agreed to support the Conservative government in a confidence and supply agreement.
- The SNP still has a significant parliamentary presence, which would be very important in a hung parliament.
- Since the Conservative and Labour parties have not won a large parliamentary majority since the 2005 general election, the importance of smaller parties is likely to remain significant.

No

- In the 2017 general election the Conservative and Labour parties won their biggest share of the popular vote since the 1970 general election.
- In the parliament elected in 2017, Labour and the Conservatives have 89% of the seats.
- Support for the Liberal Democratic Party collapsed in the 2015 and 2017 general elections.
- First-past-the-post protects the Labour and Conservative duopoly at Westminster.
- The way in which parties are funded makes it difficult for smaller political parties to break Conservative and Labour domination.

Summary

By the end of this chapter you should be able to answer the following questions:

→ What are the key functions of political parties?

→ How convincing is the case for state funding of political parties?

→ What are the main traditions and policies of the Conservative, Labour and Liberal Democratic parties?

→ How significant are divisions within the main political parties?

→ How significant are the policy differences between the main political parties?

→ Why do smaller parties find it difficult to achieve representation at Westminster?

→ How much influence do smaller parties have in UK politics?

→ Which party system model best fits UK politics today?

Practice questions

Source-based question

We will rebuild the public realm and create a genuinely mixed economy for the twenty-first century. And after a decade of austerity, the next Labour government will confront the challenge of rebuilding our public services. This year marks the 70th anniversary of the NHS … Its founder, Nye Bevan … described a free health service as 'pure socialism'. And so it is. We all contribute through our taxes so that it's there for all whenever we need it.

We'll put another 10,000 police officers back on our streets, playing a vital role in tackling crime and making people safer. But if we want to reduce crime, more police are only part of the solution. Every study tells us that investing in young people and communities is key, and crime thrives amid economic failure. So under Labour there will be no more left-behind areas and no more forgotten communities. Inequality is not just a matter of incomes. It's about having a real say too. That's why we are not only determined to rebuild our economy, communities and public services, but also to democratise them, and change the way our economic system is run in the interests of the majority.

Ten years ago this month, the whole edifice of greed-is-good deregulated financial Capitalism … came crashing to earth with devastating consequences. But instead of making essential changes to a broken economic system, the political and corporate establishment strained every sinew to bail out and prop up the system that led to the crash in the first place. Labour is offering a real alternative to the people of Britain. A radical plan to rebuild and transform our country … Investing in Britain after years of austerity and neglect and bringing our country together after a decade of division.

Source: Adapted from Jeremy Corbyn's speech to the Labour Party Conference, 26 September 2018

https://labour.org.uk/press/jeremy-corbyn-speaking-labour-party-conference-today/

Using the source, evaluate the view that the Labour Party today has completely abandoned the principles of New Labour.

In your response you must:
- *compare and contrast the different opinions in the source*
- *examine and debate these views in a balanced way*
- *analyse and evaluate only the information presented in the source* (30)

Evaluative questions

1 Evaluate the extent to which the main political parties disagree over policies and ideas. *You must consider this view and the alternative to this view in a balanced way.* (30)

2 Evaluate the extent to which political parties should be funded by the state. *You must consider this view and the alternative to this view in a balanced way.* (30)

3 Evaluate the extent to which the United Kingdom has become a multiparty democracy. *You must consider this view and the alternative to this view in a balanced way.* (30)

3 Electoral systems

First-past-the-post (FPTP) has been used for UK elections, in some form, for centuries. Over this time, however, there has been extensive reform — to constituency boundaries, the extent of the franchise and the ballot itself — to remedy complaints of corruption in the system and to reflect changing political attitudes.

Nineteenth-century Acts reformed the electoral system, with Prime Minister Gladstone insisting that:

> '… whatever might be the effect on the House from some points of view, it was past doubt that the two Reform Acts had made the House far more adequate to express the wants and wishes of the nation as a whole.'

These reforms continued into the twentieth century with the extension of the franchise to women and 18-year-olds, and in recent decades FPTP itself has come under increasing criticism for the notable flaws that it has. The criticisms have been sharper since the introduction and successful use of other electoral systems in the UK:

- The additional member system (AMS) in Wales and Scotland and for the London Assembly
- The single transferable vote (STV) in Northern Ireland
- The supplementary vote (SV) for London mayors

Across the UK polling stations open from 7 a.m. to 10 p.m. on the day of a general election

Nonetheless, FPTP has both clear benefits and numerous supporters. During the alternative vote (AV) referendum campaign of 2011, Prime Minister Cameron protested: 'Britain is in real danger of exchanging an electoral system that works for one we would come to regret profoundly.'

Elections in the UK

In a liberal democracy such as the UK, holding free and fair elections which allow true competition between parties is an expectation of its citizens. Elections give citizens an opportunity to hold their elected representatives **accountable** for their actions over their previous term in office, and to use their vote to try and shape the policies of the nation going forwards.

There is a vast array of elections that take place across the UK at different intervals using different electoral systems (Figure 3.1). Each election is an opportunity for citizens to participate, although not every citizen can participate in every election. The regional assemblies are elected only by citizens in those regions.

Key term

Accountability Literally, to be held responsible for your actions. In a political sense, citizens judge their elected representatives for their policies, votes and actions over their time in office.

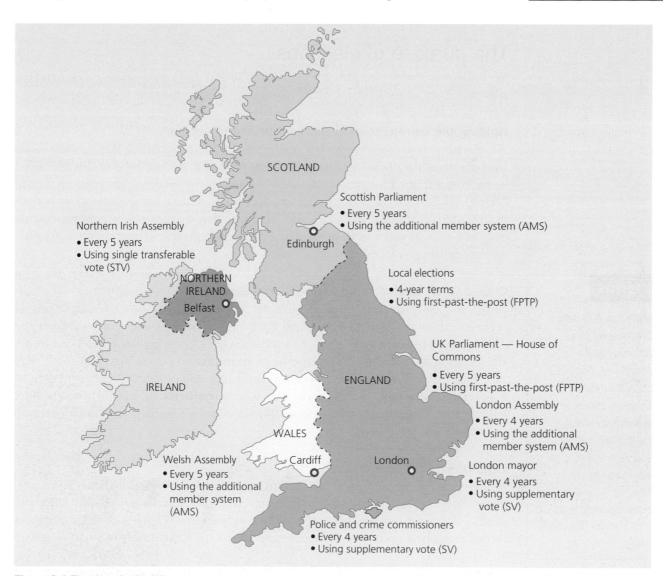

Figure 3.1 Elections in the UK

To hold an election, an electoral system must be chosen and used. In the simplest terms, an electoral system takes votes cast by citizens and turns these into seats or offices won. There are many electoral systems which can be employed to achieve this, and the processes each one uses are slightly different, often leading to different outcomes. Table 3.1 differentiates between elections, electoral systems and party systems.

Table 3.1 Elections, electoral systems and party systems

Elections (in the UK)	Electoral system	Party system
• An opportunity for citizens to cast a vote for their elected representatives • A feature of liberal and representative democracy • A way in which governments are both held accountable and chosen	• A process by which the votes cast can be translated into elected officials or seats • A variety of systems are available, broadly falling into three types — proportional, plurality and majoritarian	• The number of parties that have a realistic chance of forming government • A result of the electoral process that is chosen, not a choice in itself

The purpose of elections

To understand why elections are features of liberal and representative democracies, it is important to understand what holding an election is meant to achieve.

Holding the current elected representatives to account

An election allows for the current office holders to be judged on their performance over the time they have been in office. For most UK elected offices, this is either a 4- or 5-year term. This ensures there are consequences for the actions that an elected official takes while in office, most importantly that they can be voted out if their representatives are unhappy. This should ensure that there is a clear communication between official and voters, as ensuring they feel represented and happy is the only way to ensure re-election.

Choosing an elected representative and government

In all the elections on the map (Figure 3.1), voters are choosing politicians to represent their views. Candidates will campaign either on their personal beliefs and policies or, if they are a member of a party, on the policies in their party's manifesto. By winning an election, this person has a **mandate** to act on behalf of those who voted. In most UK elections, the election of individuals leads to the formation of a government, usually by the party that won a **majority** of seats in that election. Failing this, a number of parties may choose to work together, forming a coalition in order to govern.

Legitimising political power

A government formed as a product of a free and fair election is a 'legitimate' government. This means that it has the right to exercise power and authority (Table 3.2) over an area and the people within it. When such a government introduces a new policy, or changes an old one, it has the right to do so, having won an election.

Table 3.2 Power and authority

Authority	Power
• The rightful exercising of power, granted to a government in an election • For example, Theresa May had the authority to carry out Brexit negotiations for the UK following the 2017 election	• The ability to actually carry out government action • For example, May's ability to achieve the deal she wanted in the Brexit negotiations was hampered by the lack of a majority, a divided party and the deal that the EU desired to achieve

Essential to gaining **legitimacy** is the **participation** of voters. If the **turnout** is too low, the election result will not effectively represent the views of the public, thereby undermining the legitimacy of the government elected.

Also essential to legitimacy is the competition of an election — there must be competing parties or individuals for voters to choose between.

The coalition of the Conservative Party and Liberal Democrat Party between 2010 and 2015 is useful when considering legitimacy. On the one hand, neither party won the election outright, undermining their legitimacy. On the other hand, the two parties together commanded an overall vote of 59%. This clear majority, unusual in UK politics, arguably increased their legitimacy.

Limiting the power of elected representatives

Not only do elections legitimise a government, they also serve to limit it. Part of the limitations placed on the government is knowing that it will face election again in a period of years. However, elections also result in the election of representatives who do not form government. These are still legitimately elected officials, and they therefore form the opposition. They can use this position to scrutinise and challenge government policy.

Development of political policy

As part of an election, most parties or candidates publish a manifesto. This is a document outlining the policies the party will implement if elected. Public opinion through the election can shape these policies, and ultimately the winner of an election is usually chosen on these policies.

During the 2017 general election, the Conservative Party advanced a policy which would require people to sell their homes to pay for social care in old age. This was dubbed the 'dementia tax' by those opposed to it. Such was the public anger surrounding this policy that the Conservative Party abandoned it during the election campaign, demonstrating the public influence over party policy.

David Cameron and Nick Clegg after forming a coalition in 2010. This was the first coalition to govern the UK since the resignation of Winston Churchill's wartime coalition in 1945

Selection of a political elite

In the UK, parties can decide who runs in an election under their party name. They choose those they think mostly likely to win elections and be successful as elected officials. Once all elected representatives are chosen, some of these will be included in the formation of a government. This political elite is then responsible for the smooth running of a country; the election provides an opportunity to ensure they are capable and competent at doing so.

Different electoral systems

The electoral systems in the UK fall broadly into three categories — majoritarian, plurality and proportional (Table 3.3).

Table 3.3 Categories of electoral system

	Majoritarian	Plurality	Proportional
Meaning	• A majority is 50%+1 to win • This may refer to the number of votes needed to win a seat • Alternatively, it may refer to the number of seats needed to form a government • Likely to produce a two-party system	• A plurality of votes is having more votes than anyone else, thus winning but not having an overall majority • In a plurality system, no majority is required to win a seat • Likely to produce a two-party system	• A proportional system allocates seats in a manner which roughly reflects the percentage of votes gained by a party • No purely proportional systems are used in the UK, but a number of systems used are more proportional than FPTP • Likely to produce a multiparty system
System	• Supplementary vote (SV)	• First-past-the-post (FPTP)	• Additional member system (AMS) • Single transferable vote (STV)

Sometimes these distinctions become blurred. For example, to win an individual seat in a constituency under FPTP, a candidate needs only to gain a *plurality* of the vote. To form a government under this system, however, a government is usually expected to win a *majority* of the seats available in the House of Commons.

Plurality systems

First-past-the-post

FPTP is used for UK general elections. These should occur at a fixed point every 5 years after the Fixed-Term Parliaments Act 2011. However, this Act does have a provision to allow for an election to occur should two-thirds of MPs vote for one. This is what happened in 2017 when the issue of Brexit became particularly divisive, explaining why two general elections occurred within 3 years.

How it works

At constituency level

- The UK is divided into 650 geographical areas called constituencies. Each **constituency** contains an electorate of approximately 70,000 people, although this does vary quite widely across the UK.
- Each constituency is represented by one seat, held by a single MP, in the House of Commons. These are therefore known as **single-member constituencies**.
- Each party will select a candidate to run for election within a constituency.
- The voters of a constituency cast a single ballot, choosing between the candidates put forward. To do this, they simply put an 'X' in a box next to their candidate of choice on the ballot paper.
- The candidate with the most votes wins that constituency seat and becomes its elected representative.

The ballot paper for FPTP is simple (Figure 3.2). Candidates are listed alphabetically by their surname. If they are standing on behalf of a party, the party logo appears on the right. It is important to remember that in each constituency, voters are electing a *local MP*. While many of them may choose to vote on the basis of their party preference, they are actually voting for a person.

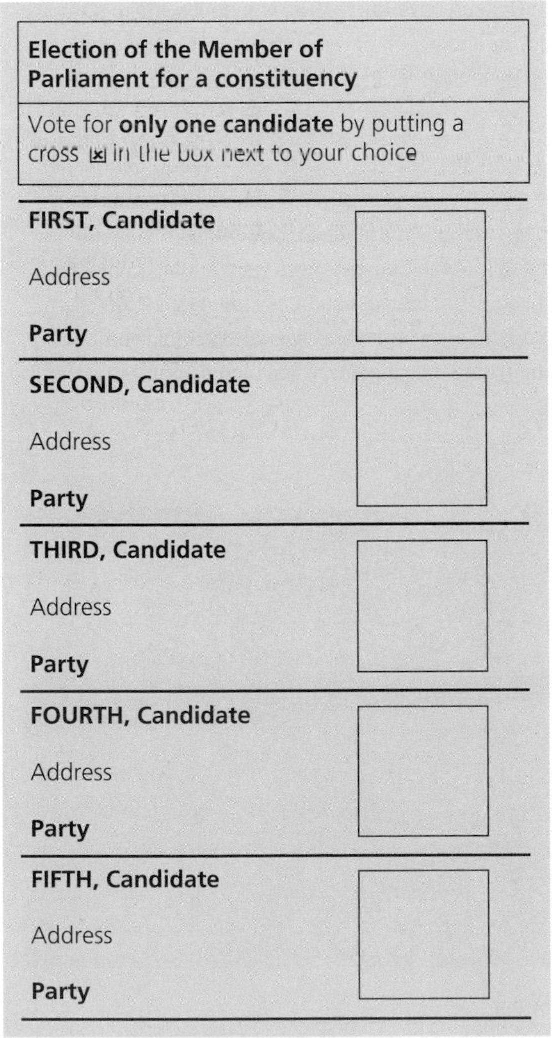

> ### Key terms
>
> **Constituency** A geographical area containing voters who elect a representative to act on their behalf.
>
> **Single-member constituency** A constituency which is represented by just one elected individual.

Election of the Member of Parliament for a constituency

Vote for **only one candidate** by putting a cross ☒ in the box next to your choice

FIRST, Candidate

Address

Party

SECOND, Candidate

Address

Party

THIRD, Candidate

Address

Party

FOURTH, Candidate

Address

Party

FIFTH, Candidate

Address

Party

Figure 3.2 A ballot paper for FPTP

At national level

- The winning candidate in each constituency is sent to Parliament to be an MP.
- The party with a majority of MPs — currently at least 326 out of 650 — can then form the government.
- If no party has a majority, two or more parties may choose to form a coalition and work together, or the leading party might choose to form a **minority government**.

In focus

Boundary Commissions review, 2018

In the UK, the boundaries of each constituency are decided by the Boundary Commissions. There are four separate Boundary Commissions, for England, Scotland, Wales and Northern Ireland. Each is an independent body that tries to ensure constituencies contain a roughly equal number of voters so that everyone eligible to vote is represented equally in Parliament.

From 2016 to 2018, the Boundary Commissions carried out a review of constituency boundaries after Parliament decided to reduce the number of MPs from 650 to 600. They reported their findings in September 2018.

The Boundary Commissions are governed by legislation which affects what they can suggest for the constituency boundaries. The electorate of each constituency must be within 5% of that of the average constituency in the UK. In the 2018 review, this meant each constituency had to have +/− 5% of 74,769. Two constituencies each must be allocated to the Isle of Wight and the Scottish Islands, regardless of population. Each constituency is also not allowed to be more than 13,000 square kilometres. The Boundary Commissions do not consider voting patterns with areas, which means the review would not have solved the problem of safe seats.

The proposals were submitted to Parliament in September 2018. They caused much anger and frustration from both Labour and Conservative Party MPs, who found their constituency boundaries had been changed, endangering their chances of re-election, or in some cases amalgamated.

The Labour Party accused the Conservatives of 'an undemocratic power grab', with some studies suggesting the new boundaries would have given the Conservatives a majority of seats if they had been used in the 2017 election, rather than the minority that they did get. Some Conservatives were equally concerned over the movement of their constituency boundaries. Boris Johnson's constituency boundaries would now include a heavily Labour-leaning area, making any re-election campaign far more challenging.

The Isle of Wight has two constituencies in spite of its relatively small population

The effects of using FPTP

While the results of each election vary according to the votes cast, using FPTP is likely to result in a number of common outcomes. While these outcomes can be assessed as either positive or negative, or in some cases a little of both, it is important to recognise that these are simply *outcomes*, the likely consequences of choosing to use FPTP, rather than advantages and disadvantages.

A two-party system

FPTP generally leads to a two-party system due to it being a plurality system based within constituencies. As all that is needed to win a seat within a constituency is to gain more votes than the person who came second, the winner can gain a whole seat with just a small proportion of the vote. Those who come second, third or below gain nothing at all. This is known as a 'winner-takes-all' system. In 2015, Alasdair McDonnell of the SDLP in Northern Ireland broke a record which had stood since 1922. He achieved just 24.5% of the vote in his constituency of Belfast South and yet won the seat. In North East Fife in 2017, the seat was won by the SNP by just two votes after three recounts (and the Liberal Democrats requested a fourth!). Despite this tiny difference in the vote gained by the two parties, the SNP took the seat and the Liberal Democrats walked away with nothing.

As a result of its 'winner-takes-all' nature, FPTP favours parties which can command a reasonable concentration of support across a large geographical area. In the UK, this means that Labour and the Conservatives benefit from the use of FPTP. Smaller parties find it difficult to compete at this level, given the expense of the campaign and the broad ideologies of the two major parties. Where third parties do compete, and are successful, they tend to find that they have a significantly smaller number of the seats available, so reducing the influence they can have in Parliament.

'Winner's bonus'

The 'winner's bonus' is not a literal bonus, rather it is the outcome that FPTP tends to over-reward the winning party in an election. For example, in 1997 Labour gained 43% of the national vote but 63% of the seats, and in 2015 the Conservatives gained 37% of the vote but 51% of the seats. The reason for this is that these figures are the national totals, whereas the reality of election day is that 650 small constituency-based elections are taking place. Regardless of the percentage of the vote they receive, the winner of each seat gains the whole seat. Therefore, while the Conservative or Labour Party may win each seat with just a plurality of the vote, by taking the whole seat they are effectively over-rewarded. When this is tallied on a national scale, it often results in a higher percentage of seats being gained by the winning party than the percentage of the vote it won.

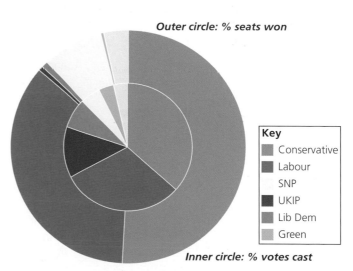

Outer circle: % seats won

Key
- Conservative
- Labour
- SNP
- UKIP
- Lib Dem
- Green

Inner circle: % votes cast

Figure 3.3 FPTP has a tendency to over-represent the winning party in an election at the expense of the smaller parties

In Figure 3.3, the inner circle represents the percentage of votes cast while the outer circle represents the percentage of seats won. This has both advantages — such as creating a government which is easily able to pass legislation — and disadvantages — such as the exclusion of minority voices.

Theresa May greets Arlene Foster, leader of the DUP, outside Downing Street in 2017, following the DUP's agreement to support May's minority government through a confidence and supply agreement

Strong, single-party government

Usually, FPTP will return a single party with a majority of the seats in the House of Commons. However, the last three elections in the UK — 2010, 2015 and 2017 — have been notable for their unpredictability and for the relative lack of single-party dominance. Nonetheless, in one of these three elections, 2015, a majority was gained by the Conservatives, even though it was a small one. In the other two elections, the Conservatives narrowly missed a majority and yet managed to create a working government. In 2010, they achieved this through a coalition with the Liberal Democrats and in 2017 through a **confidence and supply** agreement with the Democratic Unionist Party (DUP). More usually, however, the two-party nature of FPTP and the 'winner's bonus' usually mean that one party gains a clear, outright majority and is therefore able to form a strong and stable government, meaning it can pass laws with relative ease and appear unlikely to face an unexpected election.

Key term

Confidence and supply An agreement where one party agrees to support another in votes in supply (money) and votes of no confidence.

In focus

The nature of UK government

Choosing to use FPTP has a number of expected outcomes, including that it usually returns a strong single-party government to power. However, the elections of the 2010s have challenged this traditionally expected effect (Table 3.4).

Table 3.4 General elections — 2010, 2015 and 2017

Date	Details
2010	Seats won: Conservatives 306, Labour 258, Liberal Democrats 57 With no overall majority gained by any single party, the Conservatives and Liberal Democrats came together to form a coalition government. They formed a cabinet made up of MPs from both parties and created the Coalition Agreement, which effectively became their manifesto
2015	Seats won: Conservatives 331, Labour 232, SNP 56 The Conservative Party achieved a small overall majority and formed a single-party government, forming a cabinet of just its own party's MPs and with a mandate to carry out its own manifesto
2017	Seats won: Conservatives 318, Labour 262, DUP 10 With no overall majority gained, the Conservative Party formed a minority government but with an agreement of confidence and supply from the DUP. This meant that the DUP would promise support to the Conservatives on two issues — any vote of confidence in the government and any issue of 'supply' (monetary or budget issues)

Following each of these elections, a different type of government formed, only one of which was the traditionally expected single-party government when using FPTP.

Table 3.5 sets out the differences between a **coalition** and a confidence and supply arrangement.

Table 3.5 Coalition compared with confidence and supply

Coalition	Confidence and supply
• A formal agreement between two or more parties, with both forming the government • Results in the creation of joint party policies and goals for the duration of the coalition and an expectation of support for these policies from the elected representatives of both parties • The government, including the cabinet, will be formed from members of all parties in the coalition	• A more informal agreement between the governing party and one other • Results in an agreement to support the government on issues of 'confidence' and 'supply' in return for government support on specific issues important to the other party. Beyond this, there is no expectation of support • The government, including the cabinet, will be formed of members from one party

Safe seats and swing seats

As a result of the 'winner-takes-all' nature of FPTP, a number of the constituencies become **safe seats**. This means that a particular party can almost guarantee victory in a particular seat, therefore making it 'safe'. Usually, this is a result of a concentration of voters with loyalty to one specific party being grouped together in one constituency.

In contrast, some seats are **marginal** or swing seats. These are seats where the voter loyalty within a constituency is more evenly split between parties, with the result that the likely winner of the seat is more difficult to determine.

Figure 3.4 highlights both the number of swing seats and the number of safe seats in three recent general elections. Those seats won with a lower percentage margin are the swing seats, and those won with a higher percentage margin are safe seats. It is clear that the number of safe and swing seats changes with each election and this may be due to population change, party policy change or other factors that affect voting behaviour. In the 2017 general election, there was an increase in the number of both very marginal and very safe seats.

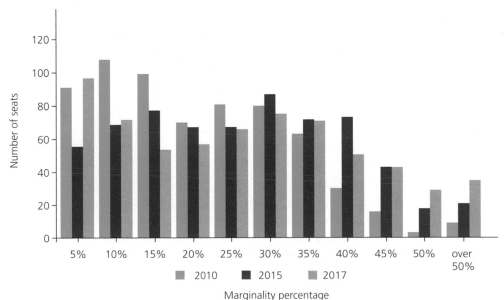

Figure 3.4 The number of swing and safe seats in the three general elections 2010, 2015 and 2017

How safe is safe?

In 1979 Bristol West was a safe Conservative seat, with Labour lagging 20% behind. Since 1997 it has been won by both Labour and the Liberal Democrats. In 2017 it became one of the safest Labour seats in the country, with Labour winning 47,213 votes against 9,877 for the Conservatives and 9,216 for the Liberal Democrats.

Can you find any other striking examples of safe seats changing hands? To what extent does this suggest that FPTP restricts voter choice by creating safe seats?

The advantages and disadvantages of FPTP

Many of the outcomes of FPTP can be judged to be positive or negative. It is important to be clear against what criteria these judgements are being made, however. Some might be positive for one group and negative for another (Table 3.6). For example, safe seats are positive for the major UK parties but negative for third and minority parties.

Table 3.6 Summary of the advantages and disadvantages of FPTP

Traditional advantages	Traditional disadvantages
Simplicity	**Lack of voter choice**
It is a simple system to use for the voters, rather than a mathematical formula, and produces a quick result. Voters therefore know how the system works and how their vote will be counted, which should increase turnout and reduce **spoiled ballots**	The resulting two-party system gives voters a lack of real choice, leading to reduced turnout or tactical voting
Strong government	**Unequal vote value**
It should produce a strong, single-party government able to effectively lead the country, rather than needing a compromise of parties	With uneven constituency sizes as well as the creation of safe and swing seats, the vote of one person can be far more valuable than that of another, depending on where they live, undermining key principles of democracy
MP–constituency link	**No majority needed**
It gives a clear link between each area and a representative, providing effective local representation and clear accountability to constituents	To win in a constituency, only a plurality is needed, meaning more people in total can vote against the winning candidate than for them, undermining legitimacy and wasting the votes of those who vote for a losing candidate
Centrist policies	**Disproportionate result**
With third parties struggling to gain success under FPTP, it keeps extremist parties out of office. Voters are given a clear choice between the two main parties and therefore the direction in which they believe the country should move. FPTP keeps out extremists	Compared to the percentage of the vote they receive, the two main parties are over-represented, usually through the winner's bonus, while other parties are under-represented

Key term

Spoiled ballot A ballot that is filled in incorrectly and therefore ignored. This may be unintentional or it may be an intentional protest by the voter.

Advantages of FPTP

Simplicity

FPTP is a simple system for the voter and for electoral administration, which allows for a cost-effective election which delivers a quick and legitimate result. The simplicity of putting an 'X' in a box and the seat being won by the person with the most votes should encourage people to turn out and vote as they can easily understand how the system works. This helps to underpin the legitimacy of the electoral system and the result. Even when a voter casts their ballot for a losing candidate, by taking part in the election they are expressing their consent to the use of FPTP as a method by which a government can be elected.

Strong government

Traditionally, FPTP has been praised for providing the country with a clear legitimate winner. The 'winner's bonus' of FPTP has usually provided the victorious party with a parliamentary majority, giving it a mandate to fulfil its manifesto commitments. By reducing the chance of coalition government, FPTP also ensures that the winning party does not have to compromise its manifesto promises without the consent of the voters. It has also generally ensured that the government has a majority with which it can pass legislation over the coming years, enabling it to make the changes that the public voted for.

MP–constituency link

The division of the UK into 650 constituencies means that each area has a local MP to represent it directly in Parliament. FPTP takes place in small, single-member constituencies. This means that the voters in a constituency can have a direct effect on the result in their area, and the MP elected has clear accountability to their constituency. Usually, MPs will have a constituency office and hold surgeries to keep in touch with their constituents. As well as having party loyalty, therefore, an elected official is more likely to be interested in remedying local issues in their constituency in order to ensure their re-election, which supports the principles of a representative democracy.

Centrist policies

With FPTP encouraging a two-party system, the main parties produce policies covering the political central ground in UK politics. The policies that are likely to be included in their manifestos are those that they believe will be popular and therefore will win them a high number of votes. They therefore ensure that the majority of the UK population is represented while excluding the policies and electoral success of minor, more extremist parties on the right or left wing of the political spectrum.

Disadvantages of FPTP

Lack of voter choice

The simplicity of FPTP is achieved through the 'winner-takes-all' aspect of the system. This means that for many voters, the only real choice is between Labour and the Conservatives, as these are the only two parties likely to get enough votes to have a realistic chance of winning the seat. Knowing this might actually decrease turnout in an election or lead to voters choosing to vote tactically, both of which undermine the legitimacy of the result. Voting tactically means that voters are not expressing their own desire at the ballot box. Rather they are considering the most likely outcome in their constituency and working out how to achieve the *least bad* outcome for themselves. For example, a Liberal Democrat supporter may choose to vote for Labour as their *least bad* outcome in a choice between Labour and the Conservatives.

In 2015 and 2017, new technology was used to create websites like Vote Swap. Voters could pledge to swap their votes with others in the country depending on how safe their own constituency was and dependent on the outcome they were trying to achieve. This relied on trust, as the UK has a secret ballot, and could be seen as a way of manipulating democracy.

In 2015 civil rights activist Peter Tatchell joined hundreds of protesters opposite the Houses of Parliament to call for voting reform in the UK

Unequal vote value

To achieve a strong, single-party government, the 'winner-takes-all' system results in votes being valued unequally, which undermines the democratic principle of 'one person, one vote'. If a person lives in a safe seat, their vote is effectively worth less than that of someone in a swing seat. They might want to vote for the party that is likely to win the seat, in which case their vote is largely ineffective as so many other people in their constituency are voting for that party. Or, they may wish to vote for a different party, which is so unlikely to win that their vote is also worthless. In contrast, in a swing seat, if just a few voters switch whom they vote for, it can dramatically affect the outcome in that seat, thereby giving each voter more power. The unequal power attached to votes across the UK undermines the principles of both representative and liberal democracy.

A lack of a majority

The election that takes place in each constituency does not require the winning candidate to have a majority, merely a plurality. In fact, most elected representatives will not have won a majority in their constituency election. If the winning candidate has less than 50% of the overall vote cast, then more people in total actually voted against them than voted for them, which goes some way to undermining the legitimacy of the winning candidate. It also means that a vast number of voters in each constituency will be represented by someone of a party or ideology for which they did not vote. These voters may therefore feel under-represented in Parliament.

Disproportionate result

FPTP gives a disproportionate result which over-represents the main parties and under-represents the other parties. The exclusion of such parties, however, is not in keeping with the principles of free and fair elections or effective representation of the voters. Not only does it reduce voter choice in an election, but it also creates artificial majorities for the main parties, which does not necessarily reflect the political beliefs of the nation. By reducing the competition in elections, the legitimacy of the result could be undermined.

In focus

Edmund Burke

Conservative philosopher Edmund Burke argued for the importance of tradition and empiricism and an expectation of gradual, organic change. He believed that institutions that had long existed should be respected. The arguments surrounding the reform of FPTP largely revolve around replacing it not reforming it, which is contrary to Burke's philosophy.

Developments in the twenty-first century

The advantages and disadvantages of FPTP have seen some new challenges in the twenty-first century:

- An increase in the number of safe seats — Figure 3.5 shows a significant jump in the number of safe seats in recent elections. In 2015, 21 seats were won by more than 50% and, in 2017, 35 seats. While there was also a jump in the number of swing seats, this simply reinforces the increased inequality in the value of a vote across the UK.

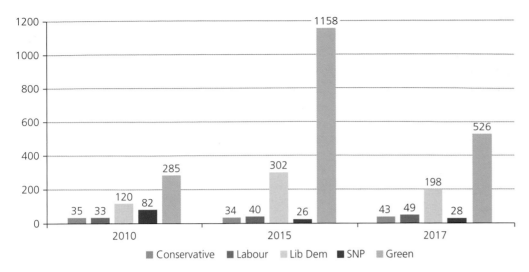

Figure 3.5 Average number of votes needed per seat won (000s) — 2010, 2015 and 2017 general elections

- FPTP can create disproportionate results — With more votes being cast for third parties, the disproportionate nature of the result has been more noticeable. In 2015, UKIP gained nearly 4 million votes (12.6%) but gained only one seat, while the SNP gained 1.5 million votes (4.7%) but gained 56 seats. In the 2015 general election, and again in 2017, a different party won the election in each of the countries within the UK. This is in addition to the disproportionate results gained for the two main parties that has always existed.

- Failure to deliver a strong, single-party government — A notable number of elections in the twenty-first century have seen a challenge to the traditional argument that FPTP produces a strong and stable government, with the production of small majorities, a minority government and a coalition. The 2017 election saw the Conservatives and Labour together gaining over 82% of the national vote, and in fact the Conservatives gained an extra 5.5% of the vote compared to their vote gained in 2015. Regardless, FPTP did not return a party with a clear majority.

Proportional electoral systems

Following the election of Labour in 1997, a number of key constitutional reforms were passed aimed at democratising and modernising the UK political landscape. This included the creation of a Scottish Parliament and a Welsh Assembly, along with negotiations for re-establishing a devolved body in Northern Ireland. Each of these bodies would use a proportional electoral system to elect members.

It is important to note that these elections have nothing at all to do with the UK general election — they happen at different times and elect different representatives to different bodies.

The additional member system (AMS)

Used for elections to the Scottish Parliament at Holyrood and the Welsh Assembly at the Senedd, the **additional member system** is the only system in the UK which gives voters two independent votes to cast — one for the voter's local representative and one for their regional representatives.

Key term

Additional member system (AMS) An electoral system which uses two votes, one for a local representative and one for regional representatives, with the aim of producing a more proportional result.

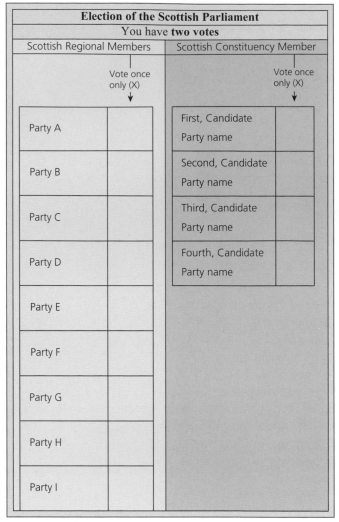

Election of the Scottish Parliament	
You have two votes	
Scottish Regional Members	Scottish Constituency Member
Vote once only (X)	Vote once only (X)
Party A	First, Candidate / Party name
Party B	Second, Candidate / Party name
Party C	Third, Candidate / Party name
Party D	Fourth, Candidate / Party name
Party E	
Party F	
Party G	
Party H	
Party I	

Figure 3.6 An example of a ballot paper using AMS

How it works

When a voter goes to the polls in AMS, they are presented with two different ballots. On each one they must cast their vote with a simple 'X' in a box. However, on the constituency vote they are electing a person, whereas in the regional vote they are casting their vote for a party. There is no need for them to vote for the same party on both ballots.

Figure 3.6 shows the choices a voter in the Scottish Parliamentary elections has to make. On the right, they elect their constituency Member of the Scottish Parliament (MSP) and on the left they cast a vote for a party in order to elect their regional MSPs.

The constituency vote

This first part of the election works in exactly the same way that FPTP works in UK general elections.

- The first ballots which are counted are those cast for a constituency representative.
- The whole of Scotland is divided into 73 small single-member constituencies and the whole of Wales is divided into 40 small single-member constituencies — these are different constituencies to those used in a general election.
- Each constituency elects a single representative on a plurality, 'winner-takes-all' basis.
- Those elected are given a seat in either the Scottish Parliament or the Welsh Assembly, and the first ballots are now effectively thrown away.

The regional vote

This second part of the election works more proportionally, and is designed to correct some of the problems of FPTP.

- The whole of Scotland and Wales are divided into large multi-member constituencies — eight regions in Scotland, each with seven elected members, and five regions in Wales, each with four elected members.
- Each party running for election draws up a list of candidates for each region, ranking them in the order they will be elected.
- The second ballots are counted within each region.
- To decide who gets the first seat, this system uses the d'Hondt formula. The inclusion of '+1' is the maths necessary to make the formula work; it is *not* an extra seat.

$$\frac{\text{Number of regional votes gained for a given party}}{\text{Number of seats a given party has gained} + 1}$$

- Once this formula is completed for every party, the first seat is allocated to the party with the highest number resulting from this equation.
- This process is repeated, until all seats in a region are allocated to a party. The party gives the seats it has won to the correct number of candidates from the top of its list downwards.

Each person in Scotland is therefore represented by a local MSP in their constituency, seven further MSPs in their region (see Figure 3.7), as well as the MP who they elect to send to Parliament.

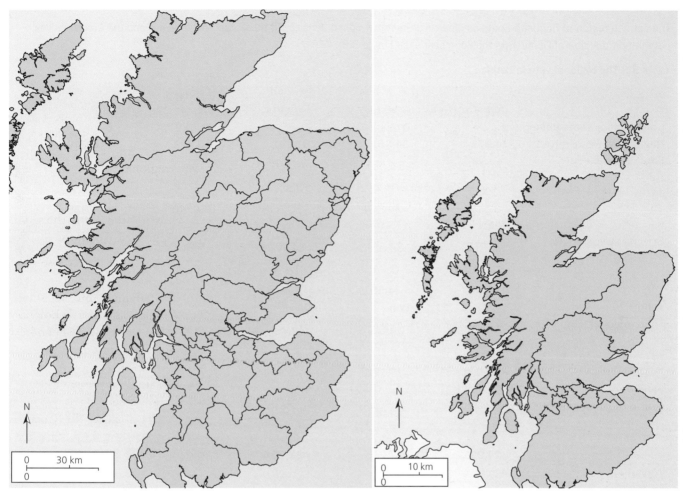

Figure 3.7 The 73 single-member constituencies in Scotland (left) and the eight regions (right)

The 2016 Scottish election results (Table 3.7) demonstrate that the parties which do not do well in the first part of the AMS process have a chance to do well in the second part. The Conservatives traditionally have low levels of support spread across Scotland, and therefore often do not gain enough votes to win in constituencies, but AMS allows them to do better in the proportional element of the system.

Table 3.7 Scottish election results, 2016

	Constituency vote	Seats gained	Regional vote	Seats gained
SNP	46.5%	59	41.7%	4
Conservatives	22%	7	23%	24
Labour	23%	3	19%	21
Liberal Democrats	8%	4	5%	1
Green	1%	0	7%	6

The Lothian region of Scotland

The Lothian region of Scotland contains nine single-member constituencies. Of these, the SNP took six, and the Conservatives, Labour and the Liberal Democrats took one seat each (Table 3.8).

Table 3.8 The regional vote in Lothian

	Conservatives	Green	Labour	Liberal Democrats	SNP
Constituency seats gained	1	0	1	1	6
Regional votes received	74,972	34,551	67,991	18,479	118,546
First regional seat	$\frac{74{,}972}{1+1}$ =37,486	$\frac{34{,}551}{0+1}$ =34,551	$\frac{67{,}991}{1+1}$ =33,996	$\frac{18{,}479}{1+1}$ =9,240	$\frac{118{,}546}{6+1}$ =16,935
Winner?	Win				
Second regional seat	$\frac{74{,}972}{2+1}$ =24,991	$\frac{34{,}551}{0+1}$ =34,551	$\frac{67{,}991}{1+1}$ =33,996	$\frac{18{,}479}{1+1}$ =9,240	$\frac{118{,}546}{6+1}$ =16,935
Winner?		Win			
Third regional seat	$\frac{74{,}972}{2+1}$ =24,991	$\frac{34{,}551}{1+1}$ =17,276	$\frac{67{,}991}{1+1}$ =33,996	$\frac{18{,}479}{1+1}$ =9,240	$\frac{118{,}546}{6+1}$ =16,935
Winner?			Win		
Fourth regional seat	$\frac{74{,}972}{2+1}$ =24,991	$\frac{34{,}551}{1+1}$ =17,276	$\frac{67{,}991}{2+1}$ =22,664	$\frac{18{,}479}{1+1}$ =9,240	$\frac{118{,}546}{6+1}$ =16,935
Winner?	Win				
Fifth regional seat	$\frac{74{,}972}{3+1}$ =18,743	$\frac{34{,}551}{1+1}$ =17,276	$\frac{67{,}991}{2+1}$ =22,664	$\frac{18{,}479}{1+1}$ =9,240	$\frac{118{,}546}{6+1}$ =16,935
Winner?			Win		
Sixth regional seat	$\frac{74{,}972}{3+1}$ =18,743	$\frac{34{,}551}{1+1}$ =17,276	$\frac{67{,}991}{3+1}$ =16,998	$\frac{18{,}479}{1+1}$ =9,240	$\frac{118{,}546}{6+1}$ =16,935
Winner?	Win				
Seventh regional seat	$\frac{74{,}972}{4+1}$ =14,994	$\frac{34{,}551}{1+1}$ =17,276	$\frac{67{,}991}{3+1}$ =16,998	$\frac{18{,}479}{1+1}$ =9,240	$\frac{118{,}546}{6+1}$ =16,935
Winner?		Win			

Source: Data from www.maths.lancs.ac.uk/jameson/scotelec2016.pdf

Edinburgh, capital of Scotland, is situated in the Lothian region. Since 1999 it has been the seat of the Scottish parliament at Holyrood

Table 3.8 demonstrates how the d'Hondt formula works. One seat at a time, the mathematical formula is worked out and one seat is allocated. This seat is then added to that party's total seats gained, and the process is repeated. Note: to make sense of the table you need to read the rows stage by stage, from the first regional seat down to the seventh regional seat.

Advantages and disadvantages of AMS

The pros and cons of AMS are summarised in Table 3.9.

Table 3.9 Advantages and disadvantages of AMS

Advantages	Disadvantages
Proportional result The second stage of AMS tries to correct the problems of FPTP. The more seats a party gains in the constituency vote, the more difficult it is for it to gain regional seats as its votes will be divided by a higher number. This reduces the wasted votes and ensures more parties have a chance of being represented	**More complicated** Although the process of voting is simple, what happens next is not. This can put voters off, as they may feel that their vote will be mathematically manipulated. This may therefore reduce turnout
Split-ticket voting Voters have more choice with two votes to cast, and they can choose to exercise their two votes for different parties (split ticket). This also encourages more parties to run, especially in the regional ballot	**An unlikely single-party government** The more proportional nature of AMS means single-party governments are harder to achieve, meaning coalitions are more likely. This means governments may be weaker and find it more difficult to pass the policies on which they campaigned
A government with broad popularity In order to form a single-party government, a party must have broad popularity across a whole country, not just in concentrated pockets. If coalitions are formed, a great number of parties can have an input on policy. This supports greater legitimacy of the government	**The first round** The constituency vote of AMS is conducted using FPTP. Therefore this carries with it the same disadvantages that FPTP has
Greater representation With all areas being represented by a constituency and regional representatives, there is more chance for the voters that someone who shares their ideology represents them, potentially increasing turnout	**Different types of representatives** AMS creates two tiers of representatives, a constituency and a regional MSP. This can cause tension and confusion for the voters and blur accountability
	Party control In the regional vote, the party controls the order of its list of candidates — voters only have the choice to support its list or not. It could be argued that this gives excessive influence to the party leadership

The effects of using AMS

Using AMS is likely to result in a multiparty system as the proportional nature of this system allows for smaller parties to have some, if limited, success. This in turn is likely to result in a coalition government as it can be difficult for one party to gain an outright majority. In Scotland, the SNP did manage to achieve an outright majority in 2011, although all of the other governments formed in Wales and Scotland have either been coalition or minority governments. Safe seats and swing seats are still a feature of the constituency vote of AMS, but this is less evident in the regional vote because this element is proportional.

The single transferable vote (STV)

Used for elections to the Northern Irish Assembly, the **single transferable vote (STV)** is the only system in the UK which allows for **ordinal voting**. This allows a voter to rank candidates in order of preference, beginning at '1' and going through as many of the candidates as they wish to rank.

How it works

- Northern Ireland is divided into 18 large, multi-member regions, each electing six representatives to send to the Northern Irish Assembly.
- The voter is given a ballot paper with all the candidates running in their region. This may include multiple candidates running for the same party. They cast their ballot by numbering candidates 1, 2, 3, and so on.
- Once the election is over, the total number of ballots cast in each region is counted.
- In order to win, a candidate needs to achieve the 'Droop quota':

$$\left(\frac{\text{Total number of valid votes cast in a region}}{\text{Number of seats available in a region} + 1} \right) + 1$$

- Any candidates who have achieved the Droop quota are automatically given a seat.
- Any votes that they achieved over this number are redistributed according to any second preferences. If any more candidates now have the Droop quota, they too are given a seat.
- If there are seats remaining and no one else has reached the Droop quota, the candidate with the fewest votes is eliminated and their votes are redistributed.
- This process continues until all available seats are filled.

> ### Key terms
>
> **Single transferable vote (STV)** A voting system in which voters express their preference, ranking candidates in order. To win, a candidate needs to achieve the 'Droop quota'.
>
> **Ordinal voting** A vote cast in which the voter ranks candidates in order of preference, ranking as few or as many candidates as they wish.

The Northern Ireland Assembly Senate Chamber at Stormont

Figure 3.8 shows how the ballot for the Northern Irish Assembly elections allows voters to express their preferences by ranking as many candidates as they would like, including ranking multiple candidates from the same party.

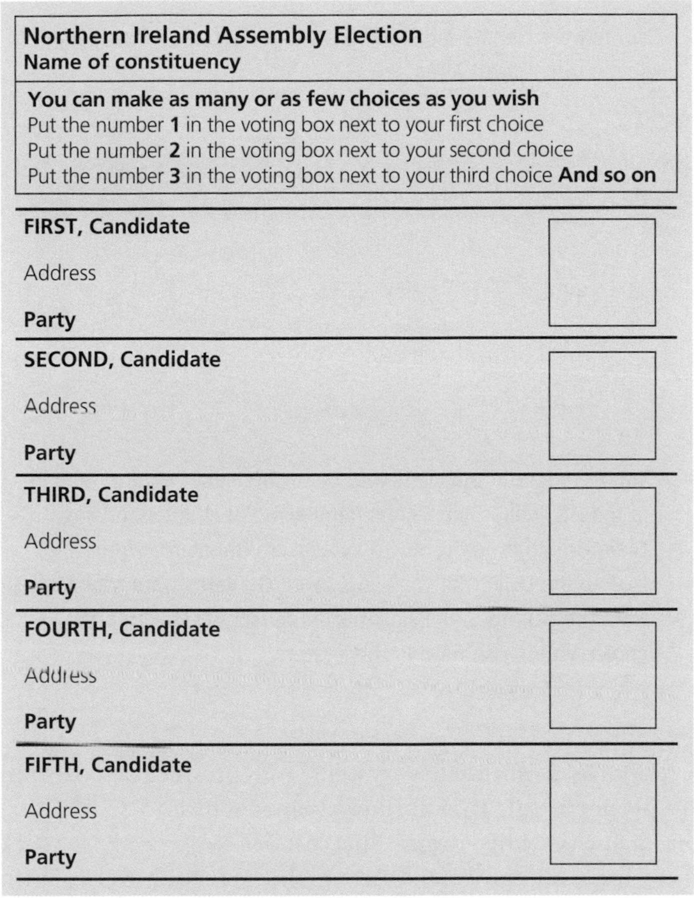

| Northern Ireland Assembly Election |
| Name of constituency |

You can make as many or as few choices as you wish
Put the number **1** in the voting box next to your first choice
Put the number **2** in the voting box next to your second choice
Put the number **3** in the voting box next to your third choice **And so on**

FIRST, Candidate

Address

Party

SECOND, Candidate

Address

Party

THIRD, Candidate

Address

Party

FOURTH, Candidate

Address

Party

FIFTH, Candidate

Address

Party

Figure 3.8 An example of a ballot paper using STV

The Northern Irish Assembly results in 2017 (Table 3.10) demonstrate a closer correlation than most other electoral systems in the UK between the percentage of votes cast for each party and the percentage of the seats it gained. This means votes are of more equal value and there is less incentive for voters to vote tactically.

Table 3.10 Northern Irish Assembly results, 2017

	First preference votes	Number of seats gained	Percentage of seats gained
DUP	28%	28	31%
Sinn Féin	28%	27	30%
SDLP	12%	12	13%
UUP	13%	10	11%
Others	18%	13	14%

Vote transfers in 2016

Under the Droop quota, votes are redistributed according to the preferences expressed by the voters. In 2016, 179,287 votes were transferred. Table 3.11 is an excerpt of just some of those transferred votes.

Table 3.11 Transferred votes, Northern Irish Assembly election, 2016

Votes transferred from → / Votes transferred to ↓	Democratic Unionist Party	Sinn Féin	UKIP	Ulster Unionist Party
Democratic Unionist Party	16,680	111	1,699	4,795
Sinn Féin	49	15,687	65	212
UKIP	174	31	0	531
Ulster Unionist Party	8,378	224	1,644	10,835

Vote transfers within the same party occur when one of its candidates wins, but has more votes than the Droop quota. If these excess votes have as their next preference a candidate from the same party then these votes are effectively transferred within that party. Table 3.11 also highlights the preferential voting exercised for parties of a similar ideology.

The Democratic Unionists and Ulster Unionists want to remain in the UK, while Sinn Féin is Republican. It is not surprising, therefore, that nearly 5,000 votes were transferred from the UUP to the DUP, while only just over 200 votes were transferred from the UUP to Sinn Féin. This demonstrates the greater choice voters can have in this system.

The effects of using STV

Using STV is likely to result in a multiparty system and produce a coalition government. Being highly proportional, it is unlikely that it will lead to any one party gaining an outright majority. This means that parties will need to work together after the election to form an agreement on which they can govern. With only multi-member constituencies in this electoral process, the likelihood of safe seats is significantly reduced and the value of each vote is more uniform.

Advantages and disadvantages of STV

The pros and cons of the STV system are summarised in Table 3.12.

Table 3.12 Advantages and disadvantages of STV

Advantages	Disadvantages
Proportional result STV is the most proportional system used within the UK, delivering a result which has a close correlation between the percentage of the vote cast and the percentage of seats gained, increasing the legitimacy of the result	**More complicated** Like AMS, although the process of voting is simple, what happens next is not, which may reduce turnout
Voter choice Voters have a great degree of choice, not only between parties, but also within parties. They may support one particular party but if it puts forward a candidate who the voters do not like, they have the choice to vote for someone else from that party	**An unlikely single-party government** In Northern Ireland, the Good Friday Agreement means there has to be a coalition in government. However, even if this was not the case, the proportional nature of STV means a coalition is a likely result, which could be weaker than a single-party government
Greater representation Like AMS, the multi-member constituencies mean a voter is likely to have someone elected who shares their ideology or beliefs	**Constituency link** With no local elected representatives as in FPTP or AMS, and large multi-member constituencies, the link between elected representatives and their local area is weaker

A different electoral system

Much research has been conducted on how the UK general election would look if another electoral system were used. If the 2017 election had been conducted using a different system, there might have been other outcomes, as shown in Table 3.13.

Table 3.13 Possible different outcomes of the 2017 general election under three electoral systems

	FPTP	AMS	STV
Conservative	317	273	283
Labour	262	260	297
SNP	35	21	18
Liberal Democrats	12	39	29
Plaid Cymru	4	4	3
Green Party	1	7	1
UKIP	0	11	1

These results do not, of course, account for the fact that under a different system a voter may use their vote differently.

How can these figures be used to support and oppose the use of FPTP for UK general elections?

Majoritarian systems

Following a referendum in 1998, Londoners voted to change the way that London was governed, and this included having an elected mayor. To elect this position, the **supplementary vote (SV)** system would be used, requiring the office holder to have a majority of the vote. In 2000, the first election took place and was won by the then independent candidate Ken Livingstone. Since then, elections have taken place every 4 years, with three different people holding the office of mayor of London.

The way in which the supplementary vote operates means that Sadiq Khan can claim a strong personal mandate as London mayor, having won 56.8% of the vote on the second round

Election of the Mayor

Vote once (X) in column one for your first choice
Vote once (X) in column two for your second choice

	column one first choice	column two second choice
1 FIRST, Candidate Party	☐	☐
2 SECOND, Candidate Party	☐	☐
3 THIRD, Candidate Party	☐	☐
4 FOURTH, Candidate Party	☐	☐
5 FIFTH, Candidate Party	☐	☐
6 SIXTH, Candidate Party	☐	☐

Figure 3.9 An example of a ballot paper for a mayoral election (SV)

Supplementary vote (SV)
How it works

- London is treated as one large constituency for the election of the London mayor.
- Candidates are given a ballot paper with all of the candidates listed and two columns — one for the voter's first choice and one for their second choice. The voter puts one 'X' in each column to vote.
- All of the first-choice ballots are counted. If anyone has a majority, they win the election.
- If no one has a majority, all but the top two candidates are eliminated in one go. The second preferences for all of the eliminated candidates are taken into account and the votes redistributed. If both a voter's first- and second-choice candidate have been eliminated, then their vote is ignored.
- With only two candidates left and all votes redistributed, one of them must now have a majority — this person is the winner.

Figure 3.9 shows how the ballot for the mayor of London allows voters to express a first and second preference.

In 2016 the mayoral election saw a turnout of just 45%, or around 2.5 million Londoners (Table 3.14). If voters choose to express no second preference, or if their second preference is for an eliminated candidate, their influence is reduced. Nearly 400,000 voters expressed no second preference.

Table 3.14 The London mayoral election, 2016

	First preference votes (%)	Second preference votes (%)	Overall (%)
Sadiq Khan (Labour)	44	66	57
Zac Goldsmith (Conservative)	35	34	43
Sian Berry (Green)	6		
Caroline Pidgeon (Liberal Democrat)	5		
Peter Whittle (UKIP)	4		
Others	6		

The effects of using SV

Using SV is likely to result in a two-party system and produce a strong, single-party government. London is not a good example of this as there is only one seat available. However, these results can be used to infer what would happen if SV was used across the UK — the elimination of all but the top two candidates for the second round is likely to result in a similar two-party dominance to that produced by FPTP, or potentially make this dominance even more likely.

Advantages and disadvantages of SV

The pros and cons of the SV system are summarised in Table 3.15.

Table 3.15 Advantages and disadvantages of SV

Advantages	Disadvantages
Majority result SV ensures that the winning candidate has a clear majority of the votes, increasing their legitimacy, while still keeping extremist parties out of influence. This should lead to a strong and stable single-party government	**Two-party dominance** The elimination of all but two candidates in one go means that third parties are unlikely to do well and the result is not proportional. This might encourage a tactical use of the second preference rather than providing better choice for voters, or discourage some from turning out to vote at all
Voter choice Voters have more choice than in FPTP, knowing that they can vote for a smaller party with their first preference if they wish, but still using their second preference to try and ensure that their vote is not wasted	**A false majority** A candidate needs only to gain a majority of the 'valid vote', meaning the votes that count. In the second round, the vote of anyone with no second preference or whose second preference has been eliminated is not counted, meaning the winning candidate might not have a true majority
Simple system Unlike the proportional systems, SV is relatively easy to understand both in how votes are cast but also how they are counted afterwards	**Wasted votes** As with FPTP, there are a large number of wasted votes which have little or no impact on the outcome of the election

FPTP compared

One way in which FPTP can be compared with other systems is by looking at the features and effects of each of the electoral systems used in the UK (Table 3.16). These different elements produce advantages and disadvantages for each system and form the basis of debates over the potential reform or replacement of FPTP.

Table 3.16 Overview of the features of the electoral systems used in the UK

System	Type of system	Type of constituency	Number of votes	Type of vote	Voting for	Likely resulting party system	Likely government formed	Used in
FPTP	Plurality	Single-member	1	Single choice	A single person	Two-party	Single party	UK general election
AMS	Proportional	Single- and multi-member	2	Single choice	Vote 1: a person Vote 2: a party	Multiparty	Coalition	Scottish Parliament and Welsh Assembly elections
STV	Proportional	Multi-member	1	Ordinal voting	A single person	Multiparty	Coalition	Northern Irish Assembly election
SV	Majoritarian	Single-member	1	First- and second-choice	A single person	Two-party	Single party	London mayoral election

Stretch and challenge

The Jenkins Commission

Following Labour's election in 1997, the Jenkins Commission was set up to look into replacements for FPTP.

Research the recommendations of the Jenkins Commission. What reasons could be given for these recommendations never having been implemented?

It is also possible to compare FPTP to other electoral systems by looking at the actual results they have produced in each country (Table 3.17).

Table 3.17 Overview of election results under different systems in different parts of the UK

FPTP	SV	STV	AMS	AMS
UK general elections	London mayoral elections	Northern Irish elections	Scottish elections	Welsh elections
2001 Labour majority government — 413 seats with 41% of the national vote	2000 Ken Livingston (Independent) won with 39% of first-round votes, and 59% after the second round	2003 Election took place but the Assembly suspended. Largest parties were DUP and UUP	2003 Coalition of Labour and Liberal Democrats — a total of 67 seats with 50% of the constituency vote and 41% of the regional vote	2003 Labour government — 30 seats with 40% of the constituency vote and 37% of the regional vote
2005 Labour majority government — 355 seats with 35% of the national vote	2004 Ken Livingston (Labour) won with 37% of first-round votes, and 55% after the second round	2007 Coalition of DUP and Sinn Féin (with UUP, SDLP and Alliance) — a total of 64 seats with 56% of the national vote	2007 SNP minority government with the Green Party — a total of 49 seats with 33% of the constituency vote and 35% of the regional vote	2007 Coalition of Labour and Plaid Cymru — a total of 41 seats with 55% of the constituency vote and 51% of the regional vote
2010 Coalition of Conservatives and Liberal Democrats — a total of 363 seats with 59% of the national vote	2008 Boris Johnson (Conservative) won with 43% of first-round votes, and 53% after the second round	2011 Coalition of DUP and Sinn Féin (with UUP, SDLP and Alliance) — a total of 67 seats with 57% of the national vote	2011 SNP majority government — 69 seats with 45% of the constituency vote and 44% of the regional vote	2011 Labour government — 30 seats with 42% of the constituency vote and 37% of the regional vote
2015 Conservative majority government — 330 seats with 37% of the national vote	2012 Boris Johnson (Conservative) won with 44% of first-round votes, and 52% after the second round	2016 Coalition of DUP and Sinn Féin — a total of 66 seats with 53% of the national vote	2016 SNP minority government — 63 seats with 47% of the constituency vote and 42% of the regional vote	2016 Coalition of Labour and Liberal Democrats — a total of 34 seats with 42% of the constituency vote and 38% of the regional vote
2017 Conservative minority government — 317 seats with 42% of the national vote	2016 Sadiq Khan (Labour) won with 44% of first-round votes, and 57% after the second round	2017 No coalition agreement reached. Largest parties were DUP and Sinn Féin		

The impact of UK electoral systems

The use of different electoral systems across the UK has had a range of outcomes. Not only are there differences between systems, there have also been differences within the same system over time (see Table 3.17).

Impact on governments and the type of government

The introduction of proportional systems has led, as expected, to a greater number of coalition or minority governments being formed in the regions using them. However, as Northern Ireland has to have a coalition government as part of the Good Friday Agreement, the data collected from its elections must be viewed through this lens. Equally, while Scotland and Wales have experienced coalition governments, they have also experienced majority governments, even under their proportional systems. That these systems have created strong and stable, single-party governments has fuelled discussions over whether systems like AMS could be used to replace FPTP.

- In both Wales and Scotland, there has been a further impact on their governments. As a result of being able to legislate successfully over their own regions, both countries pressed for further power to be devolved to them.
- For Wales this meant gaining primary legislative powers and changing from a 'conferred matters' model to a 'reserved matters' model of government, as Scotland.
- For Scotland, this meant pressure for independence and an independence referendum. The outcome of the referendum initially quelled this pressure. However, given the result of the Brexit referendum — in which the UK voted to leave the EU, but Scotland as a nation voted to remain — the issue of Scottish independence was reignited.

Aside from Northern Ireland, the governments that have been created have proven to be stable. In Northern Ireland, the problems that have occurred have been less as a result of the electoral system and more to do with the historical tensions that exist within the region.

Impact on parties and party systems

The number of parties successfully competing in elections and within government has increased as a result of the newly introduced proportional systems. In Wales, Scotland and Northern Ireland, nationalist or unionist parties (SNP, Plaid Cymru, DUP and Sinn Féin) have gained influence and been able to be part of governments in their respective countries or provinces. However, these systems have also allowed notable success for other parties too. The Conservatives, which since the prime ministership of Margaret Thatcher have performed poorly in Scotland, have been able to pick up seats, even becoming the second largest party in the Scottish Parliament due to the proportional system. AMS has allowed the Conservatives' widely spread support to be translated into seats at regional level; they do, however, still perform less well at constituency level in Scotland.

In some of the devolved bodies, it could be argued that small parties have been over-represented. In 2007, with the SNP winning 47 seats and Labour winning 46, an SNP agreement with the Green Party, which had just two seats, allowed the SNP to form a minority government. In this situation, small parties have become 'king-makers', similar to the role of the Liberal Democrats in the 2010 UK general election — this means they exercise power far beyond that which their electoral success suggests they should have.

Figure 3.10 illustrates the changing fortunes of third parties in Scottish, Welsh and Northern Irish elections since 1998/9 and the multiparty systems that exist in the devolved assemblies, in which there are a number of parties that have a realistic chance of forming a government.

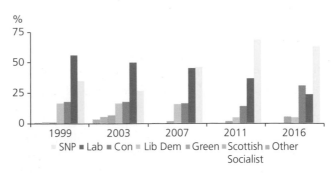

(a) Scottish Parliament

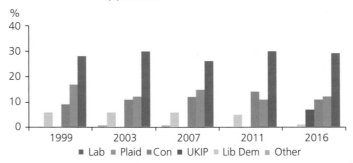

(b) National Assembly for Wales

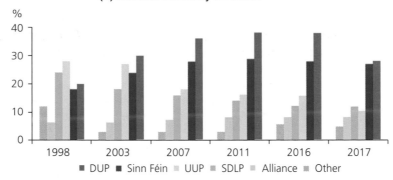

(c) Northern Irish Assembly

Figure 3.10 Elections since 1999

These successes have had a wider impact — they have led to the recognition and success of more minor parties in the UK general election. For example, the SNP was able to capture 56 seats in 2015, replacing Labour as the dominant force in Scotland. UKIP demonstrated a significant, if short-lived, ability to attract a large volume of voters. Perhaps the most visible impact of this widening of party politics has been at the televised leaders' debates prior to an election. Used for the first time in 2010 with just three party leaders, one of the debates in 2015 featured seven different party leaders. The 2017 election does suggest that the electoral success of these parties still has limitations, with the Conservatives and Labour gaining 82% of the vote between them. That said, the pressure that third parties can exert on the major parties can create a policy influence if not power.

Impact on voters and voter choice

The use of differing electoral systems can theoretically help to improve voter turnout by eliminating some of the problems associated with FPTP that may depress turnout, such as wasted votes and safe seats. However, it can be difficult to demonstrate this as turnout for a regional election does not necessarily represent the likely turnout for a general election. In many of the devolved bodies, turnout has been lower than that seen in the UK general election. While this could be attributed to the complexity of the systems, it could also be due to a reduced importance placed on them in view of the limited powers of devolved bodies. Extrapolating answers from this data is therefore fraught with danger because these systems have not been used in a nationwide election.

It is clear, however, that voters have had greater choice offered to them in all of the electoral systems that have been introduced. This includes SV which, while majoritarian, allows voters two preferences, meaning they can vote however they wish with their first vote and still use the second for one of the two major UK parties which are likely to win. The proportional systems have gone further than this, not only offering greater choice, with AMS having two votes and STV offering ordinal voting, but also reducing the votes that are wasted in an election or the likelihood of safe seats occurring. They have also improved voter choice in representation. In multi-member constituencies, voters have a choice of representative they can lobby in order to get their voice heard.

Debate

Should FPTP be replaced for UK general elections?

Yes

- Recent elections demonstrate that FPTP is no longer even fulfilling the traditional strengths that it promised, such as a strong, single-party government.
- FPTP produces a poor result regardless of your view — its lack of proportionality is increasingly evident and this does not fit with the principles of representative democracy, and it does not deliver either MPs or a government with a majority of the votes cast.
- The government that it does deliver can be argued to lack legitimacy and yet possess huge power: what Lord Hailsham referred to as 'an elective dictatorship'. Even governments with small majorities have been able to push through policy with little regard for the opposition view.
- The inequality in voter value across the UK does not fit with the principle of 'one person, one vote' and is not going to be remedied simply by moving constituency boundaries in 2020.
- Beyond this inequality, many votes are wasted, meaning they have little or no impact on the electoral outcome. This undermines legitimacy, encourages tactical voting and may discourage turnout, all of which undermine democratic principles.
- The two-party system represents a lack of true competition in UK elections, which undermines liberal and pluralist democratic principles. The only accountability that voters can often exercise is to choose the other major party, which is not a great deal of choice.

No

- It is widely understood by the public, not just in terms of how the ballot works but also how the winner of an election is calculated. As a result of this, an educated public is more likely to turn out to vote, which improves the legitimacy of the resulting government.
- The governments that it has produced have largely been 'strong and stable'. The 2010 coalition lasted for the full term of a parliament.
- It is possible for smaller parties to do well, as the SNP demonstrated in 2015, while at the same time it can keep parties with more extreme political views out of office. While UKIP gained nearly 4 million votes but only one seat in 2015, its impact was still seen through the adoption of its major policy by the Conservative Party. This allows for the best of both worlds.
- The clear choice for voters in a two-party system, and the likelihood of a single-party government, make it easier for the voters to hold a government to account simply by voting for the other major party.
- Proportional systems weaken or remove the link between geographical areas and the people who represent them, which is a key feature of FPTP. This link allows for effective local representation of the whole of the UK in Parliament.

Should FPTP be replaced?

Given the successful use of other systems across the UK, and the drawbacks of FPTP in the twenty-first century, there have been growing questions over whether the FPTP system should now be replaced for UK general elections. Although a referendum was held on this issue in 2011, it only gave the public the option of FPTP or the alternative vote (AV). AV is very similar to SV, except that voters can express more than two preferences, and instead of eliminating all but the top two candidates, the bottom-placed candidates are eliminated one at a time until one person has a majority. While the public voted against this proposal, this did not mean they rejected electoral reform outright, but rather that they rejected AV. After two more contentious elections in 2015 and 2017, the questions over the use of FPTP have not gone away.

Referendums

Referendums have gained huge prominence in UK political life through the twenty-first century. Once a relatively rare occurrence, they have been used since 2000 to:

- give more power to the Welsh Assembly
- consider replacing FPTP
- give Scotland a vote on independence
- give the UK public a vote on leaving the European Union

Indeed, the understanding and acceptance of referendums as part of UK political life is such that there have been several public campaigns for referendums to happen. This includes calls for a second referendum on Scottish independence and a 'People's Vote' referendum which would allow the electorate to approve or disapprove the final Brexit settlement.

Figure 3.11 shows how a referendum offers voters a straight binary choice on the issue on which the referendum is held.

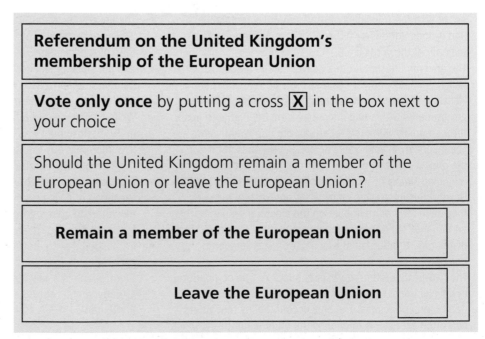

Figure 3.11 A referendum ballot paper

The UK-wide referendum on the position of the UK in the EU courted notable controversy. Not only was it a huge issue to be given just two choices, 'Remain a member of the European Union' or 'Leave the European Union', one of the campaigns was later fined for breaking electoral law. A subsequent Supreme Court case (see Chapter 8) was needed to ensure the decision would be enforced by Parliament, and not by the government alone.

Why call a referendum?

The role of referendums in UK politics has changed very little even as they have become more accepted.

- A government might call a referendum in response to public pressure. In 2014, under pressure from the majority SNP government in Scotland, the government allowed a referendum on Scottish independence to take place. In 2015, part of the general election campaign became the issue of the UK in the EU. With UKIP arguing for leaving the EU and promising a referendum, the Conservative Party eventually offered one too, fearing the loss of its voters to UKIP.
- Referendums can help to resolve controversial issues dividing a party. By handing over responsibility for a decision to the people, a party can absolve itself of the decision-making and therefore avoid arguments between factions of the party. This has been true to some extent of the Conservative Party. With the party divided between 'Remainers' and 'Brexiteers', a referendum should have helped to solve this issue. Unfortunately for the Conservative Party, once the referendum took place, the party then became further divided over the type of Brexit that should take place, so this is not always successful.
- A referendum might also be called as part of an agreement between parties. The AV referendum of 2011 was part of the coalition agreement between the Conservatives and the Liberal Democrats.
- Finally, referendums can lend legitimacy to large, constitutional changes in the UK. They have mostly been used when the location of power and sovereignty might be affected, although not all such decisions have seen a referendum. Changing the electoral system, giving more power to devolved bodies and other similar issues all influence where power lies in the UK. Some issues involving the movement of power, such as the creation of the UK Supreme Court, were not subject to a referendum. However, the referendums that have been held have all been on substantial constitutional issues.

The referendum on the UK's membership of the EU created political problems across the British political system, undermining the power of the prime minister, dividing parties and creating constitutional crises

Referendums in the UK

There have been only three nationwide referendums in the UK, although there were substantial calls for two more throughout 2018, including mass petitions and protests to support these calls. There have been a number of regional referendums, however. Table 3.18 gives details of all the referendums held since 1975.

Table 3.18 Referendums in the UK since 1975

Date	Location	Issue	Yes (%)	No (%)	Turnout (%)	Commentary
1975	UK	Remaining in the EEC	67.2	32.8	63.2	This was the first UK-wide referendum. In campaigning for it, Prime Minister Harold Wilson's pamphlet said, 'The Government will accept *your* verdict'
1979	Wales	Creating a Welsh Parliament	20.3	79.7	58.3	
1979	Scotland	Creating a Scottish Parliament	51.6	48.4	63.7	40% of the overall electorate needed to vote 'Yes' for this to be enacted. Accounting for turnout, only 33% voted 'Yes', therefore the referendum was ignored
1997	Scotland	Creating a Scottish Parliament ...	74.3	25.7	60.4	The Labour manifesto in 1997 committed to giving both Scotland and Wales a referendum over whether power should be devolved to them. As a result of both countries' 'yes' vote, the Scottish Parliament and the National Assembly for Wales were established
		... with tax-varying powers	63.5	36.5	60.4	
1997	Wales	Creating a Welsh Parliament	50.3	49.7	50.1	
1998	Northern Ireland	Approving the Good Friday Agreement	71.1	28.9	81.0	This was held as a result of the Northern Ireland Peace Process
1998	London	Creating an elected mayor	72.0	28.0	34.0	This was held as part of Labour's push for the democratisation of the UK
2011	Wales	Primary legislative powers for Wales	63.5	36.5	35.6	The result helped to begin to bring Wales more in line with the Scottish Parliament
2011	UK	Replacing FPTP with AV	32.1	67.9	42.2	Held due to the coalition agreement between the Conservatives and Liberal Democrats
2014	Scotland	Scottish independence	44.7	55.3	84.6	Held due to pressure from the Scottish government. 16- and 17-year-olds were allowed to vote
2016	UK	Leave or remain in the EU	Leave: 51.9	Remain: 48.1	72.2	Held due to a promise made by the Conservatives in the 2015 general election

The consequences of referendums in the UK

A considerable number of the referendums held across the UK have resulted in notable political change. However, Parliament is sovereign so governments do not have to follow the decision of the voters. This became a big issue following the Brexit referendum. MPs such as Dominic Grieve claimed 'the [EU] referendum was an advisory referendum', whereas John Redwood claimed 'this was not an advisory referendum'. Parliamentary sovereignty means no referendum can truly be legally binding. Even if Parliament passed a law saying that a referendum was, it could simply pass another law to contradict this later on because sovereignty rests with Parliament. However, the political pressure placed on the government to abide by the result after a referendum is considerable. Giving the public a choice and then ignoring the outcome casts questions of legitimacy and accountability on the government. Nonetheless, this remains an issue with Brexit: while some have claimed the referendum showed the will of the people, others argued that the campaigns — both Remain and Leave — were not truthful in their campaigning.

Referendums and the Electoral Commission

Following the UK-wide 2016 referendum, the Electoral Commission fined the Leave campaign for breaking electoral law.

Conclusions of the investigation

- Vote Leave's referendum spending was £7,449,079.34, exceeding its statutory spending limit of £7 million.
- Vote Leave's spending return was inaccurate in respect of 43 items of spending, totalling £236,501.44. Eight payments of over £200 in Vote Leave's return did not have an invoice or receipt with them. These payments came to £12,849.99.
- As an unregistered campaigner, BeLeave exceeded its spending limit of £10,000 by more than £666,000.
- Vote Leave failed to comply with an investigation notice issued by the commission.
- In total, the levels of fines were £61,000 for Vote Leave.

Does this data suggest that referendums are fundamentally flawed? In cases such as this, are the results of the referendum conducted legitimate?

One notable consequence of referendum use in the UK has been the public's expectation of more referendums. Indeed, since the UK constitution is uncodified and unentrenched, the use of referendums for issues concerning the reform of the constitution has arguably become a convention. However, conventions can be broken, and the expectations of the public cannot always be met.

In 2018 and 2019 as the consequences of Brexit became clearer, public pressure mounted for another referendum on whether or not the UK should exit the European Union. However, Theresa May consistently opposed this, arguing that not to deliver on the result of the 2016 referendum would threaten social cohesion, by ignoring the democratic will of the people.

Although the 2016 EU referendum achieved the highest turnout (72.2%) in a national election since 1992, the campaign was marred by allegations of lies and scaremongering on both sides

The way in which the expectation of more referendums increases the reliance on direct democracy (Table 3.19) has the potential to cause considerable conflict between the public and their elected representatives. This is especially true in the light of misleading campaigns, as the UK's representative democracy hinges on the 'trustee model' — elected officials being allowed to use their conscience to act in the best interests of the governed on the basis of being fully informed.

Table 3.19 Referendums and elections

Referendum	Election
A vote on a single, narrow issue	A vote on a wide range of policy issues
A 'yes' or 'no' vote	A choice of options is available for the voter
Called when the government wishes	Called at set intervals as defined by law
The result is not legally binding	The result is legally binding
An example of direct democracy	An example of representative democracy

Are referendums good for the UK?

Yes	No
They can encourage participation and education, as shown in the Scottish independence and Brexit referendums, which enhances legitimacy and consent in the political system.	Turnout for some referendums has been low, such as the AV referendum, which undermines the legitimacy of the decision and the effectiveness of direct democracy.

Yes

- They can encourage participation and education, as shown in the Scottish independence and Brexit referendums, which enhances legitimacy and consent in the political system.
- They have provided a clear answer to political issues and the results have been successfully implemented, such as the creation of devolved bodies.
- They have enhanced liberal democracy by serving as a way to limit the power of the government.
- The management of referendums is overseen by the independent Electoral Commission in the same manner as elections. This limits government manipulation of them.
- They have enhanced representation in the UK by allowing popular sovereignty to be directly expressed.
- As an accepted constitutional convention, they provide another way in which the public can engage in politics between elections, and ensure a responsive government with a mandate to act.
- As referendums are advisory, Parliament remains sovereign and can implement the decision in an effective manner. Although the public voted to leave the EU, Parliament decides on the manner of the withdrawal.

No

- Turnout for some referendums has been low, such as the AV referendum, which undermines the legitimacy of the decision and the effectiveness of direct democracy.
- Close results can be more divisive rather than settling an issue, as seen in Brexit and the Scottish independence referendum.
- The campaigns surrounding some referendums have been misleading, raising questions over the legitimacy of the result.
- The government decides if and when to call a referendum, which concentrates power in the government rather than limiting it.
- They have undermined representative democracy in the UK, challenging key principles of the 'trustee model' in which elected representatives act in the best interests of the electorate on the basis of the consent given at an election.
- The issues raised are often complex, with voters lacking the necessary information to make a fully informed decision and the question being too complex to reduce to a 'yes' or 'no' choice.
- Parliamentary sovereignty is undermined in reality as, having offered a referendum, there is a lot of political pressure for the government to honour the will of the people.

Summary

By the end of this chapter you should be able to answer the following questions:

→ Which electoral system in the UK best fulfils the functions of an election?

→ What are the different types of electoral systems used in the UK?

→ What is the most significant factor in assessing the effectiveness of an electoral system?

→ Have the uses of other electoral systems demonstrated the necessity of replacing FPTP?

→ To what extent have the different electoral systems resulted in different outcomes?

→ How significant has the use of referendums been in the UK?

→ To what extent do referendums undermine democracy in the UK?

→ What factors influence the calling of a referendum?

Source-based question

This source comments on the effect of differing electoral systems in the UK.

Some of the advantages of proportional systems are said to be:

- that the outcomes are proportional at a national level, appealing to people's sense of fairness and ensuring that everyone's vote counts in some way
- voters have more choice as more parties have the chance of being elected. Minority interests can be represented in Parliament
- voter turnout tends to be around five percentage points higher in countries with a form of PR, including List PR
- government tends to be by coalition (or through a minority government supported in Parliament by an agreement with other parties). This means that a wider range of interests are represented in government and that parliaments tend to have a stronger hold over the executive
- it is possible to maintain constituency links under the AMS or STV

The arguments against proportional systems are said to be:

- the prevalence of party list systems, in whole or in part (as in the Additional Member System), makes the candidate and representative remote from the voter, compared with single-member constituencies
- where party lists are combined with constituency members in the UK experience, there is a tendency for conflict between the two types of representative
- the tendency towards coalition or minority governments can have a number of negative effects. It can take a long time to form a government; governments may be indecisive on policy agendas; small parties can have significant power in coalition formations; and parties which have become unpopular with the electorate may be able to retain a stake in power
- voters may not really know what policies they are voting for, as successful parties are those that are able to negotiate the best deals in coalitions as they are being formed
- there may be stagnation over time, with the same parties regularly forming governments. This may lead to more extreme parties forming in order to express grievances

Source: 'The Governance of Britain. Review of Voting Systems: The experience of new voting systems in the United Kingdom since 1997', Ministry of Justice, 2008

Using the source, evaluate the view that a proportional system is now the best option for replacing FPTP for UK general elections.

In your response you must:
- *compare and contrast different opinions in the source*
- *examine and debate these views in a balanced way*
- *analyse and evaluate only the information presented in the source* (30)

Evaluative questions

1 Evaluate the view that the use of referendums in the UK should be increased. *You must consider this view and the alternative to this view in a balanced way.* (30)
2 Evaluate the view that the electoral systems used in the UK have created a multiparty system. *You must consider this view and the alternative to this view in a balanced way.* (30)
3 Evaluate the view that FPTP is the most effective electoral system for promoting representative democracy. *You must consider this view and the alternative to this view in a balanced way.* (30)

4 Voting behaviour and the media

Before embarking on the study of why people vote in the way that they do, it is important to address the popular misconception that the working class always vote Labour and that the middle and upper classes are invariably Conservative voters. Like any misconception, there is an element of truth in this. In the 1951 general election, for example, the Conservative Party under Winston Churchill succeeded in defeating Clement Attlee and Labour by mobilising middle-class support, which just managed to give Churchill a majority in the House of Commons.

However, the outcomes of general elections are influenced by a huge variety of other factors and it would be simplistic to argue that the public can always be relied on to vote according to class-based allegiance. Margaret Thatcher won three general elections (1979, 1983 and 1987) with significant amounts of working-class support, and in the 2017 general election Theresa May won shock victories in traditional working-class seats, while Jeremy Corbyn did unexpectedly well in prosperous middle-class seats, some of which, like Canterbury, had never returned a Labour MP.

The diversity of the British electorate makes any generalisations about its voting intentions rash and unhelpful

The question of whether we vote according to our social class is further complicated by the reasons why voters of all classes might choose to vote for the Liberal/Liberal Democrat parties, the nationalist parties and UKIP. The variations *within* social classes highlighted in Table 4.1 further demonstrate why it is so important to avoid generalisations when examining voting trends. Indeed, the more one studies voting behaviour, the more one appreciates that the reasons why we vote as we do are determined by a vast range of rational and possibly even irrational factors.

Table 4.1 Social class composition

Class	Composition and description
A	Higher managerial, professional (judges, top civil servants, company directors) Upper middle class
B	Middle managers, professionals (teachers, lawyers, accountants) Middle class
C1	Clerical workers, junior managerial roles, shop owners Lower middle class
C2	Skilled workers (builders, electricians, hairdressers) Aspirational working class
D	Semi-skilled, unskilled factory workers Working class
E	Casual workers, long-term unemployed, those elderly who rely solely on the state pension Working class

In order to engage with this topic you need to familiarise yourself with the significance of at least three general elections. The case studies in this chapter focus on the 1979, 1997 and 2017 general elections. You should be prepared to study these in great depth, although you are advised to familiarise yourself with the significance of as many general elections since 1945 as you can, as this will add conviction to your writing. It is compulsory that you cover the 2017 general election.

Social factors

Class-based voting and partisan dealignment

From 1945 until 1970, general elections were defined by the effectiveness with which the Labour and Conservative parties succeeded in mobilising their core support. The Conservatives generally relied on the support of A, B and C1 voters, with Labour's core support among C2, D and E voters. In the 1964 general election, for example, Labour's Harold Wilson won 64% of the votes of DE voters, while the Conservative prime minister, Alec Douglas-Home, won 78% of the support of AB voters.

However, the 1970 general election, in which the Conservative leader Edward Heath achieved a surprise victory over Harold Wilson, demonstrated that issue voting (see page 118) could determine the result of a general election as much as class-based voting. In this election, the Conservatives won a large number of traditional Labour seats because, following Enoch Powell's 'Rivers of Blood' speech in 1968, significant numbers of the white working class felt that immigration would be more tightly controlled by the Conservatives. The decline of class-based voting is also known as **partisan dealignment** and, since the 1970s, the results of general

> ### Key term
>
> **Partisan dealignment**
> Refers to the way in which voters since the 1970s have abandoned traditional party loyalties and have instead made their voting choices based on a range of factors including governing competence, the salience of core issues and economic self-interest.

Public anger at the consequences of the 'Winter of Discontent' led to significant class dealignment in the 1979 general election

elections have often been determined by striking examples of voting based on the government's competence and the salience (importance) of specific issues rather than according to class.

For example, in the 1979 general election, Margaret Thatcher startled political commentators by launching the Conservative campaign in Labour-supporting Cardiff. In fact, this was a clever attempt to disassociate the party from being too middle class. Indeed, the campaign's resulting focus on controlling inflation and confronting trade union power following the excessive number of strikes during the so-called 'Winter of Discontent' was so popular that there was an 11% swing to the Conservatives by C2 voters and a 9% swing by DE voters.

Like Thatcher, Tony Blair was highly successful at broadening Labour's appeal far beyond its core support. He increased Labour's share of the vote in all social categories, as well as winning a majority of support in all age groups with the progressive appeal of New Labour. In the 2017 general election, Jeremy Corbyn made dramatic inroads into the AB social category, while Theresa May made striking gains among DE voters. This was due to pro-Europeans in higher social classes wanting to punish the Conservatives for Brexit by voting Labour, while large numbers of DE voters felt the Conservatives would be more likely to deliver Brexit and control immigration.

Region

All of the national parties can claim a significant concentration of support in certain parts of the country (Table 4.2). This focus of support is to a great extent due to economic and social factors.

● The South East is the most prosperous region in the UK, with high levels of home ownership and little tradition of heavy industrial trade unionism. The Conservatives do disproportionately well here. The ethnically white rural parts of the UK are also classic Conservative territory, whether this is East Anglia, Devon, Cumbria or Northumberland.

- Labour, on the other hand, dominates ethnically-diverse big cities with large working-class populations and major centres of industrial production such as South Wales, Merseyside, Greater Manchester and Tyne and Wear.
- As a general rule, the industrial North of England is more likely to vote Labour and the South of England Conservative.

The Liberal Democrats have fared disproportionately badly out of the UK's first-past-the-post (FPTP) electoral system, because they have fewer areas of concentrated support. However, even liberalism has its heartlands in the Celtic fringes of the South West, rural Wales and the far north of Scotland, where there is a long tradition of small-scale non-conformist artisans who do not identify with either of the main political parties. Since 1950, Orkney and Shetland, for example, has always returned a Liberal/Liberal Democrat MP to Westminster.

Table 4.2 General election 2017 – voting by region

	Labour (%)	Conservative (%)	Liberal Democrat (%)	Scottish National Party / Plaid Cymru (%)
London	55	33	9	
Midlands	42	50	4	
Southern England	29	54	11	
Northern England	53	37	5	
Scotland	27	29	7	37
Wales	49	34	5	10

In every general election, therefore, the majority of seats do not change hands, because of the inbuilt majority that a party has in a particular region. Even though the 2017 general election was highly volatile, only 71 out of 650 seats changed hands — just 11% of the total number.

The key battlegrounds which have disproportionately decided the result of general elections have generally been London and the Midlands, where Labour and Conservatives have focused their resources on winning key marginal seats. However, recent general elections have challenged a number of accepted principles of regional voting behaviour. This suggests that voter dealignment is influencing both class and regional voting as the public increasingly votes according to issues rather than traditional loyalties. This can be seen most notably in Scotland, but also in London.

Scotland

The industrial areas of Scotland traditionally provided Labour with large parliamentary support, while the Conservatives, Liberals/Liberal Democrats and the Scottish National Party (SNP) gained significantly fewer seats. Indeed, so unpopular had the Conservatives become in Scotland that they won no seats there in the 1997 general election. However, the way in which the Scottish National Party has become the largest party at Holyrood, and ran such a high-profile independence campaign during the 2014 referendum, has completely changed the political landscape of Scotland.

In the 2015 general election, the SNP won 56 of the 59 Scottish seats at Westminster. The 2017 general election then provided another shock result, with the Conservatives, under the charismatic and gutsy Ruth Davidson, winning 13 seats to become the second biggest Scottish party. Table 4.3 highlights just how unstable and unpredictable Scottish politics has become during recent general elections.

Table 4.3 The results of general elections in Scotland in 2010, 2015 and 2017

General election	Labour	Scottish National Party	Liberal Democrat	Conservative
2010	41 seats	6 seats	11 seats	1 seat
2015	1 seat	56 seats	1 seat	1 seat
2017	7 seats	35 seats	4 seats	13 seats

London

The soaring cost of home ownership, as well as dramatic levels of inequality, have significantly damaged Conservative fortunes in Greater London. The way in which the capital voted decisively to Remain in the 2016 EU referendum has further damaged the Conservative Party in London since voters associated it most closely with euroscepticism. The multicultural and metropolitan values that Labour espouses have further entrenched its support in the capital. Table 4.4 illustrates how in recent years London has become increasingly Labour-dominated.

Table 4.4 The results of general elections in London in 2010, 2015 and 2017

General election	Labour	Conservative	Liberal Democrat
2010	38 seats	28 seats	7 seats
2015	45 seats	27 seats	1 seat
2017	49 seats	21 seats	3 seats

The fact that there were a number of surprise constituency results in 2017 suggests that voter dealignment across the country may increasingly challenge the traditional dominance of political parties in certain regions. The Conservatives' association with Brexit and their stricter controls on immigration provided them with unexpected victories in traditional working-class seats such as Mansfield, which had been Labour since 1923. Conversely, Labour's more cosmopolitan outlook and more consistent opposition to Brexit in the EU referendum enabled it to win seats like Canterbury, which had been Conservative since 1918.

Age

The influence of age on how we vote is significant. The Conservative Party's support is strongest among older voters, while the Labour and Liberal/Liberal Democrat parties have generally won the support of younger voters. This is because the Conservative Party has traditionally emphasised policies which appeal more to older voters, such as lower taxation, strong national defence, law and order, and, in recent years, has been significantly more eurosceptic than Labour and the Liberal Democrats. These sorts of policies have a particular appeal to older property-owning voters, who tend to favour security and stability and, having more financial responsibilities and savings than younger voters, are often keen for their taxes to be kept as low as possible. In the 2017 general election, for example, older people who had paid off their mortgages were significantly more likely to vote Conservative, while younger people who rented were much more likely to vote Labour (Table 4.5).

Younger voters are more likely to be concerned with issues such as social justice and the environment and so are more likely to favour Labour, the Liberal Democrats and the Greens. In 2017, for example, Jeremy Corbyn successfully connected with

Table 4.5 General election 2017 — voting by property status

	Conservative (%)	Labour (%)
Owned	55	30
Owned with mortgage	43	40
Private renter	31	54
Social renter	26	57

young people by emphasising that Labour was on the side of 'the many, not the few'. His pledge to abolish tuition fees further entrenched Labour support among the young, as did his idealistic commitment to resolving world problems through international organs of global governance such as the United Nations.

Table 4.6 illustrates how significant age is in determining how we vote, with 47 being the pivotal age at which voters are most likely to switch from supporting Labour to supporting the Conservatives.

Table 4.6 General election 2017 — voting by age

Age	Labour (%)	Conservative (%)
18–24	62	27
25–34	56	37
35–44	49	33
45–54	40	43
55–64	34	51
65+	25	61

Labour's focus on social justice, environmentalism and its less hardline approach to Brexit has made it a popular choice for young people

In terms of electoral success, the Conservative Party has historically benefited from the greater support that it has among older people because older people are more likely to vote. Younger people may be more attracted to radical ideas but they have been less likely to vote, so providing the Conservatives with an inbuilt advantage. However, in the 2017 general election, Jeremy Corbyn's youth-focused campaign did encourage more young people to vote than in any general election since 1992, but even in 2017 there was still a significant imbalance with older voters more likely to cast their ballots. As Table 4.7 illustrates, the tendency of older people to vote more regularly than younger voters favours the Conservative Party, as does the growing age of the UK's population.

Table 4.7 General election 2017 — voting turnout

Age group	Proportion of the UK population (%)	Turnout
18–24-year-olds	5	54% voted
65+ year-olds	18	71% voted

Labour and the Conservatives have been at their most successful when they have been able to reach beyond their core age support. In 1997, for example, Labour achieved a 5% lead over the Conservatives among voters aged 65+, helping Tony Blair to his landslide victory, while in Margaret Thatcher's 1979 general election victory the Conservatives achieved a 1% lead over Labour among 18–24-year-olds.

Enoch Powell's opposition to mass immigration and the UK's membership of the EEC/EU has had a major impact on right-wing conservatism

Ethnicity

The impact of ethnicity in determining voting behaviour is also significant. Historically, since Commonwealth immigrant communities were generally within the C2, D and E classes, they were more likely to vote Labour because of its high spending on the welfare state and close association with the trade union movement. The commitment that Labour has shown towards multiculturalism and the way in which Labour introduced the first Race Relations Acts in 1965, 1968 and 1976 to outlaw discrimination have further provided it with a strong historical connection with immigrant communities. On the other hand, the influence of Enoch Powell — whose 'Rivers of Blood' speech in 1968 called for an end to Commonwealth immigration — on some elements within the Conservative Party has often made it seem hostile to immigrant communities.

In the 2017 general election, Jeremy Corbyn's strong empathy for immigrant communities contributed to Labour winning 49 of the 73 seats in Greater London, which has a population of just 45% white British. The result in East Ham, which has a non-white population of 77%, making it the most ethnically diverse constituency in the UK, is especially revealing (Table 4.8).

Table 4.8 East Ham 2017 general election

Party	Share of the vote (%)
Labour	83.2
Conservative	12.8
Liberal Democrat	1.2
UKIP	1.2
Green	0.8

The Conservatives, on the other hand, held just five of the 75 most ethnically diverse constituencies in the UK in the 2017 general election. The way in which ethnic minorities voted in the 2017 general election demonstrates Labour's clear advantage over the Conservatives (Table 4.9).

Table 4.9 General election 2017 — how ethnic minorities voted

Party	Share of ethnic minority vote (%)	Share of national vote (%)
Labour	73	40
Conservative	19	42
Liberal Democrat	6	8

Education

The impact of education on determining voting behaviour significantly changed in the 2017 general election. Those with higher educational qualifications comprise the top social brackets and have traditionally been more likely to vote Conservative. However, in 2017, there was a remarkable change in voting patterns, with the Conservatives increasing their support among those in the lowest social bands with fewest educational qualifications and Labour achieving higher levels of support among those with degrees in the top brackets. This unusual result may, of course, be an anomaly. However, it may also be part of a long-term trend in which the Conservatives have closely aligned themselves with stricter controls on immigration, thereby increasing their support among white working-class voters who feel threatened by globalisation and so decisively voted Brexit in the 2016 referendum. On the other hand, Labour's more liberal approach to immigration and its more nuanced approach to Brexit have dramatically increased its support among better educated more cosmopolitan voters who voted Remain in 2016 and have been dismayed by what they see as Conservative insularity.

David Goodhart, in *The Road to Somewhere* (2017), has contrasted the less educated 'somewheres', who are rooted to their communities through lack of opportunities, with the better educated 'anywheres', who have the educational qualifications to take advantage of globalisation. In 2017, it seems as though Labour generated much increased support among the 'anywheres', while the Conservatives achieved their own breakthrough with the 'somewheres' (Table 4.10).

Table 4.10 General election 2017 — the significance of higher educational qualifications

Education	Labour (%)	Conservative (%)
Degree or higher	48	33
Other qualifications	39	46
No qualifications	35	52

Gender

The influence of gender in determining the result of general elections has changed since the end of the Second World War. From 1945 until the 1980s Labour's close association with male-dominated trade unionism and its reputation for allowing inflation to spiral, so hitting family finances, provided the Conservatives with a powerful opportunity to appeal to the housewives' vote. In the 1959 general election, Harold Macmillan associated Conservative prosperity and stability with a happy family life. Then, in 1970, Edward Heath defeated Harold Wilson by pledging to reduce the cost of living, thereby winning significant support among housewives. In 1979 Margaret Thatcher similarly articulated women's concerns that Labour governments had allowed inflation to undermine family finances and that irresponsible trade unionism was pulling society apart.

Table 4.11 1979 general election — how men and women voted

Gender	Conservative (%)	Labour (%)	Liberal (%)
Female	47	35	15
Male	43	40	13

However, the Conservatives' traditional lead among female voters has been challenged by Labour. This is perhaps because the Conservative Party's emphasis on strong national defence and its growing association with euroscepticism may have contrasted unfavourably for some women with Labour's focus on education, social care and the National Health Service (Table 4.12).

Table 4.12 How males and females voted in the 2015 and 2017 elections

Election	Conservative (%)	Labour (%)	Liberal Democrat (%)
2015 general election	Male 38 Female 37	Male 30 Female 33	Male 8 Female 8
2017 general election	Male 44 Female 43	Male 40 Female 42	Male 7 Female 8

Although the overall gap is minimal, it is striking that among younger voters in the 2017 general election women were dramatically more likely to vote Labour than Conservative. Among 18–24-year-old voters, just 18% of women voted Conservative and 73% voted Labour, whereas 36% of men in this age group voted Conservative and 52% Labour. However, this is a much more striking imbalance than in other recent elections so the result may have been caused by a reaction against certain male Conservative politicians! It could still be that, as men and women increasingly play similar roles in the family and workplace, so the gender gap may diminish as a factor determining voting behaviour.

Key term

Valence factor Refers to the relative success or failure of a government's policies. Voters who vote according to valence factors are making their decision based on whether they are satisfied or dissatisfied with the government's performance.

Political context

Although social factors are significant, the political context in which a general election is held is of defining importance. This is because the electorate will make decisions based on a number of judgements about the governing and opposition parties.

The factors that inform these judgements are based on the competency and effectiveness of the government and are called **valence factors**. With the decline of class-based voting, valence factors become more significant in determining the result of a general election.

Governing competence

Especially with the decline of traditional voting loyalties since the 1970s and the rise of partisan dealignment, a core reason why voters choose to vote in the way they do involves a valence judgement on the effectiveness of the government. If swing voters are reassured that the government is competent then they will be less likely to vote for opposition parties. Alternatively, if the government seems unable to cope with the challenges it faces, this will encourage swing voters to vote in a new government, either because they believe another party to be more likely to govern well or as a protest vote.

A Conservative poster from the 1959 general election depicting a happy family at home and the line 'Life's better with the Conservatives — don't let Labour ruin it' is an example of how the valence influence of competency can be utilised by a governing party to achieve victory. On that occasion, the remarkable prosperity achieved under the Conservatives rewarded Macmillan with a 100-seat majority over the Labour leader, Hugh Gaitskell.

Table 4.13 shows how valence issues of **governing competency** have helped governments to both win and lose general elections.

<table>
<tr><td>Key term</td></tr>
</table>

Governing competency The extent to which the government is regarded as having been capable and competent. If it is viewed as having failed in government this will encourage the public to vote for a change.

Table 4.13 The influence of governing competency in general elections

Successful governments	Unsuccessful governments
1959 Economic prosperity and a wider availability of consumer goods contributed to Harold Macmillan increasing the Conservatives' parliamentary majority to over 100. Macmillan's calm sense of authority and the way in which he took political advantage of rising living standards, claiming 'most of our people have never had it so good', gave voters little reason to change government	**1964** The short-lived Conservative government of Alec Douglas-Home had not been able to disassociate itself from the failures and scandals of the last years of the Macmillan government. These included Charles de Gaulle vetoing Macmillan's attempt to join the EEC, Macmillan's desperate decision to sack a third of his cabinet in the 'Night of the Long Knives', and the Profumo affair, which highlighted scandal, intrigue and deception at the heart of government. Harold Wilson and the Labour Party were thus well placed to end what they called 'thirteen wasted years of Conservative government'
1966 After 2 years in power, Harold Wilson's Labour government still looked energetic and focused and industrial unrest was limited. Facing a new and untried leader of the opposition, Edward Heath, Wilson called a snap election and dramatically increased his parliamentary majority to over 100	**February 1974** When Edward Heath called a snap general election he did so in response to another miners' strike, which threatened more severe industrial disruption. His decision to use a general election to assert the government's authority led to this being referred to as the 'Who governs Britain' general election. Many voters, however, saw this as evidence that an incompetent government had lost control of the nation
1983 Although unemployment levels remained stubbornly high, Margaret Thatcher's Conservative government had successfully brought inflation down, fulfilling its manifesto commitment. Her leadership during the Falklands War (1982) and the unity of her cabinet further reinforced the government's reputation for strength of purpose	**1979** The inability of the Labour prime minister, James Callaghan, to stop the dramatic escalation of strikes during the Winter of Discontent undermined public faith in his government. This was made worse by the way in which his attempts to reassure the country were misquoted in the press as 'Crisis? What crisis?' Swing voters consequently voted Conservative because they thought Margaret Thatcher more likely to confront the growing power of trade unionism

Leadership

As voters have become more prepared to vote imaginatively rather than according to their social class, the image that the party leader projects has become increasingly important. Some prime ministers, such as Harold Macmillan in the 1959 general election, have won convincingly because they were able to present themselves as coolly competent and in charge of events.

In the 1983 general election, Margaret Thatcher's reputation for strong and focused leadership contrasted with Michael Foot's left-wing intellectualism, which had little appeal beyond Labour's core vote. For example, Thatcher faced down one-nation rebels at the 1980 Conservative Party conference, saying: 'You turn if you want to. The lady's not for turning', and sent a task force to recover the Falklands from an invasion by Argentina in 1982. Foot, in contrast, although a brilliant orator, failed to inspire widespread backing. In 1983 he looked his 70 years, and has been described by Andrew Marr as 'a would-be parliamentary revolutionary detained in a secondhand bookshop'.

The 1979 Conservative campaign focused on Labour's failure to deliver on its core values, such as maintaining high levels of employment

In 2001, Tony Blair dominated the political landscape by the charismatic force of his personality and so there was little reason to vote for a weak and divided opposition under William Hague.

Opposition leaders

Sometimes opposition leaders can generate support by capturing the mood of the nation. In 1970, Edward Heath's dogged principles successfully contrasted with a growing distaste for Harold Wilson's misplaced presidentialism and reputation for duplicity. Similarly, in the 1979 general election campaign, Margaret Thatcher was presented as a sensible and forthright 'housewife' who, like much of the rest of the nation, was no longer prepared to tolerate excessive trade union power. In 1997, the energy of Tony Blair's campaign and his attractive self-confidence had huge appeal in the country in contrast to John Major's reputation for dithering weak leadership. Successful opposition leaders are thus able to set the agenda of an election to their advantage.

- Winston Churchill, 1951 general election — Churchill successfully campaigned on a manifesto pledge to 'set the people free', promising to end rationing and reduce the middle classes' tax burden. He also won support by contrasting one-nation Conservative values with the class-based socialism of the Attlee government.
- Margaret Thatcher, 1979 general election — Although personally less popular than Labour prime minister James Callaghan, Thatcher successfully focused the general election on the government's failure to confront the growing power of trade unionism.
- David Cameron, 2010 general election — In 2010, David Cameron succeeded in focusing the general election on the huge increase in the national debt under Gordon Brown. This was presented as Labour's weakest point and contributed to Brown's defeat. That Cameron did not achieve a parliamentary majority was due to a strong showing by the Liberal Democrats under Nick Clegg.

By associating a socialist government with 'the Gestapo' in the 1945 general election, Churchill completely misjudged the mood of the country. His 1951 campaign was much more successful in winning back traditional middle-class Conservative voters

On the other hand, some opposition leaders can fail to engage with the public and may even lose support as the campaign continues. In 1959 Hugh Gaitskell could not compete with Macmillan's effortless charm, while in both 1987 and 1992 Neil Kinnock could not convince enough swing voters that he possessed the gravitas necessary to be prime minister. In 2015, Ed Miliband also failed to inspire the confidence of the electorate.

- Neil Kinnock, 1992 general election — Having lost to Margaret Thatcher in 1987, Neil Kinnock was confident of defeating John Major in 1992. However, the triumphant presidentialism of his campaign grated with core swing voters. The Sheffield rally just days before the election saw Kinnock become incoherent with excitement. His repeated 'We're all right, we're all right' shocked enough voters back to the Conservatives to give Major a slim victory.
- Michael Howard, 2005 general election — In the 2005 general election, Michael Howard succeeded in reducing Tony Blair's majority. However, lingering memories of Anne Widdecombe's jibe that 'there was something of the night' about him meant that he could not inspire widespread popular support for the Conservatives. His support for the Iraq War (2003) also ensured that the anti-war vote went to the Liberal Democrats under Charles Kennedy.

- Ed Miliband, 2005 general election — Miliband failed to persuade enough voters that he had the strength of character to be prime minister. An attempt to provide him with greater stature by having him publicly unveil a 9-foot stone tablet with his campaign promises carved into it backfired when it was ridiculed as the 'Edstone' and 'the heaviest suicide note in history'.

Liberal/Liberal Democrat and minority party leadership

Although every modern prime minister has been a member of either the Conservative Party or the Labour Party, the leadership of other political parties has often been important in determining the result of a general election. The 1964, February 1974 and 2010 general elections all demonstrate how a strong showing by the leader of the Liberal/Liberal Democrat parties can have a significant impact on the result.

- 1964 general election — Although Harold Wilson had expected to win a decisive victory over Conservative prime minister Alec Douglas-Home, in fact Labour only managed a four-seat majority. This is because Liberal leader Jo Grimond's energetic campaign appealed to young people. The Liberal vote consequently increased by 5.3%, while the swing to Labour was only 0.2%.
- February 1974 general election — In the 'who governs Britain?' general election, Jeremy Thorpe provided a brilliantly exciting alternative to voters' tired familiarity with Edward Heath and Harold Wilson. As a result, the Liberals increased their share of the vote by 11.8%. By holding the balance of power, Thorpe was able to force the resignation of Edward Heath as prime minister.
- 2010 general election — This was the first election in which televised leaders' debates were held in the UK. Nick Clegg's engaging personality made him the clear winner, forcing both Gordon Brown and David Cameron to admit, 'I agree with Nick.' The Liberal Democrats' party political broadcasts also focused on Clegg's trustworthiness. The 57 Liberal Democrat MPs elected to Parliament denied Cameron a majority, leading to the first coalition government since 1945.

The impact of Nigel Farage as UKIP leader in the 2015 general election was also significant. Although UKIP was expected to win votes at the expense of the Conservatives, Farage's relentless focus on immigration made it a pivotal issue among the working class and so took potential votes away from Labour, helping the Conservatives to win key marginal seats. This is clearly demonstrated in the results for the Vale of Clwyd, for example (Table 4.14). Although UKIP only won Clacton, its success in achieving 12.6% of the popular vote had a major influence in determining the result.

Table 4.14 The influence of UKIP in the Vale of Clwyd constituency

2010 general election (% of votes won)	2015 general election (% of votes won)
Labour 42.3	Conservative 39
Conservative 35.2	Labour 38.4
Liberal Democrat 12.6	UKIP 13
Plaid Cymru 5.8	Plaid Cymru 7.1
UKIP 1.4	Liberal Democrat 2.6

In Scotland an extraordinarily effective campaign by SNP leader Nicola Sturgeon in the 2015 general election led to Labour losing 40 seats north of the border, undermining Ed Miliband's hopes of forming a government. Two years later, Ruth Davidson, leader of the Scottish Conservatives, ran a highly effective campaign which won the Conservatives 13 Scottish seats. This was the highest number since 1983 and without them Theresa May would not have been able to form a government.

The popularity of the party leader

Although, as we have seen, a party leader can be very important in winning support for their party, this does not mean that they need to have positive approval ratings across the electorate. As Table 4.15 illustrates, a party leader can have negative approval ratings but still achieve highly if they are able to define to their advantage the issues on which a general election is fought.

Table 4.15 The popularity of party leaders and how they fared in the 1979, 2015 and 2017 elections

General election	Party leader
1979	Although James Callaghan was significantly more popular than Margaret Thatcher, she still managed to win the general election by focusing on the competence of the government and the need for change
2015	Although UKIP leader Nigel Farage had the worst approval rating of any party leader, he succeeded in making immigration a key issue in the election, dramatically increasing UKIP's vote among the working class
2017	When the general election was announced, YouGov found that 50% of voters thought Theresa May would make the best prime minister compared to just 14% for Jeremy Corbyn and 36% undecided. Although Corbyn never achieved as good approval ratings as May, his much more optimistic campaign increased the Labour share of the vote by 9.6%

The campaign

The way in which a party campaigns can be significant in determining the result of a general election. The socialist rhetoric of the Labour Party's campaign in 1983 appealed only to its core vote and failed to engage middle-class swing voters who were beginning to benefit from the tax cuts of the Thatcher government. In 1992, John Major salvaged the Conservative campaign by taking to his soap box to appeal directly to the voters. This old-style electioneering provided a welcome contrast to the stage-managed Neil Kinnock campaign and provided the Conservatives with an unexpected general election victory. In the 2017 general election, Jeremy Corbyn campaigned in a similarly traditional fashion across the nation, taking the Labour case directly to the people, in marked contrast to Theresa May's lacklustre and highly controlled campaign.

However, even a carefully choreographed campaign can fail if the electorate is not persuaded by the manifesto or the leader. In 1987, for example, Peter Mandelson brilliantly organised Labour's campaign, including an inspiring television commercial focusing on Neil Kinnock. All media critics agreed that the campaign was much superior to the Conservatives' and yet Labour was decisively defeated as Thatcher was perceived to be much the stronger leader and voters were unprepared to trust Labour and Kinnock with either the economy or defence.

In the 1992 general election, John Major altered the dynamic of the campaign by taking his case directly to the voters, in often rowdy public meetings

Do campaigns influence the result of a general election?

Yes

- Although some campaigns may simply reinforce existing attitudes, others may challenge them, especially if it is a tight race. The growth of partisan dealignment suggests that campaigns do increasingly matter as voters have become much more flexible in their voting intentions.
- In the February 1974 general election, the Liberal Party under Jeremy Thorpe cleverly exploited widespread discontent with both Edward Heath and Harold Wilson, especially among first-time voters. In an effective campaign address a few days before the vote, Thorpe called on Liberal voters: 'Stand firm. Don't be bullied. Together we can make history and heal the self-inflicted wounds of Britain.' As a result the Liberal share of the vote increased by 11.8%.
- In 1992 John Major's decision to abandon stage-managed events and take his soap box to town centres was in marked contrasted to Neil Kinnock's hubris at the Sheffield rally. This changed the dynamic of the general election, providing the Conservatives with an unexpected victory.
- In 2010 a strong Liberal Democrat campaign, including Nick Clegg's impressive performance in the televised debates, significantly increased Liberal Democrat support, mostly at the expense of the Conservatives, leading to a hung parliament and a Conservative–Liberal Democrat coalition.
- In 2017 Jeremy Corbyn's optimistic rallies and popular manifesto commitments such as ending tuition fees contrasted sharply with Theresa May's uninspiring campaign appearances and the widespread unpopularity of the 'dementia tax'. As a result, Labour dramatically increased its support as the campaign progressed, from less than 30% of the vote at the beginning to achieving 40% in the general election.

No

- According to some political commentators the influence of the campaign can be exaggerated, since voters will generally have *already* made up their mind how they are going to vote.
- In the 1950s and 1960s the class allegiance that political parties could depend on meant that campaigns made little difference in swaying the majority of voters. For example, the 1955 and 1959 general election campaigns simply confirmed expected Conservative victories under Anthony Eden and Harold Macmillan.
- Even some modern campaigns have made little significant impact on people's voting intentions.
- Although Harold Wilson's dynamic and presidential campaign in 1964 was supposed to make him appeal to the voters as a British John F. Kennedy, in fact Alec Douglas-Home's low-key dogged earnestness proved more appealing. In the end Wilson only increased Labour's share of the vote by 0.2% on Hugh Gaitskell's lacklustre performance in 1959.
- In 1970 Edward Heath's campaign was dismissed as bland and uninspiring and plans had been drawn up by Conservative grandees to force his resignation when he lost. His surprise victory over Harold Wilson was completely unexpected.
- In 1987, although Labour ran a dynamic and much praised modern campaign showcasing Neil Kinnock as a strong potential prime minister, the Conservatives won a third election victory, with a 102-seat majority.
- In 1997 John Major decided on a long campaign in the hope that he would be able to reduce Tony Blair's huge lead in the polls. However, Blair remained stubbornly far ahead and the polls hardly changed.
- In spite of a poor Conservative campaign in the 2017 general election, the Conservatives still managed to increase their share of the vote from 36.9% in 2015 to 42.4% in 2017. This equalled the share of the vote that Margaret Thatcher achieved in the 1983 general election in a much stronger campaign.

Are voting trends a problem for UK democracy?

Yes

- In the 1992 general election, 77% of the electorate voted. In the 1997 general election, it fell to 71% and since then the turnout in general elections has been significantly lower as **disillusion** with politicians has increased.
- This disillusion was caused by concerns that in a period of Blairite consensus politics voting hardly mattered since the policies of the main parties were so similar.
- In 2001, for example, just 59% of the electorate voted and in 2005 it was only 61%.
- Disillusion has been especially associated with young people and poorer social categories, sometimes known as 'left behind' voters.
- In 2005 only 34% of young people aged 18–24 voted.
- In the 2015 general election, the ten seats with the fewest people voting were all in the lowest income bracket. The smallest turnout was Manchester Central with only a 44% poll.
- The failure of young people and poorer DE social classes to vote has given the Conservative Party an advantage in general elections since it has been able to rely on the vote of more prosperous and older voters.
- It has also been claimed that the disengagement of poorer social classes has meant there has been less urgency to represent their interests at Westminster.

No

- Political **apathy** *was* a major concern in the 2001 and 2005 general elections. The disengagement of the electorate was due to this being a period of consensus politics and Blair's victory being widely assumed. This discouraged voting rather than indicated any long-term trends.
- Voting steadily increased in the next three elections, in which the differences between the parties were more striking:
  2010: 65%
  2015: 66%
  2017: 69%
- The 2017 general election result, although disappointing by the standard of 1992, was the highest turnout in a general election since 1997.
- The surge of interest in Jeremy Corbyn also ensured that in 2017 the vote among the 18–24 age group was closer to 60%. Although still lower than other age brackets this is a big increase on 2005 and shows that young people will vote when big issues are at stake.
- Concerns that the Conservatives have been unfairly advantaged by political apathy among DE voters may become less politically significant as the Conservatives increasingly challenge Labour for votes in this category.
- Jeremy Corbyn's 'For the Many, Not the Few' campaign demonstrates that, in spite of lower than average turnout by poorer voters, their interests are not necessarily ignored by political leaders.

> **Key terms**
>
> **Disillusion/apathy** The number of people voting in general elections is generally lower than it was up to the 1990s. In particular, poorer voters and young people vote significantly less than the older and more prosperous because they can feel less engaged in the political process.

The manifesto

In its **manifesto**, a political party will explain the policies upon which it will govern. It is unlikely that voters will engage with all the elements of a manifesto. However, it is important that a manifesto is carefully composed since certain popular policies may help swing the result, while unpopular or confusing policies can help to undermine a campaign. Two examples demonstrate the influence of a party's manifesto, the Labour Party's manifestos of 1987 and 1992:

> **Key term**
>
> **Manifesto** In a general election each political party will launch its manifesto, in which it sets out the policies it will introduce if it forms a government.

- In 1987 the Labour Party manifesto did not commit to the UK's nuclear deterrent. This enabled the Conservatives to claim that Labour could not be trusted on defence, their campaign poster boldly stating 'LABOUR'S POLICY ON ARMS' next to an image of a surrendering solder.
- In 1992 the Labour manifesto commitment to increase public spending allowed the Conservatives to claim successfully that a Labour government would mean a 'tax bombshell' for every family.

On both these occasions the Labour manifesto helped contribute to the Conservative victory.

In the 2017 general election, however, the Conservative Party's manifesto pledged that if elderly people receiving NHS care at home had assets of more than £100,000, then the excess would contribute to the cost of their care after their deaths. Although the plan was supposed to provide a fairer system of care, it was quickly labelled a 'dementia tax' by the press and the Conservative campaign stalled as it became embroiled in defending the policy. Meanwhile, Labour's manifesto commitment to abolish tuition fees provided the party with a dramatic boost from young and first-time voters, while its promise of an end to austerity and the introduction of higher taxes for the top 5% of the population had broad popular appeal.

Issue/instrumental voting

As a result of partisan and class dealignment, voters, as well as making decisions on the competence of the government, can choose to vote on the salience (importance) to them of certain issues. This can also be referred to as instrumental voting and suggests that voters *do* study a party's manifesto and make decisions based on how they respond to particular issues.

This is why political parties will often establish focus groups to investigate which issues the public feels most strongly about so they can tailor their manifesto to take advantage of this. In other words, general elections can also be determined by voters making a rational choice based on their individual self-interest.

In 1983, for example, Conservative warnings that a Labour government under Michael Foot would reverse the right-to-buy scheme contributed to Margaret Thatcher's landslide re-election by encouraging the aspirational working class to vote Conservative to protect their properties. In 2015, immigration was an unexpected core issue for many voters, contributing to the remarkable increase in UKIP's vote from 3.1% in 2005 to 12.6%. More recently, in 2017, a core issue which determined the general election was where the leading parties stood on Brexit, while Labour's commitment to abolishing tuition fees provided a strong incentive for younger voters to vote Labour.

However, in some general elections instrumental voting can be considerably less important than the government's reputation for competence. For example, in the 1997 general election Labour enjoyed a 11% swing among AB voters even though they were most likely to be affected by the windfall tax on privatised utilities. This suggests that the perceived incompetence of the government of John Major was the valence factor that mattered more than economic self-interest.

The influence of the media

Opinion polls

Although political parties want to achieve a lead in the polls, the impact of polls on voters' intentions can be controversial, especially in close general elections. For example, in 1992 most opinion polls suggested that support for Labour was growing at the expense of the Conservatives. This may then have encouraged a higher poll for the Conservatives as wavering voters decided to vote for the government rather than chance a Labour administration under Neil Kinnock.

In 2015, opinion polls consistently predicted a close race between Labour and the Conservatives. This enabled the Conservatives to warn against the possibility of an unstable Labour–SNP coalition. The growing likelihood of Ed Miliband becoming prime minister also encouraged the Conservative vote to turn out, providing the Conservatives with another surprise victory.

The way in which the Conservative campaign in the 2015 general election focused on the possibility of a Labour/SNP coalition was highly effective in mobilising support for the Conservatives

On the other hand, in 2017, most opinion polls gave the Conservatives a commanding lead over Labour, which may have reduced the urgency with which the Conservatives campaigned, especially in marginal constituencies. Some pro-European Conservatives may even have voted Labour in protest at Brexit since they viewed the prospect of this leading to a Corbyn government as such a remote possibility.

The press

The press has traditionally claimed that it plays a significant role in determining the result of general elections. *The Sun*, for example, in 1992, ruthlessly ridiculed Neil Kinnock as unfit to be prime minister and, when John Major won the general election, boasted, 'It's The Sun Wot Won It'. However, at the next general election in 1997, it firmly positioned itself behind Tony Blair, commenting on his landslide victory that 'It Was The Sun That Swung It'. The *Daily Mail*, *Daily Express* and *Daily Telegraph* have always been strident in encouraging their readerships to vote Conservative, leaving the Mirror Group newspapers as the only consistently Labour-supporting tabloids.

Although it is difficult to prove that *The Sun* swung the 1992 general election to the Conservatives, the paper's relentless attacks on Neil Kinnock certainly undermined his credibility as a potential prime minister. As opposition leader, Tony Blair cultivated strong relations with Rupert Murdoch, owner of *The Sun,* and in the 1997 general election the paper then came out in favour of Labour. However, in the 2017 general election, in spite of relentless tabloid attacks led by *The Sun,* the *Daily Mail* and the *Daily Express* on Jeremy Corbyn, there was a 9.6% swing to Labour.

To what extent do you think this means that the impact of the press on the result of general elections has been exaggerated? Explain your answer fully.

As leader of the opposition Tony Blair worked hard to win the support of Rupert Murdoch's News International newspapers and was rewarded handsomely by their support

However, according to some political commentators, the press has exaggerated its influence since its headlines often simply *reinforce* the voting intentions of its readers. In short, a Conservative voter is likely to buy the *Daily Mail* because of its right-wing political views rather than be influenced by them.

The rapid decline in the circulation of newspapers (Table 4.16) as people access information from the internet has, of course, been vital in reducing their impact on general elections. The result of the 2017 general election further suggests that the importance of the press is declining. Although Jeremy Corbyn was ridiculed in most of the mass-circulation newspapers, apart from the *Daily Mirror* and *Sunday Mirror,* Labour increased its share of the vote by 9.6%.

Table 4.16 The circulation figures of major newspapers

Title	January 1992	January 1997	January 2017
The Sun	3,570,562	3,877.097	1,666,175
Daily Mirror	2,900,000	2,442,078	724,888
Daily Mail	1,675,453	2,344,183	1,511,357
Daily Express	1,524,786	1,241,336	392,526
Daily Telegraph	1,038,138	1,129,777	472,258

Television

The importance of television has remained more consistent. In contrast to the USA where television channels favour either the Republican or the Democrat Party, the BBC and ITN report the news impartially. However, the way in which politicians can use television to their advantage, or become victims of it, is highly significant. Table 4.17 shows the changing relationship that three prime ministers have had with television and the media, while Table 4.18 illustrates the influence of televised leader debates.

Table 4.17 Three prime ministers and the media

Prime minister	Relationship with the media
Harold Macmillan	As prime minister from 1957 to 1963, Macmillan initially used television to his advantage, appearing on the BBC with President Eisenhower for a mutually-congratulatory 'informal' chat just 2 months before the 1959 general election. However, the rise of satirical programmes such as *That Was the Week that Was* found him an easy Edwardian figure to mock and, in the wake of the media frenzy caused by the Profumo scandal (1963), he resigned
Margaret Thatcher	Margaret Thatcher understood the power of the media to project power. As prime minister, she softened her voice; wore bolder, less fussy outfits and favoured appearing on sympathetic programmes like Radio 2's *The Jimmy Young Show*. She also appreciated the significance of a memorable soundbite, cutting off an eager journalist from questioning the significance of the recapture of South Georgia in 1982: 'Just rejoice at that news and congratulate our forces and the marines … rejoice.' By the end of her premiership, however, her stridency on television had become an electoral liability
Tony Blair	It was during Tony Blair's years as leader of the Labour Party that 'spin' became a dominant influence in UK politics. Blair's press secretary, Alastair Campbell, intuitively understood the importance of 'spinning' a favourable news story, while on television Blair was calm, reassuring and statesmanlike, such as during his 'People's Princess' tribute on the morning of Diana's death in 1997. However, the failures of the Iraq War and controversies such as the suicide of David Kelly and the cash for honours scandal increasingly undermined New Labour's positive relationship with the media

Table 4.18 Televised leader debates

General election	Influence of television debate
2010	The decision to give Nick Clegg equal coverage with Gordon Brown and David Cameron provided the Liberal Democrats with a powerful election platform. The way in which both Brown and Cameron admitted 'I agree with Nick' boosted the Liberal Democrat campaign, which had been lagging badly in the polls
2015	The seven party leaders debated together in 2015. Although there was no clear winner, Nigel Farage used his airtime to boost UKIP's support among 'left-behind' DE-category voters. When Ed Miliband warned him not to criticise the studio audience for being handpicked liberals, Farage responded, 'No, the real audience is at home actually.'
2017	Theresa May's decision not to join the leader debates provided opposition parties with the opportunity to ridicule her without her being able to respond. As Caroline Lucas, leader of the Green Party, put it, 'You don't say it's the most important election of our lifetime and not be bothered to show up.'

Social media

The way in which voters are being increasingly influenced by social media also suggests that the role of the media is rapidly changing how general elections are fought. In 2017 Labour activists used Facebook, Twitter, hashtags and WhatsApp cascades to spread Labour's message across the internet. This was a highly effective way of campaigning, as the population increasingly accesses news and shares ideas through social media. As a result of this trend all political parties will have to engage with this new medium rather than relying on terrestrial election broadcasts, pamphlets through letter boxes and the support of loyal newspapers.

One of Momentum's campaign films, *Daddy, Why Do You Hate Me?*, was watched 5.4 million times in just 2 days. Conversely, the Conservatives' presence on the internet was much more hesitant, with Jeremy Corbyn's Facebook and Twitter followers at least three times greater than Theresa May's. The way, too, in which Corbyn's vilification in the newspapers mattered less than his dominance on the internet suggests that 2017 may have been a watershed general election, pointing the way to a new sort of social media-focused election campaign.

As the UK's first female prime minister, Margaret Thatcher used power dressing to project a strong image of commanding leadership

Case studies of three general elections

1979 general election

The loss of a vote of confidence in the House of Commons in March 1979 forced James Callaghan to call an immediate general election. Although Callaghan's approval ratings were high, large-scale industrial unrest during the preceding Winter of Discontent undermined his government's authority. The Conservative campaign exploited discontent with trade union strike action and benefited from extensive support from the press.

Governing competence

The 1979 general election demonstrates how social factors can combine with valence issues of governing competency and issue voting to determine the result. Although James Callaghan was personally popular, his minority government had only managed to survive with the support of the Liberals and the nationalist parties. In the autumn of 1978, Callaghan decided not to call a general election even though Labour was ahead of the Conservative Party in most opinion polls. This proved to be a mistake since in the winter that followed his government faced a highly damaging series of strikes by public sector workers unprepared to accept the government's 5% pay cap. These included ambulance drivers, refuse collectors, water and sewerage workers and, notoriously, gravediggers in Liverpool.

According to the press, this had become Britain's Winter of Discontent and the weakness of the government was further shown when, abandoned by its Liberal and nationalist supporters, it lost a parliamentary vote of confidence, so forcing Callaghan to call a sudden general election. The dominant issue on which the Conservatives campaigned would be the record of the government, especially its failure to confront excessive trade union pay claims.

In focus

Negative news

The way in which the media cover an event can be highly significant in the outcome of a general election. On his return from Guadeloupe, Callaghan had dismissed a description of the country being in chaos. The next day *The Sun* headline was 'Crisis? What crisis?' It was this headline, rather than what Callaghan *actually* said, that influenced how people voted and subsequently provided the basis for a powerful Conservative election broadcast.

Reporter: 'What is your general approach, in view of the mounting chaos in the country at the moment?'

James Callaghan: 'Well, that's a judgement that you are making. I promise you that if you look at it from outside, and perhaps you're taking rather a parochial view at the moment, I don't think that other people in the world would share the view that there is mounting chaos.'

James Callaghan, Heathrow Airport, 10 January 1979

During the campaign, Callaghan's steady optimism, for which he had earned the nickname Sunny Jim, failed to resonate with voters, who felt that he was underestimating the way in which trade unions were demanding more pay for their members, so driving up inflation. In particular, the way in which he had attempted to calm the nation on his return from a Commonwealth summit in Guadeloupe in January 1979, by refusing to accept there was a crisis, made him appear complacent and out of touch. The fact that the 67-year-old Callaghan had played a leading role in every Labour government since 1964 also made it difficult for him to persuade floating voters that he was now the right prime minister to successfully confront the growing influence of the trade unions.

The campaign

Even before the campaign begun, the Conservatives focused on Labour's record in power, in particular its inability to control excessive trade union pay claims, bring down inflation and reduce unemployment. Valence issues of governing competence were thus vital in the Conservative victory.

In addition, the Conservatives emphasised that they were a party of national unity with common sense and practical solutions to the growing power of trade unions.

The positive way in which the press covered the Conservative campaign further reinforced the message among voters that Mrs Thatcher would offer a fresh approach to the defining issue of trade union influence. This helped to increase the Conservative vote in a number of social groupings which had traditionally been more likely to vote Labour. The narrowing of the Conservative poll lead as the general election loomed closer is also likely to have boosted Thatcher's fortunes by encouraging her supporters to turn out to vote. The high turnout in the 1979 general election (76%) is likely to have helped the Conservatives more than Labour.

The Conservatives also gained votes from the Liberal Party which, by propping up Callaghan in the Lib–Lab Pact, lost some of its traditional middle-class support. The imminent trial of its former leader, Jeremy Thorpe, for conspiracy to murder his former lover further damaged Liberal fortunes, especially as Thorpe was still standing in the election. Voters were therefore much less inclined to vote Liberal as a protest vote and so the Conservatives were the main beneficiaries (Table 4.19).

Table 4.19 Result of the 1979 general election

	Number of seats	% of popular vote	Increase/loss of seats	Positive or negative swing (%)
Conservative	339	43.9	62+	8.1+
Labour	269	36.9	−50	−2.3
Liberal	11	13.8	−2	−4.5

The social breakdown of the general election illustrates just how much class dealignment had taken place, with Conservative support dramatically increasing across all social classes — the biggest swing being among Labour's traditional core C2 voters. Indeed, in the October 1974 general election, Labour had led the Conservatives 23% among C2 voters. By 1979 both parties were neck and neck with C2 voters (Table 4.20).

Table 4.20 Social breakdown of the 1979 election compared with the October 1974 general election

Social class of voters	October 1974 general election (%)	1979 general election (%)
AB	Conservative 56 Labour 19 Liberal 21	Conservative 59 Labour 24 Liberal 15
C2	Conservative 26 Labour 49 Liberal 20	Conservative 41 Labour 41 Liberal 15
DE	Conservative 22 Labour 57 Liberal 16	Conservative 34 Labour 49 Liberal 13

The Conservatives also significantly increased their support among women, as well as registering a huge increase in support among younger voters (Table 4.21).

Table 4.21 Women and young voters in the October 1974 and 1979 elections

	October 1974 general election (%)	1979 general election (%)
Women	Conservative 39 Labour 38 Liberal 20	Conservative 47 Labour 35 Liberal 15
18–24-year-old voters	Conservative 24 Labour 42 Liberal 27	Conservative 42 Labour 41 Liberal 12

All of this evidence suggests that the way in which the Conservatives focused on the central issue of growing trade union power and governing competency was highly effective in persuading large numbers of Labour voters to abandon their traditional loyalties.

1997 general election

In 1997 the Conservatives had been in power for 18 years. The Major government was divided over Europe and associated with sleaze and incompetence. This contrasted with the dynamism and unity associated with Tony Blair and New Labour. With Labour 20% ahead in most opinion polls at the beginning of the campaign, even the most optimistic Conservatives found it difficult to believe they could win this general election.

Governing competence

Having narrowly won the 1992 general election, John Major's 1992–97 government quickly became associated with incompetence, disunity and corruption. Major's reputation for weak leadership was then brilliantly exploited by Tony Blair who, as the dynamic leader of New Labour, provided an exciting contrast to an increasingly unpopular prime minister.

Like Callaghan in 1979, Major was defeated in 1997 because he could not persuade the electorate that his party was fit to govern. As early as 1992 the government had lost its reputation for economic competence when it abandoned the European exchange rate mechanism (ERM) on 'Black Wednesday'. The resulting dramatic rise in interest rates hit mortgage owners the most and, even when the economy began to recover, the Conservatives never regained the economic trust of the electorate.

The Conservative Party was also divided over the European Union. Major only just managed to get the Maastricht Bill, which further increased European unity, through the House of Commons against opposition from his eurosceptic backbenchers. The resignation of a number of ministers over allegations of sleaze further damaged the government's reputation. In addition to this, the government's slow response to 'mad cow' disease, together with claims that ministers had colluded in the illegal sale of arms to Iraq, undermined the government's credibility.

Tony Blair and New Labour

Although attempts to make the Labour Party more attractive to middle-class voters had begun under Neil Kinnock, he lost both the 1987 and 1992 general elections. The sudden death of his successor, John Smith, in 1994 then led to Tony Blair taking over as Labour leader. Blair's youthful energy and charisma further drove forward the modernisation of Labour, based on the principles of an inclusive 'stakeholder society'. Clause IV of the Labour Party constitution was amended so that Labour no longer committed itself to nationalisation. Blair also moved to the centre by promising not to increase income tax, while he even challenged the Conservatives' traditional lead on law and order by promising 'to be tough on crime, tough on the causes of crime'.

Tony Blair proved to be a highly effective campaigner in the 1997 general election when his charisma was at its strongest

The campaign

Tony Blair's press secretary, Alastair Campbell, ran a tightly disciplined campaign, which showcased Blair as a youthful and energetic leader whose progressive centre-ground policies were in sharp contrast to Major's reputation for weak and uninspiring leadership. The presidential way in which Blair campaigned might have damaged a less charismatic leader, but in 1997 this sort of leadership was exactly what the electorate wanted.

The 'pledge card' that Labour campaigned on in 1997 also gave coherence to its campaign and was a way of persuading voters that Labour could be trusted in government after 18 years in opposition.

> ## Labour's 1997 pledge card
> - Cut class sizes to 30 or under for 5-, 6- and 7-year-olds
> - Halve the time between arrest and punishment for persistent young offenders
> - Cut NHS waiting lists
> - Take 250,000 young people off benefits and into work
> - No rise in income tax, VAT on fuel to be cut to 5%, interest rates and inflation to be kept as low as possible

Labour's party election broadcasts were also optimistic and inspiring, reaching out far beyond Labour's core vote. Just 3 days before the general election its 'angel taxi driver' broadcast offered a moving vision of how life could be so much better under Labour, fitting in with its campaign song 'Things can only get better'. Labour's promises of dramatic constitutional reforms, including devolution and House of Lords reform, also resonated with Liberal Democrat voters, helping Labour to win seats which might otherwise have gone Liberal Democrat.

At the same time, Labour was in the unusual position of having the support of *The Sun*, which in 1997 still had a circulation of almost 4 million. It is important to note, though, that *The Sun* switched allegiance to Labour only when Labour already had a commanding lead in the polls. Its support, therefore, was significant only in reinforcing Labour's lead over the Conservatives.

In contrast, the Conservative campaign was hampered by the government's inability to escape its reputation for corruption and disunity. The journalist Martin Bell stood as an anti-sleaze candidate against Neil Hamilton, who had resigned from the government over allegations that he had taken 'cash for questions'. This created huge negative publicity for the government.

The high-profile campaign of the Referendum Party also meant that Conservative divisions over Europe remained more prominent than Major would have wished. To make matters worse, the Conservatives' disastrous 'New Labour New Danger' campaign, focusing on Blair's 'demon eyes', entirely misjudged the mood of the nation. Five years of constant media attacks on Major's competence also made his leadership an electoral liability in a way that it had not been in 1992.

The results

The scale of Blair's general election victory meant that the Conservatives scored their lowest share of the popular vote since the leadership of the Duke of Wellington in 1832 (Table 4.22).

Table 4.22 Results of the 1997 general election

Party	Number of seats	% of popular vote	Increase/loss of seats	Positive or negative swing (%)
Labour	418	43.2	145+	+8.8
Conservative	165	30.7	−178	−11.2
Liberal Democrat	46	16.8	28+	−1

Table 4.23 shows how Labour was able to dramatically increase its share of the vote in all social categories by presenting itself as a progressive party under a dynamic leader, in contrast to a discredited Conservative government. It is, however, noteworthy that in spite of its broad inclusive appeal Labour in 1997 still performed by far the best among C2 and DE voters, while the Conservatives managed to keep a substantial lead among AB voters.

Table 4.23 1997 general election – social class voting trends

Social class	Labour (%)	Conservative (%)	Swing to Labour since 1992 general election (%)
AB	31	41	11
C1	39	37	14
C2	50	31	9
DE	59	21	9

Labour also increased its share of the vote in all parts of the UK, including traditional Conservative heartlands, and won the most votes in every age group, indicating the broad inclusive appeal of New Labour across all social, geographical and age categories.

2017 general election

On 18 April 2017 when Theresa May announced that she was going to call a general election on 8 June, she was so far ahead in the polls that some suggested she might achieve a 200-seat majority in the House of Commons. However, like her Conservative predecessor Edward Heath, who also shocked the nation when he called a snap general election in February 1974, Theresa May did not achieve the result she wanted or expected.

The unexpected 2017 general election provided a remarkable result, and confirmed some assumptions about voting behaviour in the UK.

- Class and partisan dealignment continued as the electorate voted more imaginatively than ever before.
- The way in which the campaign was fought was highly significant in determining the result.
- The television debates were influential, indicating that party leadership is highly significant.

However, the result also questioned a number of key assumptions:

- The hostility of the press towards Jeremy Corbyn made no difference to the result.
- Issues mattered more than the perceived competence of the party leaders.
- Young people are not necessarily apathetic and disillusioned with politics.
- The Conservative and Labour share of the vote was the biggest since 1970, challenging the assumption that the UK has entered a period of multiparty politics.

The 2017 general election also demonstrated a dramatic increase in the role of social media in determining the result. This suggests that in future all political parties are going to have to utilise social media as a core way of engaging with the electorate.

The campaign

According to the political journalist Andrew Rawnsley, the Conservatives ran 'the worst campaign in living memory', based on the assumption that the electorate would regard Labour under Jeremy Corbyn as unelectable. The Conservative manifesto was composed by Theresa May's key political advisers, Fiona Hill and Nick Timothy, and failed to inspire excitement. Even worse, proposals to make wealthier pensioners pay a share of the cost of NHS homecare was quickly labelled the 'dementia tax' and disastrously stalled the campaign. The Labour manifesto was much more enthusiastically received, especially the pledges to abolish tuition fees, increase spending on the police and not increase direct taxes for the 95% of the population earning less than £80,000 per annum. After 7 years of austerity, Corbyn's anti-austerity message was well received, especially as Labour promised to balance the budget by an 'excessive pay levy' on annual incomes above £330,000.

The focus of the Conservative campaign on Theresa May as a powerful leader who offered 'strong and stable' leadership also backfired, as she gave a series of lacklustre, stage-managed, emotionless speeches in which she lived up to media criticisms of her as the 'Maybot'. *Daily Mail* sketch writer Quentin Letts even called her a

One of Theresa May's highly stage-managed presentations to hand-picked Conservative voters in the 2017 general election

Before the 2017 general election, Jeremy Corbyn had appeared at a number of musical festivals, such as Glastonbury, where young people were attracted both to his policies and his authenticity

'glumbucket'. Her decision not to attend the televised leader debates was further damaging, enabling Caroline Lucas, leader of the Green Party, to claim 'the first rule of leadership is to turn up'.

In contrast, the Labour election team took Jeremy Corbyn directly to the people, where he proved to be a highly successful campaigner in large public meetings. He purposefully engaged with young voters, providing the campaign with a growing sense of energy and dynamism. Labour's campaign slogan of 'For the Many, Not the Few' also had a resonance which the Conservative campaign could not match. So impressive was Corbyn on the campaign trail that by the end of the campaign he had drawn equal with Theresa May in most opinion polls. His interview with grime star JME during the campaign and his appearance on the cover of *NME* both contributed to Labour's success among young voters.

By surrounding herself with Conservative supporters in invitation–only rallies, Theresa May ignored the lesson of John Major in 1992 who had won the election by taking his message directly to the people. Labour strategists avoided Corbyn giving too many interviews on detailed Labour policy and instead arranged a nationwide series of public meetings which were widely covered in the media and showed the Labour leader at his most engaging.

The 2017 general election also demonstrated the declining role of the press in general elections. *The Sun*, the *Daily Mail* and the *Daily Express*, in particular, ran especially vehement attacks on the Labour leadership. However, although the tabloid attacks on Corbyn were even more lurid than those on Ed Miliband in 2015, Labour increased its share of the vote by a staggering 9.6%:

● Attempts by the *Daily Mail* to associate Jeremy Corbyn, John McDonnell and Diane Abbott with IRA terrorism had little traction with voters since only older ones had strong memories of the 'Troubles'.

- *The Sun*'s headline on the day of the 2017 general election was reminiscent of its 1992 headline: 'If Kinnock wins today will the last person to leave Britain please turn out the lights'. However, 'Don't chuck Britain in the cor-bin' had no discernable impact on the result of the 2017 general election.

Governing competence and issue voting

Theresa May expected to be re-elected on a substantially increased majority because she would be able to contrast the competence of her government with a 'coalition of chaos' led by Jeremy Corbyn. Instead, voters ignored gaffs by prominent Labour frontbenchers, such as Diane Abbott, and focused less on valence issues of competence than on specific issues.

Brexit was the core issue on which the general election was fought, with a major swing to the Conservatives among more economically vulnerable DE voters who felt the Conservatives would be more likely to impose the toughest controls on immigration, while much more pro-European AB voters and younger voters favoured Labour as more likely to negotiate a softer Brexit.

Young people also voted Labour in large numbers because of its commitment to abolish tuition fees. In Scotland, the defining issue was Nicola Sturgeon's controversial commitment to a second referendum on independence, which mobilised a surge by the unionist parties, especially the Conservatives. In London, glaring wealth inequalities made Labour's slogan 'For the Many, Not the Few' especially appealing, leading to significant Labour gains.

The salience of issues in this election, especially Brexit, led to highly surprising results. By the end of the campaign the Conservatives had squandered their 20% poll lead and on the day of the general election Labour achieved a 9.6% swing — the biggest to any party since 1945. In spite of this the Conservatives also increased their share of the vote by 5.5%, giving them their biggest percentage share of the popular vote since 1983.

An analysis of geographical, social and demographic trends demonstrates how volatile the general election was, with the Conservatives doing well in those parts of England and Wales which voted Brexit and Labour achieving highly in Remain areas. Table 4.24 illustrates this with a detailed comparison of the results in two Midlands constituencies.

Table 4.24 A comparison of Leave and Remain Midlands constituencies

Warwick and Leamington Spa	North Warwickshire
Voted 59% Remain in the 2016 EU referendum	Voted 67% Leave in the 2016 EU referendum
2015 general election: • Conservative 47.9% • Labour 34.9% • UKIP 8.9% • Liberal Democrat 5%	2015 general election: • Conservative 42.3% • Labour 36% • UKIP 17.4% • Liberal Democrat 2.1%
2017 general election: • Labour 46.7% • Conservative 44.4% • Liberal Democrat 5.2% • UKIP 1.5%	2017 general election: • Conservative 56.9% • Labour 38.9% • Liberal Democrat 2.2%

Meanwhile in Scotland the salient issue was the SNP's commitment to a second independence referendum, which dramatically undermined its support in areas that had voted against independence in 2014. Stirling, for example, voted 60% for 'Better Together' and in 2017 the Conservatives won the seat. Moray voted 57.6% 'Better Together' in 2014 and in 2017 the deputy leader of the SNP, Angus Robertson, lost his seat to the Conservatives (Table 4.25).

Table 4.25 Results of Stirling and Moray at 2015 and 2017 general elections

Stirling	Moray
Voted 60% No in the 2014 independence referendum	Voted 57.6% No in the 2014 independence referendum
2015 general election: • SNP 45.6% • Labour 25.5% • Conservative 23.1%	2015 general election: • SNP 49.5% • Conservative 31.1% • Labour 9.9%
2017 general election: • Conservative 37.1% • SNP 36.8% • Labour 22.1%	2017 general election: • Conservative 47.5% • SNP 38.8% • Labour 10.9%

Class dealignment was also highly significant in the 2017 general election, with Labour dramatically increasing its support among pro-European AB voters, while the Conservatives achieved their best ever showing among more eurosceptic DE voters (Tables 4.26 and 4.27).

Table 4.26 EU referendum 2016 — voting by social class (%)

	AB	C1	C2	DE
Leave	43	51	64	64
Remain	57	49	36	36

Table 4.27 A comparison of social class voting in the 2015 and 2017 general elections (before and after the Brexit referendum)

2015 general election			2017 general election		
Social class	Conservative (%)	Labour (%)	Social class	Conservative (%)	Labour (%)
AB	44	28	AB	46	38
C1	38	30	C1	41	43
C2	36	31	C2	47	40
DE	29	37	DE	41	44

The salience of Brexit as the core issue in this general election is further demonstrated by the way in which different age groups voted. Labour increased its share of the vote among pro-European younger voters, as did the Conservatives among older more eurosceptic voters (Tables 4.28 and 4.29).

Table 4.28 EU referendum 2016 — how the youngest and oldest voted

Age	Remain (%)	Leave (%)
18–24	71	29
65+	36	64

Table 4.29 Voting according to age in the 2015 and 2017 general elections

| | 2015 general election | | | 2017 general election | |
Age	Conservative (%)	Labour (%)	Age	Conservative (%)	Labour (%)
18–24	27	43	18–24	18	67
25–34	33	36	25–34	22	58
35–44	35	35	35–44	30	50
45–54	36	33	45–54	40	39
55–64	37	31	55–64	47	33
65+	47	23	65+	59	23

The results

The results of the 2017 general election are laid out in Table 4.30.

Table 4.30 Results of the 2017 general election

	Number of seats	% of popular vote	Increase/loss of seats	Positive or negative swing
Conservative	317	42.4	–13	+5.5%
Labour	262	40	+30	+9.6%
Liberal Democrat	12	7.4	+4	–0.5%
Scottish National Party	35		–21	–1.7%

Summary

By the end of this chapter you should be able to answer the following questions:
→ What is the significance of social factors in general elections?
→ To what extent has party/class dealignment taken place?
→ Are general elections determined by issue voting?
→ What is the significance of party campaigns in determining the result of a general election?
→ How important is the role of the media in a general election and has that role changed?
→ How important is governing competency in determining the result of a general election?
→ What is the significance of party manifestos in a general election?
→ How important is the party leader in a general election?

Source-based question

Theresa May called a snap general election in April in order to try to increase the Conservative majority so that she could have a strengthened mandate for Brexit talks. The Conservatives pitched May as a 'strong and stable' leader in contrast to the 'coalition of chaos' under Jeremy Corbyn.

However, May's plan for a 'hard Brexit' was not favoured by voters, who preferred the 'soft Brexit' proposed by Corbyn. Polls suggested that voters also liked the left-wing policies of Corbyn's manifesto such as more money for the NHS and renationalisation of key industries. May's manifesto was received much more negatively; one of her policies being denounced as a 'dementia tax'. Corbyn also had more favourable media exposure, for example in television interviews that May didn't attend.

Young people had a large role in the increased popularity of Labour. On election day the 18–24s turned out in large numbers to back Corbyn. The voting preferences of university areas particularly demonstrated this.

Source: Online article, 2017

Using the source, evaluate the view that campaigns are the most important factor in determining the result of a general election.

In your response you must:
- *compare and contrast the different opinions in the source*
- *examine and debate these views in a balanced way*
- *analyse and evaluate only the information presented in the source* (30)

Evaluative questions

1. Evaluate the extent to which the result of general elections in the UK is determined by government competence. *You must consider this view and the alternative to this view in a balanced way.* (30)
2. Evaluate the extent to which the image of the party leader is the most significant factor in determining the result of a general election. *You must consider this view and the alternative to this view in a balanced way.* (30)
3. Evaluate the extent to which the media play the key role in deciding the result of a general election. *You must consider this view and the alternative to this view in a balanced way.* (30)

Key term

Constitution A constitution determines where power is located within a nation state and the rules by which it is governed. It also establishes the extent of the government's authority and the rights that its citizens possess.

The nature of the UK constitution

The UK **constitution** has developed differently to the constitutions of most other nation states. This is because, since the Norman Conquest in 1066, there has not been a historical event which has entirely altered the principles on which the nation is governed. Even after the establishment of a Protectorate under Oliver Cromwell in 1653, Cromwell still had to try to work with Parliament, and in 1657 he had to reject the offer of the Crown himself. Following Cromwell's death the monarchy was re-established under Charles II in 1660.

Parliament Acts 1911 and 1949
As a result of the House of Lords' refusal to pass David Lloyd George's People's Budget, the Liberal prime minister H.H. Asquith (1908–16) threatened that he would ask King George V (1910–35) to flood the House of Lords with Liberal peers if it did not accept limits on its powers. The House of Lords relented, and in the 1911 Parliament Act the Lords lost its right of veto. Henceforth the Lords would not be able to amend financial bills such as the Budget, while it would be able to delay other bills for only 2 years. The 1949 Parliament Act reduced the Lords' right of delay from 2 years to 1 year. The two Parliament Acts established the democratic legitimacy of Parliament by asserting the primacy of the Commons over the Lords

Magna Carta Act 1215
By forcing King John (1199–1216) to accept the 63 clauses of Magna Carta, the barons placed limits on the power of the monarchy. This established the principle that the Crown is not above the law. Magna Carta also contains the first statement of the principle of habeas corpus, that one cannot be punished without due process of law

Act of Settlement 1701
The Act of Settlement confirmed the primacy of Parliament over the Crown by declaring that Parliament had the authority to determine the succession to the throne. The Act of Settlement also confirmed judicial independence by stating that a judge can be removed only on the agreement of both houses of Parliament

The Bill of Rights Act 1689
In 1688, the last Stuart King, James II, was overthrown in the Glorious Revolution because it was claimed he was trying to establish an absolutist monarchy. When Parliament offered the Crown to James II's daughter Mary and her husband William of Orange, they had to accept the Bill of Rights, which gave legal force to 'certain ancient rights and liberties'. These included the summoning of regular parliaments, free elections, no taxation without the consent of Parliament and parliamentary freedom of speech

Act of Union 1707
Although England, Wales and Scotland had shared the same monarch since 1603, the Act of Union united the Parliament of Scotland with that of England and Wales. This created the United Kingdom, although the independence of Scottish law was preserved

European Communities Act 1972
In 1972, the Conservative government of Edward Heath (1970–74) successfully steered the European Communities Act through Parliament. As a result of the Act, the UK joined the European Economic Community (from 1993 the European Union) on 1 January 1973. In 1991 in the Factortame case (see Chapter 8), the principle that, in cases of overlap, European law would take precedence over domestic law, was established

Figure 5.1 Key events in the development of the constitution

The development of the British constitution has been evolutionary, involving no irrevocable breaks with the past. This is in contrast to the history of countries such as France and the USA, in both of which a revolutionary event led to the complete overthrow of the previous government and the establishment of a codified constitution setting out the principles by which the government would operate and the rights which its citizens would possess.

The events in Figure 5.1 demonstrate how power in Britain has *gradually* moved away from the Crown to Parliament and, within Parliament, to the democratically elected House of Commons, without a single revolutionary upheaval. As a result, the British monarchy has become a constitutional monarchy, which means that it holds limited power according to the rule of law. As the power of the Crown has been reduced, the rights of the public have been secured by a series of landmark decisions, court cases and Acts of Parliament.

Synoptic link

John Locke (1632–1704)

The Bill of Rights (1689) is based on the principle that the right of the Crown to govern derives from a contract made with Parliament that it will govern according to the rule of law. The acceptance by William and Mary of the Bill of Rights established the principle of a constitutional monarchy.

The core liberal thinker John Locke provides a philosophical justification for limited government according to the rule of law in his *Two Treatises on Government* (1689). According to Locke:

'Men being, as has been said, by nature, all free, equal and independent, no one can be put out of this estate, and subjected to the political power of another, without his own consent.'

This links to Component 1, Core Political Ideas (page 246).

Key terms

Uncodified/codified
When a constitution is codified, it is contained in one single document which is entrenched and is superior to all other law. An uncodified constitution derives from a variety of sources and, since it is not entrenched, does not represent a higher law.

Unentrenched/entrenched
Codified constitutions entrench constitutional rules, making it impossible for them to be altered without complicated procedures requiring the agreement of more than just the legislature. When a constitution is unentrenched, like that of the UK, then the way in which the state is governed and the rights of its citizens can be changed simply by an Act of Parliament.

According to the great constitutional theorist, A.V. Dicey, the 'twin pillars' on which Britain's **uncodified** constitution is based are that Parliament is the supreme law-making body and that government must be according to the rule of law.

Since the UK constitution is uncodified, it is also **unentrenched**. This means that, unlike the majority of nation states, which have a **codified** constitution, the UK does not possess a single document that establishes the rights of its citizens and the limits on government and so can be said to represent ultimate power in the state. Instead, Parliament, as the sovereign law-making body, can enact any legislation for which there is a parliamentary majority and which would not be deemed unconstitutional, such as extending the lifetime of a parliament beyond 5 years.

As a result of **parliamentary sovereignty**, the rights of British citizens are not protected by the higher law of the constitution as they are in, for example the USA. Instead, the rights of British citizens have traditionally been seen as being negative rights, in that we are free to do whatever has not been forbidden by Parliament. In spite of the UK's lack of a codified constitution, our civil liberties are protected by:

- the principle that the government should act according to the **rule of law**
- the independence of the judiciary from the government and the way in which judges interpret the law according to the principles of natural justice

According to Thomas Paine — who in 1776 published *Common Sense*, which encouraged the American colonies to declare their independence — obedience to the rule of law means the difference between autocratic and free government, 'For as in absolute governments the King is law, so in free countries the law ought to be king; and there ought to be no other'.

Since Parliament is the supreme law-making body, the UK can be said to be a **unitary** state. This is because Parliament has absolute authority to enact any legislation. This contrasts with **federal** states like the USA, in which the states have certain powers which the central government cannot override. The devolution of power from Westminster to the Scottish Parliament and the National Assembly for Wales could be seen as challenging the principle that the UK is a unitary state. However, at least in theory and in certain circumstances, these devolved powers could be reclaimed by Parliament, as has been shown by the way in which Parliament enacted the European Union (Notification of Withdrawal) Act in 2017, beginning the process by which the UK reclaimed sovereign power from the European Union.

The sources of the UK constitution

Since its development has been evolutionary, the UK does not possess a codified constitution. There has not been one moment when the existing political system has been completely replaced with a new one, leading to the drawing up of a codified constitution setting out the new powers of the government and the rights of its citizens.

Instead, the British constitution has *gradually* developed over 800 years since Magna Carta. Sir Robin Butler, Cabinet Secretary (1988–98), even joked that the British constitution is 'something we make up as we go along'. The UK, therefore, has an uncodified constitution deriving from a variety of different sources rather than being contained in one document. The main sources of the UK constitution are as follows.

Statute law

Momentous Acts of Parliament contribute to the UK's uncodified constitution. For example, the Parliament Act 1911, which removed the House of Lords' right of veto, is of key constitutional significance because it established the principle that Parliament should reflect the democratic will of the public expressed through the House of Commons. Another parliamentary statute of enduring importance is the Representation of the People Act 1928, by which the UK adopted universal suffrage.

Since the election of the Blair government in 1997, a number of reforming Acts of Parliament have led to the further development of the British constitution (Table 5.1).

Table 5.1 Reforming Acts of Parliament

Act	Explanation
Scotland Act 1998	Following the 1997 referendum in which Scotland voted in favour of devolution, the Scotland Act re-established a Scottish Parliament
Human Rights Act 1998	The Human Rights Act incorporates the European Convention on Human Rights (ECHR) into British law. As a result, public bodies, including the government, are expected to act in accordance with the ECHR and judges should interpret the law according to the principles of the ECHR
Equality Act 2010	The Equality Act codifies into one parliamentary statute all previous anti-discriminatory legislation, so providing the positive right of equal treatment
Marriage (Same Sex Couples) Act 2013	This Act legalises same-sex marriage and represents a pivotal step in the development of LGBT rights

Common law

The way in which the judiciary interprets the meaning of the law contributes to the development of case law. This is especially important on occasions when **statute law** is lacking or unclear. The precedents set in such cases are so far-reaching that they can be said to contribute to the constitution as **common law**. Table 5.2 gives some examples.

Table 5.2 Some landmark common law cases

Case	Explanation
Bushell's case (1670)	In this case, the presiding judge instructed the jury to find two Quakers guilty of unlawful assembly. The jury refused to do this and so were fined for contempt of court. One juror, Edward Bushell, refused to pay the fine and in the resulting case Sir John Vaughan declared in favour of the jury, stating that a judge 'may try to open the eyes of the jurors, but not to lead them by the nose'. Bushell's case represents a landmark case protecting the independence of a jury
Entick v *Carrington* (1765)	When agents working for a member of the government, the Earl of Halifax, ransacked the home of the anti-government publicist James Entick searching for incriminating evidence, Entick sued for damages. The presiding judge, Lord Camden, found in favour of Entick, declaring that, '... if this is law it would be found in our books, but no such law ever existed in this country; our law holds the property of every man so sacred, that no man can set his foot upon his neighbour's close without his leave'. The principle of *Entick* v *Carrington*, that the executive cannot infringe the civil liberties of its citizens without legal justification, established an enduring precedent that protects British citizens from arbitrary and autocratic government
Somerset v *Stewart* (1772)	When a black slave, James Somerset, was imprisoned by Charles Stewart for having escaped, lawyers acting for Somerset claimed he had been illegally imprisoned. In his judgement, Lord Mansfield stated that nothing in English statute law justified slavery and so Somerset could not be enslaved: 'It is so odious, that nothing can be suffered to support it, but positive law.' The case is momentous because it challenged the legitimacy of slavery in common law long before its abolition by Act of Parliament (1833). Mansfield appreciated just how controversial his decision would be, but he reminded the court, 'We cannot in any of these points direct the law; the law must rule us.' This set an important precedent that the courts must always dispense justice *whatever the consequences*

Key terms

Statute law A parliamentary bill which has been approved by both houses of Parliament and then given the royal assent. In the UK, there is no authority greater than statute law.

Common law Refers to the judgements made by judges in important legal cases. Sometimes referred to as 'judge-made law', common law cases set precedents to be followed in future cases.

Convention A convention represents the accustomed way in which political activity is carried out. Conventions do not legally have to be carried out. Instead their constitutional significance derives from the force of tradition.

Conventions

Although they are not recognised in statute law, a number of **conventions** have developed which, like common law, have achieved the force of constitutional precedence.

- There is, for example, no legal requirement that a member of the House of Lords cannot be prime minister. However, in 1963, Lord Home recognised that this would be constitutionally unacceptable, and he resigned his peerage so that he could fight a by-election to enter the House of Commons as Sir Alec Douglas-Home.

- According to the Salisbury Convention, the House of Lords does not oppose the second or third reading of legislation that was in the winning party's manifesto. This convention was named after Robert Gascoyne-Cecil, the fifth Marquess of Salisbury (1893–1972). The convention dates back to the Labour government of 1945–51 when Lord Salisbury, the leader of the Conservative Party in the House of Lords, accepted that the House of Lords would not use its Conservative majority to try to wreck Labour's manifesto commitments since Labour had been democratically endorsed by the electorate.

- The principle of collective ministerial responsibility is, likewise, a convention which has developed as a way of ensuring that governments survive rather than fragment.

- In 2003, by allowing the House of Commons to vote on whether to support military action against Iraq, Tony Blair established the convention that henceforth Parliament should be consulted over the large-scale commitment of British forces to military operations.

- Another convention that has developed in recent years is that the public should be consulted in a referendum in order to legitimise proposed changes to the constitution.

Sir Alec Douglas-Home renounced his peerage so that he could enter the House of Commons. He became prime minister in October 1963

Landmark decisions

Like conventions, some historical events are so momentous that they contribute towards the constitution.

- Magna Carta (1215), for example, by recognising that limits can be placed on the authority of the Crown, has played a major role in the development of the principle of the rule of law.
- The Petition of Right (1628), which Parliament presented to King Charles I, sets out core rights including freedom from arbitrary imprisonment and the requirement that Parliament grant taxation.
- The Bill of Rights (1689) asserts the subordination of the Crown to Parliament, as well as condemning 'illegal and cruel punishments'.

Authoritative works

There are a small number of influential works that are said to be part of the constitution.

- The way in which Walter Bagehot, in *The English Constitution* (1867), explains the relationship between the monarchy, the legislature and the executive makes this work a core constitutional text.
- A.V. Dicey's *Introduction to the Law of the Constitution* (1885) is similarly important because of the way in which Dicey explains how the British constitution rests upon the 'twin pillars' of parliamentary sovereignty and the rule of law.
- Erskine May (1815–86), a clerk of the House of Commons, published *Parliamentary Practice* in 1844. It explains in minute detail how Parliament operates and is now in its 24th updated edition. It is so authoritative that it is regarded as being part of the UK constitution. In March 2019 the speaker of the House of Commons, John Bercow, used principles established by Erskine May to stop Theresa May reintroducing her Brexit deal into parliament in an unchanged state.

Since the constitution is constantly evolving, new **authoritative works** can become part of the constitution. For example, in 2010, the cabinet secretary, Gus O'Donnell, produced such a complete guide to how a coalition government should be established that it has achieved constitutional significance.

Treaties

As a result of the European Communities Act 1972, the UK accepted the Treaty of Accession which the prime minister, Edward Heath, had negotiated. This made the UK a signatory to the Treaty of Rome (1957) and meant that the UK accepted all existing European Community law. The UK has subsequently ratified a number of other EU **treaties** such as the Single European Act, the Maastricht Treaty and the Lisbon Treaty, as a result of which UK law has been significantly changed. The impact on the UK constitution of membership of the EU will remain substantial, since the European Union (Withdrawal) Act 2018 transfers all existing EU law into domestic law. According to the government, this will ensure that there is no 'black hole in our statute book'.

Relations between the sources of the UK constitution

Since the UK constitution derives from so many different sources, there can be competing jurisdictions between them. Parliamentary statute law has traditionally been seen as the ultimate source of authority, since an Act of Parliament can supersede even landmark decisions such as Magna Carta. A parliamentary statute also takes precedence over works of authority, conventions and the common law. However, in

<aside>

Key terms

Authoritative works
Texts of such profound and enduring political significance that they contribute to the constitution of the United Kingdom.

Treaty A written agreement made between two or more political entities. Following the acceptance of the Treaty of Accession in 1972, the UK's constitution was radically changed since Parliament agreed to adopt legislation that had been enacted elsewhere.

</aside>

the Factortame case (1991), the Law Lords declared that, in cases where the EU had legislated, EU law took precedence over domestic law. Although this did put limits on parliamentary sovereignty this was only in areas where the UK had pooled sovereignty with the EU. In those areas where the UK retained sovereignty, such as negotiating treaties, parliamentary statute remained supreme, which is why Westminster was able to enact legislation withdrawing the UK from the European Union.

The development of the constitution since 1997

The Blair government (1997–2007)

Although at the beginning of the twentieth century the Asquith government (1908–16) profoundly changed the constitution by asserting the primacy of the House of Commons over the House of Lords, for most of the rest of the century the reform of the constitution was not a major political issue. However, the election of the government of Tony Blair in 1997 changed all that. Blair was a modernising and progressive Labour leader, with a parliamentary majority of 179 seats, facing a weak Conservative opposition which had just gone down to its biggest general election defeat since 1832.

For Blair, the British constitution was urgently in need of reform and New Labour would address this problem. Power was too centralised in Westminster and the rights of the citizens were insufficiently protected. Since the government was so remote and unaccountable, the public had become disengaged from politics. Democracy would be invigorated by an extensive programme of constitutional reform. As Blair put it, 'modernisation is the key'.

> 'We wish to change politics itself, to bridge the gap between governed and government and to try to address the deep-seated and damaging disaffection with politics which has grown up in recent years.'
>
> Tony Blair, May 1996

Synoptic link

The reform of UK democracy links to Component 1, UK Politics (see pages 11–24).

His constitutional reform programme thus focused on the following connected themes:

- **Decentralisation** Since so much power had been focused on Westminster (especially during the prime ministership of Margaret Thatcher 1979–90), power should be devolved back to the people. Scotland and Wales would be offered their own elected governments, and cities and towns would be given the opportunity to elect their own mayors.
- **Democratisation** The public should be given more influence over decision making through the greater use of referendums on important constitutional issues. In order to encourage greater democracy, the House of Lords would be reformed.
- **Transparency** In order to encourage greater trust in government, the role of the senior judiciary would be reformed. A Freedom of Information Act would also open up government, making it more accountable to the public.
- **Rights protection** Since British citizens' human rights were not protected by a codified constitution, the government committed to incorporating the European Convention on Human Rights (ECHR) into British law. This would provide the judiciary with an important new statute, protecting and advancing the public's civil liberties.

Devolution/local government

Labour's flagship constitutional reform in 1997 was devolution. This would provide Scotland and Wales with greater powers to govern themselves. In 1997, referendums were held in Scotland and Wales over whether they wished to have their own elected governments. Scotland voted by a large majority in favour of having its own parliament, while Wales voted in favour of its own assembly by a tiny margin. In 1998, as part of the Good Friday Agreement, Northern Ireland also voted in a referendum in favour of power sharing between unionists and republicans in a devolved assembly.

The aim of these reforms was to provide the constituent parts of the UK with greater self-determination. Establishing new legislatures and executives in Edinburgh, Cardiff and Belfast would ensure that policies could be more exactly suited to the needs of the people of Scotland, Wales and Northern Ireland. Plans to move towards English devolution were stalled when, in 2004, the North East rejected proposals for a regional assembly in a referendum by 78% to 22%.

The government also provided many towns, cities and regions with the opportunity to elect their own mayors, which was designed to make local government more accountable to the public. In 1998, London voted in a referendum in favour of a Greater London Authority comprising an elected mayor of London and a London Assembly, which can veto the mayor's proposals with a two-thirds majority. The Local Government Act 2000 then enabled local authorities to offer their voters a referendum over whether they wanted their own directly elected mayors.

Synoptic link

Blair's modernisation of the UK constitution links to the progressive principles of New Labour. This links to Component 2, UK Government (see pages 51–52).

Supporters of the principle of elected mayors argue that they encourage greater accountability and transparency in local government, while David Cameron claimed that they can 'galvanise action'. However, by 2016, the electorate had rejected an elected mayor in 37 of the 53 referendums that were called. There are also concerns that, far from encouraging local democracy, mayors are frequently elected on a small turnout of the vote, so undermining their legitimacy. In 2017, for example, Andy Street became the elected mayor of the West Midlands but the turnout was a disappointing 26.7%, while in the same year Andy Burnham won the Greater Manchester mayoral election on a turnout of 28.9%. In London voting levels have been higher but in 2016 Sadiq Khan was elected on a turnout of only 45.3%.

All the main political parties support decentralisation of power away from Westminster. Andy Burnham was elected mayor of Greater Manchester in 2017, having left frontline national politics

House of Lords reform

In 1999, when the government introduced legislation to reform the Upper House, 1,330 peers were eligible to attend the House of Lords. The majority were hereditary peers, which meant that their right to sit in the House of Lords derived from their membership of one of the aristocratic families of the UK. The hereditary peers outnumbered the life peers, who had been appointed to the Lords as a result of their service to the nation.

The hereditary principle undermined the legitimacy of the House of Lords and so the government determined to remove the right of the hereditary peers to attend. This meant that the life peers became, by far, the biggest group in the House of Lords. However, in order to persuade the House of Lords to accept this reform, the government compromised by allowing the hereditary peers to elect 92 of their number who would continue to sit in the House of Lords.

The reform of the House of Lords affected its membership rather than its powers. The government's intention was to make it a more professional body by ensuring that membership became based on merit and accomplishment rather than birth. In 2000, a House of Lords Appointments Commission was established, which would nominate a small proportion of new life peers.

These reforms have raised the self-confidence of the House of Lords. However, they have also been highly controversial. Although the government intended the House of Lords Act 1999 to be a first-stage reform, nothing was done to introduce an elected element into the House of Lords. This means that, although the House of Lords can now claim greater expertise, it still lacks democratic legitimacy. In addition, the majority of life peers are still appointed on the recommendation of the prime minister, as a result of which critics claim that too many appointments to the Lords are made through political patronage.

In focus

House of Lords reform

The way in which the House of Lords was reformed in 1999 did not reduce the influence that the prime minister has on the appointment of life peers. Indeed, during his first government (1997–2001) Blair appointed 203 life peers. Although life peers are expected to be appointed on merit, there is, for any prime minister, the temptation to appoint political allies and party supporters to the House of Lords. The Conservative leader William Hague (1997–2001) accused Blair of creating a 'house of cronies', and in 2006 the prime minister was questioned by police over allegations that donors to the Labour Party had subsequently been awarded life peerages. This quickly became known as the 'cash for honours' scandal. Although no charges were brought against Blair, it demonstrates how the way in which the 1999 reforms made the Lords an almost wholly appointed chamber could encourage political cronyism. David Cameron was also widely criticised for his resignation honours list, in which he appointed 13 Conservative life peers and just one Labour life peer. It could be claimed that House of Lords reform has failed to provide the upper chamber with greater legitimacy, since the appointment process remains dominated by the prime minister.

Shami Chakrabarti, the former director of human rights group Liberty, was the only Labour life peer in David Cameron's resignation honours list

Electoral reform

Although Tony Blair, as leader of the opposition, had expressed interest in electoral reform for Westminster elections, the massive parliamentary majority Labour achieved in the 1997 general election considerably reduced his enthusiasm. Although the government did commission a report, tasking Roy Jenkins, the former Labour minister and founder of the Social Democrat Party, to investigate alternatives to first-past-the-post (FPTP), it ignored the report's recommendation that FPTP should be replaced with a form of the alternative vote (AV).

Labour was, however, prepared to adopt new electoral systems for the new devolved assemblies and elected mayors and regional assemblies in order to encourage voter choice and ensure a fairer balance of influence. The Scottish Parliament and Welsh Assembly would be elected by means of the additional member system (AMS) and the Northern Ireland Assembly by the single transferable vote (STV). The AMS would also be used for elections to the London Assembly and the supplementary vote (SV) would be used to elect mayors.

Blair's record on electoral reform was thus unimpressive, with some cynics even suggesting that the government had decided to put political expediency before principle by ignoring the strong case for electoral reform at Westminster.

The Human Rights Act

In 1998 the Human Rights Act (HRA) was passed, which incorporated the European Convention on Human Rights into British law. The HRA came into force in 2000 and is important because, for the first time, it *positively* states the rights that British citizens can claim. Supporters of the Act also argue that it has provided the judiciary with important new powers to protect our civil liberties in ways that previously would not have been possible. In the Laporte case (2006), for example, Article 8 of the HRA, the right to a private life, and Article 10, the right to freedom of expression, were used to show that the police had acted illegally when they stopped 120 anti-Iraq War protestors from reaching RAF Fairford in 2003. In another landmark decision involving Article 8 of the HRA, intrusive press coverage of the supermodel Naomi Campbell in a rehabilitation clinic was declared illegal (2004).

Incorporating the ECHR into British law has also led to the better protection of our civil liberties:

- Public bodies, such as the government, are now expected to act in accordance with the HRA.
- When Parliament legislates, it should do so, as much as possible, in accordance with the principles of the HRA.

However, the constitutional significance of the Human Rights Act should not be exaggerated. Since it is an Act of Parliament, it does not represent the sort of higher constitutional law to be found in, for example, the US Bill of Rights. Parliament therefore has the right to repeal the Act, and, since no parliament may bind its successor, Parliament can still enact legislation even if it conflicts with the HRA. In such circumstances, the judiciary would issue a formal statement of incompatibility but the new law would still stand. Article 15 of the HRA also gives the government the right to suspend, or derogate from, certain of its provisions, as the Blair government did after the terrorist attacks on Washington DC and New York in 2001.

The limitations of the HRA are illustrated by the Belmarsh case (2004). Following the terrorist attacks on the USA, the Blair government suspended Article 5, the

Synoptic link

The significance of the Human Rights Act links to Component 1, UK Politics (see pages 32–36).

right to liberty, so that it could keep foreign terrorist suspects in custody without charge. Parliament also enacted the Anti-Terrorism, Crime and Security Act 2001, which gave the government the authority to keep foreign terrorist suspects in prison indefinitely.

In the resulting Belmarsh case, the judges issued a formal statement of incompatibility, declaring that the Anti-Terrorism, Crime and Security Act was contrary to Article 14, freedom from discrimination, of the HRA since *foreign* suspects were being treated differently to *British* suspects. The government initially ignored the ruling, which it had the right to do, but then decided to release the suspects because of the unfavourable publicity. Soon after, though, Parliament enacted the Prevention of Terrorism Act 2005, which allowed the government to limit the freedom of movement of *all* terrorist suspects through control orders.

The limitations of the HRA can be seen in Tony Blair's comments in 2005 that the government would not be bound by the Act in confronting terrorism and extremism: 'Should legal obstacles arise we will legislate further, including if necessary amending the Human Rights Act.'

Supreme Court

The last major constitutional reform of the Blair government was the Constitutional Reform Act 2005. Although the judiciary should be independent from the legislature and the executive, there were a number of anomalies in the constitution. The Lord Chancellor was not only head of the judiciary but was also a member of the cabinet (executive) and presided over the House of Lords (the legislature). The most senior judges also sat in the House of Lords (although they did not vote on legislation), making it the final court of appeal.

In order to guarantee the separation of powers, the Constitutional Reform Act achieved the following:

- It ended the House of Lords' judicial function and in its place established the Supreme Court. The Supreme Court opened in 2009 and the way in which its members dispense justice has proved more transparent and conspicuous than that of the Law Lords.
- In order to make the appointment of judges more transparent, the Lord Chancellor's right to nominate judges was transferred to a Judicial Appointments Committee, which now makes recommendations to the justice secretary.
- The Lord Chancellor's role presiding over the House of Lords was removed and the new head of the judiciary became the non-political Lord Chief Justice. The Lord Chancellor's functions merged with those of the justice secretary.

The coalition government (2010–15)

The government of Gordon Brown (2007–10) was so preoccupied with confronting the global economic crisis that it did not introduce any further major constitutional reforms. However, the Conservative–Liberal Democrat coalition (2010–15) did much more to further reform the constitution. David Cameron was more open to change than former Conservative leaders. However, he also had to make constitutional reform a leading priority if he was going to be able to bring the Liberal Democrats, committed to updating the constitution, into coalition government. According to its deputy prime minister, Nick Clegg, the coalition would be responsible for 'the biggest shake-up of our democracy since 1832'.

Fixed-term Parliaments Act 2011

A major royal prerogative power of the prime minister has traditionally been deciding the date of a general election. This would have been a highly contentious decision for a coalition prime minister to have taken and so the Fixed-term Parliaments Act legislated that a general election should be held exactly 5 years after the last general election. As well as providing the government with greater stability, the Act also made it more difficult for a prime minister to call a snap general election at a time of their choosing.

However, the Act *does* allow a general election if the government loses a vote of confidence and a new government which has the confidence of the House of Commons cannot be established or if a two-thirds majority of the House of Commons agrees to a general election. In 2017, Theresa May was able to call a general election — the only difference was that she had to do this with the consent of Parliament rather than by using the royal prerogative. The day after she announced her intention to call a snap general election, Parliament ratified her decision by a majority of 522–13. The significance of this constitutional change is therefore minimal.

Electoral reform

Since the Labour and Conservative parties benefit most from first-past-the-post, electoral reform at Westminster is not a priority for either party. The Blair government ignored the recommendations of the Jenkins Commission Report (1998) to replace FPTP with a new system based on the alternative vote.

However, providing the opportunity for electoral reform was the price that David Cameron had to pay if he was to be able to form a coalition with the Liberal Democrats in 2010. The coalition agreement therefore stated that the government would call a referendum offering the public the opportunity to replace FPTP with the AV. In the 2011 referendum, opponents of change successfully portrayed the AV system as complicated and lacking in transparency. David Cameron even called it 'undemocratic, obscure, unfair and crazy', and the electorate voted 68% to 32% in favour of retaining FPTP on a turnout of just 42%.

Critics of Nick Clegg subsequently claimed that he should have negotiated for a referendum on the additional member system or the single transferable vote. These options might have been more appealing, and so Cameron had readily agreed to a referendum on the AV, knowing it would be unlikely to generate much support. Whether or not this is a fair criticism, there is no doubt that the case for electoral reform was strongly put back by this convincing endorsement of FPTP.

Parliamentary reform

Possibly the coalition's most positive legacy was in giving backbench MPs more influence and addressing the government's dominance of the House of Commons. Most of the recommendations of the Wright Committee (2009) were enacted. The most significant points are as follows.

- A Parliamentary Backbench Committee was established to give backbench MPs more control over what is debated in Parliament.
- The membership of select committees would no longer be determined by the whips. Instead the membership and chairs would be elected by MPs in a secret ballot. This has increased the legitimacy of select committees and made them more self-confident when scrutinising government.

- In order to address criticisms that Parliament was alien and irrelevant to people's everyday lives, it was important to reconnect Parliament with the public. To this end, electronic petitions were introduced, which allow the public to directly lobby Parliament. Parliament does not have to legislate on these issues, but if an e-petition reaches 100,000 signatures the issue is very likely to be debated.

In focus

The coalition and House of Lords reform

The extent to which the House of Lords should be reformed is a highly controversial constitutional question. Since Tony Blair had not introduced legislation to provide the House of Lords with a democratic element, Nick Clegg was determined to provide the 'flawed institution' with democratic legitimacy. However, his proposals were defeated by a backbench rebellion by 91 Conservative MPs and Clegg was forced to drop his proposals.

The most significant reform of the House of Lords which was enacted during the coalition was actually a private member's bill, which for the first time allows members of the Lords to resign or retire, while those who regularly fail to attend or have been imprisoned can be excluded (House of Lords Reform Act 2014).

Further devolution

Like the Blair government, the coalition was keen to decentralise power in order to bring decision making closer to the public.

- In a referendum in 2011, Wales voted in favour of its Assembly being given primary legislative power in some areas. These provisions were enacted by the Wales Act 2014, which also provided for a future referendum over whether Wales could be given some control over income tax.
- Further powers were also devolved to Scotland, including the right to vary income tax by up to 10p. The Scottish government was also given the authority to borrow up to £5 billion.

Elected police commissioners

A further example of decentralisation was the coalition's introduction of elected police and crime commissioners, who would be accountable to the public for regional policing. However, the turnout in elections for police and crime commissioners has been so low that there are concerns that they lack a sufficient democratic mandate to legitimately carry out their functions (Table 5.3).

Table 5.3 Police and crime commissioner elections, 2016

Dyfed-Powys Police	49.1% — highest national turnout
Durham Constabulary	17.7% — lowest national turnout

Power of recall

In order to help restore trust in politicians, the Recall of MPs Act was passed in 2015. Its aim is to make MPs more accountable by allowing their constituents to demand a by-election if an MP is sentenced to prison or is suspended from the House of Commons for more than 21 days. For a recall petition to be successful, 10% of constituents must sign it.

In 2018, the Democratic Unionist MP Ian Paisley was suspended from Parliament for not disclosing a holiday that he had taken at the expense of the Sri Lankan government and subsequently lobbying on its behalf when it was accused of human rights abuses. As a result of this, Paisley became the first MP to be subject to a recall petition. He survived as an MP since the petition was signed by only 9.4% of his constituents rather than the 10% needed to trigger a by-election.

Conservative governments (2015–)

David Cameron's success in the 2015 general election was the first Conservative general election victory since 1992. Although no longer governing in coalition with the Liberal Democrats, the Conservatives introduced a number of measures which significantly impacted on the constitution. Some of these reforms were a response to political circumstances.

- In 2014, for example, David Cameron promised extensive new powers to the Scottish Parliament and government if Scotland rejected independence. These were consequently introduced in the Scotland Act 2016 and provided Scotland with what have been called 'devo-max' powers.
- Similarly, the referendum on whether the UK should continue to be a member of the European Union was a Conservative manifesto commitment in the 2015 general election, which David Cameron then had to deliver on.

Other constitutional reforms carried more conviction. Like Tony Blair, Cameron and his chancellor of the exchequer, George Osborne, were in favour of decentralising power to local government. Elected mayors were duly introduced, without referendums, in the West Midlands, Greater Manchester, West of England, Tees Valley, Cambridgeshire and Peterborough, and Liverpool City Region. The powers of these new 'metropolitan mayors' are extensive, covering areas such as housing, welfare and transport. Greater Manchester's elected mayor, for example, is responsible for a £6 billion social care and health budget.

The government also addressed the West Lothian question. Since the establishment of the Welsh Assembly and the Scottish Parliament, concerns had been raised that since England did not have its own parliament then Scotland and Wales were being unduly advantaged by this constitutional arrangement. After all, MPs from Scotland, Wales and Northern Ireland still attended Westminster, where they could vote on legislation which affected England. MPs for English constituencies at Westminster, on the other hand, could not vote on issues that were now controlled by the Scottish Parliament, Northern Ireland Assembly and Welsh Assembly. As a result of this unfair constitutional anomaly, a Legislative Grand Committee has been established. Its membership reflects the composition of the parties in England and its consent is necessary if legislation which affects only England is to pass. This procedure has been in operation since 2015 and is known as English Votes for English Laws (EVEL).

The impact of devolution on the United Kingdom

In the 1997 general election, Labour committed itself to providing Wales and Scotland with referendums on whether they wanted powers to be devolved to them from Westminster. Scotland, which had had its own parliament until the Act of Union in 1707, voted decisively in favour of the restoration of a Scottish Parliament. Wales, which had less of a political sense of its own identity, only narrowly supported the establishment of a Welsh Assembly. The results of the relevant referendums are shown in Table 5.4.

Table 5.4 Results of the referendums on devolving power to Scotland and Wales, 1997

Scotland	Wales
Yes to devolution — 74.3%	Yes to devolution — 50.3%
No to devolution — 25.7%	No to devolution — 49.7%
Turnout — 60.1%	Turnout — 50.2%

According to Tony Blair, **devolution** was an essential part of New Labour's programme of constitutional modernisation since it would bring decision making closer to the people. It would also, Blair hoped, strengthen the United Kingdom by satisfying nationalist demands for greater self-determination. As he put it, 'Let Scotland and Wales do what they do best locally. Let the UK do what it is right to do together.' However, devolution has not always progressed in the way that Blair predicted.

- The Scottish National Party has replaced Labour as the dominant force in the Scottish Parliament and used its influence to successfully press for a Scottish independence referendum in 2014.
- The way in which Scotland and Wales have acquired new devolved powers suggests that devolution is an ongoing process, which could result in the unitary nature of the British state being replaced by a quasi-federal arrangement.
- The asymmetrical nature of devolution has raised questions about why England has not also been granted devolved powers, as well as why Scotland has been granted more political autonomy than Wales or Northern Ireland. This has all contributed to an unbalanced sharing of political power within the UK.

Scotland

The Scotland Act 1998, which established the Scottish Parliament and executive, devolved a number of primary legislative powers from Westminster to Scotland. These included:

- local government
- housing
- environment
- law and order
- education
- health
- income tax varying powers of 3p in the pound

These powers have been used to develop a distinctly Scottish approach to a number of far-reaching domestic issues. Powers not devolved to Scotland are said to be 'reserved' to Westminster.

- Scotland was the first member of the UK to ban smoking in public places.
- Scotland's Freedom of Information Act 2002 provides its citizens with more extensive rights of scrutiny of public bodies.
- Scotland did not introduce tuition fees and offers free university education to Scottish residents.
- In 2016, the Scottish government ended the right of council tenants to purchase the houses they live in.

However, the Scotland Act 1998 also stated that Westminster retained reserved powers over issues such as foreign policy, defence, immigration and monetary policy, since if Scotland had control over these policies it would essentially be a nation state.

The 2016 Scotland Act recognises the Scottish Parliament and government as a permanent fixture of the British constitution

Initially, as expected, Labour was the biggest party in the Scottish Parliament. However, when the Scottish National Party (SNP) won the 2011 election, it was able to form a majority administration which was committed to holding a referendum on Scottish independence. In the Edinburgh Agreement (2012) the Cameron government agreed to the referendum since, although it was not a reserved power, the SNP government could claim an electoral mandate to call one.

During the Scottish independence referendum campaign in 2014, a surge in support for independence led to the leaders of the main political parties (David Cameron, Nick Clegg and Ed Miliband) all promising 'extensive new powers' to Scotland if independence was rejected. Two days before the referendum, with Leave and Remain neck and neck, the *Daily Record* published on its front page the commitment of the three main UK party leaders to greater devolution for Scotland in the event of a Remain victory. The 'Vow' has provided the justification for the devolution of further reserved powers to Scotland (Table 5.5).

Table 5.5 Result of the independence for Scotland referendum, 2014

No to independence	55.3%
Yes to independence	44.7%
Turnout	84.6%

As a result of this commitment, the Smith Commission was established, which recommended that significant new powers be devolved to the Scottish Parliament and executive. These recommendations formed the basis of the Scotland Act 2016, which transfers more reserved powers to Scotland over a wide range of domestic areas, including:

- varying the rate of income tax by up to 10p in the pound
- having the right to receive 50% of the proceeds of VAT gathered in Scotland
- determining abortion laws
- deciding air passenger duty
- determining speed limits

Significantly, the Act states that the Scottish Parliament and executive are now permanent features of the UK constitution, which can only be abolished by a referendum. This implies that Scotland now enjoys more than just devolved powers and that the UK is much closer to becoming a quasi-federal state, with Westminster unable to abolish the Scottish Parliament and executive by Act of Parliament.

Whether or not the devolution of more powers to Scotland will ultimately lead to separation or satisfy demands for more self-government is, of course, open to question. The journalist Andrew Marr has likened England and Scotland to having become 'like a piece of pizza which is being pulled apart and only connected by strings of molten cheese'. The result of the 2016 EU referendum, in which Scotland voted decisively to remain in the EU, may indeed encourage further demands for independence (Table 5.6).

Table 5.6 Result of the 2016 EU referendum

	Remain (%)	Leave (%)
Scotland	62	38
England	46.6	53.4
Wales	47.5	52.5
Northern Ireland	55.8	44.2

On the other hand, the 2017 general election, in which support for the SNP noticeably declined, suggests that there is still considerable support for the Union in Scotland (Table 5.7). Whether New Labour's commitment to devolution will strengthen the United Kingdom or encourage its dismemberment remains extremely uncertain.

Table 5.7 Results of the 2015 and 2017 general elections in Scotland

2015 general election	2017 general election
Scottish National Party — 56 seats (50%)	Scottish National Party — 35 seats (36.9%)
Conservative — 1 seat (14.9%)	Conservative — 13 seats (28.6%)
Labour — 1 seat (24.3%)	Labour — 7 seats (27.1%)
Liberal Democrats — 1 seat (7.5%)	Liberal Democrats — 4 seats (6.8%)

Wales

Although Wales possesses its own distinct culture, the independence movement has had significantly less of an impact in Wales than it has in Scotland. This may be because Wales was absorbed into the English state in the medieval period and so did not develop a distinct legal system, while medieval and Tudor monarchs often boasted of their Welsh ancestry.

> FLUELLEN: and I do believe your majesty takes no scorn to wear the leek upon Saint Tavy's day.
>
> KING HENRY V: I wear it for a memorable honour; For I am Welsh, you know, good countryman.
>
> William Shakespeare, *Henry V*

The Labour Party also has very firm roots in English-speaking South Wales and Plaid Cymru (the 'Party of Wales') has generally won most of its support in the Welsh-speaking parts of North Wales. As a result of this, Welsh nationalism has not been able to unite the country in the same way that Scottish nationalism was able to in the 2015 general election (Table 5.8).

Table 5.8 General election support for Plaid Cymru

Election	Number of seats and % of the vote in Wales
1987 general election	3 seats (7.9%)
1997 general election	4 seats (10%)
2017 general election	4 seats (10.4%)

In the 1997 referendum, therefore, Wales was offered less extensive devolved powers than Scotland. The Government of Wales Act established a Welsh National Assembly and a Welsh executive, but Wales, unlike Scotland, was not granted any legislative or financial powers. Instead, Wales was simply given administrative powers in areas such as education, health, transport and agriculture. In effect, this meant that Wales was just being given the power to decide how to implement Acts of Parliament which had been passed at Westminster.

Like Scotland, however, Wales has steadily been granted more devolved powers. This is not because of a surge in support for Welsh nationalism. It has been more to do with ensuring that the granting of so much devolved power to Scotland is not allowed to create a totally uneven balance of power in the United Kingdom. The coalition, and the Conservative government elected in 2015, were also committed to encouraging regional initiative and so this provided further justification for increasing the authority of the Welsh Assembly and executive.

The Government of Wales Act 2006 recognised the importance of the executive by separating it from the legislature, gave it limited powers of primary legislation and provided for another referendum to be held on whether Wales should be allowed further devolved powers. The referendum was held in 2011 and, although the turnout was a disappointing 35.4%, there was a decisive vote in favour of Wales being given the power to enact its own legislation over all areas where power has been devolved to it, including education and health (Table 5.9).

Mark Drakeford, First Minister of Wales since 2018

Table 5.9 Welsh referendum 2011: Do you want the Assembly now to be able to make laws on *all* matters in the 20 subject areas it has powers for?

Yes	63.5%
No	36.5%

As a result of the referendum, the Wales Act 2014 devolved more power to Wales, including:

- control of a number of taxes, including stamp duty, land tax and landfill tax
- changing the name of the Welsh Assembly Government to the Welsh Government, symbolising its significance

The Wales Act 2014 also provided for a referendum over whether Wales should be given partial control of income tax. However, in 2015, the chancellor of the exchequer, George Osborne, as part of the government's commitment to decentralising power in order to encourage initiative, announced that Wales would be given this power without the need for a referendum.

The Wales Act 2017 gave Wales the right to vary income tax by up to 10p in the pound, as well as giving the Welsh Assembly new primary legislative powers over electoral arrangements, transport and energy. Like the Scotland Act 2016, it also stated that the Welsh government is a permanent feature of the UK constitution which can no longer be abolished simply by an Act of the Westminster Parliament. Instead, their abolition would also require the consent of the Welsh people in a referendum. In 2018, the Assembly unanimously decided that it should, by 2021, be known as the Welsh Parliament.

Although Wales has acquired significantly greater devolved powers, this has not been associated with any notable growth in support for an independent Wales. However, the way in which the permanence of the devolution settlement has been recognised in both Wales and Scotland does suggest that the unitary nature of the UK constitution is gradually being replaced with a more federal structure in which the central government's sovereignty is restricted by the permanent transfer of powers to two constituent parts of the United Kingdom.

Northern Ireland

The history of devolution in Northern Ireland has been very different to that of Scotland and Wales. As a result of the partition of Ireland in 1922, Northern Ireland was given its own Parliament. This lasted until 1972, when the government of Edward Heath imposed direct rule on Northern Ireland because of escalating violence. The Catholic (mainly Nationalist) minority felt that their rights were being ignored by the Protestant–Unionist-dominated assembly and so the decision to suspend devolved power was a practical attempt to try to end the conflict.

By the 1990s the John Major government opened covert negotiations with Sinn Féin, which had historic links with the IRA, in order to achieve a political settlement. In 1997, Tony Blair gave the peace process renewed momentum and in the Good Friday Agreement (1998) negotiated a power-sharing assembly which would fairly represent both Unionist and Nationalist sentiment. In May 1998, the Agreement was strongly endorsed by the peoples of Northern Ireland and the Republic of Ireland in two separate referendums.

Devolution in Northern Ireland is thus inseparable from the peace process and is based on the principle that if Unionists and Nationalists can work together in a devolved assembly then this will stop Northern Ireland reverting to sectarian violence. The decision to elect the Northern Ireland Assembly by the single transferable vote was also taken in order to provide as much choice to the electorate as possible and so make it more difficult for one party to dominate.

The way in which the executive comprises the leader of the largest party as the first minister and the leader of the second largest party as the deputy first minister is also meant to ensure stability. This is because they possess equal powers and if one resigns the other must also resign, ensuring that there is a strong incentive for both sides to work together.

A number of devolved legislative powers have been given to the Northern Ireland Assembly over an extensive number of areas, including:

- education
- agriculture
- transport
- policing
- housing
- health and social services

However, ongoing tension between the Republican and Unionist communities has meant that devolution to Northern Ireland has been a much less smooth process than in Scotland and Wales.

- From 2002 to 2007, the assembly was suspended because of continued conflict between Unionists and Nationalists.
- In 2007, the assembly reopened after a surprise agreement was reached between the Democratic Unionist Party (DUP) and Sinn Féin. Ian Paisley (1926–2014), the leader of the DUP, became first minister and Martin McGuinness (1950–2017) of Sinn Féin became deputy first minister. After years of violent hostility, the close relationship which they established led to them being known as the 'Chuckle Brothers'.
- In 2017, the assembly was again suspended and direct rule was imposed from Westminster when the DUP refused to support Nationalist demands for an Irish Language Act.

The relationship between Northern Ireland and Westminster is very different to that of Scotland and Wales because Northern Ireland is still so divided between Nationalist and Unionist opinion. Its devolved institutions of government are unlikely to be part of the development of a more federal United Kingdom, since the Unionist majority is still so committed to the principles of a unitary constitution.

The unlikely rapport Paisley (centre) and McGuinness (right) achieved led to a breakthrough in the Northern Ireland peace process

In what ways could the UK constitution be further reformed?

Although there has been considerable constitutional reform since 1997, critics argue that too many of the reforms have been half measures which have not fully addressed the problems they were meant to resolve. For example:

- Devolution has been granted to Scotland, Wales and Northern Ireland but not to England.
- The House of Lords has lost most of its hereditary peers but it still lacks democratic legitimacy.
- The European Convention on Human Rights has been incorporated into British law but UK citizens' rights have not been entrenched in a codified constitution.

An elected House of Lords

Although the House of Lords still lacks an elected element, opponents of further reform argue that a mainly appointed chamber has major advantages.

- As a mainly revising chamber it contains experts in every field and so the scrutinising work of committees of the House of Lords is held in high regard.
- In cases of dispute, the House of Commons will always prevail because it possesses democratic legitimacy.
- If both chambers were elected, there would be the potential for gridlock because both would be able to claim a democratic mandate.

Electoral reform at Westminster

A major argument in favour of electoral reform has been that the UK is becoming a multiparty democracy and so the electoral system should be reformed in order to provide minority parties with fairer representation. For example, in the 2015 general election, UKIP and the Greens won almost 5 million votes and only secured two seats. However, in the 2017 general election the Conservative and Labour parties won 82.4% of the popular vote. This was their highest combined share since 1970 and suggests that two-party dominance may not in fact be over. In these circumstances the case for electoral reform at Westminster might, therefore, appear less urgent.

Should devolution be extended to England and the regions?

Arguments in favour of English devolution

The devolution of power to Scotland, Wales and Northern Ireland has created an unusual situation in which three of the four constituent parts of the UK (Scotland, Wales and Northern Ireland) now have extensive rights of self-government. It has been claimed that this is an unfair constitutional arrangement which gives English citizens fewer rights of self-determination. The issue could be resolved by the establishment of an English Parliament or English regional assemblies, reflecting the wishes of the different parts of England. Supporters of English devolution make the following arguments.

- England is, by far, the most populous nation in the United Kingdom and yet its citizens are the only ones without their own government.
- In a referendum in 2011, Wales voted in favour of having more devolved powers, and the Scotland Act 2016 recognised the permanence of the Scottish Parliament and executive. This suggests that there is a popular case for devolution and that it is illogical for England not to be granted the same rights.
- Devolution has, so far, created an asymmetric United Kingdom, leading to resentment that England's interests are being taken less seriously than those of Scotland, Wales and Northern Ireland. The Barnett formula, for example, by which public funding is allocated across the UK, has always meant that spending per capita in England is less than in other parts of the UK. Devolution to England could resolve issues such as this.
- There is a strong sense of regional identity in parts of England, such as Cornwall and Yorkshire, which would make regional assemblies popular and relevant. In 2015, Cornwall became the first county to be given devolved powers, including control of investment and bus services. According to David Cameron, this reform marked 'a major shift for the people who live and work in Cornwall — putting power in their hands'.

- The establishment of elected mayors also shows how power can be decentralised. Both models could provide a template for how English devolution could be introduced.

Arguments against English devolution

- Critics of English devolution argue that there is very little positive demand for reform. In spite of the asymmetric development of the UK's constitutional arrangements, most English people are content that their interests are sufficiently represented by the Westminster Parliament.
- The introduction of English Votes for English Laws (EVEL) since 2015 has substantially addressed the West Lothian issue, whereby MPs representing Scotland, Wales and Northern Ireland could legislate on issues that only concerned England.
- The establishment of an English Parliament could challenge the authority of the Westminster Parliament. Since Westminster brings together MPs from across the whole country, any reduction in its power and prestige could threaten the survival of the UK.
- Not all parts of England have a strong sense of regional identity. Even the North East, which does have a strong sense of regional identity, rejected the opportunity to have its own assembly by 78% to 22% in 2004.
- Further devolution would create another layer of government and experience suggests that this could create a democratic overload which would undermine the legitimacy of the result. The turnout for elected mayors and police commissioners has been disappointing, and elections for the Scottish Parliament and Welsh Assembly have never reached a 60% turnout (Table 5.10). In England, where a sense of nationhood is much weaker, there is considerable danger that elected bodies would fail to achieve a necessary electoral mandate.

Table 5.10 Turnout in Scottish and Welsh elections, 1999 and 2016

1999	2016
Turnout in the election for the National Assembly for Wales: 46%	Turnout in the election for the National Assembly for Wales: 45.3%
Turnout in the election for the Scottish Parliament: 59.1%	Turnout in the election for the Scottish Parliament: 55.6%

How convincing is the case for a codified UK constitution?

The United Kingdom is one of only five countries in the world that does not possess a codified constitution. The others are Israel, Saudi Arabia, Canada and New Zealand. As a result, the UK does not have a higher constitutional law which the legislature must respect and so there are few constitutional limitations on the sort of legislation which the UK Parliament could enact.

Critics of the UK's uncodified constitution argue that the rights of British citizens need the protection of an entrenched Bill of Rights. In 1976, Lord Hailsham warned that the UK was in danger of becoming an 'elective dictatorship' because there were so few constraints on the influence of the government. The way in which a number of Acts of Parliament, such as the Investigatory Powers Act 2016, have significantly extended the power of government by restricting civil liberties would have been made considerably more difficult if citizens' rights were entrenched in a codified constitution.

> **Synoptic link**
>
> The tension between individual and collective rights is covered in Component 1, UK Politics (see pages 34–36).

A codified constitution would also clarify the relationship between the constituent parts of the United Kingdom and determine the exact location of sovereignty within the British political system. The lack of clarity over where power lies in the UK constitution is illustrated by the Gina Miller case (2017), in which the Supreme Court declared that the royal prerogative did not enable the government to negotiate withdrawal from the European Union without Parliament being consulted.

The way in which a government can introduce legislation that can change the constitution to its advantage has also been likened to a sports team being able to manipulate the rules of the game as it is being played. In 1999, there *was* a strong case for the removal of the hereditary peers from the House of Lords. However, there is no doubt, too, that this reform benefited the Blair government since the hereditary peers had provided the House of Lords with an inbuilt Conservative majority. There have also been claims that the introduction of EVEL by the Cameron government

Synoptic link

The importance of the state providing security for its citizens is a key element of traditional conservatism. This links to Component 1, Core Political Ideas (see pages 44–45).

In focus

Fighting fire with fire?

On 7 July 2005, a London bus was blown up by a suicide bomber. Thirteen passengers died in the explosion. On the same day, there were three other coordinated explosions on the London Underground. A total of 52 people were murdered in these atrocities.

In 2008, Geoff Hoon, who had been secretary of state for defence during the 2003 Iraq War, commented that 'the biggest civil liberty of all is not to be killed by a terrorist'. According to Hoon, the terrorist threat justifies Parliament in legislating to increase government power to combat terrorism and extremism. The uncodified nature of the British constitution has allowed governments to radically change the relationship between the government and its citizens by Acts of Parliament. Since Parliament is sovereign and there is no higher law of the constitution, the judiciary cannot strike down any such legislation as 'unconstitutional'. The following Acts of Parliament have been especially controversial:

- **Serious Organised Crime and Police Act 2005** As a result of this Act the right to protest outside Parliament has been considerably restricted. Critics of the Act argue that it denies the public an essential civil liberty, which is to protest their grievances at the legislature.
- **Counter Terrorism and Security Act 2015** The way in which this Act requires universities and schools to monitor debate and deny a platform to speakers who could encourage radicalisation has been criticised by some as an infringement of freedom of speech.

- **Investigatory Powers Act 2016** The increased authority this Act gives to the intelligence services to carry out electronic surveillance of private individuals has led civil liberties groups to label it 'the snoopers' charter'.

Civil liberties groups, such as Charter 88 and Liberty, claim that these statutes allow the government to act in an arbitrary fashion and so provide a strong argument for the codification of UK citizens' civil liberties in a Bill of Rights. This would make it much more difficult for the government to extend its power in the way that it has been able to. Sir Keir Starmer MP, for example, was highly critical of Theresa May's promise to change the law in any way necessary to combat terrorism, warning against 'throwing away the very values that are at the heart of our democracy and everything we believe in'.

Opponents of an entrenched constitution respond that parliamentary sovereignty enables the government to quickly react to crises and emergencies by legislating in an appropriate fashion. This is important if the collective rights of society are to be protected. If these Acts of Parliament are unpopular they can also be repealed by a future parliament. In 2010, for example, the coalition introduced legislation to repeal the Act of Parliament which had introduced identity cards. An uncodified constitution, it could be argued, is the most democratic form of constitution because it places power in the hands of Parliament and the electorate.

was politically motivated, since the Conservatives have generally won most of their seats in England (Table 5.11). The principle of English Votes for English Laws, as well as helping to resolve the West Lothian issue, will make it easier for Conservative governments, and harder for Labour governments, to pass legislation that affects only England.

Table 5.11 General election results in England, 2015 and 2017

2015 general election	2017 general election
317 Conservative MPs	296 Conservative MPs
205 Labour MPs	226 Labour MPs
7 Liberal Democrat MPs	8 Liberal Democrat MPs

In focus

David Cameron and the EU referendum

In 2013, David Cameron promised an in/out referendum on the UK's membership of the European Union. Critics of Cameron argue that he only offered a referendum in order to reduce support for UKIP in the upcoming general election and so to encourage a Conservative victory. If the UK constitution had been codified and entrenched, it has been suggested that Cameron would not have been able to gamble with the constitution for political advantage in the way that he did. Supporters of the UK's uncodified constitution argue that its flexibility enabled Cameron to respond to growing concerns about European integration, so proving how democratically accountable an uncodified constitution is.

However, supporters of the UK's uncodified constitution respond that the evolutionary development of the constitution has enabled it to keep pace with social and political change in a way that would have been much more difficult if the constitution was codified. Since the Westminster Parliament is not bound by a codified constitution, it has the flexibility to pass any legislation for which it has a parliamentary majority. This makes the British constitution highly democratic and responsive to the changing nature of society in a way that a codified constitution is not.

- For example, in the 1960s Parliament could quickly legislate to legalise homosexuality and abortion and abolish capital punishment without the need for a long and complicated constitutional procedure.
- More recently single-sex marriage and the rights of transgender people have been recognised by parliamentary statute.

A codified constitution, on the other hand, can become fossilised. In the USA, the 12th Amendment of the Constitution for the election of the president by the Electoral College has been strongly criticised for being not being suited to the way in which the demography of the USA has developed. This, like the 2nd Amendment, which protects the 'right of the people to keep and bear Arms', could only be changed by means of another constitutional amendment.

Should the UK have a codified constitution with an entrenched Bill of Rights?

Yes

- A codified constitution would represent a higher constitutional law, which would entrench the British people's civil liberties and so protect them from arbitrary government.
- The Human Rights Act 1998 does not do this because it is an Act of Parliament and so parliament can suspend its provisions or repeal it.
- The authority of the Supreme Court would be enhanced since it would be able to quash laws which it deemed 'unconstitutional' by referring to the higher law of the constitution.
- A codified constitution would clarify the relationship between the various branches of government and establish where sovereignty lies.
- The rights of minorities could be recognised in a codified constitution. This is especially important in a multicultural society, in which many alternative lifestyles exist.
- By codifying rights, the public could become more politically engaged since they would know what their relationship with the government is.

No

- The uncodified nature of the British constitution means that it is very flexible and can quickly respond to changing social, political and security circumstances.
- An uncodified constitution is more democratic because it puts power in the hands of elected representatives who are accountable to the electorate, rather than unelected judges.
- Civil liberties are adequately protected by common law and by the Human Rights Act 1998 and the Equality Act 2010. The judiciary has successfully used both of these Acts to protect and develop civil liberties.
- A codified constitution reflects the social and political attitudes of the people who composed it. It cannot keep pace with the way in which society changes in the way that an uncodified constitution can.
- The lack of certainty and ambiguity in the British constitution is an advantage since it has allowed for the changing relationship between England, Scotland, Wales and Northern Ireland in response to the will of the public. This would have been more difficult to achieve if the constitution had been codified.

Summary

By the end of this chapter you should be able to answer the following questions:
- → What are the main sources of the UK constitution?
- → Why has the UK constitution developed in an evolutionary rather than a revolutionary fashion?
- → What are the differences between a codified and an uncodified constitution?
- → How effective have the constitutional reforms introduced since 1997 been?
- → In what ways has devolution impacted on the United Kingdom?
- → How convincing is the case for further constitutional reform?
- → Should devolution be extended to England?
- → To what extent has the location of sovereignty changed in the United Kingdom?
- → How convincing is the case for the codification of the British constitution?
- → To what extent are further constitutional reforms required?

Source-based question

The virtues of a written constitution are clarity and definiteness. The virtue of an unwritten constitution is flexibility. The vices of each are the opposites of the respective virtues. Critics of written constitutions point to the difficulty of amending the constitution. Critics of unwritten constitutions point to their vulnerability to changing interpretations from which there is no appeal, the changes prompted perhaps by political self-interest.

A written constitution constrains government in ways that an unwritten constitution does not. The government is subject to it, whereas with an unwritten constitution it is the constitution which is subject to the government; the government can choose to alter it or interpret it in ways that suit itself. A written constitution is therefore an important safeguard against abuses by government of their powers, not least because it would entrench civil liberties and the due processes of law.

This last is one of the chief considerations in favour of a written constitution. In the UK, the Human Rights Act (HRA) goes some way to entrenching citizens' liberties, but because it does not give the Supreme Court power to strike down legislation, or restrain government action which is at odds with the HRA, the effect is not as powerful as a fully written constitution.

Adapted from A.C. Grayling, http://politics.co.uk, 16 October 2017

Using the source, evaluate the view that the UK constitution should be codified.

In your response you must:
- *Compare and contrast the different opinions in the source*
- *Examine and debate these views in a balanced way*
- *Analyse and evaluate only the information presented in the source* (30)

Evaluative questions

1 Evaluate the extent to which constitutional reforms introduced since 1997 have been successful in achieving their objectives. *In your answer you should draw on relevant knowledge and understanding of the study of Component 1 UK Politics and Core Political Ideas and consider this view and the alternative to this view in a balanced way.* (30)

2 Evaluate the arguments in favour of the codification of the UK constitution. *In your answer you should draw on relevant knowledge and understanding of the study of Component 1 UK Politics and Core Political Ideas and consider this view and the alternative to this view in a balanced way.* (30)

3 Evaluate the extent to which devolution has caused more problems than it has resolved. *In your answer you should draw on relevant knowledge and understanding of the study of Component 1 UK Politics and Core Political Ideas and consider this view and the alternative to this view in a balanced way.* (30)

6 Parliament

The origins and development of the UK Parliament

The origins of the British **Parliament** can be traced far back into medieval history. King Henry III, like his father King John, did not want to share power, provoking conflict with the nobility led by Simon de Montfort. Eventually, Henry was captured at the battles of Lewes in 1264 and Simon de Montfort summoned representatives of the nobility and senior churchmen, together with two knights from each county and two burgesses from leading towns, to meet at Westminster Hall in 1265. By broadening the membership *beyond* the nobility, the de Montfort Parliament is often seen as being the first English Parliament.

The main events in the development of the British Parliament from 1265 to the present day are outlined in Figure 6.1.

During the seventeenth century both Houses of Parliament increasingly asserted their authority against the Crown and in 1689, following the Glorious Revolution, William III accepted the Bill of Rights, which established the principle of parliamentary supremacy.

Key term

Parliament The UK Parliament comprises the House of Commons and the House of Lords and possesses supreme legislative authority. It also scrutinises the work of government and represents the diverse interests of the United Kingdom. Parliament also provides the membership of the government.

King Henry III (1216–72) and his parliament. Although Henry wished to rule as an absolute monarch, opposition from the nobility forced him to summon parliament against his will

The de Montfort Parliament 1265
The decision of the nobleman Simon de Montfort to summon commoners as well as nobles and churchmen to Westminster Hall in 1265 to discuss reforms is generally seen as the first recognisable parliament

The Bill of Rights 1689
The agreement of King William III (1689–1702) to Parliament's Bill of Rights established the principle of parliamentary sovereignty

Extension of the franchise — 1832, 1867, 1884, 1918, 1928 and 1969
These parliamentary reform acts gradually extended the franchise until in 1928 the principle of universal franchise was established when the vote was given to everyone over the age of 21. In 1969 the voting age was reduced to 18

Parliament Acts 1911 and 1949
The 1911 Act established the principle that the House of Lords, as an unelected body, could only delay, not veto, legislation that the House of Commons had passed. In 1949 the Lords' delaying power was reduced to 1 year

House of Lords Act 1999
All but 92 hereditary peers were removed from the House of Lords. As a result, most members of the Lords are life peers, which has made the House of Lords more assertive in its dealings with the House of Commons

Figure 6.1 Key events in the development of the UK Parliament

As the franchise was extended during the nineteenth century, the legitimacy of the elected House of Commons grew at the expense of the unelected House of Lords. The supremacy of the Commons over the Lords was not, however, achieved until the early twentieth century, when the attempt by the House of Lords to veto the 'People's Budget' led to the Parliament Act 1911. This abolished the Lords' right of veto over legislation that had passed the Commons. In future the Lords would only be able to delay legislation for 2 years. In 1949, another Parliament Act reduced this to just 1 year.

Although British democracy has evolved over many centuries, this has occurred without the codification of the British constitution. In most countries, political upheavals have provoked the establishment of codified constitutions which have set limits on government and established the rights of citizens. This has not been the case in Britain and so there is no authority greater than that of the British Parliament. As a result, Parliament is the nation's supreme law-making body and so the judiciary cannot strike down an Act of Parliament because of the principle of parliamentary sovereignty.

The UK has a parliamentary, rather than a presidential, form of government. This means that the voters elect the House of Commons, and the executive is then selected from its membership together with some members appointed from the House of Lords. In this way, the executive and the legislature are fused. As a result, the executive cannot claim its own authority. Instead its power derives from the support of the House of Commons and, if that support is withdrawn through the loss of a vote of confidence, then the government must resign.

The House of Commons and the House of Lords

The composition of the House of Commons

The **House of Commons** is the democratically elected chamber of Parliament. Each Member of Parliament (MP) represents the interests of his or her constituency. The way in which constituencies are allocated is designed to ensure that all parts of the UK can claim roughly equal representation within the House of Commons. Table 6.1 shows the composition of the House of Commons in 2017.

Table 6.1 The House of Commons elected in 2017 (650 MPs)

Region	Number of seats/MPs
England	533
Scotland	59
Wales	40
Northern Ireland	18

Ever since the development of the party system during the eighteenth and nineteenth centuries, the vast majority of MPs elected to Parliament represent a political party. There have been some examples of independent candidates being returned to Parliament. In 2001 and 2005, Dr Richard Taylor won the seat of Wyre Forest on a manifesto commitment to keep open Accident and Emergency facilities at Kidderminster Hospital. However, such instances are rare and often depend on local conditions which may count against the established parties.

The way in which the chamber of the House of Commons is designed emphasises the adversarial nature of British politics

Frontbench and backbench MPs

MPs can be divided into frontbench and backbench MPs. MPs who have been invited by the prime minister to join the government as senior ministers, junior ministers or permanent private secretaries are all bound by the principle of collective ministerial responsibility. This means that they present, and must publicly support, government policy from the front benches. The main opposition party will also have its own shadow frontbench team, whose members will scrutinise their government counterparts. Like the government front bench, they are also required to support their party's leadership.

Party whips

All the main political parties will appoint whips in order to maintain party discipline. MPs are elected on a party manifesto. However, they also represent the interests of their constituencies and, as Edmund Burke explained in the eighteenth century, should also act according to their 'judgement'. As a result of this, the parliamentary leadership needs to keep as tight control as possible of its MPs since, without it, their control of the party could break down. The Whips' Office is thus an essential part of the House of Commons. Whips will encourage their MPs to support the party line, as well as reporting back any potential large-scale rebellions which might encourage the party leadership to modify its position in order to avoid defeat. On especially important issues, a three-line whip will be issued which will require MPs to attend a vote (division) and to vote according to the demands of the leadership. If MPs refuse to do this they may have the party whip withdrawn from them, which means they lose their membership of the parliamentary party.

In focus

The role of the whips in a tight vote

The whips are particularly important when a government has a small parliamentary majority or is trying to survive as a minority administration. In these circumstances all the political parties' whips have to work hard to ensure that in tight parliamentary votes they have the best chance of winning. From 1976 to 1979, the Callaghan government had to survive without a parliamentary majority. This meant that there were a number of very close votes in which Labour and Conservative whips struggled to ensure that every possible one of their MPs went through the division lobbies.

- In one famous incident, the Conservative MP Michael Heseltine furiously brandished the mace when he felt that Labour had unfairly won a division by one vote.
- On another occasion, Conservative MP Roger Sims was late for a parliamentary vote, enabling the government to win by one vote. This provoked a somewhat menacing response from the Conservative Whips' Office: 'It's the sort of thing that happens to us all — *just once.*' Eventually, the government fell when a vote of no confidence proposed by the leader of the Conservatives, Margaret Thatcher, was passed by 311 to 310 votes.

The speaker of the House of Commons

There is one MP whose role it is to be impartial. This is the speaker of the House of Commons, who does not engage in political debate. Instead his or her role is to ensure that Parliament functions as effectively as possible. Speakers of the House of Commons are generally experienced MPs who can claim the respect of MPs on all sides of the House. The speaker arranges parliamentary business with the leaders of the main political parties, ensures that proper procedure is followed and presides over debates in the House of Commons. The speaker also has a disciplinary function and if MPs are deliberately abusive or disobedient they can be suspended. Since the election of John Bercow in 2009, the speaker has been elected by a secret ballot of all MPs. Once elected, they are then ceremonially dragged to the Speaker's Chair and, at the beginning of each new parliament, must seek re-election, although this is usually just a formality.

In focus

The speaker of the House of Commons

As speaker of the House of Commons since 2009, John Bercow has stood up for the rights of Parliament against the executive. He has supported a number of reforms to increase the powers of backbench MPs to scrutinise government. For example, the government has been made more accountable to Parliament since MPs are now allowed to ask many more 'urgent questions' which ministers must respond to the same day. His criticisms of government attempts to dominate parliamentary time also won him the support of many backbench MPs. In 2018 he reacted furiously when the government attempted to limit the time provided for an opposition day debate on the Grenfell Tower disaster.

Some of his actions, however, have been controversial. He has been accused of acting beyond his authority when he expressed his opposition to President Trump addressing Parliament. Some Brexit-supporting MPs have further criticised Bercow for allegedly breaking precedent by allowing, in January 2019, Conservative Remain MP Dominic Grieve to successfully table an amendment to a government motion giving Parliament more control over the timetable for Brexit.

In March 2019, Bercow stood up for the rights of Parliament against the executive when he stopped Theresa May from re-introducing her unamended Brexit deal into the House of Commons. He did this by quoting the parliamentary rule established by Erskine May in 1844 that 'A motion or an amendment which is the same, in substance, as a question which has been decided during a session, may not be brought forward again during that same session'.

The leader of the official opposition

The role of the leader of the official opposition is to ensure that the policies of the government are thoroughly scrutinised, while convincing the public that the official opposition is an alternative government in waiting. In order to do this, the opposition has been able since the 1970s to claim Short money from public funds to finance the leader of the opposition's office and help with parliamentary business. The leader of the opposition is also given the right to ask six questions at Prime Minister's Question Time (PMQT). This is a particularly important role since it enables the leader of the opposition to put high-profile pressure on the prime minister by highlighting any failures of policy and offering their own political solutions. The leader of the opposition will also select a shadow cabinet, whose task it is to hold the government accountable as well as persuading the electorate that they could be trusted in government.

The composition of the House of Lords

Although the **House of Lords** is referred to as 'the upper chamber', its authority is considerably less than that of the House of Commons. This is because it is an appointed chamber and so cannot claim the democratic legitimacy that the House of Commons can.

Throughout most of its history the House of Lords was primarily composed of peers, whose claim to membership was based on their possession of a hereditary noble title, as well as a much smaller number of bishops representing the Church of England. These two groups comprised the 'lords temporal' and the 'lords spiritual'. However, the expansion of the franchise during the nineteenth century meant

Key term

House of Lords The unelected chamber of the Westminster Parliament. Composed of life peers, elected hereditary peers and Anglican bishops, it does not possess democratic legitimacy and so its main focus is on scrutinising the work of the House of Commons.

The Queen in the House of Lords during the state opening of parliament

that the influence of the House of Lords declined as the authority of the House of Commons increased. For example, when Queen Victoria granted Benjamin Disraeli the hereditary title of Earl of Beaconsfield, he quipped, 'I am dead; dead but in the Elysian fields.' The Parliament Act 1911 further diminished the power of the House of Lords by removing its right to veto legislation passed by the House of Commons.

In 1958, the Life Peerages Act was passed, which gave the prime minister the authority to nominate life peers (of both sexes) to the House of Lords. Life peers do not pass on their title, and their appointment to the Lords is based on the public service that they have provided the nation. This opening up of the membership of the House of Lords to people who had distinguished themselves in the service of their country gave the upper house a new sort of professional legitimacy.

In 1999, the Labour government of Tony Blair took reform of the House of Lords considerably further by removing the right of the 750 hereditary peers to continue sitting in the upper house. However, in order to avoid a confrontation with the Lords, Blair agreed to a compromise, whereby 92 hereditary peers could be elected to the Lords by the hereditary peerage.

that the Lords plays an important role in the legislative process. When a bill leaves the House of Commons it is sent to the House of Lords, where it will be examined in detail in the chamber of the House of Lords and in committee stage. Here the expertise of the Lords is important in working through the implications of a bill and refining its contents, and any member of the Lords can propose an amendment. This is why the primary purpose of the Lords is seen as being a revising chamber.

The Commons does not have to accept the advice of the Lords. However, because of the Lords' professional expertise, their advice is politically influential and the amendments that they make can often be accepted as improving the quality of a bill. Since members of the Lords can sit for life, and a significant number of them are crossbenchers, they are also less influenced by the dictates of the whips and so can address the merits and demerits of legislation with a more open mind. The way in which the two chambers negotiate over proposed amendments to legislation before it receives the royal assent is often referred to as 'parliamentary ping-pong'.

Heavy defeats in the House of Lords may even persuade the government to reconsider whether to modify or even continue with legislation. This is especially the case if legislation has only passed the House of Commons with a small majority and the legislation is clearly controversial.

- In 2008, clauses in the Counter Terrorism Bill to enable terror suspects to be held for 42 days without charge were decisively defeated in the Lords by 191 votes. Since these proposals had only passed the Commons by nine votes, Gordon Brown decided to drop them from the bill.
- The way in which the House of Lords voted in favour of a number of far-reaching amendments to the EU (Withdrawal) Bill was especially important in focusing Theresa May's government on a softer Brexit. This is because, as prime minister of a minority government, she was not sure of the support of the House of Commons to overturn these amendments.

Anti-Brexit protestors celebrate another government defeat in the Lords, which made Theresa May's attempts to achieve parliamentary support for Brexit even more difficult

However, as a result of the Parliament Acts 1911 and 1949, the government can still pass legislation over the objections of the House of Lords. In 2000, for example, the Sexual Offences Amendment Act 2000, which reduced the legal age for gay sex from 18 to 16, easily passed the House of Commons. The Lords' opposition to the bill was overridden when the government invoked the 1911 and 1949 Parliament Acts to give the bill royal assent, effectively bypassing the Lords.

Scrutiny

The House of Lords scrutinises the work of government in oral questions to ministers and through committees. As a result of the expertise of its members, the committee work of the House of Lords is especially highly regarded. Instead of monitoring specific departments, committees concentrate on major political issues. Some of the committees are permanent and others are set up on an ad hoc basis to deal with more specific issues (Table 6.5). In 2018, new committees were established on the issues of the rural economy and regenerating seaside towns. Their reports are, of course, non-binding but they carry a great deal of weight.

Table 6.5 House of Lords committees

Permanent House of Lords committees	Temporary House of Lords committees
European Union Committee	Artificial Intelligence Committee
Science and Technology Committee	Citizenship and Civic Engagement Committee
International Relations Committee	Intergenerational Fairness and Provision Committee
Constitution Committee	Regenerating Seaside Towns Committee
Economic Affairs Committee	Rural Economy Committee
Communications Committee	Secondary Legislation Scrutiny Committee

There are also a small number of joint committees of the House of Commons and the House of Lords, such as the Joint Committee on Human Rights which has produced significant reports on free speech in universities and the wrongful detention and deportation of members of the 'Windrush generation'.

The House of Lords and secondary (delegated) legislation

Since secondary legislation does not require the same scrutiny as primary legislation, it is important that it is as thoroughly examined as possible. The House of Commons has limited time to do this and so the House of Lords Secondary Legislation Scrutiny Committee is very significant in highlighting areas of concern which might then be raised in debate in the chamber of the House of Lords. George Osborne's use of secondary legislation to cut tax credits, for example, was the subject of detailed criticism in the Lords

Legitimation, representation, providing government and debate

Since the Lords is unelected, it cannot claim a legitimising function. This also means that it does not have a representative role in a democratic sense, although the ancient tradition that the Lords represents the spiritual as well as the temporal realm is acknowledged by the presence of the bishops of the Church of England. In addition to providing government ministers, one of the most important functions of the House of Lords is to debate issues. This can help to significantly raise the profile of an issue. In 2018, for example, following the killing of a large number of Palestinians in the Gaza Strip by Israeli military forces, Lord Steel proposed a debate, 'that this House takes note of the situation in the Palestinian Territories'.

The comparative powers of the House of Commons and the House of Lords

The powers of the House of Commons

The House of Commons has the sole right to defeat a bill. It also possesses the exclusive right to dismiss the government if it loses a vote of confidence. This is because the government's legitimacy derives from the consent of Parliament as representatives of the nation and if that consent is withdrawn then the government can no longer claim a mandate to govern.

In 1979, for example, the Labour government of James Callaghan had managed to survive for 3 years as a minority administration. However, in March that year the government lost a vote of confidence by 310–311 votes. Callaghan immediately asked the Queen to dissolve Parliament, telling the House of Commons, 'Mr Speaker, now that the House of Commons has declared itself, we shall take our case to the country.'

The powers of the House of Lords

Tony Benn once claimed that 'the House of Lords is the British Outer Mongolia for retired politicians' and it is certainly true that the Lords does not have the same powers as the House of Commons. As long ago as 1867 Walter Bagehot, in *The English Constitution*, contrasted the 'efficient' part of government which was the House of Commons with the merely 'dignified' which was the House of Lords.

However, the House of Lords also has advantages that the House of Commons lacks. Since members of the Lords do not have the same constituency duties as MPs, they can devote more of their time to scrutiny. The fact that they are not elected also means that they are more able to act independently since they are not so bound by their party's manifesto. The large number of crossbenchers also makes it more difficult for a government to dominate the House of Lords.

Although prime ministerial appointments to the House of Lords have been accused of cronyism, it is important to appreciate that the vast majority of appointments are non-controversial. Most life peers appointed to the Lords are there because of their achievements and the specialist understanding that they can offer.

Table 6.6 profiles three distinguished members of the House of Lords.

Table 6.6 Three examples of specialist expertise in the House of Lords

Baroness Chakrabarti	Lord Winston	Baron Shinkwin
Shami Chakrabarti is a barrister and was director of the civil liberties pressure group Liberty from 2003 to 2016. In 2016 she was nominated a life peer in David Cameron's resignation honours list. As Jeremy Corbyn's shadow attorney general, she often speaks on issues connected with civil liberties and women's rights	Robert Winston has been a Labour member of the House of Lords since 1995. A brilliant embryologist who pioneered in-vitro fertilisation (IVF), he has chaired the House of Lords Select Committee on Science and Technology. He has argued in the House of Lords that science teaching in primary schools needs to be improved	Kevin Shinkwin spent most of his career in the voluntary/charity sector. He was created a life peer in 2015 and sits as a Conservative. Born with osteogenesis imperfecta, he is especially concerned to advance equal treatment of disabled people. He has criticised the UK's abortion laws as a 'licence to kill for the crime of being disabled'

The House of Lords also offers a unique opportunity for former members of the House of Commons to continue in public service, enabling their accumulated political experience to be used to advise government.

Lord Fowler served as Margaret Thatcher's secretary of state for health from 1981 to 1987. By explaining that HIV/AIDS could be passed on by any sexual encounter in the 'Don't die of ignorance' campaign, he made combatting it much more effective, as well as disassociating AIDS from being a 'gay epidemic'. As a member of the House of Lords, Fowler went on to chair a committee on AIDS/HIV in 2010–11 which reported that government AIDS-prevention measures had become 'woefully inadequate'. In 2014, he wrote *AIDS: Don't Die of Prejudice* and in 2016, he was overwhelmingly elected Lord Speaker.

In focus

Life after death

In 1984, on his ninetieth birthday, the former prime minister Harold Macmillan (1894–1986) re-entered Parliament as the Earl of Stockton 60 years after he was first elected an MP. This made him feel, he said, like a 'political Rip van Winkle'. In his maiden speech, he attacked Margaret Thatcher's handling of the miners' strike – 'it is pointless and we cannot afford this sort of thing' – and for the last 2 years of his life he once again became a significant political figure, stirring up debate within the Conservative Party about the political direction it should take.

A summary of the functions and powers of the House of Commons and the House of Lords is given in Table 6.7.

Table 6.7 A comparison of the relative functions and powers of the House of Commons and the House of Lords.

The House of Commons	The House of Lords
• Represents the nation and is accountable to it in a general election • Can dismiss the government in a vote of confidence • Must agree to the Budget • Legitimises important decisions such as the dissolution of parliament and, by convention, the commitment of the UK to major military operations • The executive requires the consent of the House of Commons for legislation to be enacted • Scrutinises legislation in parliamentary debate and Public Bill Committees • House of Commons select committees monitor the work of government departments	• Can delay legislation for one parliamentary session but cannot veto it. According to the Salisbury Convention, if proposed legislation has been included in the winning party's electoral manifesto it will not oppose it • Since the Parliament Acts 1911 and 1949 do not extend to statutory instruments, the Lords, theoretically, still maintains a veto over them • The Lords' main work is as a revising chamber: offering amendments to legislation and scrutinising the work of government through committees, ministerial questions and parliamentary debate • If the House of Commons voted to extend the life of a parliament beyond 5 years the House of Lords could constitutionally reject this proposal. This provides a way in which the Lords is able to protect civil liberties in the UK

The stages of a bill through Parliament

A bill can be introduced in either the House of Commons or the House of Lords. In whichever house it is introduced, it follows a similar route, as shown in Figure 6.2.

First reading
The bill is formally presented to Parliament by the relevant minister. There is no discussion at this point.

Second reading
This is the stage at which the main *principles* of the bill are debated. The government front bench will introduce the bill. The opposition front bench and backbenchers will then respond and a vote will be taken. The government can expect to win this vote — the last bill to be defeated at this stage was the Shops Bill in 1986.

Committee stage
The bill will next be considered by a House of Commons Public Bill Committee, or, if it began in the House of Lords, by the whole chamber. It is at this point that amendments will be proposed to the legislation. In the House of Commons each Public Bill will have its own committee set up to scrutinise its detail. The Budget and bills of constitutional significance such as the EU (Withdrawal) Bill are scrutinised by a Committee of the Whole House in the chamber of the House of Commons.

Report stage
The bill, and any amendments added to it, are now debated and votes taken upon them. Further amendments can be proposed by MPs who were not on the Public Bill Committee.

Third reading/Transfer
The amended bill will be further debated before being transferred to the other house, where it will go through the same stages. No votes are allowed at this stage.

Royal assent
Once a bill has passed both chambers it will receive the royal assent. Should the House of Lords refuse to support a bill it can still become law by the government invoking the Parliament Acts 1911 and 1949.

Figure 6.2 The passage of a bill through Parliament

How Parliament interacts with the executive

The role and significance of backbenchers in both houses

Backbenchers in both the House of Commons and the House of Lords are protected by parliamentary privilege. This principle dates back to the Bill of Rights in 1689, which states, 'that the freedom of speech and debates or proceedings in Parliament ought not to be impeached or questioned in any court or place out of Parliament'. As a result of this, parliamentarians are free to raise any issue they wish in Westminster without fear of being prosecuted in the courts for libel or defamation of character.

Key term

Backbenchers Members of the House of Commons and House of Lords who are not members of either the government front bench or the opposition front bench. They are not bound by collective ministerial responsibility and so are more independent, although they are expected to obey the party whip.

The main roles of backbench MPs are to represent the interests of their constituents, scrutinise the work of government, consider the merits of legislation, legitimise certain government decisions such as committing British troops to military action, and raise issues that they regard as significant.

- MPs can make a significant impact in Parliament by effectively representing the interests of their constituents. In order to achieve 'redress of grievance' for them, MPs can ask questions in the chamber of the House of Commons and question ministers on their behalf. MPs have often used end-of-day adjournment debates to raise these sorts of questions. In 2018, for example, Sir Peter Bottomley MP used the opportunity of an adjournment debate to demand a full enquiry into the case of former police Sergeant Gurpal Virdi, who had been taken to court over a historic case of sexual abuse and acquitted.
- The Backbench Business Committee was established in 2010 and provides backbench MPs with 35 days a year in which they can control parliamentary business. MPs can ask to raise any question for debate with the committee, providing MPs with opportunities to raise issues for debate in the House of Commons. In 2018, some of the debates the committee arranged included the importance of refugee family reunion, perinatal mental illness and forced adoption in the UK.
- In 2015, a Petitions Committee was created which took over the task of scheduling debates on petitions. Most of these are e-petitions which have reached 100,000 signatures. In 2018, the committee arranged debates on the proposed abolition of the House of Lords, changing the GCSE English literature exam from a closed-book to an open-book assessment and banning the sale of animal fur in the UK.
- MPs can also raise issues which they personally feel are important and require greater public appreciation. During a debate on the UN International Day for the Elimination of Violence against Women in 2016, Michelle Thomson MP publicly spoke about being raped in order to help break the taboo about sharing this kind of information.

In focus

Supporting a cause

Luciana Berger MP has campaigned extensively to raise awareness of food poverty in the UK. She has produced a film, *Breadline Britain*, and secured the first parliamentary debate on food banks. A victim of anti-Semitism, she has also spoken out in the House of Commons against anti-Semitism within the Labour Party. In February 2019 she was one of eight Labour MPs who left the party to establish Change UK (The Independent Group).

Luciana Berger

'As I said in Parliament Square outside this place — it pains me to say this as the proud parliamentary chair of the Jewish Labour Movement — in 2018, anti-Semitism is now more commonplace, more conspicuous and more corrosive within the Labour party.'

Hansard, 18 April 2018

- The extent to which backbenchers wield influence depends on the size of the government's parliamentary majority. Tony Blair won landslide parliamentary majorities in the 1997 and 2001 general elections. As a result, he could survive even very large rebellions by his backbenchers. In 2003, for example, 139 Labour MPs voted against involvement in the Iraq War, but Blair still won the parliamentary vote. However, Labour's majority dipped to 66 in the 2005 general election and Blair subsequently failed to introduce 90-day detention for terrorist suspects when 49 Labour MPs voted against the government.
- If a government has a very small or non-existent parliamentary majority then backbenchers will be at their most influential as the whips, on both sides, will need to make concessions in order to secure their support. Having lost her parliamentary majority in the 2017 general election, Theresa May had to 'manage' rather than 'lead' Brexit in order to create as much cross-party support for her strategy as possible.

Stretch and challenge

Representatives or delegates?

- The EU (Withdrawal) Bill passed its crucial second reading in the House of Commons by 326–290 votes on 11 September 2017.
- In August 2018, Frank Field MP resigned the Labour whip after 39 years as a Labour MP.

According to the Conservative political philosopher and MP, Edmund Burke, 'Your representative owes you, not his industry only, but his judgement; and he betrays instead of serving you if he sacrifices it to your opinion.' This principle has provided MPs with the independence to do what they think is right in the House of Commons.

However, the increased use of referendums has given the public greater direct power over shaping political decisions and, although the result of a referendum is not binding on Parliament, many pro-European MPs decided to support Brexit against their own beliefs.

Frank Field had been the MP for Birkenhead since 1979. Always a maverick Labour MP, Field supported stricter controls of immigration and supported Brexit. In 2018, objections from local party members that he was acting contrary to their wishes triggered a vote of confidence in him, which he lost. Field then resigned the Labour whip, blaming a 'culture of intolerance, nastiness and intimidation' in constituency Labour parties.

In what ways do these two cases suggest that the independence of MPs may be being eroded?

Backbenchers in the House of Lords can introduce Private Member's Bills — Lord Hayward, for example, has spoken frequently in the House of Lords about excessive plastic packaging — but their primary function is one of scrutiny. They do this in parliamentary debate on legislation by questioning ministers and on House of Lords permanent and temporary committees. The independence of the House of Lords and the political and professional experience of its members mean that the scrutiny its backbenchers provide is highly regarded.

Do backbenchers play an important role in the House of Commons?

Yes

- Backbenchers on select committees play an important role scrutinising the work of government departments.
- The Liaison Committee (chairs of all select committees) holds the prime minister accountable for policy development and implementation.
- MPs can provide 'redress of grievance' for their constituents by raising cases in the House of Commons.
- MPs can raise public awareness of issues such as growing anti-Semitism in the Labour Party (Luciana Berger) and speaking out about rape (Michelle Thomson).
- Backbenchers can introduce Private Member's Bills. Some of these, such as Dan Byles' House of Lords Reform Act 2014, can be very significant.
- The Backbench Business Committee has provided MPs with more control over the parliamentary agenda, enabling them to choose more topics for debate.
- MPs can dismiss the executive with a vote of no confidence (1979, James Callaghan).
- MPs can make amendments to legislation on Public Bill Committees.
- MPs have an important legitimising role: deciding whether to commit British forces to military action and whether to agree to an early dissolution of Parliament.
- Since backbenchers are not bound by collective ministerial responsibility, they can oppose their whips over legislation.
- Especially when the government has a small or non-existent parliamentary majority, MPs can exact concessions from the executive in order to win their support for legislation.
- If the government is not confident it has the support of enough backbenchers it can drop legislation. In 2005, having lost a Commons vote when 49 Labour MPs disobeyed a three-line whip, the Blair government abandoned proposals to allow terrorist suspects to be held for 90 days without charge.
- By March 2019, backbenchers had defeated Theresa May's Brexit deal three times. MPs also voted to reject a no-deal Brexit, as well as temporarily taking control of the Brexit agenda to see if they could agree on a way forward.

No

- The government can ignore the advice of select committees (the Foreign Affairs Select Committee advised against any military intervention in Syria).
- MPs are expected to obey the party whip. Ambitious MPs who aspire to a frontbench position can become 'lobby fodder'.
- A vote of no confidence can only be called in exceptional circumstances when the government is vulnerable to defeat.
- Public Bill Committees are whipped and so opposition amendments are unlikely to be accepted.
- Most Private Member's Bills fail because of insufficient parliamentary time being made available for them.
- In spite of the establishment of the Backbench Business Committee, the government still dominates most of the parliamentary agenda.
- The government's increasing use of secondary (delegated) legislation to change laws has negatively impacted on MPs' legislative function.
- The rise of political activism among Labour constituency parties has meant that MPs are increasingly expected to represent the wishes of their local party in the House of Commons rather than the Burkean principle that they should act according to their conscience.
- In exceptional circumstances, the royal prerogative allows the prime minister to commit British forces to military action without a parliamentary vote.
- Although MPs can initiate debates and vote in favour of e-petitions, this does not mean that the government has got to act on or support these proposals.
- If the government has a large parliamentary majority it will have an inbuilt majority of backbench support. It will thus be able to survive even large backbench rebellions.

Scrutinising Brexit

The way in which the House of Lords proposed 15 amendments to the government's EU (Withdrawal) Bill was criticised in the *Daily Mail* for challenging the outcome of the EU referendum. According to Jacob Rees-Mogg MP, the Lords were 'cavalier' with the constitution in some of their amendments. However, the Brexit minister, Lord Callanan, thanked the Lords for their amendments:

'Although I regret the number of defeats I am grateful to those many Lords who I think have worked constructively to improve the Bill … This House has done its duty as a revising chamber. The Bill has been scrutinised.'

In total the EU (Withdrawal) Bill was scrutinised in Parliament for 272 hours — 112 hours in the Commons and 160 hours in the Lords. During the parliamentary 'ping-pong' between the two houses the government accepted one of the Lords' amendments and made concessions on eight of them.

The role and significance of the opposition

In one of his novels, *Coningsby* (1844), Benjamin Disraeli stated that 'no government can be long secure without a formidable opposition'. According to the Conservative MP and philosopher Edmund Burke, 'He that wrestles with us strengthens our nerves, and sharpens our skill. Our antagonist is our helper.'

These two quotations encapsulate the importance of **opposition** parties in British politics. Without a strong opposition, the government does not have to justify its policies and this encourages complacent and even incompetent government. The opposition parties should therefore:

- ensure that the government justifies its legislative programme and executive decisions
- create a public debate by providing reasoned arguments why they cannot support the decisions of the government
- in the case of the biggest opposition party, known as Her Majesty's Most Loyal Opposition, be prepared to provide an alternative government-in-waiting in case the prime minister seeks an early dissolution of Parliament (as happened in 2017)
- use their various front bench spokespeople to focus on the government department that they are shadowing, exposing any failures of policy implementation
- in the case of the leader of the opposition, use the opportunity of the weekly PMQT to present himself or herself as having the political stature to be the prime minister-in-waiting

There are a variety of ways in which opposition parties can achieve these objectives:

- The parliamentary timetable allows 20 opposition days when the opposition parties can choose the subjects for debate in the House of Commons. These provide an important opportunity to make the government debate issues which the opposition believes are important. The main opposition party chooses the motion for debate on 17 of them. Only once since 1978, however, has an opposition day motion been victorious. This was in 2009 when a Liberal Democrat motion condemning Gordon Brown's refusal to guarantee UK residency rights to Gurkha veterans was passed by 267 to 246 votes with 27 Labour MPs voting against the government. This defeat was so embarrassing to the government that the policy was changed.
- As we have seen, opposition MPs scrutinise proposed government legislation in Public Bill Committees and offer amendments.

Key term

Opposition The second-largest party in the House of Commons constitutes Her Majesty's Most Loyal Opposition. The opposition front bench shadows the government front bench and scrutinises its decisions. It uses its role in Parliament to persuade the electorate that it is a potential government-in-waiting.

- Shadow ministers are expected to expose the mistakes and failures of their opposite numbers in government. A strongly interrogative shadow minister has an important role in highlighting failings of government policy development and implementation.
- Especially if the government has a small or non-existent parliamentary majority, opposition parties can also work closely with the more independent-minded House of Lords to uncover failures in government policy and to delay legislation. The large number of amendments which the House of Lords made to the EU (Withdrawal) Bill helped to encourage opposition within the Commons to a hard Brexit.
- In parliamentary debate, for example on the Budget and proposed government legislation, opposition parties play a very important role in forcing the government to justify its policies

---

In focus

The *Windrush* generation

The controversy over the '*Windrush* generation' demonstrates how the opposition can hold the government accountable for its policies. Claims that the Home Office was seeking to deport immigrants who had not got appropriate documentation would, the opposition argued, impact on elderly immigrants and their children who had spent their whole lives in the United Kingdom without the right documentation. On 23 April 2018, the shadow home secretary, Diane Abbott, put the case against the home secretary, Amber Rudd, very strongly:

The *Windrush* scandal demonstrates how the opposition can force the government on to the defensive on an issue about which the public feels very strongly

'These cases cannot come as a surprise to her because many of my Opposition colleagues have been pursuing individual cases for some time. She is behaving as though it is a shock to her that her officials are implementing regulations in the way that she intended them to be implemented. The Home Secretary must understand that the buck ultimately stops with her.'

On 30 April 2018, Amber Rudd resigned as home secretary, admitting that she had 'inadvertently misled Parliament'. Following Rudd's resignation, Abbott upped the pressure on the government, telling protestors, 'All roads lead back to Theresa May.'

Ministerial question time and prime minister's questions

Ministerial questions

As the executive sits within the legislature it can be regularly questioned, in both chambers, so that it can be held accountable for government policy. In the House of Commons, from Monday to Thursday an hour of parliamentary business time is set aside for oral questions to be put to ministers. In the House of Lords, half an hour is devoted to oral ministerial questions on the same days, although questions are directed to the government rather than to a specific department. Ministers must also respond to written questions within a week, if they are asked in the Commons, and within 2 weeks if they are asked in the Lords. According to the Ministerial Code of Conduct, 'Ministers should be as open as possible with Parliament and the public, refusing to provide information only when disclosure would not be in the public interest.'

Prime minister's questions

The prime minister is expected to attend the House of Commons every Wednesday between 12 noon and 12:30 p.m. to respond to questions from the chamber. This provides an important opportunity for the prime minister to be held accountable for government policy. On these occasions, the leader of the opposition is able to ask six questions, so it is important for both the prime minister and the leader of the opposition that they present themselves as effectively as possible. The leader of the next biggest party is given two questions to ask and then MPs have an opportunity to ask their own questions.

In 2015, Sir Gerald Kaufman MP, who was first elected an MP in 1970, said that Prime Minister's Question Time had become 'an exchange of pointless and useless declamations'. The way, too, in which the governing party's MPs ask the sorts of questions which enable the prime minister to take the credit for government successes has also led to some MPs calling it 'Gardeners' Question Time' because there are so many 'planted questions'. However, supporters of PMQT respond that it provides the opportunity for Parliament to interrogate the prime minister on a weekly basis in a way that is alien to presidential systems in which the executive is much less regularly accountable to the legislature. PMQT can also provide a powerful spotlight on the record of the prime minister, as well as enabling the prime minister to expose any inadequacies in the opposition.

Stretch and challenge

PMQT

Jeremy Corbyn: Yesterday, we learned that in 2010, the Home Office destroyed landing cards for a generation of Commonwealth citizens and so have told people, 'We can't find you in our system.' Did the Prime Minister, the then Home Secretary, sign off that decision?'

The prime minister: No, the decision to destroy the landing cards was taken in 2009 under a Labour Government.

Jeremy Corbyn: All the evidence — (interruption).

Mr Speaker: I said the Prime Minister must be heard. The Leader of the Opposition must be heard, and will be.

Mr Corbyn: All the evidence suggests — (interruption).

Mr Speaker: Order. There was a lot of this yesterday — very noisy and extremely stupid barracking. It must stop now. That is the end of the matter. The public absolutely despise that type of behaviour, from wherever in the House it takes place. Cut it out and grow up!

Hansard, 18 April 2018

Using this exchange, and others you can find, to what extent do you think that Prime Minister's Question Time provides a useful parliamentary function?

Summary

By the end of this chapter you should be able to answer the following questions:
- → What are the differences between the membership and the powers of the House of Commons and the House of Lords?
- → What are the functions of the House of Commons and how well does it fulfil them?
- → What are the functions of the House of Lords and how well does it fulfil them?
- → By what stages is a parliamentary bill enacted?
- → What obstacles to success do Private Member's Bills encounter?
- → How effective are parliamentary backbenchers?
- → How effective are opposition parties in holding government accountable?
- → Does Prime Minister's Question Time fulfil a useful function?

Source-based question

A petition, which reached 150,000 signatures, has called for a referendum on the abolition of the House of Lords. According to the petition, 'The House of Lords is a place of patronage where unelected and unaccountable individuals hold a disproportionate amount of influence and power which can be used to frustrate the elected representatives of the people.'

There are 665 eligible life peers in the chamber who are appointed by the Queen on the advice of the prime minister. There are also 90 hereditary peers and 26 bishops. With all these peers, the House of Lords is one of the world's largest decision-making bodies. The Conservatives have the most peers, followed by Labour, the Liberal Democrats and a small number from minor parties. There are also 181 crossbenchers who are not affiliated with any party. The members are expected to critique bills that have been approved by the House of Commons, and though they can't stop laws from being passed, they can cause delays and make amendments, which then have to be sent back to the House of Commons for approval.

Some argue that having unelected peers in British politics is undemocratic, whereas others argue that the House of Lords works well and guards against populist governments. Elected Lords would find it difficult to stand against public opinion, but unelected Lords are free to do this. Unelected peers also provide expertise, and can be, for example, trade union leaders, judges and academics.

Source: Online newspaper, 2018

Using the source, evaluate the view that the House of Lords provides a useful parliamentary function.

In your response you must:
- *compare and contrast the different opinions in the source*
- *examine and debate these views in a balanced way*
- *analyse and evaluate only the information presented in the source* (30)

Evaluative questions

1 Evaluate the extent to which Parliament is able to effectively scrutinise the work of government. *In your answer you should draw on relevant knowledge and understanding of the study of Component 1 UK Politics and Core Political Ideas and consider this view and the alternative to this view in a balanced way.* (30)

2 Evaluate the extent to which backbenchers in the House of Commons play a significant political role. *In your answer you should draw on relevant knowledge and understanding of the study of Component 1 UK Politics and Core Political Ideas and consider this view and the alternative to this view in a balanced way.* (30)

3 Evaluate the extent to which the House of Commons effectively fulfils its representative function. *In your answer you should draw on relevant knowledge and understanding of the study of Component 1 UK Politics and Core Political Ideas and consider this view and the alternative to this view in a balanced way.* (30)

Prime minister and the executive

The structure, role and powers of the executive

The structure and role of the executive

The **executive** is another term for the government. In the British system of parliamentary democracy the members of the government sit within the legislature and are accountable to it. The most important elements of the executive are the prime minister and the cabinet. The cabinet comprises the heads of the departments of state such as the home secretary and the foreign secretary, as well as the chief whip. In addition to this, more junior ministers are also members of the government, although they do not generally attend cabinet.

The executive is also served by senior civil servants, who run the administration of the departments of state and implement government policies. The most important of these is the chief secretary to the cabinet, the country's most senior civil servant, who provides impartial guidance to the prime minister as well as taking the minutes of cabinet meetings. A prime minister will also take advice from key political advisers who work for him or her in institutions such as the Cabinet Office and the Policy Unit at 10 Downing Street.

In 2010, David Cameron became prime minister of the first British coalition government since the establishment of Churchill's wartime coalition in 1940

It is their job to advise the government on the development of policy ideas and initiatives. The **core executive** comprises those ministers, senior civil servants and political advisers whom the prime minister freely confides in when developing policy.

The executive governs the nation in the following ways:

- It introduces into Parliament proposals for new legislation based on the manifesto that it fought the general election on. These comprise the Queen's Speech, which is delivered at the state opening of each new parliament to both the Commons and the Lords.
- It introduces legislation into Parliament in response to changing circumstances. This is known as 'the doctor's mandate' and the Queen's Speech always makes reference to this with the sentence, 'Other measures will be laid before you.'
- It introduces a Budget which will determine how the government proposes to raise revenue. This will be presented to Parliament in the autumn and will have been drawn up by the chancellor of the exchequer in negotiation with the prime minister.
- It can also introduce **secondary** or **delegated legislation**. This means that when legislation has already been passed by Parliament it can be modified by the government without the need for new primary legislation. Statutory instruments, sometimes known as Henry VIII clauses, are used to make these changes and have been criticised for being undemocratic as they seek to bypass full parliamentary scrutiny and debate. In 2016 statutory instruments were deployed to abolish maintenance grants for university students and to allow fracking to take place in national parks.

The sources of power of the prime minister

The authority of the prime minister derives from the fact that he or she has been asked by the Queen to form a government on her behalf. The individual appointed by the monarch to be prime minister will have been selected because they are able to command the support of the majority of MPs in the House of Commons.

It is highly likely that the prime minister will be the leader of the largest party in the House of Commons. In 1990, for example, when John Major replaced Margaret Thatcher as leader of the Conservative Party, he also became prime minister. In exceptional circumstances, though, an individual can be appointed prime minister without leading their party. In 1940, George VI asked Winston Churchill to form a government since, although he was not the leader of the Conservative Party, the King was confident that only Churchill would be able to establish an all-party wartime coalition government.

There is also a convention that the prime minister should be a member of the House of Commons. When Lord Home formed a government following the resignation of Harold Macmillan in 1963, he renounced his peerage and fought a by-election to secure a seat in the House of Commons.

A prime minister can be asked by the monarch to form a government having won a general election or because they are replacing a prime minister who has resigned office. Since 1976, five of the last eight prime ministers (James Callaghan, John Major, Gordon Brown, Theresa May and Boris Johnson) became prime minister following the resignation of their predecessor.

The powers of the prime minister

The prime minister, as the head of the executive, exercises the royal prerogative. These executive powers derive from the monarchy, but are exercised on the monarch's behalf by the prime minister. As a result of the transfer of **royal prerogative** powers, the prime minister:

- determines the membership of the government, including the cabinet and cabinet committees
- makes senior appointments to the civil service and judiciary
- appoints life peers to the House of Lords
- negotiates foreign treaties
- directs military forces in combat
- decides whether to launch Trident missiles

The government also shares in the prime minister's royal prerogative. For example, in 2013 the Ministry of Justice requested a posthumous royal pardon for Alan Turing. Turing cracked the German enigma code in the Second World War but in 1952 was convicted of gross indecency with another man.

The prime minister is also the key figure in casting the narrative of their government. Margaret Thatcher, for example, defined the free-market principles and uncompromising spirit of her governments, while during David Cameron's prime-ministership, the Conservatives became increasingly socially liberal, legislating in favour of same-sex marriage.

The role of government departments

As well as the prime minister, the government comprises **cabinet** and junior **ministers**. Cabinet ministers will generally be in charge of departments of state, such as the Treasury, Home Office, Foreign Office, Education or Transport. The function of **government departments** is to manage that particular area of government and to develop policy.

In addition to this, each ministerial team will make proposals for legislation concerning their department. This will include the introduction of major primary legislation into Parliament and also the amending of existing legislation, known as secondary or delegated legislation.

The key figures in a department are the secretary of state, who takes ultimate responsibility for the department, and then his or her junior ministers, who are also bound by the principle of collective ministerial responsibility. Each department will be able to rely on the support of the civil service, headed by a chief secretary. Unlike political advisers, the civil service is defined by the principles of neutrality, anonymity and permanence, which means that civil servants should provide impartial advice, to any government, on policy development and implementation. They are therefore not expected to be held accountable for the actions of a department since the overall focus of policy and administration should have been determined by elected politicians.

Ministerial responsibility

Individual ministerial responsibility

According to the principle of **individual ministerial responsibility**, ministers are accountable to Parliament for the actions of their department. This means that ministers must respond honestly to questions asked by members of the legislature. They should, therefore, when required, justify the actions of their department during parliamentary debate, in written responses and by appearing before select committees.

Individual ministerial responsibility also means that a minister should take personal responsibility for serious mistakes that occur within his or her department and of which they should have been aware.

The extent to which a minister can be held personally responsible for all major errors that take place within their department is, however, controversial. Harry S. Truman (US president, 1945–53) had a sign on his desk in the Oval Office with the words, 'The buck stops here', and on a number of occasions secretaries of state have resigned office when their departments have been seriously at fault in terms of either administration or policy.

Key term

Individual ministerial responsibility The principle that members of the cabinet take ultimate responsibility for what occurs within their department, including both administrative and policy failures. They are also individually responsible to the prime minister for their personal conduct.

Administrative failure

In 1954, Sir Thomas Dugdale resigned as minister of agriculture over the Crichel Down affair, when his department failed to return land to its rightful owner after it had been compulsorily purchased to be a bombing range before the Second World War. Although Dugdale's civil servants were the ones mostly at fault, Dugdale resigned, telling Parliament, 'I, as minister, must accept full responsibility for any mistakes and inefficiency of officials in my department, just as, when my officials bring off any successes on my behalf, I take full credit for them.'

Policy failure

In 1982, Lord Carrington resigned as foreign secretary from Margaret Thatcher's government in the immediate aftermath of Argentina's invasion of the Falklands. The reason for his resignation was that the Foreign Office should have been more aware of Argentina's intentions and should have made clearer what the response of the British government would be to any military intervention. In his resignation letter, he wrote:

> 'The Argentine invasion of the Falkland Islands has led to strong criticism in Parliament and in the press of the Government's policy. In my view, much of the criticism is unfounded. But I have been responsible for the conduct of that policy and I think it right that I should resign.'

There have also, however, been a number of occasions when ministers have held on to office in spite of intense parliamentary and media criticism of the actions of their department. In these circumstances they have often argued that they were not personally responsible for the actions of those working in their department or that the policy that they were responsible for was the policy of the *whole* government and they did not have to take any individual responsibility for its failings.

Having first entered government under Churchill, Lord Carrington was one of Thatcher's most trusted ministers

Hanging in there

Norman Lamont, Chancellor of the Exchequer, 1992

On 'Black Wednesday' the Major government was forced to abandon the European exchange rate mechanism (ERM), having raised interest rates by a staggering 5% in a desperate attempt to retain membership. As chancellor of the exchequer, Lamont was most closely associated with the crisis.

Lamont, however, refused to resign because the policy he was pursuing was also that of the prime minister. He claimed that, since Major had not resigned, neither should he.

Michael Howard, Home Secretary, 1995

As home secretary, Michael Howard was widely criticised for not resigning following a series of mass breakouts from Parkhurst jail. Instead, Howard sacked the director general of the Prisons Service, Derek Lewis, since he had been in operational control of the policy which had led to the escapes. Lewis subsequently won a case of wrongful dismissal against Howard.

Given the way in which the government increasingly delegates services to non-civil service agencies, it has become easier for ministers to distance themselves from departmental failures.

The continuing political significance of individual ministerial responsibility should not be ignored though. In 2002, Tony Blair's education secretary, Estelle Morris, was caught up in a political crisis over who should take responsibility for A-level grade-fixing. In a remarkably frank resignation letter to the prime minister, she admitted that in 'some recent situations I have been involved in, I have not felt I have been as effective as I should be, or as effective as you need me to be'.

In 2018, Theresa May's home secretary, Amber Rudd, resigned when she admitted that she had not told the truth to the House of Commons when she stated that there were no Home Office targets for removing illegal immigrants. In reality these targets did exist but in her resignation letter to the prime minister, Rudd claimed that she had not been sufficiently aware of them, leading to her inadvertently misleading the House of Commons. This resignation demonstrates the importance of a minister being fully aware of what is happening within their department so that they can honestly represent it to Parliament.

A minister can also be held accountable for their personal conduct and if this brings the government into disrepute they are expected to take responsibility for their actions and resign. The opening paragraph of the Ministerial Code of Conduct makes clear that, 'Ministers of the Crown are expected to maintain high standards of public behaviour and to behave in a way that upholds the highest standards of propriety.' Even ministers who might have preferred to try to cling on to power have often had to resign because of the intensity with which the media will speculate on their future in an era of '24-hour news'.

Synoptic link

There are numerous examples of the media influencing the political fortunes of politicians. This links to Component 1, UK Politics (see pages 119–21).

Amber Rudd

'It is with great regret that I am resigning as Home Secretary. I feel it is necessary to do so because I inadvertently misled the Home Affairs Select Committee over targets for removal of illegal immigrants during their questions on Windrush. Since appearing before the select committee, I have reviewed the advice I was given on this issue and become aware of information provided to my office which makes mention of targets. I should have been aware of this, and I take full responsibility for the fact that I was not.'

Amber Rudd in her resignation letter to Theresa May, 29 April 2018

Newspaper headlines the day after Amber Rudd's resignation

'It is of paramount importance that ministers give accurate and truthful information to Parliament, correcting any inadvertent error at the earliest opportunity. Ministers who knowingly mislead Parliament will be expected to offer their resignation to the prime minister.'

Ministerial Code of Conduct, 2018

With reference to this passage from the Ministerial Code of Conduct, why did Amber Rudd feel she had to resign from the government in April 2018? In what ways did her resignation damage Theresa May? Find other examples of ministerial resignations significantly weakening a government. Why was this?

When the private goes public

Chris Huhne, Energy Secretary, 2012

Chris Huhne was forced to resign from the coalition government over media claims that he had perverted the course of justice by colluding with his former wife, Vicky Pryce, so that she took responsibility for his speeding offence. Both were convicted and sent to prison for the crime.

Michael Fallon, Defence Secretary, 2017

The surprise resignation of Michael Fallon from Theresa May's government was caused by his acceptance that in the past his behaviour towards women had 'fallen below the high standards that we require of the Armed Forces'. In order to limit the political impact of any allegations being publicly made against him, he resigned from the government.

Priti Patel, Overseas Development Secretary, 2017

Priti Patel resigned from Theresa May's government over a series of unofficial private meetings that she had had with Israeli ministers, including the prime minister, Benjamin Netanyahu.

Patel's failure to report the meetings also put her directly in contravention of the code's requirement that 'any significant content should be passed back to the department as soon as possible after the event'.

Collective ministerial responsibility All members of the government must publicly support the government and should not disclose the contents of private ministerial discussions. If the administration is defeated on a vote of confidence, this convention also states that all members of the government must resign.

Collective ministerial responsibility

According to the principle of **collective ministerial responsibility**, if the government loses a vote of confidence in the House of Commons, the whole government must resign. This memorably happened on 28 March 1979 when the Labour government of James Callaghan lost a vote of confidence by 311 to 310 votes, precipitating a sudden general election.

- Collective ministerial responsibility also requires that discussions within cabinet must be kept secret in order to maintain the integrity of government.
- A core aspect of collective ministerial responsibility is that members of the government must support agreed policies even if in private they may have been highly critical of them. This is important in maintaining the unity of the government since without it the government would appear weak and divided. In political terms, unity represents strength and so collective ministerial responsibility is fundamental to the survival of the government. If collective responsibility did not operate, the authority of the prime minister would be greatly undermined.
- If a minister cannot bring themself to publicly agree with a government policy or the way in which government is being run then they have no choice but to resign and return to the back benches. This has happened on numerous occasions, with varied consequences for the authority of the prime minister.

In focus

High-profile ministerial resignations over collective responsibility

Peter Thorneycroft, Chancellor of the Exchequer, 1958

In 1958, the chancellor of the exchequer, Peter Thorneycroft, resigned from the Macmillan government because he could not publicly support what he regarded as the excessive public spending of the government. Two other Treasury ministers, Enoch Powell and Nigel Birch, resigned with him. Macmillan dismissed the resignations as 'little local difficulties' and the government went on to win the 1959 general election by a landslide.

Geoffrey Howe, Leader of the House of Commons and Deputy Prime Minister, 1990

The pro-European Geoffrey Howe resigned from the Thatcher government on 1 November 1990, just 2 days after Margaret Thatcher delivered her famous assault on European federalism in her 'No, no, no' speech. In his resignation speech to the House of Commons on 13 November, Howe explained that he could no longer serve under an increasingly eurosceptic prime minister. Howe's resignation prompted the leadership challenge of Michael Heseltine and by the end of November Thatcher had been forced from office.

Robin Cook, Leader of the House of Commons, 2003

In 2003, Robin Cook resigned from Tony Blair's government over its preparations for war against Iraq. Cook was unconvinced by claims that Saddam Hussein was a threat to the UK's national interests and in his resignation speech explained that, 'I intend to join those tomorrow night who will vote against military action now. It is for that reason, and for that reason alone, and with a heavy heart, that I resign from the government.' Jeremy Corbyn, among others, lent him his support. The UK continued its preparations for war and Blair won a third general election victory in 2005.

The extent to which collective ministerial responsibility always operates can, however, be contested. Ministers have been known to leak criticisms of their own government. John Major did not trust a number of eurosceptic members of his cabinet, whom he rightly believed were briefing the press against him behind his back. He was even caught on microphone confiding to the journalist Michael Brunson:

> 'Oh, I can bring in other people into the Cabinet, that is right, but where do you think most of this poison has come from? It is coming from the dispossessed and the never-possessed. You and I can both think of ex-ministers who are going around causing all sorts of trouble. Would you like three more of the bastards out there?'

Stretch and challenge

Harold Wilson (left) with Tony Benn at the Labour Party conference, 1971

In 1974, three members of Harold Wilson's government, Tony Benn, Judith Hart and Joan Lestor, backed a resolution by Labour's National Executive Council condemning the government's decision to agree to joint UK/South African naval exercises as a 'gross error'. A furious Wilson reminded them that if they were not prepared to abide by collective ministerial responsibility then he would acknowledge this 'as a decision on your part that you did not wish to continue as a member of this administration. I should of course much regret such a decision but I should accept it.' They did not resign.

Why is the principle of collective ministerial responsibility so important to effective government?

In 2010, a Conservative–Liberal Democrat coalition was established, although they had, of course, been campaigning against each other on separate manifestos during the general election. Therefore, over certain issues the cabinet would have to be allowed to disagree. The compromise that was worked out was that on areas covered in the Coalition Agreement, collective ministerial responsibility would operate, but in areas not covered by the agreement it would not operate. For example, Trident renewal and the construction of new nuclear power stations, both of which the Liberal Democrats had vigorously opposed in the general election, were not part of the Coalition Agreement and so collective responsibility would not apply. The Conservatives and Liberal Democrats also campaigned on different sides on the alternative vote (AV) referendum in 2011. Following President Assad's use of chemical weapons, David Cameron argued for a military response, which the deputy prime minister, Nick Clegg, opposed.

The EEC/EU

The two referendums that have been called on the UK's membership of the European Economic Community/European Union also demonstrate the limits of collective ministerial responsibility.

In 1975, the Labour government of Harold Wilson was so divided over membership of the EEC that Wilson had to abandon collective ministerial responsibility in order to allow members of his government to campaign on different sides, even though the stated policy of the government was to remain in the EEC. So profound were these divisions that the eurosceptic Tony Benn and the pro-European Roy Jenkins even debated the issue on television. Indeed, Wilson's failure to keep his cabinet united over continued membership of the EEC prompted a cartoon in the *Express* newspaper which suggested that some of Wilson's most reliable support for Europe came from the Conservative and Liberal parties rather than his own cabinet.

In 2016, David Cameron faced exactly the same problem as Harold Wilson. Having promised a referendum on continued membership of the EU, Cameron knew that if he demanded eurosceptic members of his cabinet, such as Michael Gove and Chris Grayling, support membership then he would suffer a series of high-profile resignations. Consequently, he suspended collective ministerial responsibility on this issue, allowing members of the cabinet such as Iain Duncan Smith (Work and Pensions) and Theresa Villiers (Northern Ireland) to campaign against membership even though the policy of the government was to remain.

As foreign secretary in Theresa May's government, Boris Johnson frequently criticised her Brexit plans and instead put forward his own proposals. When, for example, May said she favoured a customs partnership with the EU, Johnson told the *Daily Mail* that the plan was 'totally untried and would make it very, very difficult to do free trade deals'. May's reliance on Brexit MPs would, however, have made it difficult to sack Johnson as such a high-profile supporter of Brexit and so he continued to play an ambivalent role within government until his resignation.

Synoptic link

In early 2019 Theresa May's government suffered three enormous parliamentary defeats when eurosceptic Conservative MPs rebelled over her Brexit deal proposals. This shows how divided the Conservative Party has become over Brexit and links to Component 1, UK Politics (see pages 44–49).

In focus

Brexit and collective responsibility

David Davis resigned from the government following a key meeting of the cabinet at Chequers to determine government policy on Brexit. The decision to pursue closer ties with the EU was, for Davis, 'a compromise too far' and in his resignation letter he stated that 'national interest requires a Secretary of State in my department that is an enthusiastic believer in your approach, and not merely a reluctant conscript'.

Boris Johnson resigned from the government just hours after Davis. In his resignation letter, Johnson provided a classic statement of how collective responsibility operates:

'On Friday I acknowledged that my side of the argument were too few to prevail, and congratulated you on at least reaching a cabinet decision on the way forward. As I said then, the government now has a song to sing. The trouble is that I have practised the words over the weekend and find that they stick in the throat. We must have collective responsibility. Since I cannot in all conscience champion these proposals, I have sadly concluded that I must go.'

Boris Johnson, resignation letter, 9 July 2018

Party divisions over the consequences of the 2016 EU referendum have strained collective ministerial responsibility to breaking point. In March 2019 three government ministers (Amber Rudd, David Gauke and Greg Clark) said they would defy the government by voting against the prospect of a no-deal Brexit. When parliament debated a motion to reject a no-deal Brexit *under any circumstances*, 13 government ministers defied collective ministerial responsibility by disobeying their whips and abstaining. It is likely that in more normal political circumstances, collective ministerial responsibility will once again function effectively.

The prime minister and the cabinet

The functions of the cabinet

The cabinet consists of 20–25 senior government ministers who generally head large departments of state. It usually meets once a week for no more than 2 hours, on a Thursday morning, although in a crisis it can also be summoned. The prime minister sets the agenda, chairs and sums up the meeting and then approves the cabinet secretary's minutes. Votes are not taken and, although there can be intense debate and disagreement *within* cabinet, the prime minister will expect all present to publicly support the government's decisions and policies based on the principle of collective ministerial responsibility. If a member of the cabinet cannot *publicly* agree to a policy determined by cabinet they should have to resign and join the back benches, where they will be free to criticise the government.

The cabinet has a number of important roles:

- Since many decisions are taken elsewhere within the executive, a core function of the cabinet is to approve them, so providing them with the seal of government policy. This is an important way of maintaining the unity of the government. The cabinet provides the key forum in which government policies are legitimised.
- The cabinet will also determine key issues of policy. In 1976, James Callaghan allowed the cabinet to freely debate whether or not to accept a loan from the International Monetary Fund. All sides were given the opportunity to present their cases on the understanding that at the end of the process a consensus would be reached and *that* would be government policy. In 2018, May summoned the cabinet to Chequers, the prime minister's country retreat, in order to determine what the government's bargaining position should be in the final stages of Brexit.
- A key role of cabinet is to decide how the government will determine business. If controversial legislation is going to be introduced into Parliament, the cabinet will need to discuss how it is best presented and ministers will need to know when they should be available on the front benches to enthusiastically support it. The chief whip will also explain whether there is likely to be a sufficient government majority if a bill is especially contentious and so the cabinet may debate any concessions they may need to make in order to win parliamentary support.
- Occasionally, if a dispute between two departments of state is proving impossible to resolve, then the issue may be brought to cabinet as a final court of appeal in order to resolve it. This was particularly significant when departmental conflicts had to be resolved during the 2010–15 coalition.

- Prime ministers also appoint cabinet committees to develop and implement specific policy. This can be an effective way of enhancing prime ministerial authority, since the prime minister determines the membership and decides the number and remit of the committees. Theresa May, for example, took the chair of the European Union Exit and Trade Committee and the National Security Council. The decisions of cabinet committees possess the same legitimacy as decisions of the full cabinet.

How is the cabinet selected?

Deciding who is in the cabinet is an important way in which a prime minister puts their own stamp upon government. However, even here, the prime minister does not have a completely free hand. As Walter Bagehot put it in his seminal work *The English Constitution* (1867), 'The position of most men in Parliament forbids their being invited to the cabinet; the position of a few men ensures their being invited.' In other words there will be some high-profile 'big beasts' whose exclusion would be politically impossible, while other members of the legislature would never aspire to high office.

A prime minister will be under great pressure to include in their cabinet influential colleagues and dominant personalities. Harold Wilson knew that George Brown, whom he had defeated for the party leadership, was rated more highly than him by many Labour supporters — 'Better George Brown drunk than Harold Wilson sober' — and so he appointed him deputy prime minister. In 1997, it would have been inconceivable for Tony Blair not to appoint Gordon Brown as chancellor of the exchequer, given his grasp of economics and the agreement they had reached at Granita restaurant in 1994 to share the two top jobs in government.

A prime minister will also want to stamp their authority on cabinet by advancing to senior positions key allies whom they can rely on to provide unwavering support in a crisis.

- Margaret Thatcher relied totally on the advice and support of William Whitelaw, her first home secretary, while she advanced to key positions politicians like Norman Tebbit (Employment) and Cecil Parkinson (Party Chairman), who loyally shared her political views.
- After his second landslide general election victory, Tony Blair advanced the careers of Labour modernisers, such as Alan Johnson (Education) and Alan Milburn (Health) in order to provide his government with continued reforming momentum.
- When she became prime minister in 2016, Theresa May was determined to remove the 'Notting Hill' public school 'chumocracy' that David Cameron had cultivated. She therefore sacked George Osborne as chancellor of the exchequer in order to make her administration appear less elitist.

A prime minister can be well advised to also include potential rivals in government, since this binds them to collective ministerial responsibility so they cannot publicly criticise the government. By rewarding them with high office they may even be able to cultivate their loyalty. Although they had a stormy relationship, Blair knew that having Gordon Brown in his cabinet was much safer than having him on the back benches. Margaret Thatcher was considerably weakened when Michael Heseltine resigned from her government. From 2016 to 2018, Theresa May managed to ignore Boris Johnson's rather broad interpretation of collective ministerial responsibility on the understanding that her position was made safer by having him inside government than outside.

Party unity is vital, so a prime minister will need to balance their cabinet in order to avoid alienating certain sections of the party. This is well exemplified by Tony Blair's inclusion of John Prescott, who served as deputy prime minister from 1997 to 2007. Prescott was from the working-class left of the Labour Party and had had a career in the merchant navy (he was personal steward to Sir Anthony Eden on the voyage he took after the Suez Crisis). He gained influence as a militant member of the National Union of Seamen and then entered Parliament. By appointing Prescott to such a prominent role in government, Blair was able to reassure the left of the party that New Labour had not entirely abandoned its socialist ideology. Similarly, and even after her third general election victory in 1987, Margaret Thatcher appreciated the importance of keeping one-nation Conservatives in her cabinet, such as Douglas Hurd.

The maintenance of party unity was especially important to Theresa May when she became prime minister in the immediate aftermath of the Brexit referendum. Since the Conservative Party was split down the middle over Brexit she had to give prominent cabinet positions to both Remain and Leave politicians (Table 7.1).

Table 7.1 Remain and Leave MPs in May's first cabinet, 2016

Remain	Leave
Philip Hammond: chancellor of the exchequer	Boris Johnson: foreign secretary
Amber Rudd: home secretary	David Davis: Brexit secretary

However, when there is a coalition the prime minister's right to appoint is severely restricted. In 2010, for example, David Cameron, as part of the Coalition Agreement, had to appoint Nick Clegg as deputy prime minister and give the Liberal Democrats five out of the 22 seats in cabinet.

Theresa May took the significant step of saying that she wanted a cabinet that 'looks more like the country it serves'. She advanced more females and ethnic minorities through appointments to the cabinet than any previous prime minister. Her determination that the cabinet should reflect the diversity of the UK may make future prime ministers more likely to feel the need to balance their cabinets in the same way.

How significant is the cabinet?

There are two conflicting interpretations of the influence of the cabinet in British politics. According to Walter Bagehot in *The English Constitution*, the cabinet is 'the most powerful body in the state' and the prime minister, rather than dominating it, is essentially first among equals.

However, it has also been claimed that the relatively large size of the cabinet precludes constructive debate. This supports the view that it is more of a rubber stamp for policies which have already been determined elsewhere in the core executive rather than a sounding board for new ideas.

Especially since the government of Harold Wilson in the 1960s, the centrality of the cabinet in government (**cabinet government**) has been questioned. This is because prime ministers have acquired so many other sources of advice and information, and are now treated so presidentially by the media, that they will already have decided the focus and direction of their government without needing to talk it through cabinet. As a result of this it has been claimed that the UK now has a system of **prime-ministerial government** rather than cabinet government.

Key terms

Cabinet government A type of government in which the cabinet plays the key role in the development of policy. It provides a direct contrast to the prime-ministerial model of government.

Prime-ministerial government A model of government in which the prime minister is dominant and the cabinet is relegated to a subordinate decision-making role.

The expansion of the prime minister's Private Office has, in particular, provided an enhanced engine of government. In 1974, on his return to office, Harold Wilson set up the Policy Unit in Downing Street in order to provide him with his own support and advice in developing political strategy. Tony Blair introduced a number of initiatives to further increase control from the centre, and the most important phrase in government, it was half joked, became 'Tony wants':

- The position of chief of staff was established to coordinate government policy. Jonathan Powell, who held the position under Blair, explained that his appointment demonstrated 'a change from a feudal system of barons to a more Napoleonic system'. His successors have all retained this role.
- The establishment of the Prime Minister's Strategy Unit and Prime Minister's Delivery Unit further challenged the autonomy of cabinet ministers by setting their departments targets and monitoring their performance. Although David Cameron abolished both roles because of fears of micro-management, he strengthened the Policy and Implementation Unit in order to ensure more coordinated government.
- The Press Office under Alastair Campbell became more prominent in government, ensuring that Downing Street had more control over how news stories were presented and responded to.

It would be wrong though to dismiss the influence of cabinet. Every cabinet is composed of the most powerful and influential members of a political party and a prime minister would be unwise to ignore the weight of political experience that the cabinet can provide. Members of the cabinet are also likely to be ambitious, and those heading powerful departments like the Home Office or Foreign Office are still likened to feudal barons with the independent authority to challenge a prime minister. In 2018, Jeremy Hunt actually refused Theresa May's attempt to move him from the then Department of Health and even managed to expand his role to being health and social care secretary.

It is also important to remember that each prime minister will approach cabinet differently. Tony Blair, for example, had a clear vision of what he wanted to achieve as prime minister, as well as strong parliamentary majorities, and so the role of the cabinet became more focused on how to report decisions that had already been made elsewhere.

In contrast, the more pragmatic John Major, after the 1992 general election, had only a 21-seat majority and a divided party and so had to work hard to establish a unity of approach in cabinet in order to hold his government together. Theresa May, similarly, had to balance a cabinet which was highly divided over Brexit, as well as coping with the fallout of her loss of a parliamentary majority in the 2017 general election. She, therefore, lacked the political capital to be able to dominate cabinet.

In short, it would be unhelpful to generalise about the influence of the cabinet in British politics. Much of the influence that it does, or does not, wield will depend on the personality of the prime minister and political circumstances.

Does the cabinet play a central role in British government?

Yes

- During political crises a prime minister will need to discuss all the options open to them with the cabinet, since the cabinet contains the accumulated wisdom of the government.
- Following the Argentinean invasion of the Falklands in April 1982, Margaret Thatcher summoned an emergency meeting of the cabinet to discuss all the diplomatic and military options open to the government.
- In April 2018, Theresa May called an urgent meeting to discuss a military response to the Syrian government's presumed use of chemical weapons. It was particularly important that she knew she could rely on the support of the cabinet because she was not intending to consult the House of Commons.
- When there is a controversial issue to be resolved, cabinet agreement is vital in order to ensure that the government is united. In 1976, James Callaghan's cabinet thoroughly discussed the IMF loan, while John Major's cabinet met in emergency sessions during the Black Wednesday economic crisis in 1992.
- In 2018, Theresa May summoned the whole cabinet to Chequers in order to achieve a united approach to the sort of Brexit the government would pursue.
- On some occasions, cabinet can challenge the authority of the prime minister. In 1969, a cabinet revolt stopped Harold Wilson from placing legal restraints on growing trade union power when it rejected the White Paper 'In Place of Strife'.
- In 1990, the failure of the cabinet to offer Margaret Thatcher its full support during Michael Heseltine's leadership challenge prompted her resignation.

No

- Although Harold Macmillan presented an image of calm unflappability, he had a clear political agenda that he wanted to achieve. In just 6 years he appointed four chancellors of the exchequer, closely monitoring their approach to economic policy. On the appointment of his last chancellor of the exchequer, Reginald Maudling, Macmillan noted in his diary: 'To my great pleasure (and surprise) the Treasury are now adopting my views.' (10 August 1962)
- Harold Wilson liked to make decisions through a small body of core advisers in his Downing Street flat. This was known as the 'kitchen cabinet' and included key friends and allies such as his secretary Marcia Williams, press secretary Joe Haines and political adviser Bernard Donoughue.
- Edward Heath saw himself as an efficient moderniser and so made key decisions with trusted advisers such as cabinet secretary Sir Robert Armstrong and his political secretary, Douglas Hurd.
- Margaret Thatcher also had a clear political vision of what she wanted to achieve and, especially towards the end of her prime-ministership, pushed issues such as the poll tax through cabinet with insufficient discussion. The way in which she discouraged discussion during the Westland crisis also highlights her sometimes imperious and arrogant approach to cabinet government.
- Tony Blair liked to make decisions quickly and was impatient with long discussions. He therefore discouraged cabinet discussion, preferring to have *already* made key decisions with ministers in bilateral meetings. This has often been referred to as 'sofa government'.

Two examples of how prime ministers can approach cabinet

The IMF loan, 1976

In 1976 the Labour government was in turmoil over whether to accept a loan from the International Monetary Fund with its accompanying demands for stringent cuts in public spending. The chancellor of the exchequer, Denis Healey, argued that there was no alternative to the loan. However, Callaghan needed to prove that the government was united on the issue and so allowed the cabinet to fully debate the issue. The leading opponent of the loan, Tony Benn, noted in his diary on 1 December 1976 that Callaghan told the cabinet, 'we shall have to rally to the majority view, *whatever it is*, or it will not be possible for me to carry on'.

The Westland Affair, 1986

During 1985 and 1986, the Department of State for Trade and Industry and the Department of Defence clashed over whether a British firm, Westland Helicopters, should be taken over by an American or European bid. The dispute proved so irreconcilable that it went to cabinet to be resolved. However, the defence secretary, Michael Heseltine, complained that Margaret Thatcher's obvious bias towards the American business undermined genuine cabinet debate and he spectacularly resigned during a meeting of the cabinet on 9 January 1986, allegedly stating, 'I can no longer be a member of this cabinet.'

To what extent is the prime minister the dominant force in politics?

The authority that a prime minister wields depends greatly on the circumstances in which they hold office. Harold Macmillan once quipped to a journalist that the power of the prime minister depends on 'events, dear boy, events', while Harold Wilson commented that 'a week is a long time in politics'. It is important, therefore, to appreciate that although prime ministers can decisively move on the political agenda, they can also fall victim to a changing political environment.

In focus

'Events, dear boy, events'

In 1962, Harold Macmillan determined to give new energy to his government by sacking a third of his cabinet, including his chancellor of the exchequer, Selwyn Lloyd. Far from enhancing his authority, the decision gave the impression that Macmillan had lost his deft political touch and was in panic. The young Liberal MP Jeremy Thorpe claimed, 'greater love hath no man than he lay down his friends for his life' and Macmillan's reputation never recovered as the press went from referring to him as 'Supermac' to 'Mac the knife'. A year later, the Profumo scandal, in which Macmillan's secretary of state for war, John Profumo, was forced to resign over an affair with Christine Keeler which seemed to threaten national security, further undermined Macmillan's authority and, following emergency surgery, he decided to resign office in October 1963.

Edward Heath

Edward Heath (1970–74) had a dominant personality, a loyal cabinet and a workable parliamentary majority and was determined to modernise the UK. His most significant achievement was using the prestige of his office to negotiate the UK's entry into the EEC in 1973. However, his authority was challenged by a remarkable series of misfortunes. Miners' strikes in 1972 and then again in 1974 threatened the nation's energy supplies, while a dramatic rise in the cost of oil led to a huge increase in global inflation, undermining the government's economic strategy. Faced by mounting industrial unrest, Heath called a snap general election in February 1974 which he lost by four seats to Harold Wilson.

James Callaghan

Following the resignation of Harold Wilson, James Callaghan became prime minister in 1976. Popular in the party and with a strong personal approval rating in the nation, he quickly stamped his authority on government. At the 1976 Labour Party conference, he challenged the postwar economic consensus, telling delegates:

> 'The cosy world we were told would go on for ever, where full employment would be guaranteed by a stroke of the Chancellor's pen, cutting taxes, deficit spending; that cosy world is gone.'

The result of the speech was a sudden and dramatic change in government policy from high spending to deflationary measures. This commitment to deflation proved to be effective in starting to bring down inflation.

Callaghan, however, decided not to call a general election in the autumn of 1978, which he was widely expected to win. That winter the authority of his government was challenged by a series of damaging strikes and quickly became known as the Winter of Discontent. Abandoned by the Liberal Party and the nationalist parties, his minority government eventually lost a vote of confidence in the House of Commons, forcing Callaghan to call a general election at the worst possible time for the survival of his government.

Although James Callaghan skilfully managed to hold together the left and the right of the Labour Party, his failure to control trade union pay claims contributed to his defeat in the 1979 general election

John Major

When he replaced Margaret Thatcher as prime minister in 1990, John Major quickly changed the dynamic of the Conservative government. He ditched the unpopular poll tax and was widely praised for the way in which he negotiated an opt-out from the social chapter in the Maastricht Treaty. However, Major achieved only a 21-seat majority in the 1992 general election. This gave eurosceptic Conservative MPs the opportunity to disrupt ratification of the treaty, exposing growing divisions within the Conservative Party.

In June 1995, John Major resigned the leadership of the Conservative Party, telling his eurosceptic critics to either 'put up or shut up'. One member of his cabinet, John Redwood, decided to take up the challenge, winning the support of 89 MPs to Major's 218 in a leadership ballot, further exposing the divisions and highlighting Major's declining authority as prime minister.

A few hours after the result of the EU referendum was announced, a stunned David Cameron announced that he would resign as prime minister

Allegations of ministerial sleaze and constant media criticism, together with Tony Blair's combative leadership of the Labour Party, further contributed to his decline.

David Cameron

As coalition prime minister, 2010–15, David Cameron succeeded in introducing major cuts to public expenditure as part of the government's austerity programme. He also put the weight of his authority behind legislation allowing same-sex marriage in spite of the opposition of large numbers of more traditionalist Conservative MPs. Coalition government placed significant restraints on Cameron's freedom of manoeuvre, however. As part of the Coalition Agreement he had to allow a referendum on electoral reform in 2011 and he failed to reform parliamentary boundaries when the Liberal Democrats withdrew their support. His failure to persuade Parliament to support bombing President Assad in 2013, following the use of chemical weapons in Syria, further demonstrated the limits on his authority.

Cameron's promise to call a referendum on the UK's membership of the EU probably helped to keep the Conservative Party united and helped him win the 2015 general election. However, the surprise vote for Brexit which provoked Cameron's immediate resignation on 24 June 2016 highlight just how much a prime minister cannot always control events. Cameron had campaigned hard for 'Remain' and the victory for 'Leave' meant, he said, that it would not be right for him to 'be the captain that steers our country to its next destination'.

Synoptic link

The outcome of a general election can dramatically impact on the authority of a prime minister. This links to Component 1, UK Politics (see pages 122–32).

Debate

Did coalition government, 2010–15, strengthen David Cameron as prime minister?

Yes

- As David Cameron won only 306 seats in the 2010 general election and needed 326 seats to form a majority administration, the support of the 57 Liberal Democrat MPs provided him with the parliamentary votes he needed to form a stable government.
- The Coalition Agreement with Nick Clegg enabled Cameron to fulfil most of his manifesto commitments, especially his austerity proposals to reduce public spending.
- Collective ministerial responsibility would apply to all areas of policy agreed in the Coalition Agreement.
- In spite of differences between the two parties, the coalition lasted for 5 years, helped by the passing of the Fixed Term Parliaments Act 2011 which set the date for the 2015 general election.

No

- As a result of the Coalition Agreement, Cameron had to give cabinet positions to five Liberal Democrats, including Nick Clegg as deputy prime minister.
- Cameron had to agree to a referendum on the Additional Vote as part of the Coalition Agreement. His plans to redraw parliamentary boundaries were also scuppered by Liberal Democrat opposition.
- As no party had won the general election, leading to a coalition, the House of Lords suspended the Salisbury Convention so that it could oppose measures in the governing parties' manifestos.
- In order to ensure the effective functioning of cabinet, the Quad was established, in which agreement on core policies *first* had to be agreed by Cameron and his chancellor of the exchequer, George Osborne, together with Nick Clegg and Danny Alexander, the Liberal Democrat chief secretary to the cabinet.

Presidents in all but name?

A number of political commentators regard the position of the prime minister as becoming increasingly presidential. According to this model, prime ministers have become so dominant in cabinet, and the media have become so obsessed with their characters, that their personal charisma and influence have enabled them to dominate decision making as pseudo-presidential figures.

The presidentialism of British politics can be traced back to the 1960s, when Harold Wilson, as an admirer of President John Kennedy, confidently utilised television to reach out directly to the public, creating a close relationship between him and the voters. He clearly understood, too, the political power of a good photo opportunity and took the initiative in being regularly pictured with 1960s celebrities such as the Beatles and the cast of *Coronation Street*.

The political writer Michael Foley has linked the presidential model to what he has termed 'spatial leadership', in which a prime minister creates their own space by distancing him- or herself from their party and thereby securing a personal mandate directly from the public in much the same way as a president does. This therefore enables a prime minister to rise above party and, in a presidential manner, appeal directly to the people.

The development of the media has also provided more opportunities for prime ministers to act in a presidential manner. In particular, the media's appetite for celebrity news and their enthusiastic coverage of personal interventions in global crises have further increased the constant spotlight on the prime minister, rather than the government, in a highly presidential fashion. Like Wilson, Margaret Thatcher and Tony Blair demonstrated presidential tendencies, as they both had a distinctive political style and knew how to use the media to reach beyond established party loyalties to those who did not traditionally see themselves as either Conservative or Labour supporters.

During both the Falklands War (1982) and the miners' strike (1984–85) it was Thatcher, rather than her cabinet, who provided the leadership that the media and the public focused on.

Stretch and challenge

'I am not talking about failure, I am talking about my supreme confidence in the British fleet … superlative ships, excellent equipment, the most highly trained professional group of men, the most honourable and brave members of Her Majesty's Service. Failure? Do you remember what Queen Victoria once said? "Failure — the possibilities do not exist." That is the way we must look at it, with all our professionalism, all our flair and every single bit of native cunning, every single bit of professionalism and all our equipment and we must go out calmly, quietly, to succeed.'

Margaret Thatcher, television interview, 5 April 1982,
as the Task Force was being sent to recover the Falklands

The death of Princess Diana on 31 August 1997 stunned the nation. Displaying extraordinary empathy, Blair sensitively articulated the mood of the public in his 'People's Princess' speech.

'We know how difficult things were for her from time to time. I am sure we can only guess that. But people everywhere, not just here in Britain, kept faith with Princess Diana. They liked her, they loved her, they regarded her as one of the people. She was the People's Princess and that is how she will stay, how she will remain in our hearts and our memories for ever.'

Find other examples of prime ministers effectively representing the mood of the nation. Do you think all prime ministers are equally able to do this? Does this suggest that the office of prime minister is becoming more presidential?

- Blair's rhetoric was also highly personal, emphasising his moral focus, which further raised his status and developed his relationship with the public above less ideologically driven politicians. He also frequently referred to government policy as though it was his own. For example: 'the people entrusted me with the task of leading their country' and 'this is the Britain I offer you'.
- The energy with which he intervened in all aspects of government policy (sometimes over the authority of the minister concerned) further focused attention on Blair rather than his government. In particular, Blair's high-profile personal interventions were crucial in driving forward the Northern Ireland peace process: 'This is not a time for soundbites. We feel the weight of history upon us.'
- In the weeks leading up to the invasion of Iraq in 2003, Blair, characteristically, put the case for war *directly* to the public through television discussions and debates, thereby reaching beyond Parliament straight to the people.

According to the presidential model, the cabinet becomes almost irrelevant to decision making in the same way as its role is more marginal in the USA. This is because the prime minister can increasingly afford to ignore the cabinet because they have their own popular mandate directly from the people through public acclamation and so have less need to have their policies legitimised by cabinet.

Blair further enhanced the more presidential atmosphere in Downing Street by more closely modelling it on the White House. In the process, the new position of chief of staff was established and the prime minister's Private Office and Cabinet Office were enlarged to provide greater control from the centre and more 'joined-up' government.

Although a less presidential prime minister than Blair, David Cameron understood how to use the media spotlight to firmly associate certain key decisions with himself rather than his government. On a number of occasions, he acted in a presidential fashion by associating his personal authority with a specific policy. He notably did this when he very publicly and personally put forward the case for gay marriage. Then in the 2014 Scottish referendum and the 2016 EU referendum Cameron deployed the personal prestige of his office to back 'Better Together' and 'Remain'.

The way in which the 2010, 2015 and 2017 general election campaigns all included televised leaders' debates has further made UK politics more presidential by firmly putting the leadership qualities of the candidates on public display. Such debates have been integral to US politics since the Kennedy/Nixon debates in 1960, but have been a significant innovation in the UK's system of parliamentary democracy.

However, it would be misleading to suggest that prime ministers are essentially now presidents. Some prime ministers can connect highly effectively with the public. However, the UK is a parliamentary democracy and government is based on the principle of collective ministerial responsibility. This means that a British prime minister, unlike an American president, possesses no electoral mandate from the public. Instead their authority depends on having a parliamentary majority and maintaining the support of their parliamentary party. In 1979, for example, James Callaghan was forced to call a general election when he lost a vote of confidence in the House of Commons and, in 1990, Margaret Thatcher resigned as prime minister when she lost the support of her cabinet. Both events occurred because the UK is a parliamentary democracy. They could not have occurred in the USA, where a president can only be forced to resign for committing 'high crimes and misdemeanours' in defiance of the Constitution.

A British prime minister is, therefore, constitutionally incapable of being a president, although, as we have seen, certain prime ministers can display presidential characteristics if their character and political circumstances permit.

- Many other prime ministers are personally ill-suited to a presidential role or are so politically weak that presidentialism is impossible. For example, John Major's collegiate approach to politics was resolutely non-presidential and, after 1992, his declining parliamentary majority and growing divisions within his party would anyway have made it impossible for him to project a presidential image.
- Gordon Brown was another uncharismatic prime minister, whose attempts to speak directly to the nation were ruthlessly parodied by the comedian Rory Bremner. Indeed, such was his lack of charisma that his colleague Robin Cook once commented that he had 'a face like a wet winter's morning in Fife'.
- Theresa May, initially, displayed presidential characteristics when she became prime minister in 2016, but her failure to engage with the public during the 2017 general election and the humiliating loss of her parliamentary majority ensured that she was unable to govern in a presidential fashion.

Whether or not a prime minister acts in a presidential manner depends very much on his or her personality and power base. Indeed, prime ministers should beware of trying to act in too presidential a manner since this is likely to antagonise the House of Commons, from where they derive their political power. To claim, therefore, that UK politics has become more presidential is an overstatement, since whether or not this is the case depends entirely on the contemporary political situation.

Constitutional differences between presidents and prime ministers

Table 7.2 lists the main constitutional differences between presidents and prime ministers.

Table 7.2 The main constitutional differences between presidents and prime ministers

Prime ministers	Presidents
A British prime minister is not directly elected by the public. In a general election the electorate votes for an MP, and the party leader who has the confidence of the legislature becomes prime minister	In **presidential governments**, the executive is elected separately from the legislature, which means that a president possesses their own personal electoral mandate
The prime minister is accountable to the legislature and so their government can be dismissed by Parliament if they lose a vote of confidence	Since a president is separately elected from the legislature, they are not accountable to the legislature
Although a prime minister is head of government, they are not head of state. In the UK the head of state is the monarch, although most of their governing powers are now devolved to the prime minister	A president combines the role of head of government with head of state
The prime minister works closely with the cabinet. Its membership is selected by the prime minister from the legislature and it regularly meets under the chairmanship of the prime minister. As a result of the principle of collective ministerial responsibility, the prime minister will want to achieve consensus within the cabinet	The president selects the cabinet from outside the legislature. It meets much less frequently than the British cabinet and is rarely chaired by the president. It plays more of an advisory role rather than a central role in American politics

A close analysis of the prime ministerships of Harold Wilson, Margaret Thatcher, Tony Blair and Theresa May provides a powerful insight into the nature and extent of prime ministerial power and how much the nature of the relationship between the prime minister and cabinet can depend on forces beyond their control.

Key term

Presidential government
The presidentialism of UK politics suggests that there is now a greater focus on the prime minister as representative of the nation. It implies a close personal relationship between the leader and the public not normally associated with parliamentary democracy.

Case study

Harold Wilson

Harold Wilson is often regarded as a highly presidential prime minister who liked to ignore cabinet and would make key decisions regarding policy within a small group of trusted advisers known as his 'kitchen cabinet'. Ted Short, Wilson's chief whip, even called Wilson's cabinet 'the doodling cabinet' since so little of importance was discussed in it. In her diaries, Barbara Castle, one of the most prominent members of his cabinet, frequently vented her frustration that Wilson had already decided with his closest advisers what to do before cabinet even met.

Richard Crossman, another leading member of Wilson's cabinet, was similarly critical, in his diaries and in his book *The Myth of Cabinet Government* (1972), of the way in which Wilson bypassed cabinet. 'So Cabinet as a Cabinet is meeting less and is less effectively controlling policy than ever before,' he wrote on 9 March 1969.

However, although Wilson liked to give the *impression* of presidentialism, in reality he was prime minister of a party which was strongly divided between left and right and his cabinet was full of extraordinarily strong and combative figures, many of whom wanted his job. His dominance of the cabinet and his control of events can be exaggerated, as the following examples demonstrate.

- In 1969 Wilson came into conflict with his cabinet over his plans to introduce legal restrictions on the power of the trade unions. This was naturally going to be controversial for a Labour government and the White Paper 'In Place of Strife', introduced by the employment secretary Barbara Castle, led to a furious row in cabinet. Opposition from a majority of the cabinet, led by home secretary James Callaghan, eventually forced Wilson into a humiliating climb-down.

Although Harold Wilson is often seen as a presidential prime minister, on key issues he had to adapt his policies in the face of cabinet opposition

'It became clear that Harold's self-confidence, complacency, bounce and good temper were all breaking down. At one point he said, "Well, you're all giving this up because it's unpopular" … He was a little man, for the first time dragged down to our level. It was painful because in a sense he was sabotaged and utterly nonplussed.'

Richard Crossman's diary, 17 June 1969

- One of the key reasons why Wilson succeeded in winning the February 1974 general election had been by promising a referendum on British membership of the EEC. By 1975 Wilson, following limited renegotiation of the terms of British membership, was prepared to support Britain's continued membership. However, many Labour MPs opposed membership of the EEC, a special conference of the Labour Party had also demanded withdrawal and the cabinet remained divided on the issue of membership. As a result of this Wilson *had* to allow a free vote by cabinet, acknowledging that on this important issue he could not enforce the principle of collective ministerial responsibility.

Case study

Margaret Thatcher

Margaret Thatcher had a complex relationship with her cabinet. Although she had a very clear sense of purpose, when she initially became prime minister she appreciated the importance of thoroughly discussing issues in cabinet in order to maintain government consensus. This was especially important because she had to balance her supporters with those who were associated with her predecessor, Edward Heath, and more one-nation elements within the party.

- In 1981 Thatcher allowed extensive cabinet debate about Geoffrey Howe's controversial tax-raising Budget.
- When Argentina invaded the Falklands in 1982, Thatcher called an emergency meeting of the cabinet to debate the feasibility of sending a task force to recover the Falklands from Argentinean occupation.

In focus

Margaret Thatcher and the cabinet

Although Margaret Thatcher boasted, 'I don't mind how much my Ministers talk, so long as they do what I say', in reality she was much more politically astute than that. In his memoirs, *Kind of Blue*, Kenneth Clarke recalls, 'Although Margaret could speak for at least half of any cabinet meeting and was a poor chairman on that account, she did let other ministers express their views and could be prevailed upon to change her mind or even, occasionally, be overruled.

Margaret Thatcher with her cabinet, 1983. Her growing unwillingness to debate controversial issues, like the poll tax, in cabinet eventually contributed to her downfall

---

- However, following her victories over Argentina (1982) and the miners (1984–85) Thatcher became increasingly assertive in cabinet. In 1986, during the Westland crisis, Michal Heseltine resigned as her defence secretary on the grounds that his opinion was no longer being listened to. Instead she preferred to make decisions with a small group of key advisers who shared her political opinions.
- This failure to consult cabinet proved to be Thatcher's downfall. In 1989, her chancellor of the exchequer, Nigel Lawson, resigned because he complained she was listening to her special economics adviser, Alan Walters, more than him. This high-profile resignation significantly undermined her authority.
- Her increasingly eurosceptic speeches also put her so at odds with the majority of her cabinet that her deputy prime minister, Geoffrey Howe, resigned, prompting Michael Heseltine to challenge her for the party leadership.
- When Heseltine won the support of enough Conservative MPs to take his leadership challenge to a second round, Thatcher needed the support of the cabinet to survive. However, having been taken for granted for so long, one by one the cabinet told her she should resign because she would lose. As Thatcher put it, 'it was treachery with a smile'.
- In the end, although she had promised to 'let her name go forward for the second ballot', Thatcher was left with no choice but to announce her resignation on 22 November 1990.

Case study

Tony Blair

Like Margaret Thatcher, Tony Blair possessed great self-confidence and a very clear vision of what he wanted to achieve as prime minister. In the 1997 general election he also achieved a massive parliamentary majority of 179, which gave him an extraordinary personal mandate to implement change. Blair's commitment to the centrist third way also provided his government with strong philosophical foundations. More than any other postwar British prime minister, Blair enjoyed, too, a strong rapport with the British people, which reached far beyond traditional party loyalties and further persuaded him that cabinet was insignificant in policy development.

Blair's approach was, therefore, highly presidential and his government has often been referred to as a 'command prime-ministership', in which the cabinet was so diminished that it was just notified of decisions that had already been made in the prime minister's Private Office. This has also been referred to as a 'sofa government', in which Blair made key decisions in bilateral meetings with senior ministers and key advisers such as Jonathan Powell, his chief of staff, and Alastair Campbell, his press secretary.

Tony Blair, prime minister 1997–2007. Critics claim that the limitations of Blair's presidential style of government were exposed by the lack of cabinet debate over the invasion of Iraq in 2003

- Even before his first cabinet had met, Blair and his chancellor of the exchequer, Gordon Brown, decided to give interest-raising powers to the Bank of England. This was a momentous political decision which was designed to encourage economic stability by stopping the government from manipulating interest rates to its advantage. When Robin Butler, the chief secretary to the cabinet, asked if the prime minister would like to discuss this decision with the cabinet first, Blair responded, 'They'll agree'.
- Blair was personally in favour of building the Millennium Dome so, even though this was strenuously opposed in cabinet, he ignored his colleagues' reservations and plans continued for the building of the Dome.
- Preparations for the Iraq War in 2003 provide the most striking evidence for the way in which the cabinet was not consulted by Blair on key issues. The publication of the Chilcot Report in 2016 shows how Blair failed to consult the cabinet about the advisability of war and that most members of his government accepted the decision to invade Iraq as a *fait accompli*.
- However, even Blair's dominance of cabinet was not total. Part of the deal whereby Gordon Brown would not challenge Blair for the leadership of the Labour Party in 1994 was that Brown would have full control of the British economy. Even though Blair was keen to join the European single currency, Brown continually roadblocked this by demanding that his 'five tests' for membership first be fulfilled.
- Like Margaret Thatcher, Blair's control of cabinet diminished as his authority waned. Controversies over the legality of the Iraq War and the political fallout of the 2005 general election, which Blair won with only 35.2% of the popular vote (the lowest a single-party government had ever achieved), took Blair from being an electoral asset to being an electoral liability. The cabinet increasingly looked to Gordon Brown to provide the government with a new dynamic, especially since in 2005 the youthful David Cameron had taken over the leadership of the Conservative Party. In September 2006, having squandered his effortless control of cabinet, Blair announced that he would resign as prime minister within a year.

Case study

Theresa May

When Theresa May became prime minister in 2016, she was expected to provide firm leadership. Having survived 6 years in the notoriously challenging role of home secretary, she had won the support of 61% of the parliamentary Conservative Party in the second ballot of the leadership contest and in her first speech as prime minister she provided a clear vision of what she wanted her government to achieve. Jeremy Corbyn's abysmal poll ratings further suggested that she would be able to dominate domestic politics.

Theresa May, like every Conservative prime minister since Margaret Thatcher, saw her authority undermined by party divisions over Europe

- Her ruthless reorganisation of cabinet quickly stamped May's authority on the new government, especially the sacking of George Osborne as chancellor of the exchequer and his replacement with her long-time ally, Philip Hammond. Another of May's key supporters, Amber Rudd, took over as home secretary.

- Theresa May also put her personal prestige behind controversial commitments such as the reintroduction of grammar schools, allowing a free vote on fox hunting and repealing the Human Rights Act in favour of a British Bill of Rights.

- The decision to call a snap general election was not discussed in cabinet. Instead the decision was taken by Theresa May with her trusted joint chiefs of staff, Nick Timothy and Fiona Hill. The Conservative manifesto was then drawn up by Downing Street with no input from the cabinet.

- However, even at the height of her popularity there were significant constraints on her authority since she had to balance her government so that both Remain and Leave Conservatives were given important ministerial roles.

- Her unexpectedly poor campaigning in the 2017 general election dramatically diminished her authority because she was personally associated with the government's loss of its parliamentary majority. This impacted on her ability to command the loyalty of her cabinet, especially since Jeremy Corbyn had achieved a 9.6% swing to Labour.

- Lacking a parliamentary majority, and with a disunited party, May's ambitious plans for more grammar schools, a free vote on fox hunting and the repeal of the Human Rights Act then had to be scrapped as the government instead had to focus all of its energy on achieving Brexit.

- As prime minister of a minority government, Theresa May also had to rely on the support of the Democratic Unionist Party, which added new constraints to her freedom of action.

- In addition, as the date for the UK to exit the EU came closer, the difficulty of reconciling differing interpretations of Brexit became increasingly apparent. The resignations of David Davis as Brexit secretary and Boris Johnson as foreign secretary after the cabinet decision to pursue a softer Brexit, further exposed the divisions within the party, challenging her authority. Boris Johnson's resignation letter, in particular, was meant to wound May: 'Brexit should be about opportunity and hope. It should be a chance to do things differently, to be more nimble and dynamic, and to maximise the particular advantage of the UK as an open, outward-looking global economy. That dream is dying, suffocated by needless self-doubt.' Massive parliamentary defeats of her Brexit deal proposals in January and March 2019 further undermined her grip on power.

- Under increasing pressure from within the Conservative Party, Theresa May announced in May 2019 that she would step down as party leader and prime minister. On 24 July 2019 Boris Johnson replaced her as PM, having been decisively elected Conservative Party leader.

Summary

By the end of this chapter you should be able to answer the following questions:

→ What are the main powers of the prime minister?

→ From where do those powers come?

→ What factors influence the prime minister's selection of the cabinet?

→ What is the significance of individual and collective ministerial responsibility?

→ For what reasons do ministers resign?

→ What factors determine the influence that a prime minister can wield?

→ Why are some prime ministers more powerful than others?

→ What are the differences between presidential and prime-ministerial government?

→ To what extent can British prime ministers be presidential?

Practice questions

Source-based question

The prime minister has the power to determine government policy by being:

● head of the government, responsible for its strategic direction and armed with the power of patronage arising from the exercise of the royal prerogative

● party leader, responsible for party management and discipline

● the government's principal media spokesperson

● able to manage the agenda of the cabinet

Through the judicious deployment of these powers the prime minister can lead government provided ministers are willing, or can be coerced, to follow. A prime minister's influence also ebbs and flows considerably; for example, at her peak a naturally autocratic Margaret Thatcher exerted more influence than the more emollient John Major. Tony Blair was a more assertive prime minister than James Callaghan. In general, however, the array of powers and privileges a British prime minister possesses allows them to head up one of the most centralised systems of executive government in the western world. However, the extent to which they can use this power is determined by such factors as parliamentary majority, their backbench and frontbench popularity and their news media profile.

Source: Adapted from Richard Heffernan (2000), 'Presidentialization in the United Kingdom', **www.tinyurl.com/y3ba3ltk**

Using the source, evaluate the view that the prime minister is the dominant force in British politics.

In your response you must:

● *compare and contrast the different opinions in the source*

● *examine and debate these views in a balanced way*

● *analyse and evaluate only the information presented in the source* (30)

Evaluative questions

1 Evaluate the view that the cabinet plays an insignificant role in British politics. *In your answer you should draw on relevant knowledge and understanding of the study of Component 1 UK Politics and Core Political Ideas and consider this view and the alternative to this view in a balanced way.* (30)

2 Evaluate the view that a prime minister's main priority when selecting a cabinet is to advance his or her political allies. *In your answer you should draw on relevant knowledge and understanding of the study of Component 1 UK Politics and Core Political Ideas and consider this view and the alternative to this view in a balanced way.* (30)

3 Evaluate the view that the prime minister is now a president in all but name. *In your answer you should draw on relevant knowledge and understanding of the study of Component 1 UK Politics and Core Political Ideas and consider this view and the alternative to this view in a balanced way.* (30)

Relations between branches

The impact of the Supreme Court on legislative and policy-making processes

The role and composition of the Supreme Court

Key term

Supreme Court
Established in 2009, the Supreme Court is the highest court of appeal in the UK. Its 12 justices comprise the most senior judges in the country and its judgements can carry great legal, constitutional and political significance.

The judiciary represents the courts and judges, who dispense justice throughout the United Kingdom. Lower courts such as Crown Courts and Magistrates' Courts resolve cases. The judgements that are reached in more senior courts, such as the High Court, Court of Appeal and **Supreme Court**, are especially important because they set legal precedents which can then be referred to in subsequent cases. This is a key function of the more senior courts.

Although Parliament enacts legislation, the meaning and relevance of those laws have to be worked out by judges. This is because, in a particular case, it may not be certain how an Act of Parliament should be interpreted. Indeed, there may not even be a relevant Act of Parliament to refer to. The way in which senior judges interpret Acts of Parliament and resolve cases thus creates a legal precedent, known as case law or judge-made law, which judges will be expected to follow in subsequent cases. This provides the basis for British common law, in which the decisions of senior judges in previous cases achieve the force of precedence. As Bishop Benjamin Hoadly (1676–1761) put it: 'Whoever hath an absolute authority to interpret any written or spoken laws, it is he who is truly the lawgiver and not the person who first wrote or spake them.'

Lady Hale (front row) has been president of the Supreme Court since 2017

As the final court of appeal in the United Kingdom, the judgements reached by the UK Supreme Court are of profound importance. Important cases, in which the meaning of the law is uncertain, are judged by the Supreme Court and the decisions that it reaches have to be followed in future cases.

The UK Supreme Court is a relatively new court. The highest court of appeal in the UK had been the House of Lords, where the 12 Law Lords delivered judgements in the Appellate Committee. However, the fact that the most senior judges in the UK sat in the House of Lords breached the principle of the 'separation of powers', whereby the judiciary ought to be separate from the legislature. Therefore, as part of the Blair government's commitment to modernising the British constitution, the Constitutional Reform Act 2005 was passed. This removed the Law Lords from the House of Lords and, in its place, established the Supreme Court.

- The 12 most senior judges in the UK now sit in the Supreme Court and are called Justices of the Supreme Court. The head of the Supreme Court is known as its President.
- The work of the new Supreme Court is more open to public scrutiny than had been the case with the Appellate Committee.
- The jurisdiction of the Supreme Court reaches across the UK and it is the highest court of appeal for all civil cases. It is also the final court of appeal for all criminal cases in England, Wales and Northern Ireland. In Scotland, the High Court of the Justiciary, in most cases, fulfils this role.
- The Supreme Court is the final court of appeal when there is a judicial review of how the government has acted.
- The Supreme Court also has the authority to determine whether an issue ought to be under the jurisdiction of the British government or a devolved body.
- The membership of the Supreme Court is determined by a five-member Selection Commission made up of the most senior judges in the UK. Their nominations are then passed to the justice secretary for approval, who has one opportunity to reject a nomination. Once agreed, the prime minister will ask the monarch to make the appointment.

It is, of course, vital that the Justices of the Supreme Court are independent of the legislature and the executive. The rule of law depends on judges not being influenced by the government. Instead the decisions that they reach should be entirely based on the principles of justice. Judges are also expected to be neutral, which means that their judgements should never be influenced by any social or political prejudice.

The neutrality and independence of the Supreme Court

Critics of the Supreme Court's ability to provide justice argue that its membership is so privileged that the decisions it makes are unlikely to reflect the way in which the law impacts on modern society. Most Justices of the Supreme Court have been privately educated and attended Oxford or Cambridge universities, and so these rarefied experiences could make them ill-suited to interpreting the law in a contemporary setting. In short, might the privileges and prejudices of their class hinder the justices of the Supreme Court from being neutral? Men also dominate the Supreme Court. In 2019, for example, there were just three female justices on it, further making it an unrepresentative body.

Stretch and challenge

Analyse the gender mix and educational background of the Supreme Court justices. Does this suggest that the Supreme Court is highly unrepresentative of contemporary British society? Explain whether or not you think this matters.

That the members of the Supreme Court are generally from such an elite background has traditionally led to claims that they tend to favour the Establishment. In 1977, John Griffith, a radical socialist academic, argued in *The Politics of the Judiciary* that socially and politically conservative judges always favour the status quo. One of the most famous judges of the twentieth century, Lord Denning (1899–1999) sided with the government on a number of occasions. In the Hosenball case (1977), for example, he boldly asserted, 'In some parts of the world national security has been used as an excuse for all sorts of infringements of individual liberty. But not in England.'

In focus

Do judges represent the Establishment?

Judges have often been stereotyped as representing the interests of what is called 'the Establishment'. This suggests that, as privileged members of the social elite, they tend to look more favourably upon members of their own class. A famous example of this is the way in which Justice Cantley presided over the trial at the Old Bailey in 1979 of former Liberal leader Jeremy Thorpe for conspiracy to murder Norman Scott. It has been alleged that Cantley's summing up to the jury was especially prejudiced against Norman Scott, the key prosecution witness, who, as a gay stable boy, was definitely not part of the Establishment: 'He is a crook, a fraud, a sponger, a whiner and a parasite ... but of course, he could still be telling the truth ...' Thorpe and his co-defendants were all acquitted.

Synoptic link

The effectiveness of the Supreme Court in protecting civil liberties links to Component 1, UK Politics (see pages 35–36).

The government also retains some political influence over the appointment of Justices of the Supreme Court. The Constitutional Reform Act 2005 merged the position of Lord Chancellor with that of justice secretary. The justice secretary, who does not need to have a legal background, is a member of the cabinet. Despite this, the selection committee for new Justices of the Supreme Court has to pass their recommendations to the justice secretary, who can request further information and retains the right to reject a nominee. This power would only be used in exceptional circumstances and only one nomination can be rejected, but it does show how there is not a complete separation of powers in the UK. Once the justice secretary is satisfied then the prime minister will ask the monarch to make the appointment.

The high-profile involvement of the Supreme Court in cases concerning the government also risks it being pulled into major political disputes, which could compromise its neutrality. This was particularly the case over Brexit, as well as in major decisions involving the interpretation of human rights legislation.

In what ways can the Supreme Court claim to be independent and neutral?

- Opened in 2009, the UK Supreme Court is housed in Middlesex Guildhall and directly faces Parliament on Westminster Square. This physical separation from Parliament is in itself an important statement of the court's political independence.
- Judges in the UK are not permitted to be members of a political party. A barrister or solicitor may be a member of a political party and may pursue a political career but, once appointed, a judge must abandon any political ambitions and associations.
- The salaries of judges are not determined by Parliament. Instead the government follows the recommendations of the Senior Salaries Review Body and payment is made directly from the Consolidated Fund. This mechanism ensures that no government could seek to influence the judiciary through providing it with financial incentives to look favourably on its policies.
- Since the Act of Settlement in 1701, which established the Protestant succession to the Crown, a senior judge can only be removed by a resolution passed by both houses of Parliament. This means that they have, in effect, security of tenure and so cannot be removed from office by the government. As a result of this, judges can act according to how they think the law should be interpreted without fearing the consequence of loss of office.
- The Constitutional Reform Act 2005 further promoted the independence of the senior judiciary by removing the Law Lords from the Appellate Committee of the House of Lords and establishing the Supreme Court as a separate institution from the legislature.
- The Constitutional Reform Act 2005 was also designed to make appointments to the judiciary more transparent. Previously, the Lord Chancellor had advised the prime minister through 'secret soundings' of senior judges. This, it could be argued, led to a self-perpetuating socially elitist judiciary. In its place a new Judicial Appointments Commission was established, which selects judges on their merit and good character, as well as considering the importance of encouraging diversity within the judiciary.
- Appointments to the Supreme Court are decided by a specially summoned five-person selection committee comprising the Lord President of the Supreme Court, a senior judge and representatives of the Judicial Appointments Commission of England and Wales, Scotland and Northern Ireland. If candidates for the Supreme Court are deemed to be of equal merit then the selection committee may 'prefer one candidate over the other for the purpose of increasing diversity within the group of persons who are judges in the court'. This is in contrast to the USA, where the president appoints the membership of the Supreme Court with the consent of the Senate. The influence that the president has over nominations to the US Supreme Court makes it a more politically partisan body than the UK Supreme Court.
- Since court cases are generally open to the public and judgements are in the public domain, any prejudice or bias shown by a judge would be quickly publicised in the media.
- When a case is being heard, it is said to be 'sub judice'. This means that Parliament cannot express an opinion as this would breach the separation of powers and undermine **judicial independence**. If a member of the legislature or executive did express an opinion this would be contempt of court.

> ## Key term
>
> **Judicial independence**
> A central principle of the rule of law is that judges must be independent of control or persuasion by the executive or the legislative. Judges can only fairly administer justice if they are free to act without government pressure.

The claim that socially conservative judges are likely to support the government may have once been true. However, recent cases suggest that the Supreme Court has been quite prepared to confront Parliament and the executive. In the Gina Miller case, for example, it declared that the government did not have the authority to begin the process of beginning the withdrawal from the European Union. When MPs claimed that parliamentary privilege meant they could not be tried in the criminal court, the Supreme Court denied their appeal. Indeed, some politicians have claimed that the Supreme Court has become *too* socially liberal. Labour home secretary David Blunkett (2001–04) was especially critical of senior judges for stopping him limiting the rights of asylum seekers: 'I just want judges that live in the same real world as the rest of us.'

The way in which the Supreme Court has reached decisions in controversial cases involving the government and human rights, far from compromising its independence, has demonstrated the willingness of its justices to confront the government if they believe it is acting beyond its authority or not according to the principles of justice. Table 8.1 gives two such examples.

Table 8.1 Two high-profile Supreme Court cases

Al Rawi and others v *The Security Service and others* (2011)	*R (on the application of UNISON)* v *Lord Chancellor* (2017)
When former detainees of the American prison Guantánamo Bay claimed that the British security services shared responsibility for their imprisonment and ill treatment, the British government argued that the evidence of the heads of security should not be given in public in case it breached national security. The Supreme Court decided in favour of the detainees, stating, 'A closed material procedure … involves a departure from the principle of open and natural justice which are essential features of a common law trial.'	In 2017 the trade union UNISON brought a case to the Supreme Court declaring that the government's introduction of employment tribunal fees was unlawful. The Supreme Court agreed that the fees risked denying justice to those on low incomes and so were discriminatory. In their judgement the justices declared, 'The Fees Order is unlawful … because it has the effect of denying access to justice. Since it had that effect as soon as it was made, it was therefore unlawful and must be quashed.'

The Supreme Court and parliamentary privilege

According to the principle of parliamentary privilege, Members of Parliament cannot be prosecuted in civil and criminal courts for the actions they take or the statements they make as part of their parliamentary duties within the Palace of Westminster.

In the case of *R v Chaytor and others* (2010) three MPs – David Chaytor, Jim Devine and Elliot Morley – claimed that they could not be tried in the Crown Court on the charge of false accounting of their parliamentary expenses. This was because these actions had taken place as part of their parliamentary duties and so were covered by parliamentary privilege.

The Supreme Court, however, ruled that parliamentary privilege did not extend to criminal offences which take place within Westminster:

'The Houses of Parliament and their dependencies are in England and so the criminal law of England applies to what is done there. The most famous illustration of this elementary point is, perhaps, the murder of the Prime Minister, Mr Spencer Percival, in the lobby of the House of Commons in 1812. John Bellingham was arrested, prosecuted, tried for murder at the Old Bailey, convicted and executed — all according to the common law of England … To come to the present case — if a Member of Parliament dishonestly, with a view to gain for himself, submitted a claim form which to his knowledge was false in a material particular, the law of England would apply.'

David Chaytor MP, Jim Devine MP and Elliot Morley MP all received prison sentences for false accounting.

To what extent does the Supreme Court influence the executive and Parliament?

Since the UK does not have a codified constitution, the Supreme Court cannot refer to a higher constitutional law when delivering its judgements. This makes the British Supreme Court less powerful than the Supreme Courts of countries which have a codified constitution. In the USA, for example, judges are able to strike down laws if they conflict with the higher law of the Constitution.

However, the Supreme Court still has important constitutional and political functions including:

- Determining the meaning of the law, so setting judicial precedents which must be followed in future cases.
- Deciding whether a public body, including the government, has acted beyond its authority.
- Establishing where sovereignty is located within the UK.
- Declaring when government has acted in defiance of the Human Rights Act.

Determining the meaning of the law

As the final court of appeal, the decisions of the Supreme Court carry greater weight in developing the meaning of the law. In *R v Jogee* (2016), the Supreme Court overturned the principle of 'joint enterprise', which was established in common law whereby those who were part of a group which incited a murder could be convicted of the crime in the same way as the one who had actually done the killing. Instead, the Supreme Court stated that there had to be '*intent* to kill' shown if members of a group were all to be held guilty of murder. In a number of other cases the Supreme Court has also had to determine the extent to which the Human Rights Act impacts on the individual's relationship with the state.

The Supreme Court and human rights

P v Cheshire West and Cheshire Council (2014)

The judgements of the Supreme Court play a vital role in determining the meaning of human rights legislation, including the significance and impact of the Human Rights Act.

In the case of 'P', a man with Down's syndrome and cerebral palsy was placed with social services, who limited his personal freedom as part of his care. In a powerful judgement, with far-reaching consequences for the care of mentally disabled people, Lady Hale stated:

> 'Far from disability entitling the state to deny such people human rights rather it places upon the state (and upon others) the duty to make reasonable accommodation to cater for the special needs of those with disabilities ... Those rights include the right to personal liberty which is guaranteed by Article 5 of the European Convention ... If it would be a deprivation of my liberty to be obliged to live in a particular place subject to constant monitoring and control and unable to move away without permission even if such an opportunity became available then it must also be a deprivation of the liberty of a disabled person. The fact that my living arrangements are comfortable, and indeed make my life as enjoyable as it could possibly be, should make no difference. A gilded cage is still a cage.'

Establishing whether a public body has acted ultra vires

During a judicial review of the actions of a public body, the Supreme Court can decide whether the body has acted beyond its authority (**ultra vires**). For example, in 2016, the Supreme Court stated that when he was justice secretary, Chris Grayling had acted ultra vires when he amended the Legal Aid Act to restrict civil legal aid to people who had lived continuously abroad for 12 months. The Supreme Court stated that a decision as important as this should have been debated in Parliament and so Grayling had not had the authority to introduce it through secondary legislation.

Key term

Ultra vires The principle that one has 'acted beyond one's authority'. If the courts rule that a public body has acted beyond its authority then these actions can be quashed because they have not been legally carried out.

Determining the location of sovereignty in the United Kingdom

Given the way in which the location of sovereignty in the UK can be disputed, the role of the Supreme Court in establishing where sovereign power lies is crucial. This has been notably demonstrated in the Gina Miller case (2017).

Sovereignty: the Gina Miller case

R. Miller v Secretary of State for Exiting the European Union (2017)

The consequences of the Gina Miller case for Brexit negotiations were profound

The Gina Miller case demonstrates the constitutional significance of the Supreme Court. Following the EU referendum on 23 June 2016, the government claimed that it could begin the process of leaving the European Union through the exercise of the royal prerogative. However, on 24 January 2017, the Supreme Court, by a majority of 8–3, upheld an earlier decision taken in the High Court which stated that the government did not have the authority to do this. This was because Parliament in 1972 had enacted the legislation which had taken the UK into the EU and so it was Parliament's responsibility to enact legislation to remove the UK from membership of the EU. In addition, since withdrawal would remove certain legal rights from UK citizens this could not be done without the consent of Parliament. As the President of the Supreme Court, Lord Neuberger, stated in the Supreme Court's judgement:

> 'Withdrawal effects a fundamental change by cutting off the source of EU law, as well as changing legal rights … The UK's constitutional arrangements require such changes to be clearly authorised by Parliament.'

The fact that the High Court and then the Supreme Court had both declared that Parliament must consent to the government opening negotiations to withdraw from the EU was seen by some supporters of Brexit as an attempt to subvert the result of the referendum. The *Daily Mail* ran a highly controversial front cover condemning as 'enemies of the people' the High Court judges who stated that Parliament must be consulted. Neither court was doing this. Instead, the Gina Miller case clarified the following vital constitutional principles:

- The Supreme Court can determine the occasions on which the government can deploy the royal prerogative.
- The government must consult Parliament if it seeks to abolish rights which Parliament has already bestowed.
- Claims by the government that the vote to leave the EU in the 2016 referendum gave the government the right to begin the process was illegal, since the result of a referendum is legally non-binding.

The way in which the Miller case upheld parliamentary sovereignty against claims that the result of a referendum could empower the government to ignore Parliament makes it one of the most significant constitutional decisions of recent years.

Declarations of incompatibility with the Human Rights Act

Due to the principle of parliamentary sovereignty, the judges cannot strike down an Act of Parliament. However, the Human Rights Act states that 'so far as it is possible to do so, primary legislation and subordinate legislation must be read and given effect in a way which is compatible with the Convention rights'. As a result, there is the expectation that Parliament should legislate in accordance with the European Convention on Human Rights. If this is not possible then the judges can issue a formal statement of incompatibility, which will put significant pressure on the government to amend the law.

The Belmarsh case (2004) provides a classic example of this. In 2004, the Blair government used the powers given to it by the Anti-Terrorism Crime and Security Act 2001 to hold *foreign* terrorist suspects indefinitely without trial. The Law Lords declared that that was discriminatory according to the European Convention on Human Rights since British terrorist suspects were not being treated in the same way. The government accepted the ruling. However, soon after, Parliament legislated to introduce control orders, which enabled the government to monitor the whereabouts of foreign terrorist suspects in a different manner. This shows that, although a declaration of incompatibility can have significant moral influence, Parliament's power to circumvent the judiciary is still great.

Debate

Is the Supreme Court influential?

Yes

- The Supreme Court is the UK's most senior court and final court of appeal.
- The Justices of the Supreme Court are the most senior judges in the UK and their interpretation of the meaning of the law is final.
- If the Supreme Court declares a formal statement of incompatibility between an Act of Parliament and the European Convention on Human Rights, that will put significant political pressure on the government to amend the law.
- The Supreme Court also determines the location of sovereignty in the UK and can declare when a public body has acted illegally by acting beyond its authority (ultra vires).

No

- Since the UK Parliament is legally sovereign, the Supreme Court cannot strike down an Act of Parliament.
- The Supreme Court cannot initiate cases. It only determines cases which are brought to it.
- The government could ignore a declaration of incompatibility.
- Although the Supreme Court interprets the meaning of the law, it is also bound by what the law states.
- Although the Supreme Court can quash the decision of a public body for acting beyond its authority, Parliament could then legislate to give that body the legal powers which it did not have before.

The relationship between the executive and Parliament

Factors determining the influence and effectiveness of Parliament on the executive

In the British parliamentary system, the executive sits within Parliament. The executive and the legislature are thus fused. As a result of parliamentary sovereignty, the executive is accountable to the House of Commons since it represents the will of the British people expressed through the MPs they elect.

In spite of this, it has often been claimed that Parliament is ineffective at holding the government accountable for its actions. Lord Hailsham, a leading Conservative lawyer and politician, even claimed that the executive had so much power that it could be called an '**elective dictatorship**'. This is because:

- The government exerts a great deal of control over parliamentary business. This limits opportunities for the opposition to debate government legislation.
- Since Public Bill Committees always have a government majority and are whipped, it is unusual for the opposition to be able to significantly amend legislation at committee stage.
- A government with a large parliamentary majority should be able to rely on the support of its MPs to pass the legislative programme it wishes.
- The government can change the law using secondary legislation, over which the House of Commons has much less power of scrutiny.
- The prime minister possesses extensive powers of patronage. Government whips will, therefore, be able to offer ambitious backbenchers opportunities to join the government or withhold any chance of advancement. This is a powerful way in which the government can encourage loyalty.
- The royal prerogative means that the prime minister does not legally have to consult Parliament on the use of British military forces, as Theresa May showed in 2018 when she did not seek parliamentary approval for air strikes on Syrian chemical installations.
- According to the Salisbury Convention, the House of Lords should not attempt to stop government legislation that was in the winning party's manifesto, since this would obstruct what the public had voted for.

However, the relationship between Parliament and the executive is not static. It changes depending on circumstances. For example, a minority government or one with a small parliamentary majority will find it much more difficult to pass its legislative programme, especially if it cannot rely on the loyalty of its backbenchers. When this is the case, both houses of Parliament can become more assertive. Equally, if the opposition is united around a strong leader who is widely expected to win the next general election then this can undermine the confidence of the government.

Examples of weak parliamentary influence

- **1979–87** Margaret Thatcher's determined leadership of the Conservative Party contrasted with divisions within Labour, which led to the party fracturing and the foundation of the Social Democratic Party in 1981. This meant that the Conservatives were facing a split opposition and, in 1983, having won the Falklands War, Thatcher increased her parliamentary majority to 144. In these circumstances, neither Michael Foot (1980–83) nor Neil Kinnock (1983–92) was able to effectively challenge her policies in the House of Commons.

> **Key term**
>
> **Elective dictatorship**
> In 1976, Lord Hailsham stated that the ability of a British government to dominate Parliament meant it was essentially an elective dictatorship.

> **Synoptic link**
>
> The authority of a prime minister depends greatly on how united their party is. This links to Component 1, UK Politics (see pages 44–56).

The European Union

The aims of the EU

The **European Union (EU)** can be traced back to the Schuman Declaration (1950) when, in the aftermath of the Second World War, the French foreign secretary, Robert Schuman, proposed that France and Germany pool their production of coal and steel under one supranational authority, which other West European states would be free to join:

'By pooling basic production and by instituting a new High Authority, whose decisions will bind France, Germany and many other countries, this proposal will lead to the realisation of the first concrete foundation of a European federation indispensable to the preservation of peace.'

For 4 days every month the European Parliament moves from Brussels to Strasbourg. Critics of the European Union use this as evidence of the EU's wastefulness and inefficiency

The idea was that by removing coal and steel production from national control, war between member states of the European Coal and Steel Community (ECSC) would be made impossible.

The ECSC provided the basis for the European Economic Community (EEC), which was established by the Treaty of Rome in 1957. The opening paragraph of the Treaty of Rome lays down that the aim of the EEC should be 'an ever closer union among the peoples of Europe'. All subsequent treaties between its member states have increased the process towards fuller European integration. According to the principle of pooling sovereignty, member states would achieve greater political influence by sharing power within a much larger political organisation.

As well as greater pooling of sovereignty through deeper interconnectedness, the EEC/EU has significantly increased its membership across the continent. By 2013 it had increased to 28 member states from six in 1957.

The aims of integration and expansion are to encourage peace, prosperity and liberal democracy across Europe, so banishing the prospect of war by eliminating the national differences and jealousies which can encourage conflict. As Table 8.2 demonstrates, the deepening of the relationship between member states and the widening of the EU to cover most of Europe have taken place in step.

Table 8.2 The enlargement of the EEC/EU

Deepening	Widening
Treaties and agreements	**Expansion of the EEC/EU**
1957 The European Economic Community is established by the Treaty of Rome	1973 UK, Ireland and Denmark join
1985 The Schengen Agreement establishes the principle of passport-free travel across most member states of the European Union	1981 Greece joins
1986 The Single European Act commits the European Economic Community to the creation of a single internal market	1986 Spain and Portugal join
1992 The Maastricht Treaty establishes the European Union with a common citizenship. It commits members to pursuing a common foreign and security policy and launches plans for a single European currency	1995 Austria, Sweden and Finland join
1997 The Amsterdam Treaty incorporates the Schengen Agreement (omitting the UK and Ireland) and Social Chapter into EU law	2004 Malta, Cyprus, Estonia, Lithuania, Latvia, Poland, Czech Republic, Slovakia, Slovenia and Hungary join
2000 The Nice Treaty further reduces occasions when member states can use their national veto by increasing opportunities for qualified majority voting	2007 Bulgaria and Romania join
2002 The European single currency is launched into circulation as national currencies are withdrawn in the eurozone	2013 Croatia joins
2007 The Lisbon Treaty provides the EU with its own diplomatic corps and creates the new positions of a full-time EU President and High Representative for Foreign Affairs and Security Policy in order to give the EU the potential for greater international influence	

The four freedoms

The core economic aspiration of European integration is expressed in the '**four freedoms**' which were laid down in the original Treaty of Rome and envisaged a European single market. The Single European Act and the Lisbon Treaty have further recognised the centrality of a fully functioning single market to European integration. Under the four freedoms, among member states there should be:

- the free movement of goods: member states should not impose tariffs on goods from another member state, so creating a customs union
- the free movement of services: businesses should be able to open up and operate in any member state
- the free movement of capital: capital should be able to move freely throughout the member states
- the free movement of people: no internal barriers should stop citizens of the EU working in any member state and being able to claim the same social benefits

By eliminating national barriers, members of the EU would achieve so much prosperity through interconnectedness that war between them would be unthinkable. The liberal principle of Frédéric Bastiat (1801–50), that 'if goods do not cross borders, armies will', is thus of central importance to European integration.

In addition to economic integration, the EU has pursued 'ever closer union' in terms of social, political and monetary unity, as well developing closer foreign policy and defence objectives.

> **Key term**
>
> **Four freedoms** The free movement of goods, services, capital and people through which European economic unity is to be achieved.

Monetary union

At the Maastricht Treaty (1992) the principle of monetary union was agreed. This established that European integration would aspire to both economic and monetary union (EMU). In 1999 the euro was introduced as a trading currency and in 2002 the founding member states of the eurozone physically replaced their existing currencies with the euro. The Maastricht Treaty also created the European Central Bank to set a common interest rate for members of the eurozone. By 2019, there were 19 EU member states in the eurozone.

The European Central Bank in Frankfurt, Germany

Social unity

In the 1980s, the president of the European Commission, Jacques Delors, emphasised that European integration should also encourage workers' rights. In recognition of this, the Maastricht Treaty included the Social Chapter, which established certain rights which all workers in the EU can claim in areas such as health and safety, freedom from discrimination, equal treatment for men and women, paid holidays, working hours and conditions, and parental leave on the birth of a child.

The protection of human rights

In 2000, the Charter of Fundamental Rights of the European Union was proclaimed and became legally binding on all member states when they ratified the Lisbon Treaty in 2009. The human rights which the charter guarantees significantly overlap with the European Convention on Human Rights. The main difference is that the charter applies only to areas connected with EU law and is applied through the European Court of Justice.

Political union

Since the Single European Act 1986 all EU treaties have restricted the occasions on which nation states are able to exercise the veto in the Council of Ministers/ European Council, so advancing political integration. The Maastricht Treaty (1992) also established a common EU citizenship and, significantly, changed the name of the European Economic Community to the European Union.

Common foreign and defence policy

The Maastricht Treaty (1992) committed the EU to a common foreign and defence policy. This was advanced in practical terms by the Lisbon Treaty (2007), as it provided the EU with a legal identity so that it can negotiate on equal terms with nation states and an EU diplomatic service. Lisbon also established a full-time President of the European Council and a High Commissioner for Foreign Affairs and Security Policy, both of whom represent the EU in its dealings with other world leaders.

The European Union and the migrant crisis

The Syrian civil war, conflict in Libya, climate change and the chance for a better life have encouraged migrants from across Africa and the Middle East to attempt the dangerous journey to Europe. Unequal responses have meant that some member states have accepted more migrants than others, fuelling resentment. Fears of being swamped by an 'alien culture' have led to the rise of extremist parties across the EU and put the Schengen Agreement under enormous pressure as nation states see advantages to, once again, controlling their own borders.

In the UK, Nigel Farage deployed anti-migrant feeling to encourage support for Brexit, and hard-line governments in Hungary and Italy have established a common anti-migrant front.

Migrants at a refugee camp in Greece, 2018

In 2018, the President of the European Commission, Jean-Claude Juncker, even warned that the crisis could destroy the EU as member states looked to their own interests rather than those of Europe as a whole: 'The fragility of the EU is increasing. The cracks are growing in size.'

Has the European Union achieved its objectives?

Yes

- By 2018 the EU had expanded from six members to 28 members. Turkey, Macedonia, Albania, Serbia and Montenegro have all applied to join.
- The expansion of the EU has encouraged democracy in former Communist states in Eastern Europe.
- The European Charter of Fundamental Freedoms has entrenched core civil liberties in European law.
- The implementation of the four freedoms means that the EU is now the biggest single market in the world, providing EU citizens with the right to live, work or study in any member state.
- In 2018 the EU's gross domestic product (GDP) was worth $19.7 trillion, making the EU the second-biggest economy in the world. This represents 22% of the value of the global economy.
- The euro is the world's second reserve currency (after the US dollar).
- The EU has provided a global lead on issues such as combatting climate change and has been responsible for the most environmentally-friendly legislation in the world.

No

- The expansion of the EU has diluted its purpose, making it more difficult to achieve a united European response to contentious issues such as the Russian annexation of Crimea and the Syrian civil war.
- The commitment of member states such as Hungary and Poland to the democratic principles of the EU is disputed, undermining the EU's sense of common purpose.
- The austerity programmes demanded by the European Commission and European Central Bank in response to the euro crisis have undermined support for the EU in south European countries such as Greece, Italy, Spain and Portugal.
- The removal of barriers to the free flow of workers (one of the four freedoms) has encouraged the rise of populist parties across Europe which are committed to protecting their workforce from 'foreign' competition.
- The migrant crisis has exposed significant tensions between the liberal approach of the German and French governments and the more defensive approach of states such as Hungary and Italy.
- Little progress has been made on establishing a European sense of identity. National identities have even been strengthened as a result of austerity, the free movement of workers and the migrant crisis.

The institutions of the EU

The main institutions of the EU, such as the European Commission, the European Council and the European Central Bank, and the way in which they operate are listed in Table 8.3.

Table 8.3 The main institutions of the European Union

Institution	Description
The European Commission (supranational)	The European Commission is the government (executive) of the EU. Each member state sends a commissioner, who represents the interests of the EU rather than their own state, to its headquarters in Brussels. The Commission is responsible for developing EU policy and ensuring that it is carried through
Council of the European Union (intergovernmental/ supranational)	This is one of the legislative bodies of the EU. Here relevant government ministers decide whether or not to accept legislative proposals from the Commission. Some decisions require unanimity, although increasingly decisions are reached by qualified majority voting
European Council (intergovernmental)	The European Council convenes four times a year when the leaders of the EU and their foreign ministers meet. The Council develops EU foreign policy and makes strategic decisions concerning the future of the EU. According to the Lisbon Treaty, the European Council 'shall provide the union with the necessary impetus for its development'
The European Parliament (supranational)	The European Parliament is the EU's only directly elected body. It sits in both Brussels and Strasbourg and shares legislative and budgetary control with the Council of the European Union

The European Commission is accountable to Parliament and Parliament elects the President of the Commission |
| The European Central Bank (supranational) | Based in Frankfurt, the European Central Bank implements EU economic policy and sets a common interest rate for the members of the eurozone |
| The European Court of Justice (supranational) | The European Court of Justice is based in Luxembourg and ensures that European law is applied equally and interpreted in the same way in all member states |

The impact of the EU on the United Kingdom

From the time the UK joined the EEC in 1973 its membership was contentious. Supporters of the EU could point to the positive social and economic impact of membership, while critics of the EU responded that British membership had undermined democratic accountability, threatened Britain's existence as an independent nation state and created another layer of unnecessary bureaucracy. During the EU referendum in 2016 these were some of the arguments that the Remain and Leave sides deployed.

Benefits for the UK

- Membership of the EU has provided the UK with duty-free access to the world's second-biggest economy. Tariffs reduce trade and UK exporters benefit from being able to sell abroad more cheaply, while UK consumers benefit from cheaper EU imports. In 2016, 43% of British trade was with the EU and was worth £241 billion.

- Most economists agree that the UK economy has benefited from EU immigration. EU immigrants come to the UK to join the workforce and so contribute more to the state in taxation than they claim back in benefits. In 2013–14, non–British EU citizens living in the UK paid £14.7 billion in tax and national insurance and claimed just £2.6 billion in tax credits and child benefit.
- Over 3 million British jobs rely on trade with the EU. The Confederation of British Industry estimated, during the EU referendum, that the net benefit to the UK economy of EU membership was worth between 4% and 5% of GDP.
- As a result of the four freedoms, British entrepreneurs can set up businesses anywhere they want in the EU, students can study freely in the EU and the elderly can retire to an EU country and still receive their British pension. In 2017, 1.3 million British citizens were living in other EU countries.
- Since 1987 the EU's Erasmus programme has encouraged educational exchanges across the EU. Up to 200,000 British students have taken advantage of this to study in EU countries.
- The Social Chapter of the Maastricht Treaty, which the Blair government accepted, provides important safeguards to workers' rights such as the Working Time Directive which guarantees a maximum 48-week working year with 4 weeks' paid holiday.
- The European Charter of Fundamental Freedoms was incorporated into European Law with the Treaty of Lisbon. This has meant that when exercising European law the British government has had to act according to the charter, which has helped to increase the rights of workers and immigrants in the UK.

Around 200,000 British students have taken part in the Erasmus exchange programme

- In an increasingly multipolar world comprising huge nation states like the USA, China and Russia, the UK has best been able to assert shared values such as democracy, human rights and the rule of law through its membership of the EU.
- The EU is the world's most advanced example of a liberal approach to global politics, bringing together independent nation states into a union. From 1900 to 1950, an estimated 110 million people died in European wars. However, since 1957, the EEC/EU has encouraged peace and stability across Europe.

Arguments against membership of the EU

- British membership of the EU undermines parliamentary sovereignty. The key principle of democracy is that representatives are accountable to the public in regular elections. As a result of the pooling of sovereignty in the EU, Parliament has lost its sovereign right to legislate on behalf of the British people. In November 1991, Tony Benn MP put the democratic case against the EEC/EU, and the UK's membership of it, in the House of Commons:

> 'If democracy is destroyed in Britain it will be not the communists, Trotskyists or subversives but this House which threw it away. The rights that are entrusted to us are not for us to give away.'

- The EU has been accused of having a democratic deficit at its heart, since its government, the European Commission, is not directly elected and the EU's only directly elected body, the European Parliament, has less direct influence than most legislative assemblies.
- Critics argue that EU legislation creates another layer of unnecessary law which, since it is applicable to all members of the EU, may not serve the interests of a country's citizens. The implementation of EU regulations in the UK, the think-tank Open Europe estimates, costs £33 billion every year.
- The Common Agricultural Policy (CAP) represents 38% of the EU's budget for 2014–20. It helps to protect the livelihood of EU farmers by subsidising production and protecting them from outside non-EU competition. In 2015, the number of people working in agriculture across the EU as a whole was 4.4% of the EU's workforce. The UK employs just 1.1% of its population in agriculture and so gained proportionately less from the CAP than countries such as Romania where 25.8% of the workforce is employed in agriculture.
- Critics of the CAP also argue that, as a member of the EU, the UK has had to subsidise a protectionist scheme, which discriminates against the developing world and goes against the free-market principles on which the EU is supposed to be founded.
- Although UK trade with the EU in 2016 was 43% of total British trade, it had been 54% in 2006. This suggests that the UK has the potential to engage further in global trade rather than prioritising the European market.
- The UK contributes more to the EU than it gets directly back. This means that although it receives money back through CAP and regional grants to poorer regions of the UK such as Cornwall and South Wales, it is still a net contributor to the EU. In 2017, the UK made a net contribution of £8.9 billion to the EU.
- Attempts by the EU to integrate Europe through the promulgation of the four freedoms have had the opposite effect in member states such as the UK. Rather than encouraging a sense of European identity, it has encouraged xenophobic resentment, especially among C2, D and E voters who generally gained least from EU immigration.

Synoptic link

The way in which Brexit influenced the 2017 general election is covered in Component 1, UK Politics (see pages 127–32).

The Factortame judgement

As a result of legislation establishing a single European market, member states of the EU cannot restrict access to each other's fishing grounds. The Common Fisheries Policy of the EU also set quotas of fish that can be caught in order to preserve fish stocks. The impact of these two policies was highly unpopular in Britain's maritime fishing communities, since it allowed often larger fishing boats from other EU countries to fish British waters. Since what could be caught was now limited, this, fishermen argued, threatened the survival of the British fishing industry. The Common Fisheries Policy gained further notoriety as a result of fish being thrown back into the sea in order not to exceed quotas landed.

In 1988, the Merchant Shipping Act limited the ability of foreign vessels to fish in British waters. This was in defiance of the Common Fisheries Policy and the four freedoms of the EU, and a Spanish fishing company, Factortame, appealed to the House of Lords, which was then the highest court in the UK. In the resulting Factortame judgement, the Law Lords stated that the Merchant Shipping Act should be disapplied because EU law took precedence over national law. According to one of the judges, Lord Bridge, it has 'always been clear that it was the duty of a United Kingdom court when delivering final judgement, to override any rule of national law found to be in conflict with any directly enforceable rule of Community law'.

The significance of this judgement was crucial since it established the principle that when British and European law conflicted, European law must take precedence. Critics of the EEC/EU were outraged by the judgement. They argued that it removed the democratic principle of parliamentary sovereignty, making the UK Parliament answerable to the European Commission even if the interests of British citizens were potentially being compromised.

The EU referendum in 2016

From when it joined the EEC in 1973, the UK rarely had an easy relationship with its European partners. In the 1970s and 1980s, the Labour Party saw membership of the EEC as a barrier to socialism, while more recently a large section of the Conservative Party focused on the loss of national identity and threat to parliamentary sovereignty posed by European integration.

A major reason for the UK's historic lack of commitment to the EU is that it did not join until 16 years after it was established by the Treaty of Rome and so it had to accept rulings such as the Common Agricultural Policy, which conflicted with British interests. Britain's imperial legacy, which is still apparent in the existence of the Commonwealth, also made European integration seem less pressing. The UK, as an island nation state, has also developed separately from continental neighbours and avoided being conquered by either Napoleon or Hitler, further fostering a separate British identity.

When David Cameron pledged to hold an 'in/out' referendum on the UK's membership of the EU, it was widely expected that the UK would vote to remain in the union. The prime minister and most of the cabinet campaigned to remain,

The socioeconomic impact of EU migration on the UK

In 2004 the EU expanded from 15 to 25 member states, including eight from Eastern Europe. In 2007, Bulgaria and Romania also joined the EU. Under the principle of the four freedoms, members of the EU enjoy the right to work and claim social security in any member state. Some restrictions were placed on Romanian and Bulgarian work permits, but by 2014 these had been removed, establishing complete freedom of movement.

The socioeconomic impact of EU migration on the UK was profound. The UK's position as a member of the single market contributed to a significant increase in immigration. From 1991 to 1995, on average, immigration to the UK amounted to 37,000 people, whereas from 2013 to 2017 the figure was 277,000. By 2017, 3.8 million people living in the UK were citizens of another EU country. This represented approximately 6% of the UK's population. The largest number of EU migrants to the UK were, by far, from Poland, with over a million Poles living in the UK in 2017. UK citizens were much less likely to take advantage of the single market, with just 785,000 British nationals in 2017 living in other EU states excluding Ireland.

There is a strong case to suggest that the UK economy benefited from EU immigration. Most EU immigrants were in their twenties and took up paid employment, so contributing more to the economy than they claimed through social services. In 2018, unemployment levels in the UK were just 4% — the lowest since 1975 — which suggests that the UK was easily able to absorb EU immigrants. Fears that EU immigrants were changing the social fabric of the UK nevertheless had a powerful resonance in many non-metropolitan centres. People began to feel that their communities were being potentially changed for ever by EU migration. One in five of the population of Boston in Lincolnshire, for example, was an immigrant in 2016 and Boston voted 75.6% to leave the EU.

In 1968, Enoch Powell had warned that, as a result of Commonwealth immigration, British-born citizens would find 'their homes and neighbourhoods changed beyond recognition, their plans and prospects for the future defeated'. Almost 40 years later, in 2016, it was by appealing to fears such as these that the Leave campaign was helped to achieve victory in the EU referendum.

The 2016 EU referendum demonstrated a striking discontent between the more pro-European attitudes of many young people and the greater Euroscepticism of many older voters

as did the Labour and Liberal Democrat leadership. The Confederation of British Industry (CBI) and the Trades Union Congress (TUC) argued strongly in favour of the economic advantages of membership. The Governor of the Bank of England, Mark Carney, announced that Brexit could 'possibly include a technical recession' and the chancellor of the exchequer, George Osborne, went further, stating that Brexit would push the UK into an immediate recession costing 820,000 jobs in 2 years.

However, unlike the 1975 referendum, in which the UK voted decisively to remain in the EEC, in 2016 the strong economic arguments to remain in the EU proved less influential than expected with the electorate. Instead, the Leave campaign's focus on restoring British sovereignty was highly popular, especially among C2, D and E voters, who felt that their economic opportunities were being lost and that the social fabric of their communities was being irretrievably altered without their consent.

The morning after the EU referendum, at 4:39 a.m. on Friday 24 June, David Dimbleby confounded most polling forecasts when he announced on BBC television, 'The British people have spoken and the answer is we're out.'

The result was close but decisive: Remain 48%; Leave 52%.

It remains the case that the UK has enjoyed considerable economic benefits from membership of the EU's single market. The free flow of trade, services, capital and workers represented by the four freedoms has benefited the UK's economy and so the economic consequences of Brexit are highly controversial.

- Supporters of a 'soft' Brexit are keen to continue to be able to take advantage of as much of the single market as they can, without the complete free movement of people, while opting out of political integration. This is modelled on the sort of relationship that Norway and Switzerland have with the EU.
- Those who have favoured a 'hard' Brexit, such as Boris Johnson, have been more optimistic that the UK could entirely cut its ties from the single market and succeed in making its own trade deals in the global economy.

The location of sovereignty in the UK political system

Legal and political sovereignty

Political sovereignty refers to the sovereignty exercised by the public. This is the ultimate form of sovereignty since the legislature and executive depend on the consent of the public to govern. At each general election the British public reclaim their sovereignty when they choose their parliamentary representatives.

Legal sovereignty is the absolute right that every Parliament has to enact whatever legislation it chooses. Although Parliament's sovereignty has been given to it by the people, once it legislates there can be no power greater than an Act of Parliament.

Popular sovereignty occurs when the public expresses its sovereign will through direct democracy. The 2016 EU referendum provides a good example of the sovereign will of the people conflicting with that of parliament.

> ### Key terms
>
> **Political sovereignty**
> Means absolute authority. Since the legislature's authority derives from the public, the public may be said to exercise political sovereignty.
>
> **Legal sovereignty**
> Represents the right of Parliament to enact legislation which has absolute authority and cannot be overturned by any other body.

Parliament and legal sovereignty

According to the great constitutional expert A.V. Dicey (1835–1922), Parliament possesses the legal sovereignty to enact any law without this being overruled by any other body. As Dicey put it in his *Introduction to the Study of the Law of the Constitution* (1885), 'Parliament … has, under the English constitution, the right to make any law whatever; and, further, that no person or body is recognised by the law of England as having a right to override or set aside the legislation of Parliament.' The power of Parliament is, though, not of its own making, Dicey noted, because the House of Commons is accountable to the public in regular general elections.

The extent to which sovereignty has moved between branches

Synoptic link

The way in which the internet is providing a forum for political debate shows an important new way in which the public is able to assert its sovereign influence. This links to Component 1, UK Politics (see page 121).

Traditionally, the UK has been viewed as being a unitary state, since sovereign authority is located in one place: the Westminster Parliament. Unlike in federal systems of government such as the USA, power is not shared between the federal government and the states. Instead, Parliament has supreme legislative authority.

The fact that the UK does not have a codified constitution means that there is no law higher than parliamentary statute. Unlike American judges, British judges cannot strike down an Act of Parliament since they have no higher law of the constitution to which to appeal.

The legal doctrine of parliamentary supremacy was clearly stated in the case of *R (Jackson)* v *Attorney General* (2005) when Lord Bingham stated that the 'bedrock of the British Constitution is … the Supremacy of the Crown in Parliament'.

However, the location of sovereignty in the UK is much more complicated than this implies. Although Parliament does possess legal sovereignty, the extent to which it can exercise this in all circumstances is debatable.

Referendums

Since the election of the Blair government in 1997, a precedent has been established whereby referendums have been called to determine the opinion of the public on important constitutional questions such as Scottish independence and the UK's membership of the EU. The results of these referendums have not been legally binding since the questions have been only advisory. However, in reality, it would be constitutionally highly improbable, and dangerous, for the government to ask the public a question and then ignore the result. Referendums therefore demonstrate a de facto transfer of authority from the people's representatives in Parliament, via direct democracy, to the public. This most controversially occurred in 2016 when the public voted to leave the EU. Although it is estimated that 73% of MPs opposed Brexit, in 2017 the House of Commons consequently voted 498–114 to allow the government to open negotiations to exit the EU.

Strong executive

When a government has a large parliamentary majority there will be few legislative constraints on its authority. This was the case in 1997 when Tony Blair won a massive parliamentary majority. Blair was supported by highly favourable media coverage, and he was able to exert enormous political influence.

Devolution

Devolution also provides de facto evidence for a change in the location of sovereignty. In theory, Westminster did not lose any of its sovereign power when it devolved rather than gave away certain domestic powers to the Scottish Parliament and the Welsh and Northern Irish assemblies. This therefore means that the Westminster Parliament could legally reclaim those powers. This occurred in Northern Ireland in 2002–07 when direct rule was re-established, and ongoing difficulties in power sharing make it possible that this could temporarily occur again.

However, to do the same for Wales and Scotland would be much more difficult, since both the Scottish and Welsh governments can claim popular legitimacy. Also, the Scotland Act 2016 and the Wales Act 2017 recognise the permanence of their governments and establish that they can only be abolished as a result of a referendum in each country. As a result of this, some political commentators suggest that we are currently evolving into a quasi-federal state in which sovereign authority is increasingly being shared by the constituent members of the UK.

The debating chamber of the Scottish Parliament building, Edinburgh. The way in which its seating is configured is supposed to encourage a more consensual approach to decision making

Royal prerogative

The royal prerogative is exercised by the prime minister and means that in certain areas Parliament is not sovereign. These areas include patronage powers, such as recommendations to the Crown of life peers and Anglican bishops. The prime minister also decides who will be in the cabinet. Parliament is increasingly challenging the royal prerogative, however:

- Since debating military action in Iraq in 2003, Parliament now expects to be consulted over military action.
- As a result of the Fixed Term Parliaments Act 2011, Parliament can no longer be dissolved through the use of the royal prerogative. Instead, if a prime minister wants an early dissolution then he or she requires the support of two-thirds of the House of Commons.

The royal prerogative and military action

Since the parliamentary vote in 2003 supporting military action in Iraq, the convention has developed that the House of Commons should be consulted over the use of military force. However, this has not been set out in law and so there is no legal restraint on the prime minister *still* choosing to exercise the royal prerogative when committing British forces to conflict. For example, in 2018, Theresa May used the royal prerogative to authorise an RAF bombing raid on government targets in Syria. This demonstrates how, lacking a codified constitution clearly setting out the relationship between the branches of government, the location of sovereign authority in the UK can be difficult to determine.

The Crown in time of national emergency

Although the monarch generally asks the party leader with a majority of MPs in the House of Commons to form a government on their behalf, if there was an absence of clear political leadership in time of national crisis then the monarch would be constitutionally able to appoint a prime minister of their choosing. This happened in 1940 when Neville

Chamberlain resigned following the Nazi *Blitzkrieg* on Norway and Denmark. There were a number of possible replacements, including the foreign secretary, Lord Halifax. However, King George VI asked Winston Churchill to form a government on his behalf since he felt that he best represented the will of the nation to oppose Hitler.

The EU

As a member of the EEC/EU, the UK pooled its sovereignty with other member states. Where European law was established, the UK had to accept the supremacy of European law over domestic law. This principle was recognised in British law by the Factortame case (1991), which stated that in cases of conflict British courts must implement European law over British law.

However, the question as to what extent this meant that parliamentary sovereignty had been compromised was solved when, as a result of the vote to leave the EU in 2016, Parliament began the process of enacting legislation which would repeal the laws under which the UK had joined the EEC in 1973. This demonstrates that, although the UK pooled its sovereignty as a member of the EEC/EU, Parliament always retained the sovereign right to legislate to restore full parliamentary sovereignty on the principle that no parliament may bind its successor.

Human Rights Act 1998

In cases involving the protection of civil liberties, British courts can refer to the Human Rights Act 1998, which incorporates the European Convention on Human Rights into British law. However, the Human Rights Act (HRA) still falls far short of being a codified constitution which really would limit Parliament's sovereignty. As it stands, the HRA is no different from any other Act of Parliament and so parts of it can be suspended — as occurred when Article 5 was suspended after 9/11, enabling the government to hold foreign terrorist suspects indefinitely without trial. An Act of Parliament can also still become law if it is in defiance of the terms of the HRA on the principle that no parliament may bind its successor. In these circumstances, the judiciary should acknowledge the contradiction by issuing a formal statement of incompatibility, but the Supreme Court could not strike down the legislation.

Synoptic link

The constitutional significance of the HRA links to Component 1, UK Politics (see pages 33–36).

Prisoner voting, the European Convention on Human Rights and parliamentary sovereignty

The conflict between parliamentary sovereignty and the European Convention on Human Rights is demonstrated by Parliament's unwillingness to allow inmates of UK prisons to vote in elections. According to the European Court of Human Rights in Strasbourg, the British government has been acting in defiance of their human rights by forbidding prisoners to vote.

However, in 2011 when the House of Commons voted on the issue of allowing prisoners to vote, the motion was defeated 234–22. In 2017 a compromise was reached, which allows a tiny number of prisoners to vote. In this case, Parliament has demonstrated that its sovereignty is intact even in cases involving the jurisdiction of the European Court of Human Rights.

Globalisation

It could be argued that membership of international organisations such as the International Criminal Court and the International Court of Justice, as well as the impact of globalisation, has restricted UK sovereignty. For example, the UK is expected to obey the trading rules of the World Trade Organization, and is committed to the principle of Article 5 of NATO's constitution that an attack on one member state represents an attack on all member states.

UK governments can also not control capital flows and flights, suggesting that the UK government's sovereign control of the economy is practically restricted.

Debate

Is the Westminster Parliament sovereign?

Yes

- Parliament legislated to leave the EU. This means that even when the UK was part of the EU, in spite of the Factortame case, Parliament reserved the right to enact legislation to repeal UK membership.
- Since the UK does not possess a codified constitution, there is no law higher than parliamentary statute. The Supreme Court may not, therefore, strike down an Act of Parliament.
- Although the European Convention on Human Rights has been enacted through the Human Rights Act, it is no different legally to any other Act of Parliament so it can be suspended or repealed.
- Parliament could, in theory, abolish the devolved assemblies by Act of Parliament.
- Parliament is not legally bound by the result of a referendum.

No

- The devolved governments of Wales and Scotland can only be abolished by parliament following referendums calling for their removal.
- There is now a convention that major constitutional decisions should be agreed by the public in referendums rather than by Parliament.
- Parliament accepted the result of the EU referendum in 2016, although most MPs disagreed with it. This suggests that the political sovereignty of the public is superior to that of the Westminster Parliament.
- The Westminster Parliament is not sovereign in those areas involving the prime minister's exercise of the royal prerogative.
- Although the UK does not have a codified constitution, there is a growing expectation that parliamentary legislation should conform to the principles of the European Convention on Human Rights.

Summary

By the end of this chapter you should be able to answer the following questions:

→ What is the role of the Supreme Court?

→ Why is judicial independence important and how is it secured?

→ How effective is the Supreme Court in protecting civil liberties?

→ Why is the location of sovereignty in the UK difficult to determine?

→ How effective is Parliament in holding government accountable?

→ What factors explain the extent to which the legislature can control the executive?

→ Has the balance of power shifted from the executive to the legislature?

→ To what extent is the UK Parliament sovereign?

→ In what ways did EU membership impact on the UK?

→ To what extent is the EU a successful organisation?

Practice questions

Source-based question

Parliamentary sovereignty is a principle of the UK constitution. It makes Parliament the supreme legal authority in the UK, which can create or end any law. Generally, the courts cannot overrule its legislation and no Parliament can pass laws that future Parliaments cannot change. Parliamentary sovereignty is the most important part of the UK constitution.

People often refer to the UK having an 'unwritten constitution' but that's not strictly true. It may not exist in a single text, like in the USA or Germany, but large parts of it are written down, much of it in the laws passed in Parliament — known as statute law.

Over the years, Parliament has passed laws that limit the application of parliamentary sovereignty. These laws reflect political developments both within and outside the UK.

They include:
- the devolution of power to bodies like the Scottish Parliament and Welsh Assembly
- the Human Rights Act 1998
- the UK's entry to the European Union in 1973
- the decision to establish a UK Supreme Court in 2009, which ended the House of Lords' function as the UK's final court of appeal

These developments do not fundamentally undermine the principle of parliamentary sovereignty, since Parliament can repeal any of the laws implementing these changes.

Source: Adapted from 'Parliament's Authority', **www.parliament.uk**

Using the source, evaluate the view that the Westminster Parliament exercises full sovereignty in the UK.

In your response you must:
- *compare and contrast the different opinions in the source*
- *examine and debate these views in a balanced way*
- *analyse and evaluate only the information presented in the source* (30)

Evaluative questions

1 Evaluate the extent to which the Supreme Court is important in limiting the power of the executive/legislature. *In your answer you should draw on relevant knowledge and understanding of the study of Component 1 UK Politics and Core Political Ideas and consider this view and the alternative to this view in a balanced way.* (30)

2 Evaluate the extent to which the Westminster Parliament has become more effective in holding the government accountable. *In your answer you should draw on relevant knowledge and understanding of the study of Component 1 UK Politics and Core Political Ideas and consider this view and the alternative to this view in a balanced way.* (30)

3 Evaluate the extent to which the European Union's influence on the UK has been more positive than negative. *In your answer you should draw on relevant knowledge and understanding of the study of Component 1 UK Politics and Core Political Ideas and consider this view and the alternative to this view in a balanced way.* (30)

THEME 2

POLITICAL IDEAS

9 Liberalism

Classical liberalism

The political ideas of classical liberalism are most commonly associated with the age of Enlightenment in the eighteenth century, when rationalistic ideas of science and philosophy challenged the traditional religious order and divinely ordained monarchical government.

Classical liberals' ideas have been influential across the Western world. They can be summarised as follows:

- Government by consent
- Guarantee of individual freedom
- Representative democracy
- A limited role for the state within society and the economy
- Individuals are born with natural rights

Modern liberalism

Modern liberalism argued for an increased role of the state within society and the economy. For some, it enhanced individual freedom and was a logical continuation of the ideas of classical liberalism. For others, such as neo-liberals, this was a betrayal of classical liberalism's core ideas.

Liberalism, in both its classical and modern forms, is seen by many as the most influential ideology in the world today. It informs the political systems of both the USA and the European Union.

Core ideas and principles

Individualism

The preservation of individual rights and freedoms above any claims by the state or groupings within society are of paramount importance to liberals. John Locke (1632–1704) focused on the individual rights of man. Locke believed in **foundational equality**: that man's natural state was one of freedom and in particular freedom from unnecessary external interference by the state. Locke and J.S. Mill (1806–73) perceived individuals as capable of intellectually informed ideas but as self-interested and mutually indifferent to each other.

Modern liberalism's perception of individualism differs from that of classical liberalism. Modern liberalism argues that classical liberalism underplays the inequality of society. Society is not equal and some individuals have a distinct advantage over others. Likewise the idea that individuals are autonomous is also overstated. John Rawls (1921–2002) argued that one's societal position and particular circumstance (race, gender, social class, innate intelligence, etc.) were of huge importance in determining whether an individual thrived or underachieved within society. Therefore, individuals can have both innate advantages and disadvantages that play a sizeable role in their eventual fate. The negative freedom practised by classical liberalism only exacerbates these inequalities rather than addressing them. Modern liberalism therefore critiques classical liberalism's '**egotistical individualism**' (Table 9.1).

Table 9.1 Attitudes towards individualism

Classical liberalism's attitude	Modern liberalism's attitude
An individual's primary motivation is for egotistical individualism, which is concerned with maximising their own utility (their personal worth or value) so that they can thrive to the best of their ability	T.H. Green (1836–82) was an early advocate of modern liberalism, who argued for positive freedom whereby the state practises a form of **developmental individualism** to help make society a fairer place
The freedom of the individual is sacrosanct. Society would be atomistic: a collection of autonomous individuals	Modern liberals can broadly agree with classical liberals on the concept of self-reliance but argue that the state must offer a 'hand up' if every individual is to achieve this goal
The state should be small, limited to maintaining law and order and protecting society from invasion, so that it does not infringe on individual freedom and respects **formal equality**. This limited interference is sometimes called negative freedom	The influence of modern liberalism's ideas of developmental individualism can be seen in the expansion of state involvement and welfare provision in Western democracies after the Second World War
Classical liberalism influenced the American revolutionaries who refer specifically to 'life, liberty and the pursuit of happiness' in the American Declaration of Independence. These are human rights that the state must uphold and protect	Modern liberals would agree that 'life, liberty and the pursuit of happiness' are human rights. However, whereas classical liberals argue for a minimal state to ensure these values, modern liberals believe that only an interventionist state can guarantee such freedoms

Liberalism is also associated with individual tolerance, a concept that has developed over time. Locke, writing in the seventeenth century, focused on respecting alternative religious and political views, while Mary Wollstonecraft (1759–97) and

Key terms

Foundational equality
A fundamental liberal belief that all individuals are born with natural rights which entitle them to liberty, the pursuit of happiness and avoidance of pain. In a liberal state this translates into the rule of law, where all individuals are treated equally under the law.

Egotistical individualism
The belief that individual freedom is associated with a rational sense of self-reliance and self-interest.

Developmental individualism Both classical and modern liberals think that individuals must help themselves to improve. Classical liberals think the state should interfere as little as possible in this process, whereas modern liberals believe that the state, by intervening, can assist in individuals' development (e.g. a state-run education system).

Formal equality Similar to foundational equality, formal equality is a wider concept, supported by all liberals. It includes equality under the law but also the principle that every individual is entitled to equal treatment in society. It also includes the idea of equality of opportunity and the abolition of artificial social distinctions such as gender inequality.

Betty Friedan (1921–2006) argued for a toleration of men towards women, calling for an end to sexual discrimination within society. In the twenty-first century, individual tolerance has been extended towards homosexuals and more recently transgendered individuals.

Freedom/liberty

The concept of freedom has evolved as liberalism has developed over the centuries.

Early liberals resented how authoritarian government and absolute monarchies retained full legitimacy, often at the expense of their subjects' freedoms.

- Freedom is therefore intimately connected with the law, for, as Locke argued, 'where there is no law there is no liberty'.
- Freedom is a natural right; Locke asserted that the role of government was the protection of man's right to 'life, liberty and estate'. The state is needed to mediate between competing individuals to enforce order, to protect property rights and to prevent breach of contracts and fraud.
- Absolute monarchies were illegitimate and Locke argued for a state constructed by **social contract** where individuals are governed by consent. This idea was based on the rationalistic proposition that individuals would enter into a social contract to allow the state to act as a neutral umpire to resolve clashes. If the state broke the contract by not protecting or enhancing natural rights then the people were within their rights to withdraw their consent and replace the government. For many classical liberals the American Revolution was a perfect example of a broken contract between the ruled and the rulers.
- The state would practise **limited government** so that the individual might enjoy the maximum amount of freedom within a legal framework. This freedom gave heavy emphasis to the economic sphere of society and the doctrine of **laissez-faire capitalism** as advocated by Adam Smith in *The Wealth of Nations* (1776).

Key thinker

John Locke (1632–1704)

Locke is seen as one of the principal thinkers of classical liberalism, with his key work being *Two Treatises of Government* (1689).

Locke's main ideas

- The state was not created by God, nor is the monarchy legitimised by the 'divine right of kings'. Rather the state is created via a social contract between the rulers and the ruled: the principle of government by consent.
- Prior to the existence of the state, humans existed in a state of nature, a phrase and concept Locke borrowed from Thomas Hobbes (see Chapter 10). Locke argued that within the state of nature the human race was underpinned by 'natural laws', 'natural liberties' and 'natural rights'. The freedoms were extremely desirable and so the state must not encroach on them.
- The 'state of law' that Locke envisaged would see the state resolve disputes between individuals more equitably than can be achieved within a state of nature.
- The state should be limited in how it interferes in society and economy. This limited government would ensure that the state always represented the interests of the governed and always required their ongoing consent. The state should be limited under the principle of constitutionalism with a clear separation of powers to prevent an abuse of power.
- There should be tolerance between alternative religious and political views.

John Stuart Mill (1806–73)

Mill is considered to be one of the greatest philosophers of all time and his ideas influence both classical and modern liberalism. His key work is *On Liberty* (1859).

Mill's main ideas

- Mill argued for restraint by the state, leaving individuals to be free to take whatever actions they judged fit, provided this did not harm others. This latter point became known as the **harm principle**.
- Mill distinguished between 'self-regarding' actions (such as religious worship or freedom of speech), which do not impinge on the freedom of others and should be tolerated, and 'other regarding' actions (involving violent or riotous behaviour), which clearly do 'harm' and infringe the freedom of others and should not be tolerated by a liberal state.
- Mill argued that the state should be tolerant of diverse opinions. This attitude has been paraphrased by Evelyn Beatrice Hall: 'I disapprove of what you say, but I will defend to the death your right to say it.'
- Mill believed that individual liberty was essential for the development of the individual in terms of creativity, culture and intellect. If individuals were able to develop their individualism, the whole of society would benefit.
- He opposed popular democracy, where the interests of the few could be crushed by the interests of the majority. As an alternative, he supported the idea of representative democracy with, as Locke had proposed, limited government. The representatives would aggregate all the demands of individuals with society to create a broad consensus for decision making rather than strictly following the will of the majority.
- Although Mill argued that government should interfere as little as possible in society and the economy, he later modified his views, arguing that the state must intervene to help individuals attain developmental individualism. This would be achieved via the state facilitating education. He saw these ideas, which influenced modern liberalism, as a natural continuation of classical liberalism and not a contradiction.

> **Key term**
>
> **Harm principle** The idea that the state is justified in interfering with individual freedom when it is to prevent some citizens doing harm to others.

J.S. Mill broadened what liberalism meant by freedom:

- Advocating freedom of speech, thought and religion, unless these pose a direct threat to others, is an idea that became known as negative freedom.
- Individuals should be free from interference even if this means that they are harming themselves, for example suicide should not be a crime. Contemporary neo-liberals use Mill's ideas to justify why individuals should be free to take drugs that are currently illegal, arguing that it is their choice and not the state's.

Classical liberalism's conception of freedom is atomistic: made up of individuals with their own interests. There is no broader 'public interest' or 'common good' that individuals have to serve. People succeed or fail in society on their own efforts. The state should not provide welfare as this will just make individuals dependent on the state. This rugged individualism will make society more dynamic as individuals have to succeed on their own merits and efforts.

Mill moved from a strictly classical liberal approach to a more modern liberal approach when he advocated that the state had a moral right to educate individuals. These ideas changed the way liberals thought about freedom, the role of the state and the nature of society:

- T.H. Green broadened Mill's ideas when he argued that society was organic (not atomistic as classical liberals believed), that there *was* a common good and that public interest coexisted with individual interests. Limited state intervention was necessary to facilitate developmental individualism, which would increase individuals' capacity to be free.
- Whereas the negative freedom of classical liberalism focused on a freedom from the state, Green argued that this did not recognise that freedom could be threatened by social and material disadvantage within society and the economy.
- Green supported positive freedom that allowed individuals to achieve their aspirations by the state assisting their development.
- Similarly, Rawls argued for a larger role for the state in society and the economy. This 'enabling' state would ensure an individual's life chances were not determined by their status at birth. These levels of intervention would involve more taxation and state spending to ensure equality of opportunity via developmental individualism.

Table 9.2 Negative freedom vs positive freedom

Negative freedom/liberty	Positive freedom/liberty
• A conception of freedom that defines itself as an absence of constraint • Liberal philosopher Isaiah Berlin (1909–97) described it as 'freedom from' rather than 'freedom to' • Advocates of negative freedom want freedom from government interference wherever possible • Classical liberals and neo-liberals prefer negative freedom and a minimal state	• A conception of freedom which sees the state playing a positive role to assist individuals to achieve their dreams and aspirations and develop as individuals • A state-funded educational system would be an example of positive freedom • Modern liberals prefer positive freedom and an enabling state

Finally, Carole Pateman (b. 1940) and others have criticised liberalism for having a conception of freedom that is male-centric to the exclusion of women. Although Pateman is correct that many (male) writers of liberal ideas fall into this category, it is not entirely fair as liberalism has acknowledged female rights:

- J.S. Mill's *The Subjection of Women* (1869) argued for votes for women decades before enfranchisement was achieved.
- Wollstonecraft championed formal equality in society, in terms of women pursuing a career, playing a role in the economy and having legal and property rights. She also argued that women were equally as rational as men, as 'the mind has no gender'. If they did not appear equal it was because most women had been denied the same educational opportunities.
- Friedan championed equality of opportunity to a far greater and in a more explicit sense than Wollstonecraft in the middle years of the twentieth century.

The state: a necessary evil

The liberal attitude to the state, its size, role and limits, is critical to an understanding of the development of liberalism in the last 400 years. Classical liberalism set the parameters by arguing for a **minimal state** (which contemporary neo-liberals support), which was subsequently altered by modern liberals to an **enabling state**.

Classical liberalism

The traditional liberal position is that the state is a necessary evil. Although classical liberalism (and its modern-day counterpart, neo-liberalism) advocates egotistical individualism within society and a laissez-faire attitude towards the economy, it never went as far as individualistic anarchism (see Chapter 12) in arguing that there should be no state at all. The state must protect 'life, liberty and estate'. The state must intervene to uphold the rule of law and to protect society from foreign invasion. These interventions require institutions such as police forces, armies, laws and a judiciary to uphold the laws.

The kind of liberal state that Locke advocated was in direct contrast to the absolute monarchies that dominated Europe when he was writing. Power in these countries was dominated by monarchs who received legitimacy via the religious belief of the 'divine right of kings', which asserted that the sovereign was ordained to rule by God. Locke disagreed with such an irrational interpretation of God's will, arguing instead for government by consent, whereby the state would be the result of a social contract enshrining the natural state of freedom into the law of government. Individuals would enter into such a social contract voluntarily and consensually, whereby government was subject to the consent of the people and in return individuals would agree to obey its laws. This would ensure that 'government should always be the servant, and not master, of the people'. The state should be organised in the following ways:

- It should be based on rational ideas rather than traditional ideas. A constitutional government would therefore replace an arbitrary government and traditional monarchy.
- Government should be based on the principle of limited government by limiting its power and its jurisdiction (Table 9.3).

> ## Key terms
>
> **Minimal state** A concept associated with classical liberalism and modern neo-liberalism. It suggests that in a free society, the state must be strongly controlled and should have a minimal breadth of functions. If the state has too many functions it is likely to interfere with individual liberties. The concept is also associated with laissez-faire capitalism.
>
> **Enabling state** A state that does not necessarily provide for people directly but creates the conditions where people can help themselves. Education provision for all is a key example.

Table 9.3 How do classical liberals wish to limit government?

By limiting power	• Power should be divided between different branches of government. The separation of powers idea was posited by the French philosopher Montesquieu and would see three branches of government — legislative, executive and judiciary — separated from each other. Each of these three branches would have the ability to act as a check on the others • The state should be based on Locke's principle of 'government by consent'. This would be done through constitutional agreements and government that is constantly accountable to the people via regular elections • These principles influenced the creation of the US Constitution (see Chapter 17)
By limiting jurisdiction	• Individuals should be protected by law from actions that might harm their individual liberty. Economically, the state should protect property rights, oversee the enforcement of legal contracts by the law, and regulate monopoly power which would operate against the interests of consumers • The state should operate under the rule of law, whereby all citizens would enjoy foundational equality
By limiting the electorate	• Classical liberals were in favour of a representative democracy rather than a direct, popular democracy • J.S. Mill believed that only those with an appropriate formal education should be allowed to vote • J.S. Mill feared that a popular democracy might lead to a 'tyranny of the majority'

Modern liberalism

Although J.S. Mill is strongly associated with classical liberalism, he later adapted his view of limited government to allow for state intervention to assist the poor who were experiencing injustice in society and the economy. T.H. Green continued to reinterpret the role of the state so that it had a larger role in both society and the economy:

- The state should promote **equality of opportunity** through education and reductions in the influence of inherited privilege.
- The state should organise welfare to help those unable to defend themselves against deprivation, such as the unemployed, the chronically sick and the elderly.
- John Maynard Keynes' (1883–1946) key work, *The General Theory of Employment, Interest and Money*, was a rational construct that argued against Smith's laissez-faire economics. The state, Keynes argued, was capable of managing the economy so as to secure full employment. Keynes, a modern liberal, wished to rectify the negative consequences of economic downturns as he felt mass employment negated individual freedom. These economic ideas are known as **Keynesianism**.
- Recent liberals such as Rawls argue that the state should also take a more proactive role in reducing inequality within society and preventing social injustice.
- Friedan argued that the state was the structure in which to guarantee societal and economic equality of opportunity for women.

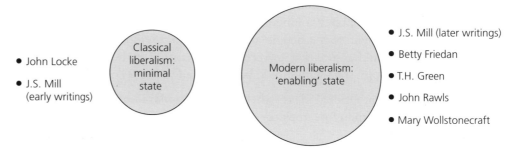

Figure 9.1 How big do liberals think the state should be?

- John Locke
- J.S. Mill (early writings)

Classical liberalism: minimal state

Modern liberalism: 'enabling' state

- J.S. Mill (later writings)
- Betty Friedan
- T.H. Green
- John Rawls
- Mary Wollstonecraft

Rationalism

The Enlightenment was an intellectual movement of the eighteenth century inspired by scientists and philosophers such as Francis Bacon, Isaac Newton, René Descartes and Immanuel Kant. What united them in their ideas was a positive view of human nature, particularly concerning rationality, as they believed that humans were capable of reason and logic. As Locke argued, 'Reason must be our last Judge and Guide in every Thing.'

Unlike conservatives, whose belief in intellectual imperfection meant that they doubted humans possessed such aptitudes, liberals believed that rationalism enabled individuals to both define their own best interests and make their own moral choices, free from external authorities such as the state and the Church. Whereas conservatives fear intellectual fallibility and cling to empiricism, customs and tradition to guide them, liberals have far more confidence in their intellectual ability to construct theories to create a progressive society (Table 9.4).

Table 9.4 How have classical and modern liberalism have been influenced by rationalistic ideas?

Classical liberalism	Modern liberalism
Locke's ideas of constitutional and representative government (as opposed to monarchical government), proved hugely influential to England's Glorious Revolution of 1688 and to the UK Bill of Rights of 1689 (see Chapter 5) as well as to the American Constitution (see Chapter 17)	T.H. Green's positive freedom, which urged state intervention to assist individual freedom, was a key rationalistic updating of classical liberalism that informed the ideas of a state-sponsored welfare state
Adam Smith's *The Wealth of Nations* is one of the most important expressions of economic theory within liberalism. Smith argued that capitalism functions best when the state takes a laissez-faire approach. These ideas resonate today with the Trump administration's flirtation with tariffs and protected markets being criticised because they contradict the principles of Adam Smith	Mill's later ideas such as universal education anticipated Green's positive freedom by arguing that the state must be an enabling state, facilitating developmental individualism. However, modern liberals agree with classical liberals on the desirability of a free-market economy
Mill's concept of negative liberty/freedom has been hugely influential in countries such as the UK and USA in determining the parameters of state intervention, the autonomy of the individual and the atomistic nature of the society	Keynesian economics, although differing entirely from laissez-faire economics, was equally rationalistic in its conception
	Rawls' ideas of equality and social justice (which we discuss further in the next section) is a perfect example of abstract rational thought

---

Synoptic link

Both the UK Bill of Rights (1689) and the US Bill of Rights (1791) were influenced by Locke's idea that government should only exist if there is an agreement between the state and the people. Individuals have innate rights and there are limits to the state's jurisdiction on an individual that should be protected by law. In the USA these are fundamental laws and entrenched, while in the UK such rights (that are also found in the Human Rights Act 1998) are statute law and hold no higher legal authority and can therefore be altered or repealed by a future parliament. This links to Component 2, UK Government (see page 135).

Equality and social justice

Liberalism was initially focused on foundational equality (the premise that all individuals are born with equal rights) and the rule of law so that no individual could be exempt from society's strictures. (For more on the rule of law, see page 136.)

- There are numerous examples of foundational equality in practice today such as the US Bill of Rights and the UK's Human Rights Act, both of which legally protect what liberals consider to be the natural and inalienable rights of individuals.
- Discussing what constitutes foundational equality has been problematic for classical liberals, who largely ignored (apart from Mill) gender and racial inequality. Modern liberalism is the strand of liberalism most associated with supporting full foundational equality.

Martin Luther King during his famous Lincoln Memorial Address on 28 August 1963

— Wollstonecraft argued forcefully in the eighteenth century that women were denied equality in terms of property ownership and political representation.

— Wollstonecraft also argued that women were discriminated against within the workplace as they were denied access to many professions. This theme was continued by Friedan, who argued for legal and economic parity and workplace equality of opportunity in the second half of the twentieth century.

— Martin Luther King and the civil rights movement demonstrated that the judicial interpretation of the US Constitution was failing to acknowledge all races equally. The Civil Rights Act of 1964 and the Voting Rights Act of 1965 began the process of creating true foundational equality and equality of opportunity for all races within the USA.

— Modern liberals still champion women and racial minorities, but also groups that the earlier modern liberals would not have considered (such as homosexuals) or even imagined (in the case of transsexuals).

Mary Wollstonecraft (1759–97)

Wollstonecraft's most important publication, *A Vindication of the Rights of Women* (1792), is rooted in liberal philosophy.

Wollstonecraft's main ideas

- Wollstonecraft had a positive view of human nature, viewing men and women as equally rational. She argued that this truth was ignored by contemporary state and society as woman were denied formal equality under the law, which gave them considerably fewer rights than men within society.

- All citizens should enjoy equality under the law and be free from discrimination. Wollstonecraft campaigned for a change in the law to give women more rights in terms of employment and property ownership, as well as retaining legal freedoms when they were married — all areas of difficulty for women when she was writing.

- Wollstonecraft supported formal equality and the social contract ideas of Locke. She viewed the divine rights of kings as an 'absurdity' and was a vocal supporter of both the American Revolution of 1776 and the French Revolution of 1789, arguing for republicanism.

Betty Friedan (1921–2006)

Betty Friedan's ideas are influenced by both classical liberalism (the importance of individualism) and modern liberalism (the enabling state) for how woman can achieve equality of opportunity with men. Her key works are *The Feminine Mystique* (1963) and *The Second Stage* (1983).

Friedan's main ideas

- Friedan argued strongly for individual freedom. In particular, she believed that individuals should be free to be able to achieve their potential. Like Mary Wollstonecraft, she argued that gender was a serious hindrance to women as they were constantly discriminated against in society.
- She believed that women were the principal victims of a lack of opportunity and restricted opportunities within society because of patriarchal attitudes. (For a more detailed discussion of patriarchy, see Chapter 14.)
- Friedan was influenced by classical liberalism in her belief that if the state allowed equality of opportunity then women's individual efforts could achieve the successful combination of marriage, motherhood and career.
- Friedan was also influenced by the ideas of modern liberalism and, like Rawls, she felt that if utilised properly an enabling state could assist women in being free. The state was the vehicle with which to counter dominant patriarchal values that discriminate against women, and to ensure foundational equality and equality of opportunity in both society and the economy. This would include state benefits for single, divorced or widowed mothers.

Modern liberals argue that foundational equality in itself is not enough to guarantee equality of opportunity, and that to guarantee true social justice individuals must have access to a full welfare state encompassing education, healthcare, the minimum wage and welfare provisions. T.H. Green's ideas directly influenced the Beveridge Report, which was the intellectual basis for the postwar welfare state in the UK.

Rawls, one most important exponents of modern liberalism, constructed a rational model which he described in his major work, *A Theory of Justice* (1971), to demonstrate not just the need for social justice, but the inherent logic of it:

- Using an abstract 'veil of ignorance', Rawls posited that if individuals were asked to choose what type of society an individual would prefer and were ignorant of their own circumstances, they would choose a society with little inequality.
- The veil of ignorance was a rationalistic idea based on what Rawls described as a 'purely hypothetical situation. Nothing resembling it need ever take place'.
- Rawls' conception of social justice (he used the term 'distributive justice') was that inequality in a modern capitalist-based society could be justified as long as those who do well economically do not do so at the expense of the least well-off in society. In other words, individuals should not be allowed to prosper at the expense of others.
- Although society was a **meritocracy** and would produce unequal outcomes, all individuals would have an equality of opportunity as the state would intervene, via a welfare state, to allow everyone equal life chances.

Key term

Meritocracy A principle that suggests that although inequality is natural in a free society, in a just society those with greater abilities, drive, creativity and work ethics deserve more rewards than those who do not have those qualities.

John Rawls (1921–2002)

Rawls is considered the most important exponent of modern liberalism of the twentieth century, with his key work being *A Theory of Justice* (1971).

Rawls' main ideas

- Rawls' key idea was 'justice and fairness', and he believed that everyone would agree to an enabling state (and positive freedom) if they were in a position of ignorance.
- An enabling state would provide a welfare state (including health and education). Rawls' theory neatly implies that classical liberals (under a hypothetical veil of ignorance and thus oblivious to their personal circumstances) would choose an interventionary state to guarantee equality of opportunity, rather than a limited state that did not.
- To the traditional idea of foundational equality, Rawls added the need for social and economic equality. He argued that a just society must provide equality of opportunity for everyone and this could only be achieved by the state taking a larger role within society. This would be funded from progressive taxation.
- Robert Nozick (1938–2002) (see Chapter 10) argued that Rawls' ideas were a betrayal of liberalism and that Rawls' demands for an interventionary state had more in common with socialism than liberalism. Nozick's ideas are part neo-liberalism, which can be seen as a modern version of classical liberalism and as a reaction to modern liberal and socialist ideas.

Liberal democracy

When Locke was writing in the seventeenth century, many governments in Europe were monarchies and the state was run by authoritarian elites. Locke's ideas were therefore a reaction to his perception of illegitimate government, enforced on the people rather than being given freely. The concept of liberal democracy is underpinned by the social contract theory of Locke, whereby the government only holds power in trust for the people whom it serves. Government, Locke argued in his book *Two Treatises of Government* (1689), should be by consent as this was the only legitimate basis for authority.

Liberal democracy was initially representative democracy, which offered only a very limited form of democracy. This was the case in the early years of the USA, where only male property owners were allowed to vote.

- Edmund Burke, who many claim was as much a liberal thinker as he was a conservative thinker, also argued for the importance of representative democracy, asserting that a voter elected a representative to make decisions based on his own judgement and not that of the electorate. 'Your representative owes you, not his industry only, but his judgement; and he betrays, instead of serving you, if he sacrifices it to your opinion.'
- Mill, like the US Founding Fathers, feared the dominance of the working class if they were given the vote. In his work *Considerations on Representative Government*, he argued for plural votes for the educated and wealthy to prevent his own class being swept aside by the proletariat.
- Mill, like Locke and Wollstonecraft, has therefore been categorised as favouring elite democracy, whereby the Establishment exercises the real power and has significantly more influence than the ordinary voter.

Such ideas have given way to full emancipation in Western democracies, and modern liberals accept that each individual should have a vote. However, the defining feature of liberal democracy, both classical and modern, is that it involves more than just free and fair elections. It also includes safeguards of individual freedoms, particularly against the tyranny of the majority. Barbara Goodwin argues that there are six key points of liberal democratic theory and the influence of both classical and modern liberal thinkers is clearly evident (Table 9.5).

Table 9.5 Key points of liberal democratic theory

Supremacy of the people	• While classical liberals accept this as a broad concept of the social contract, this does not equate to full democratic representation • Modern liberals are insistent that supremacy of the people means that every adult should have the vote • However, the US Electoral College remains as a filter against the 'tyranny of the majority' in the USA (see Chapter 17)
The consent of the governed as the basis of legitimacy	• A concept that unites both forms of liberalism — elections provide frequent opportunities for the governed to register their consent
The rule of law and peaceful methods of conflict resolution	• The rule of law forms part of the social contract between the governed and the governors
The existence of a common good or public interest	• Classical liberalism struggles with such concepts as it views society as atomistic and therefore any collective will is difficult for classical liberals to support • The developmental individualism of Mill and T.H. Green and the social justice of Rawls base their version of society on more collective aims such as a welfare state
The value of the individual as a rational, moral, active citizen	• Both strands of liberalism can accept this definition
Political equality and equal civil rights for all individuals	• Classical and modern liberalism are united on this • Friedan championed the rights of women in both respects, while Rawls' theory of justice argued that not only were such rights a necessity it was also a rational choice for individuals to make when attempting to ascertain the principles of a society

Different views and tensions within liberalism

The ideological nature of classical and modern liberalism means that these ideas are difficult to reconcile as each posits a fundamentally different understanding of what constitutes:

● freedom and the individual

which in turn informs:

● the role of the state in regard to society and the economy

Freedom and the individual

Liberalism's attitudes towards freedom are polarised, as classical liberalism and modern liberalism have fundamentally different definitions of what constitutes freedom.

Classical liberalism

Classical liberalism views freedom in a negative sense, which involves freedom from constraint and interference where possible.

- J.S. Mill argued that an individual's actions should be unencumbered unless they directly negatively affect others, in a theory that has become known as the 'harm principle'.
- This led Mill (like Locke) to advocate a strong belief in tolerance of the views and actions of others. Mill therefore advocated a society where there was freedom of thought, discussion, religion and assembly.

Locke and Mill advocated egotistical individualism, whereby individuals were self-reliant, self-interested and rational. Mill argued that individuals were sovereign beings capable of free will and therefore should organise their own lives. Such individuals would not only be freer in a negative freedom-based society, but minimal encroachments would facilitate their development as individuals. These ideas influenced the Founding Fathers in their creation of the US Constitution, with the saying 'when government grows, our liberty withers' being attributed to Thomas Jefferson.

Locke argued that men's lives were their own and arbitrary government would enslave them. This idea was expanded by Isaiah Berlin, who argued that when modern liberals expand the role of the state for paternalistic functions they do so at the expense of individual liberty. The paternalistic aspect of state intervention, for classical liberals (and neo-liberals), is therefore oppressive, as the examples below illustrate:

- Compulsory welfare states require taxation, and while individuals are free to opt out of these services they cannot opt out of paying the taxation that funds them.
- J.S. Mill argued that the individual had the right to non-interference, even if their actions caused them individual harm. This is as relevant now as in Mill's time, with neo-liberals such as Robert Nozick arguing that individuals have the right to consume drugs or end their own life if they so wish.
- Perhaps the most memorable example is the so-called Spanner Case (1990), which was named after the arresting officer. Fifteen homosexual men were convicted of assault occasioning actual bodily harm, even though all the injured parties were engaged in acts of consensual sadomasochism. One doubts that J.S. Mill had such trysts in mind when he wrote that, 'Over himself, over his own mind and body, the Individual is sovereign,' but this case illustrates the state encroaching on individual freedom.

Modern liberalism

Modern liberalism can be seen as both a continuation and a contradiction to classical liberalism. J.S. Mill has sometime been called a transitional liberal, as his later ideas advocated aspects of developmental individualism, such as universal education, which implies positive freedom as the state would have to facilitate such a development. However, it is T.H. Green and Rawls who are most associated with the development of modern liberalism and the broader understanding of freedom and individuality. Green asserted that freedom was not just to be left alone, but that it should also be viewed positively, with the creation of constructive assistance to encourage individual freedom.

Modern liberals can broadly agree with classical liberals on the concept of self-reliance, but argue that the state must offer a 'hand up' if every individual is to achieve this goal. The problem with negative freedom is that the lack of assistance from the state only compounds social and economic disadvantage. Positive freedom evens the playing field, so that all individuals can enjoy similar equality of opportunity and social justice.

Green's ideas provided the ideological and intellectual template for the UK's postwar welfare state. They also informed Rawls' *A Theory of Justice* argument, in which Rawls maintained that societal position and particular circumstance (race, gender, social class, innate intelligence) were of huge importance in whether an individual thrived or failed. Rawls' conclusions led him to advocate a substantial increase in the role of the state.

For liberal feminists such as Friedan, both strands of liberalism have been cited in terms of women achieving parity with men in society. Citing Mill's harm principle, she successfully built on the ideas of Wollstonecraft to demonstrate that the freedoms of women were being harmed by sexual discrimination that was inconsistent with the social contractual agreement made in the US Constitution.

The enabling state offers a hand-up

Neo-liberalism

While modern liberals can argue that their version of liberalism is a continuation of classical liberalism in classifying freedom and individualism, neo-liberals, best described as contemporary versions of classical liberals, would disagree. To them, modern liberalism is a betrayal of the core values of the limited state and egotistical individualism. Nozick's and Rand's ideas (see Chapter 10) were both influenced by the classical liberal Immanuel Kant (1724–1804), a German Enlightenment thinker who argued that individuals in society should not be treated as a thing or a resource.

Neo-liberal ideas of reducing the size of the state, free markets and laissez-faire economics were aspects of both Thatcher's and Reagan's administrations. However, it would be incorrect to describe these politicians as neo-liberal, as both were also influenced by neo-conservative ideas. (For a more detailed discussion of both neo-liberalism and neo-conservatism, see Chapter 10.)

The role of the state in economy and society

All aspects of liberalism subscribe to a **mechanistic theory of the state**, as if it were a machine to serve the individual. As we have discussed, classical liberals believe that the role of the state should be strictly limited to maintaining law and order, property rights and securing the society from invasion. The optimal size of the government is therefore small. Modern liberals, on the other hand, argue that the state should create conditions of freedom to allow individuals to reach their full potential.

Key term

Mechanistic theory of the state The idea that the state is not organic but was created by individuals to serve them and act in their interests. Classical and modern liberals differ in their definitions of what these best interests are.

The ideas of J.S. Mill are often associated with classical liberalism and he remains a much quoted philosopher for contemporary neo-liberals. However, his later ideas also anticipated modern liberalism and as a key thinker he illustrates the tensions within liberal thought when attempting to balance human individuality and autonomy while also furthering developmental individualism in relation to a more interventionist state (Figure 9.2).

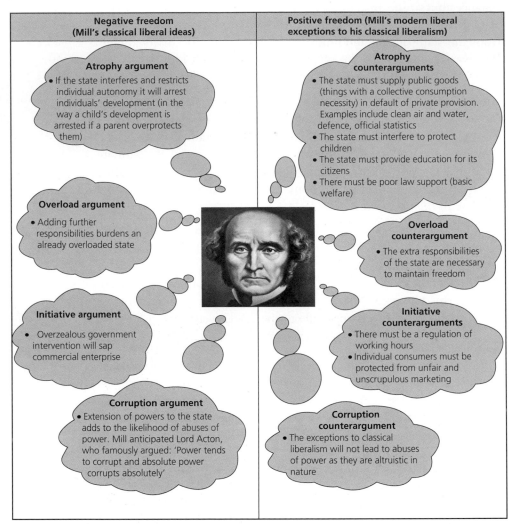

Figure 9.2 J.S. Mill and the role of the state — negative freedom (classical liberal ideas) vs positive freedom (modern liberal exceptions to his classical liberalism)

If one looks at the development of Mill's ideas on the involvement of the state it is possible to argue that modern liberalism was the natural continuation and evolution of classical liberalism. This is very much what thinkers like T.H. Green believed, arguing in the latter half of the nineteenth century that the question that should be preoccupying liberalism was no longer about state and society leaving the individual alone, but whether the state was assisting the individual in fulfilling their potential.

T.H. Green argued that liberty and freedom as defined by classical liberalism was worthless if individuals lacked the capacity to exercise those liberties. Green argued that the social constraints on freedom were manifest and the state must recognise the existence of common duties as a way of promoting individuals' capacities. Modern liberalism therefore advocates an enabling state, which facilitates individuals to be truly free by reaching their potential.

Such ideas were influential on Asquith's Liberal government:

- The Old-Age Pensions Act 1908
- The Labour Exchanges Act 1909
- The National Insurance Act 1911
- The Trade Unions Act 1913

All are examples of the state trying to facilitate the freedom of the individual: be it in providing old-age pensions, assisting the unemployed into employment, providing welfare benefits or improving workers' rights.

Modern liberalism inspired the Beveridge Report (1942), which was the intellectual foundation for the postwar welfare state and went even further than Asquith, as it proposed that the state tackle the five giants that were impeding the freedom of the individual within the UK (Table 9.6).

Table 9.6 Beveridge's 'five giants': the five evils that plague society (and impede individual freedom)

Want	Extreme poverty
Ignorance	Due to a lack of formal education
Disease	Exacerbated by the lack of free healthcare
Squalor	Poor living conditions
Idleness	Exacerbated by unemployment

Sir William Beveridge's report was inspired by modern liberalism

The development of the welfare state transformed the UK state from a limited state to an enabling state, where state intervention within society was dramatically increased. Compounded to this intervention in society (funded by increased taxation), the role of the state was also transformed by modern liberalism's preference for the state economic management of John Maynard Keynes over the laissez-faire economics of Adam Smith. Keynes argued that government could prevent economic slumps and the devastating unemployment that followed by managing demand and stimulating the economy.

Modern liberalism seemed to be in the ascendency, with this transformation of the role of the state becoming the norm in postwar Europe and America. John Rawls' *Theory of Justice* (1971) added a sophisticated rational argument that built on the work of J.S. Mill and T.H. Green. Rawls made this clear in his three principles of justice:

1 Individuals had to have the same set of absolute liberties.
2 There must be equal opportunities for all.
3 Although some inequalities were inevitable, there must be a priority to help the disadvantaged.

Rawls called the last principle the 'difference principle'. As we have discussed, Rawls proposed, via hypothetical construct, that citizens veiled from knowledge of their own circumstances would choose a society that recognised a common good, meritocratic excellence and fairness. So while Rawls recognised that a meritocracy would mean some individuals were well rewarded for their efforts, the state would have to ensure equality of opportunity, be it by supporting a minimum wage, ensuring society was free from discrimination or increasing state spending (and taxation) to fund an enabling welfare state.

Stretch and challenge

The classical liberal John Locke and the modern liberal John Rawls had different visions for the role of the state within society and the economy. Consider these quotations from them and other liberals:

'Government has no other end, but the preservation of property.'

John Locke

'The greatest danger to liberty today comes from the men who are most needed and most powerful in modern government, namely, the efficient expert administrators exclusively concerned with what they regard as the public good.'

F.A. Hayek

'Want is one only of five giants on the road of reconstruction; the others are Disease, Ignorance, Squalor, and Idleness.'

William Beveridge

'The only purpose for which power can rightfully be exercised over any member of a civilised community, against his will, is to prevent harm to others.'

J.S. Mill

'Historically one of the main defects of constitutional government has been the failure to insure the fair value of political liberty. The necessary corrective steps have not been taken, indeed, they never seem to have been seriously entertained.'

John Rawls

With reference to the quotes above, why do you think liberals disagree about the state's involvement within society and the economy?

Classical liberalism vs modern liberalism

The relationship between the two strands of liberalism is complex. Both seek to enhance individual freedom, provide equality of opportunity and support private ownership, while opposing a state-controlled economy. From a certain point of view it is possible to argue that modern liberalism is just a logical development of classical liberalism, a rational response to the demands of the industrialised world. This was certainly the perception of Mill, Green and Rawls, among others (Table 9.7).

Table 9.7 How classical and modern liberals differ in their outlook on four themes

Theme	Classical liberal outlook	Modern liberal outlook
Human nature	Individuals are rational or capable of rationality and prefer to pursue their enlightened self-interest	Individuals crave freedom but also understand that they have obligations to help others less fortunate
The state	The state should be limited and controlled by a government based on representative democracy	State intervention can be justified on the grounds of social justice, equality and social welfare, and is therefore an enabling state. The power of the state and government should be controlled by constitutional rules and robust democracy
Society	Society is naturally competitive, being made up of free individuals pursuing their own interests. Such a vison of society does not recognise collective aims such as a 'common good'	Society should embrace a degree of social welfare and social justice. Individualism should be tempered with social action and recognition of a common good
The economy	The economy should be based on free markets, free trade and a lack of state intervention	The injustices thrown up by capitalism should be reduced by the state through welfare, equality of opportunity and limited redistribution of income

However, this is not the interpretation of neo-liberals, who are the intellectual descendants of classical liberals. Neo-liberals such as Robert Nozick, Friedrich von Hayek and Milton Friedman all opposed the ideas of modern liberalism on classical liberal terms:

Robert Nozick. His book *Anarchy, State, and Utopia* (1974) was a libertarian answer to the theories of John Rawls

- Modern liberalism's belief in an expanded enabling state infringes individual liberty and erodes rugged and egotistical individualism. Rather than relying on themselves, individuals become dependent on a state that supports them from 'cradle to grave'. Hayek argued that state paternalism created a dependency culture which arrested individual development and initiative.
- Hayek also argued that the exponential cost of and demand for welfare provision would eventually bankrupt state and society. If one looks at the developed world today, many countries, including the USA and the UK, are running huge deficits because they spend more than they receive in taxation. (See these real-time world debt clocks as an illustration: **www.usdebtclock.org/world-debt-clock.html**.)
- Nozick argued that the taxation the state demanded from its citizens infringed their freedom, and he believed that 'tax, for the most part, is theft'. Nozick argued that Rawls' principles of redistribution and social justice were essentially socialism and a betrayal of liberalism's core idea of egotistical individualism.

- Nozick argued that modern liberalism betrayed the classical liberal notions of Immanuel Kant (1724–1804), who had argued that an individual should not be treated as a thing or resource. Modern liberalism contravenes such self-ownership as its enlarged state contravenes negative freedom and oppresses individuals to pay taxes, obey its intrusive laws and fight its wars.
- Milton Friedman was critical of the supposed efficacy of Keynesian economics. The state was ill-equipped to plan or intervene in the economy, and this was as true for state planners in Western democracies as it was for communist societies.
- Neo-liberalism therefore sees the role of government as being limited to controlling inflation, via a policy called 'monetarism', which emphasises the need for governments to show restraint in their role as monopolists over the supply of money. For monetarist economists like Friedman, the state's tendency to print money (as an easier alternative to raising revenue through taxes) leads only to inflation, eroding the value of private citizens' wages and savings.
- In contemporary politics, the ideas of classical liberalism inform (in part) the modern US Republican Party, while modern liberalism has a similar influence over the Democrat Party. Somewhat confusingly, when the term 'liberal' is used by politicians or the media, what they are actually referring to is modern liberalism. Even more confusingly, classical liberal ideas are often referred to as conservative (because Republicans wish to hark back to ideas that existed prior to modern liberalism).

While is it possible to argue that modern liberalism emerged like a butterfly from the larva of classical liberalism, in practical terms they are two distinct visions of liberalism. Updated by more recent thinkers and now known as neo-liberalism, the ideas of classical liberalism and modern liberalism are very much autonomous. Fundamentally these two strands of liberalism are irreconcilable in how they define freedom and the individual and the role of the state within society and the economy.

Debate

Is modern liberalism radically different to classical liberalism?

Yes

- The different strands of liberalism interpret freedom/liberty in dramatically different ways. Classical liberalism argues for negative liberty and modern liberals prefer positive liberty.
- Classical liberals argue for a minimal state; modern liberals argue for an enabling state.
- Classical liberals view taxation as an infringement of negative freedom. Modern liberals view taxation as a key process for the implementation of positive freedom.
- Classical liberals favour laissez-faire economics. Modern liberals are prepared to use Keynesian economics in certain economic situations (such as in the aftermath of a recession).
- Classical liberals prefer limited forms of democracy so that elite groups retain power. Modern liberalism embraces full representative democracy.

No

- Both strands of liberalism have a positive view of human nature and human potential.
- Both strands agree on the principle of government by consent and the concept of limited government (although their definition of what constitutes limited government differs).
- Both strands of liberalism believe in rationalism, the harm principle and tolerance of minority groups.
- Individualism is a primary goal for both strands of liberalism, they merely differ in their methods for achieving it.
- Both strands of liberalism are enthusiastic supporters of capitalism and the free market and oppose nationalisation.

Summary: key themes and key thinkers

	Human nature	The state	Society	The economy
John Locke	Humans are guided by self-interest but are concerned for others	The state should only govern by consent	Natural laws and natural rights of society predate the state	Private property is a natural right and the state's role is merely to arbitrate between individuals competing for trade and resources
Mary Wollstonecraft	Both men and women are capable of rational thought	Monarchical states should be replaced by Republican states that entrench women's rights	Society 'infantilised' women and this inhibited female individualism	Liberated women would thrive and enhance the free-market economy
John Stuart Mill	Human nature is rational but not fixed and is capable of progressing to higher levels	The state should be a representative democracy and be mindful of minority rights	Individuality should coexist with tolerance and self-improvement	Laissez-faire capitalism promotes both individual initiative and progress
John Rawls	Humans can be selfish and value individual freedom. However, they are sympathetic to those less fortunate than them	An enabling state will assist developmental individualism via public spending on services	Rawls' rationalistic 'veil of ignorance' argued that individuals would choose a society that offered opportunities for the less fortunate to improve their condition	The state's obligation to disadvantaged citizens would temper free-market capitalism
Betty Friedan	Culture has evolved so that human nature is patriarchal and discriminatory towards women (see Chapter 14)	The state should intervene in the public sphere to prevent discrimination against women (see Chapter 14)	Society is patriarchal and needs reforming	Liberated women would thrive and enhance the free-market economy. Legislation must prevent women being discriminated against in the workplace

Practice questions

1 To what extent do classical and modern liberals agree about human nature? *You must use appropriate thinkers you have studied to support your answer and consider both sides in a balanced way.* (24)

2 To what extent do classical and modern liberals disagree about the role of the state? *You must use appropriate thinkers you have studied to support your answer and consider both sides in a balanced way.* (24)

3 To what extent do classical and modern liberals agree about freedom/liberty? *You must use appropriate thinkers you have studied to support your answer and consider both sides in a balanced way.* (24)

10 Conservatism

Conservatism has traditionally sought to conserve society and has been distrustful of ideological thinking. As a political idea conservativism has developed considerably:

- **Traditional conservatism** emerged, in part, as a reaction to the rational principles of the Enlightenment in the eighteenth century. It argued that pragmatism (a practical attitude), empiricism (evidence and experience) and tradition were vital in maintaining society.
- **One-nation conservatism** developed in the late nineteenth century and evolved further in the twentieth century. One-nation conservatism advocated more state interference in both society and the economy to preserve society.
- **The New Right** emerged as a force in the 1970s. A marriage between neo-liberalism and neo-conservatism, it argued that one-nation conservatism had sanctioned too many changes to the role of the state in its interactions with society and the economy, and had lost touch with true conservative values.

On the 1651 cover of Thomas Hobbes' *Leviathan*, the king represents the state and his body represents a society made up of sovereign individuals who have willingly surrendered liberty in return for societal order

Core ideas and principles

Human imperfection

Human imperfection is a core feature of most aspects of conservatism. Thomas Hobbes (1588–1679), in his famous work *Leviathan* (1651), argued that humans are imperfect and ruthlessly self-interested. Noel O'Sullivan argued that traditional conservatism views human imperfection in three distinct categories:

- Morally imperfect: Humans are selfish creatures motivated by base impulses.
- Intellectually imperfect: Reality is beyond rational understanding. Consequently, abstract ideas or theories will always be flawed.
- Psychologically imperfect: Humans are security driven and socially dependent. We rely on tradition and culture for an identity.

Hobbes argued that human imperfection cannot be avoided.

- Humans desire power and material gratification and are distrustful of others. This is our species' natural state, which Hobbes calls the 'state of nature' — a violent, fearful place where humans are in never-ending conflict as they pursue their selfish desires.
- The 'state of nature' describes society before the existence of the state, where individuals live without laws. Here life would be little more than a struggle for power, a 'perpetual and restless desire for power and power that only ceaseth in death'. Existence would be bleak — a violent anarchy where life would be 'solitary, poor, nasty, brutish and short'.

Although Hobbes thought humans intellectually imperfect, he did not think them wholly irrational. Humans would recognise the 'state of nature' as a hell on Earth and would realise that they needed protecting from themselves. Hobbes theorised that individuals would seek a social contract: surrendering individual autonomy to a sovereign monarch, who in return would provide order through his **authority**. This would allow society to develop, and humans to live collectively and without fear. For Hobbes, human nature is also psychological in that its primary interest is self-preservation: 'the first and fundamental law of Nature, which is to seek peace and follow it'.

> **Key term**
>
> **Authority** Those in higher positions of society who are best positioned to make decisions on society's behalf. Their legitimacy comes naturally from within the hierarchy, and those below them in the hierarchy are obliged to obey.

Key thinker

Thomas Hobbes (1588–1679)

Hobbes was a philosopher linked to both conservative and liberal traditions. His work and ideas were written in response to the anarchy associated with the English Civil War (1642–51). His main ideas were discussed in his key work, *Leviathan* (1651).

Hobbes' main ideas

- Hobbes' ideas are based on how he imagined state and society to have formed.
- Humans are imperfect and selfish, with a relentless desire for the acquisition of goods and self-gratification. In this state of nature, life would be 'solitary, poor, nasty, brutish and short' and existence would be a hellish chaotic world of constant warfare.
- Human are rational enough to seek order, which can only be achieved by a social contract where individuals give up freedoms (which are meaningless in a chaotic 'state of nature') to an all-powerful sovereign. In return the sovereign grants legal and physical protection to his subjects.
- The social contract between the people establishes a sovereign and when the contract is complete individual autonomy ceases and all power is transferred to the sovereign. The sovereign is all powerful and he alone determines the rights and laws of the people. Hobbes is clear that society cannot exist before the creation of the state.

Edmund Burke (1729–97) agreed with Hobbes that humans are imperfect but disagreed considerably on the extent of this imperfection.

- Burke did not think humans are ruthlessly individualistic; rather they are naturally communal, as their imperfection compels them to band together in supportive communities.
- Burke agreed with Hobbes that humans are capable of making mistakes, but not to the same destructive levels. The scope of human reason and understanding is poor, so people are more likely to fail than succeed.
- Burke thought that decision making based on rationalistic ideas of abstract thought is ill-advised and that change should only be cautiously and empirically considered: 'Politics ought to be adjusted not to human reasonings but to human nature, of which reason is but a part and by no means the greatest part'.

Key thinker

Edmund Burke (1729–97)

Edmund Burke was a Whig MP, whose ideas have influenced both liberals and conservatives. He is now seen by many as being the father of conservatism. Burke opposed the French Revolution which, in turn, influenced his political thinking and ideas. This is reflected in his key work, *Reflections on the Revolution in France* (1790).

Burke's main ideas

- The organic society is not static and sometimes it must 'change to conserve' itself, guided by history, pragmatism and, above all, **empiricism**.
- Burke's belief in human imperfection led him to rebut the abstract ideas of Enlightenment thinkers and the rational thought that informed their thinking on political and social issues.
- The French Revolution, based on abstract principles, discarded empiricism and tradition for utopian idealism and 'philosophical abstractions' that quickly descended into violence and chaos.
- The Jacobins' quest for the ideal society failed, because they sacrificed social order for the abstract human rights of Rousseau (see Chapter 16) and Paine. (The Jacobins were radical revolutionaries who plotted the downfall of the French monarchy. They were influenced by the Enlightenment ideas of Jean-Jacques Rousseau, whose work *The Social Contract* argued against the divine right of kings, and Thomas Paine, who argued for the innate 'rights of man' in his most famous work, *Rights of Man*.)
- Interestingly, Burke was sympathetic towards the American Revolution. He believed that the colonies had been totally misgoverned by the British government and the actions of the republicans were justified. In contrast to France, when America overturned British rule it did not abandon the values, culture and traditions of the pre-existing society.

Key term

Empiricism The idea that knowledge and evidence come from real experience and not abstract theories.

The beliefs of Michael Oakeshott (1901–90) have more in common with Burke than Hobbes.

- Oakeshott argued that humans are 'fragile and fallible' but that they are capable of benevolence.
- Like Burke, Oakeshott argued that society is organic and consists of intricate customs and traditions that provide consolation, comfort and happiness.
- However, the nirvana promised by utopian societies is unobtainable, as perfection cannot be created by imperfect creatures.

Stretch and challenge

Analyse the gender mix and educational background of the Supreme Court justices. Does this suggest that the Supreme Court is highly unrepresentative of contemporary British society? Explain whether or not you think this matters.

Key thinker

Michael Oakeshott (1901–90)

Michael Oakeshott was a twentieth-century philosopher. His main ideas were discussed in his key essay, 'On Being Conservative' (1956).

Oakeshott's main ideas

- Conservatism is as much a disposition as it is a set of political ideas. The security of long-standing customs and traditions are at the core of Oakeshott's conservatism.
- 'The politics of faith': rationalism is beyond the ability of human beings because they are intellectually imperfect.
- Oakeshott explores 'the politics of scepticism': because rationalism and its doctrines are flawed, humans should put their faith in trusted tradition. Modern society is unpredictable and multifaceted; rational theories often simplify complex situations and state management, based on such a rationale, can make matters worse.
- Government should govern in the best interests of the people, grounded in pragmatism and empiricism and not guided by abstract concepts of what *should* be.

Oakeshott argues for the 'politics of faith', where decision making is grounded in empiricism and not rationalism (Table 10.1).

- Faith in rationalism is misplaced and those who act on the 'authority of' their 'own reason', rather than their experience, will fail.
- Oakeshott's conclusions on intellectual imperfection led him to argue for 'the politics of scepticism', which concluded that the implementation of abstract ideas often leads to unintended negative consequences. Rationalists underestimate the complexity of reality, failing to comprehend that in attempting to improve society or the economy they may make matters worse. Oakeshott warns us to be mindful that when rendering changes for betterment the 'cure is not worse than the disease'.

Table 10.1 Definitions of empiricism and rationalism

Empiricism	Rationalism
If the state subscribes to empiricism, the changes it makes are informed by past experience. For example, Peel's decision to remove the corn tariff in the Repeal of the Corn Laws in 1846 put the good of society above tradition. This was the time of the Irish potato famine and Peel saw from this that food must be made cheaper. Peel was informed by Burke's maxim of 'change to conserve'	If the state subscribes to rationalism, the changes it makes are informed by abstract ideas. For example, Harold Macmillan adopted Keynesian economics, which were based on a rational economic blueprint of state management rather than the long-standing tradition of laissez-faire limited government

Organic society or state

Conservatives believe that society is not created but emerges and grows, developing like an organism (Figure 10.1). Hobbes' belief that the state precedes society is vital in understanding how conservatives understand reality. The natural rights and laws favoured by John Locke (see Chapter 9) are a rationalistic conceit, as individual rights are utterly dependent on the ability of the state to maintain them. Burke agreed with Hobbes, arguing that these 'pretended rights are all extremes and in proportion as they are metaphysically true, they are morally and politically false'. Individual rights are dependent upon law and order and only the state has the authority to give individual rights a practical meaning.

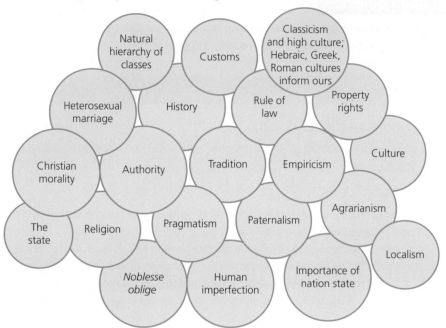

Figure 10.1 An organic society or state grows and develops naturally like a living organism; everything is interconnected

Ironically, given that conservatism is so grounded in empiricism, Hobbes' idea of a social contract is rationalistic in origin.

- Traditional conservatives such as Hobbes, Burke and Oakeshott believed that once the state provides the necessary order, society will emerge organically, maturing into a complicated organism of traditions and customs.
- Hobbes believed in an absolute monarchy, where the sovereign (the personification of the state) controlled every aspect of society (law, religion and parliament), as well as the economy (private property and taxation). However, traditional conservatives such as Burke and Oakeshott, as well as one-nation conservatives and neo-conservatives, favoured societal ideas established during the 1688 Glorious Revolution (see page 18). These ideas, which are liberal in origin, limited the power of the monarch and established the principle of parliamentary sovereignty and the idea of representative government. John Locke claimed that the purpose of *Two Treatises of Government* (1689) was to justify William III's accession to the throne.
- Burke wrote of 'little platoons' of localised communities that retain their identity and enable wider integration within the nation.

- Such communities are bound by affection and cooperation and give structure and meaning to our lives.
- The organic state, with its history, customs and tradition, is vitally important for informing both the present and the future.

Maintaining society

The multiple traditions, customs and institutions of an organic society give individuals a sense of 'rootedness' and belonging, and in return individuals have duties and obligations to maintain society.

The state is an organism that must evolve if it, and society, are to continue to flourish. Burke's idea of '**change to conserve**', where the state maintains society, has influenced not just traditional conservatives but also one-nation conservatives and neo-conservatives in the practicalities of statecraft.

- The past is to be revered and ancient institutions should not be tampered with, but if there are defects or abuses which harm the workings of the organic society they must be removed.
- Inaction can damage the organic society; the French and Russian revolutions were the consequence of disorder in society. It is for this reason that Burke argued that 'a state without the means of some change is without the means of its conservation'.

An unequal society

Some parts of the organism are more important than others and inequality is natural. The organic society is hierarchical; there is a natural order in where each individual has their place. Individuals are of unequal talents and ability, and for Hobbes, Burke and Oakeshott this was a practical reality of human existence.

- For Hobbes, society was to be ruled by an absolute monarch governing a 'commonwealth' arranged by rank and influence.
- For Burke, the aristocracy should lead as they were wiser and stronger than their inferiors and they had a responsibility for the lower orders.
- Oakeshott's championing of tradition has been seen as a justification for defending established institutions, such as the House of Lords or the Electoral College, from reform (see pages 179 and 531).

Since the mid- to late nineteenth century, all current conservative thinkers, starting with one-nation conservatives, have accepted the concept of democracy. However, society remains hierarchical, even within a modern democracy, and the paternalism of *noblesse oblige* can be found in postwar one-nation conservatism and neo-conservatism. Sometimes society must evolve but any change must be cautiously considered for fear of unintended damage.

The 'Great Chain of Being' by Didacus Valades, 1579, illustrates the conservative view (influenced by Christianity) that all life and matter is hierarchical

Key terms

Change to conserve
Society should adapt to shifting circumstances by instigating small modifications to compensate rather than rejecting change outright. These compromises will preserve the essence of society. If society does not change, it risks rebellion and/or revolution.
Noblesse oblige The duty of the society's elite, the wealthy and privileged, to look after those less fortunate.

Pragmatism

Pragmatism is a core value of conservativism. Pragmatic thinkers are informed by empiricism and have a deep distrust of the abstract theories favoured by political ideas such as liberalism and socialism.

- Burke's idea of 'change to conserve' influenced Conservative prime ministers Robert Peel and Benjamin Disraeli.
- Peel's *Tamworth Manifesto* (1834) argued that conservatism must be pragmatic and not reactionary. He put this into practice in his acceptance of the Great Reform Act of 1832, which gave middle-class men the vote for the first time, pragmatically accepting that this emerging class of the Industrial Revolution must be integrated into the political system.
- Disraeli approached the Artisan Dwellings Act 1875, which dealt with slum clearance, in a similar pragmatic fashion.

All these changes were derived from empiricism and with the aim of making society more stable.

- Later, one-nation conservatism, embodied in Conservative governments from 1951 to 1979, pragmatically accepted and continued the radical changes made to British society by Attlee's Labour government, such as state intervention in the economy and the creation of the welfare state.

Tradition

Traditions are seen as the accumulated wisdom of the past that underpin society.

- Religion is perhaps the most important tradition. Burke perceived religion as 'our comfort, and one great source of civilisation'. Moreover, religious traditions bind society together to the extent that Burke argued atheism must be supressed as it was destabilising.
- The rationalistic ideas of the Enlightenment and the rise of the secular state have, since the 1960s' social revolution, increasingly weakened Judaeo-Christian religion. Oakeshott argued that with the decline of religion, those who would once have embraced its values are now inclined towards abstract ideas and potentially harmful rationalist thinking as a kind of intellectual replacement.

For Burke, traditions were vital as they embodied continuity, which in turn advanced peacefulness: the ultimate political goal.

- Burke argued that society was a 'partnership between those who are living, those who are dead and those who are to be born'. Tradition, custom and habit should govern human action, not abstract thought.
- Accumulated wisdom is found within long-standing institutions such as the monarchy, ancient schools and universities, and communities, as well as the aforementioned religion. Humans should trust traditions to guide them. Burke called this 'wisdom without reflection'. Traditions allow individuals to feel belonging, a sense of identity reinforcing the social cohesion of society.
- Abandoning traditions is dangerous. As Oakeshott argued, 'What has stood the test of time is good and must not be lightly cast aside.' For this reason, neo-conservatives (twentieth-century conservatives influenced by traditional conservatism) are sometimes pro-religion even though they may be unbelievers, because of the societal function that it serves.

Conservatives can cite numerous examples to demonstrate the damaging consequences of when long-standing traditions are abolished in favour of rationalist replacements, such as the French and Russian revolutions. Conservative thinkers are distrustful of constitutional changes if they are, as Oakeshott has warned, based on the unproven promises of abstract theories.

Paternalism

Conservatives believe society is unequal and arranged in a natural hierarchy, in which the ruling class has a *noblesse oblige* relationship to the weaker elements. This paternal responsibility is derived from a hierarchical position of rank to help those less fortunate and who cannot act in their own interests.

- Paternalism is also a pragmatic belief, as if the state fails to counter societal problems it risks upsetting the established order and the existence of the organic society.
- Benjamin Disraeli, Conservative prime minister (1868 and 1874–80), argued for what was later called one-nation conservatism, in part influenced by the ideas of Burke.
- Consequently, the ruling elite of the late nineteenth century accepted their obligations to the new industrial working class by enacting social reforms and limited welfarism to help the poorest in society and to preserve stability.

After the Second World War, paternalistically motivated one-nation conservatives increasingly intervened in both society and economy.

As prime minister between 1957 and 1963, Harold Macmillan combined state ownership and private enterprise, continuing socialist policies. Macmillan's adoption of a mixed economy therefore reframed Disraeli's one-nation conservatism and paternalism for the twentieth century.

Neo-conservatives argued that the unintended consequences of the paternalistic welfarism of the postwar period were that those they were trying to help became hopelessly dependent on the state and that the societal obligations of traditional conservativism had been forgotten.

Neo-conservative paternalism is therefore akin to parental tough love; it acknowledges the role of the state to intervene in society but wishes to narrow the parameters and scale of its assistance.

One-nation conservatism was first conceived by Benjamin Disraeli

Libertarianism

Libertarianism is a political philosophy that emphasises negative freedom (freedom from interference) and advocates minimal state intervention.

- Libertarianism was inherent in traditional conservatism as Burke supported Adam Smith, the champion of **laissez-faire** economics. The traditional conservatism of the eighteenth century saw a minimal role for the state in society and the economy.
- It was only with the growth of the state and welfare spending that income tax in the UK became a compulsory requirement of the state on its citizens. Robert Peel reintroduced income tax in 1842 — it had briefly existed from 1799 to 1802 to pay for the Napoleonic Wars. In the USA income tax had existed on and off from 1861 (when President Lincoln signed it into law to help pay for the defeat of the Confederate states in the American Civil War) but only in 1913, with the 16th Amendment to the US Constitution, did income tax become a permanent feature.

Neo-liberals (also known as libertarians) believe in an atomistic society made up of self-interested and self-sufficient individuals. Ayn Rand (1905–82) is associated with the term 'atomistic individualism', where autonomous individuals seek rationalised self-fulfilment.

- On Rand's terms society does not exist as we are but as a loose collection of independent beings. Neo-liberals' view of human nature is quite different from the thinking of traditional conservatives.
- Neo-liberals reject pessimistic human imperfection, preferring the rationalism of the Enlightenment, that people are able to order their lives on a moral and logical basis.
- Neo-liberals like Robert Nozick (1938–2002) and Rand reject empiricism, which puts them at odds with conservative thinkers like Burke and Oakeshott.
- Neo-liberals believe in egotistical individualism, whereby the rights of the individual are more important than those of the state.
- Neo-liberals believe in negative freedom, whereby the individual should be free from as many external constraints (including the authority of religion) as possible.
- The paternalism of *noblesse oblige* restricts individuals' development as it limits choice and prevents them from learning from their mistakes.
- Neo-liberalism challenges the idea of traditional conservative hierarchies and the legitimacy of the state with all of its organic traditions. Society is atomistic and should be organised instead on meritocratic terms – Nozick argued that 'there are only individual people, different individual people, with their own lives'. The minimal state will allow the emergence and co-existences of voluntary-formed communities that individuals are free to interact with or ignore at their own discretion. The state's role is that of a nightwatchman, overseeing the rule of law and protecting the rights of individuals from criminals and foreign invaders.

Neo-liberals view the steady growth of the state from the nineteenth century as a negative development, with Nozick arguing that 'tax, for the most part, is theft' from the individual by the state.

- Neo-liberals argue for a massive reduction in tax and state spending on society as both a moral and an economic imperative for individual freedom.
- Nozick argued that the state encroaches on the lives of citizens and that welfarism creates a dependency culture, with the state 'owning' individuals.

- Neo-liberal economist Friedrich Hayek argued that expensive welfare states should be abolished as they will eventually bankrupt society. He and his disciples point to the huge deficits that developed Western economies are running.

Nozick and Rand called for a rolling back of the state's involvement in society to achieve **atomism**.

- Neo-liberals argue for **radical** deregulation and privatisation of services carried out by the state.
- Bodies regarded as obstructive to the free market, like trade unions, should have their powers curtailed.
- Nozick argued that the individual should be 'left alone' not just in the economic sphere but also in the social and cultural spheres as well. Rand's 'objectivist' philosophy saw her place the individual's 'right to choose' as paramount on issues such as abortion and homosexuality — two areas that the state at the time of her writing deemed to be immoral and illegal.
- Nozick and Rand argue that the growth of the state is the gravest contemporary threat to individual freedom.

Key thinker

Ayn Rand (1905–82)

Rand is an unusual political thinker as many of her philosophical ideas are found in works of fiction, in particular *Atlas Shrugged* (1957), as well as in her philosophical work *The Virtue of Selfishness* (1964).

Rand's main ideas

- Individuals are rational and their highest moral purpose is the achievement of personal happiness. Rand rejected human imperfection and loathed any kind of collectivism because the obligations demanded from individuals eroded their freedom. Society should be atomistic.
- The only moral purpose of society is to protect individual rights. In an atomistic society, individuals have the right to maintain property and income without being taxed for welfare spending. Individuals should maintain their lives through their own efforts; Rand opposed welfare provision, favouring voluntarism.
- Rand's belief in negative liberty provided the philosophical justification for 'rolling back the state'. Rand argued for free market economics (separating state and economy) and also a minimal role for the state in society (free from the traditional moral interference of traditional conservatives). Rand's championing of the individual meant she supported homosexuality and abortion, which were still illegal in the USA when she first began writing.
- Rand believed in 'objectivism', which is where individuals who experience negative freedom are best able to comprehend reality and achieve self-realisation and self-fulfilment. Individuals should therefore be guided by self-interest. Rand argued that there is a logic and virtue in selfishness.
- Rand's neo-liberalism, like Robert Nozick's, should not be confused with individualistic anarchism (a complete loss of government), as both require a small state to maintain free markets and social freedoms and to defend borders (see page 314).

Robert Nozick (1938–2002)

Robert Nozick was an American academic whose most famous work, *Anarchy, State and Utopia* (1974), describes his libertarian ideas.

These libertarian beliefs led him to two broad conclusions:

- 'Minarchist' government with minimal interference in the lives of individuals makes for the best society.
- The state's primary function is to protect individual human rights.

Nozick's minarchist society would allow communities to be free to practise their own particular moral codes rather than have political or religious values imposed upon them by the state.

Differing views and tensions within conservatism

Traditional conservatism

Traditional conservatism is best understood as a set of political ideas that were worked out as a response to the French Revolution of 1789, which challenged the hierarchical aristocracy of European society. Initially traditional conservatism had reactionary and pragmatic branches, but it can also be seen as a psychological disposition within all of us (Figure 10.2).

Figure 10.2 The three aspects of traditional conservatism

Traditional conservatism — reactionary

Traditional conservatism can be understood as a reactionary doctrine, partially influenced by the ideas of Hobbes, which believes in a feudal hierarchic order of society. In the eighteenth century these ideas were challenged by the ideas of the Enlightenment and the events of the French Revolution as well as by the changing dynamics of state and society caused by the consequences of the Industrial Revolution. Traditional conservativism was therefore a defensive ideology resisting the decline of aristocratic rule. As the rule of the aristocracy declined so did this aspect of conservatism. The Romanov royal family, deposed in the Russian Revolution, were one of the last examples of this kind of inflexible autocratic conservatism.

Traditional conservatism — non-reactionary

Burke was clear that conservatism must counter Enlightenment ideas, as such rationalist delusions had led to the French Revolution. Conservative ideas of hierarchy, empiricism, tradition and authority, all of which had been undermined by the ideas of the Enlightenment, must be defended as they help maintain societal equilibrium.

Unlike its reactionary strand, pragmatic or non-reactionary traditional conservatism was capable of change, but only after careful consideration. As Burke argued:

'It is with infinite caution that any man ought to venture upon pulling down an edifice which has answered in any tolerable degree for ages the common purposes of society.'

The spirit of Burke's ideas can be seen throughout the conservatism of the nineteenth century, which saw the adoption of moderate reforms to keep society stable and a commitment to the free market. Outmoded traditions that could spark revolutionary unrest were changed by careful empirical deliberation. The reforms of Robert Peel illustrate the influence of Burke, but also of Hobbes (Table 10.2).

Table 10.2 Robert Peel's reforms

The founding of the Metropolitan Police, 1829	The long-standing tradition of unpaid parish constables was failing in 1820s London. Home Secretary Robert Peel cautiously replaced an outmoded tradition, echoing the ideas of Burke. Peel argued that 'without security there can be no liberty', renewing Hobbes' belief of authority bringing order to society
The Repeal of the Corn Laws, 1846	Traditional conservatives placed the importance of the organic society above that of a free market economy and therefore practised protectionism to preserve the interests of Britain's landed aristocracy. The best example of this was the Corn Laws, a tariff issued on foreign corn which kept the price of corn artificially high. Peel acted for the good of the whole nation rather than the profit of the landed class. Moreover, Peel was 'changing to conserve' as high food prices were a cause of civil unrest and protectionism was an outmoded tradition; repealing the corn laws and adopting free trade secured societal stability and economic prosperity

Traditional conservatism — a natural disposition

Michael Oakeshott focuses on the psychological and intellectual aspects of human imperfection (implied in the ideas of Hobbes and Burke) when attempting to describe conservatism. Conservatism is a therefore a natural disposition rather than a political idea or ideology.

- Translating his view into practical politics, Oakeshott would prefer the trusted practised methods of imperfect institutions and traditions to change, arguing that: 'What has stood the test of time is good and must not be lightly cast aside.'
- Oakeshott's politics of faith argues that humans' intellectual inability to comprehend reality means that any abstract thought, divorced from experience, will be flawed. This is why rationalistic blueprints of perfect societies and state planning fail and why governments must rely on empirical informed pragmatism to govern.

While Burke argued 'change to conserve' to maintain an organic society, Oakeshott is less optimistic, arguing that political philosophy should not be expected to provide success in political activity. The reality of humankind's intellectual limitations means that we should embrace the politics of scepticism and be guided by experience. As Oakeshott argued:

'To be conservative, then, is to prefer the familiar to the unknown, to prefer the tried to the untried, fact to mystery, the actual to the possible, the limited to the unbounded, the near to the distant, the sufficient to the superabundant, the convenient to the perfect, present laughter to utopian bliss.'

Robert Peel, prime minister in 1834–35 and 1841–46, was influenced by the ideas of Hobbes and Burke

Early one-nation conservatism

By the latter half of the nineteenth century, governments were beginning to face the consequences of mass industrialisation and the call for socialist reform.

- Traditional conservative policy has always been laissez-faire within the economy and society and has seen minimal state intervention by government. However, mass industrialisation caused social inequality, which fanned the flames of possible revolution, and new ideas such as revolutionary socialism and anarchism were rational alternatives that scared traditional conservatives.
- Conservative prime minister Benjamin Disraeli drew from Burke an admiration for hierarchical aristocracy and organic society. Disraeli admired *noblesse oblige*, the wisdom inherent in traditions and the varied institutions that underpin the organic society, in particular property ownership and the Church of England.
- Moreover, like Burke, Disraeli loathed doctrines and abstract ideas supplanting empiricism. One-nation conservatism was first espoused in one of Disraeli's novels, *Sybil or the Two Nations* (1845) and is sometimes described as an updating of traditional conservatism in response to the emergence of capitalism.

Disraeli's ultimate aim was to make society secure and to do this the tensions between rich and poor must be addressed while simultaneously renewing a sense of national identity and community. Nationalism up to this point had been strongly associated with revolution: in France in 1789 and across the continent during the revolutionary upheavals of 1848.

PUNCH, OR THE LONDON CHARIVARI.—August 3, 1867.

A LEAP IN THE DARK.

The horse in this *Punch* cartoon resembles Disraeli, who is carrying Britain (personified by the goddess Britannia) into a corn field that represents the 1867 Representation of the People Act, which the government was about to pass. Britannia demonstrates her fear of this Act by covering her face, while in the background leading politicians of the day watch with concern

- Disraeli offered a form of nationalism, based on organic conservatism, where all societal classes were part of a family that was 'the nation' (see page 271).
- The elite landed class had a *noblesse oblige* responsibility to care for the rest of the people. Paraphrasing his policy, Disraeli argued that, 'the palace is not safe when the cottage is not happy'. Disraeli's reforms are influenced by empiricism and Burke's belief that society must 'change to conserve'.
- Early one-nation reforms were the Representation of the People Act 1867 and the Artisans' Dwellings Act 1875. The Representation of the People Act enfranchised large parts of the urban male working class. Conservatives traditionally fear change because the consequences are often unpredictable and can unintentionally make things worse. Disraeli had acknowledged this uncertainty by describing the Act as 'a leap in the dark'. However, he was convinced the reform would guarantee societal stability and attract new voters to the Conservative Party.

Later one-nation conservatism

One-nation conservatism from 1945 to the present day still invokes the paternal ideas of Burke and the examples of Disraeli and is most commonly associated with Harold Macmillan.

- As Churchill's housing minister, Macmillan oversaw the building of 300,000 houses a year after the Second World War.
- As well as alleviating housing pressures, Macmillan hoped to create 'a property-owning democracy' sympathetic to traditional conservative values.

As prime minister between 1957 and 1963 Macmillan championed a conservatism that steered a course between traditional conservative laissez-faire economics and the socialist collectivism of state planning which he had first discussed in *The Middle Way* (1938).

- Macmillan shared Burke's belief that preserving society was of paramount importance and he viewed the debilitating effects of unemployment as a terrible threat to stability.
- Macmillan rejected empiricism and chose the rationalistic ideas of economist John Maynard Keynes to combat this threat. His governments attempted to manage the economy in a way that no conservative administration had previously attempted.
- Contemporary conservatives were aware of this philosophical break. Macmillan's chancellor, Selwyn Lloyd, stated in 1961: 'I will deal first with growth in the economy. The controversial matter of planning at once arises. I am frightened of the word.' Lloyd was scared of abandoning traditional conservative empiricism for rationalist state management.
- The Macmillan government also demonstrated that it could abandon tradition. The Life Peerage Act (1958) was a radical break with the past which saw the creation of working 'life peers' (including female peers).
- These ideas were as much informed by modern liberalism and the enabling state (see page 250) as they were by traditional conservatism or Disraeli's empirical one-nation conservatism.
- Michael Oakeshott disapproved of this style of conservatism, as state management is rationally informed and ignores the limits of human reason.
- Modern one-nation conservatism has also embraced social liberalism, putting it at odds with traditional conservative values.

Rand was a pure libertarian and called her theory 'objectivism', a philosophy based on the rationalism of reason and scientific fact.

- The traditions that Burke, Oakeshott and all other aspects of conservative cherish are, for Rand, a nonsense.
- Objectivism argues that truth is found not in the collective beliefs of society or the unproven myth of religion, but in scientific fact.
- Rand argues for a 'virtue of selfishness' and praises egoism. For Rand, it is morally right for individuals to pursue their own dreams and objectives rather than those determined by state and society.
- Religious, socialist, fascist and democratic organic societies all demand that the individual sacrifice their own personal values for some greater good. It is wrong for any society to demand that individuals compromise their core values for some collective truth.

Unsurprisingly, Rand loathed communism, with its inherent collectivism, more than any other political idea.

Rand also argues that **altruism** is misrepresented in an organic society, as it should not be a duty dictated by the state but the rational action of an individual pursuing his or her own values.

- If individuals choose to donate money to charities providing social welfare (known as 'voluntarism') this should be as an individual's choice and not a state obligation.
- Neo-liberals argue that state-sponsored welfare spending arrests the development of atomistic individualism by making individuals dependent on the state.
- Nozick viewed welfare spending, funded by taxation, as an example of the state unfairly encroaching on individual liberty. 'The illegitimate use of a state by economic interests for their own end is based upon a pre-existing illegitimate power of the state to enrich some persons at the expense of others.'

Key term

Altruism The belief that humans are not born to be self-seeking but can display fellow feeling, sympathy for others and an instinct to help and cooperate with others.

Abolishing state intervention would allow society to rediscover its atomistic individualistic mindset. Rather than asking, What will the government do for me?, individuals would be forced to ask, What can I do for myself? While other aspects of conservatism view the state as a paternal watchman and the organic society as a reassuring communal comfort, neo-liberals view it as inhibiting the individual. Students who view school rules and sanctions as infringements on their personal autonomy can perhaps empathise with how a neo-liberal will feel about state intervention within society and the economy.

Neo-liberalism views 'selfishness' as not a vice but a virtue. When viewed through the prism of atomistic individualism, self-interest is the most rational and moral course of action that one can take. Free from the shackles and obligations of state and society, neo-liberals such as Rand and Nozick argue that human potential will be fully realised and a natural harmony will exist within human interactions.

Free-market economics

By the late 1960s and 1970s, with Keynesian state planning beginning to falter, neo-liberalism offered clear explanations for this failure, arguing that only the free market could properly allocate resources.

- The state, neo-liberals argued, was ill-equipped to plan or intervene in the economy, and this was as true for state planners in Western democracies as it was in communist societies.
- Nationalised industries, such as those common in the UK at this time, were inefficient, lacked free-market dynamism and were artificially protected from free-market competition, which in turn distorted the whole market.

According to economist Milton Friedman, the state planning inspired by Keynesian economics was inflationary, and this in turn reduced economic activity. State or government management would always lag behind and underperform the free market. As Friedman famously quipped: 'If you put the federal government in charge of the Sahara Desert, in five years there'd be a shortage of sand.'

Neo-liberalism therefore sees the role of government as being limited to controlling inflation, via a policy called 'monetarism', which emphasises the need for governments to show restraint in their role as monopolists over the supply of money.

- For monetarist economists like Friedman, the state's tendency to print money (as an easier alternative to raising revenue through taxes) led only to inflation, eroding the value of private citizens' wages and savings.
- This neo-liberal insistence on monetary restraint heavily influenced the policies of Margaret Thatcher in the UK and Ronald Reagan in the USA during the 1980s.

British Railways was the state-owned company which owned most of Great Britain's railways, until it was gradually privatised in the 1990s

Neo-liberalism's belief in minimal government intervention dictates that individuals should rise and fall on their own abilities. For neo-liberals, state intervention is flawed while the natural efficiency of the market is unquestionable. This leads neo-liberals to advocate that public services be exposed to the competitive forces of the market economy.

- In the UK, Thatcher viewed nationalised industries as inefficient and she privatised gas, electricity, water and telecoms so they could thrive in their natural habitat, the free market.
- This reduced role of the state caused tension with one-nation conservatives, as Thatcher's neo-liberal economic ideology made her indifferent to high unemployment.
- Indeed, Thatcher believed that the growing unemployment in the UK during the 1970s had been indirectly the result of state intervention — or, for her, unwarranted interference — in the economy, both by overprotecting failing industries and by allowing inflation in prices and wages that made British products uncompetitive internationally.

This was a break with the interventionist consensus that had been maintained by postwar governments, both social democratic-influenced Labour and one-nation Conservative. When in office, Thatcher passed anti-union legislation and famously took on the coal mining industry when she sanctioned the closure of uneconomic state-owned coal mines. This caused the biggest strike since before the war and a bitter conflict between police and strikers. For Thatcher, the inefficient nationalised coal mines were a market distortion and after the government won the strike she privatised the coal industry. In neo-liberal terms, she was just restoring market forces and it would have been a nonsense for the state to continue to subsidise an ailing industry.

In the UK, Thatcher also injected an element of market forces into both the NHS and education, leading to free-market business practices being adopted in state-run public services.

- This went hand in hand with the introduction of target setting and league tables, in the belief that competition among public services would improve performance.
- Likewise, it is neo-liberal influences that have attempted to check the growth of the welfare state. Friedrich von Hayek's key neo-liberal work, *The Road to Serfdom*, argues that unchecked welfare spending will bankrupt societies.
- Third way policies (see Chapter 11), such as making students contribute towards the cost of their university education and raising the age of retirement, were attempts to shrink the size of the state and were neo-liberal in origin.

Debate

To what extent do conservatives agree about the state's role in the economy?

Areas of agreement

- It is the role of the state to defend economic contracts and private property.
- It defends the existence of capitalism and the free market.
- Private property is a vitally important component of the economy as it provides psychological security for individuals within society.
- Private property reduces individuals' dependency on the state. This especially appeals to traditional conservatives and neo-liberals.

Areas of disagreement

- Neo-liberals would abolish tax; neo-conservatives and traditional conservatives argue for low taxation, while one-nation conservatives advocate higher levels of taxation.
- Most conservatives favour the free market and laissez-faire economics. One-nation conservatives are more likely to favour state intervention within the economy.
- Neo-conservatives are very sympathetic to the free market. However, they are also informed by empirically based pragmatism and supported government intervention during the economic crisis of 2008, which neo-liberals opposed.
- Neo-liberals wish to 'roll back the state', preferring an atomistic state with much reduced welfare. All other areas of conservatism believe in an organic state and, to differing degrees, welfarism.

Neo-conservatism

While neo-liberals are inspired by classical liberalism, neo-conservatives are more influenced by traditional conservativism and with:

- maintaining organic society from social fragmentation
- upholding public morality and authoritarian law and order

While neo-liberalism is concerned with reducing the involvement of the state to preserve individual liberty, neo-conservatives will increase state involvement and curtail individual freedom if they feel that it is for the good of society.

An elderly Harold Macmillan with Margaret Thatcher. Thatcher's neo-conservative tendencies meant that she respected tradition and hierarchy and so she sits, seemingly in respectful awe of her predecessor. However, her neo-liberal economic beliefs put her at odds with Macmillan's one-nation conservative politics

Neo-conservatism, state and society: a fear of social fragmentation

Neo-conservatives, like neo-liberals, celebrate capitalism as the natural economic condition. However, the free market in itself does not provide a set of values on which to base a society. Likewise, neo-conservatives have been critical of neo-liberal ideas which fragment society by failing to defend core conservative values such as religion, tradition and societal responsibility.

- For neo-conservatives, the unease started with the social and sexual revolution of the 1960s, which ushered in an age of moral relativism that has fragmented society ever since.
- The secular rejection of religion in the West, Irving Kristol (1920–2009, the 'godfather of neo-conservatism') has argued, depleted the moral and spiritual stock that binds society.

Neo-conservatives, therefore, value organic society and fundamentally reject the neo-liberal vision of atomistic individualism, which has undermined core societal values. Neo-conservatives, like traditional conservatives, believe religion, tradition, authority and duty are vital facets of the organic society. Agreeing with Burke, they argue that the preservation of society is sacrosanct.

- For neo-conservatives, the welfare reforms of the 'Great Society' in the USA and the postwar consensus in the UK created a dependency culture.
- Neo-conservatives share traditional conservatism's doubts about the morality of human nature, arguing that anti-poverty programmes failed because they ignored human imperfection, and that humans are not naturally moral or hard-working.

- Conversely, neo-conservatives also dismiss neo-liberal ideas of simply dismantling the welfare state as utterly impractical and against the paternalism that is inherent in conservative thought. A neo-conservative welfare state argues for a safety net for those who are genuinely struggling, but not handouts that erode individual responsibility.
- Unlike one-nation conservatives who allowed the welfare state to grow, almost uncontrollably, neo-conservatives wish to shrink it, simultaneously promoting conservative ideas of family values and hard work (Figure 10.4).

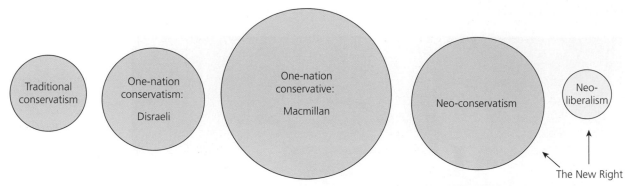

Figure 10.4 Conservatism: the size of the state in relation to society and the economy

Thatcher's 'right to buy' council houses was a neo-conservative attempt to remodel the welfare state, reduce state dependency and foster a conservative-thinking, property-owning class. Similarly, in both the USA and the UK, neo-conservatives promote traditional family structures via taxation and means-tested benefit systems. Neo-conservatives argue that individuals must also take responsibility for poverty and help themselves — the state cannot and should not do everything.

- A recent example of this thinking was the UK's Welfare Reform Act 2012, which was designed to ween benefit claimants off state reliance by incentivising them to go back to work. Its architect, the works and pension minister Iain Duncan Smith, saw this policy as a way of fixing 'broken Britain' and reintegrating an underclass that had become dislocated from the rest of society.

Public morality and authoritarian law and order

Underpinning a desire to reverse social fragmentation is a desire to uphold public morality and law and order. Neo-conservatives argue that the post-1960s decline led to immorality, leading them to promote **anti-permissiveness** and more authoritarian policing.

Neo-conservatives are critical of neo-liberalism's atomistic individualism, arguing that it has led to the rejection of communal customs and values and so helped transform Western society into a materialistic moral vacuum that ignores the ethical rights and wrongs of Christian society. Neo-conservatives, especially in the USA, are pro-religion, as it counters such moral nihilism. Religion promotes humility and a responsibility for others as well as taming what American conservative politician and theorist William Bennett has described as the 'basest appetites, passions and impulses of the citizens'.

Key term

Anti-permissiveness
A rejection, informed by Judaeo-Christian morality, that there is no right and wrong, which was dubbed 'permissiveness' by neo-conservatives. Neo-conservatives argue that sex before marriage, homosexuality, abortion and recreational drug taking, for example, are wrong. Modern one-nation Conservatives are more accepting of homosexuality, gay marriage and abortion.

- This counters Rand's idea that religion blunts rationality and infringes individual liberty.
- It also counters neo-liberals, who argue that homosexuality, abortion and recreational drug taking should be choices for the individual and not determined by the state. For neo-conservatives, these are all morally wrong and should be opposed.
- Thatcher and Reagan both had a neo-conservative-inspired 'war' on recreational drug use and advocated strict prison sentences as both a moral punishment and an authoritarian deterrent.
- Neo-conservatives therefore support a tough approach to law and order, and an extension of the state to enforce this policy.

Society must be protected from external forces as well as from internal ones. Neo-conservativism advocates hawkish foreign policy and military intervention to protect the security of the state. Examples of this would be an aggressive anti-Soviet (and therefore anti-communist) foreign policy during the Cold War; more recently, President George W. Bush and Prime Minister Tony Blair's neo-conservative-inspired foreign policy saw the USA and the UK invade Afghanistan and Iraq to combat terrorism.

Stretch and challenge

Ronald Reagan was the fortieth president of the USA (1981–89) and was heavily influenced by the policies of the New Right. Read some of his most well-known quotations:

'We don't have a trillion-dollar debt because we haven't taxed enough; we have a trillion-dollar debt because we spend too much.'

'Government's view of the economy could be summed up in a few short phrases: If it moves, tax it. If it keeps moving, regulate it. And if it stops moving, subsidize it.'

'The most terrifying words in the English language are: I'm from the government and I'm here to help.'

'Within the covers of the Bible are the answers for all the problems men face.'

'I've noticed that everyone who is for abortion has already been born.'

'We must reject the idea that every time a law's broken, society is guilty rather than the lawbreaker. It is time to restore the American precept that each individual is accountable for his actions.'

With reference to these words, state which areas of Ronald Reagan's ideas were influenced by neo-liberals and which were influenced by neo-conservatives.

The New Right: an uneasy marriage

Ayn Rand and Robert Nozick's neo-liberal ideas contradict many traditional aspects of conservatism. Rand and Nozick thought rationalism and logic infinitely superior to empiricism and the wisdom of traditions preferred by Burke and Oakeshott. Rand explicitly stated that she was *not* a conservative and like Nozick she advocated a minimal state that ignored conservative paternalism. Both perceived society as atomistic and not organic. So why is neo-liberalism now taught as an important part of conservative thought?

Divisions within both liberal and conservative ideas and the peculiarities of party politics perhaps offer the best answers. Modern liberalism's idea of the enabling state usurped the classical liberal version of the minimal state, provoking a philosophical reaction. Nozick's *Anarchy, State and Utopia* was a rebuttal to John Rawls' hugely influential modern liberal work, *A Theory of Justice* (see page 254). Some of Nozick's biggest admirers were neo-conservatives in the USA and UK, who found in neo-liberalism ideas that were consistent with Burke's traditional conservatism: a small state and laissez-faire economics. Likewise, American neo-conservatives particularly appreciated Rand's contemporary conception of individualism, which echoed the egotistical individualism inherent in the genesis of the American state.

Neo-conservatives were already worried that conservative thought was being polluted by modern liberal ideas in the USA (Rockefeller/moderate Republicans) and socialism in the UK (one-nation conservatives), and so they were highly receptive to Rand and Nozick's ideas. However, neo-conservatives could not reconcile themselves to *all* of neo-liberalism's ideas concerning human nature, state, society and economy.

- Neo-liberals believe in negative freedom and an atomistic society and so, to Nozick and Rand, the organic society of neo-conservativism is an infringement of individual liberty and autonomy. Neo-conservatives will sanction the positive freedom of a limited welfare state for societal stability, a price neo-liberals see no purpose in paying given their atomistic view of society.
- While neo-liberals wish to reduce the extent of state interference in society, neo-conservatives are willing to expand the state's authority where this might preserve stability, e.g. via authoritarian law and order policies (such as war on drugs initiatives) and hawkish foreign policy.
- Nozick's neo-liberal ideas of individual freedom led him to advocate the legalisation of hard drugs and prostitution, two ideas that offend the religious morality of neo-conservatives and contravene long-standing conservative traditions.
- Neo-conservatives are sympathetic to the rationalism inherent in free-market economics but are still informed by traditional conservative values such as pragmatism. This was demonstrated by neo-conservative Republican President George W. Bush when he supported Keynesian-style intervention during the economic crisis of 2008, a policy that neo-liberals naturally opposed.

There are neo-liberal 'libertarian' political parties in both the UK and USA, but these are fringe institutions with tiny political influence. Neo-liberal ideas (notably support for free trade and laissez-faire economics) are usually advocated by the Conservative Party in the UK and the Republican Party in the USA, which is why neo-liberalism is associated with conservatism. The New Right is a marriage of political convenience between neo-liberals and neo-conservatives which focuses on the efficacy of the free market and a loathing of the collectivist 'big state' ideas inherent in modern liberalism and socialism. In the Cold War years, the New Right was particularly united in its mutual loathing of communism. While being described as 'a conservative' angered Rand and bemused Nozick, neo-liberal ideas inform conservatism as much as they inform liberalism.

Summary: key themes and key thinkers

	Human nature	The state	Society	The economy
Thomas Hobbes	Extremely negative: Selfish humans are individualistically driven by self-interest	The state arises from a 'social contract' between sovereign and subjects. Subjects cede freedoms to an autocratic monarch to guarantee the rule of law and to avoid 'a state of war'	Society did not exist before the creation of the state. The sovereign brings order and authority. Before the creation of the state, life was 'nasty, brutish and short'	Economic activity is only possible after the creation of the state. The sovereign brings order and authority, allowing the economy to develop
Edmund Burke	Somewhat negative: Humans are morally and intellectually fallible	The state emerges and grows like an organism. Hierarchical in nature, the hereditary elite rules with paternal *noblesse oblige* for the interests of all. The state should 'change to conserve' society guided by empiricism	Society is like a multifaceted organism. Communities, traditions, customs, etc., have a symbiotic relationship	The free market is the natural organic state of the market and the state should protect laissez-faire capitalism
Michael Oakeshott	Somewhat negative: Focused on intellectual imperfection. Decisions should be grounded in empiricism not rationalism	The state should be guided by tradition and experience. Sceptical of rationalist state action. Change, if it must occur, should be guided by pragmatism and empiricism	Society is like a multifaceted organism. Communities, traditions, customs, etc., have a symbiotic relationship	The free market is the natural state of the market. State involvement should be limited to pragmatic moderation. State management or economic policies underpinned by rationalism should be avoided because of intellectual imperfection
Ayn Rand	Positive: Humans are capable of rational thought and should be 'objectivist' in pursuing self-interest	The state should play a minimal role in the life of the individual. The state should secure a free market, law and order and national security	Society pursues atomistic individualism. A collection of autonomous individuals motivated by self-fulfilment. These individuals resist state or societal obligations as they restrict individual freedom. No welfare state	Free-market capitalism with no state intervention and a privatised and deregulated economy
Robert Nozick	Positive: Individuals are rational and driven by the idea of self-ownership of their talent, abilities and labour	A minarchist state: The state should be limited to law and order, enforcement of contract and defence of the realm	Society is essentially atomistic. A collection of autonomous individuals with libertarian values. These individuals resist state or societal obligations as they restrict individual freedom. No welfare state	A minarchist state will be one of free-market capitalism with a privatised and deregulated economy

Practice questions

1 To what extent do different conservatives agree about human nature? *You must use appropriate thinkers you have studied to support your answer and consider both sides in a balanced way.* (24)

2 To what extent to different conservatives agree about the nature of society? *You must use appropriate thinkers you have studied to support your answer and consider both sides in a balanced way.* (24)

3 To what extent do different conservatives agree on pragmatism? *You must use appropriate thinkers you have studied to support your answer and consider both sides in a balanced way.* (24)

11 Socialism

The term 'socialism' was first used by Charles Fourier (1772–1837) and Robert Owen (1771–1858) in the early nineteenth century. Socialism is traditionally defined as being opposed to capitalism. In a capitalist society, economic systems are owned privately for profit, but socialism in its original conceptualisation was based on ideas of collective ownership of economic and social systems.

Like liberalism, socialism is a set of political ideas that grew out of the rationalism of the Enlightenment. It has two broad traditions: revolutionary and evolutionary socialism.

Revolutionary socialism

The most common and influential form of revolutionary socialism is derived from the ideas of Karl Marx (1818–83) and Friedrich Engels (1820–95) and is known as Marxism. It argues that socialist values cannot coexist within capitalism and therefore there must be a revolution to transform society and the economy.

Marx and Engels

Rosa Luxemburg (1871–1919) adapted the ideas of Marx and Engels for the early twentieth century and sometimes disagreed with their conclusions. The best example of this was her insistence that democracy and free elections must continue in a post-revolutionary communist society.

Evolutionary socialism

In contrast, **evolutionary socialism** argues that change should happen gradually. Democratic socialism, social democracy and the third way are all types of evolutionary socialism.

- Democratic socialism comes from the ideas of Beatrice Webb (1858–1943) and the Fabian Society, which influenced the Labour Party from its birth in 1900 and Clement Attlee's postwar government. Webb argued that **capitalism** could be gradually reformed via parliament to achieve a socialist state. Webb espoused mass nationalisation (transferring major branches of industry from private to state ownership) and state management (where private enterprise would cease and the economy would be centrally controlled) by a socialist elite to ensure social justice.
- Social democracy emerged in the 1950s. It viewed Marxism as irrelevant and democratic socialism as outdated. Inspired by the ideas of Anthony Crosland (1918–77), it values social justice above the common ownership advocated by revolutionary socialism and democratic socialism, and seeks to achieve this by working within existing capitalist systems through a redistributive welfare state.
- The 'third way' was developed in the 1990s and was inspired by the work of sociologist Anthony Giddens (b. 1938). Giddens saw his ideas as a renewal of social democracy and added a neo-liberal (see Chapter 9) element to socialism. The third way inspired New Labour prime ministers Tony Blair and Gordon Brown in the UK, Chancellor Gerhard Schröder of Germany's Social Democratic Party and US President Bill Clinton's Democratic Party.

Core ideas and principles

Common humanity

Most socialists have an optimistic view of human nature, believing individuals share a common humanity, are rational and are predisposed to cooperate. Socialists agree that human nature is not fixed but is easily shaped (for good or bad) by an individual's environment. Unlike classical and neo-liberals, who see society as a loose collection of individuals, or conservatives, who see society as an organic hierarchy, socialists perceive society as a collection of broadly equal individuals who share a common identity and collective purpose.

- Socialists find pleasure and fulfilment in work that focuses on **cooperation** and collectivism rather than individualism and competition.
- Underpinning this common humanity is a belief in **fraternity** and community.
- Socialists are united (albeit to differing degrees) in their concern about the effect that unchecked capitalism can have on the individual and this leads them to argue for an interventionist role of the state.

- Revolutionary socialism and democratic socialism are the most hostile to capitalism, while social democracy and in particular the third way argue that capitalism can be harnessed for the greater good.

Each branch of socialism shares a distinct vision of what common humanity looks like (Table 11.1).

Table 11.1 Different views of humanity within socialism

Branch of socialism	Vision of a common humanity
Revolutionary socialism	Marx and Engels argued that individuals were 'deformed' by capitalism, as the power of money corrupts those who possess it. Capitalism must therefore be abolished by a revolution instigated by the exploited working class. After a transitional period, a classless communist society would emerge, based on absolute equality (see page 292) where all social and economic activities would be done collectively. Society could then enjoy a common humanity
Democratic socialism	Webb argued for a socialist state via the ballot box. This would include **common ownership** of the means of production, achieved by extensive state nationalisation run by a socialist bureaucratic elite
Social democracy	Social democracy argued that capitalism should be reformed and not replaced, which was a significant break with democratic socialism, which envisaged a fully socialist state. Crosland had a vision of: • supporting a **mixed economy** of both nationalised state industry and privately owned companies • economic state intervention based on **Keynesian economics** to ensure permanent full employment and economic growth • the welfare state used to redistribute wealth and challenge poverty and social inequality
The third way	By the 1990s, Giddens argued that developed economies faced new challenges for the twenty-first century economy. Giddens argued for: • increased emphasis on equality of opportunity via public services, with a specific emphasis on education and twenty-first century skills • neo-liberal ideas such as the free market and self-reliance • moving away from universal welfare to more means-tested welfare (such as higher education students contributing towards the cost of their education)

Key terms

Common ownership
Common ownership is the opposite of private ownership that exists with the free-market capitalist economy. Common ownership means that the state and the public have ownership of property and economy.

Mixed economy An economic system that combines private and state enterprise.

Keynesian economics
Economist John Maynard Keynes argued that governments should stimulate economic demand in times of recession via state spending. Governments should also state manage the economy by using tax and interest rates to influence demand and prevent recessions.

Collectivism

Socialism's positive view of human nature perceives people as naturally social creatures. Generally speaking, collectivism prioritises the group over the individual. Socialists believe individuals:

- prefer to work together rather than independently
- will work far more effectively within groups than they will by their individual actions

Collectivism has been used in a variety of different ways across socialist thinking and therefore means different things to different socialists.

Utopian socialists Charles Fourier and Robert Owen argued for small-scale cooperative communities organised collectively as a way of promoting socialist values (see page 298). Marx and Engels argued on a larger scale, arguing workforces would collectively own all industry and that all agencies of society would be communal. The Soviet Union, which had been influenced by the ideas of Marx and Engels, nationalised its industry, embarked on centralised state planning and collectivised its agricultural land in the 1920s and 1930s.

Democratic socialist Beatrice Webb and the Fabian Society informed many of the collectivist policies of Attlee's Labour governments of 1945–51, in particular the use of nationalisation and top-down state management. However, Attlee's governments accepted the existence of free-market capitalism, in the form of private industry, so a fully collectivised economy and society did not come to pass.

Social democrat Anthony Crosland was suspicious of the collectivism espoused by Marx, Engels and Webb, while Giddens' third way view of collectivism showed the influence of neo-liberal ideas (Table 11.2)

Table 11.2 Two socialist positions on collectivism

Collectivist examples	Social democrat solution	Third way solution
Industrial relations	Workers belong to trade unions that have strong bargaining rights to stop exploitation	Unions should exist to preserve fair practice in the workplace. However, there must be a recognition that wages are market driven
Healthcare	A national health service provides universal care according to need. This service is 'free', paid for by general taxation	The third way advocates healthcare reform, recognising that the cost of universal healthcare is unsustainable. It supports prescription charges, and private healthcare for the rich to 'jump the queue' for non-essential healthcare
Education	Widespread comprehensive state education is available for all, providing an equality of opportunity	More equality of opportunity and spending in education. New Labour introduced academies and life-long learning courses but expected university students to help fund the cost of their tuition via fees
Key industries	The key utilities (but not private industry) are brought under government control and operate in the collective interest of all	The free market is the most efficacious way to run business. No support for renationalising state utilities

Equality

For socialists, equality is a multifaceted concept that causes tension and disagreement. However, there are three aspects of equality that socialists can agree on:

- **Foundational equality** Like liberals, socialists believe that all individuals are born with innate human rights that translate to political and legal equality.
- **Rejection of natural hierarchies** Each individual has the potential to take up any position within society to which he or she may aspire.
- **Equality of opportunity** All individuals should have access to the same life chances.

However, there are numerous disagreements among socialists about the nature of equality (Table 11.3).

Table 11.3 Socialists' ideas on various types of equality

Type of equality	Differences among socialists
Equality of opportunity Individuals are entitled to equal chances to make the best of their abilities. Positive steps should be taken to make sure that there are no artificial barriers to the progress of individual groups	**Revolutionary socialism** Marx, Engels and Rosa Luxemburg argued that equality of opportunity can only be achieved after a revolution (capitalism is so corrupt and pervasive that it is beyond reform) **Democratic socialism** Webb argued that equality of opportunity could only be achieved by reforming capitalism to the point that it is a truly socialist (i.e. common ownership) society **Social democracy** Crosland believed in a mixed economy with state management based on Keynesian ideas. He wished to break down class barriers so that they were irrelevant. He argued for progressive taxation and to allow an even distribution of opportunities via an expansive welfare state **The third way** Equality of opportunity needs to target the neediest in society: the underclass. Giddens advocated abandoning the universal welfare of Crosland's social democracy for means-tested benefits
Equality of outcome Proposes that economic rewards should be distributed to the value of an individual's contribution. In such a system the difference in rewards will be far less than it would be in a free-market economy	**Revolutionary socialism** Marx, Engels and Luxemburg dismissed equality of outcome as it presupposed that capitalism could be rid of exploitation, which they believed to be impossible **Democratic socialism** Webb argued for a gradual incremental process so that income would eventually be far more evenly distributed. This would not be absolute equality, but such income inequality that remains would be substantially fairer **Social democracy** Crosland was against pure equality of outcome as he felt it would weaken the economy by acting as a disincentive to wealth creators **The third way** Like Crosland, Giddens argued that wage equality of outcome was impracticable and a disincentive and would damage the economy
Absolute equality Suggests that all individuals should receive the same rewards as long as the contributions that are made to society are made to the best of their ability (it should be remembered that absolute equality is also understood in terms of equality of outcome, where 'fairness' is distributed to all citizens)	**Revolutionary socialism** Marx, Engels and Luxemburg believed that in an economy based on common ownership and collectivisation material rewards would be based on needs. Each individual would contribute to society and then take what they needed **Democratic socialism** Although Webb believed in high taxation to flatten the differences between classes, she did not advocate absolute equality, envisaging some wage differences **Social democracy** Crosland dismissed absolute equality as utopian (as it presupposed abundant wealth). He accepted that in a meritocratic mixed economy those who contributed more would be rewarded accordingly **The third way** Giddens dismissed absolute equality as a flawed concept and, like Crosland, accepted that inequality was a natural consequence of society

Type of equality	Differences among socialists
Equality of welfare This aspect of equality perceives society as inevitably unequal but argues that everyone should be entitled to an equal minimum standard of living, enabled by the provision of state welfare	**Revolutionary socialism** Marx, Engels and Luxemburg rejected equality of welfare for its failure to remove capitalism **Democratic socialism** Webb argued that equality of welfare would be achieved by mass nationalisation of industry. She argued that proper state management would ensure equality of welfare via an efficient redistribution of resources **Social democracy** Crosland saw the state as a neutral force that could reduce class conflict by breaking down barriers and widening opportunities: universal public services would help achieve this. He married social democracy with modern liberalism and was enthusiastic for nationalised utilities and the free-market economy **The third way** Giddens argued that high levels of social security and welfare were a disincentive to work and created a dependency culture. Benefits should be targeted at the most needy

Social class

Socialists believe that capitalism creates and reinforces harmful social class divisions that result in societal hierarchies. While socialists can agree on a broad critique of social class, they disagree on how best to rectify the problem that they have diagnosed:

- The revolutionary socialism of Marx/Engels and Luxemburg argues that problems of social class can only be resolved via a revolution.
- The evolutionary socialism of Webb (democratic socialism), Crosland (social democracy) and Giddens (third way) all have different ideas for reconciling social class division.

Marx and Engels' ideas placed social class as a core idea of socialism, arguing as follows:

- They perceived capitalists as parasites profiting from the work of an exploited workforce.
- Differences between social classes could not be reconciled within a capitalist system and therefore revolution was inevitable.
- The capitalist took the surplus value (the difference between the wages paid to the worker and the profit taken by the capitalist), alienating the worker from his labour. (Marx and Engels called the worker the 'proletariat'.)
- The state was not neutral but actively reinforced this oppressive relationship via laws, bureaucracy, police forces and the army — an idea that heavily influences anarchism (see Chapter 12).

Webb shared Marx's social class analysis. However, she argued that the nature of the state could be altered from serving capitalism to delivering a socialist state. The socialist state would introduce universal nationalisation: equality of outcome, progressive taxation and a welfare state which would significantly narrow class division.

Social democrats such as Crosland were critical of the collectively minded **utilitarianism** of Webb's ideas and the uniformity of nationalisation, which Crosland felt compromised the freedom of the individual and would 'make the socialist state' a 'dull functional nightmare'. Crosland's vision of socialism was less of a class war and more of a fairer distribution of wealth and equality of opportunity so that the individual could thrive in a society that would eventually become classless.

> **Key term**
>
> **Utilitarianism** A doctrine that states that an action is right if it promotes happiness, and that the greatest happiness of the greatest number of people is the most important principle.

Karl Marx (1818–83) and Friedrich Engels (1820–95)

Marx, and his collaborator Engels, are pivotal figures within socialism. *The Communist Manifesto* (1848) provided a radical reinterpretation of history and a revolutionary model for a utopian society.

The main ideas of Marx and Engels (see also Figure 11.1, page 299)

- Marx and Engels argued that their theories were empirical and scientifically determined (their critics argue that this is nonsense as their theories are scientifically unprovable), so as well as explaining historical change their ideas were inevitably going to occur.
- Class struggle, arising from property ownership, has existed through history. History has a final destination: communism.
- Capitalism, with its crises and recessions, will eventually leave only a tiny minority of the ruling class (whom Marx and Engels dubbed the 'bourgeoisie') benefiting from it. The vast majority of individuals will form the proletariat, who will wake up to their exploitation and achieve class consciousness.
- Marx and Engels argued that liberal democracy was a 'democratic swindle' because the state was controlled by the bourgeoisie. State and society used religion, patriotism, enfranchisement, parliament and social reforms to weaken class consciousness and the masses' mission to overthrow capitalism. However, Marx and Engels believed socialism was inevitable and that the proletariat will overthrow capitalism and a transitional phase – the dictatorship of the proletariat – will occur.
- After this transitional period, the state will wither away and a stateless communist society will emerge based on common ownership.

Crosland argued that education reinforced class division and his most famous attempt to ensure equality of opportunity was to create comprehensive schools that would cater for all abilities and break down the social segregation of grammar schools.

Giddens' position on education merely revises the aims of Crosland, arguing: 'Investment in education is an imperative of government today, a key basis of the redistribution of possibilities.'

Social democracy failed to eliminate class divisions within society. To further complicate the matter, individuals no longer see themselves in the traditional class roles that they did in the times of Marx, Engels, Luxemburg, Webb or even Crosland. Evans and Tilley argue that since the late 1970s traditional notions of class do not resonate as once they did. There is no consensus on why this is. Some, like Giddens, argue it is a breaking down of traditional class-based occupations (factory worker, coal miner, ship builder); others argue that the working class mistakenly perceive themselves as middle class (because many work in offices or call centres) even though they are lowly paid.

Wendy Bottero has argued that there exists a 'paradox of class', whereby class identification is in decline and yet the continued role of class position is nevertheless important in regard to life chances. Sutton Trust research has demonstrated that while only 7% of people attend independent schools, they dominate the higher paid professions.

Numerous studies have shown that while Crosland and Giddens were correct in arguing that education is the single most important factor in occupational attainment, the chances of obtaining a good education remain strongly influenced by class background. Evans and Tilley's research demonstrates that private education continues to be a key predictor of occupational and educational success. In the UK, while 49% of young people now attend university, poverty and inequality remain difficult to eradicate.

A group of local boys look on in curiosity at the Harrow schoolboys, 1937

Such figures would not have surprised Marx, Engels or Luxemburg, who argued that the inequalities of capitalism were beyond reform. Marxism believes that materialism dominates societal culture, ideology, politics and religion. Moreover, it prevents the subjugated from perceiving their exploitation. Whenever socialist governments have been elected, they are frustrated by the capitalist-supporting interests of the political elites that dominate the judiciary, the civil service and big business: the ability to radically change society is beyond their power. For revolutionary socialists, evolutionary socialism can only disappoint and nothing less than a socialist insurrection on an international scale can vanquish the injustice of social class.

Workers' control

All socialists agree that in an unchecked free market the capitalist will exploit the industrial worker. However, when one looks at the different branches of socialism, the concept of workers' control (where the average worker manages the workplace through workers' councils or committees) is multifaceted. Marx, Engels and Luxemburg advocate workers' control (at least for a time), whereas Webb, Crosland and Giddens do not envisage the worker seizing direct control of the economy or the means of production.

Revolutionary socialism

In the immediate aftermath of a revolution, Marx and Engels envisaged a transitional period where the formerly exploited workers were in control (see Figure 11.1). This interim stage would see society and the economy re-embracing forgotten cooperative, collective and fraternal values while removing destructive capitalist ideals. Workers' control would be a short period between the revolution and the stateless, classless, communist society and economy that would emerge from the ashes of capitalism. There would be no need for workers' control, as communism would be free from the exploitation of capitalistic competition.

Evolutionary socialism

Democratic socialist Webb did not believe in workers' control, dismissing workers as incapable of such responsibility:

> 'We do not have faith in the "average sensual man", we do not believe that he can do more than describe his grievances, we do not think that he can prescribe the remedies.'

Webb was openly critical of 1920s guild socialism, which advocated state nationalisation under workers' control, as she argued that workers lacked the intellectual capability to organise such an enterprise.

So, although Sidney Webb, Beatrice's husband, drafted Clause IV for the Labour Party with a specific aim of common ownership, the Webbs never intended that common ownership would entail workers controlling the means of production. Webb had the most negative view of human nature of all the socialist key thinkers, believing that the working class were innately intellectually inferior, and so needing guidance from paternal superiors. For Webb, the evils of capitalism:

- would not be solved by the workers but by 'the professional expert'; the working class would vote for socialism and, gradually, elected socialist governments would refashion the state so that it could manage, not oppress, the worker
- the state would 'silently change its character … from police power, to housekeeping on a national scale' — this strategy for achieving socialism would involve a highly trained elite of administrators and specialists (rather than the workers themselves) to organise society

> ### Clause IV
>
> To secure for the workers by hand or brain the full fruits of their industry and the most equitable distribution thereof that may be possible under the basis of common ownership and the means of production, distribution and exchange and the best obtainable system of popular administration and control of each industry or service.
>
> Constitution of the Labour Party, 1918

Key thinker

Beatrice Webb (1858–1943)

Beatrice Webb was a member of the Fabian Society and believed that socialism would evolve peacefully through a combination of political action and education.

Webb's main ideas

- 'The inevitability of gradualness' is an evolutionary socialist belief that parliamentary democracy and not revolution will deliver the inevitable socialist society. It is inevitable because universal suffrage leads to political equality, as democracy works in the interests of the working-class majority.
- Webb's ideas are as fundamental as revolutionary socialism, but she sought the overthrow of capitalism via the ballot box rather than revolution.
- The working class will vote for socialist parties which will begin to instigate social, economic and political reform, resulting in a socialist society.
- The expansion of the state is vital to deliver socialism. The state will develop a highly trained elite of administrators and specialists to organise the socialist society. This technocratic elite would 'impregnate all the existing forces of society'.
- Webb's *The Minority Report of the Poor Law Commission* (1909) argued for a 'national minimum of civilised life'. Many of the ideas from this report later appeared in modern liberal William Beveridge's Beveridge Report (1942) (see page 259), which was used as the intellectual basis for the modern welfare state that was introduced by the Labour governments of 1945–51. A young Beveridge was employed as a researcher on Webb's Minority Report and later wrote that his own report 'stemmed from what all of us had imbibed from the Webbs'.
- Workers' control will be achieved by evolutionary means. Revolutions are 'chaotic, inefficient and counter-productive' – an 'unpredictability' that Webb could not countenance.

Social democracy and the third way

Social democrats viewed workers' control and militant class struggle as outdated notions. Capitalism (they supposed) had largely been reformed of its most exploitative traits. Crosland was comfortable with a mixed economy, where entrepreneurs could thrive and pay taxation to fund a welfare state, but he was unwilling to sanction further nationalisation which would threaten individual liberty and be economically counterproductive. He supported the Labour leader of the late 1950s, Hugh Gaitskell, in his attempt to amend Clause IV. Gaitskell was unsuccessful in this endeavour as, for the left wing of the party, it was a core value.

Key thinker

Anthony Crosland (1918–77)

Anthony Crosland was a privately-educated Labour Party politician and Cabinet minister during the 1960s and 1970s. The ideas from his book *The Future of Socialism* (1956) influenced social democracy within the UK.

Crosland's main ideas

- Crosland criticised the Marxist view of capitalist development, arguing that it did not drive social change as the internal tensions required in Marx's dialectic of historical materialism were not present in postwar capitalism.
- Socialism is best served by the 'state-managed capitalism' of a mixed economy rather than public ownership.
- Equality of opportunity can be achieved by giving all state school students the same educational experience. Crosland judged the existing school system in Britain to be 'the most divisive, unjust and wasteful of all the social aspects of inequality'.
- Keynesian economics made state-managed capitalism a reality and society can look forward to permanent economic growth and full employment. This allows socialists to expand the welfare state and social justice.

Giddens' renewal of social democracy saw workers' control as impracticable for a similar reason to Webb and Crosland: the average worker lacked the skills or expertise to successfully lead or manage their workplace.

Giddens also argued against the mixed economy, because nationalised companies could not compete with the amount of wealth the free market creates. He shared the neo-liberal belief that free-market economies are more efficient and prosperous than either state-controlled or mixed economies (see page 303) and that it would be better to focus on channelling the proceeds of the free market towards 'the interests of social solidarity and social justice'.

Labour leader Tony Blair, who was heavily influenced by the ideas of Giddens, amended Clause IV in 1995 so that it dropped the commitment to common ownership for a vague commitment to social justice. More pertinently, Blair accepted the neo-liberal reforms of Margaret Thatcher, who had privatised in the 1980s, and did not seek to renationalise the state utilities, nationalised by Attlee's postwar Labour government.

to Giddens than to Crosland, as she had been critical of the welfare aspects of the Beveridge Report that had inspired the welfare state, concluding rather bluntly that:

'the better you treat the unemployed in the way of means, without service, the worse the evil becomes; because it is better to do nothing than to work at low wages and conditions.'

Giddens was influenced by the ideas of modern liberalism in his version of equality of opportunity, and quotes extensively from early twentieth century liberal L.T. Hobhouse, who had argued that government and state should not 'feed, house or clothe' the population, 'but should secure conditions upon which its citizens are able to win by their own effort all that is necessary to a full civic efficiency'.

Stretch and challenge

Tony Blair was Labour prime minister between 1997 and 2007 and was heavily influenced by the ideas of Anthony Giddens. Read some of his most famous quotations:

'What modernisation to me is about is not dumping principle. It's the opposite. It's retrieving what the Labour Party is really about.'

'We are a party committed to social justice.'

'Ask me my three main priorities for government, and I tell you: education, education, education.'

'Tough on crime and tough on the causes of crime'

'Britain needs successful people in business who can become rich by their success, through the money they earn.'

'New Labour does not believe it is the job of government to interfere in the ruling of business.'

'It's not a burning ambition for me to make sure that David Beckham earns less money.'

With reference to these words, identify which areas of Tony Blair's policies were influenced by the ideas of Anthony Giddens.

In focus

The ideas of democratic socialism, social democracy and the third way are all evident within the parliamentary Labour Party. However, the third way politics of New Labour have been in marked decline since 2010 and the party's current leader, Jeremy Corbyn, is an old-style democratic socialist in the tradition of Beatrice Webb.

Debate

To what extent do socialists agree about the economy?

Areas of agreement

- All forms of socialism are critical of the negative effects of capitalism.
- All forms of socialism are, to differing degrees, critical of the wasteful competition inherent within capitalism and emphasise the need for cooperation.
- All forms of socialism are committed to an economy that creates a fairer society.
- All forms of socialism envisage equality of opportunity within society.
- Evolutionary socialists all agree that capitalism can be reformed of its most exploitative tendencies.

Areas of disagreement

- Revolutionary socialists think capitalism is beyond reform. Evolutionary socialists think capitalism can be reformed (but disagree on upon how to reform it).
- Revolutionary socialists such as Marx and Engels think only mature economies can experience revolution, while Luxemburg argues that less mature economies are also capable of successful communist revolutions.
- Socialists disagree on the role of the state in organising the economy. Revolutionary socialists think the state will wither away, while evolutionary socialists disagree on how active the state must be in managing the economy.
- Evolutionary socialists disagree on how to manage the economy. Webb favours nationalisation; Crosland, a mixed economy; and Giddens prefers a neo-liberal free market.
- The third way argues for far less equality of outcome than either social democracy or democratic socialism.

Summary: key themes and key thinkers

	Human nature	The state	Society	The economy
Karl Marx and Friedrich Engels	Humans are naturally altruistic. However, capitalism instils them with a false consciousness of 'bourgeois values'	Capitalism must be destroyed by revolution. The state will be temporarily replaced by the dictatorship of the proletariat and will wither away when communism is established	Capitalism corrupts society and the elite oppress the working class, creating class conflict. A communist society will have absolute equality and societal harmony	Capitalism is corrupt and inefficient and should be replaced by an economy where resources are collectively owned and distributed according to need
Rosa Luxemburg	Human nature had been damaged by capitalism. However, humans are not perfect and parliamentary democracy is needed to prevent tyranny	Capitalism should be destroyed by revolution and replaced by a genuine democracy	Capitalism corrupts society and the elite oppress the working class, creating class conflict. A democratic communist society will provide absolute equality and social harmony	Marx's historical materialism idea is flawed as capitalism does *not* need to reach a 'final stage' before it can be abolished. Communist revolutions could happen in less economically developed societies
Beatrice Webb	Capitalism had damaged the human psyche. However, Webb believed in intellectual and moral human imperfection, particularly of the working class	The state should be used to create a socialist society. This would be achieved via universal suffrage and would be a gradual process	Society under socialist state management will produce equality of outcome	The free-market economy would be gradually nationalised as the workers obtain common ownership of the means of production
Anthony Crosland	Human nature is innately fair. Inequalities of outcome and opportunity hinder collective human progress	The state should be managed by 'meritocratic managers' and 'classless technocrats'	State management will affect societal change and create social justice and equality of welfare	Rejected Webb's gradualism and argued for a mixed economy and Keynesian capitalism. Believed capitalism had largely been reformed of its exploitative tendencies
Anthony Giddens	Human nature is shaped by socio-economic conditions. More focus on humans as both individual and collective creatures	The state should invest in social investment and infrastructure and refrain from economic and social engineering	Society will embrace equality of opportunity and communal responsibility instead of class conflict	A neo-liberal economy with a free market is more efficient than all socialist economic models and the tax revenues they generate can finance greater equality of opportunity

Practice questions

1 To what extent are different socialists committed to common ownership? *You must use appropriate thinkers you have studied to support your answer and consider both sides in a balanced way.* (24)

2 To what extent do different socialists disagree over the role of the state? *You must use appropriate thinkers you have studied to support your answer and consider both sides in a balanced way.* (24)

3 To what extent do different socialists agree about the nature of equality? *You must use appropriate thinkers you have studied to support your answer and consider both sides in a balanced way.* (24)

12 Anarchism

Anarchism is often misunderstood by those who have not studied its political ideas. 'Anarchy' is derived from the Greek *anarkhos*, which means 'without rule'. However, its most common usage in everyday speech is for a movement that propagates disorder, violence, lawlessness, confusion and chaos.

This is not how anarchists perceive themselves, however. Anarchists would argue (with some justification) that this is a misrepresentation of their ideas, which are positive and beneficial. Anarchism is a collection of ideas and movements, but a core belief of all of them is that people should be free from political authority in all forms, most notably state control.

There are two broad types of anarchism:

- **Collectivist anarchism**, which is committed to common ownership and a belief that human nature is rational, altruistic and cooperative
- **Individualist anarchism**, which argues for a society where self-interested individuals are largely free to make judgements that they feel are in their best interests

A drawing depicting the Haymarket bombing and riot, 1886

Core ideas and principles

Rejection of the state

Anarchism is united in its loathing of the role of the state in governing humanity. Democratic states only offer an illusion of freedom; the people are not sovereign — **power** is given away at the ballot box as political sovereignty lies with the ruling elite. As Emma Goldman (1869–1940) famously argued, 'If voting changed anything, they'd make it illegal.'

Authority is compulsory and **the state**'s laws must be obeyed under the coercive threat of punishment. The state restricts liberty and is oppressive, as Pierre-Joseph Proudhon (1809–65) argued:

> 'To be governed is to be watched over, inspected, spied on, directed, legislated, regimented, closed in, indoctrinated, preached at, controlled, assessed, evaluated, censored, commanded all by creatures that have neither the right, nor the wisdom, nor the virtue.'

Mikhail Bakunin (1814–76) argued that the state enslaves the governed and that 'every command slaps liberty in the face'. Max Stirner (1806–56) bluntly stated, 'We two, the state and I, are enemies.' Anarchists are therefore clear that a prerequisite for human society to thrive is that the state be removed. In the words of Peter Kropotkin (1842–1921), 'no ruling authorities … No government of man by man, no crystallization and immobility'. All would agree with Stirner's sentiment that 'I am free in *no* State'.

Power corrupts those who wield it

Anarchists have a broadly positive view of human nature, but the state and power have a corrosive effect on individuals, as Bakunin argued: 'The best of men, the most intelligent, unselfish, generous and pure, will always inevitably be corrupted.'

The state/**government** is unjust and is based on economic exploitation that reinforces and legitimises economic inequality. In 1897 the Union of Russian Socialists produced a now much imitated caricature of the pyramid of the capitalist system, which illustrates how the state organises society for the benefit of the minority at the exploitation of the majority.

Liberty

Anarchism is united in the core idea that liberty can only be achieved by abolishing the state, although collectivist and individualist anarchists differ on specific definitions of liberty.

Individualist anarchism's version of liberty

Individualist (or egoist) anarchism views the liberty/freedom of the individual from state interference as of paramount importance. Stirner pioneered this position in the nineteenth century, but anarcho-capitalists in the twentieth century have had more success at popularising its ideas (Table 12.1).

Key terms

Power Anarchists argue that the exercise of power by one person over another is unacceptable. The state uses its position to exploit individuals and this should be resisted. Anarchists believe individuals should be free to exercise power over themselves.

Authority The term is related to government and the state. Authority is the right to exercise the power granted to the state and government to carry out its duties. Anarchists view the authority exercised by the state as coercive, as individuals should be free to exercise authority over themselves.

The state This refers to the authority that is set up via a series of institutions such as sovereign, executive, legislative and judiciary to make laws and enforce order. Anarchists argue that the state uses its powers coercively to deny individuals their liberty.

Government The name of the body that controls the state. Governments can be a traditional monarchy, a dictatorship or a democracy. Anarchists view all forms of government as corrupt, to differing degrees, and that governing corrupts those who govern. Government denies individual autonomy.

Table 12.1 Egoist and anarcho-capitalist anarchism

Egoist	Max Stirner argued that individuals are self-interested egoists. To be totally free, the individual must be utterly **autonomous**. Individuals are sovereign, and for liberty to exist individuals must be free of all external influence or obligation
Anarcho-capitalist	Murray Rothbard and David Friedman argue that liberty can only be experienced by the abolition of the state, whereby individuals can enjoy negative freedom (see Chapter 9) and an atomistic society (see Chapter 10). The current functions of the state, such as the welfare state and law and order, would all be administered within an unregulated free market

Key thinker

Max Stirner (1806–56)

Johann Kasper Schmidt was a timid man, who, after a brief and unsuccessful career as a teacher, died in poverty and obscurity. His contribution to anarchism was his book *The Ego and its Own* (1844), written under the pseudonym Max Stirner, which cries out against the state's distortion of our perceptions. Stirner's main ideas are as follows.

The ego

- Philosophical ideologies and concepts such as the state, society and religion are artificial constructs that act like 'wheels in the head', causing individuals to misunderstand their actuality. These illusions are as insubstantial as 'spooks' and yet they haunt the individual as they powerfully distort true reality.
- Stirner argues that individuals must cut through the artifice of state and society to discover the truth: that the self-interested and rational individual is the centre of their own moral universe.

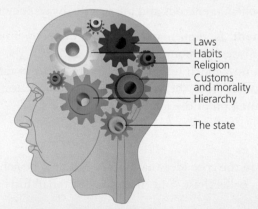

Stirner's 'wheels in the head'

The union of egoists

- The state must cease to exist if the sovereignty of the individual is to be guaranteed. Individual sovereignty would be achieved when people gain their personal 'ownness' and a realisation of the state's alienating machinations.
- Stirner's strand of anarchism is the most individualistic and nihilistic. It argues for **insurrection**, via withdrawal of labour, so that the state would wither and die.
- Stirner also argued for 'propaganda of the deed', as violence would help shake the delusion of the state's autonomy. Bakunin and Goldsmith also favoured this strategy.

Collectivist anarchist versions of liberty

Collectivist anarchism views liberty/freedom very much as a communal phenomenon.

There are several collectivist versions of liberty (Table 12.2).

Table 12.2 How different strands of collectivist anarchy view liberty

Mutualism	• Proudhon believed that as the human race developed it became capable of rational thought and an innate sense of justice. An individual's liberty was curtailed by both the state and religion • Liberty was a hybrid of socialism and individualism: a reconciliation of two distinct strands of thought. The socialist aspect envisaged an **altruistic** decentralised society where individuals unite to form cooperative working groups that together become communities of workers. The individualist aspects made clear that workers could freely enter into contracts in exchange for labour and goods • Proudhon envisaged a definite nationalistic element to liberty in that native citizens would receive preferential treatment to foreigners in all transactions • Proudhon's idea of liberty was a very male-orientated vision and would be described by feminists as patriarchal (see Chapter 14) as he perceived women as inferior, subservient and generally as ancillaries to men
Collectivist anarchism	• Bakunin believed that individuals were born with equal intelligence, moral sense and a capability for rational thought. Individual development was dictated by environment. The state threatened individual liberty by distorting human nature and the natural arrangement of society • Bakunin argued that natural laws were grounded in a belief in community. For Bakunin, society is 'the tree of freedom and liberty is its fruit'. All humans regardless of gender or nationality are equally free. The society that these state-emancipated individuals will choose will be collective, because man is a communal creature and suffers **anomie** if isolated. 'Man is born into society, just as an ant is born into an anthill or a bee into a hive.' Liberty can only be found with the solidarity of others, as there is an innate 'mutual interdependence' which manifests itself as a kind of communal individuality • Bakunin's intense belief in the sociability of individuals saw him advocate an idea of society where private property was replaced by **collectivisation**. This collectivist anarchism essentially saw liberty in socialist terms and has sometimes been described as socialism without a state
Mutual aid — anarcho-communism	• Kropotkin argued that human nature is positive and predisposed to cooperation or, as he dubbed it, '**mutual aid**'. Liberty was rooted in nature and the dominant characteristic of all creatures within a society was solidarity • Kropotkin's theories were underpinned by anthropological empirical research of successful species, which informed his anarchist theories. He argues that mutual aid was present in early settlements to the free cities of the Middle Ages. However, the rise of the state and capitalism distorted this natural condition, crushing 'individual and local life' • Once the state was abolished, liberty would be enshrined in an anarcho-communist society of voluntary associations in the form of communes, governed with equality, direct democracy and high levels of participation. Communes would be deliberately small, allowing individuals to have regular interactions and to avoid the depersonalisation of large, centralised entities. Individuals would be free to join whatever community they wished • Goldman preferred a communal individuality that echoed Kropotkin and Proudhon, whereby liberty exists via cooperation but acknowledges individualism • Goldman also viewed liberty in feminist terms, rejecting gender stereotypes and 'refusing to be a servant of God, the state, society, the husband, the family, etc.' • Goldman advocated free love, sex outside marriage and non-conventional relationships such as ménage-à-trois and lesbianism. Such behaviour was utterly taboo at the time and saw her isolated from other contemporary feminists

Key terms

Altruistic Focused on part of human nature that leads individuals to care for others and act in their interests.

Anomie If isolated from society, humans will feel intense loneliness and experience feelings of emotional dislocation.

Collectivisation The organisation of peasants into large production units where there is no private property. Individuals produce goods collectively and equally share the rewards for their labour.

Mutual aid A term used by many anarchists to mean that communities should cooperate with each other, largely in terms of trade on mutually beneficial terms rather than through a free-market mechanism.

Pierre-Joseph Proudhon (1809–65)

A brewer's son, Proudhon is credited with the first use of the word 'anarchist' in a positive sense. In his seminal text *What Is Property?* (1840), he asserted that 'property is theft'. Proudhon's main ideas are as follows.

Opposition to private property and collectivisation

- Proudhon distinguished between property, which the elite used to exploit others, and the 'possessions' of ordinary peasants and workers.
- Proudhon has been described as a libertarian socialist. His contractual system of mutualism balanced individual liberty with the rights of the commune. These ideas saw him oppose the collectivisation espoused by Bakunin as oppressive.

The rejection and overthrow of the state

- Proudhon is unique among the key thinkers as he argued for a peaceful transition to a new society rather than transition by revolutionary means.
- Proudhon's mutualist society would exist in the shell of the existing state with interconnected institutions such as a people's bank and a federation of communities cooperating with each other. Rather like Marx he saw this as a temporary arrangement and he expected the state to wither and die as mutualism took root.

Emma Goldman (1869–1940)

Emma Goldman was born in Russia in 1869. Her sympathy for anarchism was ignited when four anarchists were convicted (and executed) for throwing a bomb into a crowd of policemen during a workers' rally at Haymarket Square in Chicago in 1886. The judge of the case openly conceded that there was no evidence against them but that they were on trial simply because they were anarchists. Goldman's key work was *Anarchism and Other Essays* (1910) and her main ideas are as follows.

The state is a cold monster — it should be rejected, as it is immoral

- Goldman viewed the state as a cold monster at the core of societal violence through the twin evils of militarism and patriotism.
- Militarism includes the state's use of the police to threaten violence or imprisonment to those who dare question its law; Goldman deemed soldiers the state's indoctrinated killers.
- Patriotism fuels militarism, leading to war between competing states and 'the road to internal to universal slaughter'. Goldman argued patriotism should therefore be replaced by universal brotherhood and sisterhood.

Political participation in the state and society are corrupting and futile

- Goldman argued that all political participation by the state towards society was corrupting. She viewed Soviet communism in these terms, as society was not voluntary but a 'compulsory state communism'.
- The lack of liberty was also inherent in Western democracies, as Goldman saw the corrosive corrupting effect of power on those who wielded it.
- Goldman advocated violence and civil disobedience, industrial sabotage and general strikes, discounting reform in favour of revolution.

Anarchy is order

Anarchist society will be stateless (or, in Proudhon's case, existing in the 'shell of the state'). Table 12.3 shows how the different key thinkers of anarchism perceive order in different ways.

Table 12.3 Anarchists' perceptions of order

Max Stirner	Once free of the artifice of the state, individuals would be free to assert their own rational individualism on the world, equating to self-realisation based on self-interest
Pierre-Joseph Proudhon	Humans have an innate sense of justice and are naturally inclined to cooperate. Mutualism synthesised collectivism and individualism, allowing individuals to opt out if they so wished. Proudhon thought this would be an irregular occurrence but argued that a federal assembly could assemble (only when required) to mediate such disputes before immediately disbanding. The individuals of Proudhon's society would have a 'collective force' and this would underpin the success of society
Peter Kropotkin	Mutual aid communes would be drawn to each other by similar interests, becoming an 'interwoven network, composed of an infinite variety of groups'
Mikhail Bakunin	Bakunin only gave a sketch of how his collectivist anarchism would work, but its foundation was built on an optimistic view of human nature. He saw humans as naturally social beings, who would experience communal individuality in a federation of communes that were carefully decentralised so no one had too much power, practising collectivisation
Emma Goldman	Goldman never attempted to plan her anarchist society, but her ideas were consistent with the Kropotkin and Proudhon strands of anarcho-communism

Economic freedom

Economic freedom means different things to collectivist and individualist anarchists.

Collectivist anarchism

Proudhon argued that 'property is theft' and that the entire concept of property is a social construct to exploit the masses. The vast majority of private property is owned by the elite, while everyone else is forced to participate in an exploitative capitalist system just to pay rent. Collective anarchists seek to abolish private property for communal ownership. This would allow economic freedom to flourish, as goods and services would be priced at their true labour value and not their market value:

- Proudhon argued for mutualism (see page 317), where all the means of production would be owned collectively by the workers and society would be organised within small communities.
- Kropotkin argued for mutual aid, which although subtly different to mutualism, required common ownership and a federation of communities.
- Bakunin viewed economic freedom via collectivisation (which trespassed over individual freedom too much for Proudhon and Kropotkin to favour).
- Anarcho-syndicalism (see page 317) would see the means of production controlled by the workers rather than by individual exploitative owners.

Mikhail Bakunin (1814–76)

Born an aristocrat, Bakunin became interested in radical ideas as a young man. He was initially influenced by Marx, but broke from socialism as he disagreed with the concept of a worker's state (even if it was transitional), perceiving such an arrangement as corrupting. He left no detailed ideas of a perfect society, just a general blueprint. His key work *God and the State* was published posthumously in 1882. Bakunin's main ideas are as follows.

Propaganda by the deed

- Bakunin believed in **propaganda by the deed** to bring about revolution. This direct action would take the form of general strikes, non-payment of taxes and rent, as well as violent acts.

Human sociability

- Bakunin argued that humans are naturally sociable. He proposed abolishing society and forming collectivised communes with total economic equality.
- He believed in the concept of natural law to which all people are subject. In a stateless society, natural law would take over.
- He advocated a system of federalism in which workers and peasants would band together in voluntary communities (communes) that would vary in size.
- Communes would trade with each other on mutually negotiated terms, based on the labour value of goods instead of their market value.

Individualist anarchism

Egoism

Stirner's egoism asserts that individuals possess a sovereignty akin to a nation state. Individuals are materialists, who wish to satisfy their needs. Free of the exploitative state, these rational individuals, of similar powers and abilities, will, as autonomous creatures, reorganise the economy fairly as it will be in their self-interest to avoid social conflict.

Anarcho-capitalism

Anarcho-capitalism, unlike collectivist anarchism, favours both private property and the free market as this will ensure atomistic economic freedom. The free market will provide (more efficaciously than the corrupt and incompetent state) all public goods, including education, healthcare and infrastructure. Rational and self-interested individuals are far better at deciding what is in their best interests than the state is.

Different types of anarchism

There are several distinct subdivisions within the two broad categories of anarchism, collectivist and individualist.

Collectivist anarchism

Collectivist anarchism is committed to common economic ownership, which will nurture the altruistic and cooperative aspects of human nature that have hitherto been distorted by the oppressive state. This would end the 'surplus value' exploitation (see Chapter 11) that had oppressed workers in the capitalist system.

Collectivist anarchists believe that the free market associated with capitalism, coupled with the oppressive hierarchal nature of state/society, reinforces inequality and oppression. The free market determines the value of labour in the form of wages via supply and demand, which fails to recognise the intrinsic worth of an individual's labour. This 'exchange value' is exploitative as the state's capitalist class (who own and control the means of production) reaps the benefits of

An anarchist group during the G20 protests, 2009

economic activity while workers receive substantially smaller rewards. Collectivist anarchism has three variations: anarcho-communism, mutualism and anarcho-syndicalism.

Anarcho-communism

Kropotkin opposed private property and viewed communism as the most natural form of economic society, as wealth results from a collective effort. Thus 'all belongs to all' and 'anarchy leads to communism and communism leads to anarchy'.

Kropotkin's anthropological expertise informed his political ideas, as he made scientifically derived parallels between state/society/economy and the natural world. Kropotkin disputed Darwin's 'survival of the fittest' hypothesis and argued the reverse: that the species that cooperated thrived, whereas those that did not struggled to survive. This conclusion allowed Kropotkin to rebut Social Darwinists, such as Herbert Spencer, who had argued that the competitive nature of society and the economy was a natural state.

Kropotkin dubbed such cooperation 'mutual aid' and argued that this form of existence occurred both in Ancient Greece and in the city states of medieval Europe before capitalism corrupted human nature. He argued that if both the state and capitalism ceased to exist, the human race would revert to its natural state of altruistic mutual aid and communal **solidarity**.

- Kropotkin, viewing private property as theft and a means of exploitation, would therefore replace it with common ownership. Communes of voluntary associations practising mutual aid would band together and then form an 'interwoven network' of a wide variety of different groups.

> **Key term**
>
> **Solidarity** A feeling of common harmony and cohesion among individuals, leading them to form mutually beneficial communities and to have a communal empathy. Anarchists such as Kropotkin believe this is the natural state of the human race.

Peter Kropotkin (1842–1921)

Kropotkin was an aristocrat who grew up to despise the cruel autocracy of the tsarist state. In 1872 he converted to anarchism after observing the Jura Federation's watchmaker community, who pooled resources to live in collective harmony. His ideas were described in *Fields, Factories and Workshops* (1898) and *Mutual Aid: A Factor of Evolution* (1902). Kropotkin's main ideas are as follows:

The science of mutual aid

- Kropotkin, a respected geographer/biologist, argued from scientific observation that much of the animal kingdom was cooperative and not competitive.
- He argued that the state was beyond the reform of gradualism and nothing short of revolution could transform society and economy.
- The state would be abolished. It would become an anarcho-communist society of voluntary association in the form of communes governed with equality, direct democracy and high levels of popular participation.
- Law would be replaced by regulated relationships within the commune, where customs and free agreements would ensure harmony.
- The means of production would be collectively owned by the commune, and private property and the wage system would be abolished.
- Goods and services would be freely available and based on individual need.

Stretch and challenge

Peter Kropotkin was an anarcho-communist who believed that humans were naturally inclined to cooperate with each other. Read some of his most famous sayings:

> 'The mutual-aid tendency in man has so remote an origin, and is so deeply interwoven with all the past evolution of the human race, that it has been maintained by mankind up to the present time.'

> 'Don't compete! — competition is always injurious to the species, and you have plenty of resources to avoid it!'

> 'Under any circumstances sociability is the greatest advantage in the struggle for life.'

> 'In the long run the practice of solidarity proves much more advantageous to the species than the development of individuals endowed with predatory inclinations.'

> 'By mutual confidence and mutual aid — great deeds are done and great discoveries are made.'

With reference to the above, explain why Kropotkin preferred communal cooperation to individuals competing for the basis of a society and economy.

- Unions of communes would produce a network of cooperation that would replace the state. Laws would no longer be necessary, as a combination of customs and free agreements would create a common consensus.
- **Direct democracy** would produce unanimous decisions, but if it did not and the minority felt oppressed, they would be free to leave and start a new community.
- Kropotkin argued that there would be a free availability of goods and services and no compulsion to work, though he envisaged that mutual aid and the feeling of fraternity would make such free-riding unlikely.

Mutualism

Proudhon's theory of mutualism is another form of communist society. Like Kropotkin's anarcho-communism (mutual aid), society and the economy would not be organised by the state but would organically flourish as small communities. Capitalism would cease to exist and the means of production, land, factories, etc., would be commonly owned by the workers. Proudhon distinguished between property, which the elite used to exploit the others, and possessions, which were not exploitative.

Mutualism was a form of contractualism. Goods and services would be exchanged via a voucher system that reflected the value of labour inherent within each product or service. Pay would not be based on supply and demand, which determine wages within a capitalist society — workers would have to earn their wages by contributing. Proudhon proposed a 'people's bank' to establish and oversee the mechanics of such a system. Proudhon's contractual system would reserve the majority of liberty to the individual. The individual's rights would only be restricted in the sense that they did not intrude on the rights of the commune.

Mutualism therefore required a detailed series of explicit contracts. The economy that Proudhon envisaged would be a 'brotherhood' of small collective organisations exchanging goods and services, which would eradicate poverty as the system would provide enough for all.

Bakunin famously argued that individuals were only free if they lived in groups. However, his vision was more socialist than those of Kropotkin and Proudhon, as he envisaged the economy being organised by collectivisation.

Anarcho-syndicalism

Anarcho-**syndicalism** was a revolutionary form of anarchism that drew upon the trade unionism found in socialism. Anarcho-syndicalists envisaged a stateless society based on syndicates (trade unions) that cooperate freely with each other for mutual benefit.

Georges Sorel is seen as the most important thinker within this branch of anarchism. Sorel argued that working-class solidarity would find a meaningful expression with trade unionism and he advocated **direct action** and 'propaganda by the deed'. This would involve non-payment of taxes, bills and rents and also violence and spontaneous insurrection, via a general strike, initiating a social revolution.

Once capitalism and the state were abolished, the syndicates would become the owners of their own particular means of production. As with anarcho-communism, goods and services traded between syndicates would be priced at their true labour value and not their market value.

Key terms

Direct democracy
A system of government where the people make key decisions on behalf of the community. A decentralised process organised by small-scale communities and not the state.

Mutualism Associated with Pierre-Joseph Proudhon, this concept is of an independent association of workers cooperating and trading with each other on mutually beneficial terms.

Syndicalism A revolutionary version of trade unionism that proposes a stateless society where workers are grouped into syndicates, based on industrial occupation, which cooperate freely with each other for mutual benefit.

Direct action A reference to individuals taking proactive steps to undermine and ultimately destroy the state. Such methods include violence, civil disobedience and propaganda. Of the key thinkers, only Proudhon thought it could be achieved via peaceful means.

Key term

Utopianism An idealised and perfect society that individuals will inhabit in the future. However, utopianism can also be used in a critical sense to refer to something as being impractical and not rational.

Collectivist anarchism has been criticised for its **utopianism**, principally that its theories are rationally flawed and inconsistent (Table 12.4).

Table 12.4 Criticisms of individualist anarchism

Criticism	Explanation
Mutualism: a flawed perception of the role of the state	Proudhon's 'mutualism' argued that liberty would exist in the shell of the state. However, despite safeguards (such as a federal assembly) to ensure larger communities could not dominate smaller communities, it is difficult to disagree with Peter Marshall's assessment that such an arrangement would not see the re-emergence of the state
Mutualism: not reconciling individualism and collectivism	Proudhon struggles to reconcile the individualist and collectivist aspects of his ideas. Ultimately, the collectivist vision takes precedence as the federal assembly decision would take precedence over citizens' wishes, which undermines individual autonomy
Mutual aid: an unscientific theory	Kropotkin's 'mutual aid' has been accused of being scientifically selective and omitting examples that do not fit his theory. Likewise, his pre-capitalistic history of the ancient world and medieval city states is idealised to fit his overall hypothesis. Kropotkin's anthropological examples are also highly selective, only considering empirical evidence that fits his mutual aid theories
Mutual aid: unconsidered assumptions	Kropotkin assumes mutual aid will re-emerge once the state collapses. He does not consider that humans could well be conditioned into being state dependent after being psychologically dominated for so long. Kropotkin also fails to consider that individuals conditioned by the state to be selfish may not act altruistically once the state is vanquished
Anarcho-syndicalism: more socialist than anarchist	Anarcho-syndicalism has been criticised for being too narrow in its objectives. It is more preoccupied with democratic socialism-style struggles over wages and conditions rather than a more holistic anarchist vision of society
Federalism	Bakunin's ideas are mere sketches and lack explicit detail of how his blueprint for a new society and economy would actually work

The Christiania commune, created as a utopian community in the heart of Copenhagen

Individualist anarchism

Individualist anarchism, like classical liberalism and neo-liberalism, argues for negative freedom and individual autonomy. However, both of these strands of liberalism require a 'nightwatchman state' to uphold law and order and to enforce legal contracts. Individualist anarchists go one step further and argue that the state is no longer required.

Individualist anarchism has two broad strands: egoism and anarcho-capitalism.

This sketch of Stirner was drawn by Engels from memory, 40 years after meeting him

Egoism

Stirner's egoism posits that each individual is akin to a sovereign state, possessing an 'ownness' that means that they should enjoy complete autonomy. This, the most extreme form of individualism, meant that, unlike other anarchist key thinkers who differentiate between state and society, Stirner detested both. Egoism therefore feared collectivist anarchism, as one's individualism would be compromised by the collective expectations.

Stirner did not believe conventional state and society would cease by revolution, rather their end would occur by a spontaneous insurrection as individuals became conscious egoists and recognised the false values of state and society. The 'wheels of the mind' that distort reality would cease to turn and liberated individuals would see the world as it really is. Individuals would withdraw their labour and support from the economy, state and society. Stirner also argued for 'propaganda of the deed' as individuals broke free from their collective shackles.

- Stirner rejected conventional capitalism, arguing that work should be useful and fulfilling to the individual and that aspects of capitalism such as the factory system were akin to slavery.
- Society and the economy should be formed on voluntary agreements that are non-binding, whereby a union of egoists would form and cooperate only to the extent that it satisfied their individual wishes.
- Stirner saw it as logical for conscious egoists to make peaceful contracts and argued that this would produce harmony: 'they care best for their welfare if they unite with others'. Altruism (see Chapter 10) exists only if it is in the individual's best interest.
- Egoism is materialist and Stirner argues that individuals are driven to obtain possessions and property. Stirner maintains that the union of egoists would organise their atomistic society in such a way that everyone had enough and poverty would be eradicated. This would be done by conscious egoist bargaining and not via collective bargaining.
- Individuals are selfish, but in appealing to their selfishness it will be in everyone's interest to avoid conflict.

Anarcho-capitalism

Anarcho-capitalism has been influenced by the ideas of classical liberalism and neo-liberalism. Murray Rothbard and David Friedman are most closely associated with these ideas, which champion negative freedom and atomistic individualism. Anarcho-capitalism would see the dismantling of the state and with it the exploitative use of taxation. Rothbard, like Robert Nozick (see Chapter 10), viewed taxation as theft and argued that the state was attacking political and economic freedom. Rothbard and Friedman were both influenced by Friedrich Hayek's warnings in *The Road to Serfdom* (1944) of the dangers of the collective state bankrupting society.

Anarcho-capitalists view the world purely in free-market terms and argue that competition and the pursuit of individual self-interest give capitalism its dynamism. Private entrepreneurs are more than capable of fulfilling the state's functions: schools, hospitals, pension provision, policing, the judiciary and communal infrastructure will all be maintained by the private sector. The competition inherent in free markets will lower costs, increase choice and provide better services. Social evils such as pollution would be controlled via fines.

Rothbard saw 'greed' as individuals rationally trying to maximise their potential in a world of scarce resources. David Friedman perceived humans as economic, not social, animals. Influenced by Nozick's entitlement theory, Friedman contended that individuals have a natural sense of economic entitlement and if they work hard enough they should be free to enjoy the material rewards of their efforts. The unregulated free market is therefore the perfect habitat for the rational self-interested individual. Society does not need an overarching state, as rational, self-interested individuals will ensure 'a balance of interests' that will maintain order.

Utopian criticism of individualist anarchism

Individualist anarchism has been criticised for its utopianism, principally that its theories are rationally flawed and inconsistent (Table 12.5).

Table 12.5 Criticisms of individualist anarchism

Criticism	Explanation
Egoism's internal contradiction	Stirner's egoist ideas and arguments are not intellectually coherent as he refutes abstractions, 'wheels in the head' which induce illusions, without realising/acknowledging that his own theories on individuality and 'ownness' are just another abstraction
Egoism is vague and implausible	George Woodcock criticises the lack of practical detail in what social and economic organisation the union of egoists would take and accuses Stirner of making generalised assumptions rather than explicit explanations. It is also difficult to imagine a society of sovereign individuals not resorting to violence to settle disputes, with the powerful under no obligation to not dominate the weak. Society would resemble the 'war against all' that Hobbes described
Anarcho-capitalism is implausible	Anarcho-capitalism has been criticised for being implausible, as even neo-liberals argue for a small 'nightwatchman state', to enforce the rule of law. Neo-conservatives, who share an antipathy towards state-managed welfare states, argue that simply dismantling the state and putting all of the responsibility in the realm of the free market would be practically impossible

Debate

Is it possible to reconcile collectivist and individualist forms of anarchism?

Yes

- Both view the state as a coercive institution that must be removed (or, in Proudhon's case, exist in the shell of the state).
- Collectivist and individualist anarchism both have a broadly positive view of human nature and believe that society and the economy can function without a state.
- Collectivist and individualist anarchism claim that they can restore liberty.
- Collectivist and individualist anarchists argue that people will be able to cooperate in their particular visions of anarchist society.

No

- Collectivists and individualists disagree on the nature of liberty. Individualist forms of anarchy view collectivist anarchy's demands as an infringement of liberty.
- Although both sides agree on a positive view of human nature, individualist anarchists argue that humans are individualistic egoists whereas collectivist anarchists argue that humans are communal.
- Individualist anarchists argue that collectivist anarchism is a denial of an individual's ego.
- Individualist anarchists are suspicious that collectivist anarchism will lead to the return of the state and oppression.

Summary: key themes and key thinkers

	Human nature	The state	Society	The economy
Max Stirner	Human nature is fundamentally self-interested and individual liberty is sacrosanct	The state both denies and inhibits individualism and therefore must be abolished	Society is a false construct. Humans are all sovereign	The accumulation of property and material possession is the primary economic motivation
Pierre-Joseph Proudhon	Humans are naturally communal	The state supports capitalism and must be destroyed, preferably by peaceful means but by revolution if necessary	Society would operate by 'mutualism', whereby people are bound by social and economic relations which are mutually beneficial	Individuals would trade with each other on a mutually beneficial basis
Mikhail Bakunin	Humans are intensely social creatures and prefer collective activities	The state supports capitalism and must be destroyed by revolution	Society should be federal and national boundaries would be abolished. Society would be based on cooperation and not competition	The free market would be replaced by an exchange-based system that recognised the true value of labour and goods
Peter Kropotkin	Human nature is social, preferring collective activities	The state supports capitalism and must be destroyed by revolution	A stateless society based on small independent and internally democratic communes	Capitalism replaced by a communist system
Emma Goldman	Humans need individual liberty to be truly free	The state is part of an interlocking set of aspects of oppression, including religion and property ownership	Goldman deliberately did not plan an anarchist society but she did wish for economic, gender and racial equality	Goldman's ideas were essentially communist

Practice questions

1 To what extent does anarchism agree on human nature? *You must use appropriate thinkers you have studied to support your view.* (24)

2 To what extent do anarchists disagree on the nature of an anarchist society? *You must use appropriate thinkers you have studied to support your view.* (24)

3 To what extent is it appropriate to describe anarchism as a single movement? *You must use appropriate thinkers you have studied to support your view.* (24)

Ernst Haeckel coined the term 'ecology' in 1879 as a neutral scientific term describing the relationships between living organisms and their organic and non-organic environment. Ecologism describes a set of political ideas that are concerned with humans' harmful interaction with the environment and how this might be rectified.

Core ideas and principles

Ecology

The natural world consists of a wide variety of interconnected ecosystems. Humans behave anthropocentrically, treating the planet's finite resources as if they were unlimited, and destroying and polluting the ecosystem in a pursuit for economic growth. The human race, Aldo Leopold (1887–1948) asserts, 'hammered the artefact called civilisation' from the planet's natural state.

There are three strands of ecological thought:

- **Deep green ecology** asserts that the environment is a complex holistic web of interrelations between the organic and the non-organic. The interconnectedness of our holistic ecosystem sustains life, and humans must develop an **ecocentric** vision respecting both organic and non-organic life to preserve **biodiversity**.

Key terms

Ecocentric A nature-based rather than a human-centred system of values. It therefore gives priority to ecological balance over human wants and needs.

Biodiversity The belief that as many species of plants and animals must survive and flourish as possible to maintain the richness of nature. This will bring health and stability to the broad eco-community.

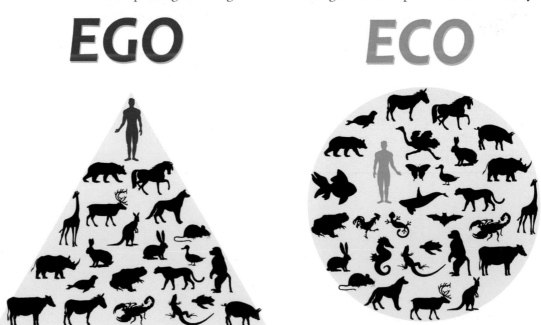

Ego vs Eco. Ego represents the dominant anthropocentric world view where humans dominate the ecosystem and are of primary importance. Eco represents the ecocentric world view of deep green ecology that argues that humans are merely part of the ecosystem and that no creature dominates

Aldo Leopold (1887–1948)

Leopold was an early pioneer of ecological thought and a holistic thinker. His key work, *A Sand County Almanac*, was published posthumously in 1949. Ecology, Leopold argues, is a study of a 'world of wounds', such is the extent of environmental damage. His main ideas were as follows:

The land ethic

- Humans should accept that the land, which incorporates 'soils, waters, plants and animals', does not belong to them. There should be biocentric equality where all beings and the community have equal value.
- Biodiversity is therefore essential to conserve endangered species and their habitats.
- 'Wilderness' landscapes free from human interference must be preserved in their natural state.

Conservation fails

- Conservation fails because it is based on an economic model where land is valued merely as a commodity of monetary worth.
- Human nature must alter so it recognises that nature is no longer perceived as a resource to be exploited.

- **Shallow green ecology** is an 'enlightened **anthropocentric**' vision whereby humans act as environmental stewards to protect the planet.
- **Social ecology** argues that environmental degradation is linked to specific social constructs that must be overturned before radical ecological change can occur. Aspects of social ecology are eco-socialism, eco-anarchism and eco-feminism.

The difference between deep green and shallow green ecology is that in shallow green anthropocentrism's ego thinks it dominates the ecosystem, while dark green has an ecocentric view and perceives humans as but an aspect of the environment.

> **Key term**
>
> **Anthropocentric** The idea that human interest is of primary importance.

Holism

Holism is a core idea of deep green ecologism and perceives every aspect of nature as being interconnected. The whole is therefore greater than the sum of its parts and the environment self-regulates beyond human understanding. Holism actively argues for biological diversity and biospherical egalitarianism, as a wide variety of species of both flora and fauna is needed to preserve the ecosystem.

Rationalistic Enlightenment thinkers disputed the idea of holism in two key ways:

1 **Mechanistic world view** Nature could be reduced to its constituent parts and then examined in isolation as if it were a machine.

2 **Dominion over nature** If nature is understood, it can be dominated by man, Francis Bacon, the Enlightenment thinker, concluded.

Carolyn Merchant (b. 1936) views such a paradigm as destructive and hubristic. Likewise, E.F. Schumacher (1911–77) argued that modern living has facilitated this myth of human ascendency as city dwellers are dislocated from the ecosystem, facilitating the idea that humans are successfully dominating nature.

> **Key term**
>
> **Mechanistic world view** In the post-Enlightenment era, the dominant view in science is that nature is like a machine where parts can be repaired or replaced in isolation from each other.

Holism's rebuttal of Enlightenment thinking

Holistic thinkers dispute these ideas as demonstrably incorrect. Leopold described holism as a land pyramid that embraces both the complexity and interconnectedness of the environment. Human ability to understand this complexity is limited, so we are best advised to practise biotic preservation, which Leopold stresses will ensure a 'harmony' within the environment.

Actions guided by a mechanistic dominance have often been disastrous for the environment. Rachel Carson's *Silent Spring* (1962) documents how American farmers mistakenly believed that the pesticide DDT was harmful only to insects and inadvertently poisoned farmland and woodland, with a devastating effect on humans and animals as well as on plant life. The failure to understand that 'everything in nature is connected to everything', as Rachel Carson (1907–64) explained, demonstrated the hubris of post-Enlightenment thinking.

> 'We poison the caddis flies in a stream and the salmon runs dwindle and die. We poison the gnats in a lake and poison travels from link to link of the food chain and soon the birds of the lake margins become its victims. We spray our elms and the following springs are silent of robin song, not because we sprayed the robins directly but because the poison traveled step by step through the now familiar elm leaf–earthworm–robin cycle … They reflect the web of life — or death — that scientists know as ecology.'
>
> Rachel Carson (1962) *Silent Spring*

Holism holds that the natural world cannot be separated into constituent parts because of this interconnectedness. Leopold articulates that humans are but an aspect of the holistic system and consideration must be given to all species and ecosystems as well as recognising the complexity of our environment. Similarly, Fritjof Capra argued that all living organisms from the microscopic to the gigantic are part of a symbiotic 'web of life'.

Key thinker

Rachel Carson (1907–64)

Linda Lear has argued that Rachel Carson's *Silent Spring* (1962) altered environmental consciousness in America, initiating the contemporary environmental movement which is now global in scale. Carson's main ideas were as follows:

State and society do not have the authority to dominate nature

- The state and society are complicit in putting economic concerns above ecological issues by facilitating big business dominating nature, anthropocentric industrialism and consumerism. Carson sardonically describes them as 'the gods of profit and production'.
- This domination has been devastating. *Silent Spring* gives numerous examples of the damage to rivers, lakes, fauna and flora from the use of the pesticide DDT.

Nature should be seen holistically

- Humans are not superior to nature and they need to develop a holistic enlightened environmental consciousness.
- Although Carson did not live to see it, DDT was finally banned in 1969.

Environmental ethics

The anthropocentric focus on conventional ethics takes precedence in guiding human interactions with the environment. Ecologists therefore seek to develop environmental ethics that are shallow green (enlightened anthropocentric) and dark green (ecocentric) in nature.

There are three broad aspects to environmental ethics: animal liberation, obligations to future generations and holistic ethics.

Animal liberation

Peter Singer argued for extending the moral community from humans to animals. Animal liberationists are not holistic as their moral extension does not extend into the whole biotic community. Rather they focus on individual species for protections — such as whales, rhinos and pangolins — rather than whole ecosystems. Animal liberation led to debate about the ethics of animal research, veganism and hunting for pleasure.

Obligations to future generations

Derek Parfit argues for further enlightened anthropocentrism, where today's decision makers preserve the environment for future generations. The actions of today affect those yet to be born; there is a moral responsibility to focus on: climate change; resource depletion; biodiversity loss, pollution and preserving ecosystems.

The pangolin in the most trafficked mammal in the world as it is highly prized for its meat and unique scales

Holistic ethics

Holistic ethics assert:

- **Holistic values** Leopold's land ethic stresses the preservation of 'the integrity, stability and beauty of the biotic community'. Arne Naess stresses the intrinsic value of all life forms, which have a richness, diversity and worth independent of their utility for human purposes.
- **The moral implications of holistic values** Leopold's land ethic states moral obligations must be extended to the whole community, including 'soils, waters, plants and animals, or collectively the land'. Arne Naess and George Sessions state that humans have no right to reduce **biocentric equality** to satisfy anthropocentric needs.

Environmental consciousness

The development of environmental ethics led ecologists to argue for a new **environmental consciousness**, although they have conflicting ideas about the nature of this consciousness.

Deep green (ecocentric) ecology

Holism

Schumacher argued that we humans must see ourselves as part of, rather than estranged from, nature. Leopold's 'land ethic' stresses that humans must become stewards of the land rather than seeking to dominate it for economic and materialistic benefit. Humans are not separate or detached from nature, but merely another strand of a complex and unfathomable web.

Biocentrism

Holism leads to biocentrism (respecting the inherent value of all living things) and environmental egalitarianism (treating every facet of nature equally). Murray Bookchin (1921–2006) believed 'ecology recognizes no hierarchy': no 'king of the beasts' or 'lowly ants'. Leopold's land thesis reiterates the prime importance of the biotic community. Naess and Sessions argued that human interference in the non-human world is damaging and is increasingly weakening biocentrism.

- A new environmental consciousness will see humans abandon **industrialism** and consumerism for small-scale **decentralised** bio-communities.
- These societies would see a decline in the standard of living measured by consumer consumption, but a higher quality of life as part of a new environmental consciousness. There are examples of such societies existing like oases in the industrialism desert.
- The Twin Oaks Community in the USA is perhaps the best known example. Its principles are influenced by deep green and social ecology. Although it is first to admit that it has not achieved utopia yet, its website and online videos give practical examples of how such a society might be organised. It also demonstrates environmental ethics and an environmental consciousness that are very different from the conventional society that most students are familiar with. Explore its website here: **www.twinoaks.org**.

Shallow green ecology

Shallow green ecology's environmental consciousness tends to be single-issue based: banning pesticides; habitat conservation; recycling; energy conservation; green energy; pollution control.

Social ecology

Social ecology's political dimension argues that humans need liberating from oppressive practices and structures before an environmental consciousness is possible. Eco-socialists focus on the removal of capitalism (see Chapter 11); eco-anarchists require the removal of the state (see Chapter 12); eco-feminists the removal of patriarchy (see Chapter 14).

Post-materialist and anti-consumerism

A new environmental consciousness will redefine how humans understand happiness. Schumacher argued that modern society equates insatiable materialism with happiness and the facilitating of such consumption is a major function of economic activity. Conventional economics is unconcerned with the ecological integrity of the land.

> **Key terms**
>
> **Industrialism** A system of large-scale production, underpinned by a belief in limitless economic growth and a faith in science and technology to deliver it.
>
> **Decentralisation** In ecological terms, this refers to societies that are based on small settlements such as communes, villages or bioregions that achieve sustainability through a high level of self-sufficiency.

Consumerism

Consumerism falsely concludes that happiness is achieved via material acquisition. Ecologists believe that consumerism offers a false consciousness and that economic activity is wasted chasing this mirage with little thought to the ecological costs involved.

All ecologists argue, to differing degrees, of a post-materialist future.

Dark green ecologists

Schumacher's Buddhist economics argues for a radical consumer post-materialist society, maximising wellbeing with the minimal amount of consumption. Humans must be liberated from their attachment to wealth and material possessions. Schumacher argues for a 'small is beautiful' descaling of the economy away from large-scale production. Similarly, Bookchin advocates bioregions and argues that a radical change of economy will facilitate a post-material society.

Small-scale societies will embrace discursive democracy, which will nurture ecological citizenship. The 'self-regarding' individual only interested in material gain is transformed into the 'other-regarding' citizen who cares for the environment. Although materially poorer, the other-regarding citizen is spiritually and ecologically happier than his materialistic predecessor. It would be a fundamentally different economic system not based on material accumulation.

Shallow green ecologists

Shallow green ecologists advocate a conserver rather than a consumer society. Individuals would consume less, lowering production and preserving resources. A more sustainable economy free of the relentless pursuit of possessions would redefine happiness in spiritual terms rather than material ones and preserve the environment.

Key thinker

E.F. Schumacher (1911–77)

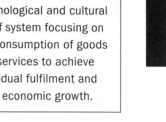

Ernst Friedrich Schumacher influenced ecological thinking by attacking traditional economics and providing a decentralised alternative with strong environmental ethics. His key work is *Small Is Beautiful: A study of economics if people mattered* (1973). His main ideas were as follows:

Traditional economics

Traditional economics are based on false premises:
- Obsession with GDP growth fuels a harmful human consciousness of consumerism and materialism, Schumacher argued 'there is more to life than GDP'.
- Humans treat natural resources as if they were infinite, which is unsustainable.

Buddhist economics

- Buddhist economics is based on wellbeing rather than consumption – humans' 'enoughness', which is essentially post-materialism.
- Schumacher envisaged small, self-sufficient communities and small-scale organisations with an economy based on strong sustainability.

Sustainability

The global economy is built on industrialism's belief in unlimited growth based on the assumption that resources are infinite. In 1972, The **Limits to Growth** (aka the Meadows Report) predicted an exhaustion of resources and ecological devastation within a hundred years. Although this was later found to be overly pessimistic, it proved to be a catalyst for global debate on sustainability.

In 1983, the United Nations formed the World Commission on Environment and Development (WCED), headed by Norwegian prime minister Gro Brundtland. In 1987, in a report commonly known as the Brundtland Report (actually entitled Our Common Future), sustainability had finally made the mainstream.

Exact definitions and methods of sustainability differ between dark green and shallow green ecologists but, broadly speaking, sustainability is committed to homeostasis and sustainable development which allows the ecological system to maintain its health over time. Homeostasis is an ecological equilibrium where the natural world is no longer degrading (losing its natural resources) and the environment is successfully renewing itself. Sustainability therefore requires the following:

- **Biodiversity** This requires the preservation of natural habitats so that the natural world can remain in a natural state for plants, animals and whole ecosystems.
- **Preservation of natural resources** Sustainability argues for a moving away from fossil-based fuels. Mining causes habitat devastation and coal use causes atmospheric pollution. Renewable energy such as wind, wave, tidal and thermal systems are more holistic resources. Increased recycling will also act as a counter to human consumption.
- **Preservation of the ecosystem** Conservation negates the degradation of the natural environment via measures such as strict quotas to prevent overfishing, planning laws and preventing the cutting down of the rainforest for industrialism objectives.
- **Pollution control** Strict limits are needed on omissions into the atmosphere, and on the pollution of seas and rivers.

Such sustainability is an example of shallow green managerialism, which requires the state to regulate society and economy at national and international levels, managing environmental problems via reform to achieve homeostasis. Deep green ecologists dismiss this as weak sustainability and remain convinced that there needs to be a radical transformation of society.

Different types of ecologism

Shallow green ecologism

Shallow green ecologists, unlike deep greens, do not require humans to undergo a dramatic shift in environmental consciousness. Shallow ecologism is reformist in nature, with ideas clustering around enlightened anthropocentrism and weak sustainability.

Enlightened anthropocentrism

Enlightened anthropocentrism is the belief that humans can live in harmony with nature through the state reforming society and the economy. This accepts limits to growth and an intergenerational responsibility on the present generation to act as a steward of nature for the benefit of future generations.

Shallow green ecologists argue for 'weak sustainability', whereby states regulate society and the economy at national and international levels, mitigating environmental problems. This interpretation of sustainability puts its faith in managerialism and green capitalism. Destructive elements of industrialism will be transformed so that market solutions can facilitate (and not hinder) environmentalism.

Managerialism and green capitalism

Developed countries need to readjust their consumption patterns to enable the environment to meet present and future needs. Environmental priorities coexist with anthropocentric social and economic needs. Examples include the following:

- The UN Department of Social and Economic Affairs, which has sponsored more than 300 sustainable development partnerships
- A string of global conferences and agreements, following the UN's formation of the WCED in 1983, designed to achieve sustainability to control air pollution, emissions, ozone depletion and global warming — most recently at the Paris Accord (agreement to combat climate change)
- Government tax breaks and investment to utilise wind, wave, thermal and nuclear power, none of which uses finite resources
- At state and local levels, widespread introductions of recycling schemes

Green capitalism has demonstrated that the market can play a positive role in preserving the environment. The free market will realise that future profit is only sustainable if environmental sustainability is achieved.

- Pressure from ethical consumers can incentivise sustainable capitalism, for example Nestlé's announcement that its palm olive supply chain will have a zero-deforestation policy.
- At state level, governments have harnessed managerialism to facilitate green capitalism, for example with taxes on air emissions the market economy incentivises industry to become sustainable.
- Finite resources such as oil and coal will increase in price and the result will be a reduction in their use and industry switching to renewables.
- The Brundtland Report argued persuasively that poverty in the developing word is correlated with environmental resource depletion, concluding that sustainable development is impossible where such human suffering exists.
- Managerialism and green capitalism facilitated the establishment of the Fairtrade label, which has sought to alleviate poverty by allowing small producers in developing countries to compete globally and achieve a fair price for their products.
- The improved economic wellbeing of workers in the developing world has facilitated better conservation of habitats in those countries.

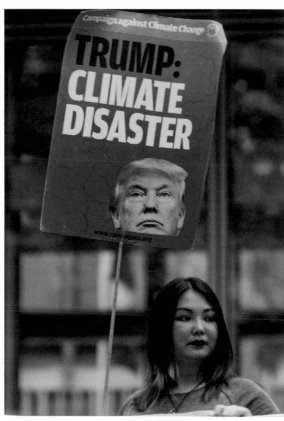

Supporters of ecology protested against Trump withdrawing the USA from the Paris Climate Agreement in June 2017

Deep green ecologism — environmental consciousness, ecocentrism and strong sustainability

The 'failure' of weak sustainability

The managerialism of shallow green weak sustainability is treated with scepticism by deep green thinkers. Ingolfur Blühdorn has argued that the sustainable development agenda championed by the Brundtland Report has withered as there is little political appetite for any substantive transformative action. The 1992 Kyoto Protocol on climate change has seen only limited participation from developed countries.

Similarly, the reaction by global leaders to the 2008 global financial crisis demonstrated unflinching commitment to the existing socioeconomic order rather than to a sustainable one. President Trump's withdrawal of the USA from the Paris Climate Agreement on 1 June 2017 illustrates the dominance of the industrialism paradigm over a new environmental consciousness.

Why do deep green ecologists oppose anthropocentrism and shallow green's 'enlightened anthropocentrism'? There are several reasons:

Continued dominance of industrialism paradigm

Trump's withdrawal from the Paris Accord confirmed that shallow ecology and weak sustainability have not delivered and that there is no coherent environmental consciousness: fossil-fuelled industrialism; exponential economic growth; the growth of fracking; and continuing materialism and consumerism remain the dominant paradigm.

Conservation fails due to anthropocentrism

The arguments for why 'conservation fails' have not changed since the time Leopold was writing: the human–environment relationship is still dictated by economic concerns. Carson's assessment that the state dominates natures and that society is in thrall of the 'gods of profit and production' still holds true today.

Ecocentrism not anthropocentrism

Ecocentrism places nature rather than humans at the centre of the world view. Deep green ecologists argue that shallow ecologism wastes its time focusing on single issues such as animal rights or fracking and should focus on promoting a radical holistic environmental consciousness.

Deep green solutions

Deep green ecologists argue that the human race must develop an environmental consciousness. This will facilitate a dramatic change in how humans choose to organise themselves, facilitating a decentralised state, society and economy which will ensure long-term environmental sustainability.

Environmental consciousness

An environmental consciousness based on holism will lead to a radical shift in environmental ethics. When this occurs, everything in the biosphere will have an intrinsic value. Humans will therefore be aware of their relationship with the land. Leopold argued that once an environmental consciousness was achieved, humans would respect 'soil, waters, plants and animals' but also understand the precarious nature of the ecosystem. Humans are not masters or stewards of nature — an enlightened anthropocentrism is a contradiction in terms.

Decentralised communities/bioregions

Deep green thinkers have therefore argued for decentralised communities/bioregions that adhere to Schumacher's 'small is beautiful' theory. Such communities would practise pastoralism — extensive livestock production in the rangelands. This would significantly safeguard natural capital and help maintain soil fertility and soil carbon, ensure water regulation and safeguard biodiversity, as well as significantly lowering emissions.

This simpler way of living, Schumacher argued, would allow a more natural relationship with rural life. Such communities would only be possible if a dramatic shift of a new environmental consciousness were achieved and the human race transcended its addiction to consumerism and industrialism. Such communities would shift the power from the central to the local, allowing collective ecological concerns to be recognised. Bioregions would be built around whole ecosystems rather than nation states.

Buddhist economics

Schumacher argued for **Buddhist economics**, which rejects the accumulation of wealth. In practical terms this would probably involve a local exchange trading system (LETS) where goods, skills and services would be exchanged within the local community. This rebalances the focus from accumulation to exchange and trade.

Population growth

Paul Ehrlich's *The Population Bomb* (1968) illustrated the simple fact that population growth is unsustainable and a clear threat to the biosphere. As Figure 13.1 illustrates, the planet's population is growing exponentially. The world population in 2019 stands at 7.7 billion; if human behaviour continues unchecked it will reach 11.2 billion by 2100. (This real-time website estimates population growth: **www.worldometers.info/world-population**.)

> **Key term**
>
> **Buddhist economics**
> E.F. Schumacher's idea which argued that people should find simpler ways of living and working with limited desires for goods and a more natural spiritual relationship with the environment.

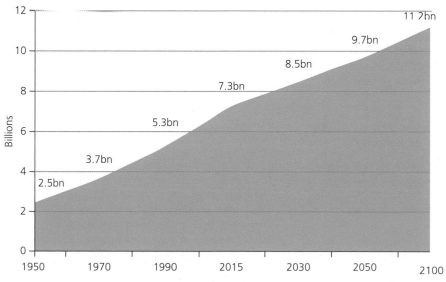

Figure 13.1 Global population growth forecast to 2100

Source: United Nations

Many countries are using more natural resources than their ecosystems can regenerate. The current level of population growth and natural resource depletion is unsustainable, and the situation is worsening as the developing countries continue to industrialise. Paul Ehrlich has argued that when 'a population becomes more wealthy it tends to consume more resources per person per year'. Many deep green ecologists shy away from population control, which contravenes individual freedom, but they are adamant that the human race must find an ecocentric way of living or else risk the planet's very existence. Table 13.1 compares the deep and shallow green beliefs.

Table 13.1 Conflict and tension between deep green and shallow green ecologists

	Deep green	Shallow green
Human nature	• Believe in ecocentrism, which argues that nature has an intrinsic value that is independent of humanity. Enlightened anthropocentrism is not radical enough • Argue that human nature must undergo a radical change to achieve an environmental consciousness (Naess and Leopold), so that humanity's environmental ethics are based on biocentric equality. Merchant blames Enlightenment ideas for making humanity think that it can dominate nature for its own selfish ends	• Believe in anthropocentrism, which argues that human nature can change and adapt so that humanity can act as a steward of nature • Argue that human nature must change its environmental consciousness for self-preservation (Carson). However, shallow greens still perceive the human race at the top of nature's hierarchy
The state	• Argue that the state is the problem and advocate decentralisation of power to bioregions (self-sufficient communities) • Dismiss managerialism as futile, as the state is still overseeing economic activity that is damaging the environment	• Believe that the state should negotiate national policy and international agreements to protect the environment • Examples of such managerialism would involve capping emissions, and quotas on fishing and finite natural resources
Society	• Reject the conventional ethics of society and argue for a break from consumerism, materialism and the mechanistic world view • Society would be decentralised and based on self-sufficient bioregions. Society would have a radically different environmental consciousness. Happiness would be equated with creative communal work that brings humanity closer to nature rather than through the consumption and the insatiable acquisition of material possessions • Peter Singer has argued that animals should receive the same rights as humans	• Argue that society should seek to protect the natural world rather than exploit it • Accept a limited concept of holism and are influenced by the ideas of Carson, who argued for the interconnectedness of human society and natural society • Enlightened anthropocentrism accepts limits to growth and that society must move beyond traditional ethics and accept the principle of intergenerational equity
The economy	• Opposed to capitalism, which it regards as consciousness that is singularly destructive to the environment. The ideas of Schumacher and Bookchin revolve around small-scale production and localism • Bioregions will recognise the limits of local ecosystems. Dark greens view green capitalism as futile • Eco-socialists and eco-anarchists both argue that private property should be abolished and replaced with common ownership	• Argue that green capitalism can use market forces to change environmental behaviour via green consumerism and green capitalism (e.g. taxes on air emissions and tax breaks on wind, wave, thermal and nuclear power) • Managerialism at state and international level has seen the creation of recycling schemes. The UN has sponsored 300 sustainable development policies

Can green capitalism solve the sustainability problem?

Yes

- With a more environmentally conscious public, consumer choice models suggest that companies will react to this demand by responding in a sustainable manner.
- If the market favours ethical environmentalism, companies will adopt sustainable activities.
- State managerialism can regulate capitalism and facilitate sustainability via laws and taxation that encourage environmentalism.

No

- Capitalism always prioritises economic growth over environmental concerns. Capitalism is motivated by profit and sustainability is expensive.
- Business pressure groups are wealthier than environmental pressure groups and have more influence on government policy, which prioritises economic growth.
- The human race in both the developed and the developing world prioritises material gain over sustainable environmentalism.

Aldo Leopold, Rachel Carson and E.F. Schumacher are three key thinkers of ecology. Read their words below.

> 'One of the penalties of an ecological education is that one lives alone in a world of wounds. Much of the damage inflicted on land is quite invisible to laymen.'
>
> Aldo Leopold

> 'Conservation is getting nowhere because it is incompatible with our Abrahamic concept of land. We abuse land because we regard it as a commodity belonging to us. When we see land as a community to which we belong, we may begin to use it with love and respect.'
>
> Aldo Leopold

> 'How could intelligent beings seek to control a few unwanted species by a method that contaminated the entire environment and brought the threat of disease and death even to their own kind?'
>
> Rachel Carson

> 'Any intelligent fool can make things bigger and more complex ... It takes a touch of genius and a lot of courage to move in the opposite direction.'
>
> E.F. Schumacher

> 'The real problems of our planet are not economic or technical, they are philosophical. The philosophy of unbridled materialism is being challenged by events.'
>
> E.F. Schumacher

With reference to the quotes above, consider why ecologists argue that the human race needs to develop a new environmental consciousness.

Social ecology

Social ecology argues that environmental degradation is linked to existing social structures and norms of behaviour. Therefore, before there is any radical environmental change there must be societal transformations. There are three forms of social ecologism: eco-socialism, eco-anarchism and eco-feminism.

Eco-socialism

Eco-socialists argue that capitalism is the root cause of environmental problems. Capitalism creates a paradigm where the environment's finite resources are plundered to satisfy the insatiable demands of industrialism, consumerism and materialism. Capitalism's desire for exponential growth and profit is relentless and comes at the expense of the environment. Capitalism commoditises nature so that natural resources are reduced to an economic value, which ignores their intrinsic worth.

Eco-socialism is critical of the green capitalism advocated by shallow green ecologists, which it dismisses as bourgeois ecology — it does not change the environmental consciousness, as profit and continual growth are prioritised over ecological concerns. President Trump withdrawing the USA from the Paris Accord in 2017 would be an example of this.

What would an eco-socialist future look like?

Eco-socialist John Bellamy Foster's reinterpretation of Marxist writings led him to conclude that there will be a 'metabolic rift' between nature and capitalist production. Foster argues that capitalism is creating a proletariat that is being oppressed economically and environmentally. An eco-socialist revolt would therefore be driven by a scarcity of resources. The new society would be based on collective and not private ownership, which would encourage humanity to use the land for the communal benefit of everyone, rather than being exploited by the few. However, as Andrew Vincent has explained, eco-socialists do not agree on the exact construction of a new society, some arguing for an enlightened eco-socialist state, while others argue for a non-state pluralist commune.

Eco-anarchism

Eco-anarchists disagree with eco-socialists on one important aspect — they believe that societal transformation must include the abolition of the state as well as capitalism. Anarchists are utterly opposed to the state, which they perceive as corrupt, whoever is in charge, meaning that society becomes an exploitative hierarchy designed to benefit a corrupt elite (see Chapter 12). They argue that communist governments have failed because their leaders, once in charge, are corrupted by power.

Eco-anarchism is most closely associated with Bookchin, who argued that the state's innate desire to dominate has led to the disastrous treatment of nature. Bookchin argues that this exploitation of the environment for selfish anthropocentric reasons has dramatically worsened since the Industrial Revolution and the expeditious development of capitalism. He argues that nature and anarchism share parallels, as both are egalitarian and non-hierarchical.

Murray Bookchin (1921–2006)

Bookchin coined 'social ecology' and discussed this concept in *Towards an Ecological Society* (1980) and *Remaking Society* (1989). His main ideas were as follows:

The environmental crisis emerges from existing social structures of oppression

- Bookchin argues that hierarchies, inherent in human state and society, facilitate ecological domination. These must be removed before ecological change can occur.
- A new anarchist society — 'ecotopia' — is needed to replace the traditional capitalistic society.
- This revolutionary approach is anarchist in nature — so no state all — based on commonly owned, small communities run with an egalitarian ethos. (See Chapter 12.)

Lessons should be learned from ecology

- Replacing capitalism would end the unsustainable consumption of resources, negating ecological degradation.
- Ecotopia would create a new rational environmental consciousness, whereby humans live in harmony with nature rather than trying to dominate it.
- Anarcho-communism would establish a new environmental ethics, abolishing private property and redistributing wealth according to need. Society would no longer be about industrialism's unsustainable pursuit of economic growth; rather, society would become non-capitalist.

What would an eco-anarchist future look like?

Bookchin championed a spontaneous popular revolution in support of anarcho-communism, which would focus on small-scale productions in the form of bioregions. Bookchin's anarcho-communist society would be an 'ecotopia' where humans are naturally cooperative. (See Chapter 12 for more on anarcho-communism.) Such a decentralised society would be organised by direct democracy, which would ensure 'living democracy' where decisions would be made locally and focus on strong sustainability. The bioregions would be naturally defined with a strong emphasis on labour-intensive organic agriculture. Peter Berg challenged nation-state borders, arguing that bioregion boundaries must be governed by environmental features.

New environmental ethics will mean that humans will enjoy a symbiotic relationship with the natural environment. Anarcho-communism would abolish private property and redistribute wealth on a needs basis. Anarchy will therefore inform the new environmental ethics, which will transform humans' environmental consciousness. Bioregions will transcend existing society's obsession with the consumerism and industrialism that have led to the domination of society.

Eco-feminism

To solve ecological problems, society must first remove patriarchy (see Chapter 14). As Merchant has argued, men are exploitative and attempt to dominate nature as they dominate women. Male Enlightenment thinkers use rationalism and science to justify their exploitation of nature. The reception that Carson's *Silent Spring* received illustrates the hostility of men towards women. Her empirically correct study was dismissed as 'emotion-fanning' and Carson herself was dismissed by hostile male critics as 'an hysterical woman'. William Bean, a contemporary critic, patronisingly wrote, '*Silent Spring* … kept reminding me of the difficulty of trying to win an argument with a woman. It cannot be done.'

Key thinker

Carolyn Merchant (1936–)

Merchant is an eco-feminist. Her most influential work is *The Death of Nature* (1976). Her main ideas are as follows:

Gender oppression is linked to ecological oppression

- Merchant links the domination of nature with patriarchy, man's wish to dominate women (see Chapter 14).
- Only by patriarchy being overthrown, facilitating an egalitarian relationship between men and women, can a new environmental consciousness be created.

Opposition to the mechanistic male view of science

- Merchant blames the Enlightenment ideas of Francis Bacon, René Descartes and Isaac Newton for altering human consciousness from a coexistence with nature paradigm to a domination of nature paradigm.
- Enlightenment ideas have led to the belief that science is superior to nature. Bacon argued that nature should be subservient to humanity.

Merchant is critical of male Enlightenment thinkers who subverted the concept of Mother Nature and remodelled environmental consciousness such that science was perceived as superior to nature and subservient to the domination of man, which, when coupled with the demands of capitalism, has led to ecological devastation.

Merchant uses the metaphor that nature is female and nature's 'womb' has yielded to the intrusive 'forceps' of science. She equates this triumph of science over nature as akin to a death, hence the title of her book *The Death of Nature* (1980). In the same vein, she argues that the allegorical sculpture by Louis-Ernest Barrias, *Nature Unveiling Herself Before Science* (1899), is a useful metaphor for how the mystery of nature has apparently been revealed to man. Nature's resources are exploited to facilitate capitalism, its resources are plundered, and women are trapped by patriarchy and forced to breed the next generation of workers.

Louis-Ernest Barrias' Art Nouveau sculpture *Nature Unveiling Herself Before Science*

What would an eco-feminist future look like?

Merchant is explicit that 'nature' is female in character. This difference feminism (see Chapter 14) argues that women's distinct feminine values are better suited to stewarding nature than the dominance of patriarchal culture. Women have also endured patriarchal dominance and male oppression, and therefore have an empathy with nature. To solve ecological problems, society must remove patriarchy, which will reconstitute societal structures. With patriarchy overthrown, there can be new environmental ethics, based on an egalitarian relationship between men and women. This new equal status between genders will allow the creation of new environmental ethics, with humans treating the environment as an equal, which will encourage coexistence and end humankind's domination over nature. Merchant describes this as a 'partnership ethic' and a 'social reconstruction'.

Summary: key themes and key thinkers

	Human nature	The state	Society	The economy
Aldo Leopold	Humans are now largely detached from the natural world and it is vital to re-establish an affinity with nature	The role of the state is to protect the environment	Industrialisation and subsequent urbanisation have separated humans from nature and damaged the natural environment	The insatiable drive for economic growth has led to a degraded natural environment
Rachel Carson	Humans do not recognise the intrinsic value of nature	The state must protect the environment, particularly rivers and seas	Society should seek to protect the natural world rather than exploit it	An unregulated economy will pollute to avoid 'unnecessary' costs. To prevent this, industry must be regulated
E.F. Schumacher	Humans are now largely detached from the natural world and it is vital to re-establish an affinity with nature	The state is overbearing and political systems should be decentralised	Small-scale societies will facilitate a stronger connection to and relationship with the natural world	The economy needs to be reorganised so that small-scale sufficiency replaces large-scale consumer capitalism
Murray Bookchin	Humans have lost their individualistic relationship with nature	The state is the enemy of both nature and liberty and should be abolished	By abolishing the state, traditional society would be replaced by an anarchist non-capitalist society that would be close to the natural world	Modern capitalism is exploitative and damaging to the environment. It must be replaced by an anarchist economy that will operate in harmony with the natural world
Carolyn Merchant	Human nature is patriarchal and exploits both women and nature	The state is controlled by men whose patriarchy exploits, dominates and harms nature	Men and women need to form equal relationships to negate patriarchy and facilitate a positive environmental consciousness	Capitalism is patriarchal and exploits natural resources. A non-patriarchal state and society will lead to the liberation of both the natural world and women

Practice questions

1. To what extent have deep green ecologists criticised shallow green ecologists? *You must use appropriate thinkers you have studied to support your answer and consider any differing views in a balanced way.* (24)

2. To what extent do ecologists agree about human nature? *You must use appropriate thinkers you have studied to support your answer and consider any differing views in a balanced way.* (24)

3. To what extent do ecologists disagree about sustainability? *You must use appropriate thinkers you have studied to support your answer and consider any differing views in a balanced way.* (24)

Feminism

Feminists argue that men have oppressed women throughout history and that this must stop. As a set of political ideas, the movement has had four waves since 1790. The movement has several broad themes:

- First-wave feminism (1790s to 1950s): liberal feminism
- Second-wave feminism (1960s to 1980s): liberal feminism; radical feminism; socialist feminism
- Third-wave feminism (1990s to early 2000s): emergence of postmodern feminism and transfeminism
- Fourth-wave feminism (early 2000s to date): further development to postmodern feminism; liberal feminism; radical feminism and transfeminism

Protesters on the London Women's March in January 2017, which took place the day after President Trump's inauguration as US president. There were an estimated 7 million people involved in protests around the world that day

Core ideas and principles

Sex and gender

Feminism differentiates between sex and gender.

Sex

Sex refers to biological differences between men and women. Humans are assigned their sex at birth: male or female. Biological differences have observable physical attributes such as external and internal anatomy, chromosomes and hormone prevalence. Within feminism there are two main debates concerning sex:

- **Difference feminism** vs **equality feminism**
- Transfeminism vs transfeminist sceptics

Difference feminism

Difference feminists argue that the biological differences between women and men are important and believe in **essentialism**. Carol Gilligan argued that biological differences affect the way that men and women think: there are specific male and female characteristics and each sex has a specific 'nature'. However, most feminists are equality feminists, arguing that women's 'nature' is socially constructed — determined by society, not biology.

Transfeminism vs sceptics

Transsexual refers to those whose gender identity differs from the biological sex that they were classified with at birth. Until the 1990s there was very little academic debate within feminism (or indeed anywhere else) about sex, as biological differences seemed to be scientifically undeniable. However, since the turn of the century, this has changed with the rise of transgenderism and the development of transfeminism. Transfeminism argues that sex is socially constructed. However, this is a minority viewpoint within global society and within feminism itself, as most feminists argue that sex is a biological fact. Prominent, radical second-wave feminist Germaine Greer has explicitly stated that transgender women are 'not women', while Sheila Jeffreys has asserted that feminism should only be for 'womyn-born-womyn'. However, Andrea Dworkin supports the socially constructed definition of sex, arguing that the state should finance sex-change operations for transsexuals.

Self-identification of sex has gone from a niche issue to one of the most prominent topics within feminism. In 2014, Denmark passed legislation to allow individuals to change their identified sex without court approval.

Gender

Gender is used to explain the 'gender roles' of men and women. The majority of feminists argue that gender roles are socially constructed and form **gender stereotypes**. Simone de Beauvoir (1908–86) argued that the biological differences between men and women had been used by a male-dominated state and society as a justification for predetermining the gender role of women. Men, de Beauvoir asserted, had successfully characterised themselves as the norm whereas women were the other, and this '**otherness**' had left women subordinate to men in society. 'Otherness' is imposed on women by men. De Beauvoir made this distinctness clear when she argued that men's domination meant that they were the 'first sex' while women were the 'second sex'.

Key terms

Difference feminism Perceives women as biologically and culturally different from men. Difference feminists argue that these differences need to be recognised and celebrated and that women need to value their distinct gender characteristics.

Equality feminism Argues for an elimination of cultural differences in the pursuit of absolute equality. Liberal, radical, socialist and postmodern feminists all have different visions of how this will be achieved in practice.

Essentialism The belief that biological differences between men and women lead to distinct differences in their fundamental natures. The fundamental nature of men and women is therefore 'natural' rather than socially constructed.

Key terms

Gender stereotype The argument that men's and women's roles are predetermined by society so that they are socialised to behave in a certain way.

Otherness Women are treated as an inferior minority who are subordinate to men in a patriarchal society.

Simone de Beauvoir (1908–86)

Drawing on her own unhappy experiences of childhood, de Beauvoir offered a powerful critique of sex and gender in *The Second Sex* (1949). De Beauvoir used existentialism to pose the question 'What is a woman?' Existentialism argues that humans have no natural nature or essence and de Beauvoir argued that men have thus created a feminine myth through which to oppress women. Her main ideas were as follows:

Sex and gender

- She argued that femininity was an artificial societal construct: 'One is not born, but rather becomes a woman.'

- She was in some ways as much a humanist as she was a feminist. 'The fact that we are human beings is infinitely more important than all the peculiarities that distinguish human beings from one another.'

Otherness

- 'Otherness' is imposed on women by men. Male domination meant that men were the 'first sex', while women were the 'second sex', as men argued that they were the norm.

Table 14.1 Examples of traditional gender stereotypes

Feminine	Masculine
Passive	Aggressive
Gentle	Tough
Sensitive	Insensitive
Emotional	Logical
Tactful	Blunt
Submissive	Dominant

Charlotte Perkins Gilman (1860–1935) argued that gender roles are socially constructed from a young age, subordinating women to the will of men. Women are socialised into thinking themselves naturally frail and weaker than men. Kate Millett (1934–2017) and bell hooks (b. 1952) both perceive social construction as beginning in childhood within the family unit. Gender roles are therefore neither natural nor inevitable (Table 14.1).

First-wave feminism

First-wave feminism extended classical liberalism's ideas about human nature and freedom of the individual so that they explicitly included women. These ideas wished for the state to reform society and economy. The two key texts at the heart of first-wave liberal feminism are Mary Wollstonecraft's *A Vindication of the Rights of Woman* (1792) and Harriet Taylor Mill's *Enfranchisement of Women* (1851). Wollstonecraft argued that women were just as rational as men and should receive the same educational opportunities. Taylor Mill argued that women should have the same right to vote as men and also play a role in the making of law.

Charlotte Perkins Gilman argued that women should have equal opportunities in the workplace and conceptualised the idea of economic independence for women.

Second-wave feminism

The key texts of second-wave feminism are Betty Friedan's *The Feminine Mystique* (1963), Kate Millett's *Sexual Politics* (1970), Germaine Greer's *The Female Eunuch* (1970) and Sheila Rowbotham's *Woman's Consciousness, Man's World* (1973). Second-wave feminism had divergent solutions to women's problems. Liberal feminists, influenced by Friedan and first-wave feminism, argued for the state to reform society and economy, allowing women equality within the public sphere of society. Radical feminists, influenced by Millett and Greer, saw the state as part of the problem and wanted radical changes to the public and private spheres of society. Socialist feminists, influenced in part by the ideas of Rowbotham, argued that only under a socialist feminist revolution could the inequalities of both capitalism and female oppression be solved. Second-wave feminism was united by one idea: that women were being oppressed by men, a concept that became known as patriarchy.

Patriarchy

Patriarchy is derived from the Greek *patriarches*, meaning 'head of the tribe'. Feminism uses the term to describe a social system supporting male domination and female subordination. Kate Millett is credited with the first analysis of patriarchy but most feminists engage with the concept. De Beauvoir argued that for the majority of human history women have been relegated to a subsidiary status by men. Different groups of feminists focus on different aspects of patriarchy.

- **Liberal feminists** Liberal feminists believe that patriarchy can be reformed by the state, and in Western society there are numerous examples: female emancipation; access to education; workplace equality; legalisation of abortion; changes in marriage and divorce law.
- **Radical feminists** Radical feminists focus on patriarchy in both public and private spheres and believe that patriarchy is too pervasive to be reformed. Instead, change must be revolutionary. Germaine Greer argued that male respect for women is an affectation as they have a deep-seated loathing of women, which is expressed by the obscenities used to describe women's sexual organs: 'women have very little idea how much men hate them'. Barbara Goodwin concludes the sheer number of domestic violence and rape cases should give women some idea of this.
- **Socialist feminists** Social feminists believe that female consciousness is created by men as part of the capitalist machine. Sheila Rowbotham (b. 1943) adopted a Marxist theory of history that concluded that women have always been oppressed and that a revolution was needed which would destroy both capitalism and patriarchy.

Third-wave feminism

Third-wave feminism expanded on the work of Millett. Sylvia Walby identified six overlapping patriarchal structures that promote **discrimination** (Table 14.2).

Table 14.2 Walby's overlapping patriarchal structures

The state	Underrepresents women in power
Household	Society conditions women to believe that their natural role is as mother/homemaker
Violence	One in four women in the UK will suffer domestic violence from men
Paid work	Women are often underpaid when they are in the same role as men. Women-centric careers also tend to be linked to gender stereotypes of nurturing, such as nursing or teaching
Sexuality	Women are made to feel that their sexual feelings are abnormal, wrong or deviant
Culture	Society reinforces roles of women, from woman being the primary carer through to objectifying how women should look. Feminists would argue that objectified and highly sexualised male fantasy versions of women are found in adverts and virtually all media, pressurising women to look a certain way and often linked to anorexia among young women

> ## Key term
>
> **Discrimination** Treating a group or an individual less favourably than another group or individual. Feminists argue that women are treated less favourably than men.

Postmodern feminism/Fourth-wave feminism

bell hooks argued that feminist discussions have primarily been from a white middle-class perspective. hooks argued women of different ethnicities and socioeconomic classes had been neglected by mainstream feminism. Fourth-wave feminists argue that patriarchy is especially **misogynistic** in the developing world, with female circumcision, forced marriage and sexual violence more prevalent than in the West.

The personal is the political

Liberal feminists focus on the **public sphere** of society (such as equal pay and conditions in the workplace), arguing that the private life of women is outside the remit of political analysis. Radical feminists refute this, arguing that 'the personal is the political' as patriarchy is prevalent in the **private sphere** of family life.

Gilman berated the misery of women's private lives and the exploitative nature of domestic roles. Societal pressure forced young girls to conform to motherhood, with gender-specific clothes and toys; Gilman argued for gender-neutral garments and playthings.

Equality feminists argue that gender stereotyping starts in infancy

Rowbotham argued that marriage was like feudalism, with women akin to serfs paying feudal dues to their husband. De Beauvoir championed contraception as it allowed women control of their bodies and the chance to avoid endless childbearing. Millett believed 'family' was a social construct and not a natural arrangement. Millett's main points were as follows:

- Patriarchy granted men ownership over their wife and children, entrenching sexism with the idea of male superiority.
- The family socialised the young into recognising masculine authority and female marginalisation within society.
- Marriage saw women lose their identity by taking their husband's surname.

Radical feminists opened private life to public scrutiny.

Kate Millett (1934–2017)

Kate Millett was an American academic and her most famous work, *Sexual Politics* (1970), is regarded as the first systematic analysis of patriarchy. Perhaps the most influential radical feminist, she challenged liberal feminism by arguing that 'the personal was the political'. Her main ideas were as follows:

Family

- Millett perceived the family unit as the foundation of patriarchal thought, as children were socialised into gender roles that they grew up perceiving as normal. Underpinning Millett's proposed solutions to patriarchy was the dismantling of the family unit for communal living and childrearing.
- Patriarchy reinforced heterosexualism as being superior to bisexual or homosexual relationships.

The portrayal of women in art and literature

- Women's gender roles were stereotyped in art and literature. Millett's analysis included a feminist deconstruction of the work of influential male writers D.H. Lawrence, Henry Miller and Norman Mailer, whom she branded sexist, misogynistic and phallocentric.

Equality feminism and difference feminism

Feminism is a splintered ideology with its different branches disagreeing on the exact nature of patriarchy and how best women should achieve parity with men in state, society and economy. However, most aspects of feminism can be housed in two different categories: equality feminism and difference feminism.

Equality feminism

The majority of feminists, be they liberal, radical, social or postmodern, are equality feminists, who believe that biological differences are inconsequential and that gender differences are socially constructed, thus holding that there are no specific feminine traits. De Beauvoir dismissed the idea of innate female characteristics as 'a myth invented by men to confine women to their oppressed state'. Women and men were essentially the same, and de Beauvoir argued that women had been dominated in part because of their bodies, 'her ovaries condemn her to live for ever on her knees'. De Beauvoir argued that contraceptives, abortion, rejection of the family and monogamy would allow women to compete with men in society.

Difference feminism

A minority of feminists, difference feminists, disagree with equality feminism, believing in essentialism, whereby biological differences *are* consequential and *do* determine gender differences.

- Difference feminism can be traced back to first-wave feminists who, while believing that women were men's intellectual equal, also believed in gender-specific characteristics.
- In the 1980s, difference feminism emerged as a rebuttal to equality feminism. Carol Gilligan, a prominent difference feminist, stated that sex was one of the most important determinants of human behaviour, positing that women are naturally more nurturing, caring and communal than men.

- Gilligan argues that there has been an assumption that there is 'a single mode of social experience and interpretation', when in fact men and women experience and interpret the world in different ways and speak with distinct voices.
- Equality feminism misunderstands these differences, leading to women attempting to replicate male behaviour while neglecting their own feminine natures.

Cultural feminism is a more extreme version of difference feminism and challenges the dominance of men in society, asserting that women's values are superior and should be promoted. Cultural feminists believe in a distinct 'female essence', which is caring and nurturing as opposed to aggressive and competitive men. Critics argue that this is inverted sexism, and if patriarchy cannot be defended neither can matriarchy.

Intersectionality

bell hooks criticised second-wave feminists for conceptualising feminism from a white middle-class perspective and college-educated background, arguing that both liberal and radical feminists largely excluded the concerns of minority groups such as 'women of colour'. hooks demonstrated the hitherto unexamined complexity of patriarchy facing black women. Black American men wanted racial equality but also to assume their 'proper place as patriarch in the home'. The black liberation movement was therefore sexist. Likewise hooks argued:

'individual black feminists despaired as we witnessed the appropriation of feminist ideology by elitist, racist, white women … organised and controlled by white women… black feminists found that sisterhood for most white women did not mean surrendering allegiance to race, class and sexual preference.'

hooks' ideas inspired Kimberlé Crenshaw's theory of **intersectionality** that challenged the notion that gender is the most important factor in understanding women's lives. Crenshaw cites the *DeGraffenreid* v *General Motors* case as a figurative example. In 1976 five black employees sued General Motors for wrongful dismissal based on discrimination. The district court viewed discrimination through the distinct lens of race and gender and dismissed the case because General Motors continued to employ black men and white women. It failed to recognise the overlapping identities that had resulted in black women being discriminated against.

Therefore, individuals can be oppressed on multiple overlapping areas such as their gender, class, race, sexuality, disability or transsexuality to name but a few. Multiple identities of women meant that the singular notion of 'sisterhood' gives way to a more communal concept of 'solidarity' according to hooks. This would allow women with different circumstances and a multiplicity of oppressions to form alliances and would reframe second-wave feminism, which argues that gender is everything.

Kimberlé Crenshaw is famous for conceptualising intersectionality

bell hooks (1952–)

hooks believed that society is full of complex relationships between different minorities. Her key work is *Ain't I a Woman: Black Women and Feminism* (1981).

hooks' main ideas

- **Women of colour** hooks broadened the feminist debate as she felt it was too focused on middle- and upper-class college-educated white women. She focused on 'women of colour' and all social classes.
- **Intersectionality** hooks' ideas greatly influenced the idea of intersectionality — a term coined by Kimberlé Crenshaw — which challenged the feminist assumption that gender was the most important factor in determining a woman's life experiences.

Stretch and challenge

The ideas of bell hooks and Kimberlé Crenshaw have helped stress the great diversity of women across cultures and the idea of intersectionality. Read some of their most famous quotes:

'Once you do away with the idea of people as fixed static entities, then you see that people can change and there is hope.'

bell hooks

'No other group in America has so had their identity socialized out of existence as have black women … when black people are talked about the focus tends to be on black men; and when women are talked about the focus tends to be on white women.'

bell hooks

'Sexism isn't a one size fits all phenomenon. It doesn't happen to black and white women in the same way.'

Kimberlé Crenshaw

'Cultural patterns of oppression are not only interrelated but are bound together and influenced by intersectional systems of society. Examples of this include race, gender, class, ability and ethnicity.'

Kimberlé Crenshaw

'Some of the worst racist tragedies in history have been perfectly legal.'

Kimberlé Crenshaw

With reference to these quotes, explain how the idea of intersectionality has expanded the feminist debate.

Different types of feminism

Key terms

Reformist Believing that society can be reformed. In a feminist context this means that negative consequences of oppression can, by legislation, gradually alter until equality is achieved.

Equality of opportunity Everyone, regardless of their gender, should have the same life chances within society.

Political equality Women should have the same rights as men to vote and to hold political office.

Gender equality Men and women should be treated the same within society. It refers to full cultural equality, which outlaws the idea that men are superior to women.

Legal equality Everyone should be treated the same in the eyes of the law. For feminists this means women should have exactly the same lawful rights as men.

Liberal feminism

Liberal feminism is **reformist** and argues that, via democratic pressure, gender stereotypes can be eliminated. Unlike radical feminists and socialist feminists, liberal feminists do not believe that there needs to be a revolutionary change in the way state, society and economy is organised. Liberal feminists focus on the public sphere (society) rather than on the private sphere (family).

Liberal feminists are influenced by the liberal values of individualism, foundational equality and **equality of opportunity** (see Chapter 9). First-wave feminists like Mary Wollstonecraft, in *A Vindication of the Rights of Women*, argued for **political equality** and that women should have the vote. The assumption was that political emancipation would lead to **gender equality** and **legal equality**, particularly in relation to the economic sphere of property ownership.

Betty Friedan's ground breaking book *The Feminist Mystique* (1963) kick-started second-wave feminism and was based on questionnaires from women with whom Friedan had graduated from college 15 years previously. The opening paragraph of the chapter 'The Problem that Has No Name' epitomised the dilemma that many women, living domestic lives as wives and mothers, felt: 'The problem lay buried, unspoken, for many years in the minds of American women. It was a strange stirring, a sense of dissatisfaction …' The question each woman was grappling with was simple, she suggested — 'Is this all?'

Like De Beauvoir, Friedan emphasised the concept of otherness and that women should be free to choose the roles they took, be it the working world dominated by men, traditional domestic roles or a combination of the two. Liberal feminists campaigned for:

- an end to discrimination and inequality in the workplace and a belief in gender equality
- an end to outdated cultural attitudes via education and an opposition to sexist language
- changes in the law to facilitate legal equality in all public spheres of society

Table 14.3 lists some liberal feminist-inspired changes in the UK. Liberal feminism was later criticised by radical feminists for its reluctance to analyse the private sphere of family life and by third-wave/postmodern feminists for its white, female, middle-class definition of feminism.

Socialist feminism

Socialist feminists argue that economics leads to gender inequality and that capitalism causes patriarchy. However, socialist feminism cannot be described as coherent as there are different branches, revolutionary and reform, and each has differing solutions and disagreements.

Reformist socialist feminism

Charlotte Perkins Gilman was an early advocate of socialist feminism, viewing collectivism and cooperation as female qualities. Gilman believed that capitalism's exploitative qualities reinforced patriarchy and that socialism would gradually succeed, allowing women and men to coexist in egalitarian society and economy. Gilman thought herself a humanist rather than a feminist, wishing parity between the sexes.

Table 14.3 Changes inspired by liberal feminism in the UK

Example of change	Details
The Married Women's Property Act 1870	Allowed women to be the legal owner of money and property. Prior to this act, all of a women's assets became her husband's upon marriage
First sitting MP, 1919	Nancy Astor became the first woman to sit in the House of Commons
Representation of the People (Equal Franchise) Act 1928	All women over 21 given the vote regardless of property ownership
Equal Pay Act 1970	Made it illegal to pay women lower rates for the same work
The Sex Discrimination Act 1975	Made it illegal to discriminate against women in work, education and training
First female prime minister, 1979	The election of a female prime minister, Margaret Thatcher, demonstrated gender equality
The Sex Discrimination (Amendment) Act 1986	Prevented discrimination against women in selection, promotion, vocational training and working conditions, and made it illegal to dismiss a woman on the basis that she had reached state pensionable age, where that age was different for men and women

Key thinker

Charlotte Perkins Gilman (1860–1935)

Gilman's 'The Yellow Wallpaper' (a short story) was influenced by the postnatal depression and unhappy marriage which helped shape her ideas. Gilman thought of herself as a humanist, but her ideas were influential to the radical and socialist feminism of the twentieth century and she anticipated 'the personal is the political' decades before it was formally conceptualised.

Gilman's main ideas

- **Sex and domestic politics** For Gilman, sex and the capitalist economy were interlinked. Women were reliant on their sexual assets to gratify their husbands, who in turn would support them financially. Gilman viewed marriage as comparable with prostitution: 'the transient trade we think evil. The bargain for life we think good'.
- **Societal pressures** Gender roles are socially constructed from a young age, and Gilman argued that children should play with gender-neutral toys. She wished to reverse this false consciousness so women would no longer see themselves as naturally frailer and weaker than men.
- **Proposed solutions** Gilman sought economic independence for women and advocated centralised nurseries and co-operative kitchens to give women freedom and autonomy.

Gilman anticipated intersectionality in arguing that gender and capitalism were interconnected forms of oppression:

- Only economic independence could give women freedom and equality with men. Motherhood should not prevent women from working outside of the home. Gilman also anticipated the personal is the political argument of radical feminism.
- She championed communal forms of living where child-rearing and housework would be shared and even professionalised, allowing women a wider role in society.

Gilman's ideas resonate with later feminists.

Revolutionary socialist feminism

Friedrich Engels was the first to argue that economics caused gender inequality and capitalism created patriarchy. Engels argued that capitalism altered pre-existing societal structures, which meant that women were needed as unpaid helpers to enable male workers to be employed in the workplace. He claimed that women were complicit both in reproducing the workforce and in socialising their children in the continuing cycle of capitalistic oppression. Women were also a **reserve army of labour**, to be cast off when they were no longer needed.

Rowbotham's book *Hidden from History* (1973) expands on Engel's theories:

- Working-class women found employment in factories where they were paid less than men, had no childcare provision and were worked 'like cattle' both at home and in the workplace.
- Rowbotham argued that men do not fully understand the nature of oppression of women: 'Men will often admit other women are oppressed but not you.'
- Rowbotham adapted Marxist historical materialism, arguing that women had always been oppressed and that their alienation from capitalism and patriarchy meant that there needed to be a 'revolution within a revolution' to destroy capitalism and patriarchy.

De Beauvoir argued that the consumptive materialism (the idea that society has become addicted to purchasing consumer goods) inherent within capitalism had weakened women's position within society.

Juliet Mitchell has argued that even the destruction of capitalism may not be enough to end patriarchy. She argues that there are four social functions that women must liberate themselves from and reframe:

1. Their role in the workforce and production
2. Their childbearing role
3. Their socialisation of children
4. Their societal position as sex objects

Mitchell therefore adds a cultural dynamic to complement the economics arguments of socialist feminism.

> ### Key term
>
> **Reserve army of labour**
> The idea that women constitute a spare workforce that can be called on as and when needed.

Key thinker

Sheila Rowbotham (1943–)

Rowbotham is an academic feminist who wrote the influential book *Woman's Consciousness, Man's World* (1973).

Rowbotham's main ideas

- **Capitalism** Rowbotham was influenced by Marx and Engels, which informs her socialist feminism. Capitalism worsened the oppression of women, forcing them to sell their labour to survive in the workplace and to cede their labour in the family home.
- **Family** Rowbotham stresses that the family performs a duel function: to subject and discipline women to the demands of capitalism and to offer a place of refuge for men from the alienation of capitalism.

Radical feminism

Liberal feminism began the second-wave of feminism and was quickly joined by radical feminism, the ideas of which rebutted liberal thinking. While liberal feminists' focus was on the public sphere, radical feminists argue that both public and private spheres must be addressed, as 'the personal is the political'. Radical feminists have all focused on different aspects of patriarchy and sexism, advocating different solutions. This has led Andrew Vincent to describe radical feminism as 'a jumble of incomprehensible views and intellectual influences'.

Kate Millett's *Sexual Politics* (1970) took a psychoanalytical approach to feminism. Millett was critical of romantic love and monogamous marriage (as aspects of patriarchy) and argued that children were socialised via the family unit and that these norms of behaviour were reinforced by religion, education, myths, art and literature. Millett's solution to ending this false consciousness was abolishing the nuclear family and replacing it with communal living and childrearing.

Radical feminism lacks cohesion; different feminists focused on different aspects of patriarchy and offered different solutions. The examples in Table 14.4 demonstrate this.

Table 14.4 Radical feminists' examples of, and solutions to, the problem of patriarchy

Examples of patriarchy	Solutions
Erin Pizzey's analysis of 'the personal is the political' focused on domestic violence in family life	Pizzey set up the first women's refuge in London in 1971, offering women and their children a refuge from domestic violence
Charlotte Bunch argued that heterosexual relationships were based on power and that lesbianism was a political choice	The nuclear family should be abolished and replaced by lesbian communities
Andrea Dworkin argued that pornography was symptomatic of men's perception of women as sex objects	
Germaine Greer argued that patriarchy had socialised women to view their sexual desires as unfeminine and to be embarrassed about their bodies. Women had been indoctrinated to believe that they must try and retain eternal youth rather than physically and emotionally embrace their age and experience	Greer argued for sexual liberation and the abandonment of traditional marriage and the male domination that this entails. She favoured communal living and childrearing Greer's views were similar to Millett's but from a more heterosexual perspective
Shulamith Firestone (adopting Marx and Engels) saw history as a dialectic struggle relating to biological difference between men and women. Patriarchy has always existed as women have been enslaved by men	Firestone's perfect society would eliminate gender distinctions and embrace androgyny (the physical characteristics of both sexes). She regarded childbirth as 'barbaric' and advocated artificial insemination, arguing that when technology advanced men might be implanted wombs and bear children. Firestone was influenced by Simone de Beauvoir and took her ideas to the next level

Erin Pizzey at her women's refuge in London, 1978

Post-feminism

Post-feminists writing in the late 1980s and early 1990s argued that most feminist goals have been achieved and that women should move on. Writers such as Camille Paglia criticised feminism for portraying women as 'victims' and argued that women needed to take responsibility for their own life and sexual conduct.

Post-feminism has been roundly criticised for examining feminism solely through a white, middle-class framework that ignores the complexity of female experience that postmodern feminism explores.

Postmodern feminism

Postmodern feminism (sometimes called fourth-wave feminism) rejects as simplistic the broad generalisations inherent within earlier feminist traditions. There are numerous other interacting factors as well as gender, as intersectionality demonstrates. Kira Cochrane argues that intersectionality 'seems to be emerging as the defining framework' of fourth-wave feminism. Patriarchy continues to adapt and find new ways to oppress women. Jennifer Baumgardner and Amy Richards argued in their *Manifesta* (2000) that successive generations will need to establish what feminism means to them. Below are just some of the themes of postmodern feminism.

Cyberpatriarchy

Kira Cochrane argues technology is a source of patriarchy and is intersectional:

- Diane Abbott received more Twitter abuse that any other MP in the 2017 general election campaign. Abbott commented on the intersectional nature of her abuse:

    'It's highly radicalised and it's also gendered because people talk about rape and they talk about my physical appearance in a way they wouldn't talk about a man. I'm abused as a female politician and as a black politician.'

- *The Great British Bake Off* winner Nadiya Hussain received intersectional discrimination with online abuse that had three overlapping forms of oppression: gender, race (Bangladeshi) and religion (Muslim).
- Natasha Walker argued that modern women are now faced with a hypersexualisation from the internet and social media. She stated that femininity has been associated with sexiness and that young girls face a highly sexualised culture that is a new form of patriarchy as it pressurises them to dress a certain way.
- Studies have shown that in the last decade girls between the ages of 12 and 18 have faced pressure and harassment from boys of the same age to send nude photos (sexting). There have even been examples of girls committing suicide after such pictures have been circulated against their will.
- In 2012 Feminista started a campaign to end cosmetic surgery advertising. According to the British Association of Aesthetic Plastic Surgeons, 90% of procedures are carried out on women.

Nadiya Hussain has been a victim of intersectional oppression

Genital mutilation

Nimko Ali set up the Daughters of Eve in 2012 to prevent genital mutilation. Genital mutilation is intersectional in at least four aspects: gender, racial, religious and historical.

Honour killings

Approximately 5,000 girls are killed by their families every year and, given the secrecy involved, the numbers may be far higher. An intersectional form of patriarchy mostly associated with Islam in India and Pakistan, it also occurs within Sikh, Hindu and Christian families according to Tom Ough who has published examples in the *Daily Telegraph*.

Transfeminism

Transfeminism is an excellent example of intersectional values as it demonstrates how complicated defining sex and gender is.

Rape and sexual assault

The One Billion Rising campaign is a mass organisation that attempts to end violence against women. The billion refers to the UN statistic that one in three women on the planet will be raped or beaten in her lifetime, which equates to one billion women. OBR's key theme is solidarity (an idea of bell hooks) as it recognises that different types of women face different threats.

- United Nations research illustrates the intersectional complexity of rape. Certain characteristics such as sexual orientation, disability status, ethnicity and country of origin can increase women's vulnerability to violence.
- A 2018 Revolt Sexual Assault report found that 70% of university respondents had experienced some sort of sexual assault, with only 10% reporting it to the police or the university. The Office of National Statistics estimated that 4% of women have experienced rape, compared to 8% of the RSA female correspondents.

Postmodern feminism in its fourth-wave incarnation is incredibly varied, ranging from academic studies to proactive and diverse groups of women defending themselves against and raising awareness of patriarchy. Table 14.5 lists examples of postmodern feminist successes in the UK.

Table 14.5 Examples of postmodern feminist successes in the UK

Example of change	Details
First National Black Conference held, 1984	An example of postmodern feminism and intersectionality
First Black Lesbian Conference held, 1984	An example of postmodern feminism and intersectionality
Prohibition of Female Circumcision Act 1985, and the Female Genital Mutilation Act 2003	The 2003 Act makes it is an offence for UK nationals or permanent UK residents to carry out female genital mutilation abroad, or to aid, abet, council or procure the carrying out of female genital mutilation, even in countries where the practice is legal
Election of first black female MP, 1987	Diane Abbott becomes the UK's first black female MP
Gender Recognition Act 2004	Allows individuals to change their sexual gender
Gender Recognition Amendment Consultation, 2017–18	If proposals go ahead, it will allow individuals to self-identify their sex

Debate

To what extent do feminists agree over the concept of patriarchy?

Areas of agreement

- Most feminists are equality feminists and use the term 'patriarchy' to define a society that is dominated by men and that seeks to oppress women.
- Gilman and de Beauvoir were among the first to identify gender stereotyping, and feminists such as Friedan and Millett explicitly defined patriarchy as a cultural and not a biological phenomenon.
- There is agreement among equality feminists that patriarchy is not a static concept.
- The majority of equality feminists agree that patriarchy must be opposed in the public sphere of society.

Areas of disagreement

- Liberal and radical feminism disagree on where to challenge patriarchy. Liberals prefer the public sphere of society, while radicals argue that patriarchy must be challenged in both public and private spheres.
- Liberal feminists believe state, society and economy can be reformed of patriarchal tendencies, while radical feminists argue there must be a revolutionary change (although there is no consensus on what this change should be).
- Post-feminists argued that most feminist goals have been achieved and that patriarchy has largely been defeated.
- Postmodern feminists argue that patriarchy is far more complicated than liberal, radical or socialist feminists have imagined because of intersectionality.

Summary: key themes and key thinkers

	Human nature	The state	Society	Economy
Charlotte Perkins Gilman	Women are equal to men and biological differences are largely irrelevant	Gilman expresses no explicit views on the role of the state	Women have historically been assigned inferior roles in society	Men dominate the economy because societal norms obligate women to a domestic role
Simone de Beauvoir	Gender differences are not natural but are the creation of men	The state reinforces a male-dominated culture which limits women's autonomy and freedom	Societal norms restrain both men and women from achieving self-realisation and true freedom of expression	Men dominate economic life which limits the life choices open to women
Kate Millett	Women are oppressed by men (patriarchy) and should free themselves by engaging in lesbian relationships	The state facilitates patriarchy	Society is patriarchal in both the public and the private spheres	Millett's ideas on the economy resemble socialism but are peripheral to her feminism
Sheila Rowbotham	Female consciousness is socially constructed by men	The state facilitates capitalism, which in turn oppresses women	Capitalist society reinforces the dominance of establishment males to the detriment of women (and the average male worker)	Women's main role in the economy is to provide a reserve army of labour
bell hooks	Women have multiple identities and therefore experience multiple forms of oppression	White men dominate the state at the expense of women	Society is a multifaceted arrangement between different minority groups. Women who are of lower class and of a racial minority are oppressed on several levels, e.g. black working-class women	Women face different levels or oppression. For example, while middle-class college-educated women face oppression but are more liberated than black working-class women

Practice questions

1 To what extent has the nature of feminism changed over time? *You must use appropriate thinkers you have studied to support your answer and consider any differing views in a balanced way.* (24)

2 To what extent does feminism address the needs of all women? *You must use appropriate thinkers you have studied to support your answer and consider any differing views in a balanced way.* (24)

3 To what extent do feminists agree over the role of the state? *You must use appropriate thinkers you have studied to support your answer and consider any differing views in a balanced way.* (24)

15 Multiculturalism

Multiculturalism is a set of political ideas that became popular in the 1960s. Increased migration from former colonies to both the UK and France after the Second World War, and the Quebec question in Canada, led to a debate on how the nation state should react to multiple cultures living in one society. Globalisation and the freedom of movement within the European Union facilitated a substantial increase in mass migration and a continuation of the multicultural debate. At its core, multiculturalism explores the relationships between majority and minority cultures and their attempts to coexist within single societies.

Core ideas and principles

Politics of recognition

Recognition relates to how cultural identities are categorised within society. Charles Taylor (b. 1931) was the first to recognise that 'nonrecognition or misrecognition can inflict harm'. Taylor used the example of the way that Africans have had a negative and demeaning image projected upon them by a dominating Caucasian society:

> '… since 1492, Europeans have projected an image of such people as somehow inferior, "uncivilized", and through the force of conquest have often been able to impose this image on the conquered.'

A bilingual sign in Quebec

Multiculturalists believe that the state should reinforce **formal equality** to remove the political, legal and social discrimination of cultural minorities by cultural majorities within society and the economy. Taylor's 'politics of recognition' requires acknowledgement of both equal dignity and equal recognition. Taylor argued that there is a universal right for all to have their identity recognised and that cultural majorities should express an 'openness and generosity of spirit' to minorities.

Equal dignity

Equal dignity requires parity between different races and cultures, so they are evenly respected. A recent example in the UK is the Muslim national holiday of Eid ul-Fitr being recognised and respected. Despite it not being a holiday that the majority culture celebrates, Muslims may take a day off work or school to celebrate a key part of their culture.

In focus

The civil rights movement in the USA during the 1960s and the Civil Rights Act 1964 are examples of equal dignity in action — guaranteed integration in education and the ending of public **segregation**. See Chapter 20 for more detail.

Equal recognition

Equal recognition is where the state recognises with laws a minority group's particular identity to enable an equal standing with the majority. Will Kymlicka (b. 1962) argued that this is important because without this recognition aspects of minority groups' ethnic heritage would be lost. Below are two examples of minority groups seeking recognition.

- Muslim women in Europe wish to wear the niqab and/or the burqa as this is their tradition. While this is recognised in the UK, it is banned in public places in France.
- In Canada, where English is the dominant language, Quebec has attempted to maintain the cultural integrity of its mainly French-speaking population as part of an English-speaking country. It has been successful in retaining its distinct heritage: French is the official language of government, business and education (for those with French heritage). Quebec is a good example of a culture that has achieved the politics of recognition.

Culture and identity

The politics of recognition inform a cultural identity and also an individual identity. Bhikhu Parekh (b. 1935) argued that human nature and identity are socially constructed, and that factors such as race, ethnicity, religion, class and gender are vitally important. Quantitative research (via the use of surveys) carried out by Tariq Modood (b. 1952) has statistically demonstrated high levels of ethnic self-identification within different ethnic **cultures**.

Key term

Culture Relates to the dominant values, beliefs, heritage and lifestyle of a particular community.

Key terms

Formal equality Where the state imposes legal equality for all individuals and groups in society. It is also described as 'equal rights'.

Segregation Where the diversity of different communities has led to separation rather than integration. Consequently, communities develop defensive attitudes and become increasingly geographically segregated. Segregation can be state driven as in South Africa in the twentieth century or the result of minority groups preferring not to integrate.

As Taylor states:

> 'It is impossible to understand ourselves and others … without understanding the communities in which we function.'

This is because:

- culture is a vital component in constructing individual identity; individuals are culturally embedded
- culture informs **identity politics**, where individual beliefs are collectively constructed within the community that they belong to — this is often described as **communitarianism**

Kymlicka and Tariq Modood have argued that communal identity is increased when individuals are confronted with differing communities to their own. Modood concluded: 'To be among those of a very different culture makes one aware of what one is *not*, and thereby sharpens our understanding of what one *is*.'

Parekh has also argued that the state must recognise the importance of identity politics when negotiating with minority cultures to understand the importance of specific ethnic and cultural belongings for informing their individual thinking. See Table 15.1 and below for examples of identity politics.

Table 15.1 Types of identity politics with examples

Identity politics	Examples
Religion	Islam; Judaism
Ethnicity	The Chinese; the Japanese
Negative historical experience	African Americans; Native Americans; Jews

In many cultures, identity politics has seen oppressed minorities reappropriate discrimination and use it to strengthen their collective identity. There are numerous examples of this:

- African Americans have turned the term 'black' into a positive statement, reappropriating the word to become a term of pride rather than derision. The 1968 Olympics saw the famous black power salute, while more recently American footballer Colin Kaepernick 'taking the knee' to the US national anthem has been a contemporary protest against 'a country that oppresses black people and people of colour'.
- The Standing Rock Sioux Tribe protested in 2017 against the North Dakota Pipeline being routed through reservation land.
- Muslim women took to the streets of Paris in 2011 to protest over the banning of the niqab and the burqa.

Colin Kaepernick (right) and his teammate take the knee

Although it can be liberating for minority groups to have their voices heard, critics have argued that focusing on one's specific cultural identity can lead to a narrow, inward-looking attitude, especially in the case of migrant groups so keen to preserve their past that they fail to engage with the culture of their new home.

Minority rights

Minority rights address the needs of specific groups within a multicultural society to be allowed preferential or specifically different treatment to facilitate their requirements as a culture. Kymlicka offered a liberal defence of minority rights influenced by the **value pluralism** of Isaiah Berlin (1909–97). Kymlicka advocated **group-differentiated rights** whereby some groups might have separate rights of their own, as long as the exercise of these rights does not harm others and does not interfere with the rights of other groups.

Different types of multiculturalism

Liberal multiculturalism

To understand liberal multiculturalism, we must explore three distinct ideas:

- The neutral state
- The principle of **tolerance**
- **Multicultural integration**

The neutral state

John Rawls (see Chapter 9) argued that the state must remain 'neutral' in its treatment of different cultures and must not promote one as being superior to another. However, Rawls had one condition, namely that when a culture practised its distinct views and freedoms it did not trespass on the views and freedoms of other cultures. Therefore, in the public sphere, individuals are expected to sign up to universalism, recognising that there are some values that are applicable to the whole society, while in the private sphere individuals are free to cultivate cultural diversity (Table 15.3).

This shallow diversity is associated with the likes of Kymlicka and Modood. Liberalism can therefore be seen as being difference-blind, where factors such as race, ethnicity, culture, gender and religion are immaterial as individuals are viewed as morally autonomous.

Table 15.3 The public and private spheres in a neutral state

The state has no right to interfere in the PRIVATE SPHERE (the individual's personal life)	The state may interfere in the PUBLIC SPHERE (the individual's public life)
This is the personal or private aspect of societal life. It involves an individual's engagement with their native language, custom, religion and culture	This is the communal aspect of social life such as the workplace and public institutions. All individuals, regardless of their culture, must respect the norms of the liberal public sphere, such as formal equality and anti-discriminatory laws

The principle of tolerance

All liberals accept the principle that tolerance is a fundamental virtue. In accordance with J.S. Mill's harm principle (see Chapter 9), liberal multiculturalists believe that all forms of activity, belief and lifestyle should be tolerated as long as they do no harm to others. Liberal multiculturalists refuse to acknowledge 'deep diversity' and individualist integration if they endanger individual autonomy and personal liberty. So whereas liberal multiculturalists could accept individualist integration that allowed someone to be exempt from Christian worship, they would not accept the likes of:

- female circumcision — illegal in the UK since 1985; and, since 2003, an offence for UK residents to have their children taken abroad to receive female genital mutilation (FGM)
- forced marriage — legislation in 2007 and 2014 has made forced marriage illegal in the UK

However, within liberalism, there is debate over what constitutes harm. Taylor argues that the state can be guilty of harming minority-group citizens by ignoring the importance of their cultural identity within society. Taylor's 'politics of recognition' argues that liberalism's focus on the individual does so at the detriment of group identity.

Liberal democracy

Liberal multiculturalists regard liberal democracy as the only system to defend the core values of liberty, tolerance and formal equality. Groups that are overtly illiberal or wish to replace liberal democracy are not tolerated. The acknowledgement of some aspects of sharia law in the UK demonstrates the 'politics of recognition' that Taylor advocated, while remaining within liberal parameters.

Sharia law

Sharia law is a set of wide-ranging principles that Muslims use to organise their daily lives within the Islamic tradition. It includes guidance on worship, marriage, economics and even hygiene, derived from the Koran (Islam's central religious text) and the rulings of Islamic scholars. Not unlike any other judicial system, the system is so complex that only specific legal experts are able to guide and judge.

Some aspects of sharia law upheld in Muslim-dominated countries create obvious tensions with liberals, for example the illegality of homosexuality and the punishments for blasphemy. Within the UK there has been some acceptance of sharia law, such as the sale of halal meat and financial products (Muslims are not allowed to profit from lending or receiving money) that complement Muslim traditions. Sharia councils are allowed to deal with business disputes and family disagreements, but crucially they cannot overrule the decisions of UK courts. The independent review into the application of sharia law in England and Wales, 2018, made quite clear that:

> 'Sharia councils have no legal status and no legal binding authority under civil law. Whilst sharia is a source of guidance for many Muslims, sharia councils have no legal jurisdiction in England and Wales.'

The same independent review, while noting the many examples of good practice of the sharia councils, also raised concern over the lack of women council members and the examples of women being treated unfavourably. One of the report's key recommendations was that the sharia councils should be brought under a traditional liberal framework so that they could be regulated as all public institutions in liberal democracies are.

16 Nationalism

Nationalism is a set of political ideas that focuses on the concept and advancement of the nation state.

- **Liberal nationalism** Liberal nationalism emerged in the eighteenth century as part of the Enlightenment. It sought to replace the monarchy with democratic political communities that were based on the nation state.
- **Conservative nationalism** Conservative nationalism emerged around the same time, as a number of thinkers saw the world naturally divided into nations based on a common language and culture.
- **Expansionist nationalism** Expansionist nationalism emerged in the nineteenth century. Some European countries viewed their nation as superior to others and they sought to colonise Africa and South America. In the twentieth century, Nazi Germany and fascist nation states sought to dominate Europe.
- **Anticolonial or postcolonial nationalism** When European powers dominated Africa and South America, indigenous populations rejected colonial rule and conceptualised anticolonial or postcolonial nationalism.

The burning of non-German books by Nazis, Berlin 1933

Core ideas and principles

Nations

All branches of nationalism stress the importance of nations, but what characteristics constitute a nation? Table 16.1 describes different traits that nations possess. Some nations will possess more of these traits than others.

Table 16.1 Characteristics of a nation

Nation trait	Definition
Language	A common language helps organically bind a nation and implies a long common history Examples: France, Germany and Italy • **Johann Gottfried von Herder** (1744–1803) argued that a nation was defined by a common language and that this allowed it to express a common culture
Culture/history	A common culture and shared history can create a collective identity and values The USA is a multinational people who share core traditions and values. The American flag is an important totem that the nation can unite around. Likewise, its Constitution and racial history inform American identity today. Despite diverse **ethnicity** the peoples of the USA have been able to create a national consciousness • **Jean-Jacques Rousseau** (1712–78) argued that only people who share a national identity can create a single consciousness robust enough to form a nation state • Herder argued that cultural nationalism means that every nation is different, with its own unique cultural character • **Giuseppe Mazzini** (1805–72) recognised the importance of a romantic idea of national spirit that is common in so many cultures • **Marcus Garvey** (1887–1940) pioneered 'black pride', which has helped enable multinational nations to come to terms with their colonial pasts and for black peoples to articulate their positive cultural contribution to the various nation states that they belong to • **Charles Maurras** (1868–1952) suggested that knowledge of a nation's culture and history can also lead to the belief that it is superior to others, such as Maurras' chauvinistic nationalism
Geography	Physical geography sets the borders for some nations, such as Great Britain and Japan. Some territories long associated with a people have a specific resonance, such as Russia whose inhabitants often describe it as the motherland
Ethnicity	Mono-ethnic nations (where the nation consists primarily of one ethnic group) such as China and Japan have an exclusive national identity which gives their culture and history a distinctness
Religion	The classic example of a nation that can exist even when the people lacked a nation state is the Jews, whose religion fed directly into a cultural history that sustained their national identity until the founding of Israel in 1948 Catholicism remains an important aspect of Spanish and Italian national identity, as does Islam in many nations of the Middle East

> **Key term**
>
> **Ethnicity** A term associated with racial identity. It stresses one's origin rather than one's specific race. It is also often used to refer to a people who are living among a people of a different origin.

Nation state

The state can be a nation or collection of territories that are organised in political community under one government. States that are made up of territories often subsume the autonomy and influence of pre-existing nations by force and coercion, declaring themselves empires.

All nation states have geographical boundaries that encompass their sovereign territory. In many countries these boundaries have shifted over time, often as a consequence of warfare. A look at a map of Europe before and after the First and Second World Wars, and again at the end of the Cold War, will show how the boundaries of states changed, how new nation states emerged and old ones ceased to exist.

Liberal nationalists argue that the world should be made up of democratic nation states that cooperate with each other as equals. **Chauvinistic nationalism** (associated with expansionist nationalism) rejects this idea and argues that some nations are superior to others; these ideas are associated with Maurras, as well as radical nationalists such as the Nazis and Fascists.

It should be remembered (it is often overlooked) that liberal nationalist nations will sometimes contradict their own liberal beliefs. The USA's Cold War foreign policy (its invasion and conduct in Vietnam in particular) and its invasion of Iraq (alongside the UK) in 2003, would be two good examples of liberal democracies not respecting the sovereignty of other nations (Vietnam) and bypassing the judgement of supranational bodies such as the United Nations (the invasion of Iraq).

> **Key term**
>
> **Chauvinistic nationalism**
> An emotionally charged form of nationalism that believes one nation is superior to other nations.

Self-determination

Self-determination is an important facet of liberal nationalism (see page 374), where nations have the right to govern themselves and be free of the internal oppression that can exist with monarchies and colonial empires. Rousseau argued that the nation state should be based on a 'general will', with society and the economy governed by the collective will of the peoples that make up the community. These republican ideas influenced the creation of France and the USA but were also adapted by Great Britain, which through reform in the nineteenth and early twentieth centuries became a fully enfranchised constitutional monarchy (see Chapter 5).

For Garvey, self-determination had a racial dimension. As an anticolonialist, he saw that European imperialism blocked self-determination and liberty in the continent of Africa. His Universal Negro Improvement Association called for black nationalism to unite all peoples of African origin.

> **Key thinker**
>
> ### Jean-Jacques Rousseau (1712–78)
>
> French revolutionary nationalists adopted Rousseau's rationalist republican ideas at the end of the eighteenth century. His key work is *The Social Contract* (1762).
>
> #### Rousseau's main ideas
>
> - Patriotism and civic pride are essential, in both the creation and the reinforcement of the nation state.
> - National identity must be the basis of the political community.
> - Only individuals who possess such a national identity would enjoy sufficient unity to create a single consciousness necessary for a nation state.
> - A national 'spirit' will unite people and form a basic democracy.

Self-determination is a contentious subject and has led to many conflicts between those wishing to achieve it and those wishing to deny it. An example of such a conflict would be Yugoslavia, which descended into violent civil war in the 1990s as different ethnic groups sought self-determination. At the conclusion of this civil war Yugoslavia ceased to exist and half a dozen separate nation states emerged from its ashes.

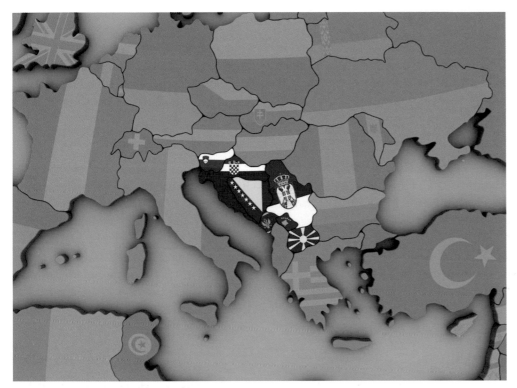

National flags of the various countries which emerged from Yugoslavia

Within the UK, Scottish nationalists wish to secede and become a fully autonomous nation state. As a liberal democracy, Scotland was granted a referendum in 2014, but the people of Scotland chose to remain with the UK (see Chapter 5). Brexit was in part about self-determination, as those who wished to leave the European Union felt that so much sovereignty had been permanently lent to the EU that the UK had lost its ability for self-determination (see Chapter 8).

Culturalism

Culturalism maintains that peoples have unique cultural identities that help define their national identity. Culturalism is grounded in deep emotional ties that are associated with the ideas of Herder and have been described as romantic and even mystical (in sharp contrast to the rationalistic ideas of Rousseau's civic nationalism, see page 375) and were originally concerned with the common culture of the German people (*Volksgeist*).

In the nineteenth century, culturalism was the preserve of those who identified as a people but lacked a nation state, such as the Germans and the Italians. In the twenty-first century, culturalism flourishes among people who feel that they have a distinctive culture that is threatened by the majority culture of the nation state (Table 16.2).

Table 16.2 Examples of minority cultures within a dominant majority culture

Minority culture	Dominant culture
Scots	English
Welsh	English
Catalans	Spain
Bretons	France
Lapps	Norway, Finland, Sweden, Russia

In each of these countries, the minority cultures wish for more cultural autonomy from the dominant culture, so Scottish and Catalan cultural nationalists wish for full independence, while Bretons wish to be recognised as a distinct nationality within France.

Cultural nationalism can be destructive when chauvinistic in nature.

● The British Empire believed its cultural values were superior to those of other cultures, and it projected its values on to indigenous peoples in terms of language, law, religion and economic practices.

● The likes of Garvey were anticolonial because of the derogatory treatment and lack of respect that Africans had been subjected to by European colonialists.

● Radical nationalists took chauvinism to the extreme, with the Nazis destroying cultures that they viewed as inferior, most particularly in their attempted genocide of European Jewry in the Holocaust. The Nazis' destruction of literature that they viewed incompatible with their culture continues to resonate as a warning from history.

Racialism

Racialism is now very much a minority viewpoint among nationalists. It argues that biological racial distinction is the most important factor of national identity. For racialists, race and culture are strongly tied together and it is natural for the world to be divided into distinct races. Racialism can be a neutral idea in that its exponents do not necessarily perceive one race as being superior to another.

Racialism is probably most recognised when it is *not* neutral. In the USA there have been examples of racialism, which in this context is called nativism. Nativism suggests that those who colonised the territory first should receive preferential treatment, forming the political elite of society and dominating social and economic discourse. In the USA this has traditionally been Caucasian Anglo-Saxon Protestants from Europe and 'inferior groupings' such as Irish and Chinese immigrants.

At its most extreme, racialism descends into pure racism and the state openly oppresses the racial groups it detests.

● In the USA before the civil rights in the 1960s, African Americans, Native Americans and other non-white groupings were routinely discriminated against in society and the economy (see Chapter 20).

● In South Africa the white minority suppressed the population by a system called **apartheid**, denying them civil rights and compounding these indignities with state-sponsored violence and persecution. Key examples are the Sharpeville massacre (1960), when police killed 69 protestors, and the Soweto uprising (1976), when police killed up to 700 secondary students who were protesting peacefully.

Key term

Apartheid A policy of segregation and discrimination on the grounds of race.

- One of the most extreme examples was the Nazis, who systematically slaughtered racial groups they deemed inferior, such Jews, Slavs, Poles, Ukrainians and Romani people (Gypsies).

Internationalism

Internationalism denies the primacy of the nation state and seeks to break down the divisions that separate peoples of different nations. There are two main types of internationalism:

- liberal internationalism
- socialist internationalism

Liberal internationalism

Liberal internationalism perceives the liberal democratic state to be the ideal model and international cooperation to be the best method of protecting liberal values. Giuseppe Mazzini's long-term aspiration was liberal internationalism, where he envisaged a united and cooperating Europe — which Europhiles today would argue is what the EU represents.

The UN is the embodiment of liberal internationalism and is not above acting against illiberal countries which harm their own people and/or threaten the freedom of another state. Such actions can take the form of economic sanctions and/or military sanctions.

The United Nations Conference Centre for Africa in Addis Ababa, Ethiopia

Progressive nationalism
A form of nationalism that connects national autonomy and pride with improvements in the state of society and the economy.

Supranationalism
Sovereignty transcending national boundaries. Within the EU, nations will often pool their sovereignty and make decisions at the European level as well as at the traditional national level. Nation states cooperate collectively as part of the United Nations and NATO (North Atlantic Treaty Organization).

Liberal internationalism A view that there should be less emphasis on national boundaries and that international cooperation is crucial to social and economic progress.

This does not mean that liberal nations will always intervene on illiberal and tyrannical nations; often to do so is financially and/or militarily impractical. In such cases liberal nations prefer to use economic sanctions (to damage the economy of the illiberal state) — recent examples would be the USA and the UK imposing sanctions on Russia and North Korea, both nation states with poor human rights records.

Liberal nationalism's promotion of democracy and societal self-determination means that is sometimes called **progressive nationalism**.

Guaranteeing liberal values

If nation states are like individuals, then the international community is like a state of nature. In Hobbesian terms (an absence of authority to maintain order), liberals fear that this could lead to conflict as the strong try to dominate the weak.

Liberal nationalism seeks to guarantee liberal values in two main ways:

- **Supranational** organisations and treaties — such as the UN, the IMF/World Bank, NATO and the EU — promote **liberal internationalism**. In Hobbesian terms, this provides the vital authority and structure to maintain international order. The UN, for example, is the supranational body through which liberal democracies will often pressure illiberal and authoritarian states with resolutions to attempt to persuade them to change their behaviour.
- Free trade helps to facilitate interdependence among sovereign nation states. One of the key arguments for the creation of the EU was to create a symbiotic supranational organisation, in which nation states' economies, laws and political relationships were so entwined that war between member states would be unthinkable.

The United Nations building in New York

Mazzini was an early liberal internationalist and these ideas were more important to him than the establishment of the Italian nation state. Mazzini's ultimate goal was a loose federation of European nation states built on liberal principles. Patriotism must never be allowed to damage 'the brotherhood of peoples which is our one overriding goal'. For liberal nationalism, the liberal values of the state are more important than the nation state itself.

Conservative nationalism

Conservative thinkers and politicians in the early nineteenth century were alarmed by liberal nationalism, as self-determination challenged the autocratic status quo and the legitimacy of empire. Conservative nationalism is not a single movement but a collective term for several different forms of nationalism that splintered from this original conservative unease.

Traditional conservative nationalism

Conservatives such as Benjamin Disraeli (1804–81) and Otto von Bismarck (1815–98) saw that nationalism could be adapted for their own particular aims. Disraeli wanted to unite Britain under a common consciousness of 'one nation', while Bismarck wished to unify the German states as a nation. Conservatives drew upon the organic need that they believe human nature has for traditions, customs, culture, history and language to facilitate a national consciousness.

Johann Gottfried von Herder believed that the world was naturally divided into distinctive nations, the cultures of which developed via shared historical and cultural experiences as well as through a shared language. These ideas influenced conservative nationalism. Herder's use of the German word *Volk* (folk) articulated a shared communal national experience and Bismarck coopted these ideas somewhat when he spoke of a ***Volksgeist*** to unite the disparate German states into a unified country.

> ### Key term
>
> ***Volksgeist*** A German expression, associated with conservatism, which refers to the spirit of the nation, a force which unites people and gives them a strong sense of national identity.

> ### Key thinker
>
> #### Johann Gottfried von Herder (1744–1803)
>
> Herder was a conservative with a romantic attachment to German nationalism and a scepticism of rationalistic ideas. His key work is *Treatise on the Origin of Language* (1772).
>
> #### Von Herder's main ideas
>
> - The national language expresses the common culture of its people, and a nation can be defined by its culture. The common culture and spirit of a people is their *Volksgeist*.
> - The German people should be defined by their language and this could form the basis of a united German people in one state. (Remember that this was at a time when 'Germany' did not exist as a nation but was a collection of individual states.)

Conservative nationalism's main goal was to preserve the nation. The social reforms of Disraeli and Bismarck (when he became German Chancellor) were as much about maintaining national unity, loyalty and pride in one's country as they were an antidote to the class politics of revolutionary socialism.

Tradition and a rose-tinted nostalgia are important aspects of conservative nationalism, reinforcing this idea of the nation state. Some contemporary examples for the UK are:

- remembering the hardships that the country has faced, such as the annual remembrance of the war dead
- a continuing fascination with the Second World War, often described as 'our finest hour'
- celebrating the royal family both past and present (the popular TV series *The Crown* demonstrating such nostalgia)
- fondly recalling key moments of collective national joy, such as the football World Cup victory of 1966 or the Olympics of 2012

The England football team celebrating their 1966 World Cup win

Conservative nationalism can sometimes be described as **exclusive nationalism** as one must be a part of collective experiences to be part of the nation. However, conservative nationalism welcomes those who integrate into the values of the nation state.

Regressive nationalism

Regressive nationalism is a more reactionary and xenophobic variant of conservative nationalism. Its key advocate was Charles Maurras, a French nationalist whose nationalism harked back to the bygone age of French glory when the country had been the most powerful nation in the world. Maurras felt France had lost its way in abandoning monarchy and embracing democracy. He described his nationalism as **integral nationalism**, which was the opposite of liberal nationalism as it placed the collective nation before individual rights. With integral nationalism, the people are merely servants of the nation and owe the monarchy their clear obedience as subjects. Moreover, Maurras perceived the French as being a superior people. His ideas have been seen as similar to fascism, and such views are often described as chauvinistic nationalism.

Key thinker

Charles Maurras (1868–1952)

Charles Maurras was an ultra-conservative French nationalist whose ideas were imbued with racism and anti-semitism. His movement, Action Française, was intensely xenophobic. His key work was *For a French Awakening* (1943).

Maurras' main ideas

- He supported hereditary monarchy, which he saw as a symbol of national pride and power, while opposing democracy.
- He advocated a regressive nationalism, which yearned for a bygone age of French glory.
- He believed that the French were a superior people and as such his views were similar to fascism (and sometimes described as chauvinistic nationalism).
- Like Mazzini, he believed in a collective identity of a people and that this was more important than individual liberty.

Key terms

Exclusive nationalism
Citizenship of a nation and national identity require an individual to enjoy a common culture, language or race with the existing members of the nation.

Regressive nationalism
A form of nationalism that looks back to an age when a nation was successful and which hopes to recreate that situation.

Integral nationalism
Associated with extreme right-wing nationalism and the ideas of Charles Maurras, integral nationalism denies the identity of the individual in favour of the interest of the whole nation.

Nativists

Nativists believe that those who colonise a territory first should receive preferential treatment. They tend to be populists who oppose political establishments that are excessively liberal and they share many of the traits of regressive nationalists. In the USA in the nineteenth century, white Anglo-Saxon Protestants had a strong sense of superiority over racial and ethnic groups whom they regarded as inferior, such as Native Americans, Mexicans, African Americans and Irish, Chinese and Jewish immigrants. Nativists often favoured economic protectionism and they are seen as anti-free trade and sceptical of globalisation. Some of President Trump's policies since his election have been described as nativist, including:

- derogatory comments towards Islam and Mexicans
- building a wall between the USA and Mexico
- the introduction of economic tariffs on trade with China and the EU

Expansionist nationalism

Expansionist nationalism can be seen as a continuation of regressive nationalism. It has a variety of different aspects, two of which are covered below.

Imperialism

Imperialism possesses elements of chauvinistic nationalism but imperial powers are now largely confined to history. In the past, national progress was seen in terms of the creation of an overseas empire of **colonial** possessions. Britain, Spain, France, Austria–Hungary, the Netherlands, Japan and Germany were all prominent examples of imperial powers. In the 1880s the great European powers stepped up their colonisation of Africa so that, by 1914, 90% of the continent was under colonial rule.

> **Key term**
>
> **Imperialism/colonialism**
> A movement involving a nation developing an overseas empire and settling its people in these conquered countries: for example, the Roman Empire; the British Empire.

Radical nationalism

Regressive nationalism was a formative influence on radical nationalists such as German Nazism, Italian fascism and Japanese nationalism. In each case the ideas were racist and used mythology to help create a national identity, Hans Günther's work on the 'purity' of the Aryan race proved a huge influence on Nazism, for example. Radical nationalists such as the Nazis claimed to be progressive, propelling the German nation forward into a powerful dominant future. However, critics correctly argue that such nationalism is based on a distorted obsession with past glories and illiberal racism.

Radical nationalism, like regressive nationalism, looks back to the past, both German Nazism and Italian fascism having a nostalgia for a simpler, more rural time and traditional family values.

Radical nationalism is also highly militaristic and chauvinistic, and such nations desire military conquest to rekindle past glories and create a sense of national unity. The Nazis, for example, wished to build a Greater Germanic Reich of the German Nation that would engulf much of Europe. In such nations the individual is absorbed into the nation, which is an example of integral nationalism.

The Nazi racial stereotype of an Aryan family

A visual example of the integral nationalist phenomenon of the individual being absorbed into the nation — but with one worker able to retain his individuality

Anti-/postcolonialism

Anticolonialism and postcolonialism are forms of nationalism, both reactions to colonial occupation.

- Anticolonial nationalism emerges when the indigenous population opposes the illegitimate supremacy of the colonial power.
- Postcolonial nationalism is concerned with the political policies that develop once independence has been achieved.

Anticolonial nationalism

Running parallel to imperial domination is the growth of the occupied nation's own sense of patriotism and an emergence of pan-Africanism (political union of all indigenous inhabitants of Africa) and pan-Arabism (political union and creation of one Arab nation), which informed postcolonial nationalism. A number of the anticolonial leaders who emerged to oppose colonial rule after the Second World War opted for a combination of socialism and nationalism to create an economy that was independent of global capitalism (Table 16.3).

Table 16.3 Selected anticolonial leaders and their responses to colonialism

Leader	Country	Colonial power	Political response to colonialism
Kwaine Nkrumah (1909–72)	Ghana	Britain	Pan-Africanism and Marxism–Leninism
Frantz Fanon (1925–61)	Algeria	France	Marxism
Mahatma Gandhi (1869–1948)	India	Britain	Liberalism and socialism
Garmel Abdel Nasser (1918–70)	Egypt	Britain/France	Pan-Arabism
Ho Chi Minh (1890–1969)	Vietnam	France	Maoist-style Marxism
Lee Kuan Yew (1923–2015)	Singapore	Britain	Conservatism
Patrice Lumumba (1925–61)	Belgian Congo (now Democratic Republic of the Congo)	Belgium	Social democracy
Julius Nyerere (1922–99)	Tanzania	Britain	Community and kinship (*Ujamaa*) and African socialism
Robert Mugabe (1924–)	Zimbabwe	Britain	Moderate Marxism
Kenneth Kaunda (1924–)	Zambia	Britain	African socialism

Postcolonial nationalism

Postcolonial nationalism is not a coherent set of ideas, but there are some common features:

- Marxist/socialist economic policies
- authoritarian governments and leadership cults
- pan-Africanism

However, it is important to recognise that these features vary and are not applicable to all postcolonial states.

Marxist/socialist economic policies

Until postcolonial nationalism, Marxists had opposed nationalism (preferring socialist internationalism). Marx and Engels viewed nationalism as a bourgeois ideology which hindered the development of a socialist consciousness. However, many postcolonial nationalists chose fundamentalist socialism as they saw it as the best way to resist international economic oppression by colonial powers. Like other examples of revolutionary socialism in practice, none of the socialist societies resembled the utopia that Marx and Engels envisaged.

Features of postcolonial socialism are as follows:

- Postcolonialist leaders were attracted to Leninism (Lenin's revision of the ideas of Marx and Engels), which critiqued economic imperialism. What good was political independence if Western multinational companies were still plundering and exploiting the resources of their former colonies?
- Postcolonialists were attracted by the cooperative and communal aspects of socialism. Before colonialism, many African nation states had been riven with internal divisions as tribal loyalties (and ensuing warfare) had greater traction than national identity. Julius Nyerere, former leader of Tanzania, proposed a policy of *Ujamaa*, which attempted to foster a sense of value of national kinship and community.
- Postcolonial leaders variously called themselves Marxists, post-Marxists or African socialists, but they all attempted to create an economy that was independent of global capitalism. Nationalisation of industry and collectivisation of agriculture were common policies in a number of postcolonial states.

Marcus Garvey's ideas of black consciousness still resonate today

Authoritarian governments and leadership cults

Many postcolonial nations have authoritarian governments on the basis that there is a need for a strong central authority to help frame a national identity long suppressed due to colonialism. This has led to leadership cults, whereby the leader becomes a symbol of national unity: Idi Amin of Uganda, Kenneth Kaunda of Zambia and, perhaps most famously, Robert Mugabe of Zimbabwe are all examples of this. Liberal critics have argued that this has led to corruption, with leaders economically exploiting their countries for their own personal gain as well as persecuting any internal opposition.

Pan-Africanism

Marcus Garvey's ideas of black pride and pan-Africanism have influenced postcolonialism within Africa. Garvey was one of the first to articulate the idea of a 'black consciousness' based on both a common ancestry of peoples in Africa and a common experience of oppression via colonialism and slavery.

- **Black pride** Garvey believed in encouraging African people to be proud of their race and to see beauty in their own kind. 'The Black skin is not a badge of shame, but rather a glorious symbol of national greatness.'
- **Pan-Africanism** Garvey argued that Africans in every part of the world must put aside cultural and ethnic differences if they are to progress. This would facilitate re-establishing cultural links within African states but also, and more ambitiously, a united Africa that could compete on the global stage with the likes of the USA and Europe. Whether this would be as a single sovereign state or as a collaboration of African states is a point of conjecture.

Marcus Garvey (1887–1940)

Garvey was a Jamaican and staunchly anticolonialist. An excellent collection of his writings and thoughts can be found in *The Philosophy and Opinions of Marcus Garvey* (1986).

Garvey's main ideas

- He perceived Ethiopia as the birthplace of all black peoples, which gave them a common identity.
- He developed a concept of **black nationalism** to unite all peoples of African origin.
- He was anticolonial, viewing imperialism as the main obstacle to the success of black nationalism.
- His ideas were a major influence on the American black consciousness movement of the 1960s.

Key term

Black nationalism A complex set of conflicting ideas on the cultural, political and economic separation felt by African-Americans from white American society. It was developed by Marcus Garvey and its most coherent idea was that of black pride: a common ancestry, culture and identity shared by all black Africans.

Discuss

What are the key distinctions within nationalism?

Liberal nationalism

- Proposes liberal democracy in new nations.
- Freedom of the individual is synonymous with freedom of the nation.
- Liberal nationalists respect the sovereignty of other legitimate states.
- The liberal state is more important than the nation. Nationalism should serve the state.

Conservative nationalism

- Stresses the organic nature of the nation rather than individualism.
- Patriotism is a key characteristic for individuals within society.
- Conservative states can be either backward-looking, seeking to preserve national traditions, or expansionist and seeking to spread their national values to other peoples.
- The state exists to serve the interests of the organic nation.

Expansionist nationalism

- The nation and its historic destiny transcend individualism and democracy.
- Expansionists do not respect the sovereignty of other nation states.
- Expansionists often have a sense of racial or national superiority over other races and nations.
- Expansionist states are often highly militaristic, stressing ideas of historic destiny and mythical heroism.

Postcolonial nationalism

- Postcolonial states are more concerned with nation-building than democracy.
- Postcolonial nation states are often subject to dictatorship in the interests of nation-building and self-preservation.
- Postcolonial nationalists often synthesise nationalism with another political creed such as socialism or religious fundamentalism. Collective values assist in creating a national community.
- Postcolonial states are often socialist in order to combat economic imperialism from international capitalism.

Summary: key themes and key thinkers

	Human nature	The state	Society	The economy
Jean-Jacques Rousseau	Rational individuals desire their own freedom	The nation is the basis of any legitimate state and is the vehicle for self-determination	Society must be based on political self-determination	Rousseau did not make a special connection between nation and economy
Johann von Herder	A collective identity based on a cultural group with a common language and history	States are only legitimate if based on the collective identity of a people who share a common language and culture	Society is socially constructed by a people who share a national heritage	Herder did not make a special connection between nation and economy
Giuseppe Mazzini	People have a romantic perception of their origins and desire liberty	The state is the romantic expression of the unity of the people	Freedom and liberty must flourish within society	Economic freedom is a consequence of societal freedom
Charles Maurras	Human nature is defined by ethnic identity	Some nation states (and their peoples) are superior to others	Society is based on shared ethnicity and some societies are superior to others	The hierarchy of states and societies leads to the economic dominance of stronger nations over weaker nations
Marcus Garvey	One's race is an important part of individual and national identity	States have been constructed to reinforce white supremacy. Black people should unite to form a black state	A black society will be free of white suppression, allowing the black race to thrive	A black state would lead to a capitalism that benefits its people and combats the economic dominance of international capitalism, which has underpinned economic imperialism

Practice questions

1 To what extent can nationalism be described as a set of inclusive ideas? *You must use appropriate thinkers you have studied to support your answer and consider any differing views in a balanced way.* (24)

2 To what extent is nationalism a set of racist ideas? *You must use appropriate thinkers you have studied to support your answer and consider any differing views in a balanced way.* (24)

3 To what extent is nationalism a cultural movement? *You must use appropriate thinkers you have studied to support your answer and consider any differing views in a balanced way.* (24)

THEME 3

US GOVERNMENT AND POLITICS

17 US Constitution and federalism

Key terms

Constitution A collection of rules, principles and conventions which outlines the political system, location of sovereignty and relationship between the government and those being governed.

Federal government The national government of the USA, consisting of three branches — Congress, the presidency and the judiciary.

Federalism A system of government in which power and sovereignty are shared between the federal government and individual states.

The US **Constitution** has been the governing document for American politics for over 200 years. It contains just over 7,000 words, including the amendments, and yet it is the source of all political power in the USA today. It provides a clear structure for **federal government**, protects the rights and liberties of US citizens, and outlines **federalism**. Despite its age, it remains important today, being the basis for Supreme Court rulings and constraining the power of the branches of US government, with both President Trump and his detractors complaining about these limits.

To fully understand the US Constitution today and to engage in the debates on how effective it really is, we must look at how it was created and what the aims were of the Founding Fathers at Philadelphia in 1787.

The origins of the Constitution

Following the Declaration of Independence in 1776, the 13 US colonies under British rule became 13 states embroiled in war with the British. The states wrote the Articles of Confederation, which created a weak federal government and ensured the sovereignty of the states. However, in the years following the War of Independence the weakness in this document became apparent. Debates were already taking place about the need for a stronger central government and rebellions against the newly formed government catalysed these debates. At Philadelphia in 1787, 55 men from 12 states assembled to try and remedy the political problems evident in the Articles of Confederation.

The Founding Fathers — a commonly used term for those who helped to shape the newly formed nation of the USA. While technically those at the Philadelphia Convention were 'Framers', many of them also signed the Declaration of Independence and contributed heavily to the drafting of the Constitution

Figure 17.1 tracks the key events from the Boston Tea Party in 1773 to the Bill of Rights in 1791.

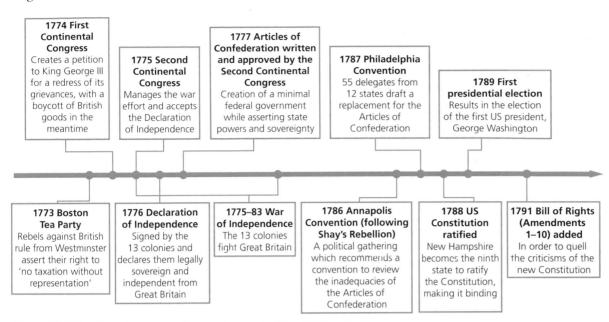

1774 First Continental Congress
Creates a petition to King George III for a redress of its grievances, with a boycott of British goods in the meantime

1775 Second Continental Congress
Manages the war effort and accepts the Declaration of Independence

1777 Articles of Confederation written and approved by the Second Continental Congress
Creation of a minimal federal government while asserting state powers and sovereignty

1787 Philadelphia Convention
55 delegates from 12 states draft a replacement for the Articles of Confederation

1789 First presidential election
Results in the election of the first US president, George Washington

1773 Boston Tea Party
Rebels against British rule from Westminster assert their right to 'no taxation without representation'

1776 Declaration of Independence
Signed by the 13 colonies and declares them legally sovereign and independent from Great Britain

1775–83 War of Independence
The 13 colonies fight Great Britain

1786 Annapolis Convention (following Shay's Rebellion)
A political gathering which recommends a convention to review the inadequacies of the Articles of Confederation

1788 US Constitution ratified
New Hampshire becomes the ninth state to ratify the Constitution, making it binding

1791 Bill of Rights (Amendments 1–10) added
In order to quell the criticisms of the new Constitution

Figure 17.1 Timeline of events in the development of the US Constitution

Synoptic link

The development of the US Constitution contrasts sharply with the evolutionary development of the UK constitution, which is far more in keeping with Burke's belief in gradual, organic change. For more on the development of the UK constitution see Component 2, UK Government (page 134) and on Burke see Component 1, Core Political Ideas (page 45).

The Philadelphia Constitutional Convention

In order to understand the principles of the US Constitution, we need to know what the Founding Fathers were trying to achieve at Philadelphia, and they by no means spoke with one voice. There were disagreements primarily about the size and scope of federal government, as well as debates over slavery (see Figure 17.2).

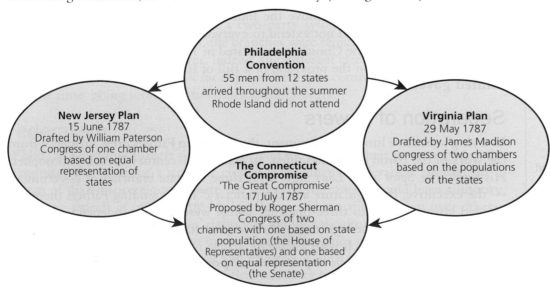

Philadelphia Convention
55 men from 12 states arrived throughout the summer Rhode Island did not attend

New Jersey Plan
15 June 1787
Drafted by William Paterson
Congress of one chamber based on equal representation of states

The Connecticut Compromise
'The Great Compromise'
17 July 1787
Proposed by Roger Sherman
Congress of two chambers with one based on state population (the House of Representatives) and one based on equal representation (the Senate)

Virginia Plan
29 May 1787
Drafted by James Madison
Congress of two chambers based on the populations of the states

Figure 17.2 Debates at the Philadelphia Convention

The nature of the US Constitution

Using these principles, at Philadelphia a new Constitution for the United States was created. Following the Declaration of Independence in 1776, Benjamin Franklin supposedly said, 'we must all hang together or most assuredly we will all hang separately'. The new Constitution intended to ensure that a stronger central government would allow just that, all of the states to 'hang together' and defend themselves from foreign threats. It is possible to see how the Founding Fathers applied these principles in the final document that they created.

Codification and entrenchment

Unlike the British constitution the new US Constitution was **codified**, meaning it was written all in one document. This means that the Constitution itself is the source of political power in the USA and any powers that federal or state governments hold are given to them by the Constitution. Over time, the meaning of the 7,000 words of the Constitution and its amendments has been altered and amended, but only through interpretation of the wording of the original document. As a codified constitution, the Constitution is **judiciable**, meaning that judges can interpret actions and laws against the Constitution to judge whether or not they are 'constitutional'.

> ### Key terms
>
> **Codification** A *single* written document containing all of the constitutional rules and principles.
>
> **Judiciable** A constitution which contains a higher form of law, and therefore allows other law to be judged against it and be deemed either 'constitutional' or 'unconstitutional'.

> ### The US Constitution outlined
>
> Article I: The Legislative Branch — outlines the structure, powers and elections of Congress
>
> Article II: The Executive Branch — outlines the structure, powers and elections of the president
>
> Article III: The Judicial Branch — outlines the structure and powers of the Supreme Court
>
> Article IV: The States — outlines the relationship between states and admittance of new states
>
> Article V: Amendments — outlines the amendment process to the US Constitution
>
> Article VI: The United States — outlines the supremacy of the Constitution
>
> Article VII: Ratification — outlines the conditions for the ratification of the US Constitution

The new constitution was also **entrenched**. This means it is difficult to amend as the document is protected by law. The US Constitution is protected by its own Article V, which outlines the amendment process. This process ensured that the Constitution could be changed in response to any emerging need, but would not be so malleable that it would change frequently. Today, there have been only 27 amendments, 10 of which were passed together in 1791, forming the Bill of Rights.

> ### Key term
>
> **Entrenched** A constitution which is protected from change through a legal process. For the US Constitution this is the two-stage amendment process, which requires supermajority approval from Congress and the states.

> ### Synoptic link
>
> Although Thomas Jefferson (1743–1826) did not oppose ratification of the US Constitution, he had considerable doubts about whether a codified constitution should be able to limit the freedom of action of future generations. The uncodified nature of the UK constitution has allowed for far greater evolution and flexibility as time has advanced than the US Constitution. This links to Component 2, UK Government (page 135).

Vagueness of the document

Given the short length of the Constitution, it is invariably vague throughout much of the document. There are debates as to why this is so, but given that the Founding Fathers had differing views on the role of states, slavery, the power of central government and the importance of a Bill of Rights, it is most likely that the more vague language allowed for compromise of the delegates and agreement of the states. This has meant that while the Constitution is codified, not every power is outlined within it.

Most commonly, the vague nature of the Constitution is seen through the difference between **enumerated powers** and **implied powers** (Table 17.2). Enumerated powers are quickly identified in the first three articles as those powers explicitly given to each branch of government. In Article I, Congress is explicitly given the power to 'lay and collect Taxes, Duties, Imports and Excises', which was an important development from the Articles of Confederation in which the central government had no power over tax and therefore relied on states for money. However, Congress is also given the power to 'make all Laws which shall be necessary and proper for carrying into Execution the foregoing Powers', meaning it had the right to make any law which allowed the members of Congress to carry out their enumerated powers. This vague clause, known as the **'necessary and proper clause'**, has been used to extend the powers of Congress over time.

Table 17.2 Comparison of enumerated and implied powers

Enumerated powers	Implied powers
• Powers that are 'enumerated' are simply those which are written down, in this case in the Constitution • They outline specifically the power a branch can exercise • The Constitution outlines in Article II that 'the President shall be Commander in Chief of the Army and Navy of the United States'. Obviously, with no air force at the time, this was not included	• These are powers which are interpreted from those laid out in the Constitution • They are gained from interpretations of the vague language of the Constitution • Following a memorandum from the Justice Department in 1947, the president is accepted as Commander in Chief of the United States Air Force, as well as of the Marines and the Coast Guard

In focus

McCulloch v *Maryland* (1819)

In 1818, the state of Maryland passed an Act which would impose a tax on banks that were not created by the Maryland government. This would have taxed the Second Bank of the United States, which Congress had created only 2 years before this, as the only bank in Maryland that was not set up by the state government. The Supreme Court was asked to judge whether Congress had the right to set up such a bank within its constitutional powers. The decision allowed for Congress' actions, effectively granting implied powers to Congress.

In the *McCulloch* v *Maryland* case, Chief Justice John Marshall wrote: '... let it be within the scope of the constitution ... [that] which are not prohibited, but consist with the letter and spirit of the constitution, are constitutional'. This supported the view that Congress, and other branches, have 'implied powers' from the Constitution in addition to those explicitly laid out.

Not all of the Constitution is as vague as the 'necessary and proper clause'. Indeed, the specificity of the 2nd Amendment (the right to bear arms) could be seen to be one of the reasons that achieving meaningful gun control has been difficult for so many presidents. It can be seen that Article I is more detailed and specific than Article II, which is not surprising given the Founding Fathers' fears of a strong executive — they gave Congress explicit and specific powers to try and ensure it could not be usurped by the president. Ironically, doing this has allowed for wider interpretation of presidential power over the last two centuries, given the more vague language in Article II, thereby expanding this branch considerably. Comparatively, Congress has found itself more restricted by the language of Article I, which is almost too specific to allow for interpretation. However, for the Constitution to have survived for over 200 years, the vagueness of the document is important in allowing it to adapt to changing circumstances and therefore remain relevant.

The constitutional framework of government

Under the Constitution, the three branches of government are given individual powers, in line with the Founding Fathers' aims to have separated powers. See Figure 17.3 for more detail.

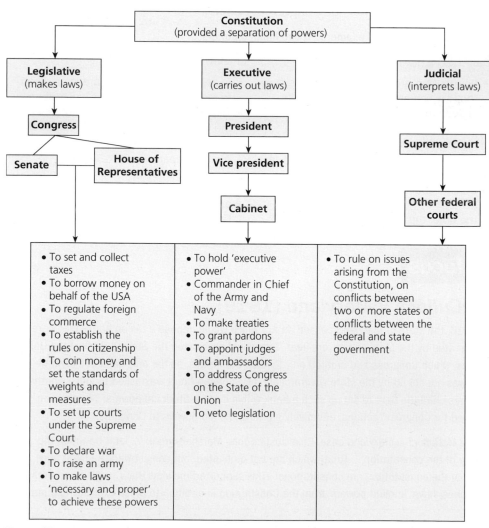

Figure 17.3 The structure and roles of the US federal government

Checks and balances in the Constitution

While the Founding Fathers aimed to follow Montesquieu's principle of 'separation of powers', Professor Richard Neustadt has argued that they did not manage this — 'rather, it created a government of separated institutions "sharing" powers.' This meant that while the three branches of government had separate personnel and, eventually, buildings, many of their powers required two branches to act together in order to exercise them. There are few truly 'separated' powers in the Constitution that just one branch of government can exercise alone. It is therefore difficult to divide the two principles of 'separation of powers' and 'checks and balances' within the Constitution (Table 17.3).

Table 17.3 Overview of checks and balances in the Constitution

Congress (legislative branch) Article I	Checks on the president: • Write legislation • Veto override • Power of the purse • Declare war • Impeachment of the president • Ratify treaties* • Ratify appointments*	Checks on the Supreme Court: • Impeachment of justices • Propose a constitutional amendment • Creation of lower courts • Ratify judicial appointments
President (executive branch) Article II	Checks on Congress: • Suggest legislation • Sign/veto legislation • Commander in Chief of the Armed Forces	Checks on the Supreme Court: • Power of the pardon • Nomination of judicial appointments
Supreme Court (judiciary) Article III	Checks on Congress: • Judicial review	Checks on the president: • Judicial review

*exercised by the Senate alone

Checks by Congress

Checks by Congress on the president

Congress has a number of constitutional powers which can limit the actions of the president, or prevent his action entirely.

- **Legislation** The key role of Congress is to produce legislation. Much of this legislation is suggested by the president at his State of the Union Address, which outlines his legislative agenda for the year. However, as the legislative branch, Congress can create, amend, delay and even reject legislation. In every State of the Union Address between 2010 and 2015, President Obama asked Congress to pass immigration reform, yet no legislation had been passed by the time he left office, much to his disappointment.
- **Veto override** Once Congress has passed a law, it goes to the president to sign, and become law, or to veto, which rejects the bill. Congress has the power to override this veto with a two-thirds vote in both houses, forcing a bill into law. The need for a **supermajority** makes achieving the veto override difficult, as it requires both parties to support it. Recent presidents usually have only a few defeats in this way, but of George W. Bush's 12 vetoes, four were overridden and attempts were made to override six more. President Obama's final veto of the Justice Against Sponsors of Terrorism Act suffered an overwhelming bipartisan defeat with only the Senate Majority Leader Harry Reid voting 'no' to the veto override.

> **Key term**
>
> **Supermajority** A required majority of more than half, usually in a vote. The US Constitution specifies supermajorities of two-thirds and three-quarters for a variety of processes.

- **Power of the purse** Congress has the right to raise taxes and spend the money raised for the national government, which is referred to as the 'power of the purse'. This should prevent the president from spending without the consent of the elected representatives. The 'appropriations clause' in Article I says: 'No Money shall be drawn from the Treasury, but in Consequence of Appropriations made by Law', so without a congressional law, money cannot be allocated for federal policies. Article I also states that **appropriations bills** — those bills that deal with tax and spending — should originate in the House of Representatives, originally the only elected house of Congress. The Senate can make amendments but cannot initiate appropriations bills. In January 2018, the US government shut down because it lacked the money to operate as a result of a dispute with President Trump over Obama's Deferred Action for Childhood Arrivals (DACA) immigration policy. While the dispute continued, Democrats in Congress held up appropriations bills, eventually leading to a government shutdown.

- **Declare war** While the president is the 'Commander in Chief' and can move troops, Congress is the only branch which can formally declare war on another nation. Congress has used this power 11 times. The last formal use followed the bombing of Pearl Harbor, after which the USA joined the Second World War, declaring war on six individual nations, the last of these six being Romania (Rumania) in 1942. Since then, Congress has been asked to authorise the use of troops, most commonly through AUMFs — the Authorisation for Use of Military Force. These ask Congress to give authorisation for the President to use his military, without formally declaring war. The AUMF that followed 9/11 authorised the use of military force against those responsible for the attack. This AUMF has been used by Bush, Obama and Trump to justify their actions in conflicts in 14 countries since 2001.

- **Impeachment** Congress can bring impeachment proceedings against a president or members of the executive branch for 'Conviction of, Treason, Bribery, or other high Crimes and Misdemeanors'. The House of Representatives is given the power to bring charges of impeachment against an individual. If this passes a simple majority vote, a formal trial is then held by the Senate. For a person to be found guilty, and therefore removed from office, a two-thirds majority vote is needed. Only two presidents have been through the whole of this process and both were found 'not guilty' — President Andrew Johnson (1868) and President Bill Clinton (1997). However, the House of Representatives has tried to bring impeachment proceedings against other presidents, most notably the Kucinich–Wexler Articles of Impeachment against President George W. Bush in 2008, which passed a vote in the House of Representatives, but languished in the Judiciary Committee until he left office.

- **Ratify treaties** (Senate only) The Senate approves treaties that have been negotiated by the president by a two-thirds vote (67 senators). The Strategic Arms Reduction Treaty (START) in 2010 passed the Senate vote by 71–26 senators. A treaty failing to get two-thirds of votes is not ratified, but the Senate can also choose not to vote on a treaty. The Arms Trade Treaty was sent to the Senate in December 2016, but with just weeks until President Trump took office, it never received a ratification vote.

- **Ratify appointments** (Senate only) Presidential appointments to the federal courts, federal government departments and ambassadors are all subject to Senate 'advise and consent'. Over 1,200 posts require Senate approval by a simple majority vote. The Senate has formally rejected nominees, such as the rejection of John Tower as the secretary of defense in 1989 following allegations of alcoholism and womanising. However, it can also shape appointments through its advice. Andrew Puzder was nominated as the secretary of labor in 2017, but withdrew following the Senate majority leader McConnell informing President Trump that he did not have the votes to ratify this appointment. Similarly, President Trump's education secretary, Betsy de Vos, only managed approval through the tie-breaking vote of Vice President Mike Pence after the Senate divided 50–50 on her ratification — such a tie-break had never been used before on the appointment of a cabinet secretary.

Checks by Congress on the Supreme Court

Congress also has constitutional powers which limit the power of the Supreme Court, or can at least shape the nature of the Court in order to try and influence its decisions.

- **Impeach justices** The process for impeaching justices is the same as the process for impeaching a president. This has happened only once for a Supreme Court justice, with Samuel Chase being found 'not guilty' of being partisan in his rulings in 1805. In other federal courts, two cases of impeachment have been brought in the twenty-first century. Samuel Kent resigned before a verdict could be reached in 2009, and Thomas Porteous was found 'guilty' of bribery and making false statements in 2010.

President Bill Clinton was found 'not guilty' of perjury (55–45) and obstruction of justice (50–50) in the Senate in 1997

- **Propose a constitutional amendment** In all Supreme Court rulings, the Court is required to judge whether an issue is constitutional or not. By changing the Constitution, a ruling of the Supreme Court can effectively be overturned, as it changes the document against which the Court has to make its judgement. This has happened only once when, in 1913, the 16th Amendment was adopted, allowing for federal income tax to be levied, after the Supreme Court had ruled to deny this in the case of *Pollock* v *Farmers' Loan & Trust Co.* (1895).
- **Creation of lower courts** Congress not only has the power to create lower courts, it also has the power to regulate the Supreme Court's role in hearing appeals from these lower courts. At its extreme, this is known as 'jurisdiction stripping' (the constitutional ability of Congress to regulate what cases the Supreme Court is allowed to hear). This has proven difficult and controversial, but remains a constitutional check attempted as recently as 2006 with the Military Commissions Act, which tried to remove from the Court the power to hear cases from Guantánamo detainees.

- **Ratify judicial appointments** (Senate only) Presidential nominations to the Supreme Court have a huge impact on the ideological make-up of the Court. A president will most likely choose a nominee with a similar ideology to his own — either conservative or liberal — and in doing so may change the ideology of the Court overall. These ratifications follow the same process as with any other presidential nominee. While this does not directly affect the power of the Supreme Court, by allowing or refusing justices on to the Court, the Senate can ensure justices are suitably qualified and, more recently, look to ensure or change the ideological balance of the Court. When Antonin Scalia died in 2016, among the reasons that the Senate did not ratify his proposed replacement, Merrick Garland, was their ideological difference — Scalia was a staunch conservative while Garland was a centrist. The ideological balance of the Court is crucial to the rulings it is likely to give.

Justice Neil Gorsuch was approved by a Senate vote of 54–45 in April 2017, with all but three Democrats voting against his nomination, and all Republicans voting in favour

Checks by the president

Checks by the president on Congress

In line with Madison's view that 'ambition must be made to counteract ambition', the president was given powers which would allow him to influence and prevent the action of Congress. This was a guard against popular democracy — a way of preventing the people electing representatives who acted only in self-interest rather than in the wider interest of the nation.

- **Suggest legislation** The US president is directly elected (notwithstanding the Electoral College), and he (or she) therefore campaigns on a platform of his own policies. With no direct legislative powers, however, the Constitution gives him the right to suggest legislation to Congress through the annual State of the Union Address. Trump asked Congress for more money for border security in 2018, in line with his promise to 'build a wall'.

- **Sign/veto legislation** The president can also choose to sign or veto legislation that is put to him from Congress, meaning it becomes law or it is returned to Congress to be amended, to be voted on again or to fail. Both President Bush and President Obama used the veto 12 times during their presidency. The threat of the veto alone can be enough to prevent Congress passing a bill to the president or to make Congress amend a bill before it passes rather than have it rejected entirely.

- **Commander in Chief of the Armed Forces** As commander in chief, the president decides on the stationing and movement of troops and the use of military weapons. When Obama sought approval from Congress for action in Syria, he clearly stated, 'I believe I have the authority to carry out this military action without specific congressional authorization', but he asked Congress nonetheless in the hopes of a stronger and more united decision.

> 'I've long believed that our power is rooted not just in our military might, but in our example as a government of the people, by the people, and for the people. And that's why I've made a second decision: I will seek authorization for the use of force from the American people's representatives in Congress.'

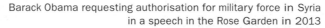

Barack Obama requesting authorisation for military force in Syria in a speech in the Rose Garden in 2013

President Obama making his speech about Syria in the Rose Garden of the White House

Checks by the president on the judiciary

The president is also given the power to check the judiciary, or at least to try to shape the ideological balance of the Supreme Court and therefore have an impact on the rulings it is likely to give.

- **Power of the pardon** The president has the constitutional right to 'grant reprieves and pardons', allowing him to excuse someone for a federal crime. This controversial power has few limits or checks upon it. On his last day in office in 2017, Obama granted 330 commutations to non-violent drug offenders, following his pardon earlier that week of Chelsea Manning, who had served 7 years for stealing state secrets.
- **Nomination of judicial appointments** In the same way that Congress can shape the Supreme Court through its ratification or rejection of nominees, the president can try and shape the Court through whom he chooses to nominate. Obama's nominated replacement for the conservative Justice Antonin Scalia was centrist Merrick Garland, whereas Trump's nominee was the more conservative Neil Gorsuch. Had Garland been appointed, the Court would have probably become more liberal, whereas with Gorsuch's appointment, the Court remained conservative.

Checks by the Supreme Court

The Supreme Court only has one power, which it uses to check both Congress and the president. This is the power of '**judicial review**' as suggested through Article III of the Constitution and fully established in *Marbury* v *Madison* (1803).

> **Key term**
>
> **Judicial review** The power of the Supreme Court to judge actions of the presidential branch or acts and actions of Congress against the Constitution. The Supreme Court can declare these acts or actions 'unconstitutional' and therefore make them 'null and void'.

- **Judicial review** The Supreme Court has the power to rule whether acts or actions of Congress or the presidency are constitutional. If it rules against Congress or the presidency, their acts or actions become null and void, meaning they no longer have any legal effect. In the case of *Boumediene* v *Bush* (2008), the Court effectively checked both the president and Congress at once, ruling the Military Commissions Act passed by Congress unconstitutional and allowing detainees held at Guantánamo Bay to challenge their detention in US courts.

The Constitution does not only lay down the framework of government in a structural sense. It also outlines the requirements to be a member of each of the branches of government.

- In order to be electable as the president, a candidate would have to be 35 years old, a natural-born US citizen and a resident of the USA for the past 14 years. Madison commented during the convention that the term 'resident' was vague, and the exact interpretation of this term is still unclear.
- For a person to be appointed to the Senate, they would have to be 30 years old, to have been a US citizen for at least 9 years and must be an inhabitant of the state that they are looking to represent in Congress. The 17th Amendment made the Senate an elected, not appointed, house but these requirements still stand for senators.
- Similarly, members of the House of Representatives must be 25 years old, have been a US citizen for 7 years and must too be an inhabitant of the state that they are looking to represent.

Government shutdowns

Since the Congressional Budget Act 1974, there have been 20 separate government shutdowns as a result of the government running out of money.

- **1976**   30 September to 11 October
- **1977**   30 September to 13 October, 31 October to 9 November, 30 November to 9 December
- **1978**   30 September to 18 October
- **1979**   30 September to 12 October
- **1981**   20 November to 23 November
- **1982**   30 September to 2 October, 17 December to 21 December
- **1983**   10 November to 14 November
- **1984**   30 September to 3 October, 3 October to 5 October
- **1986**   16 October to 18 October
- **1987**   18 December to 20 December
- **1990**   5 October to 9 October
- **1995–96** 13 November to 19 November, 5 December to 6 January
- **2013**   1 October to 17 October
- **2018**   20 January to 22 January, 9 February
- **2018–19** 22 December to 25 January

For each of these gaps, was the government at the time unified or divided? How could these shutdowns suggest that checks and balances are both effective and ineffective?

The amendment process

In order that the Constitution not become outdated, Article V outlined the process by which the Constitution could be amended (Figure 17.4). The two-stage process requires a supermajority at each vote to ensure that the Constitution is neither too flexible nor too rigid. Madison hoped that the process would 'guard equally against that extreme facility, which would render the Constitution too mutable; and against that extreme difficulty, which might perpetuate its discovered faults'. He meant that the ability to amend the Constitution was important in case of problems that emerged with it, including any abuse of political power by those who held it, but that it was important it not be changed too easily.

In order to amend the Constitution, the amendment must go through a proposal stage and a ratification stage. For each one, there are two options of how the amendment can be passed.

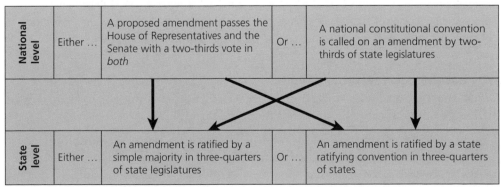

Figure 17.4 The amendment process

Of the four possible routes through which an amendment can be passed, most commonly it is passed by both houses of Congress and ratified by state legislatures. No amendment has so far been proposed by national constitutional convention and how one would even work is something that the Congressional Research Service has raised questions about. Only one amendment has ever been passed through a state constitutional convention. Out of over 11,000 proposed constitutional amendments, only 27 have passed through this process successfully, and a further six made it only through the first stage. Many amendments have been proposed over and over again, with no success. Between 1999 and 2018, a balanced budget amendment was proposed no less than 134 times, of which 18 have been proposed in the 115th Congress (2017–19).

The key amendments outlined

- **Amendments 1–10 (1791)** The Bill of Rights protecting free speech, the right to bear arms, the right to not self-incriminate, freedom from cruel and unusual punishment, and the rights of states
- **Amendments 13–15 (1865–70)** The Civil War Amendments ending slavery, guaranteeing equal protection and due process, and expanding voting rights regardless of race
- **Amendment 16 (1913)** Allows Congress to levy income tax
- **17th Amendment (1913)** Makes the Senate an elected, not appointed, house
- **18th Amendment (1919)** Prohibited the sale, transport and manufacture of alcohol
- **19th Amendment (1920)** Expands voting rights regardless of sex
- **21st Amendment (1933)** Repeals the 18th Amendment (passed by state constitutional convention)
- **22nd Amendment (1951)** Places a two-term limit on the president
- **24th Amendment (1964)** Disallows non-payment of tax as a reason to deny anyone the vote
- **25th Amendment (1967)** Allows the vice president to temporarily exercise presidential powers if the president is unable to
- **26th Amendment (1971)** Lowers the voting age to 18

Synoptic link

The US Bill of Rights was ratified by Congress in 1791 and in ten Amendments to the Constitution establishes the rights of the citizen and the limits of the federal government in the USA. The way in which the rights of the citizen are contained in one document is very different to the evolutionary way in which British civil liberties have developed. The entrenched US Bill of Rights has been the basis of calls for a UK bill of rights. UK rights are instead currently protected by a range of statute law such as the Human Rights Act. For more on the protection of rights in the UK, see page 136. This links to Component 2, UK Government.

Why are there so few amendments?

Given the clear process, and the number of amendments put forward, it can be difficult to understand why so few of them get through.

The necessity for supermajorities within the process is a big stumbling block. At both stages of an amendment, a supermajority of either two-thirds or three-quarters is needed. In the First Congress (1789–91), there were only 65 people in the House of Representatives and 26 in the Senate. This meant that just

44 House members and 18 senators needed to agree to a proposal to pass the first stage. Today, the House of Representatives has 435 members, needing 287 of them to vote together, and the Senate has 100 members, needing 67 of them to vote together. To achieve this level of consensus and compromise on an amendment is very difficult, especially in an age of two-party politics. Equally, the second stage originally needed just nine of the 13 states to agree; today that is 38 of 50 states, which is a much more challenging task. Alternatively, for both stages of an amendment, this means just a small number of House members, senators or states are able to prevent an amendment progressing.

In addition to the difficulty posed by the numbers alone, the growth of the USA is also a key factor in explaining the low number of amendments. Not only has the USA expanded geographically and numerically (from a population of 3.5 million in 1789 to over 320 million today), it has expanded culturally too and the states now vary immensely in their beliefs. Research from Colin Woodard breaks the USA down into 11 areas, which have distinct cultures, from the libertarian 'Far West' and its mistrust of big government to 'Yankeedom' and its acceptance of the 'common good' and as such being more accepting of some government intervention. Therefore, getting agreement on the need for a particular amendment is very difficult.

Diversity across the vast geography of America goes a long way to explaining the lack of amendments which have passed in the last two centuries

The advantages and disadvantages of the formal amendment process

The difficulty of passing constitutional amendments has created some problems for the US Constitution and its relevance today:

- **Difficulty in ensuring the Constitution remains up to date** There are changes in modern society which are not reflected in the Constitution due to the difficulty of adding them. Former Supreme Court Justice Stevens identified six areas of the Constitution he felt needed amending, including reforming campaign finance, the death penalty and gun control.
- **Outdated aspects of the Constitution still existing** In addition to the lack of up-to-date additions to the Constitution, there remain a good number of outdated aspects in the document itself and enforced today. In the centuries since the US Constitution was passed, the USA has changed dramatically. Its population is bigger, technology has changed and political and cultural ideas have moved on. While some of these changes have been reflected in constitutional amendments, such as changing the Senate from an appointed to an elected house, many outdated aspects remain. As part of the six amendments he felt needed making, former Supreme Court Justice Stevens felt that the 2nd Amendment should become applicable only to those serving in a militia and that capital punishment should be eliminated.

- **Ignorance of minority interests** The supermajorities needed to pass an amendment set a high threshold and should prevent the tyranny of a simple majority. However, this also results in it being difficult for a minority to bring about a change to the Constitution, meaning their rights can be ignored.

- **Power given to the Supreme Court** As the final arbiter of the US Constitution, the Supreme Court has a vast amount of power interpreting the meaning of the document. The Supreme Court has therefore been able to alter and change the Constitution considerably, yet it is unelected and unaccountable to the people. The Court's decisions can be overturned by a constitutional amendment but, given the extensive difficulty of the process, this has only happened once (the 16th Amendment). Its power is therefore largely absolute, although there are limited checks upon it (see above).

- **Tyranny of the minority** The necessity to gain supermajorities means that it is possible for just a minority of states or members of Congress to prevent an amendment from passing. The Equal Rights Amendment, which would have outlawed discrimination on the basis of sex, passed the House of Representatives in 1971 and the Senate in 1972. Despite twice extending the deadline for states to ratify the amendment, first to 1979 and then to 1982, only 37 states ever ratified the amendment, one short of the required 38. The 13 states that did not ratify the amendment accounted for only 24% of the US population at the time.

- **Despite the difficulty of the formal process, there have been mistakes** Whereas the other disadvantages deal with the difficulty of getting amendments through, it is worth noting that some amendments have made it through that perhaps should not have, bringing into question how robust the process actually is. Notably, the 18th Amendment was passed in 1920, prohibiting the sale, manufacture and transport of alcohol in response to prohibition movements that had gathered popularity in the USA. Just 13 years later this was repealed, suggesting that the process had failed in this instance to prevent a short-lived but popular trend from becoming an amendment.

There are, however, a number of advantages to having a robust amendment process and so few amendments having successfully navigated their way through it:

- **Broad support** Given the need for supermajorities, any amendments that have passed must have broad support across the USA. In a country that is so vast and diverse, it is crucial that the Constitution should reflect the political and cultural beliefs of as many Americans as possible. It is clearly impossible for the Constitution to please everyone (even the 55 delegates at Philadelphia disagreed), but having broad support ensures that the Constitution remains as relevant as possible.

- **Prevents short-lived trends becoming amendments** The arduous and difficult nature of the amendment process also helps to prevent amendments in response to unique or developing circumstances which may not stand the test of time. This can be especially important in the wake of the increased party polarisation that has been evident in the USA and in Congress over the past decades. While prohibition was arguably an error, one in over 200 years suggests the process works quite well.

- **Protects the Constitution and its principles** The principles of the Constitution as embedded in it by the Founding Fathers are what make the American democracy what it is. The acceptance of separation of powers and **republican ideals** are key to the political system of America. The challenging amendment process means the political ideals as laid down by the Founding Fathers are protected.

> **Key term**
>
> **Republican ideals** A prevention of arbitrary rule, such as monarchy or a dictator.

Synoptic link

A belief in the consent of the rule of the governed was a key idea of John Locke in his *Two Treatises of Government,* as was the strong belief in a limited government. For more on Locke see Chapter 9. This links to Component 1, Core Political Ideas (see page 246).

- **Prevents tyranny of large states and single parties** The population of the USA is large but not evenly spread. As a key principle of the Constitution, federalism should ensure that the states remain an important part of the US political system, recognising each state individually rather than simply by its population (as seen in the Connecticut Compromise). If amendments were made on population alone, the large states could dominate, making the smaller ones irrelevant and easily ignored. With the ratification stage recognising states individually, however, each has a recognisable worth as part of the US democracy. Similarly, by requiring supermajorities at the proposal level, a single party is prevented from dominating the amendment process and forcing through amendments favoured only by their supporters, such as the balanced budget amendment.

- **Few changes** The total of 27 amendments to the US Constitution can be seen as an advantage of the difficult process. Not only does it mean that most of the day-to-day governance is left to Congress or, more likely, to the individual states to decide what is best for their citizens, it also means that the principles and rights of the Constitution are clear and relatively unchanging. US citizens are acutely aware of their rights, as is evidenced by the importance of the Supreme Court in the US political system. Comparatively, UK citizens, for example, have no singular document from which to identify their rights and the power of the UK Supreme Court remains subservient, at least in theory, to the government of the day.

- **It works** While the amendment process might be arduous, a simple advantage is that 27 amendments have made it through. It has allowed amendments to pass when needed but prevented unnecessary amendments from passing.

The opening day of the Arizona Balanced Budget Amendment Planning Convention in 2017, at the Arizona House of Representatives in Phoenix

Is the amendment process effective today?

Yes

- It ensures broad support is gained for amendments. Recent mass shootings in the USA mean the suggestion of repealing the 2nd Amendment may seem obvious. However, in a 2018 YouGov poll, only 1 in 5 Americans want the 2nd Amendment repealed. It may seem unusual to European values that this is the case, but ensuring a high threshold for amendments means that the Constitution reflects as closely as possible the will of the US people.

- It ensures that amendments are well thought-through. A balanced budget amendment has been proposed 134 times since 1999 to try and ensure the US government spends only what it earns in taxes. Of those, 38 occasions came between 2011 and 2014 when Republicans controlled the House of Representatives, a figure more than double the previous two Congresses under Democratic control, making it a seemingly party political issue.

- It protects the principles of the Constitution. President Trump has described the system of checks and balances as 'archaic ... It's a really bad thing for the country', following policy defeats such as his healthcare bill and travel ban in his first 100 days. The frustration that President Trump has shown towards these principles serves to demonstrate how well protected they are.

- It prevents tyranny of the majority. The most populous five states account for nearly 37% of the US population. Hillary Clinton won California by 4 million votes in 2016, helping to explain her victory in the popular vote. The amendment process ensures that such populous states cannot simply amend the Constitution to suit themselves.

No

- Necessary amendments have been prevented, including those on campaign finance reform. The first presidential election costing over a billion dollars was in 2008, and in 2012 the candidates each raised over $1 billion. These massive sums challenge the liberal ideal of 'one man, one vote' and underpin the necessity of such an amendment.

- Outdated aspects of the Constitution remain, due to the difficulty in passing amendments. In the last five US presidential elections, the Electoral College has twice returned a different winner to the popular vote. While the Founding Fathers included the Electoral College as a guard against popular democracy, in the twenty-first century this undermines the principles of liberal democracy. (Chapter 21 covers the Electoral College in more detail.)

- It allows for minorities to be ignored. The Defense of Marriage Act 1996 defined marriage federally as being between one man and one woman. While the Supreme Court eventually invalidated this Act through its rulings in *Windsor* v *United States* (2014) and *Obergefell* v *Hodges* (2015), the chances of an amendment recognising the rights of same-sex couples is very slim, given that just 4% of American adults identify as LGBT.

- A difficult amendment process allows for a very powerful Supreme Court which can seemingly make new laws. In 2018 alone the Court issued a controversial ruling in favour of a Colorado baker who refused to make a wedding cake for an LGBT couple; ruled that cellphone location records do fall under the 4th Amendment, therefore needing a warrant to be obtained; and upheld President Trump's order which barred travellers from five Muslim-majority countries from entering the USA.

The necessity of constitutional amendments

Former Supreme Court Justice Stevens wrote a book in which he suggested six amendments necessary to the US Constitution:

1. The 2nd Amendment should be limited in its application to those serving in a militia.
2. Congress and state governments can impose campaign finance limits.
3. Capital punishment should be abolished.
4. Congressional districts should be compact and continuous, rather than gerrymandered.
5. The anti-commandeering rule, which prevents federal government forcing states to comply with federal law, should be abolished.
6. Citizens of a state should be able to bring a case against their state government if that government breaks a federal law.

For each of these proposals, identify the problem that not having these amendments poses to US democracy. Does it suggest that the codified and entrenched Constitution is too difficult to change and therefore out of date, or simply effective at upholding constitutional principles?

The constitutional key features today

Having explored what the Founding Fathers included in the Constitution, it is possible then to see how they have embedded their key features within the document, although they do not refer to them by name in it (Table 17.4).

Table 17.4 Key features of the US Constitution

Key feature	Where can it be seen in the Constitution?	An example of it working today	An example of it failing today
Limited government	• The inclusion of separation of powers and checks and balances • 10th Amendment giving states powers • The Bill of Rights guaranteeing citizens' rights	In the case of *Texas* v *US* (2016), an executive order by President Obama regarding illegal immigrants was struck down by the Supreme Court. Congress has failed to pass an immigration reform bill, which demonstrates the president's inability to make law without Congress	Both Presidents Trump and Obama launched air strikes without congressional approval — Trump on Syria and Obama on Libya
Separation of powers	• Articles I, II and III outline the individual powers of each branch of government • The 'ineligibility clause' of Article I, meaning a person can only serve in one branch of government at a given time	President Obama, Vice President Biden and Hillary Clinton all had to leave their seats in the Senate to take up roles in the executive branch	Obama negotiated the Joint Comprehensive Plan of Action (the Iran nuclear deal) limiting Iran's nuclear capabilities in return for the lifting of sanctions. As this was not labelled a 'treaty' it did not require approval from the US Senate
Checks and balances	• Numerous powers within Articles I, II and III provide checks and balances	President Trump tried to introduce his own healthcare bill in 2017, but despite having a Republican majority in both houses of Congress it failed to pass	President Obama included the USA in the Iran Nuclear Deal (JCPOA) and the Paris Climate Accord without asking for Senate approval
Bipartisanship	• The requirement for supermajorities in the amendment process, impeachment process and the veto override process • A staggered election cycle which can allow branches to be dominated by different parties	The 'Gang of Eight' in the Senate was a bipartisan group of four Democrat and four Republican senators who worked to create the bipartisan bill Border Security, Economic Opportunity and Immigration Modernization Act, which passed the Senate	Despite the bipartisan immigration bill passing in the Senate, the Republican speaker of the House of Representatives refused to allow it to even be debated in the House
Federalism	• The 10th Amendment protects states' rights • The role of the Supreme Court as the arbiter between federal and state government • The need for state approval in the amendment process • Equal representation of the states in the Senate	Marijuana remains illegal at a federal level under the Controlled Substances Act 1970, yet in nine states recreational use has been legalised by state governments and in 13 more states it has been decriminalised	Supreme Court rulings are binding on states too and in the case of *Obergefell* v *Hodges*, gay marriage was effectively legalised in all US states, including 13 states in which it had been illegal before this ruling

Whether these constitutional principles are effective or not is often dependent on political circumstances, and therefore the extent of their effectiveness varies.

- Is federal government **divided** or **unified**? When the branches of federal government are controlled by different parties, the 'checks' between branches are often more commonly used. Since the 1960s, the likelihood of a divided government and partisanship have both increased, often leading to '**gridlock**'. In times of unified government, Congress and the president are more likely to work together, but this could equally be seen to undermine the principles of limited government, with few checks being effectively used.

- When is the next election? Congressional elections occur every 2 years, with the whole of the House of Representatives and one-third of the Senate being elected. This means that congressional representatives are always mindful of the views of their constituents and the popularity of the president. When an election is looming, they are more likely to act as their constituents wish rather than as the other branches of government would wish.

- What are the national circumstances? During times of crisis, Congress is far more likely to act with deference, allowing the president to exercise greater political control. This may be during an event like 9/11, a natural disaster like Hurricane Katrina in 2005 or during an economic crisis such as the 2007 recession. This can undermine a number of constitutional principles, with the president acting with fewer limits or checks. When the national circumstances are more stable, Congress is often more assertive.

Congress passed the USA PATRIOT Act just 45 days after 9/11, granting considerable powers to the US government and especially the president. This was a response to the national outcry following the attacks

The main characteristics of US federalism

As one of the key principles of the Founding Fathers, federalism is firmly embedded within the Constitution (see Table 17.4). The newly freed states had fought for their independence and sovereignty against the British and were not willing to instantly give it up to a new federal government. Therefore the Constitution divided sovereignty between the states and the federal government, giving each distinct powers which were protected by the Constitution itself.

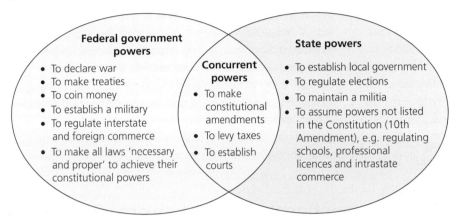

Figure 17.5 Federal and state powers laid out in the Constitution

The division of powers as laid out in the Constitution was meant both to ensure state sovereignty and also to allow for a stronger federal government to overcome the problems of the Articles of Confederation. The 10th Amendment is crucial in protecting states' power. While the federal government can only exercise the power which it has been explicitly given, the states are allowed to exercise power over anything that was listed for them plus over anything that had not been included in the Constitution. Of course, the USA has changed vastly since 1787, and this has changed the nature of the state–federal relationship (Figure 17.6).

Figure 17.6 Timeline of the development of federalism

The federal–state relationship and sanctuary cities

President Obama tried for much of his second term to achieve immigration reform in the USA. Following congressional failure to pass legislation, he resorted to using his power to pass executive orders (see Chapter 19), instructing government departments to enforce two key policies – Deferred Action for Childhood Arrivals (DACA) and Deferred Action for Parents of Americans (DAPA). These did not grant citizenship, or even a pathway to citizenship, for illegal immigrants, but did grant them a guarantee of exemption from deportation. Obama's executive orders were then reversed, however, by a US Supreme Court case in 2016 and by President Trump.

Nonetheless, a number of states or cities have defied the changes made by federal government and are seen as

'sanctuary cities' – areas which limit their cooperation with federal immigration enforcement agencies. In 2018, for example, California passed the state Senate Bill 54, prohibiting state and local law enforcement from using personnel or facilities to investigate or arrest people for federal immigration purposes. In response, President Trump threatened to withhold federal funds from sanctuary cities, but the federal courts ruled this unconstitutional in some cases. The city of Chicago sued President Trump due to his withholding of police funding over its 'sanctuary city' policies. This highlights both the tension between state and federal government, and also the reliance of federal government on states for their power.

Federalism and relationships in the twenty-first century

Through the presidencies of George W. Bush, Barack Obama and Donald Trump, the 'type' of federalism is somewhat more difficult to define. Each has given power to states but each has also expanded the reach and impact of federal government (Table 17.5).

Table 17.5 Federalism under George W. Bush, Obama and Trump

President	Development of state power	Development of federal power
George W. Bush 2001–09	• *Gonzales* v *Oregon* (2006) — effectively allowed state-sponsored euthanasia, in defiance of the US Attorney General Alberto Gonzales • Medicaid waiver given to Massachusetts to allow Governor Romney to introduce a universal health insurance program	• USA PATRIOT Act 2001 — expanded the rights of federal government to detain people and collect information about them • Medicare Prescription Drug Modernization Act 2003 — expansion of Medicare, including prescription drug benefits, cost $400 billion • Homeland Security — addition of an entirely new cabinet department • No Child Left Behind Act 2002 — allowed for uniform school testing
Barack Obama 2009–17	• Patient Protection and Affordable Care Act (PPACA, known as Obamacare) 2010 — at the states' urging, Obamacare included power over the provision of medical insurance run by the states themselves • *Texas* v *United States* (2016) — the Supreme Court struck down Obama's DAPA executive order due to the cost to states • The Cole memo — the Justice Department said it would not enforce federal restrictions on marijuana where states had legalised it except in certain circumstance, for example if firearms were involved	• PPACA (Obamacare) 2010 — expanded insurance and gave more individual rights • *Arizona* v *United States* (2012) — overturned Arizona's SB1070 law which increased state law enforcement power to enforce immigration laws • *Obergefell* v *Hodges* (2015) — the Supreme Court effectively legalised gay marriage nationally

President	Development of state power	Development of federal power
Donald Trump 2017–	• *Carpenter* v *United States* (2018) — the Supreme Court found that the federal government must obtain a warrant for a citizen's cellphone location records • Executive order minimising the economic burden of the PPACA — aimed at reversing Obamacare and giving states more control	• The Cole memo — new Attorney General Sessions rescinded the Cole memo, saying law enforcement would enforce national marijuana prohibitions • Executive order stripping federal grants from 'sanctuary cities' (later found unconstitutional)

Stretch and challenge

Marijuana and the federal government

Under President Obama, the Department of Justice issued a memo stating it would not pursue marijuana use in those states which had legalised it, other than in certain circumstances. These circumstances included where the sale or use of marijuana involved gang violence or guns. Under President Trump, the Department of Justice rescinded this memo.

> 'The Department's guidance … rests on its expectation that states and local governments that have enacted laws authorizing marijuana-related conduct will implement strong and effective regulatory and enforcement systems that will address the threat those state laws could pose to public safety, public health and other enforcement interests.'
>
> The Cole memo, 2013

> 'In the Controlled Substances Act, Congress has generally prohibited the cultivation, distribution, and possession of marijuana. It has established significant penalties for these crimes … These statutes reflect Congress's determination that marijuana is a dangerous drug and that marijuana activity is a serious crime … Given the Department's well-established principles, previous nationwide guidance specific to marijuana enforcement is unnecessary and is rescinded, effective immediately.'
>
> The Sessions memo, 2018

How far does the debate over marijuana legalisation highlight the tensions between state and federal laws? To what extent can federal government enforce its will over that of the states, and what challenges might it face in doing so?

Synoptic link

As tensions are evident within federalism, so they are within devolution in the UK. Both of these systems have experienced recent pushes from the states and devolved bodies for greater power at the same time that national governments have been expanding their own power. For more on devolution see Chapter 5. This links to Component 2, UK Government (see pages 148–53).

Despite the huge public fanfare that accompanied legislation such as No Child Left Behind or Obamacare, the federal government remains reliant on states to enforce any federal law. In 2016 alone, nine states had initiatives on their ballot papers regarding the legalisation in some form of marijuana. With marijuana 'legalised', recreationally in nine states and medically in 30, it will be difficult for President Trump's Attorney General to enforce the federal Controlled Substances Act 1970 without a considerable expense on federal law enforcement. With 50 state governments, and nearly 90,000 local governments, federal law may seem like it reduces state powers but the impact in reality can often be minimised through state interpretation and enforcement.

The extent of federalism today

Despite the importance that the Founding Fathers placed on federalism, its impact across the USA today is far from uniform. It is easy to focus only on federal government and the laws and policies it implements. For US citizens, however, the laws and policies put in by their states are often more important and impactful than those put in by federal government.

Ways in which states retain their sovereignty

- **Citizens' rights** In addition to those rights protected by the Constitution, the rights of citizens vary widely between states. States such as Alaska allow citizens to get a learner's permit for driving at age 14, while in Massachusetts a citizen must be 16 to gain a learner's permit. Equally, restrictions over issues such as abortion, euthanasia, gun control and marijuana vary hugely between the states in the USA.
- **Criminal punishment** The death penalty alone is a huge difference between the states. Currently, 30 states allow the death penalty. Between them there are five different methods of execution and each state does not use them all. Also, in Florida, Iowa and Kentucky, a convicted felon does not necessarily regain their right to vote upon release from prison.
- **Electoral regulation** Article I allows states to run their own elections. This has resulted in huge variations in electoral practice, most notably leading to the controversy over the 2000 presidential election. As of 2018, to vote in elections, states in the USA can use: a paper ballot, a paper ballot and electronic voting, a mail ballot or electronic voting alone. Furthermore, states that use electronic voting can do so with or without maintaining a paper trail, which has courted controversy after the Department of Homeland Security said that 21 states had their voting systems targeted by hackers in the 2016 election. State governments are also allowed to set the boundaries for the districts in their states, leading to court cases over '**gerrymandering**'.
- **Taxes** As well as being taxed federally, citizens are taxed by their state. These are far from uniform and citizens can find themselves paying sales tax, income tax, property tax and more. Income tax alone varies from 0% in seven states to over 13% in California.

Ways in which state sovereignty is challenged

- **Citizens' rights** Certain rights have been dictated by the federal government. The drinking age is set federally at 21, and the Supreme Court case of *Obergefell* v *Hodges* in 2015 effectively legalised same-sex marriage in every state. Equally, cases such as *Arizona* v *United States* even challenged the powers of Arizona when enforcing a federal law.
- **Criminal punishment** The Supreme Court has put numerous restrictions on the use of the death penalty while upholding the punishment more generally. Cases such as *Kennedy* v *Louisiana* (2008), *Panetti* v *Quarterman* (2007) and *Roper* v *Simmons* (2005) all limit the use of the death penalty. Indeed, as the final court of appeal, the Supreme Court can challenge the state courts in cases that it chooses to hear.

- **Electoral regulation** Numerous federal laws, and even constitutional amendments, have extended voting rights at a national level, lowering the voting age and extending voting rights regardless of sex and colour. Campaign finance laws and regulations are also set at a federal level.
- **Taxes** Not only do citizens have to pay federal income tax, states are also reliant on grants from the federal government when their own finances run low or in response to unexpected circumstances.

The federal government spent more than $100 billion on the recovery effort following Hurricane Katrina in 2005, money which would have amounted to around half of the Louisiana annual GDP

Debates around the US Constitution

The extent of democracy within the US Constitution

The Founding Fathers were far from advocates of democracy in its purest form. They were sceptical for both idealist reasons, such Madison's belief that it would allow the 'rights of the minor party [to] become insecure', and for selfish reasons. They were all men, largely privileged and educated, some were slave-owners and most were wealthy and therefore had a mistrust of popular democracy. This meant that the Constitution they produced in 1787 does not always reflect the twenty-first century understanding of democracy.

For each difference or similarity between the UK and the USA, it is important to consider which theory *best* explains why it exists. To explain some comparisons, just one theory may be appropriate. For others, more than one theory might explain a comparison and judging which theory is the best fitting is important. In both cases, there should be an explanation detailing why the theory chosen is the most appropriate.

Comparing the US and UK constitutions

On the face of it the UK constitution and the US Constitution appear so vastly different as not to be comparable. However, despite the differences in their creation and features, both fulfil the basic functions of a constitution — to outline the framework of government and the rights of the citizens (Table 17.8).

Table 17.8 Comparing the US and UK constitutions using comparative theories

Rational comparisons	• It is in the interests of the individuals within state and devolved governments to fight for their power over federal government to secure their positions
	• US citizens are used to having their rights protected through the Bill of Rights and therefore can more easily fight for them than their UK counterparts, whose rights have been determined by government
	• The separation of powers and checks and balances in the US Constitution allow its citizens greater individual influence (and a greater number of access points) than their UK counterparts
Cultural comparisons	• Cultural history explains the constitutions of both countries — the US Constitution codified as a result of a violent uprising and the UK constitution uncodified, the UK having remained relatively free of such events
	• The cultural expectation of the protection of rights is far higher in the USA than the UK
	• Amendments to the UK constitution are very much a result of cultural acceptance, whereas in the USA the cultural acceptance of necessary amendments must be demonstrated at the ballot box
	• The flexibility of both constitutions is partly a result of cultural acceptance. In the UK, there is no public pressure for codification, accepting the status quo. In the USA, the acceptance of Supreme Court rulings as informal amendments updates the Constitution
Structural comparisons	• Political processes are outlined in the constitutions of both countries, despite the difference in the nature of these constitutions
	• The nature and strength of the government in both countries, and the limitations placed upon them, are a direct consequence of the political system in each country
	• The vastly different amendment processes of the two countries are determined by the nature of their constitution
	• The location of sovereignty, with regard to both national and regional governments, is a direct result of political processes

The nature of the constitutions

In terms of features, the US and UK constitutions are vastly different (Table 17.9). Where the US Constitution is codified, the UK constitution is written across a vast range of documents including statute law, authoritative works and European treaties. This is largely a result of the creation of each constitution. In countries which have codified constitutions, the constitution tends to be a result of a civil, usually violent, uprising. For the USA this was the War of Independence in which Americans fought the British for their liberty; the resulting Constitution reflects the ideals for which they fought. Comparatively, the UK has never experienced such an uprising. Despite the civil war in the seventeenth century, the UK political system has been comparatively stable and therefore the constitution reflects a slower, more evolutionary change. For this reason, sovereignty in the USA is shared by the Constitution between the federal government and state governments, while Parliament in the UK holds legal sovereignty alone.

Table 17.9 The US Constitution vs the UK constitution

USA		UK
Written: Single document created in 1787 plus 27 subsequent amendments amounting to approximately 7,000 words. Supreme Court rulings supplement these written sources with 'interpretative amendments' Unwritten: Conventions are still commonplace within the US interpretation of the Constitution. While Article II refers to 'principal Officer[s] in each of the executive departments', it does not refer to the Cabinet, yet every president since 1789 has had a cabinet	**Sources**	Written: Numerous written sources make up the UK constitution. Most important is statute law, due to the sovereignty of Parliament. However, authoritative works and EU treaties also form part of the constitution, outlining specifically how government works Unwritten: Conventions are also an important part of the UK constitution, from how the prime minister is chosen to the expectation that the monarchy will give royal assent to laws passed by Parliament
The Founding Fathers firmly embedded the principles of limited government, separation of powers, checks and balances, bipartisanship and federalism within the Constitution, even though these are not named within the document	**Principles**	The UK operates on a principle on fused powers, with the executive being drawn from the legislature. Crucially, sovereignty resides in Parliament, which limits any truly effective checks and balances. While devolution has been developed in the past decades, the UK remains a unitary government
The Constitution is sovereign but shares power between the federal and state governments. Over time, the power of the federal government over the states appears to have grown.	**Sovereignty**	The UK Parliament is legally sovereign, and can therefore give out and take back political power. Political sovereignty may be said to reside in other places however, for example the devolved governments or the Human Rights Act
While the Constitution aimed to create three entirely separate branches of government, Neustadt suggested it was in fact 'separate institutions sharing power'	**Separation of powers**	The creation of the Supreme Court in 2005 did create a limited separation of powers in the UK, but the executive and legislative are still firmly fused, allowing executive dominance
Clear checks exist between all branches of the US federal government. This can allow for well-scrutinised policy but also for political gridlock	**Checks and balances**	The executive is drawn from the majority party in the House of Commons. This dominance allows for minimal chance of political gridlock, but also questionable effectiveness of scrutiny
The Bill of Rights and subsequent amendments to the Constitution firmly entrench the key rights of US citizens, with a powerful and independent Supreme Court able to rule to uphold these rights	**Protection of rights**	The Human Rights Act 1998 has gained moral authority and is judiciable, but the lack of sovereignty of the Supreme Court limits the extent to which rights protection can be enforced
The amendment process for the Constitution is arduous but has been used effectively. The interpretative amendments of the Supreme Court have also allowed the Constitution to be modernised as circumstances have changed	**Flexibility**	The lack of codification means that the UK constitution is very flexible and therefore can be modernised with ease, such as through a new statute law. This does, however, leave it open to abuse by a government with a large majority

Federalism vs devolution

The dispersal of power in the UK and USA looks quite similar — in the USA, states hold some power; in the UK, devolved governments in Scotland, Wales and Northern Ireland hold some power. However, the basis for these two systems is entirely different. When Ronald Reagan addressed Congress in 1981, he commented that 'all of us need to be reminded that the Federal Government did not create the States; the States created the Federal Government'. While it might not be that clear cut, certainly the Founding Fathers were both representatives of their states and worked to ensure states' interests in the creation of the US Constitution. From this a 'federal' system emerged, one in which sovereignty was shared between a central federal government and the local state governments, each having its own jurisdiction. At least originally, the states were therefore equal to the federal government. The shared sovereignty in the USA means that power — theoretically at least — flows from the states to the federal government. Comparatively in devolution in the UK, power flows out from the centre and is given to the regions, meaning it could also be taken back again by Parliament.

The UK has for centuries been 'unitary'. Unlike a 'federal' system, power is firmly centralised in one place, hence 'unitary'. This centre of power was originally the monarch but over the course of time, especially through the seventeenth century, Parliament gained power at the expense of the monarch. In more recent times, Parliament has shared the sovereignty that it has by creating devolved assemblies with jurisdiction over Scotland, Wales and Northern Ireland. However, Parliament retains the ability — at least in theory — to recall these shared powers back to Westminster. Compared to the US states, the devolved assemblies remain subservient to Parliament. This has been particularly evident through the problems that Northern Ireland experienced in 2017 and 2018, leading to a closure of the Stormont government for well over 2 years.

However, there are similarities between these two governmental systems. Despite the difference in creation, both allow for government to be more directly responsible and relevant to the citizens under its power. The freedom of the Scottish Parliament to abandon tuition fees is similar to the power of individual states to determine their education policies. Equally, both have found themselves being challenged by central government. The Scottish Parliament was not entitled to call a referendum on Scottish independence without assent from Westminster, while states have frequently found their policies challenged or overruled by either federal law or Supreme Court rulings.

Both systems are also somewhat flexible and evolutionary. While the system of federalism is codified within the Constitution, the changing nature of federalism over the past two centuries demonstrates the flexibility within this framework. States have fought for, and gained, more powers in landmark legislation such as Obamacare, while found themselves challenged through Supreme Court rulings on gay marriage and the death penalty. Equally, the UK system of devolution is flexible and continues to develop, with calls for more devolution in the form of a 'Northern powerhouse', or even Scottish independence, while at the same time removing power from the Northern Irish Assembly.

Summary

By the end of this chapter you should be able to answer the following questions:

→ What is the significance of the entrenched and codified nature of the US Constitution?
→ Is the amendment process effective at protecting the Constitution?
→ Where are the principles of the Constitution embodied within its text?
→ To what extent have checks and balances proven effective at limiting government?
→ Do the strengths of the Constitution outweigh its weaknesses today?
→ To what extent does the US Constitution obstruct government rather than empower it?
→ Does the US Constitution support or undermine democratic principles?
→ How effectively has the principle of federalism been protected?

Practice questions

1 Examine the similarities between federalism in the USA and devolution in the UK. (12)
2 Analyse the difficulties of amending the constitutions of the USA and the UK. *In your answer you must consider the relevance of at least one comparative theory.* (12)
3 Evaluate the extent to which checks and balances ensure effective government in the USA. *You must consider this view and the alternative to this view in a balanced way.* (30)

US Congress

The framework of the US Congress is laid out in Article I of the Constitution. The fact that the Founding Fathers put Congress as the first Article of the Constitution speaks to the importance they placed on it. They had fought for their freedom against King George III through the later part of the eighteenth century. Feeling that their 1774 petition of grievances had been ignored, the Founding Fathers described the king in the Declaration of Independence as 'a prince, whose character is thus marked by every act which may define a tyrant, is unfit to be ruler of a free people'.

It was this fear of **tyranny** and their experiences under British rule that perhaps explain why the Founding Fathers put Congress first in the Constitution, and so specifically outlined its powers so that they could not be removed. Congress was to be the most accountable branch to the voters, with a directly elected House of Representatives. It would protect the rights of the states within federal government and it would be able to directly challenge and limit the power of the newly formed executive.

Key term

Tyranny Oppressive or cruel rule. For the Founding Fathers, this was their experience of British rule.

The structure of Congress

Despite the anger towards British oppression, the newly formed US Congress would look remarkably similar to the UK Parliament. It would be **bicameral**, made up of the House of Representatives and the Senate. As a result of the Great Compromise, the membership of the House of Representatives would be directly elected, with each state appointing a number of representatives in line with its population.

By contrast, the Senate would be appointed by state legislatures, with each state getting two senators. The House should therefore represent **popular sovereignty**, while the Senate would ensure both a safeguard against popular sovereignty and also that every state had a voice in the new federal government regardless of its size. It also served as a protection against Congress gaining too much power alone.

The Senate became an elected chamber following the 17th Amendment in 1913. There would still be two senators from each state, each serving 6 years. This was in part over growing concerns regarding the power of big industrial monopolies to control state legislatures in the appointment of senators. The Standard Oil Company, founded by John D. Rockefeller in 1870, for example, is depicted in the *Puck* cartoon shown below as an octopus choking state legislatures and even reaching for influence in the White House.

The Standard Oil Company was founded by John D. Rockefeller in 1870. This cartoon, published in the satirical magazine *Puck* in 1904, depicts Standard Oil as an octopus choking state legislatures and reaching for influence in the White House. Concerns such as these helped to encourage the passing of the 17th Amendment

Unlike the UK Parliament, the two Houses of Congress are difficult to define as 'lower' and 'upper', especially since the addition of the 17th Amendment. Each house has unique powers such as the House's right to begin all appropriations bills and the Senate's right to ratify treaties and appointments. They also share powers, known as concurrent powers. The most important of these is their power to make legislation, which both houses exercise equally. Similarly, while the Founding Fathers make no mention of salary in the Constitution, for almost every year since 1787 House and Senate members have received equal salaries. The salary for members of the 115th Congress (2017–19) is $174,000 annually, except for the key leadership roles in both houses, which earn slightly more.

Figure 18.1 shows the growing size of Congress since 1789. Given the substantial population growth in the USA over the last 50 years, there are calls today to make the House of Representatives even larger. This would allow for members to represent smaller congressional districts and therefore provide better representation of their constituents.

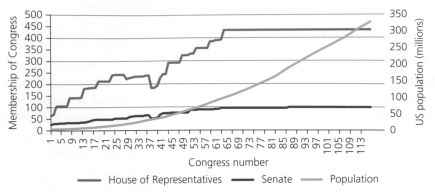

Figure 18.1 The size of Congress, 1st–115th (1789–2019)

Membership of Congress

Aside from the 17th Amendment, the constitutional structure of Congress has not really changed in the last two centuries. It has, of course, got much larger, reflecting the geographical and population growth of the USA. From the 1st Congress of just 26 senators and 65 members of the House of Representatives, Congress today is made up of 100 senators and 435 members of the House of Representatives (Table 18.1).

The Apportionment Act 1911 sets the number of members in the House of Representatives at 435. The population at the time was approximately 92 million, meaning an average of one House of Representative member for each 215,000 Americans. Today, with a population of 328 million, each House member represents an average of around 750,000 Americans.

Table 18.1 The House of Representatives and the Senate

House of Representatives		Senate
435 voting Congressmen and Congresswomen, plus six non-voting members including the member for Washington DC and those representing the American protectorates such as Guam	**Total membership**	**100 senators** with the vice president casting the deciding vote in the event of a tie
Reflective of the population of each state In the 115th Congress, seven states have only one member as their populations are around 1 million people or fewer. California has the most members, with 53 members for its population of nearly 40 million	**Number per state**	**2 senators** The longer-serving senator from a state is referred to as the 'senior senator', and the shorter-serving as the 'junior senator'
Congressional district, as drawn by the state government and redrawn every 10 years after the census	**Constituency**	Each senator represents **the whole state**
The whole House is up for election every **2 years**. There is no limit on the number of terms that can be served	**Term length**	Each senator serves **6 years**, with one-third of the house up for election every 2 years. Senators are known as Class I, II or III with each 'class' up for election at the same time. In 2018, all Class I senators were up for election. There is no limit on the number of terms that can be served
• Speaker of the House (elected by the whole House from the majority party) • Majority and minority leaders • Majority and minority whips	**Key leadership roles**	• Vice president (constitutionally, they preside over the Senate) • President pro tempore • Majority and minority leaders

The election cycle

A congressional election occurs every 2 years, compared to every 4 years for the president. Each newly elected Congress is known by a number; from the 1st Congress (1789–91) to the 115th Congress (2017–19). All federal government elections use the first-past-the-post (FPTP) electoral system, which goes some way to explaining the **two-party system** that exists in the USA today. In any congressional election, every seat in the House of Representatives is up for election, in addition to one-third of the seats in the Senate. When these elections take place in the same year as a presidential election, the elections do not have a special name. However, when they take place in the middle of a presidential term, the congressional elections are known as the **midterm elections**.

The significance of incumbency

Being the **incumbent** in an election can hold significant advantages over your political challengers. Perhaps most important is the name-recognition that currently holding office brings. Elections are an expensive business — in 2016, the average campaign cost of winning a Senate seat was $10.4 million, an increase of nearly 25% on 2014. Equally, the campaign cost of winning a seat in the House of Representatives was over $1 million. To achieve this level of funding is far simpler when the candidate is already a known quantity. In 2016, incumbents in the Senate raised an average of $12,708,000 compared to just $1,599,714 on average by the challengers. This is a vicious cycle — incumbents have name recognition and therefore can raise more, and in raising more incumbents can work to further enhance their name recognition.

Incumbents also have some congressional advantages. They are provided with a website by their house on which they can easily expound on their policy beliefs, demonstrate their own policy successes and influence, as well as have a clear and simple way in which constituents can get in contact with them. They also have 'franking privileges'. This means that the cost of mailings to their constituents is provided for by Congress. While members may not use this for electoral purposes, as they are able to contact their constituents and demonstrate their work in Congress, it helps their electoral chances. This is seen through the trend for franking costs to be far higher in election years — Congress spent $24.8 million on official mail in 2012 but only half of this the year before.

The boundaries of congressional districts also help to explain the high re-election rate of incumbents. The congressional districts for the House of Representatives are drawn within each state. The party controlling each state's legislature has the opportunity to redraw these constituency boundaries every 10 years, after each census. This has led to a practice known as **gerrymandering**. This is where a state's governing party draws the boundaries of each constituency to give it an electoral advantage. This produces relatively few swing seats, further advantaging the incumbent.

In focus

How does gerrymandering work?

In the example shown in Figure 18.2, there are 25 voters: 15 'orange' voters and ten 'green' voters. However, depending on how these voters are divided up, the number of constituencies each party would gain changes substantially. In the USA, these boundaries are decided by the state government, which is controlled by a party. It is therefore in its interest to 'gerrymander' the boundaries to give it the best political circumstances for success. This has led to very oddly shaped, and sometimes not even geographically contiguous, districts.

3 green constituencies
2 orange constituencies

2 green constituencies
3 orange constituencies

1 green constituency
4 orange constituencies

0 green constituencies
5 orange constituencies

Figure 18.2 How drawing the boundaries differently can change the outcome

Figure 18.3 shows the 4th congressional district of Illinois. It is this shape to create a Hispanic-majority district. In 2016, of the 374,000 eligible voters, 211,000 of them were Hispanic.

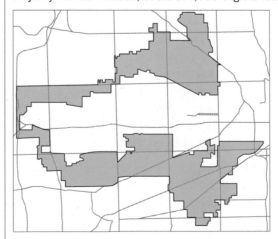

Figure 18.3 The 4th congressional district of Illinois

The result of this has been a high likelihood that a candidate running for re-election will retain their seat (Table 18.3).

Table 18.3 Incumbency rates

	House of Representatives incumbency rate (%)	Senate incumbency rate (%)
115th Congress	97	93
114th Congress	95	82
113th Congress	90	91
112th Congress	85	84
111th Congress	94	83
110th Congress	94	79

Senate elections

Every senator is known as a Class I, Class II or Class III senator. This refers to the year in which their seat will be up for election, with just one-third of the Senate up for election every 2 years. For the Founding Fathers, this arrangement would prevent individuals in the Senate gaining too much power and influence. Since the addition in 1913 of the 17th Amendment, senators are allowed to serve 6-year terms while always having to be mindful of the next election. Even though just one-third of the seats are up for election, it could change the majority in the Senate and thus drastically alter the political landscape (Table 18.4).

Table 18.4 Senate seats up for election, 2006–22

2006 Cl. I	2008 Cl. II	2010 Cl. III	2012 Cl. I	2014 Cl. II	2016 Cl. III	2018 Cl. I	2020 Cl. II	2022 Cl. III
33 seats	33 seats	34 seats	33 seats	33 seats	34 seats	33 seats	33 seats	34 seats

The impact of the election cycle

With seats in both houses up for election every 2 years, the chances of divided government in the USA are high. This means that the control of Congress and the presidency, or of the two houses of Congress, is split between two parties. This has become more common in recent history. Between 1901 and 1969, US federal government was 'divided' just 21% of the time, and in just two of the 34 Congresses in this period were the House of Representatives and the Senate controlled by different parties. From 1969 until today, however, US government has been 'divided' 72% of the time and in six of these Congresses the two houses were controlled by different parties. As a result of the last six elections, the US federal government has been divided five times, with only Obama's first Congress having a majority of Democrats in both houses (Table 18.5).

Table 18.5 The results of recent federal elections

Congress		House of Representatives		Senate			President
		Democrats elected	Republicans elected	Democrats elected	Independents (who tend to vote with ...)	Republicans elected	
110th	2007–09	233	202	49	2 (Democrat)	49	Bush
111th	2009–11	257	178	57	2 (Democrat)	41	Obama
112th	2011–13	193	242	51	2 (Democrat)	47	Obama
113th	2013–15	201	234	53	2 (Democrat)	45	Obama
114th	2015–17	188	247	44	2 (Democrat)	54	Obama
115th	2017–19	194	241	47	2 (Democrat)	51	Trump

The distribution of powers within Congress

Article I gives Congress a clear set of enumerated powers to be exercised concurrently by both houses. It also gives each house exclusive powers which can be exercised by that house alone. When comparing the two houses of Congress it is often assumed the Senate is more powerful, being subject to fewer elections, often representing more people and having ratification powers. The House of Representatives may have fewer exclusive powers, but it is potentially of far greater significance, holding the power of the purse and being able to bring impeachment charges which could remove the president from office. Ultimately, however, it is crucial to recognise that the most important powers of Congress are exercised concurrently.

In addition to these enumerated powers, Congress has assumed a number of implied powers over time. Many of these come from the necessary and proper clause of Article I, informally known as the 'elastic clause', and the **commerce clause**. The elastic clause allows Congress to make any laws which allow it to carry out its enumerated powers, while the commerce clause allows Congress to regulate foreign and interstate trade. Congress defended its power to set up a national bank in 1791 by using these implied powers. It argued that such a power was implied through Congress' power to levy and collect taxes. Founding Father Alexander Hamilton, in discussing the constitutionality of the Bank of the United States, with reference to the Constitution and Congress, commented that 'it is not denied that there are implied as well as express powers' — effectively that these were powers that allowed national government to exercise its enumerated powers.

Figure 18.4 shows the distribution of concurrent and exclusive powers in Congress. For more detail, see pages 427–31.

Alexander Hamilton features on the US $10 bill

Powers of the House of Representatives
- Power of the purse
- To bring charges of impeachment
- To choose the president if the Electoral College is deadlocked

Concurrent powers
- To create legislation
- To override the president's veto
- To propose constitutional amendments
- To declare war
- To confirm a new vice president
- Investigation

Powers of the Senate
- To ratify treaties
- To confirm appointments
- To try cases of impeachment
- To choose the vice president if the Electoral College is deadlocked

Figure 18.4 The concurrent and exclusive powers of the houses of Congress

Concurrent powers of Congress

Create legislation

The most important power of Congress is the ability to create, amend, delay and pass legislation. This is not an unlimited power, however — Congress only has this power over the areas of government laid out in the Constitution, with the states holding the power to legislate over other areas.

President Trump had to ask Congress, as the only branch that can create law, to pass legislation that would repeal and replace Obamacare. A bill was put forward by Republicans in Congress to achieve this. However, with all the Senate Democrats and nine Republicans voting against this bill, it failed to pass, much to the president's frustration. Even a vote on a partial repeal of Obamacare failed, with seven Republicans voting against it.

The original plan for Obamacare put forward by President Obama was heavily amended by Congress before passing into law. The president eventually had to issue an executive order, number 13535, to ensure that abortion would not be funded with federal money to overcome congressional disagreements on abortion, which were holding up the bill's passage.

Override the president's veto

Once a bill has passed through Congress, it requires the president's assent for it to become law. If a president vetoes a bill, Congress has the power to overturn this with a two-thirds vote in both houses. Both the veto and the veto override tend to be more commonly used when Congress is controlled by a different party to the presidency. All but one of George Bush's 12 vetoes came after he lost control of both houses of Congress, and there were override attempts on ten of these, four successfully. Equally, ten of Obama's 12 vetoes came once he had lost control of at least one house of Congress and just one of these was successfully overridden. However, the threat of the veto override can be a power in itself — in his first 6 years in office, Obama threatened 148 vetoes, yet used this power only twice.

In 2016, the congressional veto override of the 9/11 Victims Bill showed bipartisan cooperation between Republicans and Democrats. Ninety-seven senators voted to override the veto, with only Harry Reid, the Democratic minority leader, voting against. The House of Representatives voted 348–77 to override.

Stretch and challenge

The veto and immigration

In February 2018, President Trump threatened to veto any immigration bill that did not contain the 'four pillars' laid out by his administration – a path to citizenship, securing the border, an end to the green card lottery and an end to 'chain migration'.

> 'I am asking all senators, in both parties, to support the Grassley bill and to oppose any legislation that fails to fulfil these four pillars — that includes opposing any short-term "Band-Aid" approach. The overwhelming majority of American voters support a plan that fulfils the Framework's four pillars, which move us toward the safe, modern, and lawful immigration system our people deserve.'

What is the significance of such a threat to Congress and how might it affect its legislative function? How do the processes surrounding the veto override make such presidential threats significant?

Propose constitutional amendments

With a two-thirds vote in both houses, Congress can propose constitutional amendments. The last constitutional amendment to be added was in 1992, but almost as soon as the 115th Congress began in 2017, Representative Bob Goodlatte (R-VA) introduced yet another proposal for a balanced budget amendment.

Declare war

With the agreement of both houses, Congress has the power to formally declare war on another nation. This was last used to declare war on Romania (or 'Rumania' as it was in the declaration) in 1942, as part of the Second World War. In 1941, after the attack on Pearl Harbor, President Franklin D. Roosevelt addressed Congress, describing it as 'a date which will live in infamy'. He finished his speech:

> 'I, therefore, ask that Congress declare that since the unprovoked and dastardly attack by Japan on Sunday, December seventh, a state of war has existed between the United States and the Japanese Empire.'

President Roosevelt addresses Congress after Pearl Harbor is attacked

More commonly today, given the technological development of weapons in the twentieth century, Congress tries to use the powers it has over money and tax as a way to control a president's desire for military action.

Confirm a new vice president

If the office of the vice president becomes vacant during a presidential term, it must be filled. The 25th Amendment allows for a simple majority vote in both houses to confirm a new vice president. This power is most commonly used when the current vice president has to step up to the role of president, leaving their old post vacant. This may be necessary in a range of circumstances such as the assassination of the president, as in the case of John F. Kennedy in 1963, or in the event of a president resigning, such as Richard M. Nixon in 1974.

Investigation

Through an implied power of the Constitution, Congress can launch investigations into areas on which it has created legislation or may need to create legislation, and into federal programs. Congress has the power to **subpoena** witnesses in these investigations, meaning that they must attend hearings. Notable recent investigations have included reviewing 9/11 and the role of the US intelligence community and the response to Hurricane Katrina. In 2017, four different congressional committees investigated the alleged Russian interference in the 2016 presidential election, with the Republican chair, Devin Nunes (R-CA), of the House Intelligence Committee concluding that his committee 'did not determine that Trump or anyone associated with him assisted Russia's active measures campaign'.

While the reports from these investigations can highlight problems and make recommendations, as this is an implied power there is no requirement that the reports are acted on.

Key term

Subpoena The ability of Congress to order someone to attend a hearing a compel them to give evidence.

Exclusive powers of the House of Representatives

Power of the purse

The House of Representatives alone can begin appropriations bills. This gives the House considerable individual power, and power over the presidency. Each year, the president submits the annual budget for US government to the House Budget Committee to begin the approval process. In the 2018 budget, President Trump requested that the budget for the Environmental Protection Agency (EPA) be cut by one-third. Despite being of the same party as the president, House Republicans proposed cutting the EPA budget by just 6%.

It is important to remember, however, that the Senate can amend these bills and must approve them, which somewhat limits the extent of this power.

Bring charges of impeachment

The House of Representatives alone can bring charges of impeachment against the president, his officials, or justices of the federal courts. If the individual is found guilty, he or she is removed from office. This is not a criminal trial — if someone has broken the law, criminal or civil proceedings may follow, but impeachment simply removes the person from power. In 2008, Dennis Kucinich (D-OH) sponsored 35 different charges of impeachment against George W. Bush and a further three charges against Vice President Cheney. Most of these were related to the Iraq war and the resulting 'War on Terror', questioning the case for the war and accusing Bush of misleading the US public.

While this power has only been successfully used twice on the president in US history, it is a threat to any president who holds office, helping to restrain their actions.

Choose the president if the Electoral College is deadlocked

In order to win an election, the president needs to gain a simple majority in the Electoral College. Today, with 535 votes in the Electoral College, a candidate needs 270 to win. If no one manages this, the House of Representatives will choose who is to become the president. In this eventuality, each state is given a single vote to exercise, regardless of its size.

With the development of two-party politics in the USA, coupled with amendments refining the electoral process, this is a power that is now unlikely to be used. It was, however, used both in 1800 and 1824 to elect President Thomas Jefferson and President John Quincy Adams. In the election of 1800, the Electoral College returned a tie between Thomas Jefferson and Aaron Burr. After no less than 36 votes in the House of Representatives, Jefferson eventually secured an outright majority of nine votes and was declared the president.

Exclusive powers of the Senate

Ratify treaties

As a check on the president's power over foreign policy, the Senate scrutinises treaties that are made and can choose to approve or reject them by a two-thirds vote. In 2012, the Senate voted to reject the UN Convention on the Rights of Persons with Disabilities, with a number of Republicans expressing concern over the extra government regulation that it might entail. It is important to remember — as with ratification of appointments — that the Senate does not simply have to reject a treaty to be exercising this power. By scrutinising it and approving it, the Senate is also demonstrating its power.

Confirm appointments

The Senate can confirm nominees put forward by the president to the federal courts, the cabinet and ambassadorial posts, among others. This usually entails hearings by a relevant committee on the qualifications and suitability of a candidate, before a vote of the whole Senate.

President Trump had the opportunity early on in his first term to nominate two justices to the US Supreme Court. The hearings of the Senate Judiciary Committee held for his second nominee, Brett Kavanaugh, were subject to unprecedented protests objecting to his nomination, while he was questioned about his stance on abortion and the Mueller investigation into Russian election interference.

Because of Kavanaugh's stated views on abortion, senators recognised that his appointment to the Supreme Court could result in the 1973 case of *Roe* v *Wade*, which allows for abortion, being challenged. Nevertheless, Kavanaugh's nomination was confirmed

Try cases of impeachment

In a case of impeachment brought by the House of Representatives, a trial is held in the Senate and presided over by the chief justice of the Supreme Court. The House of Representatives acts as the prosecution, while the person against whom charges have been brought can mount a defence, both calling witnesses and putting forward arguments. Ultimately, a simple majority of senators is required to find the person 'guilty' or 'not guilty'. This is *not* a criminal trial, however, and the verdict simply allows an official to keep their position or to be removed from it.

The Constitution is remarkably vague about the reasons that an official can be impeached. Gerald Ford, before he became president and while he was leading a charge of impeachment for financial misconduct against Justice Douglas in 1970, commented that 'an impeachable offense is whatever a majority of the House of Representatives considers it to be at a given moment in history'.

Choose the vice president if the Electoral College is deadlocked

While the House of Representatives can choose the president in the case of Electoral College deadlock, the Senate chooses the vice president. While this seems like a lesser power than that of the House, the vice president does act as the president of the Senate, so it is logical that the Senate would select him in these circumstances. This has only ever happened twice, in 1800 and 1824.

> **Synoptic link**
>
> The exclusive powers of the Senate are far greater than those of the House of Lords as senators are elected and therefore accountable. However, the Senate has had these powers since 1787, at which point it was not an elected chamber. This links to Component 2, UK Government (pages 176–77).

The functions of Congress

Congress fulfils three main functions for federal government — legislative, representative and providing oversight of the other branches of government.

Legislation

The legislative process

The process of a bill becoming a law in Congress is lengthy and time-consuming (Figure 18.5). Bills can begin in either house of Congress, except for appropriations bills which must begin in the House of Representatives. They can pass through Congress sequentially (one house after the other) or concurrently (both houses at the same time with differences reconciled at the end).

The length of the process, coupled with a short electoral cycle of just 2 years, helps to explain why so few bills get passed by each Congress. As can be seen in Table 18.6, the percentage changes little despite the election cycle and regardless of whether government is divided or united. What this does not show, of course, is the importance of the legislation passed. For example, the passage of Obamacare had a far-reaching impact that not all legislation has.

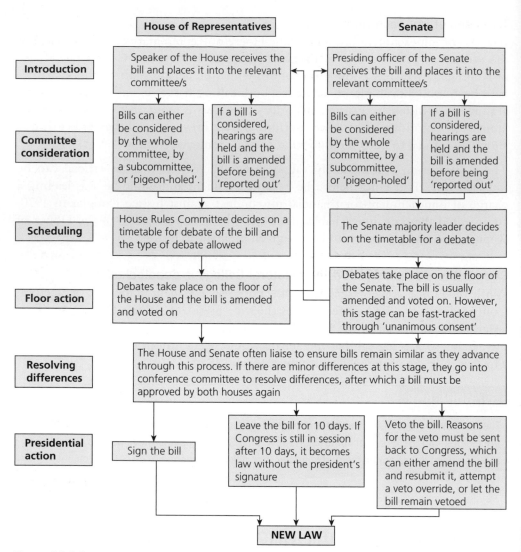

Figure 18.5 Overview of the legislative process

Table 18.6 The percentage of legislation passed

Congress	Pieces of legislation introduced	Number of bills that got a vote in at least one house	Percentage of bills that got a vote in at least one house	Enacted laws	Percentage of successfully passed laws
115th (2017–19)	10,505	813	7%	238	2%
114th (2015–17)	10,334	661	5%	329	3%
113th (2013–15)	9,184	474	4%	296	3%
112th (2011–13)	10,865	390	3%	284	2%
111th (2009–11)	11,192	601	4%	385	3%
110th (2007–09)	11,242	861	6%	460	3%

Introduction

The introductory stage of a bill is a mere formality. In either house, it is received by the leading member of that house and then placed into committee. Choices made at this stage, however, can make it more or less likely that a bill will progress through the whole process. The speaker of the House can choose to time limit a bill or not, and how many committees that bill will go into. If the speaker chooses to send the bill to more than one committee then this must be done sequentially; the bill must finish in one committee before beginning in another. This all serves to lengthen the process and potentially make it less likely that a bill will pass. Alternatively, the speaker can break up the bill and send bits of the bill to different committees. This is known as a 'split referral' and may serve to speed up the process.

In the Senate, the bill will usually go to the committee which has authority over the relevant policy area. However, while the speaker can dominate the House of Representatives, in the Senate the principle of 'unanimous consent' gives power to each individual senator. Unanimous consent means that procedures in the Senate can be set aside if no senator objects. To place a bill into more than one committee in the Senate, unanimous consent is required, limiting the power of the Senate leadership.

Committee consideration

With thousands of bills referred to committee in each Congress, very few actually make it out. Around 1 in 4 bills does make it out of committee, but many do not then get a vote in either the Senate or the House of Representatives. Table 18.6 shows that in each of the last six Congresses, the percentage of bills that got a vote on the floor of at least one chamber has always been 7% or less. This represents the amount of bills that made it out of committee in order to achieve these votes. Bills that do not make it out of committee are considered to be '**pigeon-holed**', meaning they are received by the committee but little or no further action takes place on the bill. Once the current congressional session ends, these bills simply 'die'.

Bills that *are* acted on are subject to committee hearings and are then amended by the committee. The amendments made to a bill are known as 'mark ups'. The final amended bill must pass a vote of the whole committee. On passing a vote, it is 'reported out', meaning the amended bill is sent back to the relevant house, to allow for consideration by the whole house.

> ### Key term
>
> **Pigeon-holing** A bill which is put into a congressional committee but not given any hearings or further action, therefore effectively 'dying' in committee.

Scheduling

In the House of Representatives, the timetabling is decided by the House Rules Committee. This committee is dominated by the majority party in a 2:1 ratio, and all majority party members are appointed by the speaker. This should allow for the majority party to control the passage of legislation. The House Rules Committee not only decides on when a bill is placed on to the calendar, but also under what rules it can be debated. If the debate is 'open', amendments can be made to the bill as it is being debated. Under a 'closed debate', no amendments can be made to the bill. In the Senate, a Motion to Proceed is voted on and if this receives a simple majority a bill is placed on the calendar.

By mid-2017, the House Rules Committee as appointed by Speaker Paul Ryan had set a new record — it allocated a closed rule debate for the 49th time. This was not only a record for the number of uses of the rule in one session, it also meant no legislation had been considered under the open rule up to that point of the congressional session.

Equally, the development of modern weaponry has placed greater emphasis on the presidential role of commander in chief and reduced the congressional power of the declaration of war — in a nuclear age, the declaration of war seems very finite! While Congress has wrestled to regain some of this power, passing the War Powers Act and using the Authorization for Use of Military Force (AUMF) facility to justify presidential military action, the balance of power here seems to rest squarely with the president.

Comparisons with the UK

Comparative theories

Table 18.9 Comparing the US and UK legislatures using comparative theories

Rational comparisons	• The actions of MPs and Congressmen and –women can be viewed through what is best for them and their careers — in the UK this may engender party loyalty, while in the USA this means a keen focus on constituents • The actions of leaders within Congress and Parliament can be determined by likely outcome and how that outcome might affect their own personal power — a defeat might weaken their position politically, if not literally • Both legislatures serve as springboards for future political careers. Therefore, the actions of individuals may be guided by their aspirations • The unelected nature of the House of Lords compared to the elected nature of the Senate leads to different outcomes in part due to the freedom, or not, that this gives to individuals
Cultural comparisons	• The actions of individuals within both Congress and Parliament are strongly guided by the individual's ideological coherence to their party's beliefs • The factions within parties, and the addition of caucuses in the USA, can sometimes lead to voting across party lines due to a cultural belief in an issue — this most likely occurs with moral and social issues • Both lower and upper chambers can also be compared in terms of the cultural expectations of how business is conducted. The lower houses are both more adversarial, while there are more cultural conventions about how business is conducted in the upper chambers • There is a growing expectation in both countries that the representative bodies should reflect to some extent the descriptive make-up of the electorate
Structural comparisons	• The processes that guide the legislative output of both houses are fixed and rigid. The additional impact of other processes such as the electoral system and the separation of powers within each country serve to produce vastly different legislative outputs in each country • The ability to oversee the work of government is strongly affected by the structure of each legislature — Congress being directly elected and having direct checks on the president can achieve more than Parliament, which is dominated by the ruling party • The political processes within both countries limit the influence of third parties, thereby encouraging an adversarial two-party system within both legislatures

Comparing the US and UK legislatures

On the surface, the UK and US legislatures look remarkably similar — both are bicameral, both have a two-party system, both have houses with differing powers and both have oversight of the executive branch. However, beneath this surface, not only are the powers of these two branches somewhat different, their ability to exercise power is also different. See Table 18.10 for details.

Table 18.10 Similarities and differences between the US and UK legislatures

Similarities	Differences
The 'lower' house in both legislatures controls taxation and the appropriation of money for government policies	Both houses of Congress are directly elected by the public, whereas the UK House of Lords remains unelected and unaccountable
The responsibility for the creation of legislation and indeed the legislative process is remarkably similar in both countries	The chances of 'divided government' in the UK are almost non-existent, whereas it is increasingly common in the USA
Oversight of the executive branch through a range of checks exists for both branches	Party unity in the UK is relatively high, aided by powerful whips, whereas the US system of primaries prevents whips from enforcing strict party discipline
A range of representation exists within both legislatures — of the people, the constituency, the party and lobbyists — and both suffer from similar deficiencies in this area	The speaker in the House of Commons is in theory an apolitical role, whereas the leadership in both houses of Congress is avoidably tied up with party politics
Power over foreign policy is relatively weak in Congress and Parliament, but both have attempted to regain control over this policy area	Parliament is more efficient at passing legislation owing to the fusion of the executive and legislative branches, whereas Congress passes relatively little new legislation each session
Both legislatures are able to initiate constitutional change	Parliament is sovereign, whereas sovereignty in the USA remains in the Constitution
The prevalent two-party system has helped to ensure oversight, but also worked to deepen partisanship	The executive of the UK can dominate the legislative branch, whereas separation of powers in the USA limits the power of the president in this manner

Strengths and weaknesses of each of the houses

Table 18.11 The strengths and weaknesses of the two US houses and the two UK houses

	Strengths	Weaknesses
House of Representatives	• Two-year terms ensure accountability to the voters with most members representing a smaller area and population than their Senate counterparts • Power of initiation over taxation and appropriations bills • Effectively has the power to decide on what matter an official can be impeached • The two-party system limits the impact of third parties	• Power can become concentrated in the hands of the speaker, committee chairs and House Rules Committee • Partisan politics means that few bills are passed each session • Frequent elections mean a focus on short-term change and allow for excessive influence of lobbyists • Relatively poor representation of women and minority groups
House of Commons	• Dominance by the majority party and fused powers make passing legislation quicker • The speaker is an independent referee • Five-year elections give the house the power to effect real change • Use of Parliament Acts and the Salisbury Convention allow for strong government	• Dominance by the majority party can allow for an 'elective dictatorship' and limits the effectiveness of checks on the executive • It is possible for poor legislation to be rushed through the House • Strong whips make for only limited opposition; even increasing backbench rebellions are relatively rarely successful • The two-party system limits the influence of third parties
Senate	• Longer terms allow officials to focus on making good policy and enacting change • Unique powers to ratify treaties and appointments allow for greater oversight of the executive • 'Unanimous consent' and 'unlimited debate' result in weaker party control • The power of individual senators allows for every state to have a voice that is heard	• 'Unanimous consent' allows for undue influence of a single senator • It can only ratify or reject the treaties and appointments put to it, not create its own • The use of the filibuster can lead to gridlock and is difficult to prevent • Each state having two senators under- and overvalues the importance of states across America
House of Lords	• As an unelected chamber, the Lords can focus on the long-term interests of the UK • Allows for experts to be included in policy-making, rather than charismatic politicians • Being unelected, it is more free to challenge the will of the government • It is possible to nominate a range of people to the Lords to improve representation of minority groups	• Lacking in legitimacy due to its unelected nature • Its power can be usurped through the Parliament Acts and Salisbury Convention • The large size of the Lords makes it cumbersome • The challenge it poses to the Commons is minimal as its suggestions and amendments can be ignored

Summary

By the end of this chapter you should be able to answer the following questions:

→ How significant are the Constitutional powers given to Congress?

→ Does Congress effectively represent the various groups in the USA today?

→ What are the strengths and weaknesses of the legislative process?

→ To what extent is the election cycle the biggest factor in explaining variation in congressional power?

→ Is Congress effective at holding the other branches of government to account?

→ What are the most significant factors a member of Congress will consider when deciding how to vote?

→ Does Congress fulfil the expectations set out for it in the Constitution?

→ To what extent is the US Constitution the most significant limitation on Congress?

Practice questions

1 Examine factors that explain the low legislative output of Congress and the high legislative output of Parliament. (12)

2 Analyse differences in powers of the House of Representatives and the House of Commons. *In your answer you must consider the relevance of at least one comparative theory.* (12)

3 Evaluate the extent to which congressional oversight of the president is consistently effective. *You must consider this view and the alternative to this view in a balanced way.* (30)

19 US presidency

The Founding Fathers wrote about the presidency in Article II of the newly written Constitution, reflecting the greater importance that they placed on Congress (Article I). More than just outlining the powers of the presidency, Article II also outlined restrictions to be placed on this branch, most of which would be exercised by Congress. The Founding Fathers feared tyranny by a strong executive branch, as they had experienced under the British. The Declaration of Independence (1776) had been scathing about King George III, stating:

> 'the history of the present King of Great Britain is a history of repeated injuries and usurpations, all having in direct object the establishment of an absolute Tyranny over these States.'

Article II therefore both opens and closes with restrictions to be placed on the presidential branch, from age limits for holding presidential office to the ultimate threat of impeachment, with the powers of this branch sandwiched in the middle. Thomas Jefferson hoped this Article would 'bind him [the president] down from mischief by the chains of the constitution'.

Given the size and strength of this branch today, the Founding Fathers would likely be surprised by the modern presidency. Despite the size of the bureaucracy around him, however, ultimately the president alone holds constitutional power.

The presidency and the Constitution

The Constitution lays out the requirements that must be met before someone can be the president. As well as being elected through the Electoral College, and limited to only 4-year terms, they must also be at least 35 years old, a US-born citizen, and a resident of the USA for 14 years (although whether this is consecutive or cumulative is still debated today). The age limit was added at the Philadelphia Constitutional Convention after George Mason commenting that 'his political opinions at the age of 21 were too crude and erroneous to merit an influence on public measures'.

Article II is far shorter and more vague than Article I — and this has allowed for the growth of the modern presidency. Table 19.1 provides a summary of Article II.

Table 19.1 An outline of what Article II includes in each of its four sections

Section I — Nature of the presidency	Section II — Powers of the president	Section III — Responsibilities of the president	Section IV — Impeachment
• Executive power vested in 'a President' • Four-year terms • Explanation of presidential elections • Presidential requirements — must be 35 years old, a US-born citizen and a resident of 14 years	• Commander in chief • Require the opinion of heads of departments • Pardons and reprieves • Make treaties • Appoint ambassadors, judges and officials • Recess appointments	• State of the Union address to Congress • Convene special sessions of Congress • Receive ambassadors • Faithfully execute laws	• Impeachment for 'Treason, Bribery, or other high Crimes and Misdemeanors'

Perhaps the most important part of Article II is the opening sentence, in which power is vested singularly in 'a President'. This means that even today, the president alone wields, and is accountable for, the power of this branch of government. However, despite this, the presidency today is far bigger than just one man. In order to carry out the huge number of roles required of him, the president controls the **federal bureaucracy**.

Key term

Federal bureaucracy The administrative bodies of the US presidency, consisting of departments, agencies and commissions which act under the president's direction.

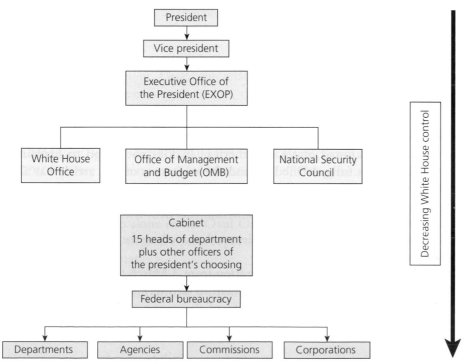

Figure 19.1 The executive branch

President Obama delivers his State of the Union address, 2015

Appointments (including recess appointments and creating a cabinet)

The president has the power to appoint around 4,000 officials, with roughly 1,200 of these needing Senate confirmation. Key among these are the appointments of Supreme Court justices and cabinet positions, which are confirmed by a simple majority vote in the Senate (Table 19.5).

Table 19.5 Presidential appointments

President	Supreme Court nominees	Notable cabinet nominees
G.H.W. Bush	• David Souter • Clarence Thomas	• Tower (Defense) — rejected by the Senate after allegations of alcoholism and womanising
Clinton	• Ruth Bader Ginsburg • Stephen Breyer	• Gober (Veteran Affairs) — withdrawn by the president following sexual misconduct allegations
G.W. Bush	• John Roberts • Harriet Miers (withdrew) • Samuel Alito	• John Bolton (UN ambassador) — eventually a recess appointment
Obama	• Sonia Sotomayor • Elena Kagan • Merrick Garland (expired)	• Judd Gregg (Commerce) — a Republican nominee who withdrew over differences with Obama
Trump	• Neil Gorsuch • Brett Kavanaugh	• Betsy de Vos (Education) — tie-breaking vote cast by Vice President Pence

As well as appointing cabinet members, the Constitution gives the president the power to 'require the Opinion, in writing, of the principal Officer in each of the executive Departments'. From this, it is implied that the president can establish his cabinet. The cabinet today must contain the heads of the 15 executive departments, but can also include other officials as the president wishes. These are often symbolic of the policy areas which he believes are a priority. See page 467 for more information about the cabinet.

Recess appointments

The president is also given the power of '**recess appointments**'. This allows the president to make temporary appointments to vacancies which would usually require Senate approval but which he cannot get because the Senate is in recess. These appointments expire at the end of the next session of Senate and the president must then either formally nominate the person he has chosen temporarily, or pick someone else to nominate. This aimed to try and prevent the president from circumventing the Senate's powers by simply waiting for the Senate to go on recess and then filling any vacancy he wanted.

President Clinton made 139 recess appointments, and President Bush made 171, including John Bolton to the role of US ambassador after his hearings in the Senate were dragged out with a Democrat filibuster. Obama made just 32 recess appointments, but his power to do so ended up being challenged in the Supreme Court.

In focus

President Obama's recess appointments

In January 2012, while Senate was in a 3-day 'recess', President Obama made four recess appointments — three to the National Labor Relations Board (NLRB) and one to the Consumer Financial Protection Bureau (CFPB). However, the Senate at this time was holding a 'pro forma' session — this meant that each day a senator would bang the gavel in the Senate Chamber so that technically the Senate was not in recess, even though no business was taking place. These appointments were challenged by Noel Canning, a distributor who the NLRB claimed had violated federal law by refusing to follow procedures. Canning challenged this ruling, claiming that the three recess appointments were invalid and so, therefore, was the ruling. The case of *NLRB* v *Canning* (2014) was heard by the Supreme Court, which found that 'the Senate is in session when it says it is' and invalidated the three recess appointments. The case also went some way to clarifying when appointments could take place, saying a recess of 10 days or longer could be considered a congressional recess.

Justice Stephen Breyer, who wrote the majority opinion in the *NLRB* v *Canning* case, said that in his opinion the Supreme Court could not ignore the pro forma sessions of the Senate and 'thus we conclude that the president lacked the power to make the recess appointments at issue here'.

These pro forma sessions were used in 2017 by the Senate to prevent President Trump from making appointments during the Senate's August break. The Senate was concerned Trump would fire his Attorney General, Jeff Sessions, and replace him with someone more willing to challenge or even remove Robert Mueller from heading the Justice Department's investigation into Russian election interference and collusion.

Executive power (including executive orders)

The vague phrasing of the opening of Article II allows a president 'executive power'. Today, this is interpreted as being able to organise the Executive Office of the President (EXOP) and carry out a range of 'executive actions'. Executive action is a catch-all term for the different things a president can do under the auspices of 'executive power' and without congressional approval. Most commonly, this includes **executive orders**, signing statements and issuing presidential memoranda.

In focus

President Obama and immigration

President Obama made numerous requests to Congress to pass immigration reform during his time in office, mentioning it in at least five of his State of the Union addresses. However, despite bipartisan efforts in the Senate, no such reform made it through Congress. In 2012, Obama used an executive memorandum to introduce DACA, protecting those who met certain conditions from deportation. In 2014, he extended this cover and introduced additional protections for parents of children born in America but who were not themselves American — the Deferred Actions for Parents of Americans (DAPA). Together, these would have protected from deportation nearly 11 million people who lacked proper documentation.

However, these 2014 additions were challenged in the Supreme Court in the case of *Texas* v *United States* (2016). The Supreme Court, lacking a member following the death of Antonin Scalia, divided 4–4 on the case, which effectively overturned Obama's executive memoranda — 'the judgement is affirmed by an equally divided Court'. In the event of a split ruling, the ruling on the case issued by a lower court is the one that stands. In this case, the lower court had ruled against President Obama, and so the divided Court upheld, or 'affirmed', that ruling.

Obama described this as 'heart-breaking for the millions of immigrants who've made their lives here'.

Key term

Signing statement A statement issued by the president regarding a bill that he has just signed into law.

Signing statements

A president can issue a **signing statement** when he signs a bill into law. It usually points out the positive or negative aspects of the bill as far as the president is concerned. This may even go so far as to allow the president to challenge aspects of a bill on constitutional grounds. When President Obama signed the National Defense Authorization Act in 2011, his signing statement highlighted the concerns that he had over the 'detention, interrogation, and prosecution of suspected terrorists' and regarding the restrictions it placed on the presidency, which conflicted with the separation of powers. His statement therefore outlined that he and his administration would interpret aspects as the bill 'to avoid … constitutional conflict'. There have been questions as to whether these statements are constitutional or not — the president is supposed to execute laws 'faithfully', not simply ignore the bits he dislikes.

Signing statements were not particularly controversial historically as they were rarely used. However, since President Reagan, the number of signing statements has notably increased (Table 19.7). This then raises questions over the power it lends to the president over legislation. The American Bar Association claimed that such statements 'undermine the rule of law and our constitutional system of separation of powers'.

Table 19.7 Increase in the number of signing statements

President	Statements	Number of these statements which objected to at least part of the law
Reagan	250	86
Bush	228	70
Clinton	381	70
Bush	161	127

Grant reprieves and pardons

The president has the right to **pardon** people, meaning he can forgive them for a federal (not state) crime, effectively making it as if the crime had never occurred. The only thing that cannot be pardoned is impeachment, which helps to explain why President Nixon resigned over the Watergate affair — in doing so, impeachment proceedings were never brought and he was able to be pardoned by his successor, President Ford. Whether a president could pardon himself has never been tested and is still a matter of debate for constitutional scholars, especially since claims by President Trump that he had the 'absolute right' to pardon himself.

This power was used en masse by President Ford and President Carter to pardon hundreds of thousands of men who had evaded the Vietnam War draft.

The granting of reprieves today has evolved to mean '**commutations**'. While pardons are usually issued after someone has served their sentence, commutations can be used to free people from a current sentence. Commutations do not change the guilt of a person but do remove or lessen the sentence that person has received.

On his last day in office, President Obama issued 330 commutations to people convicted of drug offences. This represented his view that 'the war on drugs has been an utter failure' and underlined the calls he had made during his time in office for reform of laws regarding drugs. This was the biggest number of commutations issued in one day by any president, and brought his total number of commutations to 1,715, the most of any president.

Table 19.8 The use of pardons and commutations by recent presidents — there are almost no checks on the use of this power, certainly no direct checks by Congress exist

President	Pardons	Commutations
Clinton	396	61
Bush	189	11
Obama	212	1,715
Trump (to September 2018)	7	4

Stretch and challenge

The commutation of Chelsea Manning

In 2010, while Chelsea Manning was serving in the US military, she leaked classified military intelligence to WikiLeaks. Some of the documentation released showed the atrocities of the war in Iraq and Afghanistan and Manning said she released the documents so that Americans could 'see what I was seeing' and understand the realities of the wars. She was arrested and charged with a range of crimes, including 'aiding the enemy', which carried a maximum penalty of death. In 2013 she was acquitted of this crime, but she was found guilty of the 21 remaining charges either fully or partially, and sentenced to 35 years in prison. Just days before he left office, President Obama commuted the sentence for Manning, saying that he was 'very comfortable that justice has been served'.

Does the use of a commutation in such a controversial case suggest that the president's power in this area is largely unlimited?

Key terms

Pardon The power of the president to forgive a person of a federal crime, erasing it from their criminal record.

Commutation The ability of the president to reduce the sentence issued for a crime.

Convene special sessions of Congress

The president has the power, if necessary, to call a special session of Congress, calling either or both houses of Congress back from recess. While rarely used today, it has had notable use in the past, with the entirety of Congress convened on 27 occasions and the Senate alone convened a further 46 times. For the Senate, most of these sessions have been related to its unique powers — a president needing the Senate to confirm a cabinet nominee or treaty. The whole of Congress has been recalled to deal with international situations, with Roosevelt convening a session in 1939 regarding US neutrality in what would be the Second World War, and domestic legislation, last used in 1948 by President Truman.

Commander in chief

As commander in chief, the president is constitutionally the head of the army and navy, although today this also includes the air force, marines and coast guard. The Constitution is unclear on the extent of these powers, however, except that only Congress can declare war. The powers given to the president within this role have certainly broadened over time — with war last declared in 1942, involvement of the US military globally since then has been squarely under the direction of the president.

In 1976, at a question-and-answer session in Dover, New Hampshire, Gerald Ford was asked about the extent of presidential power. He replied:

> 'Our forefathers knew you couldn't have 535 Commanders in Chief and Secretaries of State. It just wouldn't work, and it won't work. That doesn't mean that the Congress and the president shouldn't consult and work together. We have in many cases. But in the last year, there has been a tendency on the part of the Congress to limit and hamstring effective action by the president to move quickly … That is not good for the United States.'

Gerald Ford highlighted the importance of presidential power in times of national crisis

The development of new weaponry, particularly nuclear weapons, can also have an impact on this power. When wars were fought between two large armies, it was easier to understand the division of power between Congress and the president. However, with nuclear weapons being capable of mass destruction, the need for such armies is decreased but the need for a swift response is massively increased. Congress has tried to regain power in this area, passing the War Powers Resolution in 1973. This Resolution, however, has been widely interpreted as unconstitutional by presidents since then and their unwillingness to adhere to it has not been challenged.

Make treaties (including executive agreements)

The president, with the consent of the Senate, has the right to create treaties with other nations (Table 19.9). Formal treaties, such as the New Strategic Arms Reduction Treaty (New START) in 2010 require negotiation by the president and a two-thirds vote of approval in the Senate.

Executive agreements are very similar to treaties, although they do not require Senate approval. They are therefore often seen as a way around the constitutional difficulties of gaining Senate approval. President Obama brokered the Iran Nuclear Deal and the Paris Climate Change Agreement in this manner. That is not to say that they are without checks, however. Executive agreements do often require congressional approval before they are fully enforceable, usually through a joint resolution of Congress. Equally, the congressional power of the purse can also be used to control presidential action in this way.

The war on terror

Shortly after the attacks of September 11 on the World Trade Center in New York, George W. Bush addressed a joint session of Congress and used the phrase 'war on terror'. Under this guise, the USA has been involved in multiple conflicts in the Middle East in the last two decades.

- **14 September 2001** Congress passes the Authorization for Use of Military Force Against Terrorists, granting the president the right to use all 'necessary and appropriate force' against those who planned and committed the September 11 attacks.
- **October 2001** The USA, plus coalition forces, invades Afghanistan.
- **January 2002** Guantánamo Bay is established, holding suspected terrorists without trial.
- **16 October 2002** Congress passes the Authorization for Use of Military Force Against Iraq, outlining the justifications and authorisation for military involvement in Iraq.
- **March 2003** The USA, plus coalition forces, invades Iraq.

Congress tried to control the Iraq War through its power of the purse (see Chapter 17), but this failed to pass. The Supreme Court challenged detentions in Guantánamo Bay at least four times, but the camp remains open and prosecutions remain non-existent, with many detainees being released without charge. The power of the president in these areas is evidently difficult to challenge.

Presidents have also used their power over the military within the USA. Federal troops have been deployed in the case of national emergencies, such as when Hurricane Katrina hit in 2005 and during the BP Deepwater Horizon disaster in 2010. President Trump signed a proclamation in 2018 to move troops to the US–Mexico border in order to halt the crossing of illegal immigrants, saying that 'lawlessness' at the border had left him with 'no choice but to act'. Movement of such troops within the USA is not allowed under federal law unless it is authorised by Congress, but both Bush and Obama had also sent troops to the US–Mexico border.

Table 19.9 Treaties and executive agreements

President	Treaty/Agreement	Vote	Outcome
Clinton	1996 Comprehensive Nuclear Test Ban	Yeas — 48 Nays — 51	Rejected
Obama	2010 New START	Yeas — 71 Nays — 26	Passed
Obama	2012 Convention on the Rights of Persons with Disabilities	Yeas — 61 Nays — 38	Rejected
Obama	2015 Joint Comprehensive Plan of Action (JCPOA) — the Iran Nuclear Deal	As an executive agreement, no vote needed	Enforced as an executive agreement
Obama	2015 The Paris Agreement	As an executive agreement, no vote needed	Enforced as an executive agreement, although Trump has withdrawn the USA effective November 2020
Obama/Trump	2016/17 Trans-Pacific Trade Partnership	None — signed but not ratified	Trump withdrew the USA in January 2017

However, notably, while there are constitutional requirements on passing treaties, there are none regarding leaving a treaty. Even if a treaty has been approved by the Senate, a president retains the right to remove the USA from a treaty without asking the Senate — a considerable addition to his powers.

In focus

New START

The New START treaty was the third START treaty. It was agreed between Russia and the USA, with the aim of reducing the number of nuclear missile launchers and deployed nuclear warheads. President Obama and President Medvedev of Russia met in 2009 and, after rounds of talks, the treaty was finally signed in 2010. The USA and Russia still own between them almost all of the world's nuclear warheads.

Receive ambassadors

The president, as the head of state, receives ambassadors from foreign nations, appointed to be their ambassador to the USA. This power has become far more significant than it seems — by receiving ambassadors, or not, the president can use this power to recognise nations and decide with whom the USA is prepared to work.

President George Bush recognised Kosovo in 2008, while President Obama recognised Sudan in 2011, establishing diplomatic relations with these countries. Vietnam was not recognised by the USA until 1995 after an interruption of relations due to the Vietnam War.

Such receptions can cause international difficulties, however. President Obama met with the Dalai Lama four times in the White House. Given that the Dalai Lama is an exile from Tibet and a recognised campaigner for Tibetan independence, Obama's willingness to meet with him caused considerable anger from the Chinese government.

The role as the head of state and head of government

The roles of head of state and head of government are separate in many countries around the world. In constitutional monarchies such as the UK, the prime minister is the head of government while the monarch is the head of state. In republics such as France, the president is the head of state while the prime minister is the head of government.

In the USA, however, the president fulfils both of these roles. This makes it difficult to separate the powers neatly into these two roles as the Constitution does not make a distinction and there is often an overlap (Figure 19.3). Traditionally, heads of state carry out ceremonial roles, have greater oversight over foreign policy and hold the highest ranking position in their state. Heads of government deal with domestic policy, the national budget and preside over the cabinet and the executive branch.

Figure 19.3 The powers of heads of state and heads of government

Presidential powers of head of state
- Power of the pardon
- Receiving ambassadors
- Representing the USA abroad
- Ceremonial duties

Areas of overlap
- Commander in chief
- Recognising countries
- State of the Union address
- Making treaties

Presidential powers as head of government
- Chief legislator
- Chief executive

Synoptic link

In the UK, the role of head of state is carried out by the unelected queen or king, limited by the 1689 Bill of Rights. While the president in the USA is the head of state, he too is limited but by the US Constitution itself. For more on the UK Bill of Rights, see pages 134–35. This links to Component 2, UK Government.

The president as head of state

In addition to the power of the pardon and reception of ambassadors, the president carries out other functions as the head of state. He attends world summits and events such as the G7 or the G20 as a representative of the USA and to broker deals and treaties on behalf of the USA. He also carries out ceremonial duties such as the annual pardoning of the turkey or throwing the first ball of the season on the Opening Day of the US baseball season.

Every year, the president pardons a turkey, which will then not be killed and served on Thanksgiving. This is entirely ceremonial and has no constitutional basis, but has become an annual tradition at the White House

Does the USA need a monarch?

Given the extensive role that the US president has to carry out, it has been suggested that a separate head of state would be beneficial:

- It would free up presidential time with someone else carrying out ceremonial roles.
- It would allow for a non-political head of state who can act as the representative of the nation in national crises.
- It would provide a symbol of the values of the USA that was not tied up in party politics.

If the USA were to create such a role, what are the likely powers that would be given to it that are currently exercised by the president? What are the possible conflicts it would create?

The president as head of government

As the head of government, the president heads up the executive branch. He is responsible for the organisation of EXOP and presides over the cabinet and, by extension, over the federal bureaucracy. He can use executive actions to ensure that US laws are carried out effectively and has the right to sign and veto legislation as he sees fit.

The overlapping powers

A number of these powers have aspects associated with both the head of state and the head of government (see Figure 19.3), or have an impact on both foreign and domestic policy.

- **Commander in chief** As the representative of the USA to the world, and with war not having been declared since 1942, this role allows the president as the head of state to involve the USA in foreign military action. It has a domestic role too, however, more in keeping with the head of government role, with the president using troops to respond to natural disasters and crises that emerge within the USA.
- **Recognising countries** As an extension of the role of receiving ambassadors, this role is more in keeping with the global role of the president, and therefore as head of state. However, in recognising which countries the USA is willing to work with, the president effectively opens trade opportunities, which has a direct impact on the US domestic economy.
- **State of the Union address** As the chief legislator, this opportunity for the president to shape domestic policy helps him to fulfil his role as the head of government. Such speeches in other countries, however, are often given by the head of state as a more ceremonial function, such as the Queen's Speech in the UK.
- **Making treaties** Similar to recognising countries, by making treaties the president is acting as the US representative to the world, but the treaties made will often have a direct impact on the US domestic economy.

It is therefore difficult to discern an absolute distinction between these two roles for the president. However, the roles he has as head of state or those to do with foreign policy are often subject to fewer checks. Those as head of government or to do with domestic policy often have more checks from other branches of government.

Informal sources of presidential power

In addition to those powers granted by the Constitution, the president is able to use political circumstances of the day and the framework of government to develop his power.

The cabinet

Constitutionally, the cabinet has no formal power. With all executive power vested in 'a President', the cabinet is simply an advisory body for the president. Despite this, every president since 1793 has had a cabinet. Originally with just four members — State, War, Treasury and Post Office — it now consists of the heads of 15 departments, the president, the vice president and other cabinet-level executives as the president sees fit (Table 19.10). The additional members that a president chooses are often reflective either of his policy priorities or of the national circumstances in which he takes over.

Table 19.10 The cabinet members for each of the last three presidents

Executive departments (15)		
• Secretary of State • Secretary of Treasury • Secretary of Defense • Attorney General • Secretary of the Interior	• Secretary of Agriculture • Secretary of Commerce • Secretary of Labor • Secretary of Health and Human Services • Secretary of Education	• Secretary of Housing and Urban Development • Secretary of Transportation • Secretary of Energy • Secretary of Veterans Affairs • Secretary of Homeland Security
President Bush's additional cabinet members	**President Obama's additional cabinet members**	**President Trump's additional cabinet members**
• President • Vice president • Chief of staff • Environmental Protection Agency • Office of Management and Budget • Office of National Drug Control Policy • United States Trade Representative	• President • Vice president • Chief of staff • Environmental Protection Agency • Office of Management and Budget • Ambassador to the United Nations • United States Trade Representative • Council of Economic Advisers • Small Business Administration	• President • Vice president • Chief of staff • Environmental Protection Agency • Office of Management and Budget • Ambassador to the United Nations • United States Trade Representative • Director of National Intelligence • Director of the CIA • Small Business Administration

The cabinet is a source of power for the president in a number of ways. Cabinet members should be policy specialists and therefore able to offer opinions on policy and lend support to the president in his policy objectives. Tim Geithner was Obama's choice for secretary of the Treasury, having previously been the president of the Federal Reserve Bank of New York. This experience allowed Geithner to make policy suggestions as the Obama administration dealt with the recession that America was facing after the 2007 economic crash. Geithner introduced the Financial Stability Plan, committing billions of dollars to a 'lending initiative' to try and boost the economy, while requiring that banks undergo 'stress tests' to ensure that they could withstand and even prevent a future economic crash. It is this ability to manage department-level policy that is crucial for the president, who would be unable to do so across so many departments and agencies alone.

As the cabinet has no constitutional power, however, the president does maintain the final say over policy. In 2014, President Obama was concerned that Secretary of Defense Chuck Hagel was not transferring detainees out of Guantánamo Bay fast enough. Obama's national security adviser, Susan Rice, sent Hagel a memo requiring him to send transfer updates regarding detainees every 2 weeks to try to speed up the process. While Hagel publicly replied, 'I owe that to the American people, to ensure that any decision I make is, in my mind, responsible', by November of that year, he had resigned. This example highlights the president's ability not only to control policy, but also to choose to rely on his own people within EXOP, in this case Rice, rather than his appointed cabinet secretaries.

In focus

Chuck Hagel and Guantánamo Bay

Obama's choice of Chuck Hagel for secretary of defense in 2013 was always going to be subject to extraordinary scrutiny because Hagel was a Republican. Given that Obama wanted to withdraw from wars in Afghanistan and Iraq, and reduce the Defense Department budget, it gave him some bipartisan cover to have a Republican in this post. The policy aims of Obama and Hagel were not always in sync, however. In August 2014, while President Obama was comparing ISIS to a junior varsity basketball team, Hagel described it as 'an imminent threat to every interest we have'.

The real division came over Guantánamo Bay, however. While Obama pushed for the closure of Guantánamo and the transfer of detainees, Hagel was only slowly signing the release certificates necessary for the transfers. It was claimed that this added to the tension between the Obama administration and Hagel which led ultimately to the extraordinary memo from Susan Rice directing Hagel to 'provide an update on progress on detainee transfers every two weeks until further notice'. After his forced resignation, Hagel complained of White House micromanagement of the Department of Defense, saying he had to deal with White House staff 'asking fifth-level questions that the White House should not be involved in'.

Cabinet-level officials can also undertake work and roles on behalf of the president, but as a representative of his role and power. On the election of a new Mexican president in July 2018, Secretary of State Mike Pompeo was sent to meet with him

Secretary of State Mike Pompeo met Mexican president-elect Andrés Manuel López Obrador in Mexico City on 13 July 2018

to improve relations between the USA and Mexico. The president alone would be unable to attend every meeting and event required of him, so he is able to use members of the cabinet as representatives of him and his power.

In focus

Inside the Obama cabinet

As part of his drive for transparency, the Obama administration released a series of videos depicting life within his White House. One of these was *Inside the White House: The Cabinet*. In this video, Obama and his staff talk about the cabinet and raise some important points about the role and importance of the cabinet, emboldened below:

PRESIDENT OBAMA: One of the things I am most proud of is the cabinet that we have assembled. You have extraordinarily talented people in each of these fields. A lot of them are doing such a good job that **they don't meet with me much** because they're like the good students in class, they are just handling their business really well.

CHRIS LU, CABINET SECRETARY: We try and do a cabinet meeting **every two months**. The meetings run about **an hour and a half**.

CHRIS LU, CABINET SECRETARY: These are closed sessions and the president really welcomes **frank, unvarnished advice** from the advisors.

PRESIDENT OBAMA: I want, number one, to make sure that **they know they've got my ear**. The second thing is to **reinforce the real strong sense of camaraderie** that the Cabinet members have built around themselves.

GARY LOCKE, COMMERCE SECRETARY: These cabinet meetings are **an incredible way for everybody to communicate**, for everyone to really understand what the issues are and to help us all get on the same page so that we can **advance the president's priorities**.

CHRIS LU, CABINET SECRETARY: What we've typically done is **bring the press in at the end of the meeting**. The Cabinet meeting is an important **symbol** of the government at work.

HILLARY CLINTON, SECRETARY OF STATE: I think that it's [cabinet meetings] not only as important as it always was … but to some extent even more so. So that people **can look each other in the eye, they can watch the body language** and they can work together to get to the resolution of whatever the issue is.

Finally, the cabinet has a symbolic value for presidential power. Clinton famously remarked he wanted his cabinet to 'look like America'. As a singular executive, the president is likely only to appeal to a certain demographic — that might be due to their age, experience, ideology, race, sex, religion, or many other factors. Clinton's aim for greater diversity made the cabinet more representative of America, and therefore reflected a government governing for the whole of America (Figure 19.4). President Bush and President Obama continued this trend of diversity in their cabinets, although President Trump's cabinet was more male and more white than any cabinet since President Reagan. President Obama's cabinet, in contrast, remains the most diverse in history with, in 2009, seven women, four African Americans, three Asian Americans, two Hispanics, and two Republicans.

Equally, the cabinet is the symbol of 'government at work'. The media presence at cabinet meetings allows the president to project the image of his government to the public.

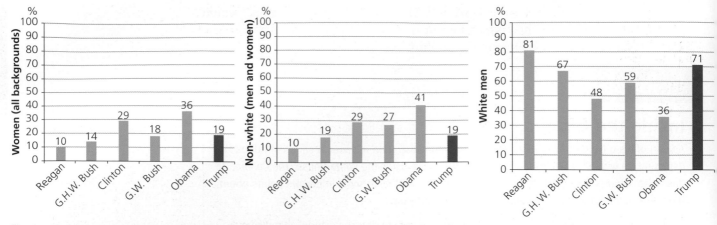

Figure 19.4 The changing diversity in the US cabinet over time. President Obama's cabinet remains the most diverse in history with, in 2009, seven women, four African Americans, three Asian Americans and two Hispanics. It also included two Republicans

---

Synoptic link

While the cabinet is an important source of power for the president, it is not a collective body as it is in the UK. Nonetheless, both cabinets can both strengthen and weaken the power of their respective executives. This links to Component 2, UK Government (pages 199–201).

Key term

Powers of persuasion
The power of the president to bargain and persuade those around him in order to achieve his policy goals.

Powers of persuasion

In 1960, Professor Richard Neustadt published a book in which he suggested that 'the power of the presidency is the **power to persuade**'. This suggestion was based on the fact that each president has the same constitutional powers and each of these powers is checked directly by Congress. The president therefore must rely on something else to achieve his policy goals — persuasion, reputation and public prestige. A president could use these skills to bargain and persuade the rival centres of power within the US political system to do as he wishes.

President Harry Truman once commented:

> 'I sit here all day trying to persuade people to do the things they ought to have sense enough to do without my persuading them. ... That's all the powers of the president amount to.'

When his successor was elected, Truman lamented: 'He will sit there, and he will say, "Do this! Do that!" And nothing will happen. Poor Ike — it won't be a bit like the army.'

Persuasion can be achieved through a variety of methods, often reliant on the image of the president and the benefits that the role brings with it:

- A president can appeal directly and morally to Congress, often through the media. Obama did this in his Rose Garden speech of 2013. In this speech, Obama maintained he was convinced of the need to take military action in Syria over its government's use of chemical weapons. He also said that, as the leader of the oldest constitutional democracy in the world, it was right that he ask Congress for its approval for such action. For President Trump, such appeals have also been made through Twitter.

President Truman receives Winston Churchill, each having represented their country's interests at the Potsdam Conference of 1945

- The White House can be used as a stage, or a '**bully pulpit**'. This means that the White House itself is a place of such importance and gravitas that speaking from it — to Congress, the press or the public — can be a way of placing pressure on those with legislative control. An address from the Oval Office can be particularly effective for this, as rather than simply representing the 'man', it represents the office of the president. President Obama used this platform to call for gun control after the San Bernardino shooting in 2015. President Trump bussed the entire Senate to the White House for a briefing on North Korea in 2017 to much the same effect.

- The president can also use his own personal gravitas more directly, through methods such as phoning congressional leaders or having personal meetings with them. At a less significant level this might be achieved by his White House staff phoning or liaising with members of Congress. Obama's deputy chief of staff Messina called senators to ensure that they would still vote to ratify Sonia Sotomayor after a difficult quote came to light during her confirmation hearings. In trying to get his tax bill passed, President Trump sent aide Kellyanne Conway to speak to whips in Congress to share information with them. More significantly, President Obama was known both to telephone and to have private meetings with Republican Speaker John Boehner to try and advance his legislative agenda.

- With a short congressional election cycle, the president might be able to offer inducements to members of Congress. This might be offering them broader policy promises to make legislation more palatable, such as Obama's promises about Syrian intervention being limited and involving no deployment of American soldiers. This might be using the actions of the executive branch to gain congressional approval. Obama deported more people than any other president in an effort to show Congress he could be trusted with immigration policy and to gain support for his proposed immigration reforms.

The more popular a president is, the more likely Congress is to listen to him; doing so may win votes and popularity for congressmen and -women themselves. A president with lower poll ratings will often find it difficult to use such powers of persuasion as they have less personal capital to expend. Much of both the power of persuasion and the public opinion of a president is also wrapped up in their personal style and charisma. Obama was well spoken and intellectual but averse to schmoozing congressional leaders, while Trump is more brash and aggressive but frequently in touch directly with the people. Both styles have advantages and disadvantages, determined by how successful a president is at utilising their own skills.

Synoptic link

Both the UK prime minister and the US president attempt to influence and control events using more informal and undefinable sources of power than those given to them through their offices alone. For more on the influence of the prime minister, see pages 205–07. This links to Component 2, UK Government.

Stretch and challenge

Powers of persuasion

'What I didn't fully appreciate, and nobody can appreciate until they're in the position, is how decentralized power is in this system. When you're in the seat and you're seeing the housing market collapse and you are seeing unemployment skyrocketing and you have a sense of what the right thing to do is, then you realize, "Okay, not only do I have to persuade my own party, not only do I have to prevent the other party from blocking what the right thing to do is, but now I can anticipate this lawsuit, this lobbying taking place, and this federal agency that technically is independent, so I can't tell them what to do. I've got the Federal Reserve, and I'm hoping that they do the right thing — and by the way, since the economy now is global, I've got to make sure that the Europeans, the Asians, the Chinese, everybody is on board." A lot of the work is not just identifying the right policy but now constantly building these ever-shifting coalitions to be able to actually implement and execute and get it done.'

Barack Obama

In order for a president to be successful, whose support might they need according to this quote from Obama? To what extent does this suggest the power of the presidency amounts to nothing more than persuasion?

Vice president

Constitutionally, the office of the vice president has only two powers — to take over the role of the president if necessary and to cast the deciding vote in the event of a tie in the Senate. The vice president has come to represent more than this, although their relevance and power varies from president to president. In the presidential election, the 'running mate' is important in 'balancing the ticket' (see Chapter 21). It is important to recognise, however, that at this point the 'running mate' is not the vice president; he or she only takes over this role on being elected and inaugurated.

- Al Gore, Jr (vice president to Bill Clinton) — As one of the president's 'most influential advisors', Gore headed the National Performance Review to reduce the cost of federal government, worked on immigration solutions and championed environmental policies.
- Richard B. Cheney (vice president to George W. Bush) — Most famously, Cheney had a huge role in responding to the 9/11 terrorist attacks and the subsequent wars, creating 'a new doctrine in which the president was accountable to no one in his decisions as commander in chief'.
- Joe Biden (vice president to Barack Obama) — When headlined in *The Atlantic* as 'The Most Influential Vice President in History?', Joe Biden claimed, 'I literally get to be the last guy in the room with the president. That's our arrangement.' His experience of over 30 years on the Senate Foreign Relations Committee afforded him expertise over the wars in Afghanistan and Iraq, as well as taking the lead on a range of economic issues.
- Mike Pence (vice president to Donald Trump) — Made headlines breaking the tie in the Senate for the first time in history on a cabinet nomination, and cast no less than six tie-breaking votes in his first year in office. Pence is less reported on than some of his vice-presidential predecessors but he holds considerable power within the White House, apparently driving the resignation of Michael Flynn as national security adviser.

President Obama and Vice President Biden had a close relationship

The modern vice presidency is certainly very different from numerous quips referring to the weakness of this role. The power of Biden, for example, was a far cry from Thomas Marshall's quote: 'Once there were two brothers. One ran away to sea, the other was elected Vice President, and nothing was ever heard of either of them again'. The power and influence of the role does depend on how much the president delegates to the holder, but this seems increasingly common and the development of the Office of the Vice President is therefore another tool that the president can use.

The Executive Office of the President

The Executive Office of the President (EXOP) are those agencies that work within, or directly for, the White House and are organised by the president himself. It is often staffed by the people he is closest to and who are very loyal to him. It is often referred to as 'The West Wing', although those working in the West Wing of the White House are more likely to be from the White House Office, rather than EXOP as a whole.

The Office of Management and Budget

The key public role of the Office of Management and Budget (OMB) is to develop the annual budget for the president for submission to Congress. It continues this monetary role, however, overseeing funding and effectiveness of federal programs and lending advice to the president on policy, budget and legal matters. As a president can only take office in January, it would be challenging for him to have a budget prepared by the first Monday in February as required by law. The OMB therefore takes the lead in drafting this, as well as briefing the president on budget and economic priorities for his first address to Congress in mid-February. With such important roles, and having around 500 staff, the director of the OMB is one of the few roles within EXOP that is subject to Senate confirmation.

The White House Transition Project outlines the importance of the OMB:

> 'OMB's knowledge and expertise strengthens the president's hand in dealings with the Congress during the annual budget process. OMB communicates with Congress at many levels through numerous channels. At the top, those Directors who were armed by mastery of numbers and policy details became the president's most effective representative and advocate in negotiations with congressional leaders. OMB's leaders have been aided in this by a small legislative affairs staff of political appointees. At lower levels, OMB staff have usually been available to their counterparts on the Hill to provide technical explanation and analysis of the president's proposals and other policy ideas.'

National Security Council

The National Security Council (NSC) advises the president on matters of national security and foreign policy. It is attended by the vice president, the secretaries of state, treasury and defense, as well as the joint chiefs of staff and the director of national intelligence, and the national security adviser. In addition to providing advice, it provides a daily security briefing for the president. The profile of the NSC often depends on the individual preferences of a president — often, it may come into conflict with the Department of Defense, as seen with the rivalry between Susan Rice, Obama's national security adviser, and Chuck Hagel (see page 468). The NSC operates out of the Situation Room, a secure conference room in the White House from which the president can action a response to a crisis.

President Trump came under criticism for his treatment of the NSC. His appointment of Steve Bannon, a senior adviser and campaign strategist, to the NSC led to accusations of politicisation of this body. In addition, he relegated the chairs of the Joint Chiefs of Staff to only attending meetings relevant to their experience and expertise, although the White House chief of staff Reince Priebus said they could attend at any time. Trump also courted controversy saying that he did not need the daily security briefing: 'I'm, like, a smart person. I don't have to be told the same thing in the same words every single day for the next eight years.' He did, however, say that Vice President Pence would be receiving the daily briefing.

White House Office

The White House Office (WHO) is headed by the president's chief of staff, and contains senior aides and advisers as the president wishes. The press secretary is the most public figure in the WHO, as they hold press briefings and often appear on the nightly news. Sean Spicer become a figure of ridicule within this role, with the actor and comedian Melissa McCarthy portraying him on *Saturday Night Live*. His replacement, Sarah Sanders, has also been a target for those making fun of the Trump administration and she found herself on the receiving end of controversial mockery at the annual Correspondents' Dinner. The president is able to appoint 'senior advisers' without Senate approval, and therefore surround himself with people whose advice he trusts the most.

This body can hold extensive power over the president if he allows. Nixon's closest advisers were referred to as the 'Berlin Wall' as they made it difficult for other advisers or indeed advice to get to the president. Supposedly, key documents in the Eisenhower administration first went for approval through his chief of staff Sherman Adams, and bore his approval, 'O.K., S.A.'. The Trump administration has seen a huge turnover of staff within the White House. Trump's second chief of staff claimed:

> 'I've been a failure at controlling the president, or a failure at controlling his tweeting, and all that. I was not brought to this job to control anything but the flow of information to our president so that he can make the best decisions.'

The presidency

The changing nature of presidential power

Presidents are seldom 'strong' or 'weak' for their entire presidency. Their power fluctuates, dependent on a range of circumstances, some of which they can control and some of which they cannot.

Elections: the electoral cycle, divided government and the electoral mandate

The success that a president has during election time can be a source of power. If he can claim a sweeping victory, this increases the strength of his **mandate** and can make his requests, especially to Congress, difficult to ignore. A president with less success, or who loses one or both houses of Congress in an election, is likely to find it more difficult to wield his presidential power. Table 19.11 gives a more detailed breakdown of votes received in recent presidential elections.

Key term

Electoral mandate The authority gained at an election by a political leader to act on behalf of their constituents, in force until the next election.

Table 19.11 Votes in presidential elections, 1992–2016

Year	Party	President	Popular vote	States carried	% popular vote	Electoral College votes
1992	Democratic	Clinton W.	44,909,889	32 + DC	43.01	370/538
	Republican	Bush H.W.	39,104,545	18	37.45	168/538
2000	Republican	Bush G.W.	50,456,002	30	47.87	271/538
	Democratic	Gore	50,999,897	20 + DC	48.38	266/538
2008	Democratic	Obama	69,498,516	28 + DC	52.93	365/538
	Republican	McCain	59,948,323	22	45.65	173/538
2016	Republican	Trump	62,984,828	30	46.09	304/538
	Democratic	Clinton H.	65,853,514	20 + DC	48.18	227/538

Part of their strength comes from the popularity they demonstrate by convincingly winning an election. Some of this is due to the **coattails effect**. This means that when a political leader does well in an election, it helps other candidates in their party by attracting votes to them too. A popularly elected president is likely to attract more support from Congress as a consequence. Conversely, if a president is unpopular, members of Congress are likely to distance themselves from the president in the midterm elections, thereby lessening his power. Donald Trump was mocked for having a short coattails effect in 2016. This meant that his popularity was not sufficient to help other Republicans gain office. This has been reflected in the subsequent difficulties he has faced getting his legislative program through Congress.

Key term

Coattails effect The ability of a president to bring out supporters for other members of his party due to his own popularity.

The extent to which a president can push his legislative agenda through Congress often depends on whether government is unified or divided. In times of divided government, the president is likely to find it more difficult to get Congress to pass his desired legislation (see Chapter 18).

National circumstances

National events can significantly either help or hinder presidential power. In the days after the 9/11 attacks, the poll ratings for George W. Bush substantially increased, largely due to the fear that Americans felt and so looking to the president as a figurehead. In contrast, George W. Bush faced criticism over his handling of the response to Hurricane Katrina, which was too slow, decreasing his poll ratings

It is not just crises: a president can often find himself with positive national circumstances that help to bolster his power, such as the blossoming economy under Bill Clinton. This is not always guaranteed, however — President Trump has made an unusual presidential record in 2018 by having an improving economy but a declining presidential approval rating.

Table 19.12 The effect of events on presidential popularity

President	Event	Detail	Effect
Clinton	Oklahoma bombing	A bomb set off in Oklahoma killed 168 people and injured more than 600	✓ Clinton was able to use the story of Richard Dean, who re-entered the building four times to rescue people, to highlight Congress' failings in allowing two government shutdowns
	Monica Lewinsky scandal	President Clinton was accused of lying under oath about his relationship with Lewinsky	✗ Clinton was subjected to impeachment as a result and only narrowly found 'not guilty', embarrassing him on a national stage
Bush Jnr.	9/11 terrorist attacks	Terrorists hijacked airliners, flying them into the Twin Towers and the Pentagon	✓ Bush's approval ratings jumped overnight and allowed him something to rally around after his poor election result in the preceding year
	Hurricane Katrina	A hurricane hit New Orleans killing nearly 2,000 people	✗ Bush's perceived slow response to this, and support of FEMA, made embarrassing national headlines
Obama	2007–08 economic crash	The economic recession that began under George Bush and continued into Obama's presidency	✗ Regardless of the policies that Obama campaigned on, he was always hampered by a need to deal with the economic crisis
	Sandy Hook shooting	20 children aged six and seven were killed in a school shooting	✓ Obama appeared as mourner-in-chief to the nation and was able to advance a gun control agenda ✗ However, ultimately little action came as a result
	Hurricane Sandy	Affecting 24 states in total, the storm badly damaged New Jersey and New York	✓ As president, Obama was able to use this event to make media headlines. At the time he was in the middle of the 2012 presidential race but this dominated media coverage, allowing Obama to gain headlines at the expense of his rival
Trump	Hurricane Maria	The hurricane hit Puerto Rico, killing around 3,000 people	✗ A slow response from Trump, and his later description of the response as a 'great success', courted controversy

Relationships with other branches of government

Congress

The president's relationship with Congress is based on more than the electoral mandate and the timing of the electoral cycle. The manner in which he exercises his constitutional powers is also important. The separation of powers in federal government should ensure compromise. Where a president is unwilling to compromise, Congress often becomes more entrenched too.

In September 2018, *Politico* ran the headline 'Congress dares Trump to shut down the government in new spending deal'. This antagonistic relationship between the two branches is to some extent a result of the looming midterm elections, but also due to the divisive nature of Trump's political ideology. His veto threats, attacks on congressional failure to repeal Obamacare and pressure to confirm Brett Kavanaugh as his Supreme Court appointment have all frustrated Congress and led to it pushing back against presidential power.

Supreme Court

The president's relationship with the Supreme Court is perhaps less changing than his relationship with Congress. His ability to pressure the Court is limited and while his nominations can considerably change the balance of the Court, vacancies do not occur at his will. However, the relationship with the Supreme Court is something that a president may well reflect upon publicly.

Obama openly criticised the Supreme Court in his 2010 State of the Union address, arguing its ruling in *Citizens United* v *Federal Elections Commission* had 'opened the floodgates' to huge volumes of money being spent in elections. Justice Samuel Alito sat in the audience shaking his head and mouthing 'not true, not true'. Obama suffered further defeats at the hands of the Supreme Court in having his DAPA

Debate

How effective is presidential accountability to Congress?

Effective

- The short election cycle of Congress and the coattails effect mean that it is highly responsive to presidential popularity. It is significantly more willing to use its powers when the president is unpopular.
- In domestic policy, Congress has significant powers to control presidential power, from passing legislation to deciding on the funding that he will be allocated.
- The Constitution gives Congress a range of checks to prevent presidential action, or ultimately remove the president if necessary.
- In times of divided government, Congress has demonstrated its willingness and ability to use powers such as the veto override, overriding presidential action.
- National crises can also dent the popularity of the president depending on his reaction, which directly affects Congress' willingness to apply checks to his power.

Ineffective

- The president's enumerated powers give him far greater power, as he is able to exercise powers alone while congressional powers often require supermajorities and bipartisanship, which are difficult to achieve.
- In foreign policy, there are significantly fewer powers that Congress has to hold the president accountable, and those that it does have are significantly weaker than its domestic powers.
- The constitutional powers of Congress are largely reactive, being able only to confirm or deny the president's choices, and in some cases being circumvented entirely.
- In times of united government, Congress is less likely to use its powers to try and limit the president, allowing him considerable power.
- In times of national crisis requiring a swift response, Congress often acts with deference to the president who, as a singular executive, can act quickly. This often gives the president large grants of power.

executive order and his recess appointments deemed unconstitutional. Equally, however, the Court upheld Obamacare and made same-sex marriage effectively legal across the whole of the USA during his time in office. These successes can hardly be attributed to the president but they do affect the relationship these two branches have in the media.

Justice Kennedy, known as the 'swing' justice on the Supreme Court, announced his retirement in 2018. This gave Trump the unusual opportunity to move the ideology of the Court, by replacing Kennedy with a justice who holds a more right-wing ideology.

Debates of the US presidency

The imperial presidency

In 1973, Arthur Schlesinger Jr. wrote a book entitled *The Imperial Presidency*, in which he discussed the growing power of the president and the lack of effective checks by Congress on this power. Today, a president is often referred to as 'imperial' when attempts by Congress to exercise its constitutional checks are either unused or ineffective. Equally, if a president is able to evade congressional checks, for example through executive orders or agreements, this too could be termed an **imperial presidency**.

By contrast, however, a president who finds it difficult to exercise his constitutional powers and appears to be weak is often known as '**imperilled**'. Such a president can also be referred to as a **lame duck**, although this has both a formal and an informal meaning:

- Formally, a 'lame duck' president is one who is not continuing in office in January, but who still holds office. He may have lost his election for second term, such as George H.W. Bush, or have served two terms, such as Obama. In either case, between the election in November and the inauguration in January, the president is known as 'lame duck' as he holds the office and constitutional powers but not the electoral mandate.
- Informally, 'a lame duck' president has come to mean one who is weak and cannot exercise his powers effectively at any point in his presidency.

George H.W. Bush and Barack Obama both formally became lame ducks following the elections in the November before they left office

It is unlikely that any president could be referred to as 'imperial' or 'imperilled' for the entirety of his presidency. The factors explored above help to explain how the powers of the president fluctuate over the course of his term in office.

A president's power can often be inferred from their poll ratings. Popular presidents tend to be more powerful, while less popular presidents find it more difficult to exercise power. Trump's low approval ratings after 100 days and 1 year help to explain the difficulties he has experienced in achieving his legislative agenda.

The president and foreign policy

As head of state, and given the constitutional powers a president has, there are a number of ways in which he has seemingly more power and fewer checks in foreign policy than in his domestic roles. This too, however, is subject to the fluctuations in presidential power over the course of a presidency. George W. Bush had huge amounts of power to involve the USA in wars in the Middle East in 2001 and 2003. However, the declining popularity of these wars, and of Bush himself, meant that Congress was increasingly willing to try and exercise control over this area by the end of Bush's term in office.

The president can attempt to control foreign policy by exercising a range of his powers:

- The creation of treaties, although these are Senate-confirmable. He could circumvent this by using executive agreements.
- The reception of ambassadors, now interpreted as the president's right to recognise nations.
- The appointment of US officials to control foreign policy. While cabinet officials such as the secretary of defense are subject to Senate approval, appointments such as the national security adviser are not. All of these officials have notable power in controlling foreign policy.
- The role of commander in chief, which has seemingly usurped Congress' power to declare war. While Congress has tried to remedy this using the power of the purse and Authorizations for Use of Military Force (AUMF), ultimately it has struggled to use this to prevent action. The War Powers Resolution has been viewed as unconstitutional by presidents since 1973 and therefore not successfully enforced.
- As the head of state, the president often finds Congress acting with deference in times of emergencies. Similar to Ford's quote regarding '535 commanders in chief', Congress allows considerable presidential freedom of action in response to a crisis, such as 9/11. By the time it tries to reclaim its power, the damage is often done.

For more powers, see page 452.

Congress can, however, endeavour to control foreign policy using its own powers:

- Using its powers over appropriations to fund or defund military action. In 2007, Democrats attempted to defund the Iraq War.
- The issuing of an AUMF, such as for the Iraq War, to secure its role in authorising military action even if it is not formally declaring war.
- It ratifies treaties and presidential appointments. When a president attempts to circumvent these powers, Congress protests and works to make headlines. The Senate did this with Obama's Iran Nuclear Deal, which Congress not only demanded a say on, but also attempted to time-limit his negotiations.
- Congress can use its legislative power to try and control foreign policy. Congress passed laws preventing President Obama allowing Syrian refugees and the release of Guantánamo Bay detainees on to US soil, thwarting the president's plans.

Synoptic link

In organised systems of government, one branch rarely acts alone. As the US president is accountable to Congress, the UK prime minister is held to account by both the houses of Parliament despite their dominance in at least the House of Commons. For more on the relationship between UK branches of government see pages 223-26. This links to Component 2, UK Government.

Who controlled the US response to the Syrian government's use of chemical weapons in 2013?

The presidency

- Obama addressed Congress from the Rose Garden, laying out his belief in the necessity of a US response and expressing his power as commander in chief.
- Obama's defense secretary, Chuck Hagel, approved plans for the use of Tomahawk missiles against Syria. They simply needed the order to fire from ships that were positioned near Syria.
- At the G20 summit in Russia, Obama tried to get other world leaders to support his proposed action in Syria, using his power as a global leader and representative of the USA.
- The information that was supplied to Congress regarding the situation in Syria was largely provided by the executive branch, even sending members to Congress to give evidence, all of which supported the president's belief in the need for action.
- Obama chose not to call Congress back into session following his Rose Garden speech, and once negotiations with Syria had begun, he called on Congress to postpone its vote.
- After a diplomatic outcome, Obama stressed publicly his willingness to act militarily if necessary.

Congress

- In the Rose Garden speech, Obama said he would allow a congressional vote to ensure full accountability for action.
- While Speaker Boehner expressed support for the military plans, he made it clear that it was Obama's responsibility to secure the votes in Congress.
- The limited action promised by Obama and the promise to not deploy soldiers reflects the long shadow cast by the Iraq War. Public opinion against this war and the short election cycle in Congress restricted the options available to Obama in this situation.
- The Senate Foreign Relations Committee held hearings on military intervention in Syria. Giving evidence, Secretary of State John Kerry again ruled out 'boots on the ground', meaning the deployment of soldiers. The committee eventually approved intervention in Syria by 10 votes to 7.
- Members of Congress were given classified briefings in preparation for a congressional vote.
- Support for military action among members of Congress was low, potentially explaining Obama's call to postpone the vote and avoid an embarrassing defeat.

Outcome: After the US threat of military action, the Syrian government responded aggressively. However, the intervention of Russia led to the Syrian government handing over its chemical weapons to Russia, while stating this was not due to US threats of military action. Following this, Syria began the process of joining the UN Chemical Weapons Convention and the destruction of its chemical weapons.

Comparisons with the UK

Comparative theories

Table 19.13 Comparing the US and the UK executives using comparative theories

Rational comparisons	• In order to advance their own policy goals, both executives can use a range of formal and informal powers — powers of patronage, removing cabinet officers, powers of persuasion • The prime minister is the head of his or her party and therefore able to advance their own goals using their party. The president serves as a de facto head of his party, thereby allowing him to expect his party in Congress also to advance his policy goals • To preserve and be able to exercise the political power given to them, executives must act in such a way as demonstrates and secures their ability to control politics in their country. This means that potentially success and failure (for example, military action) may be decided on the basis of the possible impact for the executive • The prime minister is often in a personally stronger position, usually commanding a majority in Parliament, and therefore has more freedom to act as they wish than the president, who often carries responsibility alone

Cultural comparisons	• Presidents and prime ministers are the individual focus of the electoral system in each country (even when they are not directly elected) and there is an expectation that they are powerful individuals who can control their executive branch
	• The role of the cabinet in both countries is a focus of media attention and considered to be a reflection on the head of the executive
	• The powers that either executive can gain are often a result of the media attention, poll ratings and unofficial powers that they can assume. This is especially true when considering the head of state and head of government roles, which are not clearly delineated
Structural comparisons	• The powers that each executive has are strongly determined by the constitutions and political processes of their country — theoretically giving the president a bigger list of powers, but in reality allowing great power of the prime minister through the likely majority as a result of the electoral system
	• The direct election of the president lends a stronger mandate to him than the indirectly elected office of the prime minister
	• The differing roles of head of state and head of government are a result of the different political systems used in each country

Comparing the US president and the UK prime minister

The US president and the UK prime minister have quite starkly differing roles, to some extent borne out of the vastly differing personal mandate that they hold and the different constitutional roles they are subsequently allocated. The president is directly elected and therefore holds a personal mandate, whereas the prime minister is the leader of the winning party in the House of Commons. This, however, gives the prime minister a legislative advantage of being able to dominate the legislature, both through having fused powers but also through controlling party discipline in the majority party. The president, while the figurehead of his party, may find himself facing a Congress controlled by the opposition party. Even when it is controlled by his own party, he may find that the members are more loyal to their constituents, given that they can be removed in primaries, than they are to him. The primary system also means it is difficult to enforce party discipline, further weakening the president's control over this branch of government.

These relationships cannot be predicted, however. Both Boris Johnson and Donald Trump have faced unprecedented and similar problems in trying to exercise their executive power, for entirely differing political reasons.

Accountability to the legislature

This too changes over the course of an election cycle in both the UK and the USA. However, there are a number of similar mechanisms by which an executive is held accountable:

- The passage of legislation, even when forced through, is subject to scrutiny and amendments by both houses of each legislature.
- Both legislatures are finding, and looking for, ways in which to have some greater control over foreign policy. When David Cameron gave Parliament a vote on action on Syria, Obama followed suit, suggesting he would offer Congress a vote, although this never came to fruition.
- The actions of both governments can be subject to investigations launched by the legislature.

Table 19.14 Similarities and differences between the US president and the UK prime minister

	Similarities	Differences
Head of state	• The role of commander in chief rests in theory with both the prime minister (through royal prerogative) and the president, although the legislatures in both countries have become more assertive in trying to challenge this role • Both act as the representative of their respective countries to the world, attending summits and conferences, brokering treaties and visiting foreign nations • Both the prime minister and the president carry out some, although increasingly limited, ceremonial duties	• The president is the head of state in the USA, while the monarch formally holds this role in the UK • Commanding a majority in the House of Commons means the prime minister should be able to easily gain approval for any treaty, accord or similar plan, whereas the president's treaties are subject to Senate approval. His actions to circumvent this power often come in for criticism • The president has far more exclusive powers than would usually be associated with a head of state, such as the power of the pardon and the veto. These powers, where they exist at all in the UK, are exercised by the monarch, for example the posthumous pardon of Alan Turing in 2013
Head of government	• Both are able to make nominations to their cabinet departments • Both address the legislature with an annual legislative agenda, the president at the State of the Union and the prime minister through the Queen's Speech, which is written by the government • Both are seen as the leader of their respective parties, even if the president does not hold this as a theoretical role • Both can find their respective legislatures a challenge to deal with, the president in the event of losing one or both houses, or due to his poor popularity; the prime minister due to a small majority or the House of Lords • Both have little power over the judiciary but are subject to rulings from it	• The prime minister will usually command a majority in the House of Commons, whereas the president is increasingly likely to face an opposition Congress for at least some of his time in office • The president's cabinet appointments are subject to Senate approval and yet his cabinet is not a collective body. The prime minister, by comparison, has far greater freedom over appointing cabinet secretaries, but their power once appointed exceeds that of US counterparts as they are a collective body • Rulings of the US Supreme Court can strike down presidential action as they are interpretations of the sovereign Constitution. As Parliament in the UK is sovereign, and the prime minister usually maintains control over Parliament, the powers exercised by the Supreme Court are not sovereign
Impact on government	• Both set the legislative agendas for their country, setting out their policy desires and reacting to political circumstances • Both have broad control over foreign policy, including involving their countries in military actions and treaties • Both can be challenged by the other branches of government, or their own cabinet, in trying to pass their own policy • Both have mechanisms by which they can endeavour to control their party and thereby push through their agenda	• The president is able to have a final say over legislation in a way the prime minister is not. Whereas legislation not supported by the prime minister is unlikely to pass, the president can make sure of it • The prime minister is likely to get most of their legislative agenda passed, whereas the president is likely to get only some of his legislative agenda passed • The prime minister is unlikely to face defeats and therefore more likely to lead an 'elective dictatorship'; the president could be either 'imperial' or 'imperilled' • The discipline that the prime minister can bring to bear over the government is punitive — whips and demotions — whereas the president is often restricted to more positive approaches with little in the way of party discipline available • The president is able to make a greater singular impact on the government, reshaping, hiring and firing within the executive branch. While the prime minister retains the ability to reshape the cabinet, its power in post is as a collective body, reducing the PM's singular impact

- Both can ultimately remove the executive, either through a vote of no confidence or through impeachment, although both remain rare.
- Both must retain the confidence of the legislature in order to get their legislative program through.

However, the circumstances of the UK and the USA mean that the extent of accountability does vary:

- The UK prime minister is more likely to command a majority in the legislature and also, given the fused nature of UK government, along with party control over elections, to be able to force things through. Primaries for members of Congress can divide its loyalty, and divided governments for the president have become more common.
- Equally, the extent and effectiveness of many of Parliament's powers depend on the government majority. While the ability of Congress to enforce its powers can vary, the fact that it is protected by the Constitution makes it a much greater threat to the president.
- Finally, the greatly differing length of the electoral cycle allows the prime minister a greater influence as he or she does not have to be so concerned over the opinion of the public. The frequent, short election cycle in the USA can give the effect of the 'permanent election', making Congress more reactive and therefore limiting the influence of the president.

Summary

By the end of this chapter you should be able to answer the following questions:
→ How significant are the constitutional powers given to the president?
→ Are checks and balances placed on the president ultimately effective?
→ To what extent is presidential power limited to the 'power to persuade'?
→ What is the significance of the electoral cycle in determining presidential power?
→ How do the various elements of the executive branch lend power to the president?
→ Can the president control foreign policy?
→ Are the president's powers as head of state or head of government more significant?
→ What are the most significant factors in preventing a president from achieving his aims?

Practice questions

1 Examine the differences between the cabinets of the USA and the UK. (12)
2 Analyse the factors that affect the extent of power exercised by the president and the prime minister. *In your answer you must consider the relevance of at least one comparative theory.* (12)
3 Evaluate the extent to which the main factor allowing for presidential control over foreign policy is the power of commander in chief. *You must consider this view and the alternative to this view in a balanced way.* (30)

20 US Supreme Court and civil rights

The 'powers' of the US Supreme Court, such as they are, are laid out in Article III of the Constitution. Of the three branches of government, the Supreme Court has just 369 words written about it in the Constitution, compared to over 1,000 words for the president and over 2,000 words for Congress. There has been continued historical debate over whether this was because the Supreme Court was an afterthought for the Founding Fathers or because it was intended as the least important branch of government, with no obvious answer.

The power of the Supreme Court today, however, is especially significant when compared to these humble beginnings. In Federalist Paper 78, Hamilton wrote:

> '[the rights of individuals] can be preserved in practice no other way than through the medium of courts of justice, whose duty it must be to declare all acts contrary to the manifest tenor of the Constitution void.'

For some of the Founding Fathers, then, the Supreme Court provided a final check on government, guaranteeing the rights they had lost under King George III. This is a role the Court still holds today, providing a powerful check on congressional law and presidential action.

EQUAL·JUSTICE·UNDER·LAW·

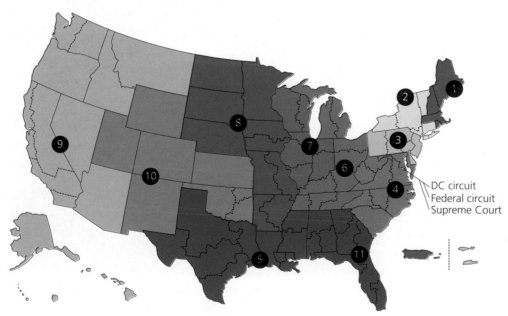

In focus

The Federalist Papers

The Federalist Papers, written by Hamilton, Madison and Jay, were a series of essays encouraging the citizens of New York to ratify the new Constitution in 1787. In Federalist Paper 78, Hamilton remarks about the Supreme Court, 'It may truly be said to have neither FORCE nor WILL, but merely judgement; and must ultimately depend upon the aid of the executive arm even for the efficacy of its judgements', suggesting a branch of more limited power than perhaps is seen today.

The nature and role of the Supreme Court

The Supreme Court and the US Constitution

Almost as soon as the Constitution was ratified, Congress passed legislation to fulfil Article III. In the brief article regarding the judiciary, the Founding Fathers left the infrastructure of the US court systems up to Congress to decide. It therefore passed the Federal Judiciary Act 1789, which allowed for the creation of the Supreme Court as called for by the Constitution, consisting of one **chief justice** and five **associate justices**.

This Act also created the courts that would sit below the Supreme Court — a district court in each state and circuit courts. Today, district courts, of which there are 94, are trial courts which deal with federal matters such as trials involving federal laws or crimes, or constitutional issues. Above them sit the circuit courts, of which there are 13. These are **appellate courts**, meaning courts of appeals. They predominantly hear appeals to the rulings of the district courts.

Key terms

Chief justice The presiding member of the Supreme Court, but who holds no additional voting power to the eight other members of the Court.

Associate justice A member of the US Supreme Court who is not the chief justice.

Appellate court A court of appeals, accepting cases for review from the courts beneath it.

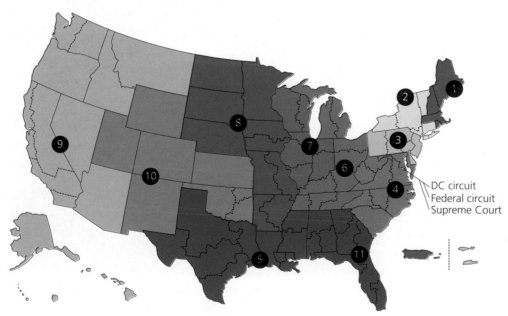

DC circuit
Federal circuit
Supreme Court

Figure 20.1 US district and circuit courts

Figure 20.1 shows the areas over which district and circuit courts have jurisdiction. Each state has at least one of the 94 district courts operating within it; a more populous state might have more than one district court, shown by the dashed lines. The numbers show the 11 circuit courts; in addition, Washington DC has a circuit court and there is one federal circuit court, making a total of 13. The Supreme Court sits above all of these courts.

The Supreme Court is also an appellate court, hearing appeals to the rulings made by the circuit courts. According to the Constitution, it also has **original jurisdiction** in certain cases. 'Original jurisdiction' is the right for a case to be heard in the first instance by the Supreme Court, without going through lower courts. For the Supreme Court, this means cases involving public ministers, two or more states, citizens of different states, or the USA. These kinds of cases are rare, with the Court having heard fewer than 200 since its creation. Most of the work of the Court is therefore created through hearing appeals from lower courts.

The number of cases that the Supreme Court hears each year has, however, been declining in recent times (Table 20.1), and continued to do so in 2017 and 2018. Today, the Court receives between 7,000 and 8,000 cases a year, of which it will hear only around 1%. As the Court can decide which cases it wishes to hear, most cases referred to it will be 'disposed of'. There is no right to have a case heard by the Supreme Court.

> **Key term**
>
> **Original jurisdiction**
> The right of the Supreme Court to be the first court to hear a case in certain circumstances, rather than a case needing to be an appeal.

This cartoon from *Puck* in 1885, captioned 'Our overworked Supreme Court', depicted the huge caseload being sent up to the Supreme Court from the lower courts. To try to reduce the workload of the Court, the Judiciary Act 1891 established the nine circuit courts, the US Courts of Appeals, to hear cases from the lower courts

Table 20.1 Supreme Court cases, 2012–17

Year	Cases sent to the Supreme Court	Cases argued in front of the Supreme Court	Cases disposed of (meaning the Supreme Court will not hear it)
2012	8,806	76	7,647
2013	8,850	77	7,547
2014	8,066	75	7,006
2015	7,535	70	6,506
2016	7,334	68	6,258
2017	7,390	83	6,192

Independence of the Supreme Court

The Constitution also aimed to make the Supreme Court independent, appearing to follow Montesquieu's advice that 'there is no liberty if the judiciary power be not separated from the legislative and executive'. There are a number of ways in which this is achieved:

- Justices are appointed for life, meaning the president or Congress cannot simply remove them if they make decisions that they do not like. This is especially important given the numerous comments made by differing presidents expressing their displeasure at voting habits of a justice they appointed. Truman declared that 'whenever you put a man on the Supreme Court, he ceases to be your friend', referring to two of his own appointees voting against him in a Supreme Court decision.
- Vacancies on the Supreme Court are only available if a current justice dies, retires or is impeached. While technically the Constitution allows Congress to change the number of justices, it has been nine since the Judiciary Act 1869. This prevents the other branches of government packing the Court with their allies.
- The Constitution prevents the salary of the justices being lowered during their time in office, protecting them from the desires of Congress and the president. In 2018, Supreme Court associate justices were paid $255,300, while the chief justice was paid $267,000. With their salary being fixed, the justices do not have to be concerned over repercussions from the president or Congress if they vote against them in a case.
- While justices are nominated by the president, the Constitution requires the Senate to approve their appointment to prevent one branch from dominating the Supreme Court and filling it with those of a similar ideology to them. It also means that the Court has an air of legitimacy, being appointed by elected representatives, but is protected from the whim of public opinion.
- Separation of powers protects the Court's independence by granting it its own power. Judicial review allows the Supreme Court to check the power of the president and Congress, while the Court itself has no power to enforce its decisions. It is therefore reliant on the other branches to carry out its decisions, making the three branches of government independent but codependent.
- The American Bar Association rates the suitability of each of the justices nominated. As industry experts rather than politically motivated, the members of the ABA help to ensure that the Court is composed of people who understand and carry out the letter of the law rather than the will of their party.

Synoptic link

The independence of judiciaries is crucial to their operation and to ensuring the power of government can be limited. The UK Supreme Court has independence guaranteed in a similar manner to that of the US Supreme Court despite the difference in the basis for its power. For more detail, see pages 215–18. This links to Component 2, UK Government.

Judicial review The power of the Supreme Court to judge actions of the presidential branch or acts and actions of Congress against the Constitution. The Supreme Court can declare these acts or actions 'unconstitutional' and therefore make them 'null and void'.

Judicial review

The Constitution allows for the power of the Supreme Court to 'extend to all cases, in law and equity, arising under this Constitution, the laws of the United States, and treaties made, or which shall be made'. Beyond this, Article III is remarkably vague. It certainly makes no mention of the power of **judicial review**. Judicial review is the power of the Supreme Court to review the laws or actions from Congress and the president and declare them unconstitutional. In doing so, these laws or actions become null and void, meaning they are no longer enforceable as they contradict the US Constitution. This power, however, is effectively taken by the Court itself, as seen in the cases of *Marbury* v *Madison* (1803) and *Fletcher* v *Peck* (1810).

In focus

Marbury v *Madison* (1803)

Shortly after its creation, the Supreme Court heard two cases in which it would grant itself the power of judicial review.

As President Adams prepared to leave office in 1801, allowing Thomas Jefferson to take over, Adams appointed a number of men to positions within the courts. Once Jefferson took office, he found that the commissions for some of these men had not been delivered and told his secretary of state, James Madison, not to allow their delivery. William Marbury, to whom one of these commissions had been promised, challenged Madison over this action in the Supreme Court. The Supreme Court, while finding in favour of Marbury, also found that it did not have the power to force the issue of his commission, ruling that part of the Federal Judiciary Act 1789 conflicted with the Constitution and was therefore unconstitutional. This was the first use of judicial review over a federal law.

> 'IT IS EMPHATICALLY THE PROVINCE AND DUTY OF THE JUDICIAL DEPARTMENT TO SAY WHAT THE LAW IS.'

The above excerpt from the *Marbury* v *Madison* ruling has become one of its most quoted lines, in which Chief Justice John Marshall effectively grants to the Supreme Court the power of judicial review over federal issues.

Fletcher v *Peck* (1810)

Just 7 years after *Marbury* v *Madison* came a second landmark case — *Fletcher* v *Peck*. In this case, the Supreme Court further extended its power of judicial review. The case arose out of a dispute over a law passed by the Georgia state legislature in 1795, which allowed for the sale of 35 million acres of land. Most of this land was sold to just four companies at a bargain price. It soon became apparent, however, that many of the Georgia legislators involved in creating and passing the law had been bribed. Following public outcry, the legislature repealed this law in 1796 and removed the land from those who had bought it.

The dispute between Fletcher and Peck came about over the issue of whether land that had been acquired under the 1795 Act could be legally sold on. Fletcher had purchased 13,000 acres of land from Peck in 1803. Fletcher then discovered that the land he had bought had originally been part of the 1795 sale that had been repealed. Fletcher therefore brought charges against Peck, claiming he had lied to him over the land.

The Supreme Court decided that the repeal of the 1795 law by the Georgia state legislature was unconstitutional. More importantly, this was the first time the Supreme Court ruled against a state law, extending its power of judicial review to state law as well as federal law.

The power of judicial review is really the only power the US Supreme Court holds today. It is, however, an important one. In deciding whether an Act or action is unconstitutional, the Supreme Court justices are responsible for interpreting the meaning of the Constitution. Additionally, as they are interpreting the sovereign document of US politics, their decisions on the meaning of the Constitution are effectively final — the only way to overturn a Supreme Court decision would be to change the document itself. It is so difficult to pass a constitutional amendment, however, that this has happened only once, with the 16th Amendment. As the future Chief Justice Charles Hughes Evans said in 1907, 'We are under a Constitution, but the Constitution is what the judges say it is.' The power of judicial review is therefore a significant one, and the cause of much conflict in US politics, both between the branches of government but also regarding how much power unelected and therefore unaccountable justices should be allowed to wield.

The appointment process for Supreme Court justices

While the Supreme Court is independent from the president and Congress, both of these branches of government play a significant role in shaping the Court. Congress not only controls the infrastructure of lower courts, but it also sets the number of justices on the Supreme Court. Since the Judiciary Act 1869, this has been one chief justice and eight associate justices. Constitutionally, the president must nominate justices for the Senate to either confirm or reject. The appointment process is shown in Table 20.2.

Table 20.2 Stages in the appointment process for Supreme Court justices

Stage	Explanation	Examples
Vacancy arises	A vacancy on the Supreme Court can only arise through death, retirement or impeachment of a current Supreme Court justice	• Death — Justice Scalia died in April 2016 and Chief Justice Rehnquist died in 2005, both while holding seats on the Supreme Court • Retirement — Justice Kennedy announced his retirement in June 2018 • Impeachment — the only Supreme Court justice to face impeachment was Samuel Chase in 1805, but he was found not guilty
Presidential nomination	The president can choose whomever he likes to fill a vacancy. It is expected, however, that the nominee will have judicial experience and will be able to pass the Senate vote. They are also likely to share the president's ideology and he may consider the Court's demographic too	• Bush and Trump both nominated justices who were likely to be conservative in their rulings (Roberts, Alito, Gorsuch and Kavanaugh), while Obama appointed those with a likely liberal outlook (Sotomayor and Kagan) • Bush also nominated Harriet Miers, who had previously worked with him but had no experience as a judge • Douglas Ginsburg withdrew his nomination in 1987 after allegations surfaced of smoking marijuana as a student
ABA rating	Not a constitutional requirement, but the American Bar Association (ABA) offers a rating of 'unqualified', 'qualified' or 'well qualified' for judicial nominees, in its professional opinion	• All but one of the current justices on the Court hold a 'well qualified' rating • Justice Clarence Thomas was only deemed to be 'qualified'. This, along with allegations of sexual harassment, made it very difficult for Thomas to be confirmed by the Senate
Senate Judiciary Committee hearings	Also not a constitutional requirement, the Senate Judiciary Committee holds hearings in which it can question the nominee. At the end of the hearings, the committee holds a vote. As it is not constitutional, this vote serves only as a recommendation to inform the whole Senate vote	• During the hearings of both Brett Kavanaugh in 2018 and Clarence Thomas in 1991, allegations of sexual misconduct were levelled at nominees. The committee was evenly split 7–7 on whether to recommend Thomas • Robert Bork was rejected by the Committee 9–5, and subsequently faced defeat in the full Senate vote • Kagan's hearings included humorous exchanges regarding where she spent her Christmas
Senate floor vote	Following the recommendatory vote from the Senate Judiciary Committee, the whole Senate must vote to confirm an appointment. Following the 2017 reforms, this vote can no longer be filibustered and requires just a simple majority	• Robert Bork was rejected in 1987 by a 42–58 vote • Clarence Thomas was narrowly approved to the Supreme Court by a 52–48 vote in 1991 • The votes of all nominees since 2006 have been dominated by party politics, compared to votes confirming justices such as Ruth Bader Ginsburg in 1993, who was confirmed 96–3

The appointment of Brett Kavanaugh

The unexpected retirement of Justice Anthony Kennedy was announced in June 2018. In his first 2 years, it appeared that Trump was going to be able to appoint two justices to the Supreme Court. The first, the appointment of Neil Gorsuch, had courted controversy as he replaced Antonin Scalia, who had died in April 2016 and whom President Obama had nominated Merrick Garland to replace. Garland's appointment was held up by the Senate, however, and nearly a year after Scalia's death Gorsuch was appointed.

The nomination to replace Kennedy would equally court controversy. In replacing Scalia with Gorsuch, the president had replaced a conservative justice with another conservative. Kennedy, however, was known as the 'swing justice' — the informal title for the justice who sits in the ideological centre of the nine. By comparison, Kavanaugh would become one of the most conservative justices on the Court and the resulting Court would be considerably more conservative in its outlook.

This made the appointment of Kavanaugh of great political interest and the events of his confirmation only highlighted, and in some cases added to, the controversy. During Kavanaugh's appointment process, allegations came from Professor Christine Blasey Ford that she had been sexually assaulted by Kavanaugh while at college. This was all the more significant given the #MeToo campaign of the preceding year. In addition to the ideological controversy, the appointment process became embroiled in these accusations. Protests took place inside and outside of Congress, as well as across the nation and in the constituency offices of members of Congress. Interest groups such as pro-choice NARAL lobbied against Kavanaugh and organised protests while media headlines and speculation abounded around the globe about the suitability of Kavanaugh's appointment.

- **10 July 2018** Kavanaugh is nominated to the Supreme Court by President Trump
- **31 August 2018** The American Bar Association issues a rating of 'well qualified' for Kavanaugh
- **4–7 September 2018** Senate Judiciary Committee hearings are held — these are dogged by protests in the committee room and accusations of sexual assault by Kavanaugh on Professor Christine Blasey Ford
- **17 September 2018** The Senate Judiciary Committee announces the nomination will not proceed until interviews of both Ford and Kavanaugh have been conducted
- **20 September 2018** The original date planned for the vote of the Senate Judiciary Committee is postponed

- **24 September 2018** Kavanaugh appears alongside his wife in an interview with Fox News denying all allegations against him
- **27 September 2018** Both Ford and Kavanaugh appear to give evidence before the Senate Judiciary Committee
- **28 September 2018** Committee member Senator Flake is caught on camera in Congress being confronted by survivors of sexual assault, challenging his support of Kavanaugh. On the same day, Kavanaugh is approved by the committee 11–10 and Trump orders an FBI investigation into the allegations
- **4 October 2018** The FBI delivers its findings to the Senate Judiciary Committee
- **6 October 2018** The Senate approves Kavanaugh's appointment 50–48, with just one Democrat voting for him; all other Democrats vote against him and all Republicans vote for him. Republican Lisa Murkowski opposes the appointment but abstains as a Republican colleague who would have voted for the appointment is absent attending his daughter's wedding
- **8 October 2018** Kavanaugh is sworn in as the 114th justice of the US Supreme Court

Over 200 protestors were arrested during the Senate hearings, with more arrests when protesters occupied the offices of Republican senators on the days after allegations of sexual assault were levelled at Kavanaugh.

Following the evidence session on 27 September, Kavanaugh was ridiculed for the anger he showed and the evidence he offered. American comedy show *Saturday Night Live* opened with a 13-minute sketch of the evidence sessions, mocking Kavanaugh. That a primetime show dedicated so much time to such a sketch speaks to the cultural impact of this process and the politicisation and political ramifications of the appointment process.

The Senate Judiciary Committee hearings into Kavanaugh led to protests both inside and outside of Congress

Presidential considerations for a judicial nominee

When a vacancy arises on the Supreme Court, the president has a number of factors to consider when choosing his nominee:

- **Judicial experience** It is expected that the nominee should have experience as a judge and be qualified in law. This was one of the key reasons that the nomination of Harriet Miers was criticised in 2005. The ABA lends the president support in this area, by rating candidates as 'well qualified', 'qualified' or 'unqualified' for the role. The only current member of the Supreme Court who was not serving on the circuit courts when appointed is Elena Kagan, who was the solicitor general for President Obama.
- **The outgoing justice** Often the president may be expected to replace a justice on a 'like-for-like' basis in terms of ideology. Certainly, these types of nominations are less likely to face extreme opposition in the Senate. However, neither Alito nor Kavanaugh can be claimed to be like-for-like replacements, both being considerably more conservative than their predecessor.
- **The demographics of the Supreme Court** A president may wish to widen the representative nature of the Supreme Court through his appointments. Obama appointed two women, doubling the number that have ever served on the Court, and appointed the first ever Hispanic person to the Court, Sonia Sotomayor.
- **The ideology of the nominee** Almost all nominees are qualified in law and usually have been a judge on a lower court. From the rulings they have made, it is possible to try and ascertain what their ideology is and whether it fits with the president's. This is not always successful but it would be rare for a president to be entirely wrong. Even in the case of Anthony Kennedy, he remained a conservative, just a moderate one. It may also be that the president listens to advice from those close to him. Kavanaugh appeared on a list of the right-wing think-tank the Heritage Foundation before Trump nominated him.

The current Court

Key term

Swing justice A justice who is in the ideological middle of the nine justices on the US Supreme Court.

While the role of the judiciary is to be neutral, in interpreting the Supreme Court it is possible to see the ideology of an individual justice. It is unlikely that a justice would describe themselves as 'conservative' or 'liberal'; however, some of the rulings they make can be categorised in this way. The justice who is placed ideologically in the middle of the nine is commonly referred to as the '**swing justice**'. In cases which seem to have an ideological split on the Court, the majority decision is often a result of which way the 'swing justice' votes. Anthony Kennedy has been the swing justice since the appointment of Samuel Alito to the Court in 2006. Before this, however, it was Sandra Day O'Connor who sat ideologically in the centre of the Court, while Kennedy was on the conservative wing. This highlights the shifting ideological nature of the Supreme Court.

The current Supreme Court includes justices who have been appointed by the last five presidents. This raises concern over the power they hold when the justices are appointed for life, yet the president who appointed them has long since lost his political mandate

The current composition of the Court is detailed in Table 20.3.

Table 20.3 The make-up of the US Supreme Court, 2019

Justice	Role	Year	Length of nomination process	ABA rating	Senate Judiciary Committee vote	Senate floor vote	Ideology
Roberts	Chief justice	2005	62 days	Well qualified	13–5	78–22	Conservative
Thomas	Associate justice	1991	99 days	Qualified	7–7	52–48	Conservative
Bader Ginsburg	Associate justice	1993	42 days	Well qualified	18–0	96–3	Liberal
Breyer	Associate justice	1994	73 days	Well qualified	18–0	87–9	Liberal
Alito	Associate justice	2006	82 days	Well qualified	10–8	58–42	Conservative
Sotomayor	Associate justice	2009	66 days	Well qualified	13–6	68–31	Liberal
Kagan	Associate justice	2010	87 days	Well qualified	13–6	63–37	Liberal
Gorsuch	Associate justice	2017	65 days	Well qualified	11–9	54–45	Conservative*
Kavanaugh	Associate justice	2018	91 days	Well qualified	11–10	50–48	Conservative*

* The ideology of these two has yet to be substantiated through their decisions on the Supreme Court

The length of the process

The process from nomination to Senate ratification takes between 2 and 3 months, sometimes longer. While this is not a problem if the vacancy has been caused by a retiree who is willing to remain on the Court during the process, it is more problematic when the process is caused by a death (or, in theory at least, by an impeachment). In this case, the Court would be left with only eight justices. In the event of a tie, the ruling of the Court from which the case was appealed would stand.

When Obama's executive order regarding DAPA (see Chapter 19) was challenged in the Supreme Court, the death of Antonin Scalia meant there were only eight justices to hear the case. The 4–4 tie resulted in Obama's executive order being struck down. Had he been able to appoint Merrick Garland to the Court, perhaps Garland would have voted with the 'liberals' on the Court and Obama's policy would have been saved. The same is true of Anthony Kennedy retiring in the summer of 2018. With Kavanaugh not confirmed until 8 October, the first week of the 2018 Supreme Court term was sat with just eight justices.

The length of the process, however, helps to ensure that candidates undergo vetting and that they are suitable for the post on the Supreme Court. Harriet Miers' withdrawal from the process was in part due to the critical reaction given to her lack of experience as a judge, with it therefore being unlikely that she would make it through the rigorous process. Given the power that judicial review gives to the Court, it is vital that the justices selected are deemed to be appropriate. The appointment process allows plenty of time for this as well as involving the expertise of a variety of bodies.

Politicisation of the process

The Constitution, and indeed the works of Montesquieu, recognised the importance of an independent Supreme Court. However, with the president nominating justices, and the Senate confirming them, the process has, predictably, become politicised. The appointments since 2006 have seen party-line votes in the Senate, with relatively few defections across the aisle. As Table 20.5 shows, those nominees put forward by Republicans have been supported by Republicans and opposed by Democrats, and vice versa. This has been irrespective of the qualifications of the candidates presented.

Table 20.5 Recent appointments to the Supreme Court

Justice	Year	Nominating president	Senate votes for		Senate votes against	
			Republicans	Democrats	Republicans	Democrats
Roberts	2005	Bush (R)	55	22	0	22
Alito	2006	Bush (R)	54	4	1	41
Sotomayor	2009	Obama (D)	9	59	31	0
Kagan	2010	Obama (D)	5	56	36	1
Gorsuch	2017	Trump (R)	51	3	0	43
Kavanaugh	2018	Trump (R)	49	1	0	48

Beyond the votes, the role of the Senate Judiciary Committee can also be questioned. During the hearings of Alito, Sotomayor, Kagan and Gorsuch, the nominees only spoke for an average of around 33% of the time over the 4 days of hearings. The rest of the time was taken up with senators talking. Given that the aim of the nomination process is to determine the suitability of a candidate, its success can be questioned when the nominee is speaking for such a relatively short time.

The president also plays a role in politicising the process. Presidents invariably try to pick someone with an ideology that aligns with their own. This is not always successful.

- Anthony Kennedy was a Ronald Reagan nominee to the Supreme Court. Having had the two previous nominees for this seat either defeated (Robert Bork, in part due to concerns over him being too conservative) or withdrawn (David Ginsburg), it was important that Reagan's next nominee be approved. In his time on the Court, Kennedy has proven to be a moderate, often voting with both the liberal and conservative wings of the Court in defiance of Reagan's own conservatism.
- Theodore Roosevelt said of his own appointment, Oliver Wendell Holmes Jr., 'I could carve out of a banana a judge with more backbone than that' after Holmes voted in a way with which Roosevelt disagreed.
- Eisenhower referred to his appointment of Chief Justice Earl Warren as 'the biggest damned-fool mistake I ever made' as Warren had been far more liberal than Eisenhower had anticipated, being responsible for some notable liberal rulings including the decision of *Brown* v *Board of Education of Topeka* (1954).

Stretch and challenge

The appointment of Sonia Sotomayor

'I would hope that a wise Latina woman with the richness of her experiences would, more often than not, reach a better conclusion than a white male who hasn't lived that life.'

This quote from Sotomayor, given in a 2001 lecture, appeared and caused controversy in her appointment process in 2009. It also spoke to her belief that having greater representation on the Supreme Court would be of benefit.

Why did this quote cause controversy? What does the quote suggest about Sotomayor's view of the role of the Supreme Court? What type of justice would such a view make Sotomayor?

In focus

Supreme Court packing plan

The power of the Supreme Court frustrated President Franklin D. Roosevelt in the 1930s. In attempting to deal with the economic depression that followed the Wall Street Crash, Roosevelt introduced the New Deal plan between 1933 and 1936. The Supreme Court, however, struck down various aspects of his plan as unconstitutional. In 1937, Roosevelt introduced the Judicial Procedures Reform Bill. The key aspect of this legislation was that it would allow the president to appoint an additional justice for each justice currently aged over 70 on the Court. With six sitting justices over the age of 70, this would have allowed Roosevelt to appoint six new justices. This was viewed as a way for him to 'pack' the Court

with those favourable to his New Deal legislation. The bill did not pass, however; in yet another Supreme Court case regarding the New Deal, one justice switched his support to the side that favoured the president, making the legislation unnecessary. After hundreds of days of being held up, the legislation ultimately failed.

The *Washington Post* had been highly critical of Roosevelt's 'court packing plan', which it saw as damaging the independence of the Court. Justice Roberts' switching sides in the *West Coast Hotel* v *Parrish* case became known as 'the switch in time that saved nine' — protecting the relative independence of the nine justices on the Court.

The role of the media and pressure groups also serves to politicise the process. The media circus that surrounds the nomination process has grown in recent years. The volume of protests against the nomination of Brett Kavanaugh, and the extent of media coverage that they garnered, underlined just how political appointments have become. During the appointment of Neil Gorsuch, donors to the Judicial Crisis Network gave $10 million to support his appointment, having given $7 million to oppose the appointment of Merrick Garland a year earlier. Even the role of the ABA can be questioned in this manner. It has no constitutional standing and its members are unaccountable, yet their rating of a candidate can have a huge effect on the chances of that candidate.

Despite this, arguably the politicisation is defensible, given the unelected and unaccountable nature of the Supreme Court. The only mandate justices could claim to have is that they were appointed by the representatives in two branches of government which they had elected. This lends them legitimacy in their role, meaning that even the more controversial decisions that the Court has made have been enforced by the other branches of government.

The Supreme Court and public policy

Public policy is simply the policy created by federal government, whether by creating new laws or through executive actions. As the Supreme Court is interpreting the Constitution, which is sovereign, its rulings are effectively sovereign. This gives it considerable power and influence over the policy that government creates, either by upholding it, striking it down or, in some cases, choosing not to hear a case at all. In each of these possibilities, the outcome could be that a Supreme Court ruling allows an existing policy to continue, removes a policy, or in some cases even creates new policy.

Table 20.6 Some recent Supreme Court rulings and their impact

Policy area	Case/s	Ruling	Impact
Elections and election spending	Citizens United v FEC (2010)	Some provisions of the Bipartisan Campaign Reform Act violate the 1st Amendment	The ruling created a new policy allowing for the development of Super-PACs, which could raise unlimited amounts for campaigning, by striking down part of a law from Congress. It was heavily criticised by President Obama at the 2010 State of the Union address, but still enforced
	McCutcheon v FEC (2014)	Caps on individual spending violates the 1st Amendment	The ruling lifted the 'aggregate cap' which limited the total amount an individual could spend in an election. It left intact a limit on how much can be contributed to an individual campaign, but removed the limit on the number of campaigns contributed to
Healthcare	NFIB v Sebelius (2011)	The individual mandate functions as a tax and therefore is within Congress' power to levy	The ruling upheld Obamacare, allowing it to continue. The law was already in place by this point, however, so the Court merely upheld a law already in existence. This decision only narrowly passed, with the four liberal justices joined by the chief justice
	King v Burwell (2015)	Subsidies for healthcare can be given to those enrolled in state healthcare exchanges or federal healthcare exchanges	The argument in the case was whether subsidies were available for those in the federal healthcare exchange. If the Court had decided 'no', it would have reduced federal subsidies by $29 billion and made healthcare unaffordable for many. In ruling 'yes', the Court upheld the key principles of Obamacare
Environment	Michigan v Environmental Protection Agency (EPA) (2015)	The EPA must consider the cost implications of enforcing the Clean Air Act, rather than simply the need to regulate	This ruling by the Supreme Court limited the interpretation allowed by the executive branch when enforcing legislation. Rather than simply regulating for Clean Air, the EPA now had to consider whether the costs could be justified, undermining Obama's environmental policy

Table 20.6 lists some areas of public policy on which the Supreme Court has ruled. There are other areas of public policy too, such as abortion, LGBTQ rights, gun control, immigration and capital punishment; these are all dealt with later in this chapter.

- In some of these cases the effect of the Supreme Court ruling is to create a new policy — *Citizens United* v *FEC* (2010) allowed for the development of Super-PACs, which would previously have been impossible due to the Bipartisan Campaign Reform Act, also known as the McCain-Feingold Act. This therefore allowed nine unelected justices to have a substantial role not only in shaping the policy surrounding elections in the USA, but also in overturning a law created by elected representatives, deeming that it conflicted with the Constitution.

- Equally, the Court can have a huge impact by upholding legislation or policy. In the two healthcare cases, the Court ruled in favour of Obamacare. This allowed the continued enforcement of this legislation, but also lent a degree of sovereignty to the law, with the Supreme Court ruling that it was within the bounds of the Constitution.

- Finally, the Court can have an impact on public policy in choosing not to hear a case. In doing so, if the case has been heard by a lower court, then the ruling of that court stands. In 2018, the Supreme Court refused to hear the case of *Planned Parenthood of Arkansas* v *Jegley*, which challenged Arkansas' strict regulation of medically-induced abortion which made it very difficult to obtain the 'abortion pill' and would have left the state with one abortion provider. In refusing to hear the case, the Supreme Court allowed this law to come into force in Arkansas, thereby shaping public policy through its inaction.

The Westboro' Baptist Church protested at the funerals of soldiers killed in action. Their protests, while controversial, were deemed to be protected under the 1st Amendment

The Supreme Court and protection of rights

Key term

Constitutional rights The rights that are explicitly identified within the Constitution and its amendments.

The rights that are protected in the Constitution are known as '**constitutional rights**'. These are by no means the only rights that a US citizen may have, as the federal or state government will have passed laws to give them additional rights, such as the driving age, drinking age and age of consent. However, the Supreme Court can only rule on those for which it can find a constitutional basis because the only role the Court has is to interpret the Constitution. Given the vague nature of the Constitution, the Court has been able to rule on a considerable range of rights over time, supporting abortion, same-sex marriage and gun rights, to name but a few.

The most notable protection of rights in the Constitution comes in the Bill of Rights. This is the first ten amendments to the Constitution, ratified all together in 1791. Subsequent amendments have added more rights to this, and Supreme Court interpretation of all of these amendments has served to protect, extend or, in some cases challenge, individual rights (Table 20.7).

Table 20.7 Amendments to the Constitution concerning rights

	Right	Case	Ruling	Impact
1st Amendment	Free speech	*Snyder* v *Phelps* (2011)	Free speech in public, even if considered offensive or causing emotional distress, is not limited	This 8–1 ruling protected free speech, even though the 'free speech of the Westboro' Baptist Church' was highly controversial. Alito, in dissent, disagreed with the ruling, saying, 'Our profound national commitment to free and open debate is not a license for the vicious verbal assault that occurred in this case'. That the only dissent was from a conservative justice demonstrates that justices consider the constitutionality of a case rather than merely their own personal ideology
	Religion	*Burwell* v *Hobby Lobby Stores* (2014)	The government (or Obamacare) cannot require employers to provide insurance cover for birth control if it conflicts with the religious beliefs of the employers	All three female justices dissented in this ruling, claiming that it limited women's rights. While the ruling only applied to a specific type of company, called 'closely held', this type of business makes up more than 90% of American businesses
2nd Amendment	Gun control	*D.C.* v *Heller* (2008)	There is a right to individual gun ownership without a connection to a militia, and for use in the home for self-defence	This was one of the first major gun control cases taken up by the Court in recent years, striking down a 1975 Act by the District of Columbia. However, the Court also ruled that the 2nd Amendment, or this ruling, was not a 'right to keep and carry any weapon whatsoever in any manner whatsoever and for whatever purpose'
		Chicago v *McDonald* (2010)	The right to keep arms for self-defence is also applicable to the states, as well as federal government law	The ruling clarified the *D.C.* v *Heller* ruling, which applied to Washington D.C., which is not a state. The justices in the majority also used the 14th Amendment to justify their decision

	Right	Case	Ruling	Impact
		Caetano v *Massachusetts* (2016)	The Court ruled that the Amendment extends to 'all instruments that constitute bearable arms, even those that were not in existence at the time of the founding'	After being arrested for possession of a stun gun, Caetano's case ended up in the Supreme Court under the 2nd Amendment. This shows a considerable interpretation of what is meant by 'arms'
4th Amendment	Searches	*Carpenter* v *U.S.* (2018)	To acquire cell phone location data amounts to a 4th Amendment search and therefore a warrant is required to access it	In a digital age, this is one of the first landmark cases that the Supreme Court has ruled on regarding privacy. It was notable also as a 5–4 decision in which four liberal justices — Bader Ginsburg, Breyer, Sotomayor and Kagan — were joined by Chief Justice John Roberts, a conservative
5th Amendment	Right to silence (Miranda rights)	*Berghuis* v *Thompkins* (2010)	A suspect simply remaining silent in an interrogation does not invoke their 5th Amendment right to silence	This ruling said that staying silent was not the same as invoking the right to remain silent. For some, this was seen as a challenge to the Court's 1966 ruling on *Miranda* v *Arizona*, from which the 'Miranda rights' come
		Salinas v *Texas* (2013)	Remaining silent before being read your Miranda rights can be used as evidence in a court of law	Having willingly answered police questions, a suspect of murder fell silent when asked about his shotgun. He had not been read his Miranda rights, so the police used this silence as evidence of guilt. The Supreme Court agreed, building on the case 3 years earlier and further eroding the Miranda rights
8th Amendment	Capital punishment	*Glossip* v *Gross* (2015)	Lethal injection using midazolam does not violate the 'cruel and unusual punishments' outlawed in the 8th Amendment	Following the botched lethal injection of Clayton Lockett 1 year earlier, Glossip argued this method of capital punishment was against the 8th Amendment. Lethal injection had already been upheld in *Baze* v *Rees* (2008) but many other Supreme Court cases placed limitations on the use of capital punishment
14th Amendment	Women's rights	*Whole Woman's Health* v *Hellerstedt* (2016)	The requirements placed on abortion centres by Texas law H.B. 2 were an 'undue burden' and therefore unconstitutional	The ruling was notable for the Supreme Court continuing to uphold the 1973 decision in *Roe* v *Wade* but also for overturning a law of a state, challenging the principles of federalism
	LGBTQ rights	*Obergefell* v *Hodges* (2015)	The right to marry is guaranteed to same-sex couples by the 14th Amendment	This ruling furthered the 2013 ruling of *United States* v *Windsor*, before which same-sex marriage was legal in only 12 states. This ruling made same-sex marriage legal in all 50 states, overturning law in 12 remaining states in which it was outlawed

Synoptic link

The strong link between the Supreme Court and the protection of rights is not necessarily reflected in the politics of the UK. There, it is more common to expect the legislature to protect rights; as Parliament is sovereign in the UK, the UK Supreme Court lacks the power that the US Supreme Court has. This links to Component 2, UK Government (see pages 219–22).

The effectiveness of rights protection

The role of an independent and neutral judiciary in protecting rights is crucial to any liberal democracy. Free of accountability to the public, such a judiciary can rule to ensure the protection of rights for all. However, the extent to which it is effective at doing this is the subject of debate.

- In a number of cases, while the rights of one group may be protected, this may be to the detriment of another. In the case of *Obergefell* v *Hodges*, the rights of the LGBTQ community were protected while the religious rights of people like Kim Davis, a clerk in Kentucky, were arguably infringed. Davis refused to issue marriage licences to same-sex couples, saying it violated her religious beliefs. She was briefly jailed for this by a district court in Kentucky, which demonstrates the impact of rulings from the Supreme Court. Conversely, in *Burwell* v *Hobby Lobby*, the religious rights of employers were placed above the rights of women.

- There is also a debate about how much power the Supreme Court actually has to protect rights. The Court hears only about 1% of the cases put to it in any year. This means the cases of the vast majority of people who may feel their rights have been infringed will never be heard by the Supreme Court. In June 2018, the Court declined to hear an appeal from a florist who had refused to make an arrangement for a same-sex couple, referring it back to the lower court. In doing so, it shied away from involvement in this controversial issue, arguably leaving the rights of some people unprotected.

Protests outside the office of Kim Davis

- Additionally, the Court has no power to enforce its rulings. Instead, it relies on the power of the president and Congress, or the states, to enforce its decisions. Controversial decisions that a president has not liked have still been enforced, such as *Citizens United* v *FEC*. However, in other cases the rulings of the Court appear to have been circumvented or ignored. In the four cases regarding Guantánamo Bay between 2004 and 2008, the Court always found in favour of the detainees. Yet the fact these cases kept coming back to the Supreme Court highlights the weakness of its ruling. In this case, Congress even passed a new law, the Military Commissions Act, to try and work around a ruling. This Act then also had to be struck down.
- Ultimately, all judicial action from the Supreme Court is bound by the Constitution. It may find it difficult to protect rights as its rulings have to be rooted in the wording of this document. In the case of *Snyder* v *Phelps*, the actions of the Westboro' Baptist Church may have appeared insensitive to the rights and feelings of the grieving family, but the Constitution clearly protects the right of free speech. In this case, it becomes difficult for the Court as it can only rule by interpreting the Constitution.

Nonetheless, a majority of the cases heard by the Supreme Court are those of significant constitutional impact, allowing the Court to use its power broadly to try and protect rights. It is unlikely that a ruling of the Court would be overtly ignored or unenforced, given the weight of importance attached to the Constitution. That it is ruling based on the document which forms the foundation of all rights in the USA gives it considerable influence in any political debate. The vagueness of the Constitution also allows a good deal of breadth in the Court's interpretation, allowing it to use the Constitution to protect rights even when they are not explicitly identified — both the right to an abortion and the right to same-sex marriage have been protected in this way. The effectiveness of the Court in this area can be challenged through the use of examples, but there are far more which suggest it has been largely effective.

The Living Constitution and originalism

In protecting rights, or indeed deciding any case before it, the Supreme Court may only use the US Constitution to judge against. In doing so, how it treats the US Constitution and how it believes it should be interpreted is crucial to the decisions it will make.

- Justices who believe that the Constitution is a living, evolutionary document believe in interpreting the words written within it more widely in the context of modern society and expectations.
- Justices who believe in 'originalism' see the meaning of the Constitution as fixed at the time of its writing, at least for judicial interpretation. They believe that it does not evolve and interpreting it as such undermines the principles codified within it by the Founding Fathers.

It is important to note that both those who believe in the 'Living Constitution' and those who believe in 'originalism' often believe that the Constitution should evolve in some way. However, for 'living constitutionalists', this can be done by the judiciary, whereas for 'originalists' this should be done through politically accountable elected branches. It is also possible to see a justice appearing to favour broader interpretation in one case, but a stricter interpretation in another.

How should the Constitution be interpreted?

As a 'Living Constitution'

- The Constitution will quickly become out of date if it is not interpreted in the light of modern developments, for example the changing beliefs on slavery or LGBTQ rights.
- Elected and accountable branches often favour the will of the majority and therefore interpretation of the Constitution can ensure minority rights are also protected.
- The Founding Fathers could not have envisaged the world which exists today and some of the words in the Constitution are meaningless without interpretation. For example, the Founding Fathers were not writing about semi-automatic rifles in the 2nd Amendment.
- The amendment process is too difficult to allow the development of the Constitution through elected branches of government.
- The principles of the Constitution can be upheld despite the wording of the document.

In an 'originalist' manner

- Interpreting the Constitution makes the Supreme Court an inherently political institution, undermining its independence and ability to check the other branches of government.
- Changes required can be left to the elected and therefore accountable branches rather than risking the misinterpretation of the original principles of the Constitution.
- People are accountable for their actions according to the law. If this law is constantly evolving and changing, it is not possible for them to know what the law is until after a judge has decided.
- The amendment process exists and has been used successfully; this is the method through which amendments should come about.
- The principles of the Constitution are not relevant. The Founding Fathers wrote the Constitution, using words and text to demonstrate meaning, and it is this meaning which should be adhered to.

An originalist interpretation

In the decision of *District of Columbia* v *Heller* in 2008, Justice Antonin Scalia wrote:

> 'The Second Amendment provides: "A well regulated Militia, being necessary to the security of a free State, the right of the people to keep and bear Arms, shall not be infringed." In interpreting this text, we are guided by the principle that "[t]he Constitution was written to be understood by the voters; its words and phrases were used in their normal and ordinary as distinguished from technical meaning." Normal meaning may of course include an idiomatic meaning, but it excludes secret or technical meanings that would not have been known to ordinary citizens in the founding generation.'

What is Scalia suggesting about the work of the Founding Fathers and the nature of the US Constitution? Given the codification of the US Constitution, what are the dangers of interpreting the document beyond the meaning advanced by Scalia?

Judicial activism and judicial restraint

In all of the cases above, the role of judicial ideology is crucial. The debate over what role the Supreme Court should have in US government stems from the unelected and unaccountable nature of the Court. This has led to two definitions being created for how justices act — 'activist' and 'restrained'.

Activism

According to President Obama, 'an activist judge was somebody who ignored the will of Congress, ignored democratic processes, and tried to impose judicial solutions on problems instead of letting the process work itself through politically'. Any justice on the Court could therefore be activist. It does not matter whether they are considered to be conservative or liberal, if they are ruling in such a way that gives a judicial solution to a problem, rather than letting Congress or the president to solve it, they are 'activist'.

- **Liberal activism** *Obergefell* v *Hodges* is a good example of liberal judicial activism. It essentially created a new policy under which same-sex marriage was legal nationally. This ruling ignored the laws of 13 states in which same-sex marriage was not allowed, but also struck down the congressional law known as DOMA, or the Defense of Marriage Act. The Court therefore overruled both state- and federally elected officials. In creating this right for the LGBTQ community nationally, the Court embodied liberal ideals of protecting rights.
- **Conservative activism** *Citizens United* v *FEC* similarly shows activism from the conservative justices. It too overturned at least part of a congressional law, the McCain-Feingold reforms. In allowing money to be seen as a form of free speech, this fits in with more conservative ideals which embrace meritocracy and a reduction in government interference in individuals' lives. Having earned the money, the individual should be free to spend it as they see fit. It is also notably an 'activist' decision as it directly contradicts a Supreme Court case from just 7 years earlier which ruled the opposite.

Restraint

Judicial restraint is when a justice sees their role on the Supreme Court in a far more limited fashion. They would believe that where possible they should allow the policy created by Congress and the president to stand. They are also more likely to look to past Court decisions to guide their current decision making. This is a principle known as **stare decisis** or 'let the decision stand'. This is based on the view that a neutral and independent Court, interpreting the same Constitution, should reach the same decision. Therefore, past Court cases should set precedents for current cases.

- **Liberal restraint** *Whole Woman's Health* v *Hellerstedt* demonstrated a continuing defence of the 1973 decision of *Roe* v *Wade*, which initially established a woman's right to an abortion. Cases on abortion have been heard since then, and while some have placed limitations on it, or allowed individual states to decide on those limitations, the unwillingness of the Court to overturn this decision remains.
- **Conservative restraint** *Glossip* v *Gross* builds on previous cases to allow the continued use of lethal injection. The case suggested that prisoners could only challenge the method of execution by providing an alternative method of execution. The Court argued it was the responsibility of the prisoner to demonstrate that the execution method caused severe pain, not the responsibility of the state.

> **Key term**
>
> **Stare decisis** A judicial principle meaning 'let the decision stand'. It means that justices should refer to, and where possible adhere to, previous Court rulings when making their decisions.

Criticisms of both judicial activism and judicial restraint are listed in Table 20.8.

Table 20.8 Criticisms of judicial activism and judicial restraint

Criticisms of judicial activism	Criticisms of judicial restraint
• The Supreme Court is unelected and is therefore unaccountable for the decisions that it makes • Allowing the Supreme Court to strike down Acts of Congress and actions of the executive branch, with only limited checks on its own power, breaches the separation of powers • Allowing the Supreme Court to strike down state laws ignores the constitutional principle of federalism and the differences that exist across the USA • The Court can overrule its own decisions, even when the Constitution has not changed, suggesting that the Court is acting politically rather than neutrally • Judicial review interprets the Constitution, meaning there are few effective checks on the Court's power as constitutional amendments are so difficult to pass	• If the Supreme Court defers to elected branches of government, this might allow laws and policies which directly contravene the Constitution to stand • Given the frequent election cycle, elected branches often shy away from dealing with controversial policy issues or focus only on the will of the majority. The Supreme Court is therefore the only branch that can deal with controversial issues or minority rights without fear of public reprisals • The codified Constitution would be outdated if the Supreme Court were not willing to interpret it with reference to modern issues • The power of judicial review, while not explicit in the Constitution, could be implied. The Court should therefore act to limit the government as the Founding Fathers intended

Checks and balances

The relationship of the Supreme Court with the other branches of federal government is governed by fewer checks and balances than the relationship between the president and Congress. The Supreme Court's only power is judicial review and while this allows it to strike down Acts of Congress or actions of the president, it hears only around 80 cases a year. The president's power to appoint justices is dependent on a vacancy occurring, something he cannot control. Congress could in theory alter the number of justices, or pass a constitutional amendment to overturn a Court decision, but both seem unlikely — the last time the number of justices changed was 1869 and the only time a constitutional amendment has been used in this way was with the passage of the 16th Amendment in 1913. The formal relationship between these branches, therefore, is far more limited than between the president and Congress.

However, this relationship is not without tension. The power of judicial review can create questions over the legitimacy of Court decisions, given the Court's unelected nature. President Obama expressed anger at the Court numerous times during his presidency, notably after the rulings regarding campaign finance and his DAPA executive order. The same is true of Congress. In 2018 the Supreme Court struck down aspects of the Voting Rights Act 1965, stating that 'our country has changed in the past 50 years'. However, while it left open the possibility of Congress passing legislation to recognise the changing political circumstances, the chance of Congress being able to do so was very limited in this partisan era. Senator Schumer recognised this difficulty, saying: 'make no mistake about it, this is a back door way to gut the Voting Rights Act'.

This tense relationship has followed decisions which have not given the outcome either the president or Congress desired. In contrast, the Court has supported and even extended the powers of these branches of government. In historic cases such as *Gibbons* v *Ogden* (1824), the Court redefined Congress' power according to the commerce clause and reinforced the extent of Congress' power, saying:

'this power, like all others vested in Congress, is complete in itself, may be exercised to its utmost extent, and acknowledges no limitations, other than are prescribed in the Constitution.'

More recently, in upholding President Trump's 'travel ban', the Supreme Court decision noted that 'the proclamation is squarely within the scope of presidential authority'.

The Supreme Court and Guantánamo Bay

Table 20.9 identifies the key cases heard by the Supreme Court over the issue of detention at Guantánamo Bay. Each time, the Court ruled against the president and for the detainees. However, each time either Congress or the president tried to find a way around these rulings. This highlights the tension between the branches of government and also the limits on the power of the Court.

Table 20.9 Cases heard by the Supreme Court over the issue of detention at Guantánamo Bay

Policy area: foreign policy/due process		
Case	Ruling	Impact
Rasul v *Bush* (2004)	Foreign detainees in Guantánamo can petition the federal government for habeas corpus, reviewing the legality of their detention	The British men involved in this case were transported to the UK before the decision was handed down
Hamdi v *Rumsfeld* (2004)	Detainees held in Guantánamo Bay have a right to due process	Hamdi was released without charge following the ruling. He was then deported to Saudi Arabia on the condition of giving up his US citizenship
Hamdan v *Rumsfeld* (2006)	Using military commissions to try detainees in Guantánamo Bay was unconstitutional, as were congressional Acts or presidential actions authorising them	The detainees could still be tried but must be tried by a court. It led to the passing of the Military Commissions Act 2006 as a reaction by the president and Congress to authorise the use of military commissions in Guantánamo Bay, thus overcoming the Supreme Court ruling. This became the focus of the 2008 case
Boumediene v *Bush* (2008)	Detainees in Guantánamo Bay have a right to try their cases in the US courts, and the Military Commissions Act 2006 was unconstitutional	This not only struck down a congressional Act, but also asserted the Court's right to rule over presidential actions in this policy area

In focus

Guantánamo Bay

Guantánamo Bay detention camp was established by President George W. Bush in 2002. It is located on the coast of Cuba. Suspected terrorists were held here in the wake of the 9/11 terrorist attacks. However, the rights of its detainees has caused controversy. Many of them are not American and they are not held on US soil. This has meant that indefinite detention, military trials and even torture have been a feature of this camp. The situation has led to considerable tension between the executive branch (looking to protect the interests of the nation) and the Supreme Court (looking to uphold the Constitution).

An imperial judiciary?

A similar debate over the Supreme Court is whether it is '**imperial**' or not. While the debate over the Court being political or judicial (below) is about its *role*, this debate is about its *power* — these two debates should not be confused or conflated. For example, that the president and Congress have a role in appointing justices has no bearing on the power of the Court, but is hugely important for discussions on the political nature of the Court. For the Supreme Court to be considered 'imperial', like the 'imperial presidency', this would mean that the Court is subject to few effective limits and has broadly unchecked power. Unlike the presidency, however, the nature of this debate is far less dependent on polls and national circumstances.

Debate

Is the Supreme Court an 'imperial judiciary'?

The Court is 'imperial'

- The Court is unelected, able to make decisions with huge impact on US government and citizens, and yet is almost entirely unaccountable.
- While justices can in theory be impeached, this process has never been used to remove a justice and only ever been used at all once, in 1805. This further advances the unaccountable nature of the Court.
- The Court's power of judicial review often amounts to the final say on any issue as it is so difficult to overturn a decision. The use of constitutional amendments to achieve this has only occurred once, in 1913.
- These decisions can also overturn the laws and actions from branches which are not only accountable, but have a mandate from the people to carry out these actions.
- These decisions have gone far beyond the original text of the Constitution and created entirely new rights, with the Court having broad powers to interpret the Constitution.
- Despite only being able to hear a limited number of cases each year, the fact that 8,000 cases are annually brought to the Court allows it a vast choice on what it wishes to rule upon.

The Court is not 'imperial'

- The Court has no way to enforce its own rulings and is entirely dependent on other branches of federal government or states to enforce its rulings or, in some cases, effectively ignore its rulings.
- The Court cannot choose cases to investigate which have not been brought before it. Even if there are Acts or actions which it considers unconstitutional, it must await a case before being able to rule on it.
- The Court's rulings can be overturned if necessary and the 16th Amendment shows that it is possible to achieve this.
- The Court has often shied away from hearing cases in which public opinion is closely divided, such as gun control cases.
- The Constitution provides the single biggest limit on the Supreme Court. Regardless of the justices' personal or political opinions, cases and decisions must be rooted in the Constitution. Even with the power to interpret this, they can only interpret what is there.
- Justices are subject to the threat of removal as they only hold their offices during times of 'good behaviour'. This should prevent justices from acting in a reckless manner.

The role of the Supreme Court

The *role* of the Supreme Court should be simply judicial — acting neutrally and with guaranteed independence, it should act merely as interpreter of the law with respect to the Constitution. However, the Court's decisions invariably have political actions. Furthermore, its decisions seem to be politically rather than judicially motivated. So, is the Supreme Court a political or a judicial body?

The Supreme Court — judicial or political?

Judicial

- The Supreme Court can only take cases with a constitutional basis and make decisions on the wording of the Constitution. The justices' personal political opinions are therefore irrelevant to the decision-making process.
- Members of the Court have legal rather than political expertise. Almost all of them have come from circuit courts and even Elena Kagan's political experience was within the Justice Department.
- The Court lacks any power to enforce the decisions it makes. Only Congress and the president, the directly elected branches of government, can enforce the decisions. The Court decisions must therefore be seen to be legitimate for them to be enforced.
- Usually upwards of two-thirds of cases are decided by a majority of more than five justices. As the Court is broadly divided into 'liberals' and 'conservatives', this suggests the justices must be basing their decisions on something other than their personal opinion. There have been numerous cases where, even in controversial and landmark decisions, a justice has seemingly voted against their known personal ideology in a case decision.
- The Court adheres to legal principles such as *stare decisis*, which helps to lend legitimacy to the decisions it makes.

Political

- The impact of many rulings is inherently political, striking down actions or acts of the elected branches of government or even, in the rare case of *Bush v Gore* (2000), effectively deciding who will be the next president.
- The appointment process to the Supreme Court is inherently political and seems to be getting more so. Since 2006, appointment votes have been more obviously divided on party lines, and the nominations of Garland and Kavanaugh were particularly contentious.
- Justices can be identified, and subsequently labelled, as 'liberal' or 'conservative', depending on which side of major decisions they align with. That it is possible to do this suggests the actions of justices are politically rather than judicially motivated, given that they are all interpreting the same evidence and the same Constitution yet reaching different conclusions.
- The Court accepts **amicus curiae** briefs — these are documents written to the Court from pressure groups trying to influence the outcome. That groups do this suggests they must believe it has some impact, but it also politicises the role of the Court.
- The Court appears to shy away from hearing some of the more controversial cases, such as a lack of gun control cases or unwillingness to hear cases about gerrymandering, suggesting its recognition of the importance of public opinion.

Race and rights in contemporary US politics

The history of race rights in the USA has often been controversial. From the three-fifths compromise in the Constitution, to the Civil War, to modern-day **affirmative action** policies, minority groups in the USA have often found they have not had the freedoms afforded to them that were afforded to their white counterparts.

Calls for **racial equality** have led to substantial changes within this policy area over time, through legal, legislative and public action.

Key terms

Affirmative action A policy that allows minority groups to be intentionally advantaged in order to begin to correct historic disadvantages.

Racial equality The idea that all races should be regarded and treated equally and be given the same legal, moral and political opportunities.

Figure 20.4 shows the total percentage of minorities in the USA according to the census. Projections into the future show that by the middle of the twenty-first century, minority groups will together make up more than half of the US population. The two biggest minority groups are African Americans and Hispanics.

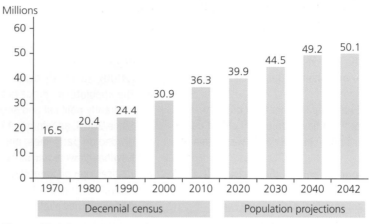

Figure 20.4 Percentage of minorities in the USA, 1970–2042

The timeline in Figure 20.5 shows major landmarks in the advance of rights for African Americans. It is difficult to trace a similar timeline for the Hispanic population. The fight for African Americans' rights revolved around slavery and its abolition. Hispanics have no such rallying cause and therefore the fight for their rights has been characterised by debates over immigration and citizenship.

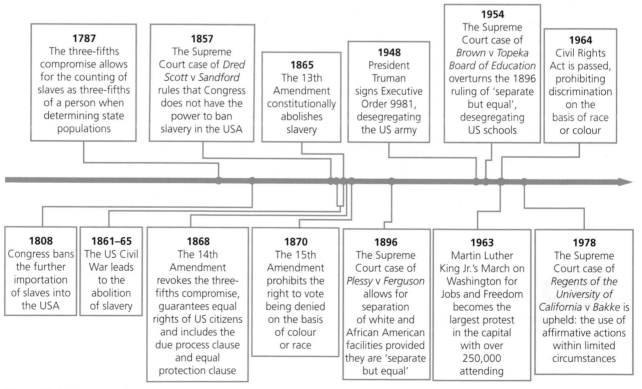

Figure 20.5 Changing African American rights

Methods of achieving change

Regardless of the minority group, the methods used to advance rights are similar. Even over time, these methods have not changed extensively. Still today, mass protesting and bringing Supreme Court cases are used to achieve change, just as they were decades ago. That these methods are still needed today gives an indication that inequality is still a part of everyday life for many Americans.

Legal action

Groups trying to effect change can and have used the US legal system in a number of ways.

- Groups themselves can bring cases to be heard before the Supreme Court. The Coalition to Defend Affirmative Action, Integration & Immigrant Rights, and Fight for Equality By Any Means Necessary (or BAMN, 'by any means necessary', for short) brought a case in 2014 challenging a ban on affirmative action in Michigan.
- Individuals can also bring such cases, but the rulings can have a wide-ranging impact. Cases on affirmative action in education and university admissions have been heard and reheard by the Supreme Court from *Brown* v *Topeka Board of Education* in 1954, to *Fisher* v *University of Texas* in both 2013 and 2016.
- Change can also be attempted through the use of amicus curiae briefs. Minority groups can submit their opinions to the Supreme Court for consideration in their cases. More than 60 amicus briefs were filed in the case of *Trump* v *Hawaii* (2018) regarding the 'travel ban', including briefs from large groups such as the National Association for the Advancement of Colored People (NAACP) and individuals such as Khizr Khan, the father of a Muslim US army captain who had been killed in action in Iraq.

Mass demonstrations and direct action

Mass demonstrations are organised to try to achieve change by showing politicians the weight of public opinion. In a representative democracy, where elected officials are dependent on the public vote for their job, such protests encourage politicians to listen in order to gain votes. Even smaller-scale direct action can achieve this by raising the media profile of a movement with a view to winning public sympathy. The March on Washington for Jobs and Freedom in 1963 was famed not only for being one of the largest ever protests in the capital, but also famously is the demonstration at which Martin Luther King Jr. gave his I Have a Dream speech:

> 'Nineteen sixty-three is not an end, but a beginning. Those who hope that the Negro needed to blow off steam and will now be content will have a rude awakening if the nation returns to business as usual. There will be neither rest nor tranquility in America until the Negro is granted his citizenship rights.'

This march was followed by King and others meeting with the president, and ultimately helped ensure that the Civil Rights Act 1964 and Voting Rights Act 1965 were passed.

The March on Washington for Jobs and Freedom, 1963

This method is still used today, often for very similar causes.

- The Black Lives Matter movement held a number of protests after the deaths of young African American men at the hands of the police.
- The Hispanic community led protests against Trump's executive order separating families.
- The 2018 Women's March drew more than 500,000 people to Washington to protest against President Trump and to fight for women's rights.

Methods such as these are often characterised as 'mass movements'. Direct action involving fewer people has also been successful in raising the profile of issues, from Rosa Park's Montgomery bus protest to the interruptions in the Senate committee room during the appointment process of Brett Kavanaugh.

Equally, groups fighting for equality may use more formal methods such as the annual conferences of pressure groups. The National Council of La Raza (now UnidosUS) dubbed Obama the 'deporter-in-chief' at its annual conference in 2014, having been disappointed by the more than 2 million people his administration had deported since taking office.

Media and social media

In the modern age, the development of technology has allowed for pressure to be placed on those in power through more indirect methods. The use of Twitter allowed for the growth of notable movements, with #BlackLivesMatter beginning on here, and the #MeToo campaign gaining considerable attention using this medium. It has also aided in the organisation of mass protests such as the Women's March in 2017 and provided a free platform to show the turnout and aims of these movements.

Affirmative action

Affirmative action first appears as a phrase in President Kennedy's Executive Order 10925, which required government contractors to 'take affirmative action to ensure that applicants are employed, and that employees are treated during employment, without regard to their race, creed, color, or national origin'. There is no singular 'affirmative action' policy, rather it allows for the traditionally disadvantaged groups to be provided with additional advantages to try and create a more equal society, whether this is through the use of race in university admissions or the use of 'busing', which transported children to schools further from their home to try and ensure schools were not racially segregated.

In the twenty-first century, affirmative action has increasingly been the subject of scrutiny, however (Table 20.10). Chief Justice John Roberts commented in 2007 that 'the way to stop discrimination on the basis of race is to stop discriminating on the basis of race', suggesting that affirmative action could itself be considered a discriminatory policy.

Table 20.10 Cases heard by the Supreme Court over the issue of affirmative action

Case	Ruling	Impact
Schuette v Coalition to Defend Affirmative Action (2014)	The ban on affirmative action in the Michigan state constitution was not unconstitutional	The immediate impact was limited, reversing a lower court decision but upholding the Michigan state constitution's ban. It was, however, one of an increasing number of cases challenging the legitimacy of affirmative action as a policy
Fisher v University of Texas (2013 and 2016)	Fisher I (2013) — The Court ruled that while race could be a consideration in university admissions, a court would need to confirm this was 'necessary' (also known as 'strict scrutiny') Fisher II (2016) — The Court found that the University of Texas admissions policy met the requirements of 'strict scrutiny'	The ruling of Fisher I, contrary to some fears, did not strike down affirmative action, but rather adhered to the principle of stare decisis, upholding the 2003 decision in Grutter v Bollinger which allowed the use of race as one factor in university admissions. However, Scalia's dissenting opinion said he would have overruled this decision if asked Fisher II upheld the use of affirmative action for university admissions. Kennedy, as the author of the majority decision, cited an amicus curiae brief in his decision, showing the importance these can have

Stretch and challenge

A study in failure: the Supreme Court or the policy of affirmative action?

The case of *Brown* v *Topeka Board of Education* in 1954 ordered schools to desegregate on the basis that they were not 'separate but equal' as demanded by the 1896 case of *Plessy* v *Ferguson*. In 2016, a federal judge ordered a school district in Mississippi to desegregate the schools in its area as it had so far failed to. The Cleveland school district in question had used policy measures to allow segregation and did not have much will to prevent segregation despite the Supreme Court ruling. In 2016 a judge ruled:

'The delay in segregation has deprived generations of students of the constitutionally-guaranteed right of an integrated education. Although no court order can right these wrongs, it is the duty of the District to ensure that not one more student suffers under this burden.'

What does this case study suggest about the power of the Supreme Court in protecting rights? Does racial equality amount to legal equality, or are there other factors to be considered?

Immigration reform

The immigration system in the USA has been the subject of numerous presidential elections. President Obama failed to achieve immigration reform through Congress, passing neither the DREAM Act nor the 'Gang of Eight's' bipartisan Border Security, Economic Opportunity, and Immigration Modernization Act 2013, which would have reformed the immigration system and given undocumented immigrants a pathway to citizenship.

He therefore turned to the use of executive orders to achieve at least some reform. Deferred Action for Childhood Arrivals (DACA) in 2012 allowed illegal immigrants who met certain conditions to remain in the USA free from the fear of deportation. Obama extended this in 2014, expanding the conditions of DACA and introducing the Deferred Action for Parents of Americans (DAPA). Together these offered protection from deportation for 11 million undocumented immigrants in the USA. It did not, however, offer them a path to citizenship. However, with key aspects of this struck down in 2016, immigration in the USA remains a highly contentious issue, especially since the election of President Trump.

With Trump's promise to 'build a wall' and increase the funding for border security, his approach to immigration has been criticised. His 2018 State of the Union address, however, like that of many of his predecessors, talked extensively about immigration reform, planning to give undocumented immigrants a pathway to citizenship alongside his more conservative policies restricting family-based immigration.

Table 20.11 details some recent Supreme Court rulings in the area of immigration.

Table 20.11 Cases heard by the Supreme Court over the issue of immigration reform

Policy area: immigration		
Case	Ruling	Impact
Texas v *U.S.* (2016)	The Court split 4–4, which meant the ruling of the lower court stood, which struck down Obama's DAPA executive order	President Obama had little success achieving immigration reform through Congress during his time in office, and this ruling struck down what he had achieved
Arizona v *U.S.* (2012)	The Court struck down key aspects of Arizona's SB 1070 law, striking down the provision that immigrants must carry registration documents because it conflicted with a federal law	The law was notable for the clash of state power versus federal power, and in which Arizona was on the losing side. It set the precedent that opportunities for state action over the issue of immigration were limited
Trump v *Hawaii* (2018)	The Court ruled that Trump's so-called 'travel ban' was not unconstitutional and fell within the remit of executive power	Immigration activists had hoped this ruling might curb presidential power in this area and believed it violated the 1st Amendment. The liberal justices on the Court argued this was religiously motivated

Equality

Table 20.12 shows the successes and failures of measures to promote equality.

Table 20.12 Measures to promote equality

Success	Failure
President Obama's Deferred Action for Childhood Arrivals (DACA) and Deferred Action for the Parents of Americans (DAPA) executive orders allowed millions of undocumented immigrants to be free from the threat of deportation	President Obama failed to get any meaningful immigration reform legislation passed, despite bipartisan support in the Senate
Numerous Supreme Court cases have upheld the policy of affirmative action, including *Fisher* v *Texas*	Segregation still remains an issue in the USA due to housing patterns. George W. Bush was accused of racism in 2005 when the federal government responded only slowly to the disaster left by Hurricane Katrina, which overwhelmingly affected the ethnic minority population of New Orleans
The election of President Obama, as well as increasing numbers of ethnic minorities represented in the Supreme Court and in Congress, shows an increasing diversity in government in the USA	The Black Lives Matter movement demonstrates the depth of inequality still felt in the USA
The focus on the growing Hispanic population, including projections that it will make up around 25% of the US population by 2045, has meant an increased attention on minority issues	The state ban on affirmative action in Michigan was upheld in *Schuette* v *Coalition to Defend Affirmative Action* (2014). In states where affirmative action has been banned, the number of ethnic minorities attending college has fallen, despite an increase in the population
Generally, ethnic minority voting turnout has increased over the past two decades, despite a slight drop more recently	The wealth gap in the USA continues to widen between white households and minority households

Representation

Representation of minorities in the federal government has increased in recent years, with more women, Hispanics and African Americans, and more, in Congress and the cabinet. Equally, both 2008 and 2016 saw female candidates on the presidential ballot — Sarah Palin and Hillary Clinton — and President Obama was the first African-American president of the USA. However, while representation has improved, it is far from representative of the demographic make-up of the USA today.

Sarah Palin and Hillary Clinton as comic book heroes in *Female Force*

Some recent Supreme Court rulings in the area of voting rights are surprising, seemingly making it more difficult for people to exercise their voting rights (Table 20.13).

Table 20.13 Cases heard by the Supreme Court on the issue of voting rights

Policy area: voting rights		
Case	Ruling	Impact
Shelby County v *Holder* (2014)	The ruling struck down aspects of the Voting Rights Act 1965, which required areas with historic records of making it difficult for minorities to vote to gain federal clearance before changing their electoral practices	Some states used this ruling to make changes to their voting regulations. North Carolina made it a requirement that photo ID was presented when voting; low-income and minority groups disproportionately lack this ID, making it impossible for them to vote
Husted v *Randolph Institute* (2018)	The ruling allowed Ohio to continue its practice of 'voter caging'. That is if someone has not voted for a while, they are sent a notice through the mail. If this is returned undelivered and the voter does not vote in the next two federal elections, they are struck from the voting register	This could have a huge effect in the 2018 midterms, with people turning up to vote only to find they had been struck from the voting register. It would also hit minority voters far more than white voters according to a brief by the NAACP

Comparisons with the UK

Comparative theories

Table 20.14 Comparing the US and UK judiciary using comparative theories

Rational comparisons	• Justices in both countries are guided by their own personal judicial philosophies. This may include advancing their own political philosophy through their rulings too • Those fighting for rights are often doing so from a point of personal inequality and using whatever access points are available to them to do this • Justices in both countries should be aware of potential legitimacy questions posed by an unelected and unaccountable Supreme Court, and they may therefore act to ensure their own power is protected
Cultural comparisons	• The cultural expectation of the protection of rights is far higher in the USA than the UK • In the USA, there is an acceptance that Supreme Court rulings are a way of informally updating the US Constitution. This is a growing feature of UK Supreme Court rulings • Neither Supreme Court has any power to enforce its rulings; the acceptance of the rulings is therefore largely based on cultural acceptance of the power of each Court even though it is unelected
Structural comparisons	• The power that each Court has is highly determined by the constitutional framework in the country, as is the independence and neutrality of the Supreme Courts • The nature of the justices in both countries is in part determined by the process by which they are appointed to the Supreme Court • The entrenched and codified Constitution in the USA gives a far stronger protection of rights than the statute law which protects rights in the UK

Comparing the US and UK Supreme Courts

Powers of the Supreme Court and the impact on politics and government

The powers of both the UK and US Supreme Court are identical — the power of judicial review. However, the location of sovereignty in each country is vastly different, which affects the impact the Courts can have.

- In the USA, the Constitution is sovereign. As the US Supreme Court is created by the Constitution, and then interprets this document, the rulings that it issues have the effect of being sovereign. This makes them very difficult to ignore or overturn and gives the Court extensive power.
- In the UK, in comparison, sovereignty resides in Parliament. While Parliament may choose to share this sovereignty, it also retains the power to take it back. The UK Supreme Court was only set up by an Act of Parliament, and therefore in theory Parliament retains the power to remove it. Certainly, the Court could be ignored by Parliament given its sovereignty.

The reality of the Courts' power, however, appears to be quite similar.

- While the UK Supreme Court has only been operating since 2009, its role in judicial review and the acceptance of its rulings have become a part of everyday political life. This was evident in the *R (Miller)* v *Secretary of State for Exiting the European Union* case in 2017. Gina Miller's challenge to the government regarding the implementation of Brexit caused huge controversy when the Court ruled that the final say for Brexit had to be given by Parliament, given its sovereignty. Despite outrage and contradictions to this from within the Conservative Party, the Court's ruling was accepted.
- Similarly, rulings of the US Supreme Court have at various times been met with anger and outrage from the president, Congress and/or states. Yet almost always, the Court's rulings are upheld.

Nonetheless, the breadth of impact of the US Court is currently far wider than that of its UK counterpart.

- The UK Court can be overruled by simply passing a new Act of Parliament. Given the fused nature of UK powers, this should not be particularly difficult to do.
- Overturning a US ruling, however, is hugely difficult, effectively granting it more power than the UK Court.
- Equally, the extent of impact on government and policy of the UK Court has so far been more limited than the USA. Some of this is due to the age of the UK Supreme Court and therefore the lack of time it has had to rule on cases.
- This is also due to the more political role of the US Supreme Court. Justices in the USA are more easily divided into 'conservatives' and 'liberals' than UK justices, referencing the impact they have on government policy.

Independence of the Supreme Court

There are notable similarities between the USA and UK that ensure the independence of the judiciary. Both countries allow the justices security of tenure, meaning that they cannot be removed by the executive or legislative branches, except in rare and limited circumstances. In both countries, the Court's independence is also protected through the separation of powers — both Courts have independent buildings, personnel and powers — allowing them to cast decisions over the actions of the other branches without interference. In the UK, however, this separation was not complete despite the Constitutional Reform Act 2005. It left the role of the Lord

Chancellor somewhat unclarified; the holder of this role today acts as the secretary of state for justice, responsible for the funding of the Supreme Court.

However, the vast difference in appointment processes serves to undermine the US Supreme Court's independence far more than in the UK.

- The highly politicised nature of the US appointment process has meant that judicial ideologies have become confusingly political. The UK judges by comparison do not have a high-profile political understanding of their personal ideologies.
- The vast funding differences have also caused controversy. The US Supreme Court bid for an annual budget of nearly $80 million in 2017, which allows it to operate with judicial clerks and relatively free of the concern it may lose money for a decision that is disliked by the government. The UK Court has been mired in difficulty almost since opening, however. The 2017 funding was around just £12 million; Lord Phillips, the first president of the UK Supreme Court, argued that the Court's budget should be ringfenced and not dependent on what the Ministry of Justice felt was appropriate.

The UK Supreme Court building in London, with a statue of Abraham Lincoln in front

Effectiveness of rights protection

The US Supreme Court has a wide ability to protect rights in the USA. Not only can it use the Bill of Rights and subsequent amendments to strike down congressional laws or presidential acts that do not protect rights, it is also able to interpret the Constitution to create new rights. As its rulings have the effect of being sovereign, it is able to exercise considerable power in this area. The UK Court by comparison is less well-established in this role. It does not have the extensive power that the US Court has and therefore the rulings that it issues are easier to circumvent, most simply by the creation of a new Act of Parliament. While this has not happened in any landmark cases, the number of such cases so far in the UK has been far fewer than in the USA.

However, the UK Court has a far greater breadth of law to interpret and protect rights. In the USA, the Supreme Court is to some extent bound by the Constitution.

This can mean that in some cases the Constitution allows for little interpretation, such as in the 2nd Amendment, or in other cases it requires considerable interpretation to be made relevant, such as in the case of *Carpenter* v *U.S.* In the UK, however, the Human Rights Act and Equality Act alone allow the Court a much broader basis to protect rights, let alone the vast array of other statutes that protect rights. Equally, while the US Court is the final court of appeals, UK citizens can also appeal to the European Court of Justice and the European Court of Human Rights, which somewhat limits the significance of the UK Supreme Court.

Effectiveness of interest groups in the protection of civil rights

The key role of pressure groups in trying to protect rights is similar in both countries — they can bring cases or they can try and influence cases, directly or indirectly. The access points available to these groups, both through the judicial process and through the political process more generally, are more numerous and established in the USA. In both countries, however, groups have brought important cases to the Court to challenge their rights; numerous examples are noted above, such as BAMN, Citizens United and Whole Woman's Health. Similar patterns have begun to emerge in the UK, with the Northern Ireland Human Rights Commission challenging the current abortion provision in Northern Ireland or the case of Ashers Baking Company, which was backed by the Christian Institute's Legal Defence Fund.

However, groups in the USA have a greater range of accepted methods of influence over the courts and therefore over the protection of rights. The ABA has a direct influence over which justices get appointed through its provision of a rating, and groups have been active in campaigning for and against the appointment of both Kavanaugh and Garland in recent years. Groups are also well versed in using amicus curiae briefs to try and influence the Court, with Kennedy even referencing one in his authorship of the majority decision in *Fisher* v *Texas* (2016). In the UK, pressure group action in this way is less established.

Summary

By the end of this chapter you should be able to answer the following questions:

→ What is the basis for the power of the US Supreme Court?
→ Has the Supreme Court appointment process become ineffective?
→ To what extent does the Supreme Court control public policy in the USA?
→ What is the significance of judicial activism and judicial restraint?
→ How effectively are the Supreme Court's neutrality and independence protected?
→ To what extent is ideology an important factor in Supreme Court decisions?
→ Has the Supreme Court effectively protected rights in the USA?
→ How far has the goal of racial equality been achieved?

Practice questions

1 Examine the basis of power for the US and UK Supreme Courts. (12)
2 Analyse the ways in which the US and UK Supreme Courts attempt to protect the rights of citizens. *In your answer you must consider the relevance of at least one comparative theory.* (12)
3 Evaluate the extent to which racial equality has been achieved in the USA today. *You must consider this view and the alternative to this view in a balanced way.* (30)

21 US democracy and participation

Since the ratification of the Constitution in 1787, debates have raged over 'democracy' in the USA. The Constitution created a 'republic', not a 'democracy', as Madison wrote in Federalist Paper #10. He argued that a large republic was advantageous as it could guard against the tyranny of the majority by having a significant number of elected representatives. Equally, he argued that the free vote of the people would prevent elections being won through 'vicious arts' and that a large republic would 'render factious combinations [parties and interest groups] less to be dreaded'. In fact the Founding Fathers warned time and again of the perils of parties.

As with so many issues at the Philadelphia Convention, however, the outcome was a result of compromise. So the Electoral College served as a compromise between congressional power and popular sovereignty. The very people who argued against parties became the organisers and leaders of the first US parties.

In a much-misquoted letter of 1816, Thomas Jefferson warned about the role of money to challenge, influence and even subvert government, saying:

> 'I hope we shall take warning from the example [of England] and crush in it's [sic] birth the aristocracy of our monied corporations which dare already to challenge our government to a trial of strength, and to bid defiance to the laws of their country.'

Despite Jefferson's hope, large corporations and wealthy organisations in the twenty-first century exercise considerable influence over the government and voters alike.

Electoral systems in the USA

The Constitution establishes, although does not name, the **Electoral College** as a method for electing the president every 4 years. States were to appoint electors who would vote for the president on behalf of that state. Together, these electors form the Electoral College and the president would be whoever gained a majority of their votes. However, the manner of elections is left to Congress and the states to decide. In 1845, Congress allocated the national Election Day as the first Tuesday after the first Monday in November, but the election that takes place on this day actually amounts to 50 state-wide elections rather than one national election.

The electoral process for presidential election

There is little in the presidential election process, other than Election Day itself, which has a fixed timing. The process itself, however, has developed far beyond the Constitution into an elaborate and lengthy event that begins years before the term for the current president is expired.

Table 21.1 is an overview of the presidential election process and when aspects of it usually occur. It is an arduous, expensive and, at times, highly personal process. Far from being a 'national' process, however, the dates of primaries, rules of elections and allocation of electors are decided by each state, leading to a vast array of electoral rules and processes in each presidential election.

Key terms

Electoral College
A body of people who cast votes on behalf of their states to formally elect the president and vice president of the USA.

Invisible primary The time between a candidate formally announcing their intention to run for presidential office and the first official primary or caucus.

Table 21.1 The presidential election process

	Month	Time until Election Day	Stage of the electoral process
Candidates *within* each party compete to be their party's nominee		18–24 months before Election Day	The **invisible primary**
	February	9 months before Election Day	Early state primaries and caucuses
	March	8 months before Election Day	'Super Tuesday'
	April–June	5–7 months before Election Day	Late state primaries and caucuses
	July	4 months before Election Day	National Party Conventions
The nominated candidates from *different* parties compete against each other	August–October	1–3 months before Election Day	The election campaign, including presidential debates
	November	First Tuesday after the first Monday in November	Election Day!
	December	1 month after Election Day	Electoral College ballots cast
	January	2 months after Election Day	Inauguration of a new president

Key terms

Primary An intraparty election to determine who will compete on the ballot for that party in the presidential election.

Caucus An intraparty town-hall-style meeting in which voters physically exercise their preferences in order to decide who will represent their party on the ballot in the presidential election.

Table 21.2 explains the difference between **primaries** and **caucuses**.

Table 21.2 Comparison of primaries and caucuses

Primaries	Caucuses
• An intraparty ballot to nominate the candidate for a party • Secret ballot • Often conducted on a state-wide basis • Used by 36 states	• An intraparty town hall meeting to nominate the candidate for a party • Voting often takes place in public • Often conducted in small local areas within a state • Used by 14 states

The invisible primary

There is no 'official' beginning to the invisible primary. It is simply the period during which potential candidates for a party compete with each other to attract attention, money and endorsements for their campaign. The competition at this point is intraparty, meaning it is a competition of candidates *within* a party. The evolution and growth of the media, especially in a digital age, and the importance of money in elections have made this an increasingly important part of the presidential campaign.

In 2016, 17 different candidates aimed to be the nominee of the Republican Party for the president. Of these, five withdrew during the invisible primary, before the first official primary had even taken place (Table 21.3). A further seven withdrew in the 20 days following the first primary on 1 February 2016.

Table 21.3 Candidates withdrawing from the race to be the nominee of the Republican Party for the presidency, 2016

Candidate	Entered the presidential race	Withdrew from the presidential race	Reason for withdrawal
George Pataki	28 May 2015	29 December 2015	Lacked public support in polls
Rick Perry	4 June 2015	11 September 2015	Lacked financial backing
Scott Walker	13 July 2015	21 September 2015	Lacked the funding to keep up with his campaign spending
Bobby Jindal	24 June 2015	17 November 2015	Lacked public support and financial backing
Lindsay Graham	1 June 2015	21 December 2015	Lacked public support in polls

Candidates have to use the invisible primary to attract public attention. This means gaining 'name recognition', being a candidate whose name is recognised by voters as a viable candidate. The success of this is often judged by the polls, and a lack of good polling can lead to a candidate withdrawing. Candidates can raise their profile through a range of events, starting with the announcement of their candidacy, which is often a big occasion drawing media attention that can help them gain recognition.

Jeb Bush, for example, announced his candidacy to great fanfare in 2015. However, he suffered bruising criticism from Donald Trump during the invisible primary, being attacked by him on Twitter more than all of the other Republican candidates combined. He withdrew from the race on 20 February 2016.

There are also televised debates held between candidates of the same party, giving them a platform to advance their own views and policies while highlighting flaws in the other candidates. In 2016, the Republican Party announced there would 12 debates, in contrast to the 20 held during the 2012 election. With so many candidates in 2016, however, fitting them all on to a single stage proved to be problematic. In 2015, the first debate in August saw ten candidates competing; in the debate before the first primary there were seven candidates and by the final debate the following March, just four remained.

Jeb Bush campaigning during the early stages of the presidential election in 2015

The invisible primary also allows candidates to attract finance. This might be donations directly from the voters themselves, which candidates call targeting the 'grassroots'. Increasingly, however, it is from **Political Action Committees (PACs)** or **Super-PACs**. PACs can donate directly to a campaign but only to a limit of $5,000. Super-PACs can spend unlimited amounts of money for or against candidates, but they cannot coordinate directly with the candidate while doing so. Attracting this money early is important for a candidate to be able to survive the long presidential campaign.

The rising cost of presidential elections means the invisible primary season is increasingly important. The data in Figure 21.1 do not take account of either inflation or the role of 'free' media attention gained by candidates — or, in 2012 and 2016, of Super-PAC spending, which may account for the drop in 2016 in official campaign spending — but it does highlight the vast cost of an election and therefore the necessity to gain significant financial backing.

Key terms

Political Action Committee (PAC) A group which can raise money to support a candidate in an election, donating a maximum of $5,000 to their campaign directly.

Super-PAC A group which can raise and spend unlimited amounts of money to support or oppose a candidate, but which is not allowed to donate directly to a campaign or coordinate with a campaign.

Figure 21.1 Spending in presidential elections, 1960–2016

■ Republican candidate   ■ Democratic candidate

Election year

Spending ($million)

Traditional wisdom suggests that the person who raises the most money is most likely to win in an election. Figure 21.2 shows the amount of money raised by Clinton and Trump through the invisible primary up to December 2016. Although Clinton raised more than Trump, estimates suggest that Trump benefited from nearly $2 billion worth of 'free' media attention due to his controversial nature, while Clinton had gained just $746 million.

Hillary Clinton spent considerably more on her presidential campaign in 2016 than Donald Trump

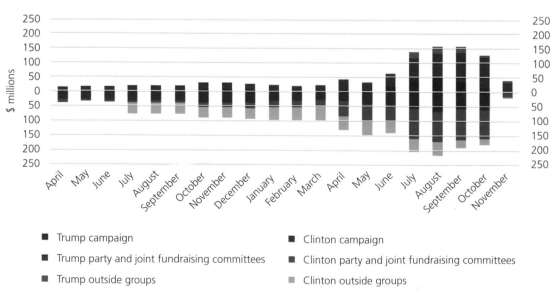

Figure 21.2 Spending in the Clinton and Trump campaigns, 2016

The importance of incumbency in a presidential election

For candidates going through the invisible primary, and indeed the rest of the electoral process, there are considerable advantages to be gained if they are the current president running for re-election (the 'incumbent'). Allan Lichtman, a presidential historian, has commented on the substantial advantages that an incumbent has:

> 'name recognition; national attention, fundraising and campaign bases; control over the instruments of government; successful campaign experience; a presumption of success; and voters' inertia and risk-aversion.'

The incumbent has the benefit of considerable name recognition, having been the president for a number of years and therefore being well known. This can make it easier for them to attract the necessary funding far earlier than their competitors. Incumbents can also point to policy successes during their first term to try and broaden their appeal and demonstrate their ability to govern, something which competitors may struggle to do.

The advantage of incumbency in terms of fundraising is shown clearly in Figure 21.3. In 2012, the incumbent Obama's ability to raise campaign funds earlier gave him a notable financial advantage over Romney, who would ultimately be his Republican competitor.

The incumbent's role and powers allow them to dominate media coverage in a way that other candidates cannot, and to take advantage of it, particularly in national situations. In 2012, in the final few weeks of the election, Hurricane Sandy hit the east coast of the USA. The ensuing media coverage of this disaster allowed Obama a huge advantage — he could act 'presidentially', touring disaster-hit areas and being photographed talking to those affected. By comparison, Romney not only faced a media blackout of sorts, with the focus pulled away from the electoral campaign, he also faced scrutiny of his policies regarding the Federal Emergency Management Agency (FEMA). Romney had previously suggested that FEMA, the agency responsible for coordinating a response to such disasters, should be closed. In the wake of Hurricane Sandy, his campaign found itself having to review his previous comments.

It is also likely that an incumbent will not face a primary challenge. This means that they do not have to spend time exposing the cracks and divisions within their own party in order to win their party's nomination. This creates a stronger party going into the election, but also reduces the amount of money it is necessary for the candidate to spend in the early stages of the election, giving them a large 'war chest' to spend later on.

However, as Lichtman points out, 'Incumbents are difficult, but not impossible, to beat.' Incumbents can also find themselves judged for their failures during their time in office, as Bush Snr. did for the weaknesses in the economy during the 1992 election. Equally, their experience on the campaign trail can mean they are held to higher standards. Obama's performance in the 2012 presidential debates was roundly criticised, with his performance unconvincing and his appearance tired, while Romney's performance was not only praised but had nothing to be compared to.

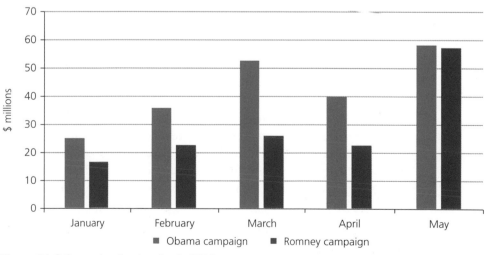

Figure 21.3 Campaign funds raised, 2012

Primaries and caucuses

In order to choose a single presidential candidate for each party, primaries and caucuses are held across the country. These are organised and held by individual parties within each state between February and June of an election year. This means there are 50 Republican primaries and caucuses and 50 Democratic primaries and caucuses each election year, plus those of third parties. In each primary or caucus, the public vote for the presidential candidate they prefer for that party. In reality, they are voting to determine whom the delegates to the National Party Convention from their state will vote for.

A primary or a caucus?

Twelve states hold caucuses and 38 states hold primaries. These are simply different ways of working out how many delegates will be allocated to each candidate.

- A caucus is a public meeting in which people vote either by moving to a part of the room for a certain candidate or through a show of hands.
- A primary is a state-wide election in which people cast a ballot for their candidate of choice.

Within each state there are further differences, most notably who is allowed to take part in a primary or a caucus.

- **Open primaries** and caucuses allow all voters in a state to take part, even if they are not a registered member of a party. Voters can take part in only *one* primary, however. Therefore they would have to decide whether to vote in the Democratic or Republican (or third party) primary or caucus. This means that a Democrat voter could choose to vote in the Republican primary and vice versa.
- **Closed primaries** and caucuses allow only voters who are registered as a party member to take part. Registered Democrats would be allowed to take part in the Democratic primary or caucus. Voters are sent a ballot only if they are registered party members and no one else can take part.
- **Semi-closed primaries** and caucuses are a hybrid of open and closed. Registered party members are allowed to take part only in their party's primary or caucus. Unregistered voters, however, are allowed to choose which party primary or caucus they want to vote in.

There are also differences in how the delegates are allocated:

- Proportionally — In all Democratic primaries and caucuses and some of the Republican ones, the delegates are allocated proportionally to the vote that a candidate receives.
- Winner-takes-all — In some Republican primaries and caucuses, the candidate with the biggest share of the vote is allocated all of the delegates for that state.
- Proportional unless a threshold is reached — In some Republican primaries and caucuses, the delegates are allocated proportionally unless one candidate wins an overwhelming amount of the vote. If one candidate reaches the 'threshold' in a state, which varies from 50% to 85% of the vote, they are allocated all of that state's delegates.

How do they work?

Primaries are quite simple in their operation. The entire state goes to the polls, the results are counted and delegates are allocated accordingly.

Key terms

Open primary A primary in which all voters in a state can take part, regardless of party membership or registration.

Closed primary A primary in which only registered party members can take part.

Semi-closed primary A primary in which registered party members and unregistered voters can take part.

Caucuses are organised differently between states and parties. In Iowa in 2016, there were Republican caucuses held at over 700 locations and Democratic caucuses held at over 1,000 locations. These took place at 8 p.m. and lasted about an hour. The votes cast in these meetings were used to work out the allocation of delegates to candidates. Overall in 2016, the Democrats had 4,763 delegates to allocate for their National Party Convention and the Republicans had 2,472.

When do they happen?

The timing of primaries and caucuses is spread across a number of months in an election year. Traditionally, New Hampshire's primary and Iowa's caucus are always the first to happen. There is an increasing trend for primaries and caucuses to be moved ever earlier — a process known as 'frontloading'. The reason for this is that for those states later in the calendar, the decision for each party can often have been finalised by the time they get a say. In 2016, Trump gained a majority of delegates on 26 May, but seven states had not held their primaries at this point, including highly populated states such as California.

The process of frontloading has led to lots of primaries and caucuses happening on the same day — this is known colloquially as 'Super Tuesday'. The largest of these was in 2008, with nearly half of the delegates for the Republicans and Democrats decided on this day, leading to it being dubbed 'Super Duper Tuesday'.

It can seem that states with earlier primaries can be more influential — by the time California voted in the 2016 Republican primary, all candidates except for Trump had suspended their campaigns.

> ### Key term
>
> **Frontloading** The movement of primaries to an earlier point in the calendar in order to give more significance to a primary or caucus within a state.

Donald Trump officially accepting the presidential nomination at the Republican National Convention in Cleveland, Ohio in 2016. National Party Conventions are attended by delegates representing their states, special guests and the media

National Party Conventions

National Party Conventions are multiday events held for each party and attended by the delegates allocated in the primaries and caucuses. They formally nominate the presidential and vice-presidential candidate for their party and hold discussions on the party policy for the coming election. Following a disastrous National Party Convention in 1968, the Democrats established the McGovern-Fraser Commission to review the nomination process of the president. The result was a system with greater importance, emphasis and openness placed on the primaries and caucuses, which previously had been of little significance. The importance of the party convention decreased in response. Today, by the time conventions are held, both the presidential and vice-presidential candidates are already well known. The process does retain both formal and informal roles, however (Table 21.4).

Table 21.4 Formal and informal roles of National Party Conventions

Formal roles	Informal roles
Selecting the party candidates for presidency While most party delegates are bound by party rules as to whom they have to vote for, this is still a process which takes place at conventions and formally acknowledges the party's nominee for president and vice president. In the vote of delegates, a simple majority of votes cast is needed to approve a candidate	**Selling the candidate** As a multimillion-dollar event with extensive television coverage, the convention allows the candidate considerable media coverage, especially of their acceptance speech. Obama's 2007 speech had an audience of around 39 million television viewers. In this speech, the nominee can talk directly to the voters and set out their campaign narrative. It can also allow some of the rising stars of the party to speak and make their mark for future campaigns, as Obama did in 2004
Adopting the party platform and policies Theoretically the party convention allows for discussion on, and amendments to, the **party platform** — this is the American equivalent of a party manifesto. While parties do take account of their members' views, the party convention today is little more than a rubber stamp for the platform. Most of the platform policy is created by 'platform committees' of each party in the days before the convention and today often this is done in collaboration with the presumptive nominee. The platforms are then simply agreed to at the convention in a vote	**Party unity** The invisible primary and primary season can be bruising. With candidates from the same party battling it out for supremacy, they often do so by pointing out the flaws in the other candidates, thereby exposing divisions within the party. The convention affords an opportunity to repair some of this damage and prepare instead to compete against an opposing party. Having lost to Obama in 2008, Clinton opened her convention speech with, 'I am honoured to be here tonight. A proud mother. A proud Democrat. A proud American. And a proud supporter of Barack Obama'

In 2016, it took the convention just 6 minutes to confirm the Republican Party platform despite concerns expressed by some of its members at the anti-LGBTQ rhetoric and policy contained within it. It passed with just a voice vote and very few objections from the floor. Similarly, despite a #NeverTrump effort by some of the Republican delegates in 2016, Trump was approved with over 1,700 delegates (69.8%) on the first ballot — comparatively, Romney won over 90% on the first ballot in 2012. In 2004, one Republican was moved to remark, 'I don't frankly see the point of spending millions and millions of dollars that amounts to a TV set that gets used for one night'.

Nevertheless, it is not uncommon at National Party Conventions today to see overt displays of party loyalty by those attending — delegates representing their states, special guests and the media — to demonstrate their enthusiasm for their party. This makes the convention something of a spectacle, which serves to attract further media attention.

The election campaign

The period between the National Party Convention and Election Day is dominated by extensive fundraising, campaign events in states and nationally televised presidential debates. As part of the campaign, events are organised for candidates across the USA. These events may not be in every state, however. The states identified as **battleground states**, where the result is not easily predictable, are likely to see far more events and far more spending by each campaign. '**Bellwether states**' are those states which historically have tended to vote for the candidate who ultimately will win the presidential election — for this reason these states see far more interest from presidential candidates.

In 2016, 94% of events by either Trump, Pence, Clinton or Kaine took place in just 12 states. (Figure 21.4 shows the number of their campaign events in each state.) This makes Governor Scott Walker's 2015 comments scarily prophetic: 'The nation as a whole is not going to elect the next president. Twelve states are.'

Key terms

Battleground state
A state in which the candidate it will support is uncertain and which therefore sees a lot of campaigning activities in order to win votes. Also known as a swing state.

Bellwether state A state which has historically tended to vote for the winning presidential candidate.

Figure 21.4 Concentration of campaigning in 12 states, 2016; the numbers indicate the number of campaign events in each state by Trump, Pence, Clinton or Kaine

Televised debates

Since 1976, there has been an expectation for candidates to take part in televised debates set against one another. Candidates who are polling at an average of 15% in national polls are eligible to take part in presidential debates. For all recent debates, this has meant there have been only two candidates — one Democrat and one Republican, with third parties failing to meet the polling requirement. Despite the hype around these debates, numerous studies have concluded 'when it comes to shifting enough votes to decide the outcome of the election, presidential debates have rarely, if ever, mattered'. In 2016, Hillary Clinton appeared to have 'won' each debate through the polling conducted afterwards, yet went on to lose the election.

Election Day and the Electoral College

After months of campaigning, Americans finally get to go to the polls in November. As with primaries, however, what really happens on Election Day is 50 separate state-wide elections, all run with different rules and processes. In each state, voters cast their ballot for the candidate of their choice. However, what they are in fact voting for is whom their state's Electoral College votes (ECVs) get allocated to. For all but two states, this is decided on a winner-takes-all basis — the candidate with the plurality of a vote in each state gets all of that state's ECVs.

The method of voting is a decision for each individual state, as is how they allocate the Electoral College votes for their state (Table 21.5). This allows for a degree of federalism but also causes controversy. The use of 'butterfly ballots' in 2000 caused such confusion that the election ended up being decided by the Supreme Court. These ballots have names down both sides and punch holes down the centre, making it difficult for people to work out how to vote for their preferred candidate.

Table 21.5 Voting methods used in different states

State	Voting methods used	Electoral College vote allocation
Colorado	Mail	Winner-takes-all
Delaware	Digital voting with no paper trail	Winner-takes-all
Maine	Paper ballot	Two votes given to the state-wide winner, one vote given to the winner in each of Maine's two congressional districts
Nevada	Digital voting with a paper trail	Winner-takes-all
Tennessee	Paper ballot, and digital voting without a paper trail	Winner-takes-all
Utah	Paper ballot, and digital voting with a paper trail	Winner-takes-all

How does the Electoral College work?

The Electoral College was included in the Constitution as a compromise. It prevented a direct election by the population, which was feared by some of the Founding Fathers. It also served the purposes of federalism, ensuring that both low- and high-population states would have a voice at national level, in much the same way the Senate would protect this in Congress.

Each state was therefore to be given a number of **Electoral College votes (ECVs)**. The number each state would be given would be the same as the number of people that that state had representing it in Congress. This meant every state had a minimum of three ECVs, as every state had at least one House of Representatives member and two senators. The number of House of Representatives members that a state is allocated is proportional to its population, therefore allocating ECVs in this way meant that it was also broadly proportional.

Sometime before the General Election, each party will select people who can exercise the ECVs in each state. These are often faithful party activists for whom this is a reward. Following the national vote, the state declares to which candidate its ECVs will be allocated. The nominated **electors** of the winning party cast their vote in the state capital on the first Monday after the second Wednesday in December. While 30 states have laws that require their delegates to cast their vote for the candidate who won the state vote, the rest do not. Delegates who do not vote as their state did are called '**faithless electors**'. The likelihood of these voters having any effect on the final outcome is minimal, but in 2016 there were ten faithless electors — three had their vote invalidated as they broke state law and had to vote again, but seven successfully cast their ballot.

To win in the Electoral College, a candidate needs to attract a majority of ECVs. Today, with 538 ECVs available, a winning candidate needs at least 270 to win. While the winner of the election should be evident after the national vote has been cast, it is not technically official until the ECVs have been cast in December.

In the 48 states that allocate their ECVs on a winner-takes-all basis, it does not matter by how much a candidate wins. Clinton won California by over 4 million more votes than Trump, but this received no recognition in the number of ECVs she received.

Synoptic links

Both the UK and the USA have notable questions over the effectiveness of their electoral processes. In the USA, the failure of the president to win the popular vote in two of the last five elections has brought controversy over the use of the Electoral College. A similar thing happened in the UK in 1951, with the Conservatives gaining fewer votes but more seats than Labour. For more on the UK voting system, see Chapter 3.

In focus

National Popular Vote Interstate Compact (NPVIC)

Given the vast criticisms that can be levelled at the Electoral College, reform of this institution is often debated. In the absence of reform, however, several states have taken it upon themselves to effect reform. They have created the National Popular Vote Interstate Compact, in which those states which are members pledge all of their ECVs to the winner of the national popular vote, regardless of the outcome in their own state. This has been adopted by 11 states and Washington DC, which together represent 172 ECVs, although it has passed through the legislatures in a further 12 states.

Debate

Should the Electoral College be reformed?

Given the flaws in the Electoral College and the advances in popular democracy since the time of the Founding Fathers, there are many arguments for and against the reform of this institution.

Yes	No
• In two of the last five presidential elections the winner of the popular vote has lost in the Electoral College, undermining modern principles of popular sovereignty and underlining the outdated nature of the institution.	• The Electoral College ensures that small states remain represented. With the US population heavily concentrated in a few big states, the role, culture and traditions of smaller states could be ignored without the Electoral College. It also helps to maintain federalism by allowing differing electoral procedures in each state.
• It effectively excludes third parties from the electoral process as the ECVs are not allocated proportionally and third-party votes tend to be thinly spread across the nation.	• The Electoral College guards against tyranny of the majority nationally. The Founding Fathers were not convinced about the wisdom of popular sovereignty and this indirect form of election disperses power away from the public.
• Small states are overrepresented in the Electoral College. California has 55 ECVs and a population of nearly 40 million. Wyoming has three ECVs and a population of 500,000. That means each ECV exercised by Wyoming represents just 195,167 people, while a Californian ECV represents over three times as many people.	• There is no consensus on what should replace the Electoral College. There are slight reforms suggested, such as the proportional allocation of ECVs, right up to abolition and replacing it with a national popular vote, plus more variations in between. This is especially problematic given the difficulty of passing a constitutional amendment generally.
• The bellwether states are effectively overrepresented as it is their votes that can change the election. The result is that a majority of states are almost ignored throughout the electoral process.	• Broadly, the Electoral College has produced a clear winner. Given the use of FPTP for US elections, the resulting two-party system means the winner has a clear majority of ECVs and therefore has a strong mandate to govern.
• That faithless electors exist undermines the very basic principles of democracy. Reform is therefore needed to maintain legitimacy in US elections.	

The two-party system

The outcome of this electoral process is a two-**party system** across the USA, which is difficult to overcome. Unlike in the UK, even politics at state level is dominated by two parties. It is not only the system that leads to this outcome, however.

- **The use of winner-takes-all** This significantly disadvantages third parties as they are awarded nothing for coming anything other than first in a state or district. Therefore, despite the threefold jump in third-party votes in 2016, they gained nothing for their achievements.
- **The nature of America** The federal nature of America, and the guarantee of a state's right to run its own election, make every election a small, single-seat election. Using a winner-takes-all electoral system in itself causes a two-party system. However, given that the USA effectively conducts a series of mini-elections on any Election Day, this problem is further exacerbated.
- **Party ideology** The two main US parties have such breadth of ideology, it is difficult for a third party to carve out any distinct policy area that is not already covered. If it were able to, it would not take much for one of the two main parties to simply assume this policy, a process known as co-optation. This means that candidates running as independents also struggle to carve out a distinct policy platform.
- **The expense of politics** US elections have become so expensive that the only parties able to really compete are those with money. Most smaller parties lack the financial muscle or membership to gain success, therefore reinforcing the two-party system.
- **The electoral rules** The rules of the presidential debate serve to exclude third parties which struggle to achieve the popularity needed in the polls. This restricts their access to what amounts to free media and undermines their legitimacy as serious parties.

Synoptic link

Two parties dominate the political landscape in both the USA and the UK, often for broadly the same reasons, including the use of a similar electoral system. For more information on the UK party system, see pages 44–56. This links to Component 2, UK Government.

Campaign finance

In Aaron Sorkin's fictionalised *West Wing*, it is remarked that money in politics is like water on a pavement — 'it finds all the cracks and crevices'. Certainly the role of money in US politics is well documented and there is little chance of it receding, given recent electoral spending. However, there have been numerous attempts to try and limit the influence of money in elections to ensure a fairer and more democratic campaign (Figure 21.5).

Key term

Campaign finance
The funds raised by a candidate or their party to support their campaign for office.

1974
FECA reformed after Watergate
The amendment creates the Federal Elections Commission to oversee and regulate election spending. It limits individual donations to a single campaign to $1,000 (with a capped aggregate total of $25,000 to all federal campaigns). It also limits campaign spending

1979
Congress amends FECA
Through further amendment of the Act, it allows for the development of **soft money** — money donated to and spent by a party rather than a candidate and therefore is not bound by campaign limits

2010
Citizens United* v *FEC
Effectively determines that money is free speech, and therefore campaign limits placed on organisations are unconstitutional. This gives rise to the creation of Super-PACs

1971
Federal Elections Campaign Act (FECA) passed
This lays out requirements for the disclosure of donations received by candidates (of over $100) and sets spending limits for candidates and their families ($50,000 for presidential elections). It also establishes matching funds

1976
***Buckley* v *Valeo* in the Supreme Court**
This ruling upholds the donation limits for elections but rules that spending caps amount to a violation of free speech

2002 Bipartisan Campaign Finance Reform Act (McCain-Feingold)
- Bans soft money donations to national parties
- Raises individual contribution limits to $2,000 (or '**hard money**') per candidate per election
- Corporations and labour unions are banned from funding issue advertisements
- Prohibits 'electioneering communications' referring to federal candidates within 60 days of a general election by corporations and labour unions
- 'Stand By Your Ad' (SBYA) provision requires candidates to endorse campaign adverts to discourage attack adverts or controversial claims

2014
McCutcheon* v *FEC
Rules that the aggregate cap placed on individuals limiting the number of candidates they can donate to within an election cycle is unconstitutional

Figure 21.5 The history of campaign finance reform

Contribution limits for individuals to candidates in 2017–18 remained at $2,700. Yet, there are other ways in which individuals can spend their money in order to try and influence an election (Table 21.6).

Table 21.6 The most common methods of raising campaign money today

Group	Can raise ...	Campaign restrictions
PACs	A $5,000 donation per campaign	Can donate directly to a campaign
527s	Unlimited amounts	Cannot call for the election or defeat of a candidate
Super-PACs	Unlimited amounts	Can call for the election or defeat of a candidate but cannot coordinate with those campaigns

A vast array of different groups have sprung up over US electoral history to raise money and try to influence elections. The most common today are shown in Table 21.6, although since the 2010 ruling in *Citizens United* v *Federal Election Commission*, which effectively allowed for the creation of Super-PACs, their role and the money they have raised have mushroomed.

Key terms

Soft money Money donated to a party, rather than a candidate, and used for 'party-building activities' rather than endorsement of a candidate directly. It is subject to few limits.

Hard money Donations directly to an electoral campaign and subject to strict limits.

Difficulty in achieving reform

Achieving campaign finance reform has proved difficult partly because those in power have benefited from the system as it stands and can therefore be reluctant to reform it, potentially making their next attempt at re-election more challenging. Where legislators have been willing to create legislation in the past, groups have simply found ways to work around this — PACs, 527s, Super-PACs all demonstrate a willingness for groups to get their voice heard through money in elections one way or another. Supreme Court rulings have also made reforming finance difficult. On numerous occasions the Court has struck down legislation limiting finance as being a challenge to the 1st Amendment free speech rights. That the Constitution is entrenched and so difficult to change means that the power of these Supreme Court rulings is relatively unrivalled. Like the Electoral College, there is also a lack of consensus about what campaign finance reform would look like. Without this bipartisan agreement, the chance of making effective legislation, let alone considering a constitutional amendment, is highly unlikely.

Debate

Is the presidential election process effective?

Yes

- The lengthy process ensures that candidates are resilient enough to withstand the demands of being the president.
- The Electoral College has served to produce a clear winner able to govern effectively despite the split nature of US political opinion.
- The primary calendar ensures that the voice of smaller states is upheld, protecting the principle of federalism.
- The ability to attract large amounts of money speaks to the character and breadth of appeal of a candidate, making them more suited to the job.
- The expectation of an acceptance speech at the National Party Conventions, plus a good performance in televised debates, highlight a skill that a good president would be expected to have — commanding and persuasive public speaking.
- It broadly works — controversies have been quickly overcome and President Bush and President Trump, who both won the Electoral College but not the popular vote, have been able to lead while being kept in check by opinion polls and Congress.
- Third parties can have a role, whether in the share of the national vote (as Ross Perot in 1992) or in trying to shape the debates of an election (as Jill Stein and Gary Johnson in 2016).
- Primaries allow voters a genuine choice. Neither Obama nor Trump were the frontrunners when the invisible primary began and yet they triumphed.

No

- The Electoral College has proven to be increasingly out of step with popular sovereignty and therefore needs reform.
- The primaries calendar effectively disenfranchises some states while overrepresenting the views of others, thereby creating an uneven form of federalism.
- The expected presidential televised debates have limited impact on the outcome of the election, and are therefore a sideshow.
- The National Party Convention, while no longer taxpayer funded, serves little democratic purpose for the voters at large.
- The amount of money required to become the president makes the process inherently elitist.
- The volume of money required also gives undue influence to interest groups and corporations over the voice of the general population.
- The length of the process creates political apathy among the voters, which can depress turnout and undermine the legitimacy of an election.
- The variety of differing voting methods has been criticised and caused controversy over election results.
- In terms of actual power, third parties are effectively excluded from the election, with the entire process creating a two-party system in which third parties have little value.
- Increasingly the role of the media is more influential than money spent, and yet this area is relatively unregulated when it comes to elections.

Parties

The Founding Fathers seemed wary of the idea of parties, or factions, and yet resigned to their existence. Jefferson shared the opinion that 'men by their constitutions are naturally divided into two parties' in 1824, an opinion that seemed to be shared by Madison in his earlier Federalist Paper #10. In fact the Founding Fathers were the creators of the first American parties. Hamilton's Federalists on one side favoured a strong national government and a relationship with England, with Jefferson and Madison's Democratic-Republican Party opposing them. This two-party system has become a hallmark of US politics, embodied today by the Democratic Party, with roots in the party of Jefferson and Madison, and the Republican Party founded in 1854.

The two main US parties do not have a distinct, coherent ideology platform. All of US politics is conducted within a more conservative part of the ideological spectrum than in the UK, but there is still a breadth of ideas and opinions across this range. Within the walls of each party there will exist a plethora of differing views on any given issue. Senator Susan Collins is a pro-choice Republican who sits of the left-hand edge of her party. Senator James Inhofe, in contrast, sits on the very right-hand edge of the Republican Party and sees very few circumstances in which abortion should be allowed; he introduced a bill into Congress that would not allow abortion to be funded by the US taxpayer.

The two major parties have a national infrastructure. The Republican National Committee (RNC) and the Democratic National Committee (DNC) head their respective parties, developing and promoting the party platform and organising fundraising. Each general election, the RNC and the DNC produce their party platform, which is then agreed upon at the National Party Convention.

Parties are also organised at state level. Each state has its own Democratic and Republican parties with their own party platforms that are both relevant to and reflective of the culture and traditions of that state. This means that although two candidates in different states might both run as a 'Democrat', their policy priorities might be entirely different.

The key ideas and principles of the Democratic and Republican parties

There are still identifiable trends within the two main parties that can be seen to be their 'principles' or ideology. This might not apply equally to every party member but it does give a broad understanding of the parties. One of the main ways in which we can identify these trends is to look at the party platforms from a general election (Table 21.7).

Table 21.7 National-level policy principles from the 2016 party platforms

	Democrats	Republicans
Ideology	Generally liberal, believing in progressive rights and some level of government intervention in both social and economic policy	Generally conservative, believing in individual rights and a limited role for the government in the economy and social policy, although a larger role in homeland security
General ideological principles	Believe in: • 'An unerring belief that we can make it [America] better' • 'Out of many, we are one' — a responsibility of society to ensure that government works for everyone • A constitutional belief in liberty and equality for all • Government intervention to ensure equality for all, in both the economy and social welfare • Being strong enough to defend the nation while seeking peace	Believe in: • American exceptionalism (the idea that the USA is uniquely 'free') • The rights of the individual, 'life, liberty and the pursuit of happiness' • An originalist interpretation of the Constitution • Limited government, separation of powers and federalism • 'Political freedom and economic freedom are indivisible' • Being strong enough to defend the nation while seeking peace
General policy belief	Support: • Women's right to choose in the case of abortion • Same-sex marriage • A level of social welfare (including healthcare) • Reform of immigration • Pro-environmental policies • Gun control • Larger government, even if that occasionally encroaches on states' rights • Access to free, or debt-free, education • Abolishing the death penalty	Support: • Restrictions on provision of and funding for abortion • Opposition to same-sex marriage • Stricter immigration policy • Pro-business policies • Gun rights • Smaller government to allow greater rights of individual states • State- and parent-run education • Tax cuts over the provision of social welfare including universal healthcare • Death penalty

The principles listed in Table 21.7 were taken from the 2016 party platforms. They demonstrate what appears to be a clear-cut division between the two major parties in the USA. These, however, are national-level policy principles. Not all elected Democrats or Republicans will agree with all of their party's principles — it will largely depend on what their constituents believe.

> ### Synoptic link
>
> The ideologies of the major parties in both the USA and the UK are underpinned by political philosophy. The Republican and Conservative parties draw heavily on key conservative thinkers; for more information, see Chapter 10. The Democratic Party draws more heavily on the liberal thinkers, as does the Labour Party to some extent; for more information see Chapter 9. The Labour Party also draws on key socialist thinkers; for more information see Chapter 11. This links to Component 1, Core Political Ideas.

The 2016 party platforms provide a useful insight into understanding specific policy differences between the Republicans and Democrats. The ideological principles of a party will often inform its policy. In explaining why the Republicans oppose universal healthcare, it is important to note that they believe in individual freedom. The provision of such healthcare would therefore remove this choice from the individual and go against the Republicans' ideological beliefs. It is also useful to compare the current platforms to previous ones. Trump made waves in 2016 for some of his more controversial views, yet in the party platform there is no great swathe of change from the 2012 platform.

Social and moral issues

Democratic and Republican stances on various social and moral issues are shown in Table 21.8, together with any change in policy between 2012 and 2016.

Table 21.8 Party policy changes on key social and moral issues

Issue	Democrats		Republicans
Death penalty	'We will abolish the death penalty, which has proven to be a cruel and unusual form of punishment. It has no place in the United States of America'	2016	'With the murder rate soaring in our great cities, we condemn the Supreme Court's erosion of the right of the people to enact capital punishment in their states'
	No promise to abolish the death penalty, just to ensure the legal system was fair	Change from 2012?	No change
Same-sex marriage	'Democrats applaud last year's decision by the Supreme Court that recognized that LGBT people — like other Americans — have the right to marry the person they love. But there is still much work to be done'	2016	'Traditional marriage and family, based on marriage between one man and one woman, is the foundation for a free society ... We condemn the Supreme Court's ruling in *U.S.* v *Windsor*, which wrongly removed the ability of Congress to define marriage policy in federal law'
	No change. They supported the repeal of the Defense of Marriage Act (DOMA), which was struck down in *United States* v *Windsor* (2014)	Change from 2012?	No change. The 2012 policy pledged to uphold DOMA
Abortion	'We believe unequivocally, like the majority of Americans, that every woman should have access to quality reproductive healthcare services, including safe and legal abortion'	2016	'We assert the sanctity of human life and affirm that the unborn child has a fundamental right to life which cannot be infringed. We support a human life amendment to the Constitution'
	No change	Change from 2012?	No change
Environment	'We are committed to getting 50 percent of our electricity from clean energy sources within a decade' 'Democrats believe that carbon dioxide, methane, and other greenhouse gases should be priced to reflect their negative externalities'	2016	'We support the development of all forms of energy that are marketable in a free economy without subsidies, including coal, oil, natural gas, nuclear power, and hydropower' 'We oppose any carbon tax'
	Reference to emissions limits rather than pricing	Change from 2012?	No mention of carbon tax
Guns	'We will expand and strengthen background checks and close dangerous loopholes in our current laws ... and keep weapons of war — such as assault weapons and large capacity ammunition magazines (LCAMs) — off our streets'	2016	'We support firearm reciprocity legislation to recognize the right of law-abiding Americans to carry firearms to protect themselves and their families in all 50 states ... We oppose ill-conceived laws that would restrict magazine capacity or ban the sale of the most popular and common modern rifle'
	No mention of magazine capacity	Change from 2012?	No change
Immigration	'Democrats believe we need to urgently fix our broken immigration system ... and create a path to citizenship for law-abiding families who are here'	2016	'Our highest priority, therefore, is to secure our borders and all ports of entry and to enforce our immigration laws'
	No change	Change from 2012?	No change

Economic issues

Democratic and Republican stances on various economic issues are shown in Table 21.9, together with any change in policy between 2012 and 2016.

Table 21.9 Party policy changes on key economic issues

Issue	Democrats		Republicans
Tax	'We believe the wealthiest Americans and largest corporations must pay their fair share of taxes. Democrats will claw back tax breaks for companies that ship jobs overseas, eliminate tax breaks for big oil and gas companies'	2016	'Republicans consider the establishment of pro-growth tax codes a moral imperative … Wherever tax rates penalize thrift or discourage investment, they must be lowered'
	No change	Change from 2012?	'We oppose tax policies that divide Americans or promote class warfare'
Minimum wage	'We should raise the federal minimum wage to $15 an hour over time and index it, give all Americans the ability to join a union regardless of where they work'	2016	'Minimum wage is an issue that should be handled at the state and local level'
	Propose a minimum wage but do not give a figure	Change from 2012?	No mention of minimum wage
Banking	'Wall Street cannot be an island unto itself, gambling trillions in risky financial instruments and making huge profits, all the while thinking that taxpayers will be there to bail them out again'	2016	'Republicans believe that no financial institution is too big to fail. We support legislation to ensure that the problems of any financial institution can be resolved through the Bankruptcy Code'
	No change	Change from 2012?	No change

Social welfare

Democratic and Republican stances on health and education are shown in Table 21.10, together with any change in policy between 2012 and 2016.

Table 21.10 Party policy changes on health and education

Issue	Democrats		Republicans
Healthcare	'Democrats believe that healthcare is a right, not a privilege, and our healthcare system should put people before profits'	2016	'It is time to repeal Obamacare and give America a much-needed tax cut … we will reduce mandates and enable insurers and providers of care to increase healthcare options and contain costs'
	No change	Change from 2012?	No change
Education	'Democrats are unified in their strong belief that every student should be able to go to college debt-free, and working families should not have to pay any tuition to go to public colleges and universities'	2016	'The federal government should not be in the business of originating student loans. In order to bring down college costs and give students access to a multitude of financing options, private sector participation in student financing should be restored'
	Commitment to affordable education rather than free	Change from 2012?	No change

A protest over gun control after the Santa Fe High School shooting, 2018

Synoptic link

While UK party conventions are held annually, compared to every 4 years in the USA, conventions in both countries have a key role in debating and confirming the policies that will be adopted by a party. For more about UK party policies and profiles, see pages 44–56. This links to Component 1, UK Politics.

The changing significance of the parties

While parties in the USA have a breadth of ideology within them, the role and significance are clear when looking at their actions in Congress. It is easy to identify party-line voting on significant issues, such as the appointment of Brett Kavanaugh in 2018. When averaged, the voting trends of members of both the Senate and the House of Representatives fall increasingly into party blocs. The sharper the divisions within Congress, the more important parties become and the less bipartisan action is seen in congressional lawmaking. This reflects the ideological shift of the US public, which too has become more polarised in the last decades.

There are factors that can limit the significance of parties in Congress, however:

- **Constituents** In a short election cycle, members of Congress must be mindful of the views of their constituents as well as their party if they wish to be re-elected. This is especially true given the nature of primaries in the USA, which allow constituents to control who makes it on to the ballot paper.
- **Congressional caucuses** These are groups of congressmen and congresswomen who share a specific common interest and come together when voting on that issue, irrespective of party lines. There is, for example, a Women's Caucus, a Black Caucus, and a Steel Caucus for those who represent states in which heavy manufacturing is a crucial part of the state economy.
- **Interest groups** It would be rare that the role of an interest group would be the publicised reason a member of Congress voted against their party. However, in an age of such expensive elections, the role of interest groups in funding both parties and individual candidates is crucial and can sometimes explain their voting behaviour.

The general trend remains, however, that since the middle of the twentieth century, the divisions between parties have widened. This serves to suggest that parties as a vehicle for ideologies have grown in importance.

Intraparty conflicts and factions

Given the breadth of ideology within US parties and the importance of state-level party organisation, it is not surprising that **factions** develop within them. These factions are not fixed, however, and often overlap with one another. Like in UK parties, the emergence and disappearance of factions changes over time in response to the key policy issues of the day.

Broadly, each party can be divided into three blocs or factions that share common ideas:

- Democrats: liberals, moderates and conservatives
- Republicans: moderates, social conservatives and fiscal conservatives

It is often possible to see where an individual sits within a party by looking both at their voting record and their support from interest groups. From time to time, named factions occur. Within the Republican Party, the Tea Party movement and the Freedom Caucus both famously represented the more right-wing element of the party's ideology.

In focus

The Freedom Caucus

The Freedom Caucus is a group of right-wing Republicans in the House of Representatives. Formed in 2015, they launched vocal challenges to Obama's immigration policy and fought to repeal the Affordable Care Act. While there was no membership list released for the group, it included enough members to make its voice heard. Speaker Boehner and his successor Speaker Ryan both tried to control this faction, but it was so disruptive that ultimately both speakers left this post — Boehner through resignation and Ryan through retirement from Congress.

John Boehner resigned in 2015, having battled with the Freedom Caucus, which considered him too moderate. Boehner described the leader of the caucus thus: 'Jordan was a terrorist as a legislator going back to his days in the Ohio House and Senate. A terrorist. A legislative terrorist.'

When Ryan took over the role of speaker, dealing with the Freedom Caucus proved just as problematic and he left the role in January 2018.

That this faction is a well-known political entity in the media highlights the significance that it has.

John Boehner found the Freedom Caucus difficult to work with despite both him and the Caucus members being drawn from the Republican Party

Democratic factions

Looking at the ratings that interest groups give to members of Congress can help to illustrate their views and where in the party they belong. The 2018 ratings in Table 21.11 demonstrate that the conservative wing of the Democrat Party is more business friendly, while the liberal wing is more focused on rights and the environment. None, however, has been awarded 0% by any of these groups, showing the breadth of ideology of each individual.

Table 21.11 Factions and ratings within the Democratic Party, 2018

	Faction		
	Liberal	Moderate	Conservative
Rating by:	Elizabeth Warren	Dianne Feinstein	Joe Manchin
United States Chamber of Commerce — supporting business	31%	49%	59%
Americans for Prosperity — supporting conservative values	5%	3%	32%
American Civil Liberties Union — supporting individual rights	94%	70%	41%
League of Conservation Voters — supporting environmental issues	94%	89%	44%

Liberals

Liberals, or progressives, within the Democratic Party are those who are on the left of their party. They are more comfortable with government intervention if it can help achieve equality in the USA and fight for the protection of the rights of everyone. Notable recent figures in this wing of the party have been Bernie Sanders, who ran against Clinton in 2016, and Elizabeth Warren, a potential presidential candidate for 2020. Sanders' 2016 campaign saw him advocate for free education, reversing *Citizens United* v *FEC*, universal healthcare and increased taxes. In 2018, 28-year-old Alexandria Ocasio-Cortez caused a 'political earthquake' within the Democrats by defeating the incumbent Congressman Joe Crowley in the New York 14th district Democratic primary. Ocasio-Cortez had worked on Sanders' campaign and described herself as a socialist.

Alexandria Ocasio-Cortez is the youngest woman ever to serve in the US Congress and is a member of the Democratic Socialists of America

In 2015, Warren led the charge against the Trans-Pacific Trade deal, calling on other progressive members of the party to rally with her against this deal. In a public video, Warren says, 'America shouldn't be signing lousy trade deals. Period … TPP isn't about helping American workers set the rules. It's about letting giant corporations rig the rules'. While they did not prevent this deal, her actions made headlines and led to numerous news stories assessing the impact of the Trans-Pacific Trade Partnership.

Moderates

Moderates are those Democratic members who sit in the centre of their party. This group is likely to hold liberal values but be willing to compromise on some of the specifics. Dianne Feinstein and Charles Schumer sit almost in the centre of their party. Feinstein, a senator from California, opposes the death penalty and supports the environment but does not support the government takeover of healthcare. In a 2017 town hall meeting, Feinstein was booed by attendees when she suggested she did not support single-payer healthcare.

The views of moderate Democrats are perhaps more liable to change over time — Feinstein previously supported the death penalty before changing her view. Considering she is the senator for California, a notably left-leaning state, her stance as a moderate is all the more interesting.

Conservatives

Conservative Democrats are those on the very right of the party. In an era of hyperpartisanship, members in this area are increasingly uncommon. These are members who would tend to be socially and morally conservative, but share agreement with the Democrats on fiscal and economic policy. Joe Manchin, the senator for West Virginia, has advocated for a measure of gun control despite his right-leaning state, but was the only Democratic vote for Brett Kavanaugh to be appointed to the Supreme Court in 2018. One of the reasons there are fewer of these members is the anger they cause among their membership in a time of partisanship — for example, Manchin was briefly suggested as a cabinet member for Trump.

Republican factions

The 2018 ratings in Table 21.12 demonstrate that the moderate wing of the Republican Party is more willing to compromise over the issue of rights as viewed by liberals, while the social conservative wing is more focused on rights from a conservative standpoint, such as anti-abortion and anti-same-sex marriage.

Table 21.12 Factions and ratings within the Republican Party, 2018

	Faction		
	Moderates	Fiscal conservatives	Social conservatives
Rating by:	Lisa Murkowski	Mitch McConnell	Ted Cruz
United States Chamber of Commerce — supporting business	91%	92%	72%
Americans for Prosperity — supporting conservative values	75%	92%	98%
American Civil Liberties Union — supporting individual rights	64%	41%	5%
League of Conservation Voters — supporting environmental issues	19%	7%	3%

Moderates

Moderates within the Republican Party tend to favour more conservative fiscal policy, looking for lower taxes and more business-friendly policies. This is often balanced, however, with a greater acceptance or tolerance of more liberal views on the issue of rights. In 2018, two Republican members of the House of Representatives opposed a provision that would ban abortion after 20 weeks, while four others in Congress support LGBTQ rights or more specifically same-sex marriage. Like conservative Democrats, however, there are increasingly fewer of these Republicans.

Fiscal conservatives

Fiscal conservatives have a keen focus on the size and cost of government, mostly with a view to cutting it down to reduce taxes and allow greater economic freedom for businesses and Americans. It is not that this faction will have either conservative or liberal views on social and moral issues, rather that these issues do not concern them in a significant way. It was these Americans who were strongly represented by Trump's promises to free the economy from government regulation, lower taxes and renegotiate those trade deals that were not in the best interests of the USA. Both the Tea Party and the Freedom Caucus have some features of fiscal conservatism, arguing for a reduction in government spending on issues such as healthcare, due to their costs rather than their moral implications.

Social conservatives

Social conservatives have a keen focus on social and moral policy issues. They are sometimes known as the '**religious right**' or the 'Christian right'. They take a conservative view on these matters, favouring the death penalty and gun rights and opposing abortion and social welfare. The opposition they have is based not on the cost of these issues, but on the moral implications of them. As the 2016 Republican platform identifies, they believe in the sanctity of life, including that of an unborn child. It was as a result of social and moral issues that the government was twice shut down in 2018, with those who favoured and opposed President Obama's Deferred Action for Childhood Arrivals (DACA) policy being unwilling to compromise. Equally, Ted Cruz's 21-hour faux-filibuster of 2013 was staged in opposition to Obamacare on an ideological, rather than a cost, basis.

> **Key term**
>
> **Religious right** A faction usually associated with the Republican Party which advances conservative views on social issues such as abortion and same-sex marriage.

> **Synoptic link**
>
> Parties dividing into factions is a result of the variation within a political ideology, and on what aspect of an ideology importance is placed. Parties in both the USA and the UK not only have factions, but these factions change and evolve over time. For more on UK party factions, see page 39. This links to Component 1, UK Politics.

Coalition of supporters for each party

When choosing how to cast their vote, a voter is likely to consider which party has policies that will be most beneficial to them. This is most likely to be determined by a range of socioeconomic and demographic factors.

The voter data from the last four presidential elections (Table 21.13) show common trends in which groups vote either Democrat or Republican. Even in 2016, the election of Donald Trump did not really change these patterns, with white people, men and older people all continuing to vote for Republicans in a majority.

Table 21.13 Breakdown of voter data from four presidential elections, 2004 to 2016 (all figures are percentages; bold text for majority opinion)

		2016		2012		2008		2004	
		Clinton	**Trump**	**Obama**	**Romney**	**Obama**	**McCain**	**Kerry**	**Bush**
Overall vote		**51**	49	**51**	47	**53**	45	48	**51**
Sex	Men	41	**52**	45	**52**	49	48	44	**55**
	Women	**54**	41	**55**	44	**56**	43	**51**	48
Race	White	37	**57**	39	**59**	43	**55**	41	**58**
	African American	**89**	8	**93**	6	**95**	4	**88**	11
	Hispanic	**66**	28	**71**	27	**67**	31	**53**	44
	Asian	**65**	27	**73**	26	**62**	35	**56**	43
	Other	**56**	36	**58**	38	**66**	31	**54**	40
Age	18–29	**55**	36	**60**	37	**66**	32	**54**	46
	30–44	**51**	41	**52**	45	**52**	46	46	**53**
	45–64	44	**52**	47	**51**	**50**	49	47	**52**
	65 and over	45	**52**	44	**56**	45	**53**	47	**52**
Religion	Protestant	39	**58**	42	**57**	45	**54**	40	**59**
	Catholic	45	**52**	**50**	48	**54**	45	47	**52**
	Jewish	**71**	24	**69**	30	**78**	21	**74**	25
	Other	**62**	29	**74**	23	**73**	22	**74**	23
Income	<$50,000	**53**	41	**60**	38	**63**	35	**57**	42
	$50,000–90,000	46	**49**	46	**52**	**50**	49	44	**56**
	$100,000 & over	47	47	44	**54**	49	49	41	**58**

Sex

Women, in every election since 1980, have voted in higher proportions than men. Traditionally, they have been more likely to support the Democratic Party than the Republican Party, although the division here is not extreme. Usually between 40% and 49% of women vote Republican, while a little over 50% vote Democratic. One of the reasons that might explain this is the Democratic sympathy towards women's issues. This does not just mean a more favourable policy towards abortion, but also with regards to other women's policy issues such as the gender pay gap and employment equality. It could also be because the Democratic Party has more female representatives in both houses of Congress and typically has more female candidates running for election. The ability to vote for someone who can descriptively represent women is therefore higher in the Democratic Party.

In 2016, 41% of women voted for Donald Trump, a notable drop on recent years. This could be attributed to his more conservative social policies that were advanced during the campaign, arguing with Clinton over abortion rights in the final presidential debate. Trump's controversial statements about women may also have served to lessen his vote from women. He commented of a Republican presidential rival that no one would have voted for her: 'Look at that face. Would anyone vote for that?' These were among the tamer comments that he made across the campaign trail. However, many women still voted for him.

Clinton offered one explanation for this:

> '[Women] will be under tremendous pressure — and I'm talking principally about white women. They will be under tremendous pressure from fathers and husbands and boyfriends and male employers not to vote for "the girl".'

This does seem to have been true to some extent according to subsequent studies of voting patterns.

Race

Turnout of the two biggest minority groups — Hispanics and African Americans — in general elections is typically far lower than the percentage of white Americans who vote. Like women, racial minorities in the USA have typically been more likely to vote for the Democrats in recent elections. It is often overlooked, however, than a significant minority of these groups do actually vote Republican. This was highlighted in 2018, with Kanye West tweeting in support of Donald Trump and Chance The Rapper also tweeting, 'Black people don't have to be Democrats'. In fact such was the support that Kanye West offered, he was received in the Oval Office by Trump in late 2018. At this meeting West commented:

> 'But there's times where, you know, it's something about, you know, I love Hillary. I love everyone, right? But the campaign "I'm with her" just didn't make me feel as a guy, that didn't get to see my dad all the time, like a guy that could play catch with his son.'

Nonetheless, policies which have typically been perceived as important to minority groups have often been championed more by Democrats than Republicans

---

Stretch and challenge

Kanye in the White House

Read the quote above from Kanye West in the Oval Office. What does this suggest about factors that affect voting behaviour in the USA? How does this link to the presidential powers of persuasion?

Interest groups

In arguing for the ratification of the Constitution, Madison made an impassioned plea:

> 'Complaints are everywhere heard from our most considerate and virtuous citizens, equally the friends of public and private faith, and of public and personal liberty, that our governments are too unstable, that the public good is disregarded in the conflicts of rival parties, and that measures are too often decided, not according to the rules of justice and the rights of the minor party, but by the superior force of an interested and overbearing majority. However anxiously we may wish that these complaints had no foundation, the evidence of known facts will not permit us to deny that they are in some degree true.'

He was lamenting the role of factions and interests over the government, and the impact of this on citizens, especially those not in the majority that he refers to. However, the role of interest groups in US politics seems as significant today as it was in 1787, if not more so, given the rising costs of elections, the growth of popular sovereignty and the increasing diversity of the US population. Significance and power must not be confused, however — the final Senate vote to confirm Brett Kavanaugh was interrupted by a disturbance from the Senate gallery of a female protestor shouting, 'I do not consent. I do not consent. Where is my representation?' Nonetheless, once the vote resumed, Kavanaugh was confirmed. This was a significant protest, but ultimately yielded little influence.

Types of interest groups

Interest groups, like pressure groups in the UK, seek to influence decision makers to create policy that is sympathetic to their cause. In the USA, the nature of government has meant that such groups can use a variety of methods and means to gain influence. The codified Constitution means that rights are protected and allows groups to use this and the Supreme Court to enact change. The federal nature of the USA means groups can choose to target districts, states and federal government in trying to achieve change.

Much like party factions, classification of US interest groups is not a simple task. In a political system with a vast array of access points and which allows for considerable significance of interest groups, they will often use whatever means they have at their disposal to be heard, which can make categorising them a challenge. There appear to be three broad types of group — single issue, professional and policy, although there is overlap between these definitions.

Single-issue interest groups

A **single-issue group** tries to gain influence over a specific issue that is very narrow in its scope. This does not necessarily mean the group has a singular campaign, but any campaigns that it does have will be on a very small area within government policy. The National Rifle Association (NRA), for example, fights for the rights of gun owners in the USA. That might be over storage of weapons, as in the Supreme Court case of *District of Columbia* v *Heller* (2008), or fighting against restrictions on magazine capacity or against an assault rifle ban. Equally, a group's campaigns may evolve in nature. In 2017, after the mass shooting in Las Vegas in which 58 people died, a national discussion began about the regulation of 'bump stocks', which can achieve a far higher rate of fire from semi-automatic weapons. All of these, however, are relevant specifically to the single-issue area of guns, under the protection of the 2nd Amendment.

Professional interest groups

Professional interest groups are similar to those categorised in UK politics as 'sectional' groups. These groups seek to represent the interests of a group of workers or professionals, or of an industry as a whole, in government legislation. They may cover a wide array of areas but within a field that is relevant to their industry. The American Farm Bureau Federation represents farmers across America. The issues that they consider to be relevant to their group, however, are more than just agricultural policy. They also campaign on immigration reform, tax and energy to name but a few. Of course the infrastructure needed to make the farming industry successful is far more than just agricultural policy. It is this broader approach in representing a professional section of society or industry that makes these 'professional' groups.

Synoptic link

UK pressure groups can be divided into sectional and causal categories. Professional groups in the USA could be defined as 'sectional', whereas a group focusing either narrowly or broadly could be defined as 'causal'. For more information on pressure groups in the UK, see pages 25–32. This links to Component 1, UK Politics.

Key term

Professional interest group An interest group which represents the interests of its members. Often these are professional associations.

Key term

Policy interest group An interest group that tries to influence a wide policy area.

Policy interest groups

Policy interest groups are similar to single-issue groups, but with greater breadth over the issues they care about. Rather than a single, small issue within a government policy, these groups are interested in an entire policy area, and in exercising influence over it. These groups are likely to represent issues such as the environment or foreign policy. Members of such groups may not be direct beneficiaries of any successes the group might have, but they share an ideological belief in their goals. Environment America looks to have an influence over the whole government policy concerning the environment, from issues such as renewable energy and global warming to wildlife conservation to clean air and water.

Some groups seem to fit in more than one of these categories. The American Israel Public Affairs Committee (AIPAC), for example, looks to promote the relationship between the USA and Israel while also campaigning on other Middle Eastern concerns, such as the war in Syria, and defence issues. As such it could arguably fit all three categories. This is shown graphically in Figure 21.8

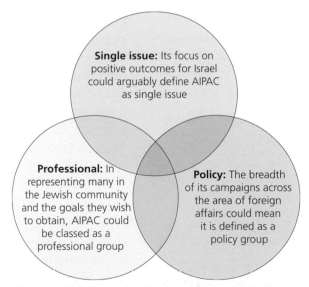

Single issue: Its focus on positive outcomes for Israel could arguably define AIPAC as single issue

Professional: In representing many in the Jewish community and the goals they wish to obtain, AIPAC could be classed as a professional group

Policy: The breadth of its campaigns across the area of foreign affairs could mean it is defined as a policy group

Figure 21.8 Categorising the American Israel Public Affairs Committee (AIPAC) interest group

Resources of interest groups

The resources that interest groups have at their disposal have a big influence on their chances of success:

Key term

Grassroots The basic or lowest level of an organisation. In US politics, this often refers to the citizens themselves.

- **Money** A group with large amounts of money will be able to contribute to election campaigns, hire expensive lobbyists and organise **grassroots** campaigns more effectively. The NRA was able to spend over $5 million on lobbying in 2017 and contributed over $700,000 to electoral campaigns in 2018. This money may be from a few big donors or from a vast membership, but without money it can be difficult to sustain influence.

- **Membership** The larger a group is the more likely it is to have an influence due to the short election cycle in the USA. This means that a group which can mobilise many voters can pose a significant threat to a member of Congress up for re-election. Who is in their membership is also important. Those with expertise in the field can help to shape campaigns, as can big donors, lawyers or professional experts.

- **Access** A group that has either access to, or the support of, a politician is more likely to be able to be heard. This may come from a retired member of Congress or it may be that former congressional staff members move into these groups. This tends to be more relevant to professional groups and lobbying groups. One report in 2018 suggested that 340 former congressional staff worked for pharmaceutical groups or their lobbying firms, thereby offering them valuable information on the legislative process but also bringing with them access to the people they used to work with.

Tactics of interest groups

Each group is unlikely to use just one tactic. They will utilise a range of methods to try and ensure that their voice is heard.

Lobbying

Lobbying is the act of seeking the ear of government. Therefore, all interest group methods could be defined as 'lobbying'. In US politics, however, lobbying is a multimillion-dollar professional industry. Professional lobbyists can provide groups with either access to politicians or with information that makes a group useful to politicians. Lobbyists can be hired directly by a group, or a group could hire a lobbying firm. This has become so important in national politics that a series of high-profile lobbying companies can be found on K Street in Washington DC. When John Boehner left his role in Congress, he took on a job at Squire Patton Boggs where he now serves as a 'strategic advisor'.

Lobbying is a big, multifaceted method. It could mean something as simple as arranging a meeting with a member of Congress to try and convince them of your arguments. It could equally be something as significant as drafting legislation and trying to win a congressional sponsor to introduce the legislation into Congress.

- In 2013, a bill passed the House of Representatives that would have rolled back part of the Dodd-Frank Act. This Act was passed in 2010 to place regulation of the financial industry in the hands of the government after the economic crash of 2007–08. The bill that the House of Representatives passed would have allowed banks to use savers' money to trade in things such as stocks, something that contributed to the crash. What was significant was that the language in the bill was almost identical to language suggested by lobbyists for Citigroup, one of America's largest banks. While this might not be the norm for most interest groups, it gives an example of just how powerful they can be, especially as some members of Congress did not even know the language was drawn up by lobbyists.

Lobbying can also mean the provision of information to Congress to try and get it to change or create favourable legislation or appointments. Cabinet appointments are a frequent target for groups as these will be the top government officials that determine policy in the areas relevant to them. President Trump's pick for attorney general was Jeff Sessions. At his hearings, both the NAACP and the National Fraternal Order of the Police gave evidence on his credentials for this role. It may be that groups are trying to influence the appointment or rejection of a candidate, or it may be that they are simply trying to build a relationship with that candidate, thereby giving them greater influence once they are appointed. Either way, the expertise these groups offer can be valuable to Congress both in legislating and in ratifying appointments.

- The NRA is so large and well organised, it has its own lobbying arm within its structure — the NRA Institute for Legislative Action (NRA-ILA). Wayne LaPierre is the CEO and executive vice president of the NRA. He is also listed as a lobbyist on Open Secrets, which tracks lobbying and spending in US politics, and has lobbied the 115th Congress on hundreds of issues. In 2013, he gave evidence directly to Congress on the issue of gun control at a hearing titled 'What should America do about gun violence?' Here, he publicly advocated for better education about gun safety, better instruction in the use of firearms by qualified instructors and better safety in schools following the massacre in Sandy Hook. He also advocated for the proper enforcement of existing firearms laws rather than the addition of new ones. These were all messages that supported the goals of the NRA, but having this status and access to Congress gave LaPierre an unparalleled stage on which to make his arguments.

Stretch and challenge

The open secret of lobbying

Soft money and hard money are well documented and one way in which interest groups can gain influence. Using the website Open Secrets, research 'dark money'.

www.opensecrets.org/dark-money

What does dark money suggest about the role of interest groups in the American democracy? Does this suggest that money is the only significant factor in a group gaining influence at all?

Report cards

Interest groups try to place pressure on politicians by issuing annual report cards on them. Members of Congress will be ranked on how well they have supported an issue in their voting record and this is publicised to the membership of an interest group and the media more widely. While these have no direct effect, the hope is that for constituents who place a high value on specific issues, if their politicians are getting poor grades, it will cost them votes.

How important a Congress member's grade is will depend on their district (Table 21.14). Senator Sanders was also given a D– in 2016 while he was campaigning for presidency. Referencing this grade proudly in a campaign event, *Politico* wrote that Sanders 'is wearing a bad grade as a badge of honor'.

Table 21.14 Interest group report cards from 2018 (2017 for the NRA) showing the support of each member of Congress for a specific issue

Interest group	Congress member			
	Sanders (D-VT)	Manchin (D-WV)	Toomey (R-PA)	Rubio (R-FL)
ACLU — supporting rights	94%	41%	11%	47%
Americans for Prosperity — supporting conservative values	5%	32%	96%	99%
NORML — supporting marijuana reform	A+	D	D	F
League of Conservation Voters — supporting environmental issues	91%	44%	7%	6%
US Chamber of Commerce — supporting business	18%	59%	85%	78%
National Rifle Association — supporting right to bear arms	D–	A	C	B

Campaign finance and electioneering

One way in which interest groups can try to gain influence is through the donation of funds to a campaign. However, direct donations are still limited by campaign finance legislation and therefore these sums pale into insignificance against the amounts many groups spend on lobbying. Of the $700,000 the NRA spent on donations in 2018, only three Democrats received any money at all from it and the maximum donated to any one candidate was less than $10,000. With the average campaign cost of winning a Senate seat in 2016 being nearly $10 million, direct campaign contributions can have only a limited impact.

Key term

Electioneering Take part in a political campaign.

Interest groups can, however, offer their 'endorsement' to candidates. This **electioneering** is not unlike the report cards as it offers an outward sign to voters that a candidate is supportive of their issue. The pro-choice group NARAL has a list of candidates it endorses on its website. If this is then an issue that is important to a voter, they can quickly see which candidates they should vote for. In 2018, the NRA publicly advocated against the re-election of Joe Manchin (D-WV) due to his stance on gun control, alongside issuing him a 2018 report card grade of D.

Grassroots activity: protests, demonstrations and direct action

Organised protests are one of the simplest and visually most effective forms of interest group action. Having a groundswell of people turning up in one location to voice their opinion will not only gain media attention, but it also demonstrates to politicians the depth of support among the public. This can also be achieved through encouraging constituents to email or write to their member of Congress to express their opinion.

The NRA has published a number of videos directly attacking conservative Democrat Joe Manchin for his stance on gun control. One video in 2013 urged its members to contact him directly to stand by his 2010 campaign promises in which he pledged to protect the 2nd Amendment but supported criminal background checks. In 2018, the NRA issued a similar video in which it claimed that 'Joe Manchin is part of the problem' and argued for his defeat in the impending elections.

Legal methods
If they have the money, and a legal reason, interest groups can launch court cases to try and advance their cause. The most significant examples of these are groups which have fought their case in the Supreme Court. Citizens United challenged the FEC's campaign finance laws, while the Coalition to Defend Affirmative Action challenged Michigan's ban on affirmative action. This requires a significant amount of funding, as well as a constitutional challenge if it is to be heard by the Supreme Court. If groups do not bring the cases themselves, they can submit amicus curiae briefs to the Supreme Court on cases that are relevant to them. (For more detail, see Chapter 20.)

Influence and significance of interest groups
The ability of a group to achieve its goals is far more than gaining headlines in the media. Equally, a group is unlikely to have used only one method to try and achieve its goals. It is therefore difficult to assess which methods are the most successful. However, there have been some notable interest group successes, failures and clashes.

Single-issue interest groups — abortion
NARAL, a pro-choice interest group, organised mass protests through its website against the appointment of Brett Kavanaugh to the US Supreme Court, as well as organising online campaigns under the banner #StopKavanaugh. It also occupied the state office of Senator Chuck Grassley in Iowa, and stormed the Senate and packed the offices of Senators Donnelly, Murkowski, Corker and Grassley to lodge its objections to Kavanaugh. Despite making headlines on MSNBC and other major news outlets, Kavanaugh was ultimately confirmed.

Professional groups — pharmaceuticals
This industry is the biggest collective spender in Washington DC lobbying, having spent over $2 billion in the last decade alone. For the most part, the influence of this money will go unseen by the public, and certainly members of Congress would not want to suggest that their votes had been bought. However, in deciding what drugs will and will not be funded and preventing cheap overseas competitors, the money spent is hugely influential and largely allows the industry to charge whatever it likes for drugs provided to Medicare and Medicaid.

Policy groups — the environment
The League of Conservation Voters (LCV) opposed the Keystone XL Pipeline, an oil pipeline that would run thousands of miles from Alberta in Canada to Houston in Texas. It spent millions of dollars on adverts advocating for and against candidates in the 2010 election cycle and spent thousands of dollars directly lobbying Congress on the issue. Nonetheless, it passed Congress and was only stopped in 2015 by a presidential veto. In 2017, when Trump became president, he used his presidential powers to allow Keystone to advance once again. This suggests, if anything, that the most the LCV achieved was a temporary halt.

A protest against Keystone Pipeline in California shows a good deal of public support for the issue

In spite of wide public support, as with much interest-group action, it is rarely apparent whether an interest group's successes and failures are a direct result of its actions or simply a case of legislators acting in accordance with their own beliefs.

Interest group activities

Marijuana Policy Project

One of the ways in which interest groups can enact change is to get an initiative on the ballot in an election. An initiative is a question put on the ballot if enough people in the state sign a petition to include it. The Marijuana Policy Project (MPP) spends time and money collecting such signatures to get initiatives on the ballot that would allow for the legalisation of marijuana in a state. In Arizona, MPP collected 50,000 signatures in just 10 weeks, and went on to collect the more than 150,000 needed by state law to get Proposition 205 on the ballot in November 2016. The initiative would allow 'individuals to possess, grow and purchase marijuana from state-licensed facilities for personal use'. Despite its initial success, the initiative was defeated in the actual election by 51.32% to 48.68%.

American Federation of Teachers

The American Federation of Teachers represented increasingly disgruntled teachers facing underfunded schools and being stripped of their pensions in 2018. In Texas, the Federation helped to organise protests for its teachers called the 'Speak Out and Stand Together' rally. Unlike elsewhere in the USA, however, they had to stop short of strike action. This is because in Texas, teachers who strike can lose their teaching certificate as they are not allowed to strike according to state law. Interest groups are therefore limited by the scope of state law.

US Chamber of Commerce

The US Chamber of Commerce headquarters

The US Chamber of Commerce is the annual biggest spender in Washington DC lobbying, although its impact is often hidden away. An instance in 2004 demonstrates its influence, however. Two businesses in Iowa had been told by the courts to pay billions of dollars for mislabelling products or deceiving customers. These cases were being appealed, and on the appeal court there was one — locally electable — vacancy. The Chamber poured money into the judicial election with the aim of getting a business-friendly justice elected. Having achieved this, when the two cases were heard, the new justice was the deciding vote on throwing the cases out.

The impact of interest groups on government

The impact that interest groups can have on government is not always apparent. It would be unlikely for any member of one of the branches of government to overtly suggest that the reason for their vote, decision or legislation was the result of pressure from one group. Not only could this appear undemocratic or unrepresentative, it could also lead to tensions with conflicting groups. Therefore, it is simpler to try and understand the methods and access points that a group could use to try and influence government. These are listed in Table 21.16.

Table 21.16 Methods and access points available to interest groups

Influencing Congress	Influencing the president	Influencing the Supreme Court
• Lobbying • Proposing legislation • Giving evidence in Congress • Record cards • Campaign donations • Attack/endorsement adverts • Organising grassroots activism • Protesting	• Lobbying • Campaign donations • Attack/endorsement adverts • Protesting	• Bringing a case to the Supreme Court • Submitting amicus curiae briefs • Some groups have a direct role in the nomination of justices (the ABA) and others lobby on this issue

Are interest groups good for democracy in the USA?

Any debate surrounding democracy will depend entirely on which type of democracy is being discussed.

	Good for democracy	Bad for democracy
Representative	✓ Interest groups can represent minority groups and their interests, which might be ignored or overlooked in a winner-takes-all system ✓ Interest groups can encourage their members to turn out in elections, increasing the legitimacy of those elected	✗ Interest groups can undermine the power of legitimately elected local representatives ✗ The power of interest groups over the legislature can work in the interest, and even overrepresentation, of the minority, rather than the majority
Liberal	✓ Interest groups can raise issues about, and work to protect, rights. This can include bringing cases to the Supreme Court ✓ Interest groups raise issues that hold government to account, thereby limiting its power ✓ A wide range of interest groups on directly competing issues are tolerated	✗ Free and fair elections can be undermined by the money that interest groups pump into elections ✗ Tolerance of more extremist groups can appear to undermine the rights of other groups ✗ Interest groups that use illegal methods undermine the rule of law
Pluralist	✓ The nature of US politics gives interest groups a greater number of access points, dispersing power ✓ Smaller interest groups have had success in gaining national attention for their issues, even if not in managing to achieve legislative change ✓ The issues raised by interest groups provide an important link between the people and government, and ensure the government is responsive	✗ Interest groups with more money seem to have a disproportionate amount of influence ✗ The same interest groups annually seem to retain influence over the political process ✗ The focus of interest group action in Washington DC centralises power

Leaders of the National Education Association and the American Federation of Teachers protesting in January 2019

Comparisons with the UK

Comparative theories

Table 21.17 Comparing democracy and participation in the USA and the UK using comparative theories

Rational comparisons	• The choices that voters make are most commonly determined by the party that is offering policies that will give the best outcome for them, demonstrated through some level of partisan dealignment as experienced in both the USA and the UK • Party-line voting is often determined by the career aspirations of those within a party • The party policies advanced in either country can be strongly influenced by the personal political beliefs of the leading individuals within each party • Factions within parties are often a reflection of the personal beliefs of individuals within a party • Pressure-group action in both countries is characterised by many groups or lobbyists trying to achieve the best outcome for them personally through whatever access point is available to them • The methods of pressure groups are often determined by the resources available to them and what they therefore need to do in order to achieve influence for their cause
Cultural comparisons	• There is some expectation that certain socioeconomic groups should vote for a certain party based on political history • The expectation of party unity is also high in both countries. Even in the USA where historically this has not been as strong, there is a striking and growing polarisation between the two major parties • Very few independents are elected as the public in both countries expects the most powerful parties to be the two major parties • The degree of internal party unity is often determined by national issues of the day, especially those which are of greatest concern to the public generally • The difficulty in achieving campaign reform in both countries is due to a lack of political motivation from those in charge • Party policies in both countries are influenced by ideological belief in certain political principles • The growing media presence in pressure-group action and vast numbers of people taking part in these group activities suggest not only shared beliefs in certain issues, but also a shared belief in the effect and influence that such groups can have
Structural comparisons	• The number of access points for pressure groups is determined by the political structure of each country, which also determines the methods and influence that the groups may be able to achieve • The voting behaviour of party members can be determined by the process in which they find themselves, including party discipline, and legislative and electoral processes • The constitutional framework of both countries determines the electoral process, and the resulting mandate gained from it for elected representatives • The party systems in both countries are a result of the choice of electoral process • Parties in both countries hold conventions or conferences to inform, develop and legitimise the policies they will go on to advance

Comparing democracy and participation in the UK and the USA

The different nature of the party systems

The nature of the party system in the USA and the UK makes for an interesting comparison. On the face of it, both countries appear to be dominated by two main parties. However, closer inspection reveals a more fluid situation in both countries. Third parties have had more notable success in the UK in recent years. Remember, however, that the breadth of ideology within the two American parties means both that there are notable factions within each party, and also that at state level the Democratic and Republican parties in one state may look very different to their own party in another state.

A two-party system?

The national legislatures of both countries are dominated by elected politicians from the Labour and Conservative parties in the UK and the Republican and Democratic parties in the USA. The inability of third parties to gain a foothold — as a product of the electoral system, high electoral costs, and co-optation of policies — has been a sustained feature of both countries.

As Table 21.18 shows, the two major parties have held a vast majority of the seats in the national legislatures in all recent elections. Even the slightly decreasing trend in the seats held by the Conservatives and Democrats still gives both parties clear dominance overall.

Table 21.18 Two-party majorities in the national legislature, UK (1983–2017) and USA (1984–2016)

Year	Total seats for Conservatives and Labour in the House of Commons	Year	Total seats for Democrats and Republicans in Congress
1983	606/650	1984	535/535
1987	605/650	1988	535/535
1992	607/651	1992	534/535
1997	583/659	1996	533/535
2001	578/659	2000	533/535
2005	553/646	2004	533/535
2010	564/650	2008	533/535
2015	562/650	2012	533/535
2017	579/650	2016	533/535

A two-and-a-half-party system?

Third parties in both countries have had a notable effect even if they have not been viable candidates for power at national level. In the UK, the Liberal Democrats won enough seats in 2010 to form a coalition with the Conservative Party, while the DUP in 2017 formed a confidence-and-supply agreement to allow a Conservative minority government to be functional. In the USA, the vote for third parties tripled in 2017, although the impact of this was limited. However, in 2000, the campaign of Ralph Nadar had a 'spoiler effect'. This means that the votes Nadar attracted in 2000 would likely have gone to Al Gore if Nadar had not stood. By splitting the more liberal vote in this manner, it made it easier for George W. Bush to win.

The growing media recognition of third parties has been a marked trend in both countries. In 2010, the first televised leaders' debates in the UK featured the leaders of three parties not two. The number of parties involved in these debates has increased in subsequent years. In the USA, the discussion over whether the Green Party and Libertarian Party leaders should be allowed to be involved was more prominent than ever in 2016.

A multiparty system?

Both the USA and the UK have a variety of third parties that have a prominent existence in their political landscape. At regional level, these parties tend to enjoy greater success. In the 2015 UK general election, a different party 'won' in each region — the Conservatives in England, Labour in Wales, the SNP in Scotland and the DUP in Northern Ireland. In the devolved bodies, third parties have done especially well. While not as dominant generally in the USA, Progressive and Independent candidates have won in recent **gubernatorial** races, while a range of third parties have had success in being elected for state legislatures.

Key term

Gubernatorial Relating to a governor — in this case, the election of a state governor.

Degree of internal unity within parties

The nature of the party structures in the UK allows them to create a far greater level of party unity than in the USA. That the party controls the candidate selection for constituency seats, let alone the power that the party leaders and whips have in controlling career progression, makes it far easier to exercise party discipline in the UK. Comparatively, in the USA, the use of primaries allows voters control over who gets a place on the ballot, with the short election cycle making this even more significant.

All parties suffer from some lack of internal unity, however. This is due to the ideological breadth of the parties — the broader they are, the more disagreement is likely to exist within them, and the two major parties in each country are quite broad. Recently, all of the major parties seem to have been embroiled not only in intraparty disagreements over specific issues, but over the very ideological direction of their party.

- Both Labour and the Democrats have seen notable political figures trying to pull their parties more towards the left — Corbyn in the UK, and Sanders in the USA.
- The Republicans and Conservatives by comparison have seen controversy over figures trying to pull their party to the right — Johnson in the UK, and Trump or even notable senators like Ted Cruz in the USA.

Significant internal arguments within the Conservative Party over Theresa May's stance on Brexit led to Boris Johnson resigning from the cabinet in July 2018. His strong criticisms from the back benches further weakened her and in July 2019 he succeeded her as prime minister

In both countries, however, the rise of adversary politics has meant that internal divisions within a party can become masked when one party is pitted against the other over a policy issue.

- Despite fractures in the Republican Party over the presidency of Donald Trump they almost all voted for the appointment of Brett Kavanaugh, while the Democrats almost all voted against.
- Equally, despite the deep divisions in the Conservative Party, in January 2019 when Jeremy Corbyn brought a motion of no confidence against Theresa May's government, all 314 Conservative MPs voted for the government and the motion was defeated by 325–306 votes.

There does seem to be a common trend that, despite internal disquiet, one's own party is better than the other one in controversial issues.

The policy profiles of the two main parties in each country

The main parties in the USA and the UK are not easily comparable — it would be oversimplistic to liken the Democrats to Labour and the Republicans to the Conservatives. The entirety of the American political landscape is to the right of that in the UK. Nonetheless, there are similarities and differences that can be identified on specific policy areas.

Table 21.19 summarises the policy commitments in the 2016 US election and 2017 UK election. There are clearly areas in which the US parties share a different view to UK parties, such as defence, or where the more left-leaning parties share a different view to the right-leaning parties, such as education. But there are also some broad similarities, such as in immigration, and notable differences, such as healthcare.

Table 21.19 Policy commitments in the 2016 US election and 2017 UK election

Policy area	Conservatives	Democrats	Labour	Republicans
Social welfare	Increase to NHS budget and means-tested pension benefits	Fight attempts to privatise Medicare	Reverse NHS privatisation and substantially increase NHS budgets	Repeal and replace Obamacare, and place limits on government funding for senior healthcare
Education	Increase overall schools budget and introduce a new funding formula	Debt-free college and no tuition fees for working-class families	Abolish university tuition fees and provide 30 hours of free childcare for two-year-olds	Restoration of private sector in student financing
Defence	Spend 0.7% of GDP on international aid and lend support to international institutions	Believe that the US military should be the strongest in the world	Spend 0.7% of GDP on international aid and spend 2% on defence	Commitment to rebuilding the US military to 'the strongest on earth'
Environment	Develop the fracking industry	Acceptance of the threat posed by climate change	Introduce clean air legislation and ban fracking	Description of climate change as a 'political mechanism'
Economy	Balanced budget by 2025 and review business rates	Introduce a multimillionaire surtax and tax relief for working- and middle-class families	Reintroduce a 50p tax and raise income tax for highest earners	Where taxes work to prevent economic growth they must be changed
Immigration	Reduce net migration to tens of thousands and tougher student visa rules	Reform the immigration system to include a path to citizenship	Wary of freedom of movement due to the impact on wages and conditions	Embrace Trump's 'build a wall' programme

Debates around campaign finance and party funding

There have been notable controversies surrounding the issues of money in politics and lobbying in both the USA and the UK in recent years. The Conservative Party was fined £70,000 in 2017 for its financial accounting in the 2015 general election, while the Obama campaign was fined $375,000 in 2013 for violating federal laws surrounding the disclosure of donations. Yet these figures pale into insignificance when compared with the spending of these parties in a general election — the Clinton campaign raised over $1 billion in 2016, while the Conservatives spent nearly £20 million in 2017. The fines, therefore, seem to be a small price to pay, literally, for breaking campaign finance laws.

Reforming laws has proved a challenge in both countries, however. In the UK, electoral spending is limited by a number of laws:

- Representation of the People Act 1983, which limits individual spending — updated in 2014 to increase the maximum spending limits to £30,700 for 'pre-candidacy expense' (the 'long campaign') and £8,700 for general election spending (the 'short campaign')
- The Political Parties, Elections and Referendums Act 2000 — requires the reporting of donations to the Electoral Commission
- Political Parties and Elections Act 2009 — requires declarations as to the source of donations over £7,500
- Transparency of Lobbying, Non-party Campaigning and Trade Union Administration Act 2014 — requires the registration of professional lobbyists and requires charities spending more than £20,000 to try and influence votes to register with the Electoral Commission

These seem to reflect similar concerns to those expressed in US politics over the costs of elections and the source of money influencing elections. However, the success of UK legislation seems to be relatively higher, despite the fines issued by the Electoral Commission, given the substantially lower election cost.

Following the referendum campaign in 2016, the Vote Leave campaign was fined by the Electoral Commission for coordination with another Brexit campaign group

Party funding

In both the USA and the UK, a debate has been raised over whether parties should be state funded to level the political playing field.

- In the USA, 'matching funds' tried to achieve this — the government matching dollar-for-dollar the donations a party receives if it acts within certain spending limits. Recent presidential candidates of both parties have found it more lucrative to ignore both the limits and the matching funds.
- In the UK, so-called 'Short money' is given to the opposition in Parliament but this is for the opposition's parliamentary expenditures rather than for elections. A share of the Public Development Grant of £2 million is available for UK parties to help them develop manifesto policies, but to be eligible a party must have at least two sitting MPs, so it does not help to promote new parties.

The arguments surrounding state funding for parties, rather than having party donors, are similar in both the USA and the UK — allowing greater third-party access, reducing the cost of elections and reducing the role of lobbying and interest groups. However, an agreement on what party funding would look like in either country is far from agreed.

The methods and influence of interest groups

Interest-group methods are similar in the USA and the UK — actions can be broadly broken down into direct action (small or large scale), legal action, electioneering and lobbying. Which of these methods is more successful in either country, however, does have some variation, because although the actions might be similar, the political landscape is not.

Supreme Court

- The entrenched political understanding of the US Supreme Court, and the power that it wields, make it much more influential than the UK Supreme Court, and therefore a more attractive proposition for interest groups to target.
- Comparatively, the weakness of the UK judiciary is that Parliament remains sovereign, therefore targeting lawmakers in Westminster is a more successful route.

Constitution

Coupled with this is the important difference in constitutions.

- The codified nature of the US Constitution guarantees individuals' rights, and this can be used to mount legal challenges.
- The UK constitution by comparison is far more flexible, making it more difficult to successfully challenge legislation, when Parliament retains the power to simply rewrite it in the face of a negative ruling.

Access points

- There are a greater number of access points in the USA than in the UK, giving interest groups either the chance to exert pressure on a wider basis, or more specifically target their campaign. The federal nature of the US political system means interest groups are more able to try and exert influence directly on lawmakers in the USA. They can choose to target individually one of the three branches of government, or go directly to state legislatures and enact change at a state level.

- Interest groups in the UK can target the devolved bodies but, as with the UK Supreme Court, ultimate power rests with Parliament.

Election cycle

- The short US election cycle creates greater opportunities for interest groups. They can directly electioneer by donating and supporting candidates, but they can also be a force to mobilise voters, which can be a threat to those running in elections if their policies are not seen to be in sync with those voters.
- The 5-year UK election cycle gives parties and candidates greater freedom to ignore groups between election years.

It is important to remember that interest groups are usually defined by their unwillingness to seek to hold political power or office themselves; instead they seek to influence those who do have power. The extent of their influence can be seen, therefore, in the successes and failures that they have in promoting their own issues and winning favourable legislation or court rulings for their cause. In both countries, the influence of individual groups often waxes and wanes with the changing fortunes of political parties and ideologies. However, the influence of groups generically over the political system can be seen today as a fact of political life.

Summary

By the end of this chapter you should be able to answer the following questions:
- → Is the presidential electoral process in need of reform?
- → Is incumbency the most significant factor in explaining electoral outcomes?
- → Have the attempts at campaign finance reform come to an end?
- → To what extent are the two major US parties ideologically coherent?
- → What is the significance of factionalism within US political parties?
- → How significant are socioeconomic factors in explaining voting patterns?
- → To what extent are interest groups beneficial for US democracy?
- → What factors determine the methods that an interest group may choose to use?

Practice questions

1. Examine the differences in the party policies of the Democratic Party and the Labour Party. (12)
2. Analyse the need for campaign finance reform in UK and US general elections. *In your answer you must consider the relevance of at least one comparative theory.* (12)
3. Evaluate the extent to which the US political system allows for the success of interest groups. *You must consider this view and the alternative to this view in a balanced way.* (30)

Acknowledgements

Photos reproduced by permission of: **p.8** wyrdlight/Alamy; **p.10** Maurice Savage/Alamy; **p.13** Leon Neal/Getty; **p.14** Rupert Rivett/Alamy; **p.17** Guy Bell/Alamy; **p.19** Mark Sinclair/Alamy; **p.20** Archive Pics/Alamy; **p.21** Dinendra Haria/Alamy; **p.24** nullplus/Adobe Stock; **p.26** Kuttig – People/Alamy; **p.28** REUTERS/Alamy; **p.29** Cliff Hide News/Alamy; **p.31** Paul Brown/Alamy; **p.33** Lordprice Collection/Alamy; **p.34** Trinity Mirror/Alamy; **p.38** AFP Contributor/Getty; **p.45** imageBROKER/Alamy; **p.46** MediaPunch Inc/Alamy; **p.49** (top) peter Jordan/Alamy, (bottom) MediaPunch Inc/Alamy; **p.50** Roger Jackson/Getty; **p.52** Dan Vincent/Alamy; **p.54** Russell Hart/Alamy; **p.57** Steven Scott Taylor/Alamy; **p.60** Jason Richardson/Alamy; **p.68** lazyllama/Adobe Stock; **p.71** epa european pressphoto agency b.v./Alamy; **p.74** Martina/Adobe Stock; **p.76** WENN Rights Ltd/Alamy; **p.80** Pete Maclaine/Alamy; **p.84** Leonid Andronov/Adobe Stock; **p.87** Stephen Barnes/Northern Ireland News/Alamy; **p.89** Mark Thomas/Alamy; **p.97** Kathy deWitt/Alamy; **p.99** David Bleeker/Alamy; **p.102** Justin Kase z12z/Alamy; **p.104** BRIAN HARRIS/Alamy; **p.107** Apex News and Pictures Agency/Alamy; **p.108** Keystone Press/Alamy; **p.112** Keystone Press/Alamy; **p.113** David Cole/Alamy; **p.115** DAVID THOMSON/Getty; **p.119** mark severn/Alamy; **p.120** Homer Sykes Archive/Alamy; **p.121** Tim Graham/Alamy; **p.125** Martin Beddall/Alamy; **p.128** Steven Scott Taylor/Alamy; **p.129** WENN Rights Ltd/Alamy; **p.132** Fotolia; **p.135** The Picture Art Collection/Alamy; **p.138** Trinity Mirror/Alamy; **p.141** PjrNews/Alamy; **p.142** Miles Willis/Alamy; **p.146** Aadvark/Alamy; **p.149** STEVE LINDRIDGE/Alamy; **p.151** christopher jones/Alamy; **p.153** Bloomberg/Getty; **p.160** Heritage Image Partnership Ltd/Alamy; **p.162** Press Association; **p.165** WENN Rights Ltd/Alamy; **p.169** ake/Adobe Stock; **p.172** Alan West/Alamy; **p.174** Imageplotter News and Sports/Alamy; **p.177** colaimages/Alamy; **p.179** ZUMA Press, Inc./Alamy; **p.181** Zefrog/Alamy; **p.185** Wiktor Szymanowicz/Shutterstock; **p.188** Shutterstock; **p.191** David Cole/Alamy; **p.195** Popperfoto/Getty; **p.201** REUTERS/Alamy; **p.203** Popperfoto/Getty; **p.204** Mark Kerrison/Alamy; **p.209** Popperfoto/Getty; **p.210** Topfoto; **p.211** Michael Olivers/Alamy; **p.212** Malcolm Park editorial/Alamy; **p.214** claire Doherty/Alamy; **p.220** Justin Kase z12z/Alamy; **p.221** Michael Tubi/Alamy; **p.227** Guy Corbishley/Alamy; **p.228** age footstock/Alamy; **p.230** tichr/Adobe Stock; **p.231** Anadolu Agency/Getty; **p.233** Andrea Ronchini/Alamy; **p.234** seb hovaguimian/Adobe Stock; **p.236** WPA Pool/Getty; **p.239** Andy Buchanan/Alamy; **p.244** Rawf8/Adobe Stock; **p.246** North Wind Picture Archive/Alamy; **p.247** DEA BIBLIOTECA AMBROSIANA/Getty; **p.252** Everett Collection Inc/Alamy (top), Ian Dagnall Computing/Alamy (bottom); **p.253** Everett Collection Historical/Alamy; **p.257** Michael Brown/Adobe Stock; **p.258** Pictorial Press Ltd/Alamy; **p.259** Pictorial Press Ltd/Alamy; **p.261** Martha Holmes/Getty; **p.264** The Picture Art Collection/Alamy; **p.266** Heritage Image Partnership Ltd/Alamy; **p.269** AF Fotografie/Alamy; **p.271** GL Archive/Alamy; **p.273** Julius Schulman/Getty; **p.275** INTERFOTO/Alamy; **p.276** Heritage Images/Topfoto; **p.281** CBW/Alamy; **p.283** Heritage Images/Topfoto; **p.288** philipk76/Adobe Stock; **p.295** Jimmy Sine/Getty; **p.296** Hulton Archive/Getty; **p.300** age footstock/Alamy; **p.304** Julius Lando/Alamy; **p.308** North Wind Picture Archives/Alamy; **p.312** Pictorial Press Ltd/Alamy; **p.314** The Granger Collection/Alamy; **p.315** Janine Wiedel Photolibrary/Alamy; **p.318** Juan Jimenez/Alamy; **p.319** INTERFOTO/Alamy; **p.322** desdemona72/Adobe Stock; **p.323** Everett Collection Inc/Alamy; **p.324** Science History Images/Alamy; **p.325** 2630ben/Adobe Stock; **p.328** ZUMA Press Inc/Alamy; **p.330** WENN Rights Ltd/Alamy; **p.335** Iris Schneider/Getty; **p.336** Godong/Alamy; **p.338** Jane Campbell/Alamy; **p.340** Pictorial Press Ltd/Alamy; **p.342** Oksana Kuzmina/Adobe Stock; **p.344** WENN Rights Ltd/Alamy; **p.345** Anthony Barboza/Getty; **p.347** Historic Collection/Alamy; **p.349** GARY DOAK/Alamy; **p.350** Hulton Deutsch/Getty; **p.351** Mark Waugh/Alamy; **p.354** Michael Matthews/Alamy; **p.357** Rex/Shutterstock; **p.361** Bloomberg/Getty; **p.362** dpa picture alliance/Alamy; **p.364** Topfoto; **p.365** peshkova/Adobe Stock; **p.366** Trinity Mirror/Alamy; **p.368** Topfoto; **p.371** Thomas Griger/Alamy; **p.372** kotoyamagami/Adobe Stock; **p.373** Images of Africa Photobank/Alamy; **p.376** Melvyn Longhurst/Alamy; **p.378** Trinity Mirror/Alamy; **p.379** Chronicle/Alamy; **p.380** Heritage Image Partnership Ltd/Alamy; **p.382** World History Archive/Alamy; **p.386** Ian Dagnall/Alamy; **p.389** Pictorial Press Ltd/Alamy; **p.395** Topfoto; **p.396** Xinhua/Alamy; **p.397** Newscom/Alamy; **p.401** (left) Daniel Dempster Photography/Alamy, (right) Spencer Platt/Getty; **p.403** AB Forces News Collection/Alamy; **p.406** PCN Photography/Alamy; **p.411** Stocktrek Images/Alamy; **p.415** Newscom/Alamy; **p.417** Fotolia; **p.420** Fotolia; **p.421** Animalparty/Wikimedia Commons; **p.426** Dmytro Synelchenko/Adobe Stock; **p.428** Bettmann/Getty; **p.430** Win McNamee/Getty; **p.438** Handout/Alamy; **p.442** AFP Contributor/Alamy; **p.444** Granger Historical Picture Archive/Alamy; **p.447** Gary/Adobe Stock (l), Fotolia (r); **p.450** Fotolia; **p.452** Fotolia; **p.454** dpa picture alliance/Alamy; **p.456** Newscom/Alamy; **p.458** Storms Media Group/Alamy; **p.462** Andia/Alamy; **p.465** World History Archive/Alamy; **p.468** Xinhua/Alamy; **p.471** Keystone Press/Alamy; **p.473** American Photo Archive/Alamy; **p.478** White House Photo/Alamy; **p.484** Kim Seidl/Adobe Stock; **p.486** J. Keppler/Alamy; **p.489** Fotolia; **p.491** ZUMA Press Inc/Alamy; **p.493** dpa picture alliance/Alamy; **p.497** WDC Photos/Alamy; **p.499** Chip Somodevilla/Getty; **p.502** Tribune Content Agency LLC/Alamy; **p.507** Friedrich Stark/Alamy; **p.512** MediaPunch Inc/Alamy; **p.515** ALLTROTS STILL-LIFE/Alamy; **p.518** LH Images/Alamy; **p.520** oneofmany/Adobe Stock; **p.523** Sean Rayford/Getty; **p.524** Stuart Sipkin/Alamy; **p.527** Xinhua/Alamy; **p.535** Joe Sohm/Getty; **p.539** michaelmond/Alamy; **p.540** Science History Images/Alamy; **p.541** lev radin/Alamy; **p.545** ZUMA Press Inc./Alamy; **p.554** Lisa Werner/Alamy; **p.555** Kristoffer Tripplaar/Alamy; **p.556** Rex/Shutterstock; **p.559** Tommy London/Alamy; **p.561** 67 photo/Alamy.

The extract on p.213 is reproduced by permission of Richard Heffernan.

Index

Note: **bold** page numbers indicate where definitions of key terms are to be found.

A

ABA (American Bar Association) rating 490, 498
Abbott, Diane 129, 130, 185, 351
abortion
  Democratic and Republican stances 537
  single-issue interest groups 553
  Supreme Court rulings 499
absolute authority
  of central government, unitary state 135
  sovereignty as 236
absolute equality 292
absolute monarchies 246, 269, 375
access points, US interest groups 555, 562–63
accountability **69**
  of executive to legislature 481–83
  of the president to Congress 477
Act of Settlement (1701) 134, 217
Act of Union (1707) 134, 148
additional member system (AMS) **81–82**, 92
adversary vs consensus politics 40
affirmative action **358, 509**, 512–13, 553
African Americans
  in Congress 440–41
  election turnout 545
  identity politics 357
  rights, advance of 510, 511–12
  wealth gap 546–47
age and voting behaviour 106–08, 131–32, 544
altruism/altruistic **280, 311**
amicus curiae briefs, US Supreme Court **508**, 509, 511
anarchism 308–21
  collectivist 315–18
  core ideas and principles 309–14
  and economic freedom 313–14
  individualist 319–20
  liberty 309–12
  perceptions of order 313
  rejection of the state 309
anarcho-capitalism 310, 314, 319–20
anarcho-communism 311, 315–16, 335
anarcho-syndicalism 313, 317, 318
Anarchy, State and Utopia (Nozick, 1974) 261, 274, 279, 286
animal liberation 325
anomie **311**

anthropocentrism **323**
  deep green ecologists' opposition to 330–31
  enlightened 325, 328–29
  represented by the Ego 322
anti-permissiveness **284**
Anti-Terrorism Crime and Security Act (2001) 34, 144, 222
anticolonial nationalism 368, 381
apartheid **372**
apathy, political 24, **117**
appellate court **485**
appointment process, US Supreme Court 489–98
  presidential nomination 398, 492
  ratification by Senate 396
  strengths and weaknesses of 495–98
appointments, presidential 456–57
  checks by Congress on 394–95
  confirmation by the Senate 430
appointments, UK
  House of Lords 142, 165–66, 176
  Supreme Court 144, 216, 217
appropriations bills **394**
Asquith, Herbert (1908–16), Liberal governments 55, 134, 140, 259
associate justices **485**, 487, 489, 493
atomism **273**
atomistic individualism
  anarcho-capitalism 319–20
  neo-conservative rejection of 283, 284
  neo-liberal view 272, 279–80, 286
Attlee, Clement 50, 291, 301
authoritarian governments, postcolonial nations 382
authoritarian law and order 284–85
authoritative works, UK constitution 139
authority **265**, 268, **309**
  of a prime minister 202–04
Authorizations for Use of Military Force (AUMF), US 394, 446, 463, 479
autonomy **310**

B

backbenchers 163, **180**
  increase in powers of 145, 225
  role and significance of 181–83
Bagehot, Walter, *The English Constitution* 139, 176, 198, 199
Bakunin, Mikhail (1814–76) 309, 313, 314, 317, 321
battleground states **529**
Bellweather states **529**

T

tactical voting 60, 79
tactics of interest groups 550–53
Tax Cuts and Jobs Act (2017) 436
taxation 272
   Conservative Party 47, 51
   Democratic and Republican stances 538, 560
   devolved bodies 146, 148, 151–52
   Labour Party 50, 53, 303, 305, 560
   Liberal Democrats' proposals 56
   as theft, Nozick 261–62, 280
   in the US 410, 411
Taylor, Charles (1931–) 354–55, 356, 362, 367
Taylor Mill, Harriet, first-wave feminism 340
televised debates
   UK 94, 114, 120–21, 207
   US 523, 529
terrorism, UK
   Acts of Parliament 34, 156
   and civil liberties 35, 36
   detention of foreign suspects without trial 35, 144,
      222, 240
   and limitations of HRA 143–44
terrorism, US 406, 463
Thatcher, Margaret (prime minister 1979–1990) 210
   1979 general election campaign 123
   compared to Theresa May 49
   free-market policies 281–82
   leadership 112, 113
   media relationship 121
   neoconservative tendencies 283, 284, 285
   weak parliamentary influence 224
Theory of Justice, A (Rawls, 1971) 253, 254, 257, 260, 286
think-tanks **31**
third parties, success of in devolved bodies 93–94, 558–59
third-wave feminism (1990s to early 2000s) 341
third way **51**, 289, 303–06
   on equality 292, 293
   influence on New Labour 304–06
   promoting community, responsibility and inclusion 304
   promotion of education and infrastructure investment 304
   recognition of free market 303–04
   view of collectivism 291
   vision of humanity 290
Thorneycroft, Peter, resignation of (1958) 194
Thorpe, Jeremy 114, 123, 202, 216
Timothy, Nick 41, 128, 212
tolerance 245–46, **360**
Toryism (traditional conservatism) 44–45
trade unions
   and anarcho-syndicalism 317
   excessive pay claims 122–23
   Labour Party relationships with 43, 53
   strike action 27, 104, 111, 122, 203, 206, 282
tradition, conservative value 270–71, 283, 366, 377
traditional conservatism 44–45, 264, 274
   as a natural disposition 275
   non-reactionary 274–75
   reactionary 274

traditional conservative nationalism 377–78
transfeminism 339, 351
transparency
   on campaign finance 561
   Freedom of Information Act 140
   inside the Obama cabinet 469
   of judiciary appointments 144, 217
treaties **139**
   European Union 139, 228–30, 233
   president's right to create 462–64, 466
   ratification by the Senate 394, 430
Truman, Harry, S. (1945–53) 191, 458, 470,
      471, 487
Trump, Donald (US president 2017–) 458
   appointment of judges 456, 496
   election campaign 524, 527, 528, 529
   executive orders 458–59
   federalism under 409
   immigration reform 427, 459, 514
   nativist policies of 379
   and the NSC daily briefing 474
   persuasive powers 470–72
   poll ratings 443, 479
   proclamations 459, 463
   protest marches against 512
   repeal of Obamacare 427
   signing of legislation 453–54
   State of the Union address 455
   support for, voter trends 543–47
   use of pardons and commutations 461
   withdrawal from Paris Accord 329, 330, 334
Turing, Alan, posthumous royal pardon 179, 190
turnout **71**
Twin Oaks Community, ecovillage 326
two-party system **423, 532**
   created by FPTP 75
   created by SV 90, 91
   erosion of in the UK 63–64
   in the US 532, 535
   US-UK comparison 558
Two Treatises of Government (Locke, 1690) 246, 254
tyranny **420**
tyranny of the minority 402, **413**

U

UKIP (United Kingdom Independence Party) 58–59, 64
ultra vires **220**
unanimous consent **437**
uncodified constitution **135**
unentrenched constitution **135**
unequal (organic) society 269
unequal vote value, disadvantage of FPTP 77, 79
unified government **406**
unitary state **136**
unity/disunity 54, 194, 199, 528, 558–59
   Labour party 54
universalism **359**
US Bill of Rights (1791) 251, 387, 390, 400, 500
utilitarianism **293**